From Honey to Ashes

*the text of this book is printed
on 100% recycled paper*

By the same author

STRUCTURAL ANTHROPOLOGY

TOTEMISM

THE SAVAGE MIND

THE SCOPE OF ANTHROPOLOGY

THE ELEMENTARY STRUCTURE OF KINSHIP

Introduction to a Science of Mythology (*Mythologiques*)

1. THE RAW AND THE COOKED

2. FROM HONEY TO ASHES

3. THE ORIGIN OF TABLE MANNERS

4. THE NAKED MAN

Claude Lévi-Strauss

FROM HONEY
to ASHES

*Introduction to a
Science of Mythology: 2*

TRANSLATED FROM THE FRENCH BY
JOHN AND DOREEN WEIGHTMAN

HARPER TORCHBOOKS

HARPER & ROW, PUBLISHERS
NEW YORK, EVANSTON, SAN FRANCISCO

Contents

Illustrations

Table of Symbols

{ △   man
{ ○   woman

△ = ○   marriage (disjunction of marriage: #)

┌──┐
△   ○   brother and sister (their disjunction ⌐//⌐)

△   ○
| |
△   ○   father and son, mother and daughter, etc.

⇒   transformation

→   is transformed into ...

↔   if and only if ...

{ :   is to ...
{ : : as ...

/   contrast

{ ≡   congruence, homology, correspondence
{ ≢   non-congruence, non-homology, non-correspondence

{ =   identity
{ ≠   difference

{ ∪   union, reunion, conjunction
{ // disunion, disjunction

f function

$x^{(-1)}$ inverted x

+, —   these signs are used with various connotations, depending on the context: plus, minus; presence, absence; first or second term of a pair of opposites.

TRANSLATORS' NOTE

All through the first two volumes of *Mythologiques*, we have translated the plural form *nous*, which is common in academic theses and learned articles in French, as 'I', because this seemed to us to give a more natural style in English. However, for reasons which he explains in the recently published Volume 4, *L'Homme nu*, the author has deliberately avoided the first person singular. To be consistent we must continue to use 'I', but we shall give an additional explanatory note at the appropriate point in Volume 4.

TO MONIQUE

Foreword

The present work, the second in a series devoted to the study of myths, continues the inquiry which was begun in *The Raw and the Cooked*. This being so, I have made a point of restating at the outset, although in a new light, information essential to readers unacquainted with the previous volume, who nevertheless wish to begin confidently on this one. It aims to show that the world of mythology is round, and therefore does not refer back to any necessary starting-point. The reader can begin where he chooses and yet be sure of completing the course, provided he heads always in the same direction and advances patiently and steadily.

Both in France and other countries, the method employed in the first volume and the findings put forward have given rise to much discussion. The time has not yet come, I think, for me to reply to what has been said. Rather than allow the argument to take a philosophical turn which would very soon have a sterilizing effect, I prefer to carry on with my task and add more evidence. Opponents and defenders alike will thus have further documents at their disposal. When the undertaking is almost completed and I have produced all my witnesses and displayed all the exhibits, the case can be heard.

For the time being, then, I will do no more than thank those who have helped me in my task. Jesus Marden dos Santos, director of the *Serviço de Meteorologia do Brasil*, Djalma Batista, director of the *Instituto Nacional de Pesquisas da Amazonia*, Dalcy de Oliviera Albuquerque, director of the *Museu Paraense Emilio Goeldi*, and Mme Claudine Berthe of the *Muséum national d'histoire naturelle* supplied invaluable meteorological or botanical information. Mme Jacqueline Bolens assisted in the assembling of the material from German sources, and translated it. Mlle Nicole Belmont helped me with documentation and illustrations.

TOWARDS HARMONY

Et encore estandi l'angre sa main tierce foiz et toucha
le miel, et le feu sailli sus la table et usa le miel sanz
faire à la table mal, et l'oudeur qui yssi du miel et
du feu fu tresdoulce.

'De l'Ystoire Asseneth', p. 10; in *Nouvelles*
Françoises en prose du XIVe siècle.
Bibl. elzévirienne, Paris, 1858

Metaphors inspired by honey are among the oldest in the French language, as well as in others of earlier date. The Vedic hymns often link milk and honey and, according to the Bible, the Promised Land was to flow with both these substances. The words of the Lord are 'sweeter than honey'. The Babylonians regarded honey as the most fitting offering for the Gods, since the latter demanded a food untouched by fire. In the *Iliad*, earthenware jars of honey were used as an offering to the dead. In other contexts, such jars served as repositories for their remains.

For several thousand years now, phrases such as *tout miel* (all honey) and *doux comme miel* (sweet as honey) have been current in Western civilization. Metaphors inspired by the use of tobacco are, on the contrary, recent and easily datable. Littré mentions only two: *cela ne vaut pas une pipe de tabac* (that is worthless) and *tomber dans le tabac* (to fall on hard times). Such slang phrases, many other variants of which could be quoted (cf. Vimaître),[1] can also be found in other languages: in English, 'not to care a tobacco for' means to care very little for somebody or something; and in Portuguese *tabaquear* means to mock or poke fun at someone (Sébillot). Among French sailors, expressions such as *il y aura du tabac* and *coup de tabac* indicate bad weather. *Coquer, fourrer, foutre, donner du tabac* and, more recently, *passer à tabac, tabasser* mean to ill-treat, bully, belabour (Rigaud, Sainéan, Lorédan-Larchey, Delvau, Giraud, Galtier-Boissière and Devaux).

Honey and tobacco are both edible substances yet neither, strictly speaking, depends in any way on cooking. For honey is made by non-human beings, the bees, who supply it ready for consumption, while the most common method of consuming tobacco places the latter, contrary to honey, not on the *hither side* of cooking but *beyond* it. It is not consumed in the raw state, as is honey, nor exposed to fire before consumption, as is the case with meat. It is burnt to ashes, so that the

[1] See Bibliography, pp. 477–92, for full information on this and other titles.

smoke thus released can be inhaled. Now, everyday speech (I am taking my examples chiefly from French, but am convinced that similar observations could be made on the basis of other languages, either directly or by a simple process of transposition) bears out the fact that the expressions *à miel* (with honey, or honey as adjective) and *à tabac* (tobacco, ditto) form a pair, and are used to convey antithetical ideas, which in turn are situated on various levels. I am not forgetting, of course, that some phrases including the word 'honey' constitute borderline cases in which the connotation becomes pejorative: 'honeyed discourse', 'honeyed words', and even *miel* alone, when used as an interjection in French, with the present participle *emmiellant*,[2] a practice which is not simply based on a similarity of sound convenient for young ladies who consider themselves to be well-bred.[3] Far from disregarding these distortions of meaning, I shall explain their existence. But even so, there would seem to be no doubt that, in Western civilization, 'honey' and 'tobacco' phrases stand in opposition to each other. In spite of a certain amount of overlapping, what I would like to call their points of semantic balance are differently placed; the 'honey' phrases are mainly eulogistic, the 'tobacco' phrases on the whole disparaging. They denote respectively abundance and dearth, luxury and poverty; and either gentleness, kindliness and serenity – 'Manare poetica mella', or unruliness, violence or confusion. Perhaps, if we had further examples to hand, we might even say that the former stand in a certain relationship to space (*tout miel* 'all honey'), the latter in a certain relationship to time (*toujours le même tabac* 'always the same old thing').

The sentence which I have used as the epigraph to this Introduction shows that the oppositional relationship we are concerned with existed, in a sense, before the two substances formed a pair. Before tobacco was even known in Europe, the 'honey fire', lit by the supernatural power of the angel, marked out the place of the absent term and anticipated its properties, which had to be those of a correlative and antithetical

---

[2] *C'est un miel* (it's a honey). This is a slang phrase, used by the Parisian lower classes indiscriminately and mostly inappropriately. If they approve of, or admire something, they say '*C'est un miel*'; equally if they go into some foul-smelling place. At the sight of a bloody combat with bare fists or knives, they will say: '*C'est un miel*' (Delvau). '*C'est un miel*: It is very pleasant and (ironically) very unpleasant' (Lorédan-Larchey). This wide semantic range is already present at least by implication in the belief held by the Greeks and Romans, and which was probably Egyptian in origin, that a swarm of bees would inevitably spring from the rotting carcass of a calf which had been asphyxiated in a confined space by the blocking up of its respiratory passages, and whose flesh had been beaten to make it disintegrate without damage to the skin (Virgil, *Georgics*, IV, vv. 299–314, 554–8).

[3] TRANSLATORS' NOTE: *Miel* and *emmiellant* are used euphemistically for *merde* and *emmerdant*.

term of liquid honey, corresponding to it point by point in the complementary scale of the dry, the burnt and the aromatic. The fact that the *Ystoire Asseneth*, from which the example is taken, is most probably the work of a late medieval Jewish author throws a still more curious light on the medieval interpretation, also Jewish nevertheless, of the verse in Leviticus prohibiting the offering of honey on altars, because of the unpleasant smell of burnt honey. At any rate, the discrepancy shows that, in medieval times and perhaps even earlier, honey was a 'marked' term in respect of fumes and smell, which were later to become the essential modes of tobacco. The fact that the oppositional relationship existed before the substances themselves, or at least before one of them, enables us to understand how it was that, as soon as tobacco became known, it combined with honey to form a pair endowed with supreme virtues. In an English play written by William Lily at the end of the sixteenth century (1597) and whose title, *The Woman in the Moone*, is not without analogies in the mythology of the New World, as will be seen in the next volume, the heroine, Pandora, wounds her lover with a sword and, seized with remorse, sends for medicinal herbs with which to dress the cut:

> Gather me balme and cooling violets,
> And of our holy herb nicotian
> And bring withall pure honey from the hive
> To heale the wound of my unhappy hand.[4]

I find this quotation particularly gratifying since it unexpectedly emphasizes the link which, by way of the previous volume, *The Raw and the Cooked*, unites the present work to *The Savage Mind*. (The French title, *La Pensée sauvage*, also means 'The Wild Pansy', a flower closely related to the violets in the quotation.) And it also testifies to a long-established connection in England between honey and tobacco, a connection which still seems to exist on the technical level. We Frenchmen tend to think that English brands of tobacco are closer to honey than our own. We often explain the affinity by imagining, rightly or wrongly, that the pale leaves of English tobacco have been macerated in honey.

Unlike Europe, South America has always been familiar with, and partaken of, both honey and tobacco. It therefore provides an especially rewarding field for the semantic study of the opposition between them, since both diachronically and synchronically, honey and tobacco

[4] Quoted by Laufer, p. 23.

can be observed there side by side over a long period. In this respect, North America seems to stand in a symmetrical relationship to the Old World, since, in recent times, that part of the Continent, apparently, was acquainted only with tobacco, honey having almost completely disappeared, whereas Europe was perfectly familiar with honey at the time when tobacco was introduced as a novelty. I shall return to this problem again later (Vol. III). It follows that tropical America, on which I drew in the previous volume to study the contrast between the two fundamental categories of cooking, the raw and the cooked, which are the constituent elements of the meal, proves also to be an appropriate area for the analysis of a second pair of opposites – honey and tobacco – in so far as these substances offer complementary characteristics; the former being infra-culinary, and the latter meta-culinary. It is along these lines that I propose to continue my research into the mythic representations of the transition from nature to culture. As I develop my inquiry and extend the area of investigation, I shall be able to follow up the previous investigation into the mythic origin of cooking, with an examination of what might be called the *peripheral adjuncts of the meal*.

In doing so, I shall, as always, keep to the plan which is prescribed by the actual contents of the myths. Neither honey, nor tobacco, nor the idea of establishing a connection between them on a logical or concrete level is to be considered as a speculative hypothesis. On the contrary, these themes are explicitly suggested by certain myths, encountered and partially studied in the course of the previous volume. To spare the reader the necessity of referring back to that work, here is a brief recapitulation.

My opening remarks in *The Raw and the Cooked*, the first volume in the series, had, as their starting-point, a story told by the Bororo Indians of central Brazil, relating to the origin of storms and rain (M_1). I began by showing that, without postulating any relationship of priority between this and other myths, it could be reduced to a transformation by inversion of a Ge myth relating to the cooking of food (M_7–M_{12}); the Ge linguistic group is geographically and culturally very close to the Bororo, and the myth exists in different tribal variants. All the myths referred to have as their central theme the story of a bird-nester, marooned at the top of a tree or a rocky cliff as the result of a quarrel with an affine (brother-in-law, sister's husband or father in a matrilineal society). In one instance, the hero punishes his persecutor by sending down rain which puts out domestic fires. In other instances, he brings back to his parents the burning log of which the jaguar was master, thereby procuring cooking fire for the human race, instead of taking it from them.

Noting that in the Ge myths and in a myth belonging to a neighbouring group (Ofaié, M_{14}), the jaguar, master of fire, occupies the position of an affine, since he married a human wife, I established the existence of a transformation which, in its regular form, is exemplified by myths belonging to Tupi tribes adjacent to the Ge: Tenetehara and Mundurucu (M_{15}, M_{16}). As in the previous instance, these myths portray a brother-in-law (or, on this occasion, several) who are 'takers' of women. But the myths with which we are now concerned do not depict an animal brother-in-law who protects and feeds the human hero personifying the group of affines, but describe a conflict between one or several superhuman heroes (demiurges and relatives) and their human affines (sisters' husbands) who refuse them food; as a result of which they changed into wild pigs, or more accurately into tayassuidae of the queixada species (*Dicotyles labiatus*), which did not exist as yet and which the natives consider to be the superior form of game, representing meat in the highest sense of the term.

So, as we move from one group of myths to the next, we see that they depict either a human hero and his relation (by marriage): the jaguar, the animal master of cooking fire; or superhuman heroes and their relations (by marriage): human hunters, the masters of meat. The jaguar, although an *animal*, behaves *courteously*: he gives food to his human brother-in-law, protects him from his wife's spitefulness and allows the stealing of cooking fire. The hunters, although *human*, behave *savagely*: they keep all the meat for their own use, and indulge in unrestrained intercourse with the wives they have been given, without offering any gifts of food in return:

(*a*) [Human/animal hero] ⇒ [Superhuman/human heroes]
(*b*) [Animal, courteous brother-in-law → eater of raw food]
⇒ [Humans, savage brothers-in-law → eaten cooked]

This double transformation is also repeated on the etiological level, since one of the groups of myths deals with the origin of the cooking of food and the other with the origin of meat; the *means* and the *matter* of cooking respectively:

(*c*) [fire] ⇒ [meat]

The two groups are not only symmetrical in structure, they also stand in a dialectical relationship to each other: meat had to exist before man could cook it; this meat, which occurs in the myths in the superior form of the flesh of the queixada, was cooked for the first time with the help of the fire obtained from the jaguar, presented in the myths as a hunter of pigs.

Having reached this stage in the demonstration, I was anxious to test its accuracy through one of its consequences. If a Bororo myth (M_1) was transformable into Ge myths (M_7–M_{12}) on the same axis, and if in turn the Ge myths were transformable into Tupi myths ($M_{15,16}$), on a different axis, the whole group could only constitute a closed set, as I had supposed, on condition that there existed other transformations situated possibly along a third axis, and allowing us to move back from the Tupi myths to the Bororo myths which were themselves a transformation of the original myth. Observing a methodological rule to which I remain systematically faithful, I had, then, to subject the two Tupi myths to a kind of filtering process in order to discover what residue, if any, of mythic material had remained unused during the previous operations.

It was at once obvious that there was such a residue and that it consisted of the series of devices used by the demiurge to change his wicked brothers-in-law into pigs. In M_{15}, he ordered his nephew to shut the culprits up inside a prison made of feathers, to which he set fire, with the result that the suffocating smoke brought about their transformation. M_{16} starts off in the same way, except that the demiurge is helped by his son, and that it is the tobacco smoke injected into the feather enclosure which plays the decisive part. A Kayapo-Kubenkranken myth about the origin of wild pigs (M_{18}), and which I had previously shown to be necessarily a derivation from the other two, or from one of them, provided a weak variant of the magic transformation, which in this instance is attributed to the use of a charm made from feathers and thorns. I therefore proposed (RC, p. 101) to arrange the magic methods in the following pattern:

[1](tobacco smoke, M_{16}), [2](feather smoke, M_{15}), [3](feather charm, M_{18})

In addition to the fact that the above arrangement is the only logically satisfying one, since it takes into account both the derivative nature of M_{18} in relation to M_{15} and M_{16} and the simultaneous presence of the smoke in M_{15} and M_{16} and the feathers in M_{15} and M_{18}, it is confirmed by a famous myth of the Cariri Indians, which was transcribed at the end of the seventeenth century by the French missionary Martin de Nantes. The Cariri myth (M_{25}) also explains the origin of wild pigs, which it attributes to the greed of the first men who begged the demiurge to let them taste this hitherto unknown meat. The demiurge took the children off to the sky and changed them into young wild pigs. Henceforth, men would be allowed to hunt the wild pig, but they would be deprived of the demiurge's company. The latter decided to stay in the sky and he arranged for tobacco to take his place on earth. In this myth, therefore, tobacco also plays a decisive role, but in an even more powerful form than in the Mundurucu version (M_{16}): from being a simple magical substance it becomes the hypostasis of a divinity (cf. M_{338}). There is, then, a series in which tobacco smoke is the weak form of personified tobacco, feather smoke the weak form of tobacco smoke, and the feather charm the weak form of feather smoke.

This much having been established, how do the Bororo describe the origin of wild pigs? One of their myths (M_{21}) explains that the animals were once men and that their wives, in order to avenge an insult, served them a stew of prickly fruits. When their throats were scratched by the prickles, the men grunted 'ú, ú, ú . . . ' and were changed into wild pigs, which utter this cry.

This myth has a two-fold claim on our attention. In the first place, the magical role played by the thorns links up with the charm made of feathers *and thorns*, which occurred in M_{18}. When looked at from this angle, it is seen to follow on after M_{18} in the series of magical transformations to which it adds a new variant, without changing the order in which the others had been arranged. But in another respect, the Bororo myth effects a reversal: instead of the incident arising from a quarrel between affines, as it does in M_{15}, M_{16} and M_{18}, it is the result of a quarrel between husbands and wives. For a discussion of this transformation, I refer the reader to the previous volume (*RC*, p. 91) where I showed it to be typical of Bororo mythology. In the present instance, it therefore results from the application of the general rule on which it depends:

(*a*) *In the case of a non-varying message* (in this instance, the origin of wild pigs):

Mundurucu, etc. $\left[\begin{array}{c} \overset{//}{\underset{\triangle \quad \bigcirc}{\rule{1cm}{0pt}}} = \triangle \end{array} \right] \Rightarrow$ Bororo $\left[\bigcirc \neq \triangle \right]$

Going one stage further, I felt compelled to ask myself whether there did not exist among the Bororo a myth reproducing the family circumstances depicted by the Mundurucu etc. myths about the origin of wild pigs, while at the same time transmitting, if not the same message, at least a transformed version of the message. I identified M_{20} as such a myth. The chief characters in it are ancestors who used to live in huts made of feathers at some distance from their brother-in-law (their sister's husband), from whom they obtained all they wanted by sending one of their younger brothers to him as a go-between (compare: M_{15}, *nephew as guest*/M_{16}, *son as go-between*).

One day they wanted some honey, but all they obtained was a thick, scummy substance, unfit for eating. This was because, in defiance of the taboos, the brother-in-law had had intercourse with his wife when it was being gathered. The wife herself added insult to injury by spying on her brothers while they were engaged in designing and making shell necklaces and beads. Because of the insult, the heroes built a pyre and threw themselves into the flames, whence they rose again in the form of birds with ornamental feathers. Later cotton, gourds and the urucú were to spring from their ashes (*RC*, pp. 92–3).

The etiological functions of this myth are at once more limited and more broadly significant than those of the Tupi myths, which also take as their starting-point a quarrel between affines; more limited since, as is often the case among the Bororo, the myth is intended to explain the origin not of one or several vegetable or animal species, but of varieties or sub-varieties. At the beginning of the myth, the birds were already in existence, otherwise the heroes could not have lived in huts made of feathers and down. But the birds which rose up from the sacrificial fire had 'prettier and more brightly coloured' plumage. Similarly, the myth makes it clear that the plants which sprang up among the ashes belonged to varieties of superior quality – for instance, a kind of urucú which gave a red unequalled for the dyeing of cotton. This initial limitation of the etiological field is accompanied by yet another. The Bororo myth does not claim to explain how one vegetable or animal species came to be available to the whole human race, or even to the tribe in general, but rather why certain varieties or sub-varieties came to belong to one particular clan or sub-clan. In this respect, the myth is particularly eloquent, not only on the subject of plants but also about the adornments designed by the heroes, and which, before they die, they divide out among the various family groups composing their clan.

Although more limited in these two respects, the Bororo myth can claim to be more broadly significant in a third, since its etiological function is, in a sense, intensified. The Tenetehara and Mundurucu myths with which I would like to compare it deal with the origin of one animal – the pig, in other words with good meat, whereas the Bororo myth deals, on the one hand, with the origin of certain birds with beautiful feathers and, on the other, with the origin of several vegetable products, also of exceptional quality.

But there is more to be said. The animal species the origin of which is traced in the Tupi myths is described purely in terms of food, whereas the animals and vegetables in the Bororo myth are described purely in their relationship to technology. The new birds are distinguished from the others by the ornamental richness of their plumage and none of the new plants have any food value: they serve only for the manufacture of useful articles and ornaments. Although the three myths, M_{15}, M_{16} and M_{20}, undoubtedly have the same starting-point, they develop contrapuntally (see the diagram on p. 26), in accordance with the second rule, complementary to the one on p. 23, and which can now be formulated as follows:

(b) *In the case of a non-varying armature* (here: $(\triangle \quad \circ = \triangle))$:

Mundurucu, etc. $\left[\text{ origin of meat } \right] \Rightarrow$ Bororo $\left[\text{ origin of cultural objects } \right]$

I can now summarize the general line of my argument. The myths about the origin of wild pigs are concerned with a kind of meat which the natives put into a superior category, and which is therefore, *par excellence*, the raw material for cooking. It is therefore legitimate, logically, to treat these myths as functions of the myths about the origin of domestic fire, the latter describing the means, the former the matter, of culinary activity. Now, just as the Bororo transform the myth about the origin of cooking fire into a myth about the origin of rain and storms – in other words, of water – we have confirmed that, with them, the myth about the origin of *meat* becomes a myth about the origin of *cultural objects*. Or, to put it another way, in the one instance we have a crude, natural material which is situated on the *hither side* of cooking and, in the other, technical and cultural activity which lies *beyond* cooking.

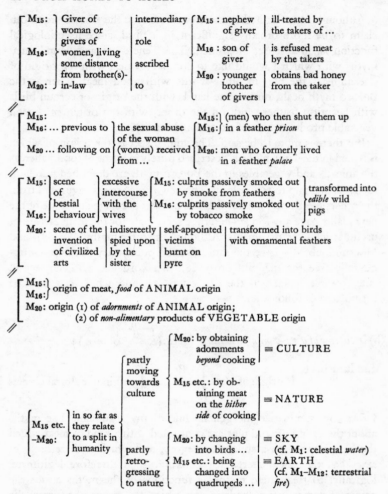

M_{15}: M_{16}: M_{20}:	Giver of woman or givers of women, living some distance from brother(s)-in-law	intermediary role ascribed to	M_{15} : nephew of giver	ill-treated by the takers of …
			M_{16} : son of giver	is refused meat by the takers
			M_{20} : younger brother of givers	obtains bad honey from the taker

//

M_{15}: M_{16}: … previous to M_{20} … following on	the sexual abuse of the woman (women) received from …	M_{15}: M_{16}: (men) who then shut them up in a feather *prison*
		M_{20}: men who formerly lived in a feather *palace*

//

M_{15}: M_{16}:	scene of bestial behaviour	excessive intercourse with the wives	M_{15}: culprits passively smoked out by smoke from feathers M_{16}: culprits passively smoked out by tobacco smoke	transformed into *edible* wild pigs
M_{20}:	scene of the invention of civilized arts	indiscreetly spied upon by the sister	self-appointed victims burnt on pyre	transformed into birds with ornamental feathers

//

M_{15}: M_{16}:	origin of meat, *food* of ANIMAL origin
M_{20}:	origin (1) of *adornments* of ANIMAL origin; (2) of *non-alimentary* products of VEGETABLE origin

//

M_{15} etc. $-M_{20}$: in so far as they relate to a split in humanity

partly moving towards culture
- M_{20}: by obtaining adornments *beyond* cooking ≡ CULTURE
- M_{15} etc.: by obtaining meat on the *hither side* of cooking ≡ NATURE

partly retrogressing to nature
- M_{20}: by changing into birds … ≡ SKY (cf. M_1: celestial *water*)
- M_{15} etc.: being changed into quadrupeds … ≡ EARTH (cf. M_1–M_{12}: terrestrial *fire*)

It is easy to show that, with this transformation, the sequence comes full circle and that the group of myths we have been dealing with is, in this respect, cyclical in character. First, we worked out the following transformation:

(*a*) Ge [origin of cooking (fire)] ⇒ $Bororo$ [origin of anti-cooking (fire) = water]

We then moved on to:

(*b*) Ge [origin of cooking fire (= *means*)] ⇒ $Tupi$ [origin of meat (= *substance*) for cooking]

The third and last transformation, which has just been determined, can be expressed as follows:

(c) *Tupi* [origin of meat (cooking substance)]⇒ *Bororo*
[origin of adornments (*anti-matter* of cooking)]

since we have seen that the adornments came from non-edible parts of animals (shells, feathers) and from plants (gourds, cotton, urucú) which have no use as food. The initial contrast between the means (of cooking) and its opposite, has therefore simply been transformed into a contrast between the substance (for cooking) and its opposite. The Bororo myths always stand in the same relationship to these two pairs of opposites.

All I have said so far was demonstrated in *The Raw and the Cooked* with the help of the same or different arguments. I now propose to deal with a different aspect of these myths, which did not need to be examined in the previous volume, or which was only mentioned incidentally. I established earlier that, in the series of magical means described by the Cariri, Mundurucu, Tenetehara and Kubenkranken myths to explain the transformation of humans into pigs, tobacco was the relevant term. We should not be surprised by the fact that no reference is made to tobacco in the Bororo myth about the origin of cultural objects, since it resembles the Tupi myths as regards its armature, and transmits an inverted message which presupposes a different vocabulary. We thus see the emergence of a new term, which is missing from the other myths: this is honey, the refusal of which, or more precisely the offer of which in the form of a variety of inferior quality, acts as the determining factor in the transformation of the heroes into birds, concurrently with their *sister's* 'incestuous' behaviour, of which the Mundurucu myth presents a symmetrical image, in the form of the excessive copulation of the husbands with their wives (who are the hero's *sisters*).

It will also be remembered that in the Bororo myth about the origin of wild pigs, which is symmetrical with the other, since in this instance, and when it is compared with the Tupi-Ge group on the same theme, the message seems to be identical and the armature inverted, an unpleasant stew (full of thorns) replaces the poor quality honey (lumpy instead of smooth). The magical means in the Bororo myths, which tend towards the moist, thus contrast with the magical means in the Ge-Tupi series (tobacco or feather smoke, feather and thorn charm) which tend towards the dry, a contrast which is congruous with the one between the Bororo myth about the origin of water and the Ge-Tupi myths about the origin of fire, that I took as my starting-point.

In actual fact, the situation is rather more complex, since only one of the two Bororo myths is entirely 'wet': this is M_{21}, in which the disagreement between husbands and wives arises in connection with fishing (fish : aquatic game, forming a triangle with the birds : celestial game in M_{20}, and the pigs : terrestrial game in M_{16} etc.) and ends with the victory of the women, thanks to a preparation of stewed fruit (stewed fruit = *vegetable* ∪ *water*/*fish* = *animal* ∪ *water*). Conversely, the dry plays an essential part in M_{20}, with the pyre on which the heroes deliberately choose to be burnt to death, and which seems to be homologous (although more emphatic in character) with the burning feathers in M_{15}, and the burning tobacco in M_{16}. But, although the terms are undeniably homologous, they are opposed to each other as regards the ultimate purposes for which they are respectively used. The burning on the pyre – of the heroes themselves, and not of a product intended for their consumption – constitutes a double 'ultra-culinary' process, which therefore has a *supplementary* relationship with its result: the appearance of adornments and ornaments which are also 'ultra-culinary', since they fall within the domain of culture, whereas cooking is a technical activity ensuring a transition between nature and culture. In M_{15} and M_{16}, on the contrary, the burning of the feathers and tobacco which is also 'ultra-culinary' in type although to a lesser degree, occurs as a *complementary* process of its result, which is the appearance of meat, a doubly 'infra-culinary' object, since it is at once the natural and preliminary condition for the existence of cooking.

This difficulty having been solved, I am now more free to emphasize the opposition between honey and tobacco which emerges from the myths for the first time at this point, and with which we shall be concerned to the end of this book. The fact that these two terms belong to the same pair of opposites was established by the exclusive presence of one or other in M_{20} and M_{16}, which, for independent reasons, I showed to be reversed as regards their message. It should be added at this point that a term correlative with the 'bad' honey – i.e. the 'bad' stewed fruit – appears in M_{21}, which is identical with M_{16} as regards its message (origin of wild pigs), but reversed as regards its armature

$$\left(\circ \neq \triangle / \triangle \overbrace{\qquad}^{-/\!/-} \circ = \triangle \right)$$ and doubly reversed (both as regards armature and message) in relation to M_{20}. Honey and stewed fruit are classed

as vegetable substances (this is obvious as regards the stewed fruit; it will be demonstrated later in the case of honey), both belonging to the category of the moist. 'Bad' honey is defined as being thick and lumpy, in contrast to good honey, which consequently is smooth and runny;[5] the 'bad' stewed fruit is full of prickles, which similarly make it thick and rough to the tongue. Honey and stewed fruit are therefore analogous; and at the same time we know that, in the series of magical means, the prickly stewed fruit comes after the feather and thorn charms in M_{18}, which is a weakened transformation of the feather smoke in M_{15}, which, in turn, stands in the same relationship to the tobacco smoke in M_{16}. Finally, as we have just seen, by broadening the series, it is possible to establish the relationship of correlation and opposition between honey and tobacco.

We thus have fresh evidence of the fact that the system revolves round the central theme of tobacco. Only tobacco worthy of the name unites properties that are normally incompatible. A Bororo myth (M_{26}) about the origin of tobacco or, to be more accurate, of the different species of fragrant leaves smoked by the Indians, describes how the latter, on trying them for the first time, pronounced some to be good and others unpleasant, according to whether the smoke was 'pungent' or not. The terms of the series of magical means whereby men were changed into animals are therefore linked. Tobacco smoke and smoke from burning feathers are both pungent, but one is foul-smelling and the other scented; stewed fruit is tasty (since people eat it in any case) but may be more or less well prepared; smooth to the palate when the prickles have been removed, or extremely prickly; honey, too, can be smooth or lumpy. So there are two kinds of smoke, two kinds of stewed fruit and two kinds of honey. Finally, in the homomorphic myths (those which have the same armature), honey and tobacco are in a relationship of symmetrical inversion.

We now find ourselves faced with an interesting problem. Tropical America offers us, in the first place, a mythological system relating to the origin of cooking, which, according to the groups considered, is presented either directly (origin of fire), or in an inverted form (origin of water). Let us therefore call the direct form of this first system S_1, and the inverted form, S_{-1}, which we shall leave aside for the moment. By turning S_1 back upon itself from the point of emergence of one of

[5] The Umutina invocation to honey – the Umutina are close cousins of the Bororo – clearly brings out the fact that fluidity is one of the main properties demanded: 'To give a lot of honey ... soft, sweet and liquid ... like water. To give honey which flows like river water, sweet as clayey water, and not to give thick honey (pollen)' (Schultz 2, p. 174).

its elements (the episodic appearance of a wild pig), I reconstituted, in *The Raw and the Cooked*, a second mythological system relating to the origin of wild pigs, that is of meat: the substance and pre-condition of cooking, just as fire was the means and instrument of cooking in the first system. The second system, which I will call S_2, I will place arbitrarily to the right of S_1 (since that was the diagrammatic form adopted in *The Raw and the Cooked*, Figure 6, p. 98). This being so, a third system relating to the origin of cultural objects, and symmetrical with S_2 in relation to S_1, will have to be placed to the left of S_1 (since meat and adornments are respectively on the hither side and on the far side of cooking, the origin of which is explained in S_1). The inverted system of S_2 will be called S_{-2}:

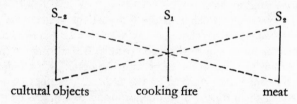

S_{-2} S_1 S_2

cultural objects   cooking fire   meat

Let us confine ourselves for a moment to the examination of what is taking place in the mythic field 'to the right' of S_1. What we see there is S_2, which I previously defined in two ways: it is a mythic system the *aim* of which is to explain the origin of wild pigs, and which uses as a *means* to this end a variety of substances, which I have shown to be combinatorial variants of tobacco smoke. Tobacco therefore emerges in S_2 as an instrumental term. But, just as S_1 (the origin of cooking) inevitably presupposes S_2 (the existence of meat) – since one is the substance used for the other – the use of tobacco as a means in S_2 presupposes its previous existence. In other words, to the right of S_2 there must be a mythological system, S_3, in which tobacco acts as the end and not just the means; which consequently consists of a group of myths about the origin of tobacco; and which, being a transformation of S_2, just as S_2 was a transformation of S_1, ought to reproduce S_1, at least on one axis, so that the group can be considered as closed on that side. Otherwise, it would be necessary to repeat the operation and look for another system, S_4, which would raise a similar query, and so on and so forth until we arrived at a positive answer, or until we lost all hope of succeeding and resigned ourselves to the view that mythology is a genre devoid of redundancy. If this were so, any attempt to create a grammar of mythology would be based on an illusion.

As it happens, I have already isolated the system, S_3, in the previous volume and confirmed that it reproduces S_1. It will suffice to recall that the myths in question are a group of Chaco myths (M_{22}, M_{23}, M_{24}) about the origin of the jaguar (a problem posed by S_1, in which the jaguar appears as master of cooking fire) and of tobacco (a problem posed by S_2). The mere fact that these two terms are found together in the same etiological field is no doubt highly significant. But the most important point is that S_3 does in fact reproduce S_1, since the story follows the same pattern in either case: it tells of a bird-nester (macaws' or parrots' nests) who becomes involved with a jaguar, either male or female (or male in the first instance and subsequently female); either friendly or hostile and, finally, either brother-in-law or wife, i.e. an affine. Furthermore, the myths in S_1 have cooking as their objective – cooking through the medium of 'constructive' fire the function of which is to make meat fit for human consumption. Similarly, the myths in S_3 have tobacco as their objective, through the medium of a destructive fire (the pyre on which the jaguar dies so that the plant springs up from its ashes). This fire is constructive only as regards tobacco, which, unlike meat, has to be burnt (= destroyed) before it can be consumed.

It is therefore clear that to the right of S_2 we have a system, S_3, which transforms it and explains it, while at the same time reproducing S_1, and that consequently the sequence is closed on that side. If we look to the left of S_1, we find S_{-2}, the *purpose* of which is to explain the origin of adornments while using honey as a *means*, and honey is a term which has been independently proved to be symmetrical with tobacco. If the group is in fact closed, we can suppose, not only that there exists to the left of S_{-2} a system S_{-3}, which establishes the existence of honey, as S_3 had already done for tobacco at the other extremity of the field, but which also, as regards content, must reproduce S_1 (although in a different perspective) in a manner symmetrical to the way in which S_3 reproduced S_1. So that S_3 and S_{-3}, each of which reproduces S_1 in its particular fashion, also reproduce each other (see diagram on p. 32).

Let us therefore set out in search of S_{-3}. As far as is known, it was among certain northern Tupi tribes that honey seems to have held the most important place in ceremonial life and religious thought. Like their Tembé relatives, the Tenetehara of Maranhão dedicated their most important festival to honey. It took place every year, at the end of the dry season, that is in September or October. Although it had not been celebrated for very many years, the Indians whom Wagley and Galvão (p. 99) visited between 1939 and 1941 flatly refused to let them hear the honey festival songs because, as they said, the rains had started and to sing out of season might bring down some supernatural punishment upon them.

The festival proper only lasted a few days, but preparations were begun six or eight months in advance. As early as March or April, the

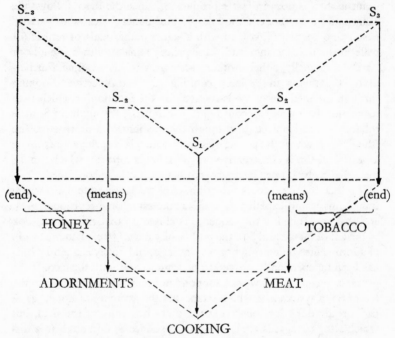

wild honey had to be gathered and stored away in gourds which were hung from the beams of a ceremonial hut, specially built for the occasion. According to the accounts available, there were between 120 and 180 gourds, each one containing more than a litre of honey. They were fastened next to each other and formed from six to eight rows. During the entire period of the honey-gathering, the villagers would assemble every night and sing songs: the women in the ceremonial hut, 'underneath the honey', the men on the dancing arena outside. It appears that the songs referred to different types of game and to the hunting techniques prescribed for each variety. The main purpose of the honey festival was to ensure successful hunting for the rest of the year.

The task of organizing the honey-gathering and the festival fell to an important member of the community, who assumed the title of 'proprietor of the feast'. When he was certain that enough honey had been gathered, he sent messengers to invite the neighbouring villages. Vast quantities of manioc soup and game were prepared and offered to the visitors. Both visitors and hosts greeted each other noisily, but as soon as the newcomers entered the ceremonial hut, the shouts and the sounding of the horns gave way to absolute silence. The men arranged themselves in groups according to their villages, and each group sang in turn. The men of the village which was acting as host were the last to sing. Then the gourds were taken down, but the contents were poured into a large jar and diluted with water before being drunk. The feast continued until all the honey had been consumed. On the morning of the last day, there was a collective hunt, followed by a feast of roasted meat (Wagley–Galvão, pp. 122–5).

There is a myth which explains the origin of the honey festival:

M_{188}. Tenetehara. 'The origin of the honey festival'

One day, Aruwé, a well-known Tenetehara hunter, found a spot where many macaws came to eat seeds from a tree. He climbed into the tree, built a hunting blind and waited. He killed many macaws. When he climbed down from his hunting blind at the end of the day, however, he saw jaguars approaching. He hid again and saw that they came to this tree to collect wild honey. When they left, he returned to his village with the macaws he had killed. He spent the next day hunting from the same tree and with the same excellent luck. He waited until after the jaguars had come and gone before leaving his blind.

One day Aruwé's brother asked him to teach him where to hunt. His brother wanted tail feathers from the red macaw to make decorations for a festival. Aruwé ... instructed him not to climb down until after the jaguars had gone. The brother ... saw the jaguars coming to the tree and, against the advice of his brother, decided to try to kill one. His first arrow missed and the jaguar climbed the tree and killed the brother.

Aruwé waited all one day and all one night for his brother to return. When he did not return he was certain that his brother had been killed by the jaguar. He returned to the spot and saw signs of the battle. He followed the jaguar's tracks which were marked with his brother's blood, until they disappeared at the opening of an ant-hill. Aruwé was a shaman ... he transformed himself into an ant and entered into the hill. Inside he saw many houses: it was the village of the jaguars. Aruwé changed himself into a man again and entered the village in search of his brother. He saw a jaguar woman there who appealed to him. He went with her into her father's house and married her. It was her father who had killed his brother and the father explained how the brother had provoked the jaguars. Aruwé lived with the jaguars for a long time.

Aruwé watched the jaguars leave the village each day for many days and return each day with gourd containers full of wild honey ... At night the jaguar people gathered near the house where they hung the honey and sang beautiful songs unknown to the Tenetehara. Aruwé learned [the dances] and the songs.

Soon afterwards, Aruwé was homesick to see his Tenetehara wife and son. He asked the jaguar people to let him go back to visit them. They agreed on condition that he take his jaguar wife with him. The couple returned to the Tenetehara village. Aruwé asked his jaguar wife to wait outside while he told his Tenetehara wife of his arrival. The Tenetehara wife was happy ... and he stayed a long time. When he went back to the ant-hill his jaguar wife had gone, and she had filled in the entrance of the ant-hill after her. Aruwé returned several times, but he never again found the jaguar village. He taught the Tenetehara how to celebrate the Honey Feast. The Honey Feast as it is celebrated nowadays was taught to the Tenetehara by Aruwé (Wagley–Galvão, pp. 143–4).

Before embarking on a discussion of this myth, I will give the Tembé version (the Tembé are a sub-group of the Tenetehara):

M_{189}. *Tembé.* '*The origin of the honey festival*'

Once upon a time, there were two brothers. One made himself a hide-out at the top of an azywaywa tree, the flowers of which the macaws used to come and eat. He had already killed a great many birds, when two jaguars appeared on the scene carrying gourds which they filled with nectar pressed from the blossom on the tree. For several days running, the hunter watched the animals without daring to kill them, but, in spite of his advice, his brother was less prudent. He shot at the jaguars, without suspecting that they were invulnerable. The animals raised a storm, which shook the tree, bringing down both the hide-out and its occupant, who was killed instantly. They carried off the corpse to the underworld, the entrance of which was as small as an ant hole, and they placed it on a wooden cross standing in bright sunshine.

The hero, after being changed into an ant, came to the jaguars' hut, where vessels full of honey were hanging. He learnt the ritual songs, and every evening he resumed his human form and danced with the jaguars; in the day-time he became an ant again.

When he returned to his village, he told his companions of all he had seen (Nim. 2, p. 294).

The two versions differ only as regards the amount of detail given, and as regards the origin of the honey which, in M_{189}, does not come from bees, but is directly expressed from the yellow flowers of the azywaywa tree, which may be the same as aiuuá-iwa, one of the lauraceae. Whatever the species, this reading is particularly instructive since, unlike our varieties of honey, those found in tropical America do not seem to be extracted mainly from flowers. But the South American Indians, who find honey chiefly in hollow tree-trunks where various kinds of bees make their nests, classify it for this reason as a vegetable. Several Tacana myths (M_{189b}, etc.) describe the unfortunate experience of a monkey, which was cruelly stung when it bit into a wasps' nest, thinking it to be a fruit (H.-H., pp. 255–8). A Karaja myth (M_{70}) tells how the first men, when they emerged from the bowels of the earth, gathered 'great quantities of fruit, bees and honey'. According to the Umutina, the first human beings were created from wild fruits and honey (Schultz 2, pp. 172, 227, 228). The same correlation is found in Europe, among the peoples of antiquity, as is proved by the following quotation from Hesiod: 'At the top of the oak-tree are acorns, in the middle, bees' (*Works and Days*, vv. 232–3) and by various Latin beliefs: in the Golden Age, the leaves of trees secreted honey and bees are still spontaneously generated from foliage and grasses (Virgil, *Georgics*, I, vv. 129–31; IV, vv. 200).

This perhaps explains why the Tupi refer to the bee as iramanha, which Nordenskiöld (5, p. 170; 6, p. 197), following Ihering, takes to mean: 'keeper of the honey' (and not producer). But, according to Chermont de Miranda, the term ira-mya means 'mother of honey'. Barbosa Rodrigues gives iramaña, without any explanatory comment, whereas Tastevin and Stradelli give ira-maia, with the suggestion that the second word is borrowed from the Portuguese *mãe*, 'mother'; Stradelli, however, is not absolutely convinced (see under 'maia, manha'), since his *Vocabulario* mentions a root, manha(na), which has the same meaning as the one proposed by Ihering.

I shall return to this question later. For the moment, it is important to stress the relationship between the Tenetehara and Tembé myths and those in the S_1 group, since it confirms my theory that myths which

Figure 1. Hunting macaws. (A drawing by Riou, based on J. Crevaux, *Voyage dans l'Amérique du Sud*, Paris, 1883, p. 263.)

have honey as their principal theme must reproduce those concerned with the origin of cooking fire, while the latter in their turn are reproduced by the myths about the origin of tobacco (S_3). In all three cases, we are concerned with a bird-nester (or hunter) going after macaws or parrots, and who discovers that one or several jaguars are at the foot of the tree or rock up which he himself has climbed. In all the myths, the jaguar is a relative by marriage, either the husband of a human wife in S_1, a wife who began by being human in S_2, or the father of a jaguar-wife in the myth with which we are now concerned. In S_1 and S_3 the jaguar eats the macaws; in S_{-3} it is the man who eats them. The *two* jaguars in S_1, one masculine and protective, the other feminine and hostile, behave differently towards the *same* man. The *single* jaguar in S_{-2} behaves in equally different ways towards the *two* men: he eats one and gives his daughter to the other. In S_3, where there is only one jaguar and one man, the duality is re-established on the diachronic level, since the jaguar was initially a human wife, who subsequently changed into a man-eating wild beast. The three systems therefore have the same armature consisting of the triad: man (or men), macaws, jaguar(s), whose different behaviour patterns ($+$, $-$) unite the following terms in groups of two:

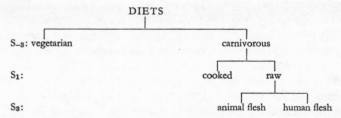

Each mythological system springs from what might be called a dietetic opposition – the raw and the cooked in S_1 (but always with reference to meat): cannibalism and another kind of carnivorous diet (parrots devoured by the woman) in S_3; lastly, in S_{-3}, a carnivorous diet (the man is defined as a killer of macaws) and a vegetarian diet (since we have seen that honey is classed among the vegetable substances). From this point of view, the three systems can be arranged as follows:

```
                          DIETS
                            |
        _____
       |                                            |
S_-3: vegetarian                               carnivorous
                                                    |
S_1:                                        _____
                                           |                |
                                        cooked             raw
                                                            |
                                                     _____
S_3:                                                |               |
                                              animal flesh    human flesh
```

In spite of this seemingly 'open' structure, the group is closed in S_3 and S_{-3}. Of the three systems only S_1 presents a static character: at the beginning, the man is an 'eater of raw food', and the jaguar an 'eater of cooked food', and at the end they simply switch roles. At the beginning of S_{-3}, on the contrary, man is carnivorous and the jaguar vegetarian, and although it succeeds in introducing man to its diet, this is only after it has changed from a vegetarian to a cannibal diet, like the woman who changed into a jaguar in S_3. Symmetrically, the 'cannibalism' of the woman in S_3 (she devours live birds) anticipates and announces her transformation into a jaguar; and as a penalty for having turned man into a food (instead of a consumer of food), the jaguar itself has to undergo the transformation into tobacco: a vegetable food (the situation is congruous with that of consumer of vegetable food in S_{-3}) which must be *reduced to ashes* before being consumed, and is therefore anti-symmetrical with the honey eaten in a *moist* form by the jaguar in S_{-3}. The group is definitely closed, but the closing is dependent on three transformations, which themselves are situated on three axes; there is an identical transformation: *cannibalistic jaguar* ⇒ *cannibalistic jaguar*; and two non-identical transformations, both referring to a vegetarian diet : *food consumed* ⇒ *consumer of food*, and : *burnt* ⇒ *moist*.

Having established the unity of the meta-system constituted by the group {S_1, S_3, S_{-3},} we can now go on to examine in greater detail the relationships between S_1 and S_{-3}; my initial intention was, in fact, to discover S_{-3} as a reproduction of S_1. In this limited perspective, I should like to make three remarks:

(1) It is a characteristic of man to be both vegetarian and carnivorous. From the vegetarian point of view, he is congruous with the macaws (which are always described in the myths as being vegetarian birds, thus forming a pair of opposites with birds of prey, cf. *RC*, p. 324). From the carnivorous point of view, man is congruous with the jaguar. From this double relationship of congruence, S_{-3} deduces a third, directly uniting the jaguars and the macaws, which are similar in respect of honey since they frequent the same tree, either with different purposes (a weak form of the rivalry in M_{188}), or with the same purpose in M_{189} where the macaws eat the flowers from which the jaguars express the nectar. The direct congruence between macaws and jaguars (derived from the two other kinds of congruence between men and macaws and men and jaguars, through the application of an argument of the type: our friends are the friends of our friends)[6] might in theory be established in two ways, either by changing the mythical macaws into carnivorous birds, or by changing the mythical jaguars into vegetarians. The first transformation would be in contradiction with the

---

[6] It is clear from this that mythic thought utilizes two distinct forms of deduction. The congruence between man and the macaw in respect of vegetarianism and between man and the jaguar in respect of carnivorousness, are deduced from empirically observed data. On the other hand, the congruence between the macaw and the jaguar, which can be inferred from the other two instances of congruence, is synthetic in character, since it is not based on experience, and is even contrary to observation. Many apparent anomalies in ethnozoology and ethnobotany can be explained, once it is realized that these systems of knowledge juxtapose conclusions arrived at by what we can, in the light of the preceding remarks, call *empirical deduction* and *transcendental deduction* (cf. my article, 'The Deduction of the Crane', in P. and E. K. Matanda, eds., *Structural Analysis of Oral Tradition* [Philadelphia: University of Pennsylvania Press, 1971]).

unequivocal position occupied by the macaws in other myths. The
second would only be in contradiction with that occupied by the jaguars
if, in S_{-3}, the latter were presented purely and simply as the masters and
originators of a vegetable food – honey. But as it happens, the myths
belonging to this group make no such statement. M_{189} is careful to
distinguish two antithetical ways of eating honey: the way adopted by
the macaws, which is *natural*, since they only eat the flowers (which, in
a sense are 'raw'), whereas the jaguars gather the honey for a *cultural*
purpose: the celebration of the honey festival. The jaguars are not
therefore 'masters of the honey', which the macaws also eat (and that
men no doubt eat too, although at this period they associated no ritual
with the process) but rather 'masters of the honey festival': i.e. initiators of a mode of culture linked furthermore with hunting); and this
confirms, rather than disproves, the part played by the jaguar as master
of another mode of culture – cooking fire – in S_1.

(2) From the point of view of kinship, a transformation occurs when
we move from S_1 to S_{-3}:

$$S_1 \begin{bmatrix} \triangle & = & \overset{\frown}{\bigcirc \quad \triangle} \\ \text{jaguar} & & \text{humans} \end{bmatrix} \Rightarrow S_{-3} \begin{bmatrix} \triangle & = & \overset{\frown}{\bigcirc \quad \triangle} \\ \text{humans} & & \text{jaguars} \end{bmatrix}$$

In other words, men are givers of women in S_1, and takers in S_{-3}.

This transformation is accompanied by another, which is concerned
with attitudes. A remarkable feature of S_1 is the indifference with
which the jaguar appears to receive the news of the murder, or wound-
ing, of his wife by the young hero whom he has adopted as his son
(*RC*, pp. 81–3). His 'profession of indifference' has an exact parallel
in S_{-3}, where the hero is easily convinced that the jaguar who killed
his brother did so in legitimate self-defence (M_{188}), or even allows himself to be so charmed by the songs and dances of the honey festival that
he forgets his original purpose in coming to visit the jaguars, which was
to find or avenge his brother (M_{189}):

(3) Finally there exists, between S_1 and S_{-3}, one last resemblance which, in this instance too, is accompanied by a difference. In both systems, the jaguar plays the part of an initiator of culture – either in respect of cooking, which requires fire, or in respect of the honey festival, which requires water. Cooked food consumed in the profane manner corresponds to the former, while raw food consumed in the sacred manner corresponds to the latter. It can also be said that, along with cooking (accompanied, in S_1, by bows and arrows and yarn), the jaguar brings material cultural benefits to man. With the honey festival, which among the northern Tupi tribes is the most important and most sacred of religious ceremonies, the jaguar brings spiritual cultural benefits. The transition is a decisive one in both instances but, significantly, in the one case it is from the raw to the cooked (and so definitively constitutive of culture), and in the other from profane rawness to sacred rawness (thereby overcoming the opposition between the natural and the supernatural, but in a non-definitive way, since the rites have to be celebrated afresh every year), and so corresponds to the bridging of wider or narrower gaps:

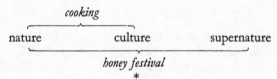

One final aspect of the meta-system remains to be considered, but it will be more clearly understandable if I first briefly recapitulate what has already been said.

Having obtained S_2 by reversing S_1, we found that there occurred in S_2, according to the group concerned, a breaking-up of the sociological armature which, in the case of a non-varying message (origin of wild pigs), takes the form: $\overset{\longmapsto\!\!/\!\!\longmapsto}{\triangle \quad \circ} = \triangle$ among the Tenetehara and the Mundurucu, whereas among the Bororo it is: $\circ \,\#\, \triangle$. When we inquired what message the sociological armature: $\overset{\longmapsto\!\!/\!\!\longmapsto}{\triangle \quad \circ} = \triangle$ in the last-mentioned group corresponded to we discovered that it was the origin of ornaments and adornments, i.e. the origin of cultural objects (S_{-2}).

Setting this finding aside for the time being, we embarked on a third stage by pointing out that the jaguar, both as an animal and as the kindly brother-in-law in S_1, was the counterpart of the pigs in S_2 – brothers-in-law (who had been changed) into animals (because) of their spiteful behaviour. S_2, however, was concerned with the origin of pigs. The question was whether or not there existed a system, S_3, which would account for the origin of the jaguars who were the protagonists in S_1. Certain Chaco myths (S_3) met this requirement and it was particularly significant that, within the same story, they should confuse the origin of the jaguar and the origin of tobacco, since this had the effect of closing the circle: in S_1, the jaguar is the means whereby cooking fire ('constructive fire') is obtained; in S_2, tobacco fire is the means whereby pigs are created (since it causes them to appear); finally, in S_3, the funeral pyre (destructive fire) is the means whereby tobacco is created, since it springs from the jaguar's body, of which it is – and no pun is intended – the 'end' (purpose). Now, tobacco fire occupies an exactly intermediary position between cooking fire and the funeral pyre: it produces a consumable substance, but only after it has been reduced to ashes (RC, pp. 83–107). At the same time as the transformation from S_2 into S_3 was being confirmed, we established three points. Firstly, S_3 reproduced S_1 in respect of the code (story of a bird-nester; a triad formed by man, macaws and the jaguar); secondly, S_3 transformed S_1 in respect of the armature, which became $\bigcirc \mathbin{\#} \triangle$ instead of

$$\underset{\triangle \qquad \bigcirc \;=\; \triangle}{\overline{\rule{0pt}{1ex}\quad}^{\;\#}\,\rceil}$$; finally, this transformation was identical with the one we observed in moving from the Tupi myths to the Bororo myth similarly concerned with the origin of pigs.

This being so, a problem arises. If, among the Bororo, the armature $\bigcirc \mathbin{\#} \triangle$ is already used in S_2, and the armature $\underset{\triangle \qquad \bigcirc \;=\; \triangle}{\overline{\rule{0pt}{1ex}\quad}^{\;\#}\,\rceil}$ in S_{-2}, what kind of family relations must these Indians resort to in order to explain the origin of tobacco? As it happens, they present a further instance of a break-up. since we find that they have two different myths relating to the origin of different species of tobacco.

These myths have already been analysed (RC, pp. 103–7), so I shall do no more than give a brief reminder of them here. One, M_{26}, describes how one kind of tobacco (*Nicotiana tabacum*) sprang up from the ashes of a snake, to which a woman had given birth after being accidentally fertilized by the blood of a boa, which her husband had killed while out hunting, and which she was helping to carry home in pieces. The other myth (M_{27}) is concerned with a species of anonaceous plant, of which the Bororo also smoke the leaves and which they call by the same name as real tobacco. These leaves were discovered by a fisherman in a fish's belly; at first, he smoked them only at night and in secret, but his companions forced him to share with them. To punish them for their gluttony in swallowing the smoke instead of exhaling it – thus depriving the spirits of the offering which was their due – the latter changed the men into otters. As regards M_{26}, I showed it (RC, p. 103) to be rigorously symmetrical with the Chaco myths about the origin of tobacco (M_{23}, M_{24}). No less significant are the connections between M_{26} and the Bororo myth about the origin of wild pigs (M_{21}), of which we have two versions: the one that has already been summarized, and another, older one, which was transcribed in 1917. In spite of some gaps and obscure passages, it transpires from this version that the women, being jealous of their husbands' success at fishing, agreed to prostitute themselves to the otters, on condition that the otters supplied them with fish. Thus the women could claim to be better at fishing than the men (Rondon, pp. 166–70). The story is the same as in the other version, except that the latter draws a veil over the relationship between the women and the otters, which seem to be prompted by less debauched motives.

Although the theme of the animal as seducer is frequent in South American mythology, we know of hardly any instances in which this particular role is ascribed to otters; it is usually fulfilled by the tapir, the jaguar, the caiman or the snake. The Bororo use the tapir as seducer but humanize it (it is a man whose clan eponym is the tapir, M_2) and we find that, in M_{26}, they use the snake, while at the same time reducing its seductive function to a minimum, since the snake in question is not alive but dead, only a section of its body is concerned, not the whole animal, and the fertilizing of the woman occurs accidentally and without her knowledge, by means of the blood (a polluting, but not a fertilizing, liquid) which drips from the piece of flesh she is carrying. Thus, in this instance, an animal which is normally a seducer has its potency reduced; and, similarly, its victim, the woman, is forgiven a sin, which here appears to be rather an effect of mischance. On the other hand, in their myth about the origin of wild pigs, the Bororo have an exceptional seducer – the otter – which plays a particularly active part with regard to the women, while they show themselves to be doubly vicious: they conclude an obscene bargain with the animals in order to get the better of the men in fishing, whereas in a properly organized society, the men catch the fish and the women merely transport it.

Why otters? In the group of Bororo myths we are now examining, they appear in two contexts. According to M_{27}, a fishing expedition, undertaken by a man, led to the discovery of tobacco through the medium of a fish, which was kept hidden from other men; and the inhaling of the tobacco smoke led to the transformation of men into otters. According to M_{21}, the transformation of the otters into men (= seducers of human wives: the Rondon version, in fact, refers to them as 'men') leads to a fishing expedition, undertaken by women, which deprives the men of fish and causes them to change into pigs, after eating stewed fruit full of prickles. There is, then, a relationship between the *direction* of one transformation: men into otters, or otters into men (in one instance, it is metonymical: it concerns *part* of the men; in the other, it is metaphorical: the otters copulate with the women *like* men) and the contents of the other transformation, relating to a substance which was swallowed when it ought to have been ejected: tobacco or stewed fruit; but either with metaphorical intent (so that the tobacco smoke could assume the *function* of an offering to the spirits) or metonymically (by the spitting out of the prickles which were *part* of the stewed fruit).

If we now remember that, in the Mundurucu myth (M_{16}) about the origin of wild pigs, the inhaled tobacco smoke (which in the Bororo myth changes men into otters) brings about their transformation into pigs (whereas, in the case of the Bororo, the prickly stewed fruit fulfilled this function), we shall be able to understand the reason for the presence of the otters, the masters of fish in the same way as the pigs are masters of terrestrial game (for evidence of this, cf. *RC*, pp. 117–18). The two species are symmetrical, granted the various transformations, which are homologous among themselves, from the *dry* to the *moist*, from *tobacco* to *stewed fruit*, from *hunting* to *fishing*, and finally from *fire* to *water*. The argument can be summarized in the two formulae:

(a) M_{16}[men ⇒ pigs], M_{27}[men ⇒ otters] $= f$[inhaled smoke]

(b) M_{21}[men ⇒ pigs] $= f$[smoke = stewed fruit], [otters ⇒ men]

Having thus – with the help of M_{16} – reduced the codes of M_{27} and M_{21} to a single unit by using their common properties which, in the case of M_{16} and M_{21}, lie in the fact that they are myths of origin about the same animal species: wild pigs, and in the case of M_{16} and M_{27}, that they have recourse to the same agent, tobacco smoke, which, when inhaled, causes the men to be changed into different animal species, we can effect the same reduction by starting with M_{26} which, like M_{27}, is a myth about the origin of tobacco. It is obvious that M_{26} is a transformation of M_{27} and M_{21} in respect of the dry and the moist: the tobacco (in M_{26}) comes from an animal corpse which has been *thrust into fire* instead of being *taken out of water*, as it is in M_{27}. And the resulting substance consists of smoke, which is good on condition that it is *pungent*,[7] and thus contrasts with the *drink* in M_{21}, which the men made the fatal mistake of believing to be good, for the simple reason that they never thought it would be *pungent*.

This two-fold transformation: [*out of water*] $\Rightarrow$ [*into fire*] and [*drink*] $\Rightarrow$ [*smoke*], is a clear inversion, in the body of Bororo mythology, of the transformation governing the transition from the Ge and Tupi myths about the origin of fire to the corresponding Bororo myth (M_1), which we know to be a myth about the origin of water. If we confine ourselves to the Bororo group (M_{21}, M_{26}, M_{27}), which is, in fact, the subject of the present discussion, the transformations which must inevitably command our attention are those correlative to the sociological armature. M_{21} describes a quarrel between husbands and wives about fishing, the women refusing to collaborate with their husbands as carriers of fish, which is the role normally assigned to them in accordance with the rules governing the division of labour between the sexes, and claiming the right to fish on their own account, like the men, and better than the men, a claim which leads them to becoming the otters' mistresses. Everything happens the other way round in M_{26}: the activity is hunting, not fishing, and the women are keen to collaborate with their husbands, since they respond to the whistling set up by the hunters some way from the village, and run to help them to carry the pieces of meat. As I have already pointed out, these docile wives have no trace of perversity. Fate alone is responsible for the fact that in totally non-erotic circumstances, one of them is contaminated, rather than seduced, by a piece of meat.[8] The fact that it is meat from a snake, a phallic animal and a seducer figuring in innumerable myths of tropical America, emphasizes still further that M_{26} is aimed very carefully at neutralizing these characteristics.

[7] M_{26}, which is marvellously explicit on this point, says that when men first encountered tobacco, they 'gathered the leaves and put them to dry; then they rolled them into cigars, which they lit and began to smoke. When the tobacco was strong, they would say: "This one is strong, it is good!" But when it wasn't strong, they would say: "It is bad, it is not pungent." ' (Colb. 3, p. 199.)

TRANSLATORS' NOTE: The French terms used by the author, and which we have translated as 'pungent', are *piquante, il pique*, which can also mean 'stinging', 'prickly' and 'sharp' (of a drink).

[8] Cf. *RC*, p. 152, n. 6, in connection with the Bororo horror of blood.

The same kind of neutralization of the quarrel between husbands and wives as that which forms the armature of M_{21} can be observed in M_{27}, although it is expressed in a different way. Let us say that, in M_{26}, the husbands and wives remain but the quarrel disappears, whereas the contrary is true in M_{27}, where the quarrel remains but the husbands and wives disappear. In M_{27}, there is definitely a quarrel, but it occurs between companions of the same sex – whose functions in respect of fishing are alike instead of being complementary. And yet one of them tries to keep for himself the miraculous result of a collective undertaking, and only decides to share it when he is discovered and cannot do otherwise.

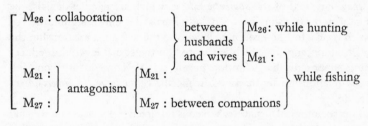

We are now in a position to reply to the question which was raised a little while ago. In order to explain the origin of tobacco, the Bororo who are, as it were, 'short' of an armature, re-use the one that has already served to explain the origin of wild pigs, and which is the same as the one employed by the Chaco tribes for the origin of tobacco: $\bigcirc \neq \triangle$, which can be generalized in the form $\bigcirc / \triangle$, contrasting with $\bigcirc \cup \triangle$. But since this armature already fulfils a different role in their myths, they vary it by taking it as far as it will go in the two possible directions: either they keep the terms and abolish the relationship: $(\bigcirc / \triangle) \Rightarrow (\bigcirc \cup \triangle)$, or they keep the relationship, and abolish the difference between the terms: $(\bigcirc / \triangle) \Rightarrow (\triangle / \triangle)$. So they imagine either collaboration between husbands and wives which is impaired from without by fate, or collaboration between individuals of the same sex which is impaired from within through a perverse action committed by one of them. As there are two solutions, there are two myths explaining the origin of tobacco, and as these solutions are reversed, the myths too are reversed in respect of vocabulary, since one species of tobacco comes from water, the other from fire.

Consequently, the transformation of the sociological armature, which is a feature of the mythical systems as a whole {S_1 (origin of fire), S_{-1} (origin of water), S_2 (origin of meat), S_{-2} (origin of cultural objects or advantages), S_3 (origin of tobacco), S_{-3} (origin of the honey festival)} is not completely exhausted by its canonical expression: $\left[\begin{smallmatrix} & \overset{\shortmid\!\!/\,\shortmid}{} & \\ \triangle & O = \triangle \end{smallmatrix} \right] \Rightarrow \left[O \neq \triangle \right]$. Beyond [O # $\triangle$], it can still produce further results. As has been established, the myths approach the disjunction between husbands and wives from two points of view: the techno-economical, since in illiterate societies there is generally a division of labour according to the sexes to bring out the full significance of the matrimonial state; and the sexual. By alternately choosing one or other viewpoint and taking it to its logical conclusion, we obtain a series of sociological terms ranging from the character of the *perverse companion* to that of the *apathetic seducer*, which are parallel denials, the first of a relationship between individuals the entire significance of which is on a techno-economic level, and the second, a relationship the entire significance of which is situated on the sexual level, the seducer being supposedly by definition purely sexual; consequently, one lies *beyond* relationship by marriage, while the other is *on the hither side* of kinship.

This sociological armature, which is refracted twice over and for that reason somewhat blurred in outline, nevertheless remains discernible throughout the Bororo myths relating to the origin of tobacco (without raising any doubts about their transformational relationship with the Chaco myths on the same theme) and it is also found in myths situated at the opposite end of the semantic field, that is in the Tembé and Tenetehara myths dealing with the origin of the honey festival (M_{188}, M_{189}). In both versions, the hero has a brother who turns out to be a *vicious companion*: a fault which brings about his disjunction. The hero then sets off in search of his brother, but he forgets about him almost immediately, on being captivated ($=$ *seduced*) by the songs and dances of the honey festival. Later he is *seduced* by the welcome given him by his own people and forgets his *jaguar/wife*, whom he cannot find anywhere when he sets off to look for her.

Having reached this point in my analysis, I could declare myself satisfied and consider that I had succeeded in bringing all the myths into 'harmony' with each other, like the instruments of an orchestra which, after the confused din of their tuning-up, begin to vibrate in unison, if there did not remain one discordant element in the meta-system that I am using, as it were, as an orchestra in order to play the score which, after a fashion, is constituted by this book. At one end of the semantic field, we find not one but two groups of myths explaining the origin of tobacco: the Chaco myths with a sociological armature [$\bigcirc \# \triangle$], which explain the origin of tobacco *in general*, for the benefit of *humanity as a whole* (from the latter point of view, the sending out of messengers to the neighbouring villages, referred to in the myths, indicates an outlook which is 'open' to the external world); and then beyond these myths, those of the Bororo, the sociological armature of which presents a doubly refracted image of the preceding armature, and which are about the origin of *particular varieties* of tobacco for the benefit of *specific clans* of a tribal society. It follows that, both as regards object and subject, the Bororo myths have a synecdochic relationship with the Chaco myths: they consider parts of the whole (a part of tobacco and part of the smokers), instead of considering the whole.

But although, at this end of the semantic field, we have too many myths at our disposal, the opposite occurs at the other end, where we have too few. Myths (M_{188}, M_{189}), which I used to make good this deficiency, are not strictly speaking, nor as might have been expected, myths about the origin of honey: they are myths about the origin of the honey *festival* – a social and religious rite and not a natural product, although the natural product is necessarily involved in the ritual. So, at this point, a group of myths about the origin of honey is missing, a group which, as one reads the diagram on p. 32 from right to left, ought to figure immediately before, or to the side of, S_{-3}. If we postulate the existence of such a group, as a working hypothesis, it follows that system S_{-3}, which is concerned with honey, is symmetrically reduplicated by system S_3, which deals with tobacco. Finally, the symmetry between S_{-3} and S_3 must conceal an obvious dissymmetry on another level: the two groups of myths about the origin of tobacco have, as I have said, a synecdochic relationship with each other, a relationship which, if we take the terms in the broader sense, is a form of metonymy. Whereas, if there are any myths about the origin of the honey proper, their relationship with the myths about the origin of honey *festival* must be that of signified to signifier, the actual honey acquiring a significance it lacks as a natural product, when it is gathered and consumed for social and religious purposes. In such a case, the relationship between the two groups of myths would be metaphorical in nature.

Such considerations determine the direction of the inquiry I am now about to undertake.

PART ONE THE DRY AND THE DAMP

Si quando sedem augustam seruataque
mella
thesauri relines, prius haustu sparsus
aquarum
ora foue, fumosque manu praetende
sequacis.

Virgil, *Georgics*, IV, vv. 228–30

1 *The Dialogue Between Honey and Tobacco*

Bees, like wasps, are hymenopterous insects, and several hundreds of species of them, arranged in groups of thirteen families or sub-families, for the most part solitary, are to be found in tropical America. But only the social bees produce honey in sufficient quantities to serve as food: *pais de mel*, 'fathers of honey', is the charming Portuguese description; they all belong to the Meliponidae family, and the *Melipona* and *Trigona* species. Unlike European bees, the Meliponidae are stingless, and they are also smaller in size. But they can be extremely troublesome because of their aggressive behaviour, which explains why one species is known colloquially as *torce cabellos*, 'hair-twister'; and they can cause even greater distress when in their tens, or even hundreds, they fasten onto the face and body of the traveller in order to suck his sweat and his nasal and ocular secretions. This explains the colloquial name for the species *Trigona duckei*: *lambe olhos*, 'lick-eyes'.

The person attacked very soon becomes infuriated by tickling sensations occurring in particularly sensitive spots – inside the ears and nostrils and in the corners of the eyes and mouth – and which it is impossible to put a stop to by means of the sudden movements we normally use to drive insects away. The bees which become heavy and, as it were, drunk with human food seem to lose the desire, and perhaps even the the ability, to fly away. Their victim, weary of beating the air to no purpose, is very soon driven to striking his face, a fatal move, because the squashed, sweat-laden corpses glue the surviving insects to the spot and act as a lure for others, which are attracted by the prospect of a further meal.

The everyday experience I have just described is enough to show that the Meliponidae have a more varied diet than European bees, and do not disdain food of animal origin. More than a century ago, Bates noted (p. 35) that the bees in the Amazonian regions fed not so much on flowers as on the sap from trees and on bird droppings. According to Schwartz (2, pp. 101–8), the Meliponidae are attracted to a great variety of substances, from nectar and pollen to decaying carcasses, urine and excrement. It is, therefore, not surprising that the honey they produce is very different, in colour and consistency as well as in taste and chemical composition, from the honey produced by the *Apis mellifica*. The honey made by the Meliponidae is often very dark, always liquid and slow to crystallize, because of its high water content. Unless it is boiled, which is a possible method of ensuring its preservation, it soon ferments and turns sour.

Ihering, from whom I have borrowed the above details (see his article, 'As abelhas sociaes indigenas') states clearly that sucrose, of which an average proportion of ten per cent is present in the honey of the *Apis mellifica*, is completely absent from the honey made by the Meliponidae, which instead contains levulose and dextrose, but in far higher proportions (30–70 per cent and 20–50 per cent respectively). As levulose has a considerably greater sweetening capacity than sucrose, the many different varieties of honey produced by the Meliponidae have a richness and subtlety difficult to describe to those who have never tasted them, and indeed can seem almost unbearably exquisite in flavour. A delight more piercing than any normally afforded by taste or smell breaks down the boundaries of sensibility, and blurs its registers, so much so that the eater of honey wonders whether he is savouring a delicacy or burning with the fire of love. These erotic overtones do not go unnoticed in the myths. On a more commonplace level, the high sugar content and powerful flavour of the varieties produced by the Meliponidae give honey a status which is not comparable with that of any other food and also mean that it has almost always to be diluted with water before it is eaten.

Certain kinds of honey, which are alkaline in composition, have a laxative effect and are dangerous. This is the case with the honey of a few species of Meliponidae, belonging to the *Trigona* sub-group, and especially the varieties of honey made by wasps (Vespidae), which are said to be equally as 'intoxicating' as the honey of a *Trigona* bee known in the State of São Paulo as *feiticeira*, 'witch', or: *vamo-nos-embora*, 'off we go' (Schwartz 2, p. 126). Other varieties of honey are definitely poisonous; for instance, the honey produced by the wasp known in Amazonia as *sissuira* (*Lecheguana colorada*, *Nectarina lecheguana*), which was probably responsible for the poisoning Saint-Hilaire suffered from (III, p. 150). This occasionally toxic effect can probably be explained by the fact that the insects have fed on poisonous species of flowers, as has been suggested in the case of *Lestrimelitta limão* (Schwartz 2, p. 178).

Be that as it may, wild honey has an attraction for Indians that no other food can equal, an attraction which, Ihering has noted, is tantamount to a passion: '*O Indio ... (e) fanatico pelo mel de pau.*' In Argentina too,

> the greatest diversion and keenest pleasure enjoyed by the rural peon is that of honey-gathering. For a spoonful of honey he is ready to work an entire day around a trunk and often endangers his life. One cannot estimate the risk which people are prepared to take in the mountains for the sake of honey. All that is needed is that a peon observe a small portal of wax or a cleft in a trunk to make him go immediately for a hatchet and to overturn or at the least destroy a beautiful trunk of the most valued species (Spegazzini, quoted by Schwartz 2, p. 158).

Before setting off to gather honey, the Ashluslay of the Chaco bleed themselves above the eyes in order to increase their luck (Nordenskiöld 4, p. 49). The Abipones, who used to live on the borders of Paraguay and Brazil, and whose distant descendants are the Caduveo of the southern part of the Mato Grosso, explained to Dobrizhoffer (Vol. II, p. 15) that they used to pluck their eyebrows very carefully, so that they would have no difficulty in following the flight of an isolated bee as it made its way to its nest: this is a method of locating with the naked eye which we shall encounter shortly in a myth belonging to a neighbouring community (p. 70).

Ihering's comment refers more particularly to *mel de pau*, or 'wood honey', which is found in two forms: in nests stuck to the surface of the trunk or hanging from a branch, and which, according to their appearance, are given picturesque names: 'manioc cake', 'tortoise shell', 'vagina', 'dog's penis', 'gourd' etc. (Rodrigues 1, p. 308, n. 1); or inside hollow trees, where certain species, chiefly the mandassaia bee (*Melipona quadrifasciata*), knead together the wax they secrete and the clay they collect to make various kinds of round 'pots' whose capacity varies from three to fifteen cubic centimetres, and which may be present in sufficient quantity to give a yield of several litres of the most deliciously flavoured honey (Figure 2).

These bees, and other species too perhaps, have been partly domesticated in certain areas. The simplest and most common method consists in leaving a certain amount of honey in the hollow tree in order to induce the swarm to return. The Paressi catch the swarm in a gourd, which they leave near the hut, and several tribes in Guiana, Colombia and Venezuela do the same, or bring back the hollow tree, suitably trimmed, and hang it parallel with the roof beams; or they may even hollow out a trunk specially (Whiffen, p. 51; Nordenskiöld 5, 6).

Mandassaia

Figure 2. Mandassaia bee (*Melipona anthidioides quadrifasciata*) and its nest. (After Ihering, cf. *loc. cit.*, under 'mandassaia'.)

The so-called 'earth' or 'toad' honey (*Trigona cupira*), which is less abundant than wood honey, is found in underground nests, with entrances often beginning a long way from the actual nests and so minute that only one insect at a time can pass through. After hours and days of patient watching in order to locate the entrance, it is necessary to dig for several hours more before obtaining a very meagre quantity of honey – about half a litre.

We can conclude from these various observations that the different kinds of honey in tropical America are found in insignificant or appreciable (but always very uneven) quantities, according to whether they are produced by earth or tree species; and that the tree species include bees and wasps whose honey is as a general rule poisonous; and finally, that the various kinds of bee honey can be either sweet or intoxicating.[1]

This three-fold division, although no doubt too simple to be an accurate reflection of the zoological reality, has the advantage of corresponding to native categories. Like other South American tribes, the Kaingang-Coroado think of bees and wasps as being opposites, bees having been created by the demiurge, and wasps by the deceiver, along with poisonous snakes, the puma and all the animals hostile to man (Borba, p. 22). It must not be forgotten that, although the Meliponidae do not sting (but sometimes bite), the wasps of tropical America include some highly poisonous species. But within this major opposition between bee honey and wasp honey, there exists another opposition, less absolute since it includes a whole series of intermediary stages, between harmless and intoxicating kinds of honey, whether these kinds are produced by different species, or derive from the same honey which varies according to whether it is eaten fresh or fermented: the taste of honey differs with the species and the time at which it is gathered, and may range from extremely sweet to acid and bitter (Schultz 2, p. 175). As we shall see later, the Amazonian tribes make a systematic use of the poisonous kinds of honey in their ritual in order to induce vomiting. The Caingang of southern Brazil consider honey as having two strongly contrasted properties. They regard honey and raw vegetables as being cold foods,[2] the only foods to be given to widowers and widows, who would be in danger of constipation and death if they ate meat or any other cooked food (Henry 1, pp. 181–2). However, other groups of this same population distinguish between two different varieties of beer made from maize: one is a simple extract of maize called 'goifa', and the other, 'quiquy', has honey added to it (this is the only use that this particular community makes of honey). The honey beer, which is 'more intoxicating' than the other sort, is drunk without food and it induces vomiting (Borba, pp. 15, 37).

This two-fold division of honey, which almost everywhere is separated into the categories of the sweet and the bitter, the harmless and

[1] It would perhaps be more accurate to say that they produce a drugged effect, and cause paralysis and depression, whereas wasp honey tends to cause nervous excitement with overtones of gaiety (Schwartz 2, p. 113). But the problems relating to the poisonous nature of the various kinds of South American honey are still far from being definitively solved.

[2] Unlike Mexicans, who classify honey among the 'warm' foods (Roys 2, p. 93).

the poisonous, even among groups who have no knowledge of fermented drinks or do not use honey in their preparation, is clearly illustrated by a Mundurucu myth, which has already been summarized and discussed (*RC*, pp. 267–8). I indicated at the time, however, that I was keeping a version of it in reserve to be examined in a different context. Here it is:

M₁₅₇ᵦ. Mundurucu. 'The origin of agriculture'

In former times, game and cultivated plants were unknown to the Mundurucu. They fed on wild tubers and tree fungi.

It was then that Karuebak, the mother of manioc, arrived and taught men the art of preparing it. One day, she ordered her nephew to clear an area of the forest, and she announced that soon bananas, cotton, caras (*Dioscorea*), maize, the three varieties of manioc, water-melons, tobacco and cane sugar would grow there. She ordered a ditch to be dug in the newly cleared area, and asked to be buried in it. Care should be taken, however, not to walk over her.

A few days later, Karuebak's nephew found that the plants listed by his aunt were growing on the place where she lay; however, he inadvertently walked on the hallowed ground, and the plants at once stopped growing. This determined the size to which they have grown ever since.

A sorcerer, displeased at not having been informed of the miracle, caused the old woman to perish in the hole where she lay. Since she was no longer there to advise them, the Indians ate manikuera raw, not knowing that this particular variety of manioc is poisonous and emetic in that form. They all died, and next morning went up into the sky where they became stars.

Other Indians, who had eaten manikuera first raw and then cooked, were transformed into honey flies. And those who licked the remains of the cooked manikuera became the kind of bees which produce bitter, emetic honey.

The first Mundurucu Indians who ate water-melons also died, since the fruit had been brought by the devil. This is why the Mundurucu call water-melons 'the devil's plants'. The surviving Indians kept the seeds and planted them, and the water-melons which grew from these seeds were harmless.

Since that time people have had no hesitation in eating them (Kruse 2, pp. 619–21. There is an almost identical variant in Kruse 3, pp. 919–20).

The version noted down by Murphy in 1952-3 and which I used in the previous volume is both remarkably similar to, and remarkably different from, those given by Kruse. The similarity lies in the contrast between two types of food, one consisting of the straightforwardly edible plants, and the other of the one or two plants which can be eaten only after undergoing a transformation. In the Murphy version, only timbó is mentioned as belonging to the second category; timbó is the fish poison the Mundurucu grow in their plantations and which, although not directly eaten as food, is consumed indirectly, as it were, in the form of the fish which it allows the Indians to catch in huge quantities. The Kruse versions quote timbó in the list of cultivated plants which were to grow from the body of old mother Karuebak, but do not enlarge upon its characteristics in the way the Murphy version does. Instead, they present two themes: the water-melons which only become edible in the second generation, after the seeds have been planted and cultivated by the Indians themselves, and the manikuera, which is also only suitable for consumption in a modified state, after it has been cooked in order to rid it of its toxicity.

Let us leave the water-melons aside for the moment (we shall come back to them later) and assume that the manikuera in M_{157b} takes the place of the timbó in M_{157}. The first men ate manikuera in three forms: raw, cooked and as left-overs, that is, without unduly straining the wording of the myth, in a rancid state and belonging to the category of the rotten. The eaters of raw manioc were changed into stars. It must be realized that, at the time, 'there was neither sky, nor Milky Way, nor Pleiades,' only mist and hardly any water. Because of the absence of sky, the souls of the dead vegetated under the roofs of the huts (Kruse 3, p. 917).

I have two observations to make in connection with this point. In the first place, the eating of raw poisonous manioc leads simultaneously to the appearance of the sky and to disjunction, for the first time, between the dead and the living. The disjunction in the form of stars is the result of an act of gluttony, since to avoid death, men ought to have postponed their meal instead of rushing at it. Here we find a link with a Bororo myth (M_{34}), which explains the origin of stars by the transformation of children who had been greedy. Now – and this is my second observation – I put forward elsewhere (RC, pp. 240-43) reasons for believing that these stars are the Pleiades. The specific mention of the Pleiades at the beginning of the Mundurucu myth gives weight to this suggestion, which will be given definitive confirmation later in the present volume. We shall in fact see that while the Pleiades represent, as it were, the first term in a series also including sweet honey and bitter honey, certain Amazonian myths associate the Pleiades directly with the poisonous honey which here occupies an intermediary position (that of poisoner) between the change undergone by the men who ate raw (poisoned) manioc and that undergone by those who ate cooked manioc and who are a danger neither to themselves nor to others and consequently occupy a neutral position between two strong positions.[3]

It follows that honey, like fish poison, occupies an ambiguous and equivocal position in the general scheme of vegetable foods. Timbó is both a poison and a means of procuring food; it is not directly edible in one form, but is indirectly edible in another. The distinction, stated explicitly in M_{157}, is replaced in M_{157b} by another more complex distinction, in which honey is both associated with, and opposed to, poison. The substitution of honey for fish poison in two very close variants of the same myth might well have some empirical foundation, since in one region of Brazil – the valley of the Rio São Francisco – the crushed nest of an aggressive species of melipona, which produces a rare and unpleasant-tasting honey (*Trigona ruficrus*), is used as fish poison with excellent results (Ihering, under 'irapoan'). But, apart from the fact that this method of fishing has not been described as existing among the Mundurucu, there is no need to assume that it was once more widespread in order to understand that the qualities attributed to honey by the myths constantly fluctuate between two extremes: either it is thought of as a food, whose richness and sweetness make it superior to all others, and therefore the object of ardent desire; or as a particularly treacherous poison, since the nature and seriousness of its effects are always unpredictable, depending, as they do, on the variety of the honey, where and when it was gathered and the circumstances in which it is eaten. But this imperceptible transition from the category of the delectable to that of the poisonous is not a feature peculiar to

---

[3] The order adopted by the myth: the poisoned > the neutral > the poisoners is puzzling only if the double contrast it observes is not noticed:

$$\begin{cases} raw : \text{mortal} \\ cooked : \text{non-mortal} \end{cases} \begin{cases} \text{fresh } (+) \\ \text{rancid } (-) \end{cases}$$

It is nevertheless remarkable that, in this pattern, the rotten appears as a *terminus ad quem* of the cooked, instead of the raw being the *terminus a quo* of the cooked, as in most of the myths of tropical America. In respect of this transformation, which is probably correlative with certain methods of preparing fermented drinks, cf. *RC*, pp. 159–60.

South American honey, since it can also be seen as a characteristic of tobacco and other plants with a similar narcotic effect.

Let us begin by noting that the South American Indians count tobacco as a 'food', along with honey and fish-poison. Colbacchini (2, p. 122, n. 4) observes that the Bororo 'do not use a special verb to denote the action of smoking a cigar; they say "okwage mea-ǧi", "eating a cigar" (literally "with the lips enjoy the cigar"), while the cigar itself is called "ké", "food" '. The Mundurucu have a myth the opening episode of which suggests the same link between tobacco and food:

M_{190}. *Mundurucu. 'The insubordinate page'*

There lived in the village of Macuparí the chief of which was Karudaiibi, a man named Wakörebö. Now Wakörebö had a wife in the village of Uaradibika, and he went there often to visit her. On one occasion he arrived when the men were all absent and only the women were in the village. He repaired to the men's house and found there a young boy whom he ordered to bring fire to light his cigarette. The boy refused, saying impudently that cigarettes were not food. Wakörebö explained to him that for men cigarettes were food, but the boy still refused to perform the errand. This angered Wakörebö so much that he picked up a stone and hurled it at the boy, striking him in the head and killing him instantly (Murphy 1, p. 108; cf. Kruse 2, p. 318).

In spite of their uneven distribution, the two species of cultivated tobacco – *Nicotiana rustica* (from Canada to Chile) and *N. tabacum* (restricted to the Amazonian basin and the West Indies) – would both seem to have come originally from the Andes, where domestic tobacco had apparently been obtained by the cross-breeding of wild species. Paradoxically enough, it seems that tobacco was not smoked in this region in pre-Columbian times, and that it was originally chewed or taken as snuff. Very soon, however, it was replaced by the leaves of the coca plant. The paradox recurs in tropical America where, even at the present time, some tribes smoke tobacco, while adjoining tribes are unacquainted with it or prohibit its use. The Nambikwara are confirmed smokers, and are hardly ever seen without a cigarette in their mouths, or slipped under a cotton arm-band or into the pierced lobe of the ear. Yet their neighbours, the Tupi-Kawahib, have such a violent dislike for tobacco that they look disapprovingly at any visitors who dare to smoke in their presence, and even on occasions come to blows with them. Such differences are not infrequent in South America, where the use of tobacco was no doubt even more sporadic in the past.

Even in those areas where tobacco is known, it is consumed in very diverse ways. When it is smoked, pipes may be used, or it may be made into cigars or cigarettes; in Panama, the lit end of the cigarette was placed in the mouth of a smoker, who blew the smoke out so that his companions could inhale it through their cupped hands. It seems that, in the pre-Columbian era, the use of pipes was rarer than the making of cigars and cigarettes.

Tobacco was also ground to a powder and sniffed up through the nose, either by one person or two people together (thanks to a small instrument with a bent nozzle which made it possible for the tobacco to be blown into the nostrils of a companion, either in its pure state or blended with other narcotic plants such as *piptadenia*); or eaten in powder form, chewed, or sucked in the form of a sticky syrup, thickened by boiling and evaporation. In several regions of Montaña and Guiana, the Indians drink tobacco after boiling the leaves, or simply leaving them to soak.

The methods of using tobacco may be very varied, but the same is true of the intended result. Tobacco is consumed either individually or collectively: either in solitude, or by two or several people together; and either purely for pleasure or for ritualistic purposes which may have to do with magic or religion. A sick man is sometimes treated by being made to inhale tobacco fumes. Or someone about to be initiated, or to become a priest or healer is purified by being made to imbibe greater or lesser quantities of tobacco juice in order to induce vomiting, followed sometimes by loss of consciousness. Lastly, tobacco is used to make offerings of leaves or smoke by which it is hoped to attract the attention of the Spirits and communicate with them.

And so, like honey, tobacco, the profane use of which allows it to be classed as a food, can in its other functions possess the exactly opposite characteristic: it can act as an emetic and even as a poison. It has been confirmed that a Mundurucu myth about the origin of honey is careful to distinguish between these two aspects. The same is true of a myth about the origin of tobacco, belonging to the Iranxé or Münkü, a small tribe who live in a region to the south of the Mundurucu:

M_{191}. *Iranxé (Münkü). 'The origin of tobacco'*

A man had behaved badly towards another man, who was determined to take his revenge. Using a fruit-gathering expedition as a pretext, the latter got his enemy to climb a tree, and there he left him, after removing the pole that had been used to make the ascent.

The prisoner, who was starving, thirsty and emaciated, caught sight of a monkey and called to it for help; the monkey agreed to bring him some water, but claimed to be too weak to help him get down. A thin, foul-smelling urubu (vulture), succeeded in rescuing him and then took him back to its home. It was the master of tobacco, of which it possessed two kinds, one good and the other poisonous. It presented them to its protégé so that he could learn to smoke the former and use the latter as a means of revenge.

When the hero returned to the village, he gave the bad tobacco to his persecutor who was seized with a fit of giddiness and changed into an ant-eater. The hero went after him and, having come upon him unawares in broad daylight when he was asleep, killed him. He invited his benefactor, the urubu, to eat its fill of the decayed corpse (Moura, pp. 52–3).

The above myth, of which we possess only this one obscure and elliptical version, is extremely interesting on several counts. It is a myth about the origin of tobacco which, as I had already postulated (and confirmed in the case of the Chaco myths on the same subject), reflects myths about the origin of fire: the hero is a fruit-picker (homologous with the bird-nester) stranded at the top of a tree and saved by a fearsome animal (ferocious like the jaguar, or revolting like the urubu) in which the hero bravely places his trust, and which is master of a cultural advantage, as yet unknown to man, that it bestows upon him: cooking fire in the one instance, tobacco in the other, which we know to be a food like cooked meat, although the way in which it is consumed places it beyond cooking.

However, the Chaco myths we used in the construction of system S_3 (origin of tobacco) were in the main a reproduction of the myths in S_1 (origin of fire), whereas M_{191} provides further evidence by being a still closer reflection of S_{-1}: i.e., the Bororo myth about the origin of water (M_1).

Let us begin by establishing this point. It will be remembered that, unlike the Ge myths about the origin of fire, the Bororo myth about the origin of wind and rain (M_1) begins with an incestuous act committed by an adolescent boy who rapes his mother and whose father is resolved on revenge. The Iranxé myth does not refer explicitly to incest, but the expression used by the informant in his dialectal Portuguese, 'Um homem fêz desonestidade, o outro ficou furioso', clearly seems to refer to some kind of sexual misdemeanour, since the normal meaning of the word 'desonestidade' in the inland districts of Brazil implies some act contrary to the rules of decency.

There is nothing in the Ge myths about the origin of fire which corresponds to the helpful monkey episode in M_{191}, but it is reminiscent of the series of three helpful animals in M_1 which help the hero to achieve success in the expedition to the aquatic realm of the souls. The link between the two myths is confirmed when we see that, in M_1, the hero overcomes the presence of water (he succeeds in crossing it), while in M_{191} he overcomes the absence of water, since the monkey brings him some kind of fruit already broken open and full of refreshing juice to alleviate his thirst. When I compared M_1 with a Sherente myth (M_{124}), which also has a thirsty hero who is helped by animals, I showed (RC, pp. 205–6) that there was a transformation allowing the transition from the monkey to the pigeon, which occupies a central position among the three helpful animals in M_1.

The jaguar, which plays the main role in system S_1 (M_7–M_{12}), is absent from M_1 and M_{191}. In both cases, it is replaced by the urubu or urubus which come to the hero's aid.

At this point, however, the problem becomes more complex. The urubus in M_1 behave ambiguously: to begin with, they show no pity (and even feed on the hero's flesh), and only later do they behave with compassion (by bringing the hero down to ground level). The same ambiguous behaviour occurs in M_{191}, but this time the animal is the monkey. To begin with, it shows compassion (by quenching the hero's thirst) but later behaves callously (by refusing to take the hero back to the ground). From the point of view of symmetry, the urubu in M_{191} corresponds more closely to the pigeon in M_1 (one is related to air, the other to water) as regards the non-ambiguous nature of their respective behaviour, since the urubu gives the hero tobacco, and the pigeon makes him a present of the rattle, and – as I shall establish later – tobacco and the rattle are linked.

There is no doubt, then, that the transition from one myth to the other is possible, although it can only be effected by means of a series of chiasmi:

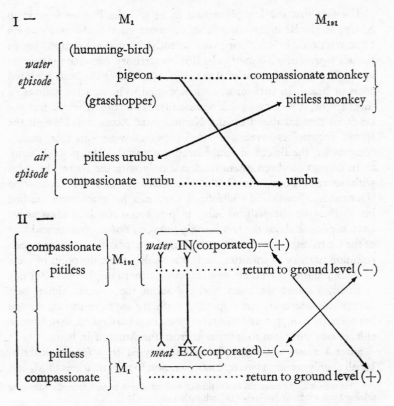

Finally, we can observe one final point of resemblance between M_{191} and M_1. In both myths (and contrary to what occurs in those in system S_1), the hero takes his revenge on his persecutor by transforming *himself* into an animal (a species of deer in M_1) or by changing the *persecutor* into an animal (an ant-eater in M_{191}). The change is either self-imposed or imposed on another, but it always ends with the death of the opponent and his being devoured, either in a fresh or rotten state, by an aquatic/cannibal (M_1) or by an aerial/carrion-eater (M_{191}). A good deal might be said about the deer/ant-eater contrast, since I have established elsewhere that these two species form a pair with the jaguar (which replaces one or other of them in S_1): either diachronically (since mythical deer were man-eating jaguars), or synchronically (since the ant-eater is the opposite of a jaguar). For more details about this two-fold argument, cf. *RC*, pp. 138–9, 188–9.

The fact that the Iranxé version in S_3 and the Bororo version in S_{-1} are so similar in structure raises ethnographical problems to which I can refer only briefly. Until very recently the vast zone stretching to the north-west of what used to be Bororo territory, between the sources of the Tapajoz and those of the Xingu, was one of the least explored areas of Brazil. In 1938–9, when I happened to be near the sources of the Tapajoz, it was impossible to reach Iranxé territory, which was not far from that inhabited by the Nambikwara, because – although the Iranxé themselves were said to be peace-loving – another hostile community, the Beiços of Pau, barred the way (L.-S. 3, p. 285). Since then, contact has been established, not only with the Iranxé, but also with several tribes – the Caiabi, the Canoeiro and the Cintalarga[4] (Dornstauder, Saake 2) – which, if they can be completely studied before they die out, will probably help to transform such ideas as we have at present about the relationship between Bororo culture and that of the Ge tribes, more especially the Tupi farther north. It has long been common practice to consider the Bororo solely from the point of view of their affinities with their western and southern neighbours. But this is chiefly because we knew nothing about the cultures along their northern borders. In this respect, the affinity we have just confirmed between their myths and those of the Iranxé, suggests that Bororo culture was also open to influences from the Amazonian basin.

Since I must, unfortunately, restrict myself to a formal analysis, I shall simply mention two features common to the armatures of M_1 and

[4] This tribe is in the headlines at the time of writing, as can be seen from the following three-column article in *France-Soir* (March 14th–15th, 1965):

120 BRAZILIANS SET UPON BY
INDIANS WITH A TASTE FOR HUMAN FLESH
(From our special permanent correspondent, Jean-Gérard Fleury.)

'Rio de Janeiro, March 13th (by cable). Alarm in Brazil: armed with bows and arrows, Indians of the formidable cannibal tribe known as "broad belts" are besieging Vilh-Na (*sic*: Vilhena?), a village with a population of 120 inhabitants which lies off the Belem–Brasilia road (?).

'An air-force plane has flown over the area to drop antidotes against the curare which the Indians use to poison the tips of their arrows.

'The "broad-belt" Indians, who are traditionally partial to human flesh, recently tried out a new recipe: they grilled a captured *gaucho*, after smearing him all over with wild honey.'

Whether or not this story is of local origin, it provides admirable illustration of the fact that the native South Americans, whether they be peasants of the Brazilian hinterland or Indians, regard honey as an extreme food, since its use in conjunction with that other extreme food, human flesh, represents a peak of horror that ordinary cannibalism would perhaps be incapable of inspiring. The Guayaki of Paraguay, who are cannibals, believe there are two kinds of food which are too strong to be eaten in their pure state – honey, to which they add water, and human flesh, which must be stewed with palm kernels (Clastres).

M_{191}, which help to explain why they are developed in the same way. Both myths are obviously etiological in character. They deal either with the origin of celestial water which puts out domestic fires, thus causing men to regress to a *pre-culinary* state, or rather (since the myth does not claim to explain the origin of cooking) to an *infra-culinary* state; or with the origin of tobacco, that is, a food which has to be burnt before it can be consumed, and whose introduction consequently implies an *ultra-culinary* use of cooking fire. M_1 therefore brings the human race back *to the hither side* of the domestic hearth, whereas M_{191} takes it *beyond*.

Both myths are off-centre in relation to the institution of the domestic hearth, and also resemble each other in another way, which similarly distinguishes them from the myths grouped together in S_1. Etiologically, they run along parallel and complementary lines. M_1 explains simultaneously how the hero becomes *master of fire* (his hearth-fire being the only one not put out by the storm), and his enemy (along with all the other inhabitants in the village) the *victim of water*. M_{191} explains simultaneously how the hero becomes *master of good tobacco*, and his enemy the *victim of bad tobacco*. But in both myths, only the appearance and consequences of the negative term are commented upon at length (involving in each instance the death of the hero's opponent), since, in M_1, the swamp where the piranhas live is a function of the rainy season, just as, in M_{191}, the transformation of the culprit into an ant-eater is a function of the enchanted tobacco, whereas the positive term receives virtually no mention.

But there is more to it than that. The pair of opposites: water $(-)$/fire $(+)$ in M_1 corresponds, as we have just seen, to the pair of opposites tobacco $(-)$/tobacco $(+)$ in M_{191}, and we know already that the latter pair of opposites also exists in the Bororo myths since they distinguish between good and bad tobacco, although the difference is based not on the nature of the tobacco but on the method of consumption:[5] tobacco, the smoke of which is exhaled, establishes a beneficent form of communication with the Spirits (whereas, in M_{191}, it is the consequence of a communication of this kind); tobacco, the smoke of which is *inhaled*, leads to the transformation of humans into animals (otters with very small eyes in M_{27}), which is precisely the fate suffered in M_{191} by the man who eats bad tobacco (he is changed into an ant-eater, an animal which, throughout the length and breadth of

[5] Cf. *RC* where I stressed on several occasions (pp. 143, 194, 272) that Bororo mythology tends to be on the side of culture.

Brazil, is frequently described in myths as a 'blocked' animal, i.e. with no mouth or no anus). In the Bororo myths, good tobacco is linked with fire (it comes from the ashes of a snake) and bad tobacco is linked with water (it is discovered in a fish's belly and causes its victims to be changed into otters, aquatic animals). The correspondence between the myths is therefore fully proved:

Iranxé [tobacco $(+)$: $(-)$] :: Bororo [$(M_1$, fire $(+)$: water $(-))$ ::
$(M_{26}$–M_{27}, tobacco $(+)$: tobacco $(-))$]

Finally, remembering the distinction, congruous with the preceding ones, between good tobacco which is pungent (*qui pique*) and bad tobacco which is not pungent, a distinction that the Bororo myth, M_{26}, introduces as a subsidiary theme, we arrive at the final confirmation of the fact that, like honey, tobacco occupies an ambiguous and equivocal position between food and poison:

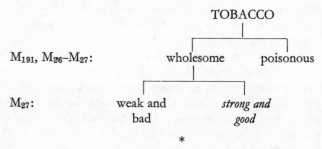

TOBACCO

M_{191}, M_{26}–M_{27}:   wholesome   poisonous

M_{27}:   weak and   *strong and*
                        bad   *good*

*

At the beginning of this book, I stressed the doubly paradoxical, yet very real nature, of the contrast in European cultures between tobacco and honey. With us, one term is indigenous, the other exotic; one very ancient, the other barely four centuries old. The existence, in South America, of a correlational and oppositional connection between honey and tobacco is to be explained, it would seem, by precisely opposite reasons. There, honey and tobacco are both indigenous, and the origin of both is lost in the dim and remote past.[6] Honey and tobacco are therefore bracketed together, not as they are in European societies because of an external contrast which underlines their complementary

[6] I am restricting my remarks for the moment to tropical America. The place occupied by honey in the thought and mythology of the Indians of North America raises problems which will be dealt with in a different context. As regards Central America and Mexico, where agriculture was highly developed in the pre-Columbian period, the observation and analysis of still surviving rites has as yet hardly begun, although their rich complexity is hinted at in the few references to them to be found in ancient or contemporary literature.

properties, but rather because of an internal contrast between opposite properties which honey and tobacco each conjugate separately and independently, since – within different registers and on different levels – each seems perpetually to oscillate between two states: that of being a supreme food and that of being a deadly poison. Furthermore, in between these two states can be found a whole series of intermediary forms, and it is particularly difficult to gauge the transitions from one to another since they depend on minute, and often imperceptible, differences relating to the quality of the commodity, the time of the harvest, the quantity consumed or the time which elapses before consumption.

These inherent uncertainties may be accompanied by others. The physiological effect of tobacco is partly that of a stimulant and partly that of a narcotic. Honey too may be a stimulant or a drug. In South America, honey and tobacco share these properties with other natural products or prepared foods. Let us consider first the case of honey. It has already been noted that South American varieties of honey are unstable and that, if they are mixed with water and left for a few days, or even a few hours, they begin to ferment spontaneously. One observer noted this phenomenon during the honey feast of the Tembé Indians: 'The honey, mixed with wax from the comb and soaked in water, ferments in the sun ... I was offered some (of this intoxicating drink); although at first I was reluctant to try it, I found it had a sweet and acid taste which was very pleasant' (Rodrigues 4, p. 32).

Whether it is eaten fresh, or in a spontaneously fermented form, honey is, then, akin to the innumerable fermented liquors which South American Indians make with manioc, maize, palm-tree sap or fruit of various kinds. In this connection, it is significant that the deliberate and systematic preparation of a fermented honey drink – let us call it mead, for the sake of simplicity – seems to have existed only to the west and south of the Amazonian basin, among the Tupi-Guarani, the southern Ge tribes, the Botocudo, the Charrua and almost all the Chaco tribes. This crescent-shaped area coincides approximately with the southern limits of beer-making with manioc and maize, while in the Chaco it borders on the zone where beer is made from algaroba (*Prosopis* sp.), which is a local development (Figure 3). It is conceivable then that mead was regarded as a substitute for manioc beer and, to a lesser degree, for maize beer. On the other hand, the map clearly shows another contrasting feature between the southern zone, where mead is predominant, and the discontinuous but essentially northern zones, where what could be called tobacco 'honey' is made, that is, where tobacco is soaked or boiled and then imbibed in a liquid or syrupy form. Just as it is important to distinguish between the two ways of consuming honey, in the fresh or the fermented form, the forms of tobacco consumption, in spite of their great variety, can be reduced to two main categories: tobacco can be consumed dry, when it is taken as snuff or smoked and, in that case, it is similar to several vegetable narcotics: *Piptadenia, Banisteriopsis, Datura*, etc. (with some of which it is occasionally mixed); or else it can be consumed moist, as a kind of jam or potion. It follows that the pairs of opposites which I used at the beginning to define the relationship between honey and tobacco (*cooked/raw, moistened/burnt, infra-culinary/super-culinary*, etc.) express only part of the truth. In reality, the situation is much more complex, since honey can exist in two forms: fresh or fermented; and tobacco, in several forms: burnt or moistened, and in the latter case, raw or cooked. It is to be expected, then, that at the two opposite ends of the semantic field under investigation, the myths about the origin of honey or tobacco, which, as I have already postulated and to some extent verified, are reduplicated in terms of the contrast between 'good' and 'bad' honey, 'good' and 'bad' tobacco, should show a second line of division, situated along a different axis, and determined not by differences affecting *natural properties*, but by differences relating to *cultural customs*. Finally, since on the one hand, 'good' honey is *sweet*, while 'good' tobacco is *strong*, and on the other hand, 'honey' in the literal sense can be eaten *raw*, whereas in most cases tobacco 'honey' is the result of the tobacco having been previously *cooked*, it is to be expected that the transformational relationships between the various types of 'honey' myths and 'tobacco' myths should take the form of a chiasmus.

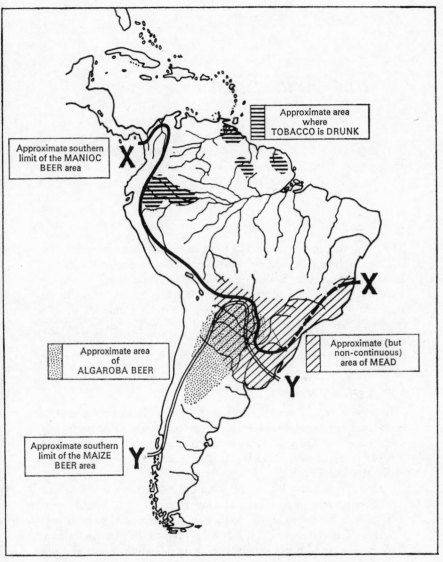

Figure 3. Beer, mead and tobacco liquor in South America. (Redrawn from *Handbook of South American Indians*, Vol. 5, pp. 533, 540.)

2 The Arid Beast

Venit enim tempus quo torridus aestuat aer
incipit et sicco fervere terra Cane.

Propertius, *Elegies*, II,
XXVIII, vv. 3–4

The S$_{-3}$ group, in the provisional form in which I have worked it out, includes only myths dealing with the origin of the honey *festival*. In order to find a myth dealing explicitly with the origin of *honey* as a natural product, we must refer to a community belonging to the southern Mato Grosso, the Ofaié-Chavanté, who numbered about a thousand individuals at the beginning of the century, but by 1948 had dwindled to a mere handful with little recollection of their traditional customs and beliefs. Their myths, couched in dialectal Portuguese, contain a great many obscure passages.

M$_{192}$. Ofaié. 'The origin of honey'

In former days, there was no honey. The wolf was the master of honey. Its children were seen to be smeared with honey from early morning, but the wolf refused to give any to the other animals. When they asked for some, it gave them araticum fruits, and claimed that this was all it had.

One day, the little land tortoise announced that it was determined to gain possession of honey. Having fitted its shell securely over its belly, it went inside the wolf's den and demanded some honey. The wolf at first denied that it had any, but as the tortoise insisted, the wolf allowed it to lie on its back with its mouth open and drink freely of the honey which flowed from a hanging gourd.

This was just a trick. Taking advantage of the fact that the tortoise was totally absorbed in its feast, the wolf got its children to gather dead wood to make a fire around the tortoise, in the hope that it could be eaten when it was cooked. But to no avail: the tortoise continued to drink its fill of the honey. It was the wolf which found the intense heat hard to bear. When the gourd was empty, the tortoise calmly got up, scattered the wood cinders, and told the wolf it ought now to give honey to all the animals.

The wolf fled. Under the tortoise's command, the animals cornered it and the prea lit a bush-fire round the place where it had taken refuge. As the circle of fire grew smaller, the animals wondered if the wolf was really there: only a partridge flew out from the flames. But the tortoise, which had continued to watch the spot where the wolf had taken refuge knew that the wolf had changed into a partridge.

So it continued to keep its eyes fixed on the partridge until the bird was out of sight. On the tortoise's orders, the animals rushed off after it. The chase lasted several days. Each time they caught up with the bird, it flew off again. After climbing onto another animal's head to get a better view, the tortoise saw the partridge change into a bee. The tortoise planted a stake to show the direction taken by the bee. The chase was resumed, but just as ineffectively. The animals had by now completely lost heart. 'No, no,' said the tortoise, 'we have been advancing for only three months and we have covered almost half the distance. Look at the stake there, behind you: it is showing us the right direction.' The animals turned round and saw that the stake had changed into a pindo palm tree (*Cocos* sp.).

They continued on and on. Finally, the tortoise announced that they would arrive at their goal the next day. And next day, sure enough, they saw the bees' 'house', the entrance of which was guarded by poisonous wasps. One after another, the birds tried to approach the house, but the wasps attacked them 'by squirting them with their fluid' and the birds fell to the ground in a daze and died. However, the smallest of them, a woodpecker (or a humming-bird?) succeeded in getting past the wasps and taking the honey. 'Well, my son,' said the tortoise, 'now we have some honey. But there is very little of it; if we eat it, there will soon be none left.' It took the honey, gave each animal a cutting (*uma muda*) so that it could make a house for itself and plant the honey. They would come back when there was enough honey for all.

A long time afterwards, the animals began to be anxious about their honey plantations, and they asked the 'maritaca' to go and see what was happening. But the heat in the honey plantations was so intense that the 'maritaca' could not get near. The next animals who agreed to make the attempt preferred to stop on the way: the parrot on a fruit tree (*mangaba*: *Hancornia speciosa*), the blue macaw in a pleasant forest; and they blamed their failure on the scorching heat. Finally, the parakeet flew so high, almost as high as the sky, that it succeeded in reaching the plantations, which were laden with honey.

When the leader of the animals had been informed, he decided to go to the plantations and see for himself. He inspected the houses: many people had eaten the honey they had been given to plant, and so had none left; others had enough, buried at ground level and easy to extract. 'This cannot last much longer,' said the leader; 'we shall soon be without honey. There is very little, in fact, hardly any at all. Wait a little and there will be enough honey for everybody.' In the meantime he had released the bees, which flew away into the forest.

Later, he called the inhabitants together and told them to take their hatchets and set off in search of honey: 'Now the forest is full of all kinds of honey: bora, mandaguari, jati, mandassaia, cagafogo – absolutely every variety. All you have to do is go and look for it, and if you do not care for one particular kind of honey, you can move on to the next tree, where you will find another. You can collect as much as you like; the supply will never be exhausted, provided you only take as much as you can carry away in the gourds and other containers you must take with you. But what you cannot take away must be left where it was for the next time, after you have carefully closed up the opening (made in the tree with an axe).'

Since then, because of this, we have had enough honey. When people go to clear the forest, they find honey. In one tree there is bora honey, in another mandaguari honey and in another jati honey. There is every variety (Ribeiro 2, pp. 124–6).

Although this is a very long myth, I have translated it almost literally, not only because its obscurity is such that any attempt to shorten it would have very soon made it incomprehensible, but also on account of its importance and the wealth of detail it contains. It expresses the standard native doctrine in respect of honey and, for this reason, dictates how all the myths to be examined subsequently should be interpreted. The reader should therefore not be surprised if the analysis of the myth proves to be difficult, and forces me temporarily to disregard certain aspects, and proceed by successive approximations, rather as if it were necessary to stand well back from the myth and reconnoitre it in outline before exploring each detail.

Let us, therefore, go straight to the main point. What is the myth about? It describes the time when animals, man's ancestors, were not in possession of honey, the form in which they first obtained it, and how they gave up this form in favour of the one that men are now familiar with.

It is not surprising that the acquisition of honey should go back to the mythical period when there was no difference between animals and men, since honey is a wild product belonging to the category of nature. As such, it must have become part of the heritage of humanity when men were still living in a 'state of nature', before any distinction was made between nature and culture, or between men and animals.

It is also quite normal that the myth should describe the original honey as a plant, which germinates, grows and ripens. As we have already seen, in the pattern of Indian thought, honey is considered as part of the vegetable kingdom; M_{192} provides fresh confirmation of this.

Nevertheless, we are not dealing here with any ordinary plant, since the first kind of honey was cultivated, and the development outlined by the myth consisted in turning it into wild honey. Here we touch on the essential point, since the originality of M_{192} is that it takes the reverse approach to that adopted by the myths about the introduction of cultivated plants, which I grouped together and studied in *The Raw and the Cooked* under numbers M_{87}–M_{92} (cf., too, M_{108} and M_{110}–M_{118}). These myths refer to a time when men knew nothing of agriculture and fed on leaves, tree fungi and rotten wood before the existence of maize was revealed to them by a celestial woman, who had taken the form of an opossum. The maize was like a tree in appearance, and grew wild in the forest. But men made the mistake of felling the tree, and they then had to share out the seeds, clear the ground for cultivation and sow maize, because the dead tree was not sufficient for their needs. This gave rise, on the one hand, to the different varieties of cultivated species (in the beginning, they had all been together on one tree) and, on the other hand, to the differences between peoples, languages and customs, which occurred when the first men dispersed in various directions.

In M_{192}, everything happens in like manner, but the other way round. Men do not need to learn about agriculture, since, as animals, they are already in possession of it and can apply it to the production

of honey, from the moment the latter falls into their hands. But cultivated honey has two disadvantages: either men do not resist the temptation to devour their honey 'in the blade', or the honey plants grow
well and are so easily harvested – in the same way as plants grown in
fields – that excessive consumption exhausts productive capacity.

As the myth then sets out to demonstrate systematically, the transformation of cultivated honey into wild honey removes these disadvantages and gives men a triple security. First, the bees become wild
and diversify into the various species; this means that there will be
several varieties of honey instead of one. Next, honey will be more
plentiful. Finally, the greed of the honey-gatherers will be limited by
the quantities it is possible to bring back; the excess honey will remain
in the nest, where it will keep until the next gathering. There is, therefore, a three-fold gain – in quality, quantity and lastingness.

There is no doubt where the originality of this myth lies: it is, one
might say, 'anti-neolithic' in outlook, and pleads in favour of an
economy based on collecting and gathering, to which it attributes the
same virtues of diversity, abundance and preservation claimed by most
of the other myths for the reverse outlook, which is a consequence of
humanity's adopting the arts of civilization. And it is honey which
provides the occasion for this extraordinary reversal. In this sense, a
myth about the origin of honey also refers to its loss.[7] Once it becomes
wild, honey is half lost, but it has to be lost in order to be saved. So
powerful is its gastronomical appeal that, were it too easily obtained,
men would partake of it too freely until the supply was exhausted.
Through the medium of the myth, honey is saying to man: 'You would
not find me, if you had not first looked for me.'

We can, then, at this point, make a curious observation, which will
recur later in connection with other myths. In the case of M_{188} and
M_{189}, we were dealing with genuine myths of origin, but they were
not wholly satisfactory, because they related to the honey festival, and
not to honey itself. And now we find ourselves faced with a new
myth concerned with honey proper, but which, in spite of appearances,
is not so much a myth about the origin of honey as about its loss, or
more precisely, one which is intent on transforming an illusory origin

[7] Compare with the following passage (M_{192b}) from the creation myth of the Caduveo:
'When the caracara (a species of falcon and an incarnation of the deceiver) saw the honey
forming in the huge gourds where it was to be had for the taking, he said to Gô-noêno-
hôdi, the demiurge: "No, this is not right, this is not the way it should be, no! Put the
honey in the middle of the tree so that men are forced to dig it out. Otherwise the lazy
creatures will not work" ' (Ribeiro 1, p. 143).

(since the initial possession of honey was tantamount to a lack of honey) into an advantageous loss (men being assured of having honey, as soon as they agree to relinquish it). The succeeding chapters of this volume will throw light on the paradox, which must be accepted as a structural feature of myths with honey as their theme.

Let us now return to the text of M_{192}. The plantations, where the primordial beasts cultivated their honey, had one extraordinary feature: the heat there was so intense that no one could approach, and only after several fruitless attempts did the animals succeed in finding a way in. In order to interpret this episode, we might be tempted to proceed by drawing an analogy with the myths about the origin of cultivated plants which explain that, before men were acquainted with vegetable foods, cooked in accordance with culture, they fed on vegetable matter which had rotted in accordance with nature. If the cultivated honey of the heroic ages is the opposite of the wild honey of today, and if, as has already been established, real honey denotes the category of the moist in correlation with, and in contrast to, tobacco which denotes the category of the burnt, must we not reverse the relationship and move the honey of olden days into the category of the dry and the burnt?

There is nothing in the myths to rule out such an interpretation, but I believe it to be incomplete, because it disregards an aspect of the problem to which, on the contrary, the honey myths constantly call attention. As I have already stressed, honey has several paradoxical features, not the least of which is the fact that, although it has a connotation with humidity in its relationship to tobacco, it is constantly associated in the myths with the dry season, for the simple reason that, like most wild products, honey is gathered and eaten fresh during that season.

There are innumerable indications to this effect. Both the northern Tupi tribes and the Karaja used to celebrate a honey festival which took place during the harvest period, that is, during August (Machado, p. 21). In the province of Chiquitos in Bolivia, wild honey was collected from June to September (d'Orbigny, quoted by Schwartz 2, p. 158). Among the Siriono of lower Bolivia honey 'is most abundant in the dry season, after the flowering of the plants and trees; therefore the drinking bouts (the drink is mead mixed with maize beer) occur during the months of August, September, October and November' (Holmberg, pp. 37–8). The Tacana Indians collect bees' wax during the dry season (H.-H., pp. 335–6). In Guayaki territory in eastern Paraguay there is no clearly defined dry season: there is, however, a cold season, at the beginning of which, in June and July, abundance of honey coincides with the distinctive colouring taken on by a certain creeper (timbó) which is said to be 'pregnant with honey' (Clastres). The Tereno of the southern Mato Grosso, in preparation for their Oheokoti festival at the beginning of April, used to devote a whole month to the gathering of large quantities of honey (Altenfelder Silva, pp. 356, 364).

We have seen that the Tembé and the Tenetehara begin collecting for their honey festival in March or April, that is, at the end of the rainy season (see above, p. 32). The myth we are now dealing with is less explicit, but even so contains two indications to this effect. The last part makes it clear that it is when people go to clear the land for cultivation that they find honey. In central Brazil, clearing operations are carried out after the rainy season, so that the felled wood can dry off for two or three months before being burnt. The sowing and planting are done immediately afterwards so as to take advantage of the first rains. Also, the scorching heat in the place where the cultivated honey is growing is described in terms of the dry season: *la tem secca brava*, 'the drought is severe'. This leads me to conclude that the old honey and the present-day honey are to be thought of not so much as antithetical terms but as terms of unequal force. Cultivated honey was a super-honey: plentiful, concentrated in one area and easy to harvest. And just as these advantages led to corresponding disadvantages, such as eating too much too quickly and using up the supply, so in this context the reference to honey in hyperbolic terms results in equally hyperbolic climatic conditions. Since honey is collected during the dry season, super-honey calls for a hyper-dry season which, like hyper-abundance and hyper-accessibility, means that enjoyment of it is practically ruled out.

The behaviour of the parrot and the macaw provides an argument in support of this second interpretation. They were sent by their companions to look for the honey, but chose to stop, one on a mangaba plant (a savannah fruit, which ripens during the dry season), the other in the refreshing shade of the forest. Both, therefore, lingered on the way in order to take advantage of the last amenities of the rainy season. The attitude of these two birds thus recalls that of the raven in the Greek myth about the origin of the constellation Corvus, which also lingers near seeds or fruit (which would ripen only at the end of the dry season), instead of bringing back the water requested by Apollo.

As a result, the raven is doomed to endure everlasting thirst; previously, he had a splendid voice, but from now on only a harsh croak was to emerge from his parched throat. It should be remembered that, according to the Tembé and Tenetehara myths about the origin of (the) honey (festival), the macaws formerly used to feed on honey, and honey is a dry season 'beverage', like the chthonian well-water in the Greek myth, as opposed to celestial water which is associated with a different period of the year. Perhaps, then, this episode of the Ofaié myth is meant to explain by omission, why the parrot and the macaw, which are fruit-eating birds, do not (or no longer) eat honey, although honey is considered to be a fruit.

I have no hesitation in thus comparing the Indian myth and the Greek myth, since in *The Raw and the Cooked*, I established that the latter was a dry-season myth and, without postulating the existence of some ancient, and unproven, link between the Old and New Worlds, I was able to show that the use of an astronomical coding imposed such strict limitations on mythic thought that it was understandable, on a purely formal level, that the myths of the Old and New World should, in certain instances, reproduce each other either directly or by inversion.

The Ofaié myth presents the 'maritaca's' failure as preceding that of the parrot and the macaw. The meaning of the word 'maritaca' is uncertain; it could be either an abbreviation of 'maritacáca', which means skunk, or a dialectal form of 'maitáca', a small parrot of the genus *Pionus*. It is difficult to be definite, especially since there exists an Amazonian form: 'maitacáca', of the word for skunk (Stradelli 1), which is identical with the name of the bird, apart from the repetition of the last syllable. In support of the theory that the word is a distortion of 'maitáca', it can be pointed out that the Ofaié, in referring to the skunk, seem to use a similar, although slightly different, word: 'jaratatáca' (M_{75}), frequent evidence of which is found in Brazil (cf. Ihering, under 'jaritacáca, jaritatáca'), and that the other animals in the same sequence are also parrots. As will appear subsequently, the skunk interpretation is not to be ruled out entirely, but the transition maitáca > maritaca is more likely from the phonetic point of view than the loss of the reduplicated syllable, and so it is this interpretation I propose to adopt.

Let us suppose, therefore, that four parrots are involved. It is immediately obvious that they can be classified in several ways. The myth stresses that the parakeet, which was successful in its mission, is the smallest of them: 'Aí foi o periquitinho, êste pequeno, voôu bem alto para cima, quasi chegou no céu ... ' It is, then, because of its small size and lightness that the parakeet can fly higher than other birds of the same species and succeeds in avoiding the scorching heat which prevails in the honey plantations. On the other hand, the macaw which tries just before the parakeet is, as is made quite clear in the text, an 'arára azul' (*Anodorhynchus hyacinthinus*): it therefore belongs to the largest variety of a family which itself includes the biggest of the psittacidae (cf. Ihering, under 'arára-una'). The parrot which has its turn before the macaw is smaller in size than the macaw; and the maitáca, which comes first, is smaller than the parrot although bigger than the parakeet which closes the cycle. So, the three birds which fail are absolutely bigger, and the one which succeeds absolutely smaller, and the first three are graded according to size, so that the major contrast is between the macaw and the parakeet:

bigger:	*smaller:*

maitáca < parrot < macaw / parakeet (< maitáca)

It should now be noted that, within the series of bigger birds, the parrot and the macaw form a functional pair: they do not even attempt to carry out their mission and prefer to take refuge, one in the *savannah*, the other in the *forest*, in close proximity to evidence of the recent end of the rainy season: juicy fruits and cool shade, whereas the other two birds are the only ones which definitely brave the drought and testify, one to its 'dry' aspect: the unbearable heat, and the other to its moist aspect: the abundance of honey.

DRY				MOIST	
maitáca		parrot	/	macaw	parakeet
(*heat*)	/	(*savannah*)		(*forest*)	/ (*honey*)
	(rainy season)			(dry season)	

Finally, if we adopt a third point of view, and think in terms of the result of the birds' mission, a different principle of classification becomes evident. Only the first and last birds bring back an actual report on the situation, although one item of information is negative in character (the bird explains that the intense heat makes it impossible to reach the plantations), and the other positive (the abundance of honey is an incentive to the animals to brave the obstacle). On the other hand, the two birds which occupy a middle position (both in size and in the narrative sequence) do not bother to go and see for themselves and merely repeat what has already been said: they therefore bring back no information:

maitáca /	parrot	macaw	/ parakeet
(—)	(o)	(o)	(+)
	no information		real information

I have spent some time over the sequence of the four birds, and for a specific purpose. The analysis of the sequence makes it possible to settle a methodological point. It shows that a sequence which the old mythography would have interpreted as a semantic redundance and a rhetorical device must, like the myth as a whole, be taken absolutely *seriously*. We are not dealing with a gratuitous enumeration, which can be dismissed with brief reference to the mystic connotation of the figure 4 in American thought. No doubt the connotation exists; but it is systematically exploited to build up a multi-dimensional system allowing the combination of synchronic and diachronic attributes, relating in the one case to structure, in the other to events, to absolute properties and relative properties, essences and functions. The demonstration I have just carried out not only throws light on the nature of mythic thought and the mechanism of its operations, by clarifying the procedures it uses to integrate methods of classification, some depending on a concept of continuity and progress (the arranging of animals in order of size, or according to the amount of information supplied, etc.), others on discontinuity and antithesis (the contrasting of largest and smallest, dry and moist, savannah and forest, etc.); it also establishes and illustrates an interpretation. The sequence just deciphered turns out to be more complex than at first appeared, and this complexity makes it possible to understand why birds of the same family which we mistakenly believed to be distinguished only by their size, and solely for the purpose of creating a fairly commonplace dramatic effect (the smallest and weakest succeeds where bigger and stronger birds fail), are also vehicles for the expression of contrasts which, as I have shown on different grounds, are an intrinsic part of the armature of the myth.

I propose, then, to apply the same kind of exhaustive analysis to the part played by two other characters: the prea and the tortoise. But before solving the problem they present, I must draw attention to one particular point.

The episode of the four birds, which relates to the *collecting* of *culti-vated* honey, reproduces the scenario of a previous episode which dealt with the *planting* of *wild* honey: in both instances, one or more abortive attempts are made before success is finally achieved. 'Tudo que é passarinho', so birds too, tried to conquer wild honey, but they were prevented from doing so by the wasps, which were guarding it and which savagely slaughtered them. Only the last and smallest of the birds succeeded: 'êste ... bem pequeno, êste menorzinho dêles', and about its identity we unfortunately cannot be certain, since the only version we possess hesitates between the woodpecker and the humming-bird. Whatever the species, the two episodes are obviously parallel.

Now, in the second episode, cultivated honey is passively unattain-able because of the heat, just as in the first episode wild honey is actively unattainable because of the wasps. But the wasps' warlike disposition is expressed in a very curious form in the myth: 'They attacked, by squirting out their fluid (*largavam aquela agua dêles*) and the animals fell down in a daze and died.' This episode may seem paradoxical in two respects. First, I have shown (*RC*, p. 314) that there is a contrast between vermin and poisonous insects, congruous with that between the rotten and the burnt, and from this point of view the wasps should not appear as a mode of water, but as a mode of fire (cf. the vernacular term *caga fogo* which corresponds to the Tupi *tataira*, 'fire honey', the name of an aggressive, stingless bee which secretes a caustic fluid: *Oxytrigona*, Schwartz 2, pp. 73–4). Secondly, this particular way of describing the wasps' attack is immediately reminiscent of the way in which certain myths belonging to the same region describe the behaviour of an entirely different animal: the skunk, which squirts its opponents with an evil-smelling fluid – a deadly poison, according to the myths (*RC*, p. 154 n. 9, and M_{75} which is another Ofaié myth; cf., too, M_5, M_{124}).

Let me recall, then, some of the conclusions that were reached about the skunk in *The Raw and the Cooked*. (1) In both North and South America, this member of the family of the mustelidae and the opossum form a pair of opposites. (2) North American myths expressly associate the opossum with the rotten, the skunk with the burnt. At the same time, the skunk is shown to have a direct affinity with the rainbow and has the power to resuscitate the dead. (3) In South America, on the other hand, it is the opossum which has an affinity with the rainbow (to the extent that, in Guiana, it is called by the same name), and just as the rainbow in South America is credited with lethal power, one of the mythical functions attributed to the opossum is the shortening of human life.

As we move from one hemisphere to the other, the respective functions of the skunk and the opossum would seem to be reversed. In the South American myths, both animals appear as rotten or putrescent creatures. But the opossum has affinities with the dry season and with the rainbow (which initiates a miniature dry season, since it heralds the end of the rainy season), and so, if the total system has any coherence, it should follow that the skunk's South American affinities place it with the rainy season.

Is it conceivable that the mythology of honey may have adapted the very general contrast between the opossum and the skunk for its own purposes, while modifying it along the lines of a more limited contrast between the bee and the wasp, which for obvious reasons would correspond more closely to its needs?

If this hypothesis were true, it would provide us with the key to the anomaly we noticed in the role that the myth assigns to the wasps, and which lies in the fact that the role is coded in terms of water instead of fire. The anomaly would be a result of the implied equation:

$$(a) \ \text{wasps}^{(-1)} \equiv \text{skunk}$$

In this case, for the *opossum/skunk* contrast to be maintained, the mythology of honey would have to contain by implication the complementary equation:

$$(b) \ \text{bee}^{(-1)} \equiv \text{opossum}$$

signifying in this instance – since bees are *producers* or *guardians* of honey (see above, p. 35) – that the opossum must be the *consumer* or *stealer* of honey.[8]

As will be seen later, this hypothesis, which I arrived at by means of deductive and *a priori* reasoning, will be fully confirmed by the myths. We can already understand why, in M_{192}, the bees are categorized as dry (the approach to them is 'scorching') and the wasps as moist (the approach to them is 'damp').

[8] In *RC*, *passim*, I emphasized the semantic position of the opossum as a polluting and foul-smelling beast. According to evidence discussed by Schwartz 2, pp. 74–8, it would seem that several meliponae are able to pollute or immobilize their enemies by means of more or less foul-smelling secretions, either for the purposes of attack or in self-defence. On the subject of the smell emitted by the meliponae, and especially the sub-species *Trigona*, cf. *ibid.*, pp. 79–81. It should also be noted that the meliponae practise what entomologists call 'brigandage', either as a full-time or as an occasional activity. It would appear that *Trigona limão* does not collect nectar and pollen from flowers, but simply steals honey from other species (Salt, p. 461).

Most important of all, these provisional findings are indispensable, if we are to make any headway with the analysis of the contents of M_{192}. The opossum does not appear in person in the myth, but the role of stealer of honey which the myth should assign to it by omission, if my hypothesis is correct, is fulfilled by two other animals: (*a*) the prea (*cavia aperea*) which sets fire to the bushes (cf. M_{56}) and whose function, as has already been suggested on quite different grounds, may be to act as a combinatory variant of the opossum (*RC*, pp. 170, 193, n. 29), since both are on the side of fire and the dry season, one actively as a fire-raiser, the other passively as a sufferer by fire (*RC*, pp. 129, 218, n. 8). (*b*) The second animal is the land tortoise (jaboti) which unmasks the wolf, master of honey, sees through its series of disguises and finally by sheer tenacity catches up with it at the spot where it had hidden all the honey, after changing into a bee.

It should be recalled at this point that an important group of myths, mostly Amazonian in origin, correlate and contrast the tortoise and the opossum as being imputrescible and putrescible: respectively, master and victim of decay (*RC*, pp. 174–6). The tortoise, even when deprived of food and buried in the ground which has been softened by the first rains, can survive for several months in a damp heat, whereas the opossum cannot withstand such heat, whether it is buried in the ground or in a fish's belly, whence it emerges permanently foul-smelling (*ibid.*). Like the prea, therefore, the tortoise forms the active pole of a pair of opposites, with the opossum as the passive pole: in relation to the dry, the prea is a fire-raiser, the opossum a sufferer by fire; in relation to the moist, the tortoise emerges victorious from the decay which kills the opossum, or for which the opossum has at least to serve as a vehicle. One detail in M_{192} confirms the triple relationship, since the myth, in also describing the tortoise in respect of the dry, uses a new transformation for this purpose: the tortoise *cannot be burnt* (this gives the triangle: fire-raiser/sufferer by fire/impervious to fire), a characteristic which is confirmed objectively by ethnography, since the wolf's trick of trying to cook the tortoise while it was lying on its back is based on a method which may seem barbarous but is still current in central Brazil: the tortoise is so difficult to kill that the peasants cook it alive among the hot wood cinders, with its own shell acting as the cooking-dish; the process may last several hours, because the poor beast takes so long to die.

We have gradually exhausted the subject matter of M_{192}. The only point which still remains to be elucidated is the part played by the wolf, the master of honey and of the araticum fruit. The araticum is a plant of the anonaceae family (*Anona montana* and neighbouring species, or perhaps *Rollinia exalbida*, which is known under the same name) and produces large fruit with farinaceous pulp and an acid flavour. Like honey, it is one of the wild products of the dry season, and so one can easily see how, in the myth, it might play the part of a honey substitute. Whether or not the reference is to the same fruit or to different kinds, this minor doublet is a common feature in the mythology of honey and as such, as we shall see, its interpretation raises no difficulty. Unfortunately, the same cannot be said of the wolf.

The animal referred to as a 'wolf' (*lobo do mato*) seems to be almost always a kind of long-legged, long-haired fox: *Chrysocion brachiurus, jubatus*; *Canis jubatus*, which is found in central and southern Brazil, and consequently in the territory of the Ofaié, who assign a major role to this animal in their myth about the origin of honey. Gilmore's observation (pp. 377–8) that 'all the native Neotropical canids are foxes, with the exception of the bush dog' (*Icticyon venaticus*), is a warning to us to pay particular attention to myths which present a fox as the master of honey, as well as to those which assign this role to other animals in almost identical terms but at the same time maintain an oppositional relationship between the animal which is master of honey and the opossum:

M97. *Mundurucu. 'Opossum and his sons-in-law'* (extract)

The opossum had one mishap after another with the series of sons-in-law he chose. The daughter then married the honey-eating fox and one day the new husband invited her to take a gourd and go hunting with him. He climbed a tree in which he spied a beehive and called out, 'Honey, honey'. The honey flowed out of the beehive and filled the gourds. When the father tried to emulate his son-in-law, he had no success and he ordered his daughter to leave the fox. (Murphy 1, p. 119. In a different version, the dove, then the humming-bird take the place of the fox, Kruse 2, pp. 628–9.)

M98. *Tenetehara. 'Opossum and his sons-in-law'* (extract)

The 'honey-monkey' walked through the forest and sucked up honey. When he arrived home, he asked his father-in-law for a knife, and punching a hole in his throat he filled up a gourd vessel with the

Figure 4. The *lobo do mato* or guará. (After Ihering, *loc. cit.*, under 'guará'.)

honey which flowed out. The opossum tried to imitate his son-in-law, and died an instant death, since, unlike the 'honey-monkey', opossums have no pouch in their throat (Wagley–Galvão, p. 153).

M₉₉. Vapidiana. 'Opossum and his sons-in-law' (extract)

The mosquito sucked the honey, then ordered his wife to pierce his body with a needle and honey flowed from his belly. But only blood came from the opossum's belly ... (Wirth 2, p. 208).

These are adequate samples of an extremely widespread type of story, and they illustrate three points. First, the nature of the animal which is master of honey may vary a great deal, from the fox to the mosquito by way of the monkey and birds. Secondly, the role of master

of honey often presents a tautological character, the animals being defined as functions of honey, instead of the opposite being the case, so
that it may be difficult to identify them: which animal exactly is the
'honey-eating fox'? And the 'honey-monkey', which has a pouch in its
throat, is surely an *alter ego* of the guariba monkey, whose hyoid bone
is hollow and cup-shaped. Any animal, then, can play the part of master
of honey, provided he has an acknowledged capacity for guzzling: in
the myths, the dove or the pigeon drink their fill of water (*RC*, p. 204);
and it is an observable fact that the humming-bird sucks nectar from
flowers and the mosquito blood from other animals, while the howler
monkey has a receptacle (actually, a resonator) in his gullet. So the
pigeon, the humming-bird and the mosquito fill their bellies, and the
monkey fills its gullet. In each instance, the real or supposed organ
creates the function (master of honey). Only the fox, which was our
starting-point, presents a problem, since it is impossible to discern
what anatomical basis there could be in its case. And yet the myth
manages to justify its function as master of honey by an external rather
than an internal device, which is cultural rather than natural: the fox
places gourds at the foot of the hive, and they fill up at his command.

The difficulty raised by the canidae as masters of honey is still further
increased by the absence, in the myths we have considered up till now,
of an animal which would be better suited to the part, if it is taken in the
literal sense and not – as in all the cases we have just looked at – in the
figurative sense. I am thinking of the irára (*Tayra barbara*), the vernacular Portuguese and Spanish names for which – papa-mel, 'honey-
eater', and melero, 'honey-merchant', speak for themselves. This
species of the mustelidae family is a nocturnal forest animal. Although
carnivorous, it is very fond of honey as is indicated by its name in
lingua geral, which is derived from the Tupi word *ira*, meaning honey;
and it attacks hives in hollow trees by burrowing through the roots or
by tearing at the trunk with its claws. A plant which the Bororo call
'the irára plant' is used in magic rites intended to ensure a good honey
harvest (*EB*, Vol. I, p. 664).

The Tacana of Bolivia give the irára an important place in their
myths. They contrast it with a honey-stealing fox which, in a story
(M_{193}), tears off a piece of the irára's flesh, thus creating the yellow
patch which stands out against the irára's black fur (H.-H., pp. 270–76).[9]

[9] The ancient Mexicans used to say of a species with a light-coloured head (*Tayra barbara
senex*) that, if the head happened to be yellow, this meant that the hunter would die, whereas
if it were white, he would have a prolonged and wretched life. It was an animal of ill-
omen (Sahagun, Book XI, Ch. 1 under 'Tzoniztac').

Since this 'fox' has just had its tail pulled off, it might be confused with the opossum, which is often referred to as a fox and which, in both North and South America, is the subject of several myths explaining how its tail became bare. One group of myths (M_{194}–M_{197}) is concerned with the adventures of a pair of twins, the Edutzi, in the land of the animal demons, from among whom they each select a wife. The irára plays a part, either as the father of the two women who are sisters, or as the second husband of one of them, the other being in that case the vampire. In order to shield its daughters from the vengeful Edutzi, the 'melero' changes them into macaws (H.-H., pp. 104–10). These myths will be examined later in a different context. I will say no more about the Tacana for the moment, except to point out that they have a group of myths (M_{198}–M_{201}) which divide the animals into two camps: caterpillar /cricket, monkey/jaguar, cricket/jaguar, fox/jaguar, cricket/melero. In spite of the uncertainty of the terms, which means that, before these myths can be interpreted correctly, the enormous body of material collected by Hissink would have to be sorted out on both the syntagmatic and paradigmatic levels, it would seem that the relevant contrasts are between animals which are respectively large and small, terrestrial and celestial (or chthonian and celestial). Generally speaking, the jaguar is the dominant member in the first camp and the cricket in the second. The melero appears twice in this group of myths either as an intermediary between the two camps, or as the cricket's chief opponent (in place of the jaguar). It is therefore the leader of the chthonian animals. Except when it is fighting the caterpillar, the cricket always wins, since it is helped by wasps which inflict painful stings on its honey-seeking rival.[10] In addition to the monkey and the cricket, the fox and the ocelot figure among the opponents of the jaguar. The fox and the ocelot have a small shaman's drum which also plays a part in the clash between the Edutzi and the melero in the group M_{194}–M_{197}. Sahagun (*loc. cit.*) compares the ocelot with a Mexican variety of the melero.

The presence of the irára or melero in a great number of the myths of eastern Bolivia is especially worthy of remark, since Brazilian and Guiana myths make little mention of this animal. With the exception of a Taulipang myth (M_{135}) about the origin of the Pleiades, which ends with a father and his children deciding to change into an araiuag: 'a quadruped similar to a fox, but with soft, shiny, black fur, a slender body, a round head and a long snout' (K.-G. 1, pp. 57–60), which could well be the irára since 'it likes honey and is not afraid of bees', there are

[10] Cf. the enemies defeated by wasps and hornets in the Popol Vuh.

very few references to it. Moving southwards, we first encounter it in Amazonia. A short myth (M_{202}) contrasts the corupira, the cannibalistic spirit of the woods, with the honey-eating irára. The irára saves an Indian from the corupira's claws, after the cunauaru frog (cf. *RC*, pp. 270–71) has rendered the same service to an Indian woman who, like the Indian, had stolen the ogre's meal. Thereafter, the ogre was to eat neither fish nor tatu. He was to eat human flesh, whereas the irára would continue to live on honey (Rodrigues 1, pp. 68–9).

The Botocudo of the Rio Doce area in eastern Brazil have two myths about the irára:

M_{203}. Botocudo. 'The origin of water'

In olden times, the humming-bird possessed all the water in the world and the animals had nothing to drink but honey. The humming-bird used to go and bathe every day, and the envious animals got the wild turkey (mutum: *Crax* sp.) to spy on it, but to no avail.

One day, the entire population was assembled round a fire. The irára arrived late, because it had been away collecting honey. It asked for some water in a low voice, and was told: 'There is none.' So it offered to give the humming-bird honey in exchange for water, but the latter refused and announced that it was going to have a bath. The irára followed it and came to the water, which was in a little hole in the rock, almost at the same time. The humming-bird jumped into the water and the irára did likewise, and splashed about so vigorously that the water spurted out in all directions, thus giving rise to streams and rivers (Nim. 9, p. 111).

The author to whom we owe the above myth observes that the same story is found among the Yamana of Tierra del Fuego, except that the humming-bird's role is reversed; it discovers the water which is being jealously guarded by the fox.

M_{204}. Botocudo. 'The origin of animals'

In olden times, animals were like humans, and were all friends. They had enough to eat. It was the irára which had the idea of setting them at variance with each other. It taught the snake to bite and kill its victims and the mosquito to suck blood. From that moment they all became beasts, including the irára, so that no one would recognize it. The sorcerer who supplied the animals with their food was unable to remedy the situation. He changed into a woodpecker and his stone axe became the bird's beak (Nim. 9, p. 112).

These myths prompt several observations. The first myth contrasts the irára, the master of honey, with the humming-bird, the master of water. It has already been observed that in South America honey and water invariably go together, since honey is always diluted before it is consumed. The original situation referred to by the myth, in which the animals in possession of honey have no water, and vice versa, is therefore 'anti-natural', or more accurately 'anti-cultural'. A myth belonging to the Kayua of southern Brazil (M₆₂) describes how the animals challenged each other to a race:

The irára, too, wanted to run in the race. It is said to carry honey on its back. The ema (*Rhea americana*) said to it: 'You will die. You live

Figure 5. The irára (*Tayra barbara*). (After A. E. Brehm, *La Vie des animaux, les Mammifères*, Vol. I, Paris, undated, p. 601.)

on honey. You want to run in the race. There is no water here. You will die of thirst ... I don't drink water, all my friends can run, I will not give them any.' After running in the race and nearly dying of thirst, the dog broke the container carried by the irára and the honey was spilt, to the irára's intense annoyance. Then the ema said to it: 'It is no use being cross, it was done in fun. We don't fight here. Go away.' And it took all the irára's honey from it (Schaden 1, p. 117).

Here too, therefore, the irára is a bad-tempered, unsatisfied animal because it has honey but no water. It is therefore an incomplete master of honey, anxious at times to wrest possession of the water it lacks from an opponent who is in possession of it (M_{203}), at other times in danger of losing the honey it possesses to a rival capable of doing without the water which it, the irára, so acutely lacks (M_{62}). In either case, it cannot accept the *status quo*: hence its role as a deceiving demiurge in M_{204}.[11]

My second observation relates specifically to M_{204}, in which the irára endows snakes with their poison, an effect which Chaco myths (M_{205}, M_{206}) attribute to the action of pimento fire or smoke (Métraux 3, pp. 19–20; 5, p. 68). Encouraged by Cardus' observation (p. 356) that the Guarayu consider tobacco to be an antidote to snake bites, let us take the following equation as a working hypothesis:

$$\text{smoked pimento} = \text{smoked tobacco}^{(-1)}$$

If we now allow that honey without water (= too strong) stands in the same extreme position in relation to diluted honey as pimento smoke does to tobacco, we shall be able to understand how the irára, the master of honey without water, can, in the Botocudo myth, play a part which is easily confused with the part that Chaco myths assign to a kind of smoke, which scorches literally (fire) or figuratively (pimento), in a total system that can be illustrated as follows:

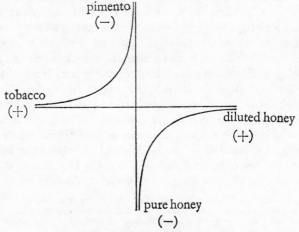

Figure 6. Tobacco, pimento, honey

[11] It is amusing to compare it with Jupiter who plays the same part of deceiving god, lavish with his malice, but niggardly as regards honey:

Ille malum virus serpentibus addidit atris
praedarique lupos iussit pontumque moveri
mellaque decussit foliis ignemque removit.

(Virgil, *Georgics*, I, vv. 129–31)

The above analogical model[12] is indirectly confirmed by the fact that, in Amazonia, a contrast exists between bad honey, which is known to induce vomiting and is used ritually for this purpose, and good tobacco, which the Tucano of Colombia say came from divine vomits. The first thus appears as the *cause* of vomiting which is intended to establish communication between men and gods, whereas the second appears as the *result* of vomiting, which already constitutes in itself a form of communication between the gods and men. Finally, it will be recalled that in M_{202}, a myth made up of two superimposable episodes, the irára intervenes as a combinatory variant of the cunauaru frog, the mistress of a hunting poison, that is, of an inedible substance which like timbó (cf. above, p. 57) is 'transformed' into game, an edible substance, whereas the irára is in possession of pure honey which, as such, is inedible but which can be transformed (by being diluted) into an edible substance.

The preceding discussion has to some extent served to clarify the mythic position of the irára. Being a master of honey, in the literal sense, the irára cannot fully carry out this function in the eyes of men, since it differs from them in eating honey without water; it therefore suffers from a deficiency which explains why other animals are chosen instead of it to fulfil the same function in the myths, although they can only claim to do so figuratively. First and foremost among these animals are the canidae. It is appropriate at this point to recall a Bororo myth (M_{46}) in the opening episode of which the irára is correlated and contrasted with other quadrupeds, some of them canidae. The myth deals with the origin of the heroes Bakororo and Ituboré, who were born of a marriage between a jaguar and a human woman. On her way to the wild beast's lair, the woman met in turn several beasts which tried to pass themselves off as the husband to whom she had been promised by her father on condition that his life be spared. These animals were, in the following order, the irára, the wild cat, the small

[12] I am stressing this characteristic because Leach has accused me of disregarding models of this type and of using exclusively binary patterns. As if the very notion of transformation of which I make constant use and which I borrowed in the first instance from d'Arcy Wentworth Thompson were not entirely dependent on analogy ...

In fact, I constantly have recourse to both types, as the reader may have noticed in connection with a different analysis (p. 79), in which I even tried to combine them. In *The Raw and the Cooked*, there were clear examples of analogical models – e.g. the graphs or diagrams, Fig. 5, p. 90; Fig. 6, p. 98; Fig. 7, p. 107; Fig. 8, p. 194; Fig. 20, p. 335, and the formulae on pp. 163, 199, 249, 250, etc. The same is true of all the diagrams in which the signs + and − denote, not the presence or absence of certain terms, but the *more* or *less* pronounced character of certain polarities which, within a single group of myths, may vary, either directly or inversely.

wolf, the great wolf, the jaguatirica or ocelot and the puma. Having unmasked them all in turn, the woman finally arrived at the jaguar's house.

In its way this episode provides a lesson in ethnozoology, since seven species are set out both in order of size and in relation to their greater or lesser resemblance to the jaguar. From the point of view of size, it is clear that

(1) wild cat < ocelot < puma < jaguar;
(2) small wolf < great wolf.

From the point of view of resemblance to the jaguar, the irára and the jaguar are furthest apart; and the irára is also much smaller than the jaguar. The most remarkable feature of the series is its miscellaneous nature in the light of modern taxonomy, since it includes one of the mustelidae, two canidae and four felidae, in other words animal families very different both in their anatomy and in their way of life. To mention only the most superficial of the differences between them, certain species have spotted or marked coats, while others are all of one colour, but may be light or dark.

But the fact that this seems to us to be a miscellaneous grouping does not necessarily mean that it appeared so to the native mind. Starting with the root iawa, the Tupi form the following nouns by the addition of suffixes: iawara, 'dog', iawarate, 'jaguar', iawacaca, 'otter', iawaru, 'wolf', iawapopé, 'fox' (Montoya), thus grouping felidae, canidae and one of the mustelidae in one and the same category. The Carib of Guiana used to classify animal species according to a principle which is far from clear, but in which it would seem that the jaguar's name, arowa, with the addition of a determinative – tortoise, jacamin bird, agouti, rat, deer, etc. – was used to designate several kinds of quadrupeds (Schomburgk, Vol. II, pp. 65–7). Consequently, as I showed in *The Raw and the Cooked* with regard to ungulates and rodents, to which the native mentality applies the same principle of classification based on the oppositional relationship of the long and the short (animals with tails/animals without tails; long snout/short snout etc.), it would seem that one of the mustelidae such as the irára must not be radically separated from animals belonging to different zoological species. In these circumstances, the fact that the myths assign the role of master of honey to various members of the canidae family would seem to arise not so much in connection with one particular species and its empirical behaviour, as in connection with a very broad ethnozoological

category including not only the irára, which we know from experience to be a master of honey, but also the canidae about which I
have yet to show that, from the semantic point of view, they are better
fitted to fulfil this role than the irára, even though the available empirical evidence does not qualify them for it as clearly as the irára. But we
must also take into account the fact that, in the myths, honey does not
appear simply as a natural product: it is heavily overlaid with connotations which, in a sense, have been superimposed upon it. In order to
control honey, which has become its own metaphor, a real but incomplete master is less well suited than one who is particularly able to
fulfil the function with the required authority, since the myths give the
function itself a figurative meaning.

In order to explain the semantic position of the canidae, we must undoubtedly look towards the Chaco. In the myths belonging to this
area, the fox occupies a leading position as the animal incarnation of a
deceiving god, who occasionally also takes on human form. Among
the Chaco myths, there exists a group in which Fox has a positive or
negative, but always strongly marked, relationship with honey. I now
propose to examine these myths which, so far, have not been studied
from this particular point of view.

M₂₀₇. Toba. 'Fox takes a wife'

After several adventures at the end of which Fox died but came back
to life again as soon as there was a slight fall of rain, he arrived at a
village in the guise of a handsome young lad ... A girl fell in love
with him ... They slept together. The girl, who was in love with him,
scratched and tore him with her nails. 'Don't scratch me like that,'
cried Fox, 'or I shall leave you. It hurts.' ... Fox cried until his cries
were those of a fox and ... the girl left him.

Another girl fell in love with [Fox] and they slept together until
morning. Fox said 'I shall go look for some food' ... In the bush
he collected sachasandias and empty honey combs. He put them
in a bag and returned home. The girl's mother took the bag and
hung it on a post. She said, 'I am going to get a gourd and mix
water and honey in it and let it ferment. I shall prepare mead for my
family. What is left will be for my son-in-law.' ... Fox said to his
wife, 'I am going to take a walk and will come later' ... Fox's
parents-in-law opened the bag and cried, 'This is not honey, these

are sachasandias ... This fellow is not a man ... – he is Fox' (Métraux 5, pp. 122–3).

M₂₀₈. *Toba. 'Fox in search of honey'*

It is said that one day Fox set out to look for wasp honey (lecheguana). He travelled for a long time with no success, and then met a bird (čelmot), which was also looking for honey and which agreed to accompany him. The bird found large quantities of honey. It climbed trees, kept a watchful eye on individual wasps in order to discover the whereabouts of their nests, and then all it had to do was to take out the honey. Fox tried to do likewise, but without success.

The bird then decided to put a spell on such a lamentable partner. It murmured some magic words: 'May a splinter of wood enter Fox's foot so that he cannot walk!' Hardly had it finished saying this when Fox, jumping down from a tree he had climbed, impaled himself on a pointed stick, and died. The bird (čelmot) went off to quench its thirst in a pond, and returned home without telling anyone what had happened.

There was a slight shower of rain and Fox came back to life. Having removed the stake, he succeeded in finding some honey which he put into his bag. As he was thirsty, he set off in the direction of a pond and jumped in without looking. The pond was dry and Fox broke his neck. Nearby a frog was digging a well. Its stomach was full of water. After a very long time, a man appeared who wanted to drink. He noticed that the pond was dry, that Fox was dead and that the frog's stomach was full of water. He pierced it with a cactus thorn; the water spurted out and spread all around, wetting Fox who came back to life again.

One day when Fox was expecting guests and preparing algaroba beer, he noticed Lizard who was sleeping at the top of a Uchan tree (*Chorisia insignis*). Fox left the beer and begged Lizard to make room for him, explaining that he liked to climb trees and that the only reason he did not usually live in the tree-tops was that he preferred to have company there. Lizard cast a spell: 'When Fox jumps may he tear his stomach!' Fox jumped in order to join Lizard and was ripped open by the thorns on the trunk of the yuchan. As he fell, his intestines came out and caught on the tree and held him suspended in mid-air. 'We shall make these entrails grow,' said Lizard, 'so that men can cut them and eat them.' This was the origin of the creeper called 'Fox Tripes', which Indians eat (Métraux 5, pp. 126–7).

In the Matako version of the same myth (M_{209a}), the deceiver, who is called Takjuaj (Tawk'wax) hangs his own intestines on the branches of the tree, where they are changed into creepers. He buries his stomach just below the surface of the ground, and it becomes a kind of melon

Figure 7. A South American fox. (After Ihering, *loc. cit.*, under 'cachorro do mato'.)

full of water. His *reyuno*[13] and his heart give rise to the smooth tasi and the prickly tasi and, under the ground, his large intestine is changed into manioc (Palavecino, p. 264).

Métraux divides this group of myths into three distinct narratives, but if we superimpose them one on the other, it is not difficult to see that they all have a common pattern. A food-collecting operation: a search for honey (probably to make mead, cf. M_{207}) or the preparation of some other fermented beverage fails because Fox does not know how to climb trees, or it succeeds only after Fox has fallen from the tree,

[13] I have been no more successful than Métraux (5, p. 128) who left the term untranslated, in discovering the meaning of this Spanish word in the local dialect. It obviously refers to a part of the body. But the anatomy of the Matako deceiver is full of surprises, as is shown by the following different version (M_{209b}) of the same myth:
'Tawkxwax climbed a yuchan and fell down head first. As he fell the thorns of the tree tore his body. He removed his stomach from his body and buried it. From it grew a plant (iletsáx), the root of which is very large and full of water. His intestines became lianas. Like a cow, Tawkxwax had two stomachs. With the second he made a plant called iwokanó' (Métraux 3, p. 19).
It is worth noting that in North America myths closely resembling the Chaco ones likewise associate an excessive use, either of parts of the body, or of trees, or plants or wild fruits and the origin of the latter with a deceiver personified by Mink or Coyote (Menomini: Hoffman, p. 164; Pawnee: Dorsey, pp. 464–5; Kiowa: Parsons, p. 42). Among the Iroquois (Hewitt, p. 710), several climbing plants with edible fruit are said to have sprung from the intestines of Tawiskaron, the god of winter. The Ojibwa believe that the demiurge's evil brother underwent the same transformation. In South America itself, the Fox reappears as a clumsy and greedy deceiver in the myths of the Uitoto (Preuss 1, pp. 574–81), and also in those of the Uro-Cipaya on the Andean plateau (Métraux 2).

but in that case the search has made him thirsty and the deceiver, behaving thoughtlessly as always, falls to his death in a waterless pond: water being the indispensable element needed to restore him to life. Fox who is *impaled* in the first episode corresponds, in the second (but with the reverse effect: wet earth instead of dry earth), to the frog whose stomach is *pierced* and, in the third, to the Fox who is disembowelled, not as a result of falling *from high to low*, as in the first two episodes, but by trying to jump *from low to high*. When Fox falls *from high to low*, he is *without honey* (first episode). When he falls to a still lower position (to the bottom of a dried-up pond), he is *without water* (second episode). Finally, when he jumps *from low to high* (third episode) he determines the appearance, *at the half-way mark*, not of honey or water, but of things which bear an extraordinary resemblance to them in the sense that, not being absolutely one or the other, they illustrate approximately the conjunction of both, which were previously in a state of disjunction: honey above in the trees, water below in the pond or in the belly of a frog which is busy digging a well. The conjunction takes the form of plants or wild fruits which, like honey (in the native system of classification), belong to the vegetable realm but, unlike honey, contain water.

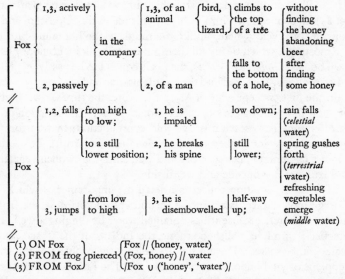

| Fox | 1,3, actively | in the company | 1,3, of an animal | bird, lizard, | climbs to the top of a tree | without finding the honey abandoning beer |
| | 2, passively | | 2, of a man | | falls to the bottom of a hole, | after finding some honey |

//

Fox	1,2, falls	from high to low;	1, he is impaled	low down;	rain falls (*celestial* water)
		to a still lower position;	2, he breaks his spine	still lower;	spring gushes forth (*terrestrial* water) refreshing
	3, jumps	from low to high	3, he is disembowelled	half-way up;	vegetables emerge (*middle* water)

//

(1) ON Fox   }
(2) FROM frog } pierced { Fox // (honey, water)
(3) FROM Fox }   { (Fox, honey) // water
                             { /Fox ∪ ('honey', 'water')/

In support of the above summary, it can be pointed out that certain themes occurring in the three episodes correspond to each other exactly. This is especially so in the case of what I would like to call the 'piercing operation': Fox is impaled on a sharp-pointed stick, the frog's stomach is pierced with a cactus spine, Fox is disembowelled by the spikes on the trunk of the yuchan tree. As will be confirmed later, this is a basic theme in honey myths, and we shall obviously have to try to find some explanation for it. But for the time being, I merely wish to emphasize three points.

In the first place, the 'piercing' has to do in each case with a natural vessel: the fox's body or the frog's body, that is – since the fox is the hero of the myth – his *own body* or some *other body*. In the first episode, his own body is a *container without content*: nothing escapes from Fox's impaled body since his stomach is empty (without honey) and he is thirsty (without water). After being restored to life by the rain, which moistens the outside of his dry, still empty and water-seeking body, Fox breaks his spine, thus introducing, by means of his *own body*, the second term of a contrast: *pierced entrails/broken bones*, the first term of which is represented by the body of another – the body of the frog, which, unlike that of Fox, then appears in the form of a *container with content*: it is full of water. This outward materialization of the container, once its internal materialization is out of the question, provides a fresh illustration of a pattern to which I have already drawn attention (p. 85), in connection with the honey episode in the 'Opossum and his sons-in-law' cycle, where, unlike the monkey, the humming-bird and the mosquito, which busily fill their gullets or bellies with honey (their own bodies *container ∪ content*), the fox is content to be passively present when the honey is poured into the gourd (his own body *container // content*).

In the first two episodes of M_{208}, therefore, the (fox's) own body is dry and the body of the other (the frog's) is wet. The function of the third episode is to solve this two-fold contradiction: by transforming his own body into other bodies (vegetables and fruit), Fox brings about a conjunction between dry and wet, since the swollen vegetables and fruit are dry outside and wet inside.

My next observation concerns a detail the importance of which will emerge more clearly later. In the second episode of M_{208}, the frog is master of water, because it has obtained water by digging a well. This practice is firmly established among the Indians of the Chaco, where water can be scarce: 'During the dry season, the problem of the water supply is of vital importance to the natives. The Lule and Vilela tribes, who used to live to the south of the Bermejo, dug deep wells or built huge reservoirs. The present-day Lengua have wells between $4\frac{1}{2}$ and six metres deep and about seventy-five centimetres wide. They are so constructed as to allow a man to go down inside by placing his feet in notches cut in opposite sides of the well wall' (Métraux 14, p. 8).

Finally, it is impossible to mention the theme of 'broaching' without reference to its inverted form, which is illustrated in other Chaco myths about Fox, particularly those belonging to the Toba and the Mataco. These myths (discussed in RC, p. 305; M_{175}) relate how the deceiver Tawkxwax, or his Toba equivalent Fox, had all the orifices of his body blocked by a wasp or a bee, which I showed – by a very different line of reasoning – to be a frog that had been transformed by inversion of the dry/damp connotations belonging respectively to the two creatures. It is clear that, in this respect, the second episode in M_{208} is a retransformation of M_{175} by means of a three-fold contrast: *dry/wet, closed/open, active/passive*, which can be reduced to the following formula:

$$M_{175}[^1BEE\ ^2which\ ^3blocks] \Rightarrow M_{208}[^1FROG\ ^2which\ is\ ^3pierced$$

corresponding to the fact that, in M_{175}, Fox has all the water he could wish for (exteriorized by the bee: in jars) but regards it with contempt, whereas in M_{208} he is deprived of water which he covets because the water is interiorized by the frog (in its body).

Another Toba myth offers a variant of the final episode of M_{208}–M_{209}:

M_{210}. *Toba. 'Fox stuffed with honey'*

Fox is fishing in the lagoon while Carancho is looking for wasp honey (lecheguana). He finds a great deal, but Fox catches no fish. His entire contribution to the midday meal consists of two poor chumuco birds.[14] Fox is annoyed at his friend's not appreciating the birds, and he refuses the honey on the ground that it is bad. Carancho casts a spell on him: 'May Fox's stomach secrete honey!' Fox does indeed discover that his excrement is full of honey, that his saliva changes into honey as soon as he spits it out, and that he is oozing honey from every pore.

Thereupon, Carancho, having made a good haul of fish, invites Fox to eat some of it. Fox begins by eating heartily, but when Carancho reveals that what he thinks is fish is really honey magically disguised, Fox is so sickened that he vomits. He notices with a certain pride that his vomit changes into water-melons: 'It is as if I were a shaman. Where I vomit, new plants grow!' (Métraux 5, pp. 138–9).

This variant is interesting in two respects. First of all, it illustrates a

[14] On these birds as an inferior form of game, see RC, p. 204.

connection, already observed among the Mundurucu, between honey
and water-melons (cf. p. 57). It will be remembered that the Mundurucu believe water-melons to come 'from the devil', and that they
were originally poisonous, until men domesticated and cultivated them
so that they became safe to eat. Now Fox, a deceiving divinity, clearly
plays the part of a 'devil' in Toba mythology. The Goajiro Indians,
who live in the extreme north of tropical America, in Venezuela, also

Figure 8. The carancho bird (*Polyborus plancus*). (After Ihering, *loc. cit.*,
under 'carancho'.)

believe the melon to be a 'diabolical' food (Wilbert 6, p. 172). The same
is true of the Tenetehara (Wagley–Galvão, p. 145). The diabolical
nature of water-melons, which is widely believed in by tribes remote
from each other and different both in language and culture, raises a
problem that we must try to solve.

At the same time, M_{210} recreates in a clearer and more vigorous form
the contrast, already present in M_{208}–M_{209}, between the unlucky fox
and its more gifted companion, which was first a bird (the čelmot),
then the lizard. The companion in question here is none other than
Carancho, i.e. the demiurge (as opposed to the deceiving Fox) who,
among the Toba, takes the form of a predatory, carrion-eating, species
of falcon, fond of larvae and insects, *Polyborus plancus*: 'It prefers

savannah lands and open spaces. It has a slightly pompous gait and when it raises its feathered crest it has a rather noble bearing, which is hardly in keeping with its very plebeian mode of life' (Ihering, under 'carancho').[15] In the myth, the demiurge is a master of fishing and of the search for honey, and Fox is furious at being inferior to him. Sickened by honey, like the corupira in the Amazonian myth, M_{202}, he has to make do with being master of water-melons.

Figure 9. Carácará birds (*Milvago chimachima*). (After Ihering, *loc. cit.*, under 'carácará'.)

It is clear that, in this instance, the water-melons are a substitute for honey and fish. What have these three sources of food in common and in what ways are they different? At the same time, what common features are there between the water-melons (*Citrullus* sp.) which spring up from Fox's vomit and the plants created from his entrails in M_{208}–M_{209}: edible creepers, tasi, manioc, and also, as it happens, the water-melon? Finally, what is the relationship with the fruit of the sachasandia tree, of which Fox is the master in M_{207}?

[15] The carancho is bigger than the carácará, another of the falconidae (*Milvago chimachima*), which plays the part of the deceiver in Caduveo mythology, cf. above, p. 74, n. 7.

Within this group, a special place must be given to manioc, which is the only cultivated plant. But at the same time it is, of all cultivated plants, the one which demands least attention and the one which does not ripen at any set season. Cuttings are planted at the beginning of the rainy season. The ground is weeded from time to time and, several months later, the plants are fully grown: between eight and eighteen months, according to the methods used. From then on, and until the crop is exhausted, they supply edible roots all through the year.[16] Since manioc requires little attention, is capable of thriving in the poorest soil, is always available and is so along with wild plants at times when other cultivated plants have already been harvested, if not eaten, it represents a non-specified source of food which is mentioned together with wild plants with a certain food value. This is because the fact that it can still be eaten during the wild fruit season is more important from the practical point of view of the native diet than its being theoretically included among the cultivated plants.

As for the sachasandia (*Capparis salicifolia*), its fruit has a sinister connotation at least for the Mataco, about whom we know a great deal, since it provides the normal means of suicide, for these Indians seem particularly prone to take their own lives. Poisoning by sachasandia brings about convulsions, foaming at the mouth, irregular beating of the heart, which stops and starts again, contractions of the throat, choking sounds, trembling and jerky contractions accompanied by violent diarrhoea. Finally the victim falls into a coma and dies fairly quickly. Prompt treatment in the form of morphine injections and the administration of an emetic has made it possible to save several Indians, who have later described their symptoms: profound depression, followed by giddiness 'as if the world were turning upside down', which forces them to lie down (Métraux 10).

It is therefore understandable that the sachasandia should figure in the Chaco diet only during periods of shortage. And even then the

[16] Whiffen's observation (p. 193) about north-west Amazonia can be generalized: 'Although manioc is planted as a rule just before the heaviest annual rainfall becomes due, there is no part of the year when some of the roots are not ready to gather.'

In support of the preceding remarks, I can also quote the following comments by Leeds (pp. 23-4): 'Thus manioc has no clear peak, is regular over the years, is storable both in raw form and in prepared forms ... is so located as not to permit of a concentration of labour at any one time and needs no massive labour for harvesting because of short harvest periods. Thus, in general, the very nature of manioc as a crop, and the labour requisites for harvesting it, require no centralized authority, and renders it possible and even probable that the management of production or distribution can be carried on without it. The same may be said on the whole, for all the hunting, fishing and gathering harvests.'

fruit must be boiled up five times in fresh water to eliminate the toxins. However, this is also true, although to a lesser extent, of most of the wild plants I have listed.

Several authors (Métraux 14, pp. 3–28; 12, pp. 246–7; Henry 2; Susnik, pp. 20–21, 48–9, 87, 104) have described in detail the cycle of economic life in the Chaco. From November until January or February, the Indians in the Pilcomayo area drink the pods of the algaroba (*Prosopis* sp.), the nourishing fruit of the chanar (*Gourleia decorticans*) and of the mistol (*Zizyphus mistol*) in the form of a lightly fermented beer. This is the period the Toba call 'kotap', which seems to have the same meaning as 'bienestar', when peccaries and coati are plump and plentiful. It is a time of feasts, merrymaking and inter-tribal visits, when bridegrooms-to-be present their future mothers-in-law with bags full of meat.

In February and March, the wild produce already mentioned is replaced by other forms: among agricultural tribes poroto del monte (*Capparis retusa*), tasi (*Morrenia odorata*) and Barbary figs (*Opuntia*) provide an addition to maize, pumpkins and water-melons. As soon as the rains stop in April, any surplus wild fruit is dried in the sun for winter use, and the plantations are made ready.

From the beginning of April to mid-June, shoals of fish swim up the rivers, heralding a season of plenty. In June and July, the streams gradually dry up, fishing becomes difficult and once more the population has to fall back on wild fruit: tasi, which has already been mentioned, and tusca (*Acacia aroma*), both of which ripen between April and September.

August and September are the months of real food shortage, when the Indians live on reserves of dried fruit, with the addition of the naranja del monte (*Capparis speciosa*), cucurbitaceae, bromeliaceae, wild tubers, an edible creeper (Phaseolus?) and the sachasandia fruit already mentioned. Because of their bitter taste, several other varieties of fruit which I mentioned previously – e.g. poroto and naranja del monte – must also be boiled in several changes of water, then dried in the sun after being crushed in a mortar. When water runs short, the Indians drink what has collected at the base of the leaves of the caraguata, one of the bromeliaceae, and chew the fleshy root of one of the euphorbiaceae.

During the dry months, the Indians scatter and lead a nomadic life, after being together in large groups during the festive season to drink algaroba beer and fish along the river banks. Families go off on their own and wander through the woods, looking for wild fruit and game. All the tribes hunt, especially the Mataco who have no access to the rivers. The great collective hunts, which are often carried out with the help of bush fires, take place chiefly during the dry season, although hunting goes on during the rest of the year as well.

The Toba, who call this period Káktapigá, lay stress in their stories on the fact that this is the time when animals are thin and lacking in the fat so necessary in the diet of the hunter. This is the time of 'hunger sickness': the mouth becomes dry and parched, and the flesh of the ema (nandu) provides a bare subsistence. Consequently, influenza is rife and unweaned children and old people die; the staple food is armadillos, and the Indians wrap themselves up well and sleep near their fires ...

It is clear from the preceding details that, although there is no real rainy season in the Chaco, where violent downpours can occur at any period in the year, the rains tend nevertheless to be concentrated between October and March (Grubb, p. 306). All the fox's plants therefore appear to be dry-season foods; this is also true of fish, and of honey which is collected chiefly during the nomadic period. However, the dry season is shown to have, alternatively, two different aspects: it is characterized by plenty and by shortage. All the myths we are dealing with relate to the dry season, which is considered either in its most favourable aspect, which is marked by a plentiful supply of fish and honey (of which, as Métraux stresses (*loc. cit.*, p. 7), Chaco Indians are very fond), or in its poorest and most distressing aspect, since most of the wild fruits gathered during the dry season are poisonous or bitter and require complicated treatment before they are safe to eat. Water-melons, which grow at the beginning of the dry season, are non-poisonous owing to the fact that they are cultivated. Under their hard outer bark, they conceal a copious supply of water and thus allow the last beneficial effects of the closing rainy season to be prolonged right into the dry season. They are a supreme and paradoxical illustration of the contrast between container and content: one being dry, the other wet;[17] and they can be used as an emblem for a deceiving god, who is also paradoxically different outside and inside.

Surely, in its way, the yuchan tree, on whose hard spikes Fox is disembowelled, is not unlike the water-melon and other juicy fruit eaten during the dry season. In Mataco and Ashluslay mythology

[17] Kruse's version of M157 (p. 56) is most eloquent on this point: 'When the fruit becomes hard, declares the mother of cultivated plants, it will be ready for eating.'

(M_{111}), the yuchan is the tree which, in former times, held all the water in the world inside its swollen trunk, and which supplied men with fish from one year's end to the next. It therefore interiorizes terrestrial water and neutralizes the contrast between the fishing season and the fishless season, just as wild fruits interiorize celestial water and thus neutralize – although only relatively, but nevertheless in an empirically verifiable manner – the contrast between the dry season and the rainy season. Later in the Guiana myths, we shall come across trees which, like the yuchan, belong to the bombax family, and it is hardly necessary to remind the reader that evidence of their being considered as the tree of life is to be found even in ancient Maya mythology. But the fact that the theme also exists in the Chaco, and in the particular form of the tree filled with water and fish, shows that, in this region, it has a peculiar link with the techno-economical substructure: the spiky dryness of the trunk, in an allegorical way, encloses the water, and the water encloses the fish, just as the dry season encloses the special period when fish become more plentiful in the rivers, and also encloses within its duration the ripening period of wild fruit, which encloses water within the volume circumscribed by its hard skin.

Finally, like fish, honey presupposes both water (with which it is diluted to make mead) and dryness. They are mediatory agents between the dry and the wet and at the same time between the high and the low, since during the dry season the dry is atmospheric in nature, hence celestial, and in the absence of rain-water must inevitably come from the earth – that is, from wells. The mediation illustrated by honey and fish is therefore the most ambitious in range, because of the gap between the terms which have to be brought together, and the most rewarding in its results, whether the latter are defined quantitatively (fish, the most plentiful of all foods), or qualitatively (honey, the most delicious of all foods). The fox manages to bring about the same mediation, although at a more mediocre level: however juicy they are, wild fruits do not take the place of water, and they give a great deal of trouble before they can be harvested and rendered fit for consumption. Finally, this makeshift mediation is achieved by the fox at an equal distance between the high and the low – it is half-way up the tree – and through the sacrifice of its middle parts since, anatomically speaking, its entrails are half-way between the high and the low.

3 The Story of the Girl Mad About Honey, Her Base Seducer and Her Timid Husband

a. IN THE CHACO

The first of the honey myths belonging to the Chaco region that we discussed (M_{207}), and in which Fox plays the chief part, hints at the intervention of a feminine partner: the young girl whom Fox seduced after he had disguised himself as a handsome boy, and whom he made a pretence of marrying. A short myth repeats this particular episode: it anticipates, in a condensed form, an important group of myths which it is possible to isolate, once we have recognized the basic pattern outlined in M_{211}, behind the various transformations:

M_{211}. Toba. 'Sick Fox'

On returning from a successful honey expedition, in which he had taken part along with the other villagers, Fox was stung by a poisonous spider. His wife called four famous healers to give him treatment. At this time Fox had human form. As he coveted his sister-in-law, who was prettier than his wife, he insisted that she should act as his nurse. He expected to be able to seduce her when they were alone together. But she would not hear of it, and denounced him to her sister who left her husband in a rage. Fox's behaviour, which was so little in keeping with the malady with which he claimed to be afflicted, finally aroused suspicion and he was unmasked (Métraux 5, pp. 139–40).

Here now are variants of the same myth, but in which the theme is treated at much greater length:

M_{212}. *Toba.* '*The girl mad about honey*' (1)

Sakhé was the daughter of the master of the Water People, and she was so fond of honey she was always begging for it. Irritated by her persistent requests, both men and women replied: 'Get married!' Even her mother, when pestered by the daughter for honey, told her it would be better if she got married.

So the young girl decided to marry Woodpecker, the famous honey-gatherer. He was, as it happened, in the woods with other birds, all busy like himself, piercing holes in the tree-trunks with their beaks in order to reach the bees' nests. Fox pretended to help them but did no more than beat the tree with his stick.

Sakhé inquired where Woodpecker was to be found. As she walked in the direction indicated, she met Fox, who tried to pass himself off as the bird. But his breast was not red, and his bag, instead of honey, contained only dirt. The young girl was not deceived; she continued on her way and finally met Woodpecker, to whom she proposed marriage. Woodpecker showed little enthusiasm, discussed the matter and said he was sure that the young girl's parents would not approve of him. Whereupon she insisted angrily: 'My mother lives alone, and does not want me any more!' Fortunately, Woodpecker had some honey, and she calmed down as she ate it. Finally, Woodpecker said: 'If it is true that your mother has sent you with this intention, I shall not be afraid to marry you. But if you are lying, how could I marry you? I am no fool!' Thereupon he came down from the tree he had climbed, carrying his bag full of honey.

Meanwhile the lazy Fox had filled his bag with sachasandia and tasi fruits, which people fall back on when they can find nothing else. Yet, during the days that followed, Fox deliberately refrained from going back to look for honey with the birds which were dissatisfied with the amount of honey gathered on their first expedition. He preferred to steal the honey he ate.

One day, Woodpecker had left his wife alone in the encampment, and Fox tried to take advantage of the situation. Pretending to have a splinter in his foot which prevented him following his companions, he went back alone to the encampment. Almost immediately on arrival there, he tried to rape the wife. But the latter, who was pregnant, fled into the woods. Fox pretended to be asleep. He felt terribly ashamed.

When Woodpecker returned, he inquired anxiously about his wife, and Fox lied to him, saying that she had just left with her mother. Woodpecker, who was a chief, ordered that a search party should be sent to find her. But the mother was not at home and the wife had disappeared. Woodpecker then shot magic arrows in several directions. Those which saw nothing came back to him. When the third arrow did not come back, Woodpecker knew that it had fallen at the spot where his wife was, and he set off to join her.

Meanwhile, Woodpecker's son (it must be assumed that he had had time to be born and grow up) had recognized his father's arrow. Along with his mother, he went to meet him; they kissed each other and wept for joy. The wife told the husband what had happened.

The wife and child reached the camp first. They handed food round, and the mother introduced the child. But the grandmother, who knew nothing of her daughter's marriage and motherhood, was surprised. 'Well, yes,' explained the daughter, 'you scolded me. I left and got married.' The old woman said not a word, and her daughter too was vexed with her because of being scolded and driven away when she had asked for honey. The child spoke up: 'My father is Woodpecker, a big chief and clever hunter and he knows how to find honey ... Don't scold me, or I'll go away.' The grandmother protested that she had no such intention and was delighted. The child agreed to go and look for his father.

Woodpecker assured his mother-in-law, who was amiability itself, that he was in need of nothing, that he did not want any algaroba beer, and that he could look after himself. He asked the old woman to be kind to her grandson, who would be his heir. He also announced his intention of having other children.

Now, Woodpecker prepared to take his revenge. He accused Fox of having lied about his lame foot. Because of him, the wife had nearly died of thirst in the woods! Fox protested, accused his victim of being over-prudish, and insisted that she had had no grounds for taking fright. He offered gifts, which Woodpecker refused. With the help of his son, he tied Fox up, and the child undertook to cut Fox's throat with his grandfather's knife. For the son had more nerve than the father (Métraux 5, pp. 146–8).

After giving this version of the myth, Métraux draws attention to several variants supplied by his informants; some of them reproduce M$_{207}$, while others resemble the version published by Palavecino. In this last version, the heroine recognizes Fox by his characteristic stench (cf. M_{103}). Fox therefore stinks like an opossum, but – if we are to go by the Toba myths – less than the skunk, since the latter hunts and kills pigs with its noxious farts, and Fox tries in vain to imitate it (M_{212b}, Métraux 5, p. 128). Once she is married to Woodpecker and lavishly provided with honey, the heroine refuses to give any to her mother. When caught unawares by Fox while bathing, she prefers to change into a capybara, rather than yield to him. From this point onwards, the Palavecino version follows a decidedly different course:

M_{213}. *Toba.* '*The girl mad about honey*' (2)

After the failure of his amorous ventures, Fox could not think how to avoid the vengeance of the outraged husband. Since the wife had disappeared, why should he not pretend to be her? So he took on the appearance of his victim and, at Woodpecker's request, undertook to delouse him, a service a wife normally performs for her husband. Fox, however, was clumsy: he injured Woodpecker with his needle, as he tried to kill the lice. Woodpecker's suspicions were aroused, and he asked an ant to bite his so-called wife in the leg. Fox uttered most unfeminine howls, which betrayed his identity. Woodpecker killed him, then, by means of magic arrows, tried to find out where his wife was hiding. After discovering from one of the arrows that she had changed into a capybara, he gave up searching for her, believing that from then on she would want for nothing. After being dried and mummified by the sun, Fox was restored to life by rain and went on his way (Palavecino, pp. 265–7).

Before examining the Mataco variants of the story of the girl mad about honey, I propose to introduce a myth about the origin, not of honey, but of mead, and one which shows how important this fermented beverage was among the Chaco Indians.

M_{214}. *Mataco.* '*The origin of mead*'

In ancient times there was no mead. An old man tried to make it with some honey ... He mixed the honey with water and left the mixture to ferment for one night. The next day he tasted it and found it very good. The other people did not want to taste the drink as they thought it might be poisonous. The old man said, 'I will drink because I am very old and if I died it would not matter.' The old man drank much of the mixture and he fell down as if dead.

That night he awoke and told the people that the beer was not a poison. The men carved a larger trough and drank all the beer they made. It was a bird who carved the first drum, and he beat it all night, and at dawn he was changed into a man (Métraux 3, p. 54).

The interest of this short myth lies in the fact that it establishes a two-fold equivalence: on the one hand between fermented honey and poison and, on the other, between the trough used for mead and the wooden drum. The first equivalence confirms my previous remarks; the importance of the second will appear at a much later stage, and I shall leave it on one side for the time being. It will be noted that the invention of the trough-drum leads to the transformation of an animal into a human, and consequently that the invention of mead brings about a transition from nature to culture. This was already obvious from my analysis of the myths about the origin of the honey (festival) (M_{188}, M_{189}); at the same time, according to a Botocudo myth which I have already discussed (M_{204}), the irára, master of honey without water (hence non-mead) is responsible for the reverse transformation of humans into animals. Another Mataco myth confirms this (M_{215}): whoever eats too much honey without water chokes and is in danger of dying. Honey and water are mutually involved with each other, and one is given in exchange for the other (Métraux 3, pp. 74–5). After stressing the importance of the correlation between honey and water in Mataco thought, we can now embark on the main myths.

M_{216}. *Mataco*. '*The girl mad about honey*' (1)

The daughter of the Sun adored honey and the larvae of bees. As she was white-skinned and pretty, she resolved to marry only an expert in the collecting of honey of the ales variety, which is very difficult to extract from hollow trees, and her father told her that Woodpecker would make an ideal husband. She therefore set off to look for him, and went deep into the forest where the sound of axes could be heard.

First, she met a bird which could not probe deep enough to get at the honey, and so she went on her way. Just when she was about to catch up with Woodpecker, she accidentally stepped on a dry branch which snapped under her weight. Woodpecker took fright and flew to the top of the tree that he was busy on. From his high perch, he asked the young girl what she wanted. She explained why she had come. Although she was pretty, Woodpecker was afraid of her. When she asked him for a drink (she knew that Woodpecker always carried a gourd full of water), he began to come down, but he was overcome with fear again and went back up to his retreat. The girl told him that she admired him and wished to have him as her husband. Finally, she persuaded Woodpecker to come down to her, and she was able to quench her thirst and eat as much honey as she wanted. The marriage took place. Tawkxwax was jealous, because he desired the girl; she, however, despised him and told him so. Every evening, when Woodpecker reached the conjugal abode, she gently deloused him with the help of a cactus thorn.

One day, during her menstrual period, she remained behind in the village, and Tawkxwax caught her unawares while she was bathing. She fled, leaving her clothes behind. T. dressed up in them and took on the appearance of a woman, whom Woodpecker believed to be his wife. He therefore asked her to delouse him as usual; but with each movement T. scraped his head. This made Woodpecker angry and aroused his suspicions. He called an ant and asked it to climb between T.'s legs: 'If you see a vulva, that's all right, but if you see a penis, sting him!' The twinge of pain caught T. unawares, so that he lifted up his skirt and revealed his true identity; he received a sound thrashing. After which, Woodpecker went off in search of his wife.

After a while he disappeared too and the sun became anxious as to his fate. Sun started to seek him. He followed his trail until his footprints disappeared in a pool. Sun threw his spear into the water and it immediately dried up. At the bottom were two *lagu* fish, one small and the other large. He managed to make the small one vomit but could find nothing in its stomach. He did the same to the large fish and in its stomach was the woodpecker. The woodpecker came to life and he changed himself into a bird. Sun's daughter disappeared forever (Métraux 3, pp. 34–6).

Another variant in the same collection (M_{217}) relates that Sun had two daughters and fed on aquatic animals – lewo – similar to caymans, the masters of wind, tempests and storms, and which were rainbows in animal form. The story continues along almost identical lines to the preceding version, except that Sun advises his daughter to get married, because he cannot supply her with the quality of honey she prefers. After unmasking the deceiver, Woodpecker kills him, then finds his wife again at her father's house, where she has, in the meantime, given birth to a child. Two days later, Sun asks his son-in-law to go and fish for lewo in the water of a lake. Woodpecker does so, but one of the aquatic monsters swallows him. The young woman begs her father to give her back her husband. Sun discovers the culprit, and orders it to restore its victim to life. Woodpecker flies out of the monster's mouth (*ibid.*, pp. 36–7).

A third version, also Mataco in origin, differs considerably from the previous versions.

M_{218}. *Mataco.* 'The girl mad about honey' (3)

In the beginning, animals were men and fed exclusively on bees' honey. Sun's youngest daughter was cross with her father, who was a great leader living on the shores of a lake, because he did not give her enough larvae to eat. On his advice, she set out in search of Woodpecker who, of all the birds, was the best honey-gatherer. Woodpecker's village was a long way away from her father's village. When she arrived at Woodpecker's house, she married him.

At the beginning of the third moon, Takjuaj (= Tawkxwax) arrived at Woodpecker's village, ostensibly to take part in the honey harvest. One day when the honey-gatherers were working a short distance away from the village, he deliberately hurt his foot on a thorn and asked Sun's daughter to carry him to the village on her back. Sitting astride her in this way, he tried to copulate with the young woman from behind. She threw him off angrily and went back to her father, the Sun.

Takjuaj was in an embarrassing situation. What would Woodpecker say when he could not find his wife? Perhaps he would try to take his revenge and kill him? He therefore decided to take on the appearance of his victim [var. he made himself clay breasts and a clay vagina]. Woodpecker returned, gave all the honey he had gathered to the woman he took to be his wife, but from the unusual manner in which Takjuaj set about eating the grub (he threaded it onto a needle) [var. from the manner in which T. deloused him], Woodpecker spotted the deception, and confirmed it by means of an ant which he sent to inspect the nether parts of the false wife [var. when bitten by the ant, T. jumped and his false attributes dropped off]. Woodpecker then beat Takjuaj to death and hid his body in a hollow tree. After which, he set off to look for his wife.

He found her at Sun's house. The latter asked him to go and find him a lewoo, for that was the only food he ate. The monster devoured the fisherman. The wife demanded to have her husband back. Sun went to the lewoo, and forced it to vomit; Woodpecker's soul flew out; from then on Woodpecker became a bird. This is the origin of Woodpeckers, as they are known today (Palavecino, pp. 257–8).

The theme of the deceiver imprisoned in a hollow tree, the importance of which will appear later, is found in another myth in the same collection:

M_{219}. *Mataco. 'The stoppered and blocked deceiver'*

During the course of his wanderings, Takjuaj noticed a mistol tree (*Zizyphus mistol*), the fallen fruit of which lay strewn on the ground. He started to eat and realized that the food was passing straight through his anus undigested; he coped with this difficulty by means of a cork made from 'pasto' (paste? straw? – cf. M_1). Having put on a little flesh, T. met the nakuó bee (= moro moro, cf. Palavecino, pp. 252–3) and asked it for some honey. The bee pretended to comply with this request, and made him enter a hollow tree full of honey, but lost no time in blocking up the opening with clay. T. remained a prisoner in the tree for a lunar month, until a violent gale tore the tree apart and set him free (Palavecino, p. 247).

This myth is reminiscent of another one (M_{175}; cf. *RC*, pp. 305–11), in which the same deceiver quarrels with a bee or wasp which blocks up all the orifices of his body. Thus the Fox, whether in human form (Mataco) or animal form (Toba), appears in the Chaco myths as a personage whose body serves as the basis for a dialectic of opening and closing, container and content, outside and inside. The piercing may be from the outside (adjunction of feminine attributes), and the closing internal (closing up of the orifices through excess in M_{175}, or through a lack in M_{219}). Fox is pierced before he is blocked up (M_{219}), or blocked up before being pierced (M_{175}): in the one instance, he is a container without any content of its own (when the food passes through his body), in the other, he is the content of another container (the hollow tree in which he is imprisoned). This links up with my previous comments on a Mundurucu myth (M_{97}; cf. above, p. 83) and on other Chaco myths (M_{208}: cf. pp. 93–5).

It is quite clear that the Mundurucu and Chaco myths throw light on each other. In the former, the canidae also play a part: as a Mundurucu hero (M_{220}), Fox ties his enemy Jaguar to a tree-trunk, on the pretext that he is *protecting him from a strong wind* (compare with M_{219}; Fox himself is imprisoned in a tree-trunk – tree = *internal prison/external prison* – from which he is eventually *freed* by a strong wind); a wasp *fails to free* Jaguar (M_{219}: a bee *succeeds in imprisoning* Fox). After which Jaguar, in order to catch Fox, hides in a *hollow tree*, where Fox forces him to betray his presence by making him believe that the hollow tree talks when it is empty, but is silent when it is protecting an occupant: this is a transposition into the acoustic code of the contrast between homogeneous container without content (the case of the talking tree) and non-homogeneous content in the container (the case of the silent tree). The symmetry between the Chaco myths and a Mundurucu myth is continued significantly in the use the latter makes of the well-known theme of the *bicho enfolhado*: the fox finally deceives the jaguar by smearing itself with honey (*external use*/*internal use*), and then rolling in dead leaves which stick to its body. Thus disguised, the fox succeeds in reaching the river to which the jaguar is trying to deny it access (Couto de Magalhães, pp. 260–64; Kruse 2, pp. 631–2). Thanks to honey (but which he puts to a non-alimentary use) Mundurucu Fox therefore succeeds in getting something to drink, whereas in the Chaco myths Fox, who is very thirsty (through having eaten too much honey), fails to find anything to drink, because the ponds are dry. Another Mundurucu myth (M_{221}), the leading characters of which are the fox and the vulture (that is, the eater of raw food as opposed to the eater of rotten food), transforms the theme of the *bicho enfolhado*: Fox, who is now victim instead of persecutor, smears his body with *wax* (/*honey*) in order to stick feathers on it (/*leaves*). Thus attired, he proposes to *fly in the air* (/*swim in water*) *so as to follow the vulture* (/*to escape from the jaguar*). But the sun melts the wax and Fox crashes to the ground and is killed, whereas, in M_{220}, the water dissolves the honey and Fox manages to survive by swimming to safety (cf. Farabee 4, p. 134). All these transformations bear witness to the fact that we are dealing with a coherent system, the logical frontiers of which follow the geographical frontiers of the Amazon basin and of the Chaco, in spite of the distance between these two areas.

But if this is the case, we are perhaps justified in trying to elucidate one detail in the Chaco myths by a corresponding detail in a Mundurucu myth. It will be remembered that a Mataco variant of the story of the girl mad about honey (M_{216}) describes the latter as being 'white-skinned and very pretty'. Now, in Mundurucu cosmogony, the moon is a metamorphosed young virgin with a very white skin (Farabee, *ibid.*, p. 138; other versions in Kruse 3, pp. 1000–1003; Murphy 1, p. 86). The parallel is all the more significant in that there exists a Guiana belief to the effect that honey runs short during the period of the full moon (Ahlbrinck, under 'nuno' §5, and 'wano' §2). The story of the girl mad about honey might therefore admit of an interpretation in terms of the astronomical code, in which the heroine (whose father, as we already know, is the Sun) could be the incarnation of the full moon, and would be all the more greedy for honey since honey is completely lacking when she is present.

In support of this negative pre-condition, I can quote a variant of M_{218}, but one which is of very remote origin since it belongs to the Pima of Arizona (M_{218b}). Coyote pretended to be wounded and insisted that his sister-in-law should carry him on her back; he took advantage of the situation to copulate with her from behind. This offensive behaviour led to the imprisonment of all the animals: that is, *game was lost* instead of *honey being lost* as in South America. Yet the North American version seems to adhere so closely to the affinity between the two themes that it uses one metaphorically to describe the other: Coyote, the liberator of game, opens wide the prison door and 'out swarmed the deer and other game animals, as pour forth the bees from a newly opened hive' (Russell, pp. 217–18). With or without reference to honey, the Chaco myths we have just examined reappear in North America, from California to the basins of the Columbia and Fraser rivers.

At this point, a further observation should be made. In M_{213}, the girl mad about honey changes into a capybara. Another Mataco version (M_{222}) tells the story of a girl mad about wasp honey, lecheguana, who is changed into a non-identified nocturnal rodent (Métraux 3, p. 57, n. 1). As is well known, the capybara (*Hydrochoerus capibara*), which is also nocturnal (Ihering, under 'capivara'), is the largest living rodent; but another rodent, smaller but still quite large and with the same habits (viscacha, according to the informant: *Lagostomus maximus?*) might well be a combinatory variant of the capybara, especially since the Bororo language, for instance, takes the name of the capybara as a model for the formulation of the names of other rodents: okiwa gives okiwareu, 'similar to the capybara' = rat.

The capybara plays a fairly minor part in the myths of tropical America. Towards the end of this volume, I shall discuss a Tacana myth (M_{302}) which attributes the origin of capybaras to the greed of a woman who had an insatiable passion for meat instead of honey. According to the Warao of Venezuela (M_{223}), the origin of the capybara dates from the transformation of disgreeable and disobedient wives (Wilbert 9, pp. 158–60), terms which are also applicable to the girl mad about honey who continually pesters her family in order to obtain the coveted delicacy.

In the Chaco itself, a cosmological myth ends with a woman being changed into a capybara:

M₂₂₄. Mocovi. 'The origin of capybaras'

In the olden days, a tree called Nalliagdigua reached from the earth right up to the sky. The souls used to climb up from branch to branch until they came to lakes and a river, where they caught large quantities of fish. One day the soul of an old woman could catch nothing, and the other souls refused to give her anything. So the old woman's soul became angry. Having changed into a capybara, she set about gnawing the base of the tree until it fell, to the distress of the entire population (Guevara, p. 62, quoted by L.-N. 6, pp. 156–67).

So, here too, the story is about a frustrated woman. But, in this last transformation, it is easy to recognize the heroine of a Mataco myth about the origin of the Pleiades (M₁₃₁ₐ): the old woman responsible for the loss of the fish and *honey*, both of which used to be available all the year round, and whose season is henceforth to be marked by the appearance of the Pleiades (*RC*, p. 241 *et seq.*). It is clearly the seasonal nature of the honey harvest that the heroine of the myths takes over, as it were, and for which she assumes responsibility.

This being so, it should also be pointed out that the Vapidiana, who live along the frontier between Guiana and Brazil, refer to the constellation Aries as 'the capybara', and that for them its appearance heralds the planting season, which is also the locust season and the time for hunting the capybara (Farabee 1, pp. 101, 103). No doubt this northern region is a long way away from the Chaco and has a different climate, and the timing of seasonal occupations is not the same in both areas. I shall return to the point later when I shall try to show that, in spite of these differences, the cycles of economic life have something in common.

The rising of Aries occurs two or three weeks before the rising of the Pleiades, whose importance in the economic and religious life of the Chaco tribes is well known. Among the Vapidiana, the triple connotation of Aries also suggests the dry season, when the ground is cleared for cultivation, vast swarms of locusts appear and the capybara is hunted: the animals are more easily spotted when rivers and lakes are low, since they live under water during the day and wait until nightfall to come out to graze on the banks.

I have found no reference to the Aries constellation in the astronomy of the Chaco tribes, of which Lehmann-Nitsche has made a detailed study. But if, on the strength of the oft-proved affinity between the Chaco and Guiana myths, we can accept the fact that the metamorphosis into a capybara contains an implicit allusion to a constellation heralding the dry season, it would be possible to integrate the two aspects, the astronomical one and meteorological one, which we discovered to be characteristic of the Chaco myths relating to the honey harvest. Looked at from this angle, the *diurnal/nocturnal* contrast in M_{222} would merely be a transposition, onto a scale of periodicity even shorter than the other two (daily, instead of monthly or seasonal) of the basic contrast between the two seasons which is, in the last analysis, the contrast between dry and wet:

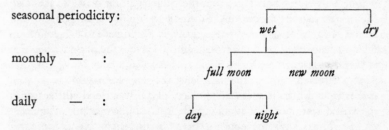

Moreover, among the Toba, the viscacha (which I suggested could be a combinatory variant of the capybara) gives its name to an unidentified constellation (L.-N. 5, pp. 195–6), so that it might be the case that each level retains the features of the other two and differs only in the order of importance it attributes to the three types of periodicity. The three types would, then, be present at each level, one overtly, the other two in a disguised form.

We can now try to get a synthetic view of the whole group of Chaco myths which have as their heroine a girl mad about honey. The heroine's father is the master of aquatic spirits (M_{212}) or the Sun (M_{216}), which feeds on aquatic animals, the originators of rain and storms (M_{217}, M_{218}), and which are assimilated to the rainbow (M_{217}). This initial contrast recalls a famous mythological theme of the Caribbean area (Central America, the West Indies and Guiana): the conflict between the Sun and the hurricane, represented in the day-time by the rainbow and at night by the Big Dipper. There too, the myth is seasonal in character since, in that part of the world, hurricanes occur from mid-July to mid-October, the period during which the Big Dipper disappears almost completely below the horizon (L.-N. 3, *passim*).

On the strength of this connection, let us suppose that, at the beginning of the myths we are examining, the dry, in the person of the Sun, prevails over the wet, represented by the aquatic animals, masters of rain, which form the Sun's diet. Everything, therefore, is taking place in the mode of the dry, and this explains why the heroine is doubly unsatisfied: diachronically speaking, she is the full moon, that is, the wet in the dry, and absence of honey in its presence; but, on the other hand, from the synchronic point of view, the presence of honey, which is associated with the dry season, is not enough; there must be water too, since honey is drunk diluted with water and, from this point of view, honey, although present, is also absent. Honey is a dual substance: diachronically it belongs to the dry; and synchronically it requires water. This is not only true from the culinary point of view; it is also the case as regards the seasonal timetable: in mythical times, according to the Mataco (M_{131a}), men fed exclusively on honey and fish, a link-up which is explained by the fact that, in the Chaco, the period when fish is plentiful lasts from the beginning of April to about May 15th, that is, it is situated right in the middle of the dry season. But as we saw earlier (p. 103), there was a time when all the water and all the fish in the world were permanently available in the hollow trunk of the tree of life. Thus, both the contrast between the seasons and the paradoxical combination, during the dry season, of the 'wet' foods (honey and wild fruits) with the absence of water were neutralized at one and the same time.

In all versions, the heroine can choose between two potential husbands: Woodpecker, a bashful fiancé, but one who possesses the secret of the conjunction between the dry and the wet: even during the search for honey in the dry season, he remains master of an inexhaustible supply of water contained in the gourd which he keeps with him all the time; in fact, he even offers water before honey.[18] In all these

18 The woodpecker's position as master of honey is based on empirical observation: 'Woodpeckers . . . attack nests of stingless bees in the neighbourhood of the flight hole, notwithstanding the fact that the bark is entirely healthy at this point, so that a search on the part of the woodpecker for larvae beneath the bark cannot be offered in explanation of the attack. A few pecks at the trunk of the tree will produce an outpouring of the bees from the nest in numbers to satisfy even a bird's appetite. Numerous specimens of a species of stingless bees were obtained from the stomach of a woodpecker, *Ceophloeus lineatus*, and as it is customary to name a species after its collector, this bee was described as *Trigona (Hypotrigona) ceophloei*. It is said that the jaty bee (*Trigona [Tetragona] jaty*) seals the entrance

respects, the fox is in direct contrast to the woodpecker: he is a brazen seducer, without any honey, which he tries to replace by dirt or by the wild fruits found during the dry season, and without water. Even when he manages to obtain honey, he still has no water and this lack leads to his downfall. The oppositional relationship between the fox and the woodpecker can therefore be given the following simplified expression: (dry − water)/(dry + water).

Between the two, the girl mad about honey occupies an ambiguous position. On the one hand, she is a vixen, since she is without honey and begs for it, or even steals it; yet on the other hand she could be like woodpecker, plentifully supplied with honey and water, if only she could stabilize her marriage with the bird. The fact that she does not do so presents a problem which will be solved later. For the moment, I merely wish to draw attention to a similarity between the heroine of the Mataco myths and the heroine of a short Amazonian myth of uncertain origin, which sheds light on one aspect of the myths I have just been examining. In the Amazonian myth (M_{103}), a young and pretty girl is impelled by hunger to set off in search of a husband. She arrives first of all at the house of the opossum, which she rejects as a husband because it stinks: she also turns down the worm-eating raven (vulture) for the same reason. Finally she comes to the abode of a species of small falcon, the inajé, which feeds her on birds and which she marries. When the vulture or urubu comes to claim the young girl, inajé breaks its skull, and its mother washes the wound with water which is too hot and scalds it. This is why the urubus are bald-headed (Couto de Magalhães, pp. 253–7).

In this myth, as in those belonging to the Chaco, the hunger felt by a young unmarried girl provides, as it were, the source of the action. It is the initial lack, to which Propp refers, which determines the subsequent events in the story. The end, too, is the same: the brazen and foul-smelling seducer is either beaten, maimed or killed (cf. M_{213}). It is true that, in M_{103}, there are three potential husbands instead of two, but this is also the case in M_{216} in which an incompetent bird, which is called čitani in Mataco, is the first to claim the heroine's hand: and in M_{213}, where the same part is played by a bird known as ciñiñi in Toba and, in Spanish, as gallineta (Palavecino, p. 266); it is

to its nest with resin to prevent woodpeckers and other birds getting into the nest' (Schwartz 2, p. 96). The woodpecker appears as master of honey in the myths of the Apinayé (Oliveira, p. 83), the Bororo (Colb. 3, p. 251) and Caingang (Henry 1, p. 144), and no doubt of many other tribes.

perhaps a species of wild hen.[19] On this slender basis, I shall try to carry the comparison further:

	Opossum	Urubu	Inajé
M_{103}: { RAW/ROTTEN	—	—	+
AIR/EARTH:	—	+	+

	Fox	Gallineta	Woodpecker
HONEY($\equiv$ RAW)/WILD			
M_{213}: { FRUITS($\equiv$ ROTTEN):	—	—	+
AIR/EARTH:	—	+	+

In the above tables, the signs + and — are assigned respectively to the first and the second term of each pair of opposites. In order to justify the congruence: wild fruits $\equiv$ rotten, we need only observe that the fox does not climb trees (except in M_{208}, where the action leads to its death), and the myths describe it as feeding on fallen wild fruits (cf. M_{219}), which are therefore already damaged, and which must also be the food of the gallineta, since the gallinaceae (supposing the bird belongs to this species) live mostly on the ground, and this particular bird is unable to gather honey, and so resembles the fox in respect of the search for food (but differs from it in being a bird with the power of flight and not an earth-bound quadruped).

The comparison between M_{103} and M_{213} confirms that on two new axes – the raw and the rotten and the high and the low – the fox and the woodpecker are also diametrically opposed to each other. What happens in the myths we are now examining? The story of the heroine's marriage is related in three episodes. Being placed, as we have seen, in an intermediary position between those occupied by her two suitors, she tries to win over one, and is herself the object of an identical attempt by the other. Finally, after her disappearance or metamorphosis, Fox, usurping the heroine's role, tries to win over Woodpecker: this is a ludicrous and non-mediatized union which is bound to come to nothing. From then on, the oscillations between the polar terms become more marked. When forced to flee by Fox, who is the dry in its pure state, the heroine – at least in one version – changes into a capybara, that is, she goes in the direction of water. Executing the opposite movement, Woodpecker goes towards the Sun (*high + dry*), which sends him to fish for sub-aquatic monsters (*low + wet*), from which he escapes only by abandoning his human form and assuming his nature

[19] I put forward my interpretation very tentatively, since Tebboth's Toba Dictionary gives 'carpinteiro (ave)' for chiñiñi. The bird should therefore be regarded as a different species of woodpecker, which is contrasted with the ordinary woodpecker for reasons unknown.

as a bird once and for all: but the bird is the woodpecker, that is, as has already been shown in RC (pp. 203–5), and can be directly inferred from its habits, a bird which finds its food under the bark of trees and therefore lives half-way between the high and the low: not a terrestrial bird like the gallinaceae, nor one which haunts the heights of the sky like the birds of prey, but one associated with the atmospheric sky and the middle region where the union of sky and water is effected (*high* + *wet*). However, a result of this transformation, which is also an instance of mediation, is that there will no longer be any human master of honey. The time is past when 'animals were men and fed exclusively on bees' honey' (M_{218}). This provides further confirmation of the fact, which was remarked upon in connection with other myths, that the mythology of honey is concerned with its loss rather than with its origin.

b. IN THE STEPPES OF CENTRAL BRAZIL

Had we not already, with the help of examples drawn from the Chaco, defined the group of myths which has the girl mad about honey as its heroine, we should no doubt be unable to find it elsewhere. Yet this group also exists in the inland areas of Brazil, and in particular among the central and eastern Ge; but in a strangely modified and depleted form, with the result that certain versions barely hint at the theme of the girl mad about honey, to which they make no more than a brief reference. In other versions it is set in so different a context that it is almost unrecognizable until behind the superficially divergent stories more exhaustive analysis reveals the single basic pattern which re-establishes their unity.

In *The Raw and the Cooked*, I referred to the first part of a myth belonging to the Apinayé and the Timbira and which I will recall now only very briefly, since what we are concerned with at the moment is its continuation. The myths tell of two giant, man-eating eagles, which used to persecute Indians and which two heroic brothers undertook to kill. One Apinayé version, in which only one eagle appears, ends with this happy outcome (Oliveira, pp. 74–5).[20] But another version goes beyond this point.

M_{142}. *Apinayé. 'The killer bird'* (continuation: cf. RC pp. 258–9)

After killing the first eagle, the two brothers Kenkutan and Akréti tackled the second. They adopted the same tactics, which consisted

[20] So do the Mehin versions (Pompeu Sobrinho, pp. 192–5; cf. *RC*, p. 258).

in taking turns in coming out into the open, so as to tire the bird which swooped down each time in vain on an elusive prey and had to climb again before making its next attack. But Kenkutan, either through clumsiness or fatigue, was not quick enough to escape from the bird, which cut off his head with one stroke of its wing and returned to its eyrie, where it remained.

Akréti was forced to abandon the fight. He picked up his brother's head, put it on the branch of a tree and set off in search of his fellow-tribesmen, who had fled in order to escape from the cannibalistic eagles. He wandered over the savannah, where he met first of all the sariema tribe (*Cariama cristata*) which had set fire to the brush wood in order to hunt lizards and rats. After introducing himself, he went on his way and met the black araras or macaws[21] which were breaking and eating the nuts of the tucum palm (*Astrocaryum tucuman*) in the burnt savannah. In response to their invitation, he shared their meal and left them. He then went deeper into the forest, where monkeys were gathering sapucaia nuts (*Lecythis ollaria*). They gave him some which he ate with them and, after inquiring of them which road would take him back to his native village, Akréti finally arrived at the water-hole used by the villagers.

Hidden behind a jatoba tree (*Hymenea courbaril*), he caught pretty Kapakwei unawares as she was finishing bathing. He introduced himself, told his story and the two young people agreed to get married.

When evening came, Kapakwei made an opening in the grass wall of the hut near her bed so that her lover could rejoin her in secret. But he was so big and strong that he almost completely destroyed the wall. Having been discovered by Kapakwei's companions, Akréti publicly revealed his identity. He announced that. he was going to hunt small birds for his mother-in-law; he actually killed four 'ostriches', which he carried back by their necks as if they were ordinary partridges.

One day, he set off with his wife in order to collect honey from a nest of wild bees. Akréti made a hole in the trunk and told Kapakwei to take out the combs. But she plunged her arm in so far that it became wedged. Saying that he would widen the hole with his axe, Akréti killed his wife and cut her up into pieces, which he roasted. On returning to the village, he offered the pieces of meat to his

[21] Nimuendaju, no doubt following the practice of his informants, uses the term in referring to the blue arara or macaw (*Anodorynchus hyacinthinus*); (cf. Nim. 7, p. 187).

relatives. One of the brothers-in-law suddenly noticed that he was eating his sister. Convinced that Akréti was a criminal, he followed his tracks back to the scene of the murder and discovered the remains of his sister, which he gathered up and buried in accordance with the demands of ritual.

The next day, taking advantage of the fact that Akréti wanted to cook *Cissus* (a plant of the grape family, cultivated by eastern Ge) in the glowing embers of a huge communal fire,[22] the women pushed him so that he fell in. An ant-hill sprang up from his ashes (Nim. 5, pp. 173-5).

At first sight, this story seems difficult to understand, since we are not told why the young husband dealt so brutally with his pretty wife, with whom he had fallen in love only a short while before. Also, the ignominious fate meted out to him by his fellow-villagers shows a lack of gratitude on their part, if we reflect that it was he who had rid them of the monsters. Finally, the link with myths in which the heroine is a girl mad about honey seems very tenuous, apart from the fact that honey has a place in the narrative.

It should, however, be noted that the story of a woman caught by the arm in a tree full of honey and who dies in this uncomfortable position is also found not far from the Chaco in the region of the Rio Beni (Nordenskiöld 5, p. 171) and among the Quechua in the north-west of the Argentine (L.-N. 8, pp. 262-6), in whose myth the woman, after being abandoned at the top of a tree laden with honey, changes into a nightjar, a bird which replaces the eagle in some versions of the Ge myth (M_{227}).

But the comparison is even more obvious, if we refer to another version of the myth belonging to the Kraho, a sub-group of the eastern Timbira, who are close neighbours of the Apinayé. The Kraho regard the two episodes – the destruction of the eagles and the hero's marriage – which in Apinayé mythology are run together, as belonging to two separate myths. Have we, then, to explain the contradiction between the great service rendered by the hero to his compatriots and their lack of compassion by an accidental confusion of two myths? To do so would be to disregard an absolute rule of structural analysis: myths do not admit of discussion, they must always be accepted *as they are*. If Nimuendaju's informant included in a single myth episodes which elsewhere

---

[22] 'Unlike the Sherente and the Canella, the men of the Apinayé tribe participate in the cooking of meat pâtés' (Nim. 5, p. 16).

belong to different myths, this can only mean that the episodes are connected by some link which it is up to us to discover and which is essential for the interpretation of both.

Here, then, is the Kraho myth which clearly corresponds to the second part of M_{142}, while at the same time depicting the heroine as a girl mad about honey:

M_{225}. *Kraho.* '*The girl mad about honey*'

An Indian set off with his wife in search of honey. The tree containing the nest had hardly been felled when the wife, yielding to her craving for honey, and heedless of her husband's pleas to allow him to finish his task, threw herself upon it. He flew into a rage, killed the gluttonous woman, cut up her body and roasted the pieces on hot stones. Then, he made a straw basket into which he put the pieces, and returned to the village. He arrived during the night and invited his mother-in-law and his sisters-in-law to eat what he said was ant-eater meat. The victim's brother arrived on the scene, tasted the meat, and at once recognized what it was. The next morning, they buried the roasted pieces of the young woman, then took the killer off into the savannah. They lit a big fire underneath a tree which they asked him to climb in order to bring down a nest of arapuã bees [*Trigona ruficrus*]. His brother-in-law then shot an arrow at him and wounded him. The man fell; they finished him off by clubbing him to death, after which they burnt his corpse in the red hot ashes (Schultz 1, pp. 155–6).

We are now beginning to understand why the hero of M_{142} killed his wife during a honey-gathering expedition. She too probably displayed excessive greed and had exasperated her husband by her gluttony. But one other point is worthy of attention. In both cases, the wife's relatives, unwittingly, eat the flesh of their daughter or sister, which is precisely the punishment meted out in other myths (M_{150}, M_{156}, M_{159}) to the wife or wives who have been seduced by a tapir and are forced to eat their lover's flesh. This, surely, can only mean that in the group dealing with the girl mad about honey, honey, a vegetable and not an animal entity, plays the part of seducer.

No doubt the development of the story cannot be exactly the same in both instances. The group in which the tapir is the seducer plays on the double meaning of the consumption of food: taken figuratively, it suggests copulation, that is, misbehaviour, but taken in the literal sense it denotes punishment. In the group dealing with the girl mad about honey, these relationships are reversed: in both instances, it is a question of the consumption of food, but in the first case – the consumption of honey – there is also an erotic connotation, as I have already suggested (p. 52) and as is confirmed, along different lines, by the comparison I am now making. The guilty girl cannot be condemned to eat her metaphorical 'seducer': this would be tantamount to gratifying her, since it is exactly what she wishes; and she obviously cannot copulate with a food (however, see M_{269}, where this idea is taken to its logical conclusion). So, the transformation: *literal seducer* ⇒ *metaphorical seducer* inevitably involves two further ones: *wife* ⇒ *parents*, and *wife who eats* ⇒ *wife who is eaten*. The fact that the parents are punished through their daughter is not, however, the result of a purely formal operation. As will be seen later, the punishment is directly motivated and, in this respect, the form and content of the story are interdependent. For the moment, I am merely concerned to point out that these successive inversions lead to another: the wives seduced by the tapir and tricked by their husbands (who make them eat their lover's flesh) take their revenge by deliberately changing into fish (M_{150}); the parents of the wife seduced by honey are tricked by their son-in-law (who makes them eat their daughter's flesh), and they take their revenge by transforming *him* willy-nilly into an ant-hill or by reducing him to ashes, that is, by pushing him in the direction of the dry and of earth, instead of towards the wet and water.

As will become clear later, this demonstration of the semantic position of honey as seducer, which has been carried out with the help of the myths, represents an important achievement. But, before going further, I should add to the Kraho version of the second episode in the Apinayé myth, the other Kraho version which refers directly to the first episode, and then consider the mutual transformational relationships between the three myths.

M_{226}. *Kraho. 'The killer bird'*

In olden times, in order to escape from the cannibalistic birds, the Indians decided to take refuge in the sky which, in those days, was not so far away from the earth. Only one old man and one old woman, who failed to set off with the rest, remained below with their two grandsons. Being afraid of the birds, they decided to live in hiding in the bush.

The two boys were called Kengunan and Akrey. Before long

Kengunan displayed magic powers which allowed him to assume the forms of all sorts of animals. One day, the two brothers decided to remain in the river until they became strong and agile enough to destroy the monsters. Their grandfather made them a platform underneath the water where they could lie down and sleep; every day he brought them some sweet potatoes on which the two heroes lived [in a Kayapo version, which is very similar to, but less detailed than, the Kraho version, the hiding-place is also under water (Banner 1, p. 52)].

After living in isolation for a long time, they reappeared big and strong, while their grandfather carried out the celebratory rites which marked the end of the young men's period of seclusion. He handed each one a sharpened stick. Thus armed, the brothers proved themselves to be prodigious hunters. At that time, animals were much bigger and heavier than they are now, yet Kengunan and Akrey killed them and brought them back without any difficulty. They pulled out the feathers of the winged creatures they slew, and changed them into birds [*id.* Kapayo version, Banner 1, p. 52].

It is at this point that the episode of the war against the cannibalistic birds occurs. It differs very little from the summary I have already given in connection with M_{142}, except that it is Akrey and not his brother who is killed and decapitated by the second bird, and his head, which is also placed in the fork of a tree, changes into the nest of an arapuã bee (cf. M_{225}).

Kenkunan avenged his brother by slaying the killer bird. He decided not to go back to his grandparents and to roam the world until he should meet with death at the hands of some unknown people ... During his travels, he encountered, in succession, the tribe of emas (*Rhea americana*: a small, three-toed ostrich) which set fire to the brush in order to be able to pick up more easily the fallen fruit of the pati palm (*Orcus* sp.; *Astrocaryum* according to Nim. 8, p. 73), then the sariema tribe (*Cariama cristata*, a smaller bird than the preceding one) which used the same tactics in hunting grasshoppers. The hero then left the savannah and entered the forest,[23] where the coati tribe (*Nasua socialis*) lit fires in order to bring to the surface the earthworms they fed on. The fires which next occurred were those lit by monkeys, which cleared the ground in order to gather the fruit of the pati palm and the jatoba tree (*Hymenea cour-*

[23] The opposition between *chapado* and *mato*, which is employed by the informant, is more accurately an opposition between open country and dense shrub-like vegetation.

baril), then those lit by tapirs looking for jatoba fruit and edible leaves.

Finally, the hero spotted a track which led to a water-hole used by an unknown tribe (the so-called coati people – the Mehin Indians – just as the name of the Kraho Indians means paca people). He remained hidden and watched a 'log' race. Later, he suddenly appeared to a young girl who had come to draw water, and engaged her in a conversation strangely reminiscent of the meeting between Golaud and Mélisande in Maeterlinck's play: 'You are a giant!' – 'I am a man like other men ... ' Kenkunan told his story: now that he had avenged his brother's death, he had but one hope which was to die at the hands of an enemy people. The young girl assured him that her people were well-disposed towards him and Kenkunan made her a proposal of marriage.

After the episode of the nocturnal visit which, as in M_{142}, revealed the hero's stature and physical strength, the latter was discovered by the villagers who greeted him warmly. It was fortunate for them that they did, since Kenkunan, armed only with his spear, displayed his gifts as a hunter. I shall return later to this section of the story.

Single-handed, Kenkunan drove back an enemy people which had encroached on the hunting grounds belonging to his adopted village. He was universally respected and lived to such a great age that it is not certain whether he died finally of sickness or old age ... (Schultz 1, pp. 93-114).

In more than one place, this version compares the childhood of Akrey and Kenkunan with the initiation rites to which young men were subject. The informant is even careful to explain that present-day adolescents spend their period of seclusion in the huts and not under water, but that their sisters or mothers look after them: when it is hot, they wash them with water drawn from the river and fatten them up with lavish quantities of sweet potatoes, cane sugar and yams (*loc. cit.*, pp. 98-9). Among the Apinayé and the Timbira, the close link between myth and ritual is clear from Nimuendaju's commentary. He even notes that the Timbira ritual of the pepyé, that is the young men's initiation ceremony, is the only one to be explained by a myth of origin. In this myth, we find the main features of the Kraho version almost word for word, and I shall restrict myself to noting the differences between them.

M₂₂₇. Timbira. 'The killer bird'

First of all, the myth is more explicit about kinship ties. The old man and old woman are respectively the father and mother of a woman who, along with her husband, was devoured by the canni-balistic bird. The grandparents took charge of the orphans when the other Indians fled.

Akrei and Kenkunan do not spend their period of seclusion under-neath the water but on a natural bridge, formed by two huge tree-trunks which had fallen across the stream. On these trunks the grand-father built a platform and a waterproof hut, in which the two boys shut themselves away (in this respect, then, the Timbira version reproduces the Apinayé version). When they reappeared after the old man had performed all the ceremonies by himself, including the ritual 'log' race, their hair was so long that it came right down to their knees. Armed with heavy clubs, the brothers killed the first bird, but the second (which was a nightjar, *Caprimulgus* sp.) cut off Akrei's head. His brother placed the head in the fork of a tree near a nest of borá bees (*Trigona clavipes*) which make their nests low down in hollow trees (Ihering, under 'vorá, borá').

Kenkunan went back to his grandparents and told them about his brother's tragic end, then he started off to try to find his fellow-tribesmen. The animals he met told him exactly which way to go. They were, in succession, emas which hunt grasshoppers, lizards and snakes by setting fire to the brush; sariemas who offered him a dish of lizards pounded together with manioc, but which the hero refused, and finally more sariemas, which were fishing with fish-poison, and whose meal he consented to share.

He hid by the spring of the village until he saw approaching the girl engaged to him since infancy. He gave her the flesh of a deer he had killed, then she returned to the village and brought him sweet potatoes.

After the incident of the nocturnal visit during which the hero smashed the hut wall because he was so big and strong, he did not incur the hostility of the men of the village, thanks to his new mother-in-law who had recognized him.

Meanwhile the grandparents had been wandering alone and aim-lessly over the savannah. When they came to a mountain which blocked their path, they decided to go round it, the man to the right, the woman to the left, and to meet on the far side. Hardly had they started off on their separate ways when they changed into ant-eaters. Hunters killed the old man, whom they did not recognize in his new form. His wife, weeping bitter tears, waited for him in vain. Finally she went on her way and disappeared (Nim. 8, pp. 179–81).

When we compare these various versions of the same myth, we note that they are on the whole fairly detailed, and also that they differ on precise points. This gives me an opportunity to settle once and for all a methodological question which has perhaps already been puzzling the reader. A short while back, I recalled a rule of structural analysis, which is that a myth should always be accepted *as it is* (p. 121). But on the very same page I may have infringed this rule by proposing to fill in what I said was a gap in the Apinayé version (M_{142}) with the help of the more precise account provided by the Kraho version (M_{225}). To be consistent, ought I not to have accepted the Apinayé version 'as it was' and allowed the episode of the young woman's murder by her husband, which is inexplicable in the context, to remain unaccountable? To overcome this objection, it is necessary to distinguish between two possibilities.

It can happen that myths belonging to different communities transmit the same message, without all being equally detailed or equally clear in expression. We therefore find ourselves in a situation comparable to that of a telephone subscriber who is rung up several times in succession by a caller giving, or repeating, the same message, in case a storm or other conversations may have caused interference with his earlier messages. Of the various messages, some will be relatively clear, others relatively indistinct. The same will be true even in the absence of background noise, if one message is given at great length whereas a second is abridged in telegraphese. In all these instances, the general sense of the messages will remain the same, although each one may contain more or less information, and a person who has heard several may legitimately rectify or complete the less satisfactory ones with the help of the more explicit.

It would be quite a different matter if one were dealing not with identical messages, each of which is transmitting a varying amount of information, but with intrinsically different messages. In this case, the quantity and quality of the information would be of less consequence than the content, and each message would have to be accepted *as it is*. We would be in danger of making the worst kind of miscalculations if, arguing from the quantitative or qualitative insufficiency of each myth, we imagined we could make good the insufficiency by combining separate messages into one single message, which would have no meaning at all, apart from that which the person receiving it might care to attribute to it.

Let us now return to the myths. When and how can we decide whether they represent identical messages, differing only in respect of the quantity or quality of the information transmitted, or whether they are messages conveying irreducible information and cannot be used to complete each other? The problem is a difficult one, and there is no hiding the fact that, in the present state of both theory and method, it is often necessary to settle the matter empirically.

But, in the particular instance with which we are concerned at the moment, we are fortunate in having at our disposal an external criterion which removes the element of uncertainty. We know that the Apinayé and the Timbira-Kraho group, which are both very similar in language and culture, are not really different communities, since their separation dates from a period sufficiently recent for the Apinayé to preserve the memory of it in their legendary tales (Nim. 5, p. 1; 8, p. 6). Consequently, the myths of these central and eastern Ge can not only be legitimately subjected to a formal treatment which brings out their common properties; their structural affinities have an objective foundation in both ethnography and history. The Ge myths form a logical group, primarily because they belong to the same family, and so it is possible to establish a system of genuine relationships between them.

It is therefore legitimate to complete some of these myths with the help of others since, only a few centuries ago at most, they were still indistinguishable. But conversely, the differences which now separate them acquire a greater value, and take on an even greater significance. For if we are dealing with myths which were the same at a relatively recent date historically, omissions or gaps can be explained by the fact that certain details have been forgotten, or certain episodes become blurred; but if the myths contradict each other, there must be some good reason for this.

After completing the myths by means of their resemblances, we must now try to discover the points on which they differ.

They all agree in recognizing the superiority of one brother over the other: one brother is stronger, more adroit, more agile; in M_{226}, he is even gifted with magic powers which allow him to change into various animals. In the Kraho and Timbira versions, the stronger brother is called Kengunan or Kenkunan; and the one who falls victim to the second bird, either through weariness or lack of dexterity, bears the name of Akrey. The Apinayé version is the only one which reverses the roles: at the very beginning of the myth, Akréti shows himself to be a prodigious hunter and a good runner; he is the one who survives the fight with the monster, whereas Kenkutan has his head cut off.

This inversion is the result of another, which itself follows on from the fact that the Apinayé are the only people to identify the hero of the myth with the husband of a woman mad about honey, who does not appear in the Timbira myths and to whom the Kraho devote a completely separate myth (M_{225}). So the Apinayé reverse the respective parts played by the two brothers because, in Apinayé mythology, but not in that of the Kraho and the Timbira, the brother who is victorious over the cannibalistic birds is doomed to come to a sad end. He murders his wife, he is killed and burnt by his relatives, and he is turned into an ant-hill. All this is in complete contrast with what happens to the hero in the Kraho myths, where he enjoys a long and glorious old age – 'like unto himself at last ... '[24] we might be tempted to say in order to emphasize that the hero's old age, the ultimate end of which the myth does not even define in concrete terms, constitutes an identical transformation (identical with itself) – and is diametrically opposed (but on a different axis) to what happens in Timbira mythology, where there is, of course, a different transformation (as in Apinayé mythology) affecting not the hero himself but his ancestors, who are changed into ant-eaters (which eat ant-hills) and not into ant-hills (which are eaten by ant-eaters). Between these two transformations, one identical, one different, one passive, one active, there occurs the pseudo-transformation of the murdered woman in M_{225}, whose body is offered to her mother and sisters *as if it were* ant-eater meat.

Every time the myths specify the genealogical position of the grandparents, they place them in the maternal line of descent. But in all other respects, the versions systematically follow a contrasting pattern of behaviour.

In the Apinayé version (M_{142}), after his brother's death, the hero leaves his grandparents and never sees them again; he sets out in search of his own people and, having found them again, he marries a compatriot who proves to be a disastrous wife.

In the Kraho version (M_{226}), the hero also leaves his grandparents

[24] TRANSLATORS' NOTE: *Tel qu'en lui-même enfin ...* the first words of Mallarmé's sonnet on Edgar Allan Poe.

and never sees them again, but he sets out in search of a hostile people at whose hands he hopes to die; and although he finally marries a girl belonging to this people, she turns out to be a perfect wife.

Finally, in the Timbira version (M_{227}), the hero is careful to return to his grandparents in order to bid them farewell before setting off to look for his own people, among whom he rediscovers and marries the girl to whom he has been betrothed since childhood. From every point of view, therefore, this last version is the one of the three with the most 'family' feeling:

	M_{142}	M_{226}	M_{227}
grandparents: revisited (+)/abandoned (−)	−	−	+
marriage with: compatriot (+)/foreigner(−)	+	−	+
wife: good (+)/bad (−)	−	+	+

Similarly, a varying fate awaits the remains of the hero's brother – that is, his head: in M_{142}, it is placed in the fork of a tree; in M_{226}, it is placed in the fork of a tree and changed into an arapuã bees' nest; in M_{227}, it is placed in the fork of a tree near a nest of borá bees. M_{142} is difficult to interpret in this respect, for we have no means of knowing whether it is really different or whether something has been omitted: does the head undergo no transformation, or did the informer deliberately omit or disregard this detail? I therefore confine my comparison to the variants M_{226} and M_{227} which, as regards their respective relationships, can be defined in two ways. First, the transformation into a bees' nest is a more strongly emphasized theme than the mere proximity of a head and a nest would seem to indicate. Next, the nest of the arapuã bee is different from the nest of the borá bee: one is a hanging nest and is therefore found outside the tree, the other is inside, in the hollow trunk; furthermore, the nest of the arapuã bees has a relatively higher position than that of the borá bees, which are also called 'treebole bees', because they nest close to the ground. Finally, the arapuã are an aggressive species, which produce a rare kind of honey, both inferior in quality and disagreeable in taste (cf. Ihering, under 'irapoã', 'vorá').

In all respects, therefore, M_{226} seems to be a more dramatic version than M_{227}. Furthermore, in this version all the contrasts seem to be amplified – the Indians escape to the sky, the two brothers go and live in seclusion at the bottom of a river, and the hero displays exceptional magic powers. It will be noted, too, that in M_{225} the arapuã nest fulfils an intermediary function: it is a *means* which brings about the death of the hero himself and not a *result* of his brother's death. In the sub-group formed by the two myths about 'the girl mad about honey', this fatal means forms a pair with the one used in M_{142}:

$$\text{means of the hero's death}: M_{142} \left[Cissus \begin{Bmatrix} \text{cultivated} \\ \text{cooked} \end{Bmatrix} \right] \Rightarrow M_{225} \left[Arapu\tilde{a} \begin{Bmatrix} \text{wild} \\ \text{raw} \end{Bmatrix} \right]$$

I end this list of differences with a brief examination of the episode relating to the hero's various encounters, which can be looked at from various standpoints: the animals encountered, the produce they live on, the hero's acceptance or rejection of their food, and finally, the affinity (often specified by the myths) existing between the animal species and their natural setting, which is either savannah or forest:

	natural setting	animals encountered	food	hero's attitude
(1) M_{142}	savannah	sariema	lizards, rats; tucum	o
	,,	black macaw	palm nuts	+
	forest	monkey	nuts of the sapucaia tree	+
(2) M_{226}	savannah	ema	pati nuts;	o
	,,	sariema	grasshoppers	o
	forest	coati	earthworms;	o
	,,	monkey	pati, jatoba;	o
	,,	tapir	jatoba, leaves	o
(3) M_{227}		ema	lizards, snakes, grasshoppers;	—
		sariema (1)	manioc and lizards;	—
		sariema (2)	fish	+

A steady contrast seems to be maintained between savannah and forest, as well as between animal food and vegetable food, except in M_{227} where the contrast is between terrestrial food and aquatic food:

$$M_{142}, M_{226}: \frac{\text{savannah}}{\text{forest}} \qquad M_{227}: \frac{\text{earth}}{\text{(savannah)}} \Big| \text{water}$$

This divergency brings us back to the root of the matter, that is, to the transformation which takes place in M_{227} (and only in M_{227}): that of the grandparents into ant-eaters, in spite of the extreme consideration

shown them by the hero. Consequently, even when the young initiate
has no desire to break with his elders, they leave him. The fact that the
grandmother alone survives in the form of an ant-eater can no doubt be
explained by the belief, which is current from the Chaco (Nino, p. 37)
to the north-west of the Amazonian basin (Wallace, p. 314), that large
ant-eaters (*Myrmecophaga jubata*) are all females. But what is the significance of the appearance, within the group we are dealing with, of a
cycle which centres in such a curious way round the ant-eater? Ant-
eaters certainly feed on ant-hills, into which the hero of M_{142} is changed;
in M_{225} this same hero offers his wife's flesh to his parents-in-law,
claiming that it is ant-eater flesh, and he thus changes them into eaters
of this animal, which his grandparents themselves are transformed into
in M_{227}.

To solve the enigma, another short myth must be introduced at this
point:

M_{228}. *Kraho*. '*The old woman who changed into an ant-eater*'

An old woman one day took her grandchildren to gather puça fruit
(unidentified; cf. Nim. 8, p. 73).[25] She took her basket and told them
to climb the tree. When the children had eaten all the ripe fruit, they
started to gather the unripe fruit which they threw at their grandmother in spite of her protests. When the children were scolded, they
changed into parakeets. The old woman, who had no teeth, remained
below alone, asking herself: 'What will become of me? What am
I going to do now?' She changed into an ant-eater, and went off to
dig up ant-hills (*cupim*). Then she disappeared into the forest
(Schultz 1, p. 160. Cf. Métraux 3, p. 60; Abreu, pp. 181–3).

This myth has an obvious transformational relationship with the
Sherente myth (M_{229}) about the origin of ant-eaters and the padi feast
(the wild fruit is generously offered by the ant-eaters instead of being
denied them; cf. Nim. 6, pp. 67–8). I shall return to the padi feast
later, but here I wish to examine other aspects of the myth.

As in M_{227}, the old woman who changes into an ant-eater is a grandmother abandoned by her grandsons. At the same time, the greedy
children who overindulge in fruit and pick them while they are still
green, offer a striking analogy with the wife mad about honey, who
also consumes her 'corn when it is green', since she devours the honey
before her husband has finished collecting it. The greedy children are

[25] According to Corrêa (Vol. II), in the State of Piauhy *pussa* is *Rauwolfia bahiensis*, one of
the Apocynaceae.

also reminiscent of the children in a Bororo myth (M_{34}), who are punished for the same misdemeanour. In this myth, the children escape to the sky and change into stars, not parakeets. But these stars are more probably Pleiades, which are sometimes called 'the Parakeets' by South American Indians. Moreover, the fate of the Kraho children is identical with the fate meted out in a Bororo myth (M_{35}) to another greedy child who is changed into a parrot because he swallows scalding fruit: that is 'overcooked', rather than green = 'too raw'. Finally, M_{228} states explicitly that the grandmother is toothless, and this appears to be also the case with the old men in M_{229} before they change into ant-eaters. They give all the fruit of the padi palm they have gathered to their daughter, explaining that they cannot chew it because it is too hard. The grandmother in M_{35} has her tongue cut out, and this makes her dumb like an ant-eater.[26]

There are still further points to be noted. The old woman, who is the victim of her descendants' greed and who changes into an ant-eater, can be compared with the heroine of the Chaco myths which we studied in the first part of this chapter: she was a young woman, not an old one; she changed into a capybara, not an ant-eater, and she was the victim both of her own gluttonous passion for honey in the literal sense, and of metaphorical gluttony (gluttony transposed onto the sexual plane) on the part of a rejected suitor. If, as I suggest, the Kraho myth M_{228} is a weak form of a myth about the origin of the stars of which M_{35} represents the strong form, we can consider it significant that M_{228} should also exist in the Chaco, but as the strong form of a myth about the origin of the stars and more particularly of the Pleiades. The fact can be deduced from M_{131a}, and especially from M_{224} in which the heroine, an old woman who is also a victim of the gluttony of her own family, changes into a capybara. The cycle of transformations is completed by another Chaco myth of Toba origin (M_{230}) which tells how men tried to climb up to heaven in order to escape from a universal fire. Some succeeded and changed into stars; others fell and found shelter in caves. When the fire died down, they came out into the open in the form of various animals; one old man had become a cayman, and an old woman an ant-eater, etc. (L.-N. 5, pp. 195–6).

It follows from my preceding observations that the transformations into ant-eater and capybara act as a pair of opposites. The first is toothless and the other, the largest of the rodents, has long teeth. Throughout

[26] The Caingang-Coroado believe both large and small ant-eaters to be dumb old men (Borba, pp. 22, 25).

the whole of tropical America, the sharp incisors of the capybara are used to make planes and engraving tools, whereas the tongue of the toothless great ant-eater is used as a file (Susnik, p. 41). It is not surprising that a contrast based on both anatomical and technological factors should be systematically exploited. The transformation into one or other animal is a function of gluttony attributable either to the self or the other, and of which kin or affines are guilty. It entails also a triple disjunction along the axes of the high and the low, the dry and the wet, youth and old age. In this last respect, the Timbira version admirably conveys what happens at each initiation: the new age

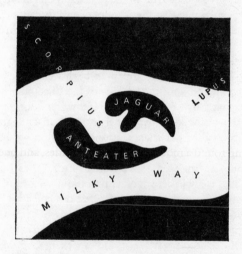

Figure 10. The fight between the jaguar and the ant-eater. (Redrawn after Nim. 12, Fig. 13, p. 142.)

group takes the place of the one immediately preceding it, and the others do likewise, with the result that the oldest group is excluded from active life, and is forced to take up its position in the centre of the village where it has no more than an advisory capacity (Nim. 8, pp. 90–92).

The contrast between the capybara and the ant-eater is confirmed when we observe that the Mocovi believe the Milky Way to be the ashes of the tree of the world, which was burnt after the old woman turned capybara had cut it down (the Bororo call the Milky Way 'Ashes of stars'). The Tucuna have a myth (M_{231}) in which the ant-eater appears in the form of a 'bag of charcoal' in the Milky Way, i.e. a negative Milky Way: dark on a light background, instead of light on a dark background. The territory of the Tucuna is far removed from that of the Ge, and still farther removed from the Chaco. But the northern Kayapo, who belong to the central Ge group, and the Bororo, who have the Kayapo on one side and the Chaco tribes on the other, have the same myth about the fight between the ant-eater and the jaguar, with exactly the same details, ($M_{232a, b}$; Banner 1, p. 45; Colb. 3, pp. 252-3): the only difference is the absence of the astronomical coding. But if we can assume that, behind the story of the fight between the ant-eater and the jaguar a latent astronomical code is constantly in operation, and in such a way that the two zones of the Milky Way devoid of stars correspond to the fighting animals, the jaguar gaining the ascendancy shortly after sunset and – since the relative positions are reversed during the night – being overcome before dawn by the ant-eater, we cannot exclude the possibility that the Iranxé myth about the origin of tobacco (M_{191}), in which the vulture replaces the jaguar as the ant-eater's opponent, may lend itself to a similar interpretation. The same could apply to the Timbira myth (M_{227}), which describes how the old man and old woman are changed into ant-eaters while they are walking round a mountain on different sides, and one of them is killed by hunters, while the other continues on its way. This example, too, suggests a nocturnal change which modifies visibility and the respective positions of celestial objects. Finally, if it were legitimate to universalize the Vapidiana identification of the Aries constellation with a capybara, it would seem still more significant that the celestial ant-eater should be a 'non-constellation' close to the Scorpion and – with a discrepancy of about three hours – in phasic contrast with Aries.

It follows from these remarks that, although the Ge myths dealing with the killer bird belong historically to the same family, they belong logically to a group of which they illustrate various transformations. This group is itself a sub-group within a broader system in which the Chaco myths about the girl mad about honey also have their place. We have shown that in the Ge myths, the girl mad about honey fulfils a logical function; whenever she appears, she personifies the *bad marriage* made by the hero, in spite of the fact that he chose his wife from among his *own people*; this is one particular combination within a permutation, the other elements of which are a *good marriage* contracted *among his own people*, and a marriage which is still *better*, although it has been contracted *among strangers,* who may even be presumed to be his enemies. This combinatory system is therefore based on the concepts of local endogamy and exogamy, and it always implies disjunction.

In M_{142} and M_{225}, the hero is unhappily married among his own people, and is disjoined by the individuals who kill him in order to avenge the murder of his wife, the woman mad about honey, and who cause the culprit to be reduced to ashes or changed into an ant-hill, the food of ant-eaters: he is thus turned into a *terrestrial object.* And when, in M_{226}, the hero rushes off in search of enemies at whose hands he can expect only death, this is because his own people have brought disjunction between himself and them by fleeing up into the sky, thus turning themselves into *celestial subjects.* Finally in M_{227}, the hero does all he can *to avoid* disjunction between himself and his own people: he is an attentive grandson, faithful to his own people and to the young girl to whom he has been betrothed since childhood. But to no avail, since his grandparents, to whom he has shown his attachment by his respectful behaviour, are deliberately disjoined from him by changing into ant-eaters, that is, into *terrestrial subjects.* The fact that the axis of disjunction is thus defined by two poles, 'sky' and 'earth', explains why the strongest versions present the initiation as taking place under water, and the weakest (in this respect) at water level. The initiation period is intended to give young men the necessary strength, not to oppose disjunction, from which there is no escape in societies where initiation leads to marriage and matrilocal residence, but to adjust themselves to it, on condition, however, that they make a suitable marriage. This, in fact, is the lesson implicit in the myths, as will be shown later.

Let us begin by sketching the outlines of the meta-group, to which belong both the Ge myths about the killer-bird and those Chaco myths concerned with the girl mad about honey. In the latter, we are concerned with a heroine who is greedy for honey and who is the daughter of Sun, the master of aquatic spirits; the poles of disjunction are therefore sky and water, and more particularly (since I have shown that we are dealing with dry-season mythology) the dry and the wet. The heroine finds herself placed between two suitors: Fox and Woodpecker, one too ardent, the other too retiring, and who later become respectively base seducer and lawful husband. As regards the search for food, they are both in the same category: they represent the gathering of wild produce; only one illustrates its generous aspect: honey and water, the other its meagre aspect: toxic fruits and absence of water. The myth ends with the (temporary) neutralization of Fox, Woodpecker's disjunction in the direction of the sky (where he definitively assumes his bird nature) and the disjunction of the heroine who vanishes, no one knows where, while still quite young or changes into a capybara, an animal belonging to the category of water.

The Apinayé myth (M_{142}) and the Kraho myth (M_{225}) present an inverted picture of the same system. Instead of being the heroine, the girl mad about honey becomes an insignificant adjunct to the hero. The hero reconciles the antithetical functions of Fox and Woodpecker, since the two characters of the *brazen seducer* and the *timid husband* are merged into one, which is that of the *bold husband*. However, the duality is re-established on two levels: on the level of economic functions, since the Ge myths simultaneously introduce hunting and the search for honey, and on that of kinship, since the two affines in M_{213} etc., one timid, the other brazen, are replaced by two relatives, a timid brother and a bold brother.

Corresponding to the heroine who has been changed into a capybara (an aquatic subject with long teeth) is a hero who has been changed into an ant-hill (terrestrial object of a toothless mammal), and one of whose kinsmen, his brother (the counterpart of the heroine's husband, an affine), survives, after being devoured by a celestial mônster (whereas the husband was eaten by an aquatic monster), in the form of a round object (his head) placed on a branch where it looks like a bees' nest (the food, situated at the half-way mark, of a bird – the woodpecker of the Chaco myths – which itself belongs to the middle world).

Between these two symmetrical and equally catastrophic versions, the Kraho myth (M_{226}) defines a point of equilibrium. The hero is an accomplished hunter whose marriage has been a success and who attains an advanced age. His 'non-metamorphosis' is indicated by his longevity and by the fact that the myth does not disclose what really happened to him in the end: 'And Kengunan spent his whole life in this village until he was no longer conscious of anything, anything at all. Then he died. And even at that time in the village where he lived, nothing further was known about Kengunan, either whether he died of an illness or of old age. He disappeared and the village remained' (Schultz 1, p. 112). This indeterminate state of permanence contrasts with the irrevocable transformations undergone by the heroine (M_{213}) or the hero (M_{142}), or again with the premature disappearance of the heroine before she has had time to reach an advanced age.

The Timbira version (M_{227}), in its turn, provides a link between the Kraho myth (M_{226}) and the Apinayé-Kraho myths (M_{142}, M_{225}):

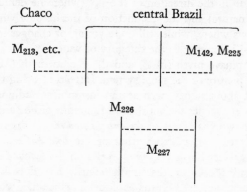

The axis of disjunction is vertical in M_{213} etc. (*sky/water*). It is horizontal in M_{142} (the search for the Indians who have gone far away), vertical in M_{225}, but only faintly stressed (the arapuã's nest in the tree, the red hot ashes below), and reversed in relation to M_{213} (the Sun above, the sub-aquatic monsters below). And whereas M_{226} brings two axes into play: one vertical (the disjunction of the Indians in the sky, while the protagonists remain on earth) the other horizontal (the horizontal disjunction of the hero searching for a distant and hostile people), in M_{227} there is only one horizontal axis of disjunction, and the vertical axis exists only in a latent state (if, as I believe, the transformation of the grandparents into ant-eaters is to be explained in terms of an astronomical coding), and comes last, whereas it occurs at the beginning of M_{226}. We can therefore confirm, in the Ge subgroup, that the Timbira version occupies an intermediary position between the other versions, and this explains the special treatment of the brother's head which is cut off by the bird. It will be remembered that the head is placed on a low branch near a nest of borá bees, whereas in the other versions a nest of arapuã bees, hanging much higher up, is connected with the hero himself (M_{225}) or with his brother (M_{226}), as the means of the death of the one, or the result of the death of the other, as has already been explained.

The Chaco myths dealing with the girl mad about honey and those of central Brazil in which the same character plays a less obvious part, are then part of the same group. Since the former, as we already know, are seasonal in character in that they describe certain kinds of economic activity and one particular period in the year, the same must also be true of the latter. The point needs now to be elaborated.

The territory occupied by the central and eastern Ge forms an almost continuous zone in central Brazil, stretching south approximately from 3–10° of latitude and west from 40–50° of longitude. Within this vast region, climatic conditions are not absolutely uniform: the north-western part borders on the Amazonian basin, the north-eastern part on the famous 'triangle' of drought, where there can be a total absence of rainfall. On the whole, however, the climate in all regions is like that of the central plateau, where there is a contrast between a rainy and a dry season. However, the various Ge tribes do not all adapt to their climatic environment in the same way.

We know something of the seasonal occupations of the northern Kayapo. Their dry season extends from May to October. The natives clear the land at the beginning of the dry season, and burn the wood at the end, by which time it has dried. As the Kayapo fish only with poison, their fishing is restricted to the season when the rivers are low, that is, from the end of July until the beginning of the rainy season. And 'since the operation ... destroys almost all the fish at one go, (it) can only take place once a year in the same river. Fish, therefore, provides only a small fraction of their food, and the fact that it is scarce makes it all the more appreciated' (Dreyfus, p. 30). Game is also scarce: 'sometimes expeditions have to be made very far afield in order to find the meat the Kayapo lack and of which they are extremely fond' (*ibid.*).

At the end of the dry season, game becomes even scarcer and sometimes there is a shortage of agricultural produce. Extra food is obtained by collecting wild fruit. In November and December, the inhabitants of the village set off in different directions to look for piqui fruit, which ripen about this time. The dry months (July to September) correspond, therefore, to a nomadic way of life which continues far into the rainy season for the gathering of the piqui fruit. But this nomadic existence does not necessarily signify a food shortage: the aim of the annual expedition, which always occurs sometime between August and September, is to 'assemble the food required for the great festivities marking the close of the rituals which take place before the rains start, and agricultural work begins again'. When an epidemic strikes the village, the Indians believe that the best remedy is to return to their nomadic existence and that the disease will be driven away if they live in the forest for a while: 'food being more plentiful – they regain strength and return in better physical condition' (*ibid.*, p. 33).

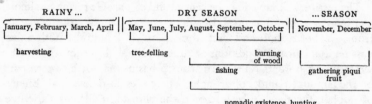

RAINY ...	DRY SEASON	... SEASON
January, February, March, April	May, June, July, August, September, October	November, December
harvesting	tree-felling	
	burning of wood	
	fishing	gathering piqui fruit
	nomadic existence, hunting	

Nimuendaju observes that the prevailing climate in Timbira country is 'noticeably drier than in the adjacent Amazonian area. Unlike the territory farther east and south-east, the country does not suffer the terrors of a drought, yet there is a definite dry season from July until December' (Nim. 8, p. 2). These details do not coincide exactly with the pattern of the ceremonial calendar, which divides the year into two halves, one corresponding in theory to the dry season, from the maize harvest in April until September, the other beginning with the agricultural work which precedes the rains, and occupying the rest of the year (cf. Nim. 3, pp. 62, 84, 86, 163). All the important feasts take place during the ritual period, the so-called dry season, and which consequently is also the period when the Indians lead a settled life. For this reason, and although the information at our disposal is not always clear, it would seem that collective hunts take place during the rainy season (Nim. 8, pp. 85-6). However, mention is also made of hunting savannah birds (emas, sariemas and falconidae) during the dry season, and of collective hunts at the end of each important ceremony (*ibid.*, pp. 69-70). Practically nothing is known about conditions in former times, but it is possible that the spatial contrast between the dry savannah and the strip of forest land bordering the streams and rivers (where fishing takes place and where the plantations are) was as important in native thought as the temporal contrast between the seasons. At any rate, observers seem to have been particularly struck by the former contrast (Nim. 8, p. 1). This may perhaps explain why the contrast between forest animals and savannah animals, which is merely mentioned in the Apinayé and Kraho myths, is concealed in the Timbira version behind another more complex contrast, which gives the following pattern for the respective foods eaten by the animals encountered by the hero:

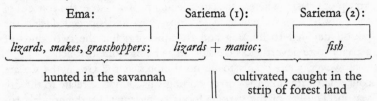

Ema:	Sariema (1):	Sariema (2):
lizards, snakes, grasshoppers;	*lizards* + *manioc*;	*fish*
hunted in the savannah	‖ cultivated, caught in the strip of forest land	

Let us move on now to the Apinayé. 'Anciently, as soon as their clearings were planted, the Apinayé marched into the steppe where they lived the nomadic life of hunters and gatherers until harvest time; only sporadically this or that family would return to the village' (Nim. 5, p. 89). During this period, certain priests had the special task of keeping a jealous watch over the growing plants, which they called 'their children'. Any woman who dared to pick anything from her field before the ban was lifted would be in danger of severe punishment. When the crops were ripe, the priests recalled the villagers from the forest. After a final collective hunt, the families returned to the village, and were at last free to use the produce of their plantations. This moment marked the beginning of the ceremonial period (*ibid.*, p. 90).

If this account of the ancient customs is accurate, what we are dealing with is a rainy season nomadism, since in central Brazil planting takes place at the end of the dry season and the crops ripen a few weeks or a few months later. Thus, the Sherente clear the ground during June and July then burn and plant during August and September, so that germination is helped by the first rains, which follow soon after (Oliveira, p. 394). This rainy-season nomadism, of which we have also found evidence among the Timbira, does not exclude dry-season nomadism, during which hunting also plays an important part, whereas fishing is a far less important activity than is the case in the Chaco. All this suggests that the contrast between the period of plenty and the period of shortage, which is so strongly marked among the Chaco tribes (much more so than the contrast between two kinds of seasons), is expressed by the central Brazilian tribes in socio-economic terms: either in the form of a sacred (ceremonial) period plus a profane period (with no ceremonies) or a nomadic period – collectively devoted to hunting and fruit-picking – plus a sedentary period, mainly taken up with agricultural work. Among the Apinayé, where it appears that agricultural tasks and the occupations associated with the nomadic way of life were carried out during the same months, there was nevertheless a contrast between them; the former, being sacred, were the prerogative of a group of priests, whereas the latter, being profane, were the concern of the population as a whole. The crops grew and ripened during the period devoted to hunting and fruit-picking, but the two kinds of activity were nevertheless considered as being quite distinct.

However, there seems to be no doubt that the Ge myths we are concerned with, like the corresponding Chaco myths, relate to the dry season. The list of the various foods being eaten by the animals encountered by the hero provides an initial indication. All the animal or vegetable products mentioned, whether savannah creatures such as snakes, lizards and grasshoppers, or fish caught during the period when the rivers are running low, or palm or sapucaia nuts or jatobá pods, are typical of the dry season. For instance, this was the season when the Botocudo of eastern Brazil gathered sapucaia nuts, which were an important element in their diet.

Both the Timbira and Apinayé Indians associated the harvesting and gathering of wild produce with the period of nomadic life in the savannah. Nevertheless, the transition from the Chaco myths to the Ge myths is marked by a transformation. In the former, honey and wild fruits are the foods gathered during the nomadic period, while game and honey occupy this position in the latter. But the reason why game replaces wild fruit is immediately obvious: the picking of wild fruit was essentially a feminine occupation among the Ge, but honey was collected by the men (Nim. 5, p. 94; 8, pp. 72–5). As regards the hierarchy of masculine occupations, it can be said that, in the Chaco, the collecting of honey was held to be more important than the picking of wild fruits, just as in central Brazil hunting was considered more important than the collecting of honey:

$$\begin{bmatrix} \text{CHACO} \\ M_{213} \text{ etc.:} \\ \text{honey} > \text{wild fruit} \end{bmatrix} \Rightarrow \begin{bmatrix} \text{CENTRAL BRAZIL} \\ M_{226}: \quad M_{142}: \\ \text{game} \quad \text{game} > \text{honey} \end{bmatrix}$$

I have examined the structure of the group from the formal point of view, and I have linked certain transformations occurring within the group to the ecological features of each region, and to various aspects of the material culture of the communities concerned. On these two levels, I have thus succeeded in solving two difficulties that were pointed out by Nimuendaju in connection with the Apinayé version (M_{142}):

Pebkumre'dy (the second phase of the initiation) represents the true initiation for warriors ... The Apinayé link its origin to the same traditional theme that the Canella (= Timbira) associate with their own initiation ritual of the pepyé: the fight between two brothers and a giant falcon. It would seem, however, that the parts played by the brothers are reversed, and I think that the final episode spread down from the north to the Apinayé and that it was added at a later date – I am referring to the story of the man who roasted his wife (Nim. 5, p. 56).

We know, however, that this story is part of the Ge heritage, since it exists as a separate myth among the Kraho Indians. In fact, where Nimuendaju saw two distinct problems, I have shown that there is only one, the different aspects of which throw light on each other. It is because the Apinayé hero (unlike the Kraho or Timbira hero) is destined to meet an ignominious death that his role must be filled by that one of the two brothers who, in the other versions, is killed in his place. It still remains to be explained why this variant requires the presence of the girl mad about honey who becomes the doomed brother's wife. After subjecting these myths to a formal analysis and studying them ethnographically, we must now consider them from a third point of view, namely that of their semantic function.

As I have pointed out on several occasions and have just recalled, the central and eastern Ge regard the fight between the two brothers and the killer-birds as the origin of the young men's initiation ceremony. The initiation rite had a two-fold character. On the one hand, it marked the fact that male adolescents had reached the status of hunters and warriors; thus, among the Apinayé, at the end of the period of seclusion, initiates received ceremonial clubs from their sponsors in exchange for game (Nim. 5, pp. 68–70). But at the same time the initiation rite was a prelude to marriage. In theory at least, the young men were still bachelors. Any young girl who bestowed her favours on one of them before initiation was ruthlessly punished; she was subjected to collective rape by the fully grown men on the day when her lover went into seclusion, and from then on was reduced to the condition of a prostitute. At the close of the initiation period, the young men all got married on the same day, as soon as the ceremony was over (Nim. 5, p. 79).

This was a particularly important event for the men since, like most Ge tribes, the Apinayé were matrilocal. On the day of the marriage, the future brothers-in-law dragged the intended husband out of his maternal hut and led him to their own maternal hut, where his wife-to-be awaited him. Marriage was always monogamous and it was considered to be an indissoluble bond, provided the young woman was a virgin. Each family undertook the responsibility of dealing with the husband or wife, as the case might be, if either should attempt to break the marriage bond. So, the teaching given to the novices every evening all through the initiation period had a distinctly pre-marital aspect: marriage was the main subject for discussion – the instructors explained how to choose a wife 'so as to forestall being fettered to a lazy and faithless woman ... ' (Nim. 5, p. 60).

The same thing was true among the Timbira: 'Formerly, a young man could not marry before completing the cycle of the initiation rites and thus attaining the status of penp, "warrior". At the end of the closing ceremony, the future mothers-in-law walked in parade, leading the young warriors, their prospective sons-in-law, on ropes' (Nim. 8, p. 200 and pl. 40a). All the marriages took place at a collective ceremony at the end of the initiation (*ibid.*, p. 122). The exhortations addressed to the novices never failed to stress the two-fold aim of the rites. During seclusion, the young men were crammed with food, so as to build up strength for competitive sports, hunting and war; not only were they constantly kept in training throughout the entire period of seclusion by means of foot-races and collective hunting expeditions, this was also the time when they were first given the kopó, a weapon half-way between a spear and a club, which is looked upon as being essentially a weapon of war throughout the whole of central Brazil.

The other aspect of the teaching given them related to marriage: how to avoid quarrels and arguments which might set the children a bad example, but also how to detect feminine shortcomings such as flightiness, laziness and untruthfulness. Lastly, the man's duties towards his parents-in-law were enumerated (Nim. 8, pp. 185–6).

The myths provide, as it were, an active commentary on these aspects of the rites. But, according to the versions, certain aspects are singled out and treated in relation to some particular eventuality. Let us look first of all at the Kraho myth about the fight with the killer-bird (M_{226}). It is centred entirely on hunting and war. The hero, Kengunan, is past-master in both these arts, which are to all intents and purposes one and the same, since he does not use bows and arrows for hunting, but only the spear-cum-club, the kopó, which is a weapon of war, although the Timbira use it on exceptional occasions in hunting the ant-eater (Nim. 8, p. 60), a practice which, incidentally, is very much in keeping with the myth's original conclusion (M_{227}).

In fact, the major part of the Kraho version consists of an enthusiastic enumeration of the qualities of a good hunter. Without a bow or a dog, he can find game where no one else can: he kills enormous quantities of game, and although the slaughtered animals are very heavy, he carries them without any difficulty. Yet he modestly declares that he has killed nothing, or only an insignificant amount of game, so as to allow his affines the surprise and credit of making the discovery for themselves. His affines only, since he is married and lives in a village belonging to another tribe where he has no blood relations. Above all, by his example, Kenkunan teaches respect for the taboos on which a successful hunt depends. The hunter must not eat the game he himself has killed or, if he eats it, he must at least postpone the act of consumption in two ways which are complementary to each other: in time, by allowing the meat to become cold; and in space, by taking care not to grasp it with his naked hands, but to pick it up on the pointed end of a stick: 'The Kraho', according to the informant, 'do not eat the first animal they have killed; but only if they have killed a lot of the same quality (= species); even then, they do not take the meat in their hands, but pick it up on a pointed stick and allow it to get cold before eating it' (Schultz 1, p. 108).

Among the Ge, therefore, the hunting rites taught to novices during initiation consist chiefly in the practice of discretion. The main object of the married hunter is to provide food for his affines, from whom, the tribe being matrilocal, he is receiving hospitality. He does so generously and modestly, being careful to disparage the game he himself has killed, and to refrain from partaking of it, or to partake of it only very moderately, while keeping the meat at a distance through the use of time and space as mediatory agents.

Now, as we have already observed, the postponement of consumption is a characteristic feature of the rites performed at the honey festival of the northern Tupi tribes, the Tembé and the Tenetehara, who are neighbours of the Ge. Instead of eating the honey immediately, they store it, and the honey, which ferments during the waiting period, becomes a *sacred, shared* beverage. It is shared with the guests from neighbouring villages, and thus helps to strengthen inter-group relations. Yet it is sacred too, since the honey festival is a religious ceremony, the aim of which is to ensure successful hunting throughout the year, and therefore has the same purpose as the Ge hunting rites.

It is possible that a similar distinction existed in the Chaco between the honey collected during the dry season and consumed immediately, and the honey intended for the preparation of mead which, as certain indications suggest, was perhaps kept in reserve, since according to Paucke (1942, pp. 95–6) among the Mocovi,

> the making of mead took place chiefly from November onwards, when the heat was intense. The beverage made from honey and fruit was drunk both day and night and the natives lived in a constant state of intoxication. More than a hundred people would be present at these feasts, which sometimes degenerated into drunken brawls.
>
> In order to prepare the mead, the dried skin of a jaguar or deer was hung up by the corners to form a pouch, into which the honey was poured along with its wax, and then water was added. In the space of three or four days, the mixture fermented naturally in the sun. Young men and bachelors, unless they were of noble birth, were not allowed to drink, and had to be content to act as cup-bearers (*ibid.*, 1943, pp. 197–8).

The weather is cold in the Chaco from July to September. The documents therefore suggest that the collective and ceremonial consumption of mead was also perhaps deferred consumption. At all events, the rites excluded certain categories of men who, like the Ge hunters, although in a different way, were entitled to take part in them only after a certain *point in time*: in this case, after a change in status.

The Caingang of southern Brazil provide a more straightforward illustration of these discriminatory behaviour patterns. One informant has given an illuminating account of an excursion into the forest with two companions in search of honey. Once a tree had been spotted, fires were lit all round it in order to stupefy the bees. Then it was felled and the trunk hollowed out with axes. As soon as the bees' nest was uncovered – 'we take out the layers of the paper-like structure and in our hunger eat the contents raw. They are sweet, rich and juicy. Now we build small fires and lay the cells against them to roast. Having eaten my fill, I receive no more. The two Indians divide the rest, the one who discovered it getting the larger share.' For, to quote the informant, 'honey constitutes a kind of free food. When a nest is discovered, anyone who happens along may share it. No one would think of making a whole meal of honey, but it is a godsend in the middle of the day' (Henry 1, pp. 161–2).

The Suya of the Rio Xingu area are also said to eat honey on the spot where it has been collected: 'All the Indians thrust their hands into the honey and licked it; they ate the combs along with the larvae and the masses of pollen. A small quantity of honey and larvae was kept in reserve and taken back to the camp' (Schultz 3, p. 319).

In contrast to this immediate consumption of fresh honey, which is shared and eaten there and then without ceremony, the Caingang practice deferred consumption in the form of mead intended primarily for affines.

A man and his cousins or brothers decide to make beer for his in-laws. They cut down cedars, hollow them for troughs and go to look for honey. After several days they have enough. They then send their wives for water to fill the troughs. The honey is poured into the water, and the water is heated with hot stones ... The woody stem of a fern called *nggign* is pounded and titrated and the red infusion mixed in the trough. This is to make the beer red; without *nggign*, say the Kaingang, the beer would not ferment. This goes on for days, and then the mouth of the trough is covered with strips of bark and the beer is left standing several days longer. When it begins to bubble, the Indians decide that it is *thô*, intoxicating or bitter, and ready to drink ... (Henry 1, p. 162).

This lengthy preparation, some details of which have been omitted, appears even more complex when it is remembered that the making of the troughs requires huge trees, the felling of which is in itself a long and difficult operation. Moreover, sometimes several of these huge trees had to be felled in order to find one without a crack through which the beer might leak. A whole team of Indians would labour arduously to drag the perfect trunk back to the village, then to hollow out the trough with rudimentary tools, there being a constant danger that a leak might occur during the operation, or worse still, after the beer has started to ferment (*ibid.*, pp. 169–70).

Among the Caingang, then, there were two ways of consuming honey: immediate consumption, without preferential distribution, and in the fresh state; long-deferred consumption, which made it possible to store up an adequate supply and to achieve the conditions necessary for the preparation of fermented honey. Now it will be remembered that, according to the informant, mead is intended for affines. In addition to the fact that the same kind of priority of distribution has a prominent place in the hunting rites in the Ge myths, certain details of the Chaco myths dealing with the girl mad about honey point to a similar conclusion.

On the day after his marriage, the deceiving fox in the Toba myths brings back poisonous fruit and empty combs. But his mother-in-law, who believes the bag to be full of honey, picks it up at once and declares, as a matter of course, that she is going to make mead for all her relatives with the honey gathered by her son-in-law (M_{207}). When Sun's daughter demands a variety of honey he is unable to find, he replies no less spontaneously: 'Get married!' (M_{216}).[27] The theme of marriage as a means of obtaining honey recurs as a leitmotiv in all the myths in this group. Here, too, then, two ways of consuming honey can be distinguished: the woman eats her fill of the fresh honey there and then; at the same time, some honey is kept in reserve and brought back, and this honey is intended for the affines.

We now understand why, in the Chaco myths, the girl mad about honey is doomed to meet with a lamentable end, i.e. is changed into an animal or disappears. Her greed and indiscretion do not provide a sufficient reason, since these defects do not prevent her from making a good marriage. It is only after her marriage that she commits the real crime: she refuses to give her mother the honey collected by her husband. This detail occurs by implication in M_{212}, and in M_{213} it is stressed in a very significant way since, in this version, a mean heroine is changed into a capybara, whereas the heroine of M_{224}, who is old instead of young, also assumes the appearance of a capybara in order to be avenged on her own people for their meanness. Consequently, the misdemeanour committed by the girl mad about honey is that she carries selfishness, greed or spite to the *extent of interrupting the cycle of food-gifts between affines*. She keeps back the honey in order to eat it herself, instead of allowing it to flow, as it were, from her husband who has gathered it to his parents who are entitled to eat it.

We already know that, from the formal point of view, all the myths we have examined so far (whether they belong to the northern Tupi, the Chaco tribes, or the central and eastern Ge), form one group. But now we understand why. All these myths transmit the same message, without necessarily using the same vocabulary or the same grammatical constructions. Some use the active, some the passive, mood. Some

[27] Among the Umutina, too, 'the honey which had been collected was always shared out according to a system based on kinship. The largest share went to the hunter's mother-in-law, and the smallest to his sons, and a little honey was set aside for those who were absent' (Schultz 2, p. 175).

explain what happens when what ought to be done is done; others adopt the reverse procedure and consider the consequences of doing the opposite of what ought to be done. Lastly, since all the myths deal with the question of bringing up young people, the central figure in the story can be a man or a woman: a bad woman who does not even benefit from having a good husband; or a good man who makes a success of his marriage even in a hostile country (but is this not always the situation of a man in a matrilocal society?); or again, a well-bred man who is guilty on three counts: he has chosen a bad woman as his wife, he has rebelled against her and has offended his affines, to whom he offers a kind of 'anti-contribution' in the form of their daughter's flesh.

Within this group, the Ge myths stand out as displaying a characteristic dialectical pattern, for each version examines the instruction given to initiates from a different angle. The hero of the Kraho version, who is a master of war and hunting, makes a success of his marriage through this fact alone, and the successful marriage is, as it were, an additional bonus. He found a good wife, because he was not afraid to seek death at the hands of strangers; and he succeeded in keeping his wife and in reaching an advanced age, because he had won the gratitude of his affines by seeing that they were plentifully supplied with food and by destroying their enemies. The Timbira version reproduces more or less the same pattern, but in a much weaker form, since here the emphasis is shifted: the relevant theme, instead of being the concluding of a marriage, is rather the revoking of a blood relationship (the grandparents are changed into ant-eaters), always in accordance with the rule that even a marriage arranged from childhood and with fellow-countrymen represents a sort of bond which is incompatible with the bond which springs from a blood relationship. As for the Apinayé version, as compared with the other two, it is weaker on four counts: the part of chief protagonist is given to the brother to whom the other versions assign a lower position; the story takes place during a honey-gathering expedition, a more humble form (as compared with hunting) of the search for food during the dry season; the teaching referred to is that relating to the choice of a wife, and not to the conduct of hunting and warfare; finally, and contrary to what happens in the other myths, the hero fails to derive benefit from this teaching, since he marries a wife who is as ill-bred as he is.

Whether explicitly referred to or not, honey plays the part of relevant feature in all the myths. The Chaco myths evolve a theory of honey which contrasts it with other wild and vegetable foods of the dry season. The Ge myths, either overtly or by omission, expound the same theory, basing it on the contrast between honey and game. Among the Ge, only the consumption of game was subject to certain ritualistic prohibitions which caused it to be deferred in time and space, whereas the consumption of honey does not seem to have been controlled by any specific rules. No doubt the Apinayé had a ritual connected with cultivated plants but, with the exception of manioc which has little or no seasonal character, these plants have no place in any mythological cycle definable in relationship to the dry season.

Finally, among the Tembé and Tenetehara, the same theory of deferred consumption is based almost entirely on honey, but only in so far as the deferred consumption of honey is seen as a means of the non-deferred consumption of game: the honey festival is put off until a certain period of the year, in order to ensure successful hunting throughout the whole year.

It follows then that, in the myths of central Brazil, the non-deferred consumption of honey (of which a woman is guilty) is the opposite of the deferred consumption of game (which redounds to a man's credit). In the Chaco, the non-deferred consumption of honey (by a woman) both resembles the non-deferred consumption of wild fruits (i.e. which are still toxic) by both sexes, and forms a contrast with the deferred consumption of honey by a man who does without it himself for the benefit of his affines.

PART TWO THE FEAST OF THE FROG

Et veterem in limo ranae cecinere querellam.

Virgil, *Georgics*, I, v. 378

1 *Variations 1, 2, 3*

In connection with the Ofaié myth about the origin of honey (M_{192}), I pointed out a progressive–regressive movement which I now see is characteristic of all the myths we have studied up till now. The Ofaié myth can be described as a myth of origin in one respect only. For the honey to which it refers bears very little resemblance to the honey with which we are now familiar. This early form of honey had an invariable and uniform flavour, and grew in plantations, like the cultivated plants. As it was within easy reach, it was eaten up when it was barely ripe. Before men could possess honey permanently and enjoy all its different varieties, cultivated honey had to disappear and be replaced by wild honey, which, although available in smaller quantities, is present in an inexhaustible supply.

The Chaco myths illustrate the same theme, more discreetly and less explicitly. In former times, honey was the only food, and it ceased to fulfil this function when the woodpecker, the master of honey, changed into a bird and abandoned human society for good. The Ge myths, on the other hand, transpose the historical sequence into terms of a contemporary contrast between hunting, which is subject to all kinds of rules and is therefore a cultural quest for food, and the collecting of honey, which, being free of all restrictions, suggests a natural means of acquiring food.

We must not be surprised then if, when we move on now to Guiana, we find there as elsewhere myths about the origin of honey, which are also concerned with its loss:

M_{233}. *Arawak. 'Why honey is so scarce now'*

In olden times bees' nests and honey were very plentiful in the bush, and there was one man in particular who had earned quite a reputation for discovering their whereabouts. One day while chopping into a hollow tree in order to extract honey from it, he heard a voice from inside calling: 'Take care! You are cutting me!' Opening the tree very carefully he discovered a beautiful woman who told him she was called Maba, 'honey', and who was the Honey-Mother, that is, the Spirit of honey. As she was quite nude, he collected some cotton which she made into a cloth, and he asked her to be his wife. She consented on condition that he never mention her name, and they lived very happily for many years. And, just in the same way that he became universally acknowledged as the best man for finding bees' nests, so she made a name for herself in the way of brewing excellent cassiri and paiwarri. No matter the number of visitors, she only had to make one jugful, and this one jugful would make them all drunk. She thus proved to be a splendid wife.

One day, however, when all the drink was finished, the husband, no doubt slightly intoxicated, went round to his many guests and expressed regret that there was no more liquor. 'The next time', he said, 'Maba will make more.' The mistake had been made and the name of his wife uttered. The woman at once changed into a bee and flew away, although he put up his hands to stop her. And with her, his luck flew away, and since that time honey has always been more or less scarce (Roth 1, pp. 204–5).

Cassiri is a kind of beer made from previously boiled manioc and 'sweet red potatoes', to which is added other manioc that has been chewed by the women and children and impregnated with saliva and cane sugar in order to speed up fermentation, a process which lasts about three days. The preparation of paiwarri is similar, except that this beer is made with previously roasted manioc cakes. It must be consumed more rapidly, since it only takes twenty-four hours to prepare and starts to turn sour after two or three days, unless freshly roasted manioc is added and the other operations repeated (Roth 2, pp. 227–38). The fact that the mother of honey is credited with the preparation of fermented beverages is all the more significant in that the Guiana Indians do not make mead: 'Wild honey may be mixed with water and drunk, but there is no record of it ever having been left to ferment' (*ibid.*, p. 227).

Yet the Indians of Guiana are well versed in the manufacture of fermented liquors from manioc, maize or various fruits. Roth mentions no less than fifteen (2, pp. 227–32). It may well be that fresh honey was sometimes added to the beverage as a sweetening agent. But as evidence of this practice is chiefly found in myths, as will be shown later, the association of fresh honey with fermented beverages can more likely be explained by the intoxicating properties of certain kinds of honey, which make them immediately comparable to fermented beverages. Whether we study the cultures of the Chaco or those of Guiana, the same correlative and oppositional relationship can be noted between fresh honey and fermented beverages, although only fresh honey is present as a constant term, the place of the other term being taken by various kinds of beer made from different substances. Only the form of the contrast is permanent, but each culture expresses it in different lexical terms.

A recent work by Wilbert (9, pp. 90–93) contains Warao variants ($M_{233b, c}$) of the myth that I have just summarized. It makes no mention of fermented beverages. The supernatural wife procures for her husband a delicious kind of water, which is in fact honey, on condition that no one else drinks any of it. But he makes the mistake of handing the gourd to a thirsty companion who is asking for a drink, and when the latter exclaims in astonishment 'But this is honey!' the wife's forbidden name is thus uttered. She pretends to go off to relieve nature, but vanishes, after changing into honey of the mohorohi bees. The man in turn changes into a swarm. The Warao version noted by Roth is very different:

M_{234}. Warao. 'Honey-bee and the sweet drinks'

There were two sisters looking after their brother and for whom they were always making cassiri, but even when they tried their best, the drink had no taste; it was never good and palatable. So the man was forever complaining and wishing he could find a woman who could make him a real sweet drink, something like honey!

One day while wandering through the bush and wishing he could find such a woman, he heard footsteps behind him. Turning round, he saw a female who said to him: 'Where are you going? You called Koroha (the honey-bee). That is my name and here I am!' The Indian told her about his own and his sisters' wishes and, when she asked him whether he thought his people would like her, he said he was quite sure they would. Koroha accordingly went home with him. The village people asked her how he had met her, but she was careful to explain to her parents-in-law that she had only come because their son had called her.

She then made the drink. And the way she made it! All she had to do was to put her finger in the water, stir it, and the drink was ready! It tasted sweet, sweet, sweet! And never before had it tasted so good. From that time onward they always had sweet drinks. And on every occasion when her husband was thirsty, Koroha brought him water into which she had dipped her little finger to make it sweet.

But at last the man got tired of all this sweet drink and began to quarrel with his wife, who protested angrily: 'You wanted sweet drinks and you called me to get them for you and now you are not satisfied. You can get them for yourself now!' With this she flew away and ever since then people have been punished by being put to all the trouble of climbing up, and cutting the honey out of the tree, and having to clean it before they can use it for sweetening purposes (Roth 1, p. 305).

It is clear that this myth is a transformation of the preceding one in respect both of kinship ties and the beverages mentioned, although in each instance the drinks are beer and honeyed water. But in each of the two myths a distinction is made between the two drinks. The honey in M_{233} is delicious and the beer perfect – that is, very strong, since it intoxicates even in tiny quantities. In M_{234}, the opposite is the case: the honeyed water is too sweet, and therefore in its way too strong, since it proves to be sickly, while the beer is weak and tasteless. Now, the good honey and good beer in M_{233} are solely the result of a conjugal union; they are supplied respectively by a husband and his wife and are offered only to 'guests', that is to an anonymous group, which remains undefined in respect of kinship.

Unlike the hero of M_{233}, a great producer of honey whose skill has made him universally famous, the hero of M_{234} is defined by his negative features. He is a consumer and not a producer and, what is more, is never satisfied. He is, in a sense, only an incidental character, and the really relevant family relationship compares and contrasts the sisters-in-law, who are producers: the husband's sisters who make the beer too weak, and the brother's wife who makes the syrup too sweet:

Furthermore, the plentiful supply of honey and the strong beer are treated by M_{233} as positively homologous terms: their coexistence is the result of a conjugal union and itself assumes the outward appearance of a logical union, whereas the (over)-plentiful honey and insipid beer in M_{234} are in a logical relationship of disunion:

$$M_{233} \text{ [beer } (+) \cup \text{ honey } (+)] \Rightarrow M_{234} \text{ [beer } (-) \mathbin{//} \text{ honey } (-)]$$

It will be remembered that, among the Caingang, who have mead instead of manioc beer as a fermented beverage, the same terms were combined more simply. Like M_{233}, the Caingang material illustrates a logical union, but one established between fresh sweet honey on the one hand and, on the other, a fermented beverage made from honey and which, according to the Caingang, is of better quality as it is more 'bitter', and which is intended for affines. Whereas the four terms of the Guiana system form two pairs of opposites – *sweet/sickly* for sweetened, non-fermented beverages, and *strong/weak* for the fermented beverages – the Caingang have only two terms forming one oppositional relationship between two beverages, which are both made from fresh or fermented honey: *sweet/bitter*. The English language, more clearly than the French, offers an approximate equivalent of this basic contrast in the distinction between *soft drink* and *hard drink*. But in French, we surely have the same contrast, transposed, however, from an alimentary coding to the language of social relationships (the terms of which, moreover, are alimentary in the first place, but are used in a figurative sense) when we correlate and contrast *lune de miel* (honeymoon) and *lune de fiel* or *lune d'absinthe* (sour moon), and thus introduce a three-fold contrast between the sweet and the bitter, the fresh and the fermented, total and exclusive conjugal union and its reinsertion into the pattern of social relationships.

In subsequent chapters, I shall show that these familiar and graphic expressions bring us much closer to the inner meaning of the myths than do formal analyses, although we cannot do without such analyses, if only as a laborious means of justifying the other method which, had it been applied straightway, would have been discredited by its naivety. Formal analyses are indispensable, for they alone make it possible to reveal the logical armature hidden beneath seemingly strange and incomprehensible stories. Only after this armature has been disclosed can we afford the luxury of returning to 'primary truths', which then appear – but on that condition alone – to merit the double meaning we give to the expression.

The *sweet/sickly* contrast, which is a feature of honey in the Guiana myths, exists elsewhere too, since we have met it in an Amazonian myth (M_{202}) in connection with the story of the ogre who was sickened by honey, and in a Chaco myth (M_{210}), the hero of which is Fox who is crammed with honey, exactly like the unfortunate Indian at the end of M_{234}. This last similarity between characters both of whom stand out as not having any clearly defined relationship to honey, inevitably draws

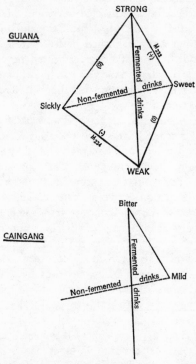

Figure 11. The oppositional system of fermented and non-fermented drinks

attention to another point of resemblance between the Guiana myths and those of the Chaco. The former depict a supernatural creature, the mistress of honey, in the guise of a shy young woman. In M_{233}, where she is completely naked, her first concern is not to offend against modesty: she has to have cotton in order to clothe herself. And, in M_{234}, she is worried about the proposal of marriage, and about the kind of welcome she will receive from her suitor's family. Is he sure that his proposal will meet with approval? As it happens, the wood-pecker in the Chaco myths replies to the proposal made to him by the girl mad about honey in exactly same way and in almost the same terms. It is therefore clear that this diffidence, which the old mythography would no doubt have regarded as a romantic embellishment, constitutes an essential feature of the pattern. When we move from the Chaco to Guiana, it becomes the central theme on which all the other relationships hinge, but which nevertheless preserves the symmetry of the pattern. We note that the Guiana myth, M_{234}, whose hero is a boy mad about honey, provides an exact counterpart to the Chaco myths about the girl mad about honey. The Chaco heroine compares the respective merits of two men: a husband and rejected suitor. The Guiana hero is in the same situation with regard to a wife and sisters. The disappointed suitor – Fox – is rejected because he shows himself to be incapable of supplying good honey, in place of which he offers only toxic fruit (too 'strong'). The sisters drive their brother to marriage because they are incapable of making good beer and can only offer him insipid beer (too weak). In both cases, the result is marriage either with a timid husband, the master of honey, or with a timid wife, the mistress of honey. But the parents of the other spouse are not allowed to enjoy the honey which from now on is in plentiful supply, either because the wife is not sick of it and wants to keep it all for herself, or because the husband is sick of it and does not want his wife to go on producing it. In conclusion, the consumer- or producer-wife changes into an animal – a capybara, or a bee. The following transformations can be noted, as we move for instance from M_{213} to M_{234}:

M_{213}:	M_{234}:
Fox	$\Rightarrow$ Sisters
Woodpecker	$\Rightarrow$ Bee
The Girl mad about honey	$\Rightarrow$ The Boy mad about honey

At this point it must be admitted that the observation I made a little while back raises a problem. If the character acting as the hero in M_{234} is a transformation of the character who is acting as the heroine in M_{213}, how can he also reproduce certain aspects of the character of the Fox? The difficulty will be overcome once I have shown that, in M_{213}, and in the other myths belonging to the same group, there is also a resemblance between Fox and the girl mad about honey, which explains how Fox had the idea of impersonating the heroine in order to deceive the latter's husband (pp. 165, 277).

In order to get to that point, I must first of all introduce a new variant from Guiana. With M_{233} and M_{234} we have by no means exhausted the group of Guiana myths about the origin of honey, all of whose transformations can be generated, that is, whose empirical contents can be deduced, by means of a single algorithm, defined by the following two operations:

It having been accepted that, in the myths of this group, the chief protagonist is an animal, the group can be established if and only if (↔):

(1) *the identity of the animal remains the same in the two consecutive myths, while its sex is reversed;*

(2) *the sex of the animal remains the same in the two consecutive myths, while its specific nature is 'reversed'.*

The homology of the two operations obviously implies the acceptance, as a previously formulated axiom, of the hypothesis that the transformation (⇒) of one animal into another always occurs within a pair of opposites. I have quoted sufficient examples in *The Raw and the Cooked* for the reader to agree with me that this axiom has at least a heuristic value.

Since, in the last version we examined (M_{234}), the chief protagonist was a bee, we shall begin our series of operations with the bee.

a. FIRST VARIATION

$$[bee \Rightarrow bee] \leftrightarrow [\bigcirc \Rightarrow \triangle]$$

Here first of all is the myth:

M_{235}. Warao. 'The honey-bee son-in-law'

A man made up a little family party to accompany him on a hunting expedition, leaving his wife and his other two daughters at home. When the hunter and his children had gone far out into the bush, they constructed a shelter in which they camped.

Next day the girl told her father she was indisposed and that she could not build the barbecue and do the cooking, since it was not permissible for her to touch the utensils. The three men went hunting alone, but returned empty-handed. The same thing happened on the succeeding afternoon, as if the young girl's condition were the cause of their bad luck.

Next morning the huntsmen went into the bush, and the girl, who was lying in her hammock in the camp, was somewhat startled on seeing a young man approach and jump in beside her, although she informed him of her condition. She fought and wrestled with him, but the boy held her firmly, assuring her that he had not the slightest intention of troubling her. She learnt that he had been in love with her for a long time, but for the moment his only intention was to rest, and he promised to ask the old man for possession of her later in the proper manner.

So they both lay there quietly in the hammock, discussing their respective prospects and affairs. The young man explained that he was a Simo-ahawara, that is, a member of the bee tribe. Now just as Simo had anticipated, the father was not at all vexed at seeing the stranger in his daughter's hammock. In fact he made not the slightest reference to her even having company.

The marriage took place the following morning and Simo told the three men to remain in their hammocks, as he would make himself responsible for supplying them with food. In an instant he killed a prodigious quantity of game which all three Indians together were unable to raise from the ground, but which he himself brought back without effort. They had plenty to last them for several months. Having dried all the meat, they started on their homeward journey, each one carrying as much as he could. Simo was so strong he carried a load five times heavier than all their loads put together. And yet he speedily caught up with them on the road.

So they all went home together, and Simo took up his residence, as was customary, at his father-in-law's place. After he had finished clearing the land and planting, his wife gave birth to a beautiful baby boy.

Now it was just about this time that his two sisters-in-law were beginning to give trouble. They had fallen in love with him and were always jumping into his hammock, but as fast as they got in he would turn them out. He neither liked nor wanted them, and complained to his wife about their conduct. Of course (as the informant remarks), there was nothing wrong in what his sisters-in-law were trying to do, because among the Warao it is no sin for a man to live with his sisters-in-law as well as his wife.

Every time the three women bathed in the river with Simo minding the baby on the bank, the sisters-in-law would try and dash spray over him. This was very wicked of them, still more so since Simo had warned them that if water should ever touch him it would act like fire, that is, first weaken then destroy him. As a matter of fact, none of the three women had ever seen him bathe: he washed himself in honey just as the little bees do. But only his wife was well aware of the reason for this, since he had told no one else who he was.

One day as he was sitting on the bank with the baby in his arms while the three women were washing themselves, the sisters-in-law succeeded in dashing water over him. He at once screamed 'I burn, I burn!', and flying away like a bee into a hollow tree, he melted into honey, and his child changed into Wau-uta, the tree-frog (Roth 1, pp. 199–201).

Let us leave the tree-frog on one side for the time being, since we shall encounter it again later. The theme of the water which burns and melts the bee-man's body can obviously be explained, as Roth observes, by the idea that a person such as the bee-man must be made of honey and wax, the first of which substances dissolves in water, while the other is melted by fire. In support of this theory, I can quote a short Amazonian myth (M_{236}), based on the same theme. After a hunter had been torn to pieces by the birds, the Spirit of the Woods glued the pieces together with wax and warned his protégé that from now on he should not drink anything hot. But the latter forgot about the injunction, the heat caused the wax to melt and his body disintegrated (Rodrigues 1, pp. 35–8).

From the point of view of kinship and the allocation of the various roles, the characters in M_{235} can be divided into three groups, which are easily illustrated by the following diagram:

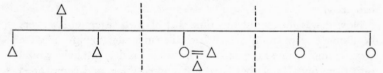

The central group consists of the heroine, her husband who will be turned into honey, and her young son who will also undergo a transformation, but into a frog.

The group on the left, which consists entirely of men, is composed of characters collectively described as unlucky hunters.

The group on the right, which is entirely feminine, comprises the two sisters-in-law. This distribution recalls the one we observed in the Chaco myths which I used in order to constitute the cycle relating to the girl mad about honey. There too we had three groups:

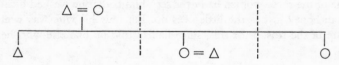

with, in the centre, Fox and the young girl he succeeded in marrying on the pretext that he would provide his parents-in-law with the honey they lacked. The group on the left, then, consists of unlucky honey-gatherers, who have not been supplied with food by their son-in-law (whereas, in M_{235}, it consists of a band of unlucky hunters, who, on the contrary, are plentifully supplied with food by their son-in-law). In both cases, the group on the right consists of one or more sisters-in-law, but only after a further reversal has been effected, since in the one instance, it is the husband who leaves his wife and tries to seduce a sister-in-law who is not at all anxious to follow him, and, in the other, the sisters-in-law who try to seduce a husband who is determined to remain faithful.

The reversal of the erotic relationship that the myth establishes between the affines is therefore itself a function of a two-fold reversal of their alimentary relationship: negative in the one instance, positive in the other; and centring either on honey or meat.

It is remarkable that Bee, in assuming the male sex in M_{235}, should become a supplier of meat (dried meat according to the myth, that is half-way between raw and cooked), whereas in M_{233} and M_{234} in which Bee was a female, she played the part of provider of honey (in a raw form) or beer (in a cooked form). But the fact is that honey, which has an alimentary significance in M_{233} and M_{234}, takes on a sexual connotation in M_{235} (all three are Guiana myths); that is, honey which is always held to be 'seductive' is literally so in the one instance and figuratively so in the other. This transformation within the Guiana group is equally apparent when M_{235} is compared with the Chaco myths, for it is clear that if we move back from the latter to the Guiana myth, the respective functions of the female affines are reversed, at the same time as there is a transition, as regards the 'seductive' connotation of honey, from the literal to the figurative sense. In the Chaco myths, the wife is mad about honey in the literal, and therefore alimentary, sense, and the sister-in-law unintentionally arouses sexual passion in her brother-in-law, Fox. In M_{235}, the opposite happens: the sisters-in-law are mad about honey, but in the figurative sense, since their sister's husband is called 'Honey', and unintentionally arouses sexual passion in them.

But in this respect, they bear a resemblance to Fox, who like them, and as a result of the same amorous approaches, causes the other characters to be changed into animals. From this point of view, the group appears to be over-determined, a circumstance which is in danger of causing some confusion in the table of commutations, where certain terms seem arbitrarily related by multiple connections. I referred to this difficulty earlier, and the time has now come to solve it.

I shall begin by observing that, in M_{235}, there are two sisters-in-law, whereas one would have been enough for the purposes of the narrative. This is also the case in the Toba myths, which I suggested could be interpreted as a reverse transformation of the Guiana myth. Might it not be accepted, as a working hypothesis, that the fact of there being two sisters expresses the ambiguity inherent in a kind of behaviour which can be interpreted in two ways: either in the literal sense, as a search for food, or figuratively, as a sexual quest, since the myth is concerned with the amatory possession of honey (that is, in this case, the possession of a character called 'Honey')? The presence of two sisters-in-law in M_{235} would mean, then, that the common role assigned to them involves two separate aspects. It is as if the purpose of one of the sisters-in-law were to interpret, in the figurative sense, the part played by the Chaco heroine, who was also mad about honey, but honey as food, whereas the other sister-in-law might be said to preserve, in the literal sense, the seductive function assigned to Fox on the sexual level, with the difference that the roles are switched: in the Chaco, Fox trying to seduce his wife's sister; in Guiana, the sisters-in-law trying to seduce Bee, their sister's husband.

This interpretation opens up interesting vistas, when we consider its sociological implications. It suggests a relationship of equivalence between a rhetorical transformation and a sociological transformation:

rhetorical level [literal sense $\Rightarrow$ figurative sense] ::

sociological level $\begin{bmatrix} \text{seduction of a woman} \\ \text{by a man} \end{bmatrix} \Rightarrow \begin{bmatrix} \text{seduction of a man} \\ \text{by a woman} \end{bmatrix}$

If it is possible to find other examples confirming this relationship, we shall be able to conclude that, in native thought, the seduction of a woman by a man belongs to the real world, and is the reverse of a symbolic or imaginary procedure. For the moment, I merely put forward the suggestion, pending the time when other myths force me to consider the problems relating to the existence and function of a rhetorical coding (see below pp. 170, 174 *ff*, 279 *ff*).

In explaining the duality of the sisters-in-law by the ambiguity of their function, I have at least succeeded in removing the confusion which was threatening to invade the table of commutations, as it may be drawn up on the basis of the Guiana myth. But we have not solved the overall problem, since it is now essential that there should be a duplicated role in the Chaco myths corresponding to the two sisters-in-law in M_{235}. This is a *sine qua non* of the completion of the transformational group.

At this juncture, then, it is appropriate to recall that, in the Chaco myths, Fox plays two parts: his own, first of all, when he tries to marry or seduce the girl mad about honey; and that of the girl herself when he tries to take her place as Woodpecker's wife after her disappearance. Fox is therefore both a man with a sexual passion for women and a girl with an (alimentary) passion for honey, and this, from the diachronic point of view, amounts to a good analytical description of the synthetic attitude attributed by M_{235} to a pair of women (analytically separate on the synchronic level), who are both mad about a man, and mad about 'Honey'.

Therefore Fox's diachronic duality clearly corresponds to the synchronic duality of the two sisters-in-law.

One last comparison must be made. In M_{235}, Bee, who is at first alive, dies after being splashed by water from a river (terrestrial water), which acts upon him as if it were fire. It will be remembered that, in the Chaco myths, Fox, who was dead and dried up as a result of the sun's heat, comes to life again when he is moistened (= splashed) by rain, that is, by celestial water. It is clear, therefore, that if, in the Chaco myths, Fox and Woodpecker are opposites, and that if Woodpecker, the master of honey in the Chaco myths, is congruous with Bee, the master of hunting in the Guiana myth, the Chaco Fox and the Guianese Bee are, not surprisingly, opposites. Each behaves differently towards a young girl who is alone and indisposed: one tries to take advantage of her condition, while the other does not do so. Fox is unlucky in his search for honey; Bee is a miraculous hunter, and is therefore half-way (not only because of his hunting ability but also because of his great strength) between the hero of the Chaco myths and the hero of the Ge myths. But this creates no problems, since we have previously established that the latter myths also stand in a transformational relationship to the Chaco 'honey' myths. But at the same time we see along what a multiplicity of axes we must distribute the transformations which make it possible to move from the Chaco myths to the Guiana myths: *honey/game, male/female, raw/cooked, spouse/affine, literal sense/figurative sense, diachrony/synchrony, dry/wet, high/low, life/death.* The great variety of axes rules out any hope of being able to grasp the group's structure intuitively with the help of diagrams which, in the present instance, would necessitate so many signs and symbols that the reading of them would complicate the explanation rather than simplify it.

b. SECOND VARIATION

$$[\triangle \Rightarrow \triangle] \leftrightarrow [\text{bee} \Rightarrow \text{frog}]$$

In assuming the male sex, Bee also changes from mistress of honey to master of hunting. His new function continues throughout his transformation into a frog, which takes place, as it were, with parity of sex. It will be remembered that the last myth had already prepared the way for this transformation since, at the same time as Bee lost his skill as a hunter and returned to his honey nature, he left a son – therefore a male – who turned into a frog. Consequently, Bee played two parts, one of which was a reversion to his original role as mistress of honey (M_{233}, M_{234}), while the other moved on towards the next transformation, the hero of which is, precisely, a male frog:

M_{237}. Arawak. 'The story of Adaba'

There were once three brothers who went out to hunt, taking their sister with them. She was left all alone in the camp while they wandered about in search of game. But they brought back nothing except an occasional powis (wild turkey, Portuguese: 'mutum', *Crax* sp.). This happened for many days.

Close to the camp a tree-frog, Adaba, lived in a hollow tree which contained a little water. One afternoon when the frog was singing 'Wang! Wang! Wang!', the young girl called out to him: 'What are you holloing for? It would be much better if you stopped that noise and brought me some game to eat!' So Adaba stopped holloing, changed himself into a man and went off into the bush. Two hours later he returned with some meat which he told the girl to cook, for her brothers were sure to return with nothing. They were greatly surprised when they did in fact return empty-handed, to see their sister busy barbecuing plenty of meat, and a strange man lying in one of their hammocks! He was a strange man indeed: he had stripes all the way down his thin legs and he wore a lapcloth: otherwise he was quite naked. Having said 'howday' to one another, Adaba asked the three brothers what the result of their hunting expedition had been and told them he would like to inspect their arrows. He burst into a hearty laugh and wiped off the fungus that was growing everywhere on them, and said that, so long as they did not remove this stuff, their arrows would never shoot straight. He then told their sister to spin a fishing line and tie it between two trees. He next told the brothers to take aim at the line, and each brother's arrow stuck into the very centre of the fishing line. Adaba himself had a curious trick in shooting with his arrow: instead of aiming at an animal direct he would point the arrow up into the sky so that in its descent it would stick into the creature's back. The brothers began to learn this method and very soon became such adepts that they never missed anything. They became so proud of themselves and of Adaba that they decided to take him home with them and make him their brother-in-law. Adaba lived a long, long time very happily with their sister.

But one day, the woman insisted on her husband following her to the pond in which she bathed. 'No,' replied Adaba, 'I never bathe in places like this, in ponds. My bathing-place is in the water-holes inside hollow trees.' So the woman dashed some of the water over him and, after doing so three times, she jumped out of the pond and rushed to seize him. But directly she put her hands on him, he turned himself into a frog again and hopped away into the hollow tree where he still is. When the sister came back home again her brothers asked where Adaba was, but all she would tell them was that he had gone away. But they happened to know how and why he had gone away so they beat their sister unmercifully. This, however, did not mend matters because Adaba never came out of the hollow tree again to bring them luck. The three brothers never brought back anything like the quantity of game they used to get when Adaba was present (Roth 1, p. 215).

The Arawak word adaba corresponds to the Tupi: cunauaru and to the Carib kobono-aru, which means a tree-frog (*Hyla venulosa*), able to eject a caustic fluid. A weak variant which is Carib in origin (M$_{237b}$) refers to the animal by the dialectical form konowaru. In this variant, which comes from the Barama river Caribs of British Guiana, the woman is unmarried and one day expresses her regret at the fact that the frog she hears singing in the bush is not a man: if he were, he would bring her back some game. The wish is no sooner uttered than it is fulfilled. The unlucky hunter mentioned later is a passing stranger, whom Konowaru cures by washing him with urine. Konowaru eventually changes back into a frog, after being splashed by his wife, in spite of his warning (Gillin, pp. 195–6).

In connection with the above variant, it should be noted that, throughout Guiana, the epidermal secretions of tree-frogs are used as a magic ointment by hunters, and their bodies enter into the making of various charms and talismans (Gillin, p. 181; Roth 1, pp. 278-9, 370; Ahlbrinck, under 'Kunawaru'; Goeje, p. 48). Ahlbrinck, who gives a Kalina variant which will be studied later, states that the Kunawaru frog usually lives in a hollow tree and that 'if there is water in the tree, it utters a cry resembling that of a young child: wa ... wa' (*ibid.*). This is clearly the same cry, of which M_{237} and M_{237b} give a phonetic transcription.

The ethnozoology of the cunauaru tree-frog was discussed in *The Raw and the Cooked* (pp. 264-5, 310). I will therefore simply mention two points. In the first place, this particular species lays its eggs in a nest made of cylindrical cells, built in a hollow tree. The cells are fashioned by the animal with resin from the breu branco (*Protium heptaphyllum*). The water which collects in the hollow cavity of the tree rises up into the cells, through the funnel-like opening at their lower end – and covers the eggs. According to popular belief, the resin is secreted by the body of the frog, and it is used as a talisman for fishing and hunting (Tastevin 2 under 'cunawara'; Stradelli 1 under 'cunuaru-icyca').

Zoology and ethnography explain, then, how the bee and the tree-frog came to form a pair of opposites, and how I was able to postulate above, as a theoretical principle, that the transformation of one into the other must inevitably appear as an inversion. Both the bee and the tree-frog do, in fact, make their nests in hollow trees. In both cases, the nest consists of cells, in which the animal lays its eggs, and the cells are fashioned out of an aromatic substance, wax or resin, which the animal secretes or is thought to secrete. It is, of course, untrue that the tree-frog itself produces the resin; it merely collects it and moulds it into shape, but something similar occurs in the case of a great number of meliponae, which build their cells with a mixture of wax and clay, the latter ingredient also being collected.

Although they are alike on all these counts, the bee and the tree-frog nevertheless differ in one essential respect, which constitutes the relevant feature of the contrast between them. The bee belongs to the category of the dry (cf. *RC*, p. 311 and M_{237}: for the bee, water is as fire), whereas the frog belongs to the category of the wet: it needs water inside its nest to make sure that the eggs are protected, so it sings when it finds water, and in the whole of tropical America (as in the rest of the world too) the croaking of the frog is a sign of rain. We can therefore formulate the equation:

$$(bee : frog) :: (dry : wet)$$

Next it must be stressed that myths and rites establish a connection between the tree-frog and success in hunting: 'It is difficult to understand the relationship, except on a basis of some original belief in the divinity of these batrachians, such as we know to have existed in other parts of the Guianas' (Roth 1, pp. 278–9). I hope it was satisfactorily shown in *The Raw and the Cooked* that the connection is to be explained by the cunauaru's ability to emit a toxic fluid, which the native mind associates with the poison used in hunting, and for the preparation of which the venom of dendrobate batrachians is sometimes used (Vellard, pp. 37, 146). As an instance of the emergence of nature within culture, the poison used in hunting or fishing thus has a particularly close affinity with the sociological character of the seducer, and this explains why, in certain myths, poison is the son of the animal which plays the part of seducer (*RC*, pp. 275–81).

As I have established at various points throughout this book, honey too must be placed in the category of seducers: either in the figurative sense, as a substance which inspires quasi-erotic desire, or in the literal sense, whenever honey is used to describe a character who is defined purely in relation to it (like *deficiency of honey* or *abundance of honey*, that is, the girl mad about honey in the Ge and Chaco myths, or Bee in the Guiana myths). It is clear, then, that the transformation of Bee, mistress of honey, into Frog, master of the poison used in hunting, can also be explained in this way.

In M_{237}, Adaba, a marvellous hunter, uses a particular technique of archery: he shoots the arrow into the air and it falls downwards onto the animal, piercing its backbone. This is not a purely imaginary device, since evidence of its use is found among tribes who are extremely expert in archery. The natives of tropical America are not all equally skilled in this respect. I have often had occasion to observe the indifferent performances of the Nambikwara, whereas the Bororo reveal an expertise which struck other observers before me: 'An Indian draws a circle of about a yard in diameter on the ground and stands one pace away from the circumference. He then shoots eight or ten arrows straight up into the air and they all fall inside the circle. Every time we happened to be present during this exercise, we felt that the arrows could not fail to fall on the archer's head; but, confident in his skill, the latter remained motionless where he stood' (Colb. 3, p. 75). In 1937 or 1938, I met a small group of fairly deprimitivized Guarani Indians in the Parana valley who, according to the demonstration they gave us, seemed to practise a similar form of archery, but in their case it was dictated by the weight of their arrows which were iron-tipped or headed with a piece of crudely fashioned iron. These unwieldy missiles had to be used at short range and were given a sharply curved flight.

We must not, therefore, exclude the possibility that experience provided the framework on which the myth embroidered. But the framework in question could hardly be more than a pretext, since the archer in the myth is not so much skilled as endowed with a magic power: he does not calculate the course of his arrows but releases them at random, as is precisely stated in a variant, to one aspect of which I have already referred. In this variant (M_{236}), the Spirit of the Woods enables a hunter to shoot birds without fail and without taking aim, but on condition that he should never let fly in the direction of a flock of birds; if he does, the companions of the slaughtered bird will take revenge. This is what happens when the hero fails to respect the prohibition. He is torn to pieces by the birds, but brought back to life by his supernatural protector who sticks the fragmented body together again with wax (p. 162).

The interest of this variant lies in the very clear distinction it makes between two possible ways of interpreting the idea of 'random shooting'; it can be taken either in the absolute sense of shooting at nothing, or in the relative sense of shooting in the general direction of a group, in which case the uncertainty is not about the *species* of the animal which will be killed, but about which *individual* animal will be killed out of several which all belong to the same, already known, species. As we have already seen, M_{236} can be brought into line with M_{235} on the basis of two homologous pairs of opposites: *water/fire, honey/wax*. The comparison with M_{237}, which itself is a transformation of M_{235}, now suggests a further comparison between M_{235} and M_{236}, this time on the rhetorical level. The contrast between the literal meaning and the figurative meaning, which emerged from the analysis of M_{235}, provides an adequate model of the contrast between the two methods of random shooting in M_{236}, one of which is prescribed, the other prohibited. Only the former corresponds to the definition of random shooting as understood in the literal sense, since, in the absence of any kind of target, it represents a genuine instance of randomness. But the latter, in which the target is at once present yet indeterminate, does not have the same degree of randomness although, like the other, it is referred to as random shooting; it can only be random in the figurative sense.

Other aspects of the Adaba myth will be more profitably discussed after I have introduced myths illustrating the next stage in the series of transformations.

c. THIRD VARIATION

$$[\text{frog} \Rightarrow \text{frog}] \leftrightarrow [\triangle \Rightarrow \bigcirc]$$

The third variation, which is illustrated by several myths of major importance, will engage our attention for longer than previous variations.

M_{238}. *Warao. 'The broken arrow'*

There was once a man who had two brothers-in-law. While he was one of the unluckiest of mortals, they invariably returned home with plenty of game. Tired of supplying both him and his wife with food, they decided to lose him away (get rid of him), and instructed him to follow a track leading to the Black Jaguar's lair. At the sight of the monster the Indian fled, but the jaguar pursued him and they both started running round and round an immense tree. The man, who ran faster, just managed to catch up with the animal's hind-quarters and cut off his heels. Black Jaguar was unable to walk at all and sat down. The Indian next shot it through the neck with an arrow, then finished the job with a knife.

Now his two brothers-in-law, knowing well how poor a hunter he was, never doubted that they had seen the last of him. They were thus greatly surprised at his arrival at the house and made excuses for having left him, alleging that there had been a misunderstanding. At first they were unwilling to believe that he had killed Black Jaguar, but the man was so insistent that they all, including their old father, agreed to follow him to the place. When they saw the ogre, the three men were so afraid that the victor had to trample on the carcass before his father-in-law would agree to approach it. As a reward for this doughty deed, the old man gave his son-in-law another of his daughters, his brothers-in-law built him a bigger house and he was henceforth recognized as headman of the village.

But the man was very anxious to have a reputation for being clever in hunting all other animals. He therefore resolved to ask Wau-uta, the tree-frog, to help him. He set out to look for the tree in which she lived and stood below it, calling out to her and begging her to show him all the things he was anxious to learn. It was nearly dark and the frog gave no answer. He continued his entreaties which, when it became quite dark, he interspersed with tears and groans, 'for he knew full well that if he cried long enough, she would come down just as a woman does when, after refusing a man once, she finally takes pity when she hears him weeping'.

As he stood waiting underneath the tree, a whole flock of birds appeared, all arranged in regular order according to size, from the smallest to the largest. One after the other, they pecked his feet with their beaks so as to make him clever in hunting. Wau-uta was beginning to take pity on him, but of course he did not know that. When the birds had finished with him, the rats came in order of their size, to be followed by the acouri, the paca, the deer, the wild pig, then the tapir. As they filed past the Indian, each animal put out its tongue and licked his feet so as to give him luck when hunting its kind. Next came the tigers, from the smallest to the largest, all going through the same performance. Last of all the snakes crept past.

This went on all through the night and it was only at daybreak that it came to a stop, when the man finally ceased his weeping. A stranger came up to him. It was Wau-uta carrying a curious looking arrow: 'So it was you making all that noise last night and keeping me awake! Look down your arm, from your shoulder to your hand!' His arm was covered with fungus and the other was just the same. The man scraped off all the fungus, for that was what had given him bad luck. Whereupon Wau-uta suggested that they should exchange arrows; hers had broken into three or four pieces and had been subsequently spliced. When he tried it in his bow, the man nevertheless succeeded in shooting at a thin vine rope hanging a long way off. Wau-uta explained to him that henceforth he must shoot into the air and in any direction he liked; and the Indian observed that, when it fell, his arrow always stuck into some animal or other: birds first of all, in the same rotation as before, then a rat, an acouri etc., finally the tapir; tigers, snakes in their proper order, exactly in the way the animals had filed past him during the night. When all this

was finished, Wau-uta told him he might keep the arrow on condition that he never divulged to anyone that it was she who had
taught him to be so good a marksman. Then they said good-bye
and parted company.

Our friend returned home to his two wives, and soon gained as
great a reputation as a provider of smoked meat as he already bore
for his bravery in killing the Black Jaguar. All did their level best
to discover the secret of his success, but he refused to tell. So they
invited him to a big beer-feast. Drink proved his undoing; he let
loose his tongue and divulged what had happened. Next morning,
after regaining consciousness, he went to fetch his arrow, the one
Wau-uta had given him, but found it replaced by his own. From that
time he lost all his luck (Roth 1, pp. 213–14).

There is a long Kalina variant of this myth (the Kalina are a Carib
group of Guiana), which provides a perfect transition from M_{237} to
M_{238}. In this particular variant (M_{239}), the protecting frog is a male
cunauaru, i.e., it is of the same species and sex as Adaba, the hero of
M_{237}. But, as in M_{238}, the frog in M_{239} plays the part of protector to an
unlucky hunter who is rescued from the cannibalistic Jaguar (instead
of killing it); it removes the maleficent fungus from the hunter's
arrows (like Adaba, but unlike Wau-uta, who discovers the fungus on
the hunter's body) and turns him into a first-class marksman (although
there is no question here of any magic arrow).

The rest of the story takes us back to M_{237}: the hero returns to his
own people but he has acquired a frog's nature through living with
batrachians. So he bathes only in 'frog's water', which is found in
hollow trees. His wife is to blame for his coming into contact with
water in which human beings wash, and as a result of this, his son and
he both turn into frogs (Ahlbrinck, under 'awarupepe', 'kunawaru').

The theme of the animals grouped according to size is still present
in this variant, but occurs in a different place, that is, during the hero's
stay with the cannibalistic Jaguar. The latter asks him how he uses
his arrows, and he replies that he kills animals, which he enumerates
according to their different families, at the same time as he displays
his arrows one after the other, in each case starting with the smallest
animal and working up to the largest. As the size of the animal quoted
increases, the Jaguar's laughter grows louder (cf. Adaba laughing when
he discovers the fungus on the arrows), for he hopes that his inter-
locutor is about to name the jaguar and thus provide him with an

excuse for devouring him. On coming to the last arrow, the hero names the tapir,[1] and the Jaguar roars with laughter for two hours, thus allowing the man time to escape.

Let us approach the myth from this angle. The entire group to which it belongs describes, alternately, or concurrently, two types of behaviour: verbal behaviour relating to a name which must not be uttered or a secret which must not be betrayed; and physical behaviour relating to bodies which must not be brought into contact with each other. M_{233}, M_{234}, M_{238} and M_{239} (first part) are concerned with verbal behaviour: it is forbidden to utter Bee's name or reproach her for having a bee's nature, to betray Wau-uta's secret or to utter the Jaguar's name. M_{235}, M_{236}, M_{237} and M_{239} (second part) are concerned with physical behaviour: the bee's or the frog's bodies must not be wet with the water human beings use to wash. In all the myths, the theme is always the harmful collocation of two terms, one of which is a living being and, according to the physical or verbal character of the conduct described, the other can be a thing or a word. We can say, then, that the idea of collocation is taken literally in the first instance, and figuratively in the second.

The term which is actively brought into contact with the other can itself have two characteristics. As a word (the proper noun) or as a sentence (the secret), it is compatible with the individual to whom it is applied. 'Bee' is unmistakably the name of the bee, 'Jaguar' that of the jaguar, and it is equally true that Maba and Wau-uta are each responsible for the benefits they confer. But when it is a question of a thing (water in this instance), then it is incompatible with the being with whom it is brought into contact: the kind of water used by humans is antipathetic both to the bee and to the frog.

Thirdly, the contact between the two terms (whether physical or verbal) can be either random or directed, according to circumstances. In M_{233} and M_{238}, the hero utters the forbidden word involuntarily and by accident. In M_{235} and M_{239}, the sisters-in-law or the woman do not know why they must not splash water onto the hero. On the other hand, in M_{239}, the hero lists the animals in order of size, starting with the smallest and working up to the largest, and only in this instance is the maleficent contact avoided. The following comparative table must therefore include this possibility, and it must also take into account the disastrous consequences of the contact, although in this case they would

---

[1] The Dutch original gives *buffel*, buffalo, but this is the term Ahlbrinck uses to denote the tapir, as the translator of the French version observes in a note in the article 'maipuri'.

be expressed as a conjunction (the jaguar would eat the man) and not by disjunction (the transformation of the supernatural woman or man into an animal):

	M$_{233}$	M$_{234}$	M$_{235}$	M$_{237}$	M$_{238}$	M$_{239}$
actual/verbal	−	−	+	+	−	+
compatible/incompatible	+	+	−	−	+	−
directed/random	−	−	−	−	−	+
contact: *brought about/avoided*	+	+	+	+	+	+
conjunction/disjunction	−	−	−	−	−	−

The purpose of this summary in diagrammatic form (in which the signs + and − denote respectively the first and second term of each pair of opposites) is merely to serve as a temporary guide. It is incomplete, because some myths are only partially present. Having reached this stage of the analysis, I must now introduce other aspects. What has already been said by no means exhausts the question of the contrast between order and randomness. If we go through the series of myths, we discover that its field of application is much vaster than the one we have explored up till now, and that it also involves an additional contrast. At the beginning, we are dealing with two-term systems: a character and the name he or she bears, an individual and something he cannot tolerate, then from M$_{238}$ onwards, two individuals who cannot tolerate each other (the hero and the jaguar). So far, then, the negative relationship constitutes a polarity, just like the positive, and subjectively random, relationship which occurs from M$_{236}$ onwards between a hunter and his game *on condition that he aims into the air*, that is, without there seeming to be any foreseeable link between the behaviour and its result: an animal will no doubt be killed, but the species to which it belongs will remain unknowable until the result is achieved. I have already drawn attention to the semi-random nature of the ultimate behavioural possibilities that M$_{236}$ is careful to forbid: if the archer shoots in the direction of a flock of birds, the uncertainty will relate to the identity of the individual bird which will be killed but not to the species, and so the conditions required by the hypothesis will no longer be fulfilled. So the other birds swoop down on the culprit and tear him to pieces.

On the other hand, a hunter who was certain of hitting something, but without knowing exactly what, cannot be considered as a perfect hunter. It is not enough to be always sure of killing something; he needs to assert his mastery over the whole range of game. The behaviour of the hero in M$_{238}$ admirably conveys this compulsion: even the fact of having killed the cannibalistic jaguar, the supreme form of game, did not necessarily mean that he was an established hunter: 'He was very anxious to have a reputation for being clever in hunting all other animals, in addition to the glory he had earned in ridding the country of the Black Jaguar' (Roth 1, p. 213). Since M_{236} shows the impossibility of escaping subjectively, and by quantitative means, from the inadequacies of a system of polarity, the solution must be at once objective and qualitative, that is, the subjectively random character of the system (from which, as M_{236} proves, there is no escape) must be counterbalanced by an objective transformation from a polar system to an ordered system.

The transformation of the polar system begins in the first episode of M_{238}. There are still no more than two contrasting terms – on the one hand, the jaguar who is an ogre, and on the other hand, the unlucky hunter who is doomed to become his prey. So what happens? The jaguar chases the hunter round a tree and their respective positions, after being clearly defined to begin with, become relative, since it is no longer certain who is running after whom, who is the hunter and who the hunted. In escaping from his pursuer, the hunter catches up with the animal from behind, and wounds it unexpectedly; all that then remains to be done is to finish it off. Although the system is still confined to two terms, it is no longer a polar system; it has become cyclical and reversible: the jaguar was stronger than the man and the man is stronger than the jaguar.

We have yet to note the transformation, at a later stage, of the two-term system, which is cyclical and not transitive, into a transitive system comprising several terms. This transformation takes place between M_{238} (first part) and M_{239} (first part) and then M_{238} (second part). This interlinking is hardly surprising since we saw that M_{239} overlaps M_{238} and also M_{237}, which is the first of the three in the cycle of transformations.

The first ordered and transitive cycle appears in M_{239} (first part), in the doubly muted form of verbal behaviour the result of which calls for negative expression: the hero *is not* eaten by the jaguar, even though the latter forced him to list all wild animals, each family in turn, beginning with the least important families, and working up from the smallest animal in each family to the largest. As the hero does not mention the jaguar (deliberately or unintentionally, we do not know) the jaguar does not kill the man, in spite of the fact, which is not mentioned in the context, that men usually kill jaguars. The hero's verbal behaviour and the imaginary hunt he mimes for the jaguar's benefit, by presenting all his arrows in turn, are replaced in M_{238} (second part) by real animal behaviour and by a hunt in the literal sense, both of which call into play a complete and ordered zoological system since, in both instances, the animals are arranged in classes, which in turn are graded from the least harmful to the most dangerous, while the animals themselves are graded within each class from the smallest to the largest. The initial contrast, which was the contrast inherent in fatality (whether the latter is negative, in the sense that terms which ought never to have been brought into contact are accidentally juxtaposed, or positive, in the sense that, during the magic hunt, the hunter is always sure of shooting some animal by chance, although it is always one that he had no precise intention of killing), is thus overcome, thanks to the emergence, *in response to a subjectively random intention, of an objectively ordered natural world*. The analysis of the myths confirms that, as I have suggested elsewhere (9, pp. 18–19, 291–3), a belief in the effectiveness of magic presupposes an act of faith in the natural order.

If we come back to the formal organization of the group of myths in question, it is clear that further remarks must now be added to complete those already made. From M_{233} to M_{235} we are dealing with a system involving two terms, the conjunction of which – imaginary if one of the terms is a name or a predicative judgment, real if it is a thing – brings about the irreversible disjunction of the other term, accompanied by negative consequences. In order to overcome the antithesis of the polarity, M_{236} at one point envisages a solution which it admits to be wrong, because the result is a negative conjunction – that of the hunter and the birds, which leads to the hero's death. M_{236} thus appears as a blind alley or a cul-de-sac, in which the literal and figurative meanings, which the earlier myths used alternately, are simultaneously blocked. In this myth, the conjunction between the man and the birds has a physical reality and must be taken in the literal sense; but as I have already shown (p. 171), it results from the fact that the hero chose to interpret the prohibition imposed on him in the figurative sense.

The first part of M_{238} transforms the polar system into a cyclical system without introducing new terms; the transformation takes place in the literal sense, since the two adversaries pursue each other materially around a tree, which is a thing. The pursuit results in a positive conjunction, the implications of which are still limited: the man gets the better of the jaguar. The cyclical and ordered system appears first of all in a verbal and figurative form in M_{239} (first part), in which it is confirmed by a positive disjunction (the man escapes from the jaguar), then in a literal and real sense in M_{238} (second part), where the confirmation is a positive conjunction with general implications: man has become the master of all forms of game.

There is one last aspect we still have to examine: the one relating to the theme of the fungus covering the arrows (M_{237}, M_{239}) or the arms (M_{238}) of the unlucky hunter. Since we know that, in fact, M_{239} illustrates a transformation intermediary between M_{237} and M_{238}, we must suppose that the fungus on the arrows, the instruments used by the hunter, is an initial approximation towards the fungus which directly affects his body, and that the transition from one to the other occurs correlatively with the transition from the still random system of M_{237} to the completely ordered system of M_{238}.

I indicated earlier that Guiana hunters often rub their arms with the secretions of certain species of frogs. The Tucuna in the Rio Solimões area observe a similar practice when undergoing treatment prescribed by a shaman. For this purpose, they use the frothy secretions, which are soluble in water, of a tree-frog with a bright green back and a white stomach (*Phyllomedusa*). When rubbed over the arms, the secretions cause vomiting, which has a cleansing effect. As we shall see further on, several tribes of the Amazonian region have recourse to certain toxic varieties of honey in order to achieve the same result. In the light of this approach, it is possible to consider the fungus referred to in the myths as a representation in reverse of the tree-frog's secretions: the latter ensure success in hunting, the former prevents it; the tree-frog removes fungus and supplies secretions. Furthermore, through a series of transformations, an indirect connection can be detected between the honey which appears at the beginning of the group and the fungus referred to at the end. We have already seen how, from the Chaco myths to the Ge myths on the one hand, and through the series of Guiana myths on the other, honey could be transformed into game; and it is now clear that, if we start with the game which is ensured by means of the frog's secretions, the latter can be changed into fungus which hinders the pursuit of game.

One observation is called for here. In the rites, the frog is the means of obtaining game in the literal sense; it plays this part through the effect of a physical contact between its body and that of the hunter. In the myths, the part played by the frog is retained but it is described in the figurative form, since the virtues of the frog are moral, not physical. This being so, the literal meaning continues to exist, but refers to the fungus which has a physical effect on the hunter's body and which, in a sense, constitutes an inverted frog. This is an important transformation, because it enables us to establish an indirect link between the group we are dealing with and a Tucuna myth, although the only point in common is, it would seem, the theme of the fungus on the hunter's body:

M_{240}. *Tucuna*. '*The mad hunter*'

A bird-catcher set his snares, but every time he went to examine them, he found he had caught nothing but a sabiá bird (a kind of thrush: one of the *Turdidae*). Yet his fellow-hunters used to bring back large birds such as the mutum (*Crax* sp.) and the jacus (*Penelope* sp.). Everyone made fun of the unlucky hunter, who was plunged into deepest gloom by these jests.

The next day, he once again caught nothing but a thrush and flew into a rage. He forced open the bird's beak, broke wind into it, letting it fly away. Almost at once the man went mad, and started to rave. What he said made no sense: 'he talked endlessly about snakes, rain and the ant-eater's neck etc.'[2] He also told his mother he was hungry, and when she brought him food he refused it, insisting that he had only just finished eating. He continued to talk until he died five days later. His corpse, which was stretched out in a hammock, became covered with mould and fungi and continued to utter a stream of nonsense. When they came to bury him, he said: 'If you bury me, fire ants will attack you!' At last they waited no more but buried him while he was talking (Nim. 13, p. 154).

I have transcribed the above myth almost literally because of the interest of the clinical picture it gives of madness. The madness takes the form of verbal behaviour and is expressed by a flood of words and confused utterances, which anticipate metaphorically the mould and fungi with which the corpse of the madman is eventually covered in the literal sense. Like the heroes of the Guiana myths, the madman is an unlucky hunter. But whereas the Guiana heroes claim that they are being victimized and address verbal complaints to the animals, he behaves in a physically aggressive manner towards the animals, and for this he is punished by a metaphorical fungus: madness, which is the *consequence* of his absurd behaviour, whereas his Guiana counterparts got rid of real fungus, which was the *cause* of their enforced inaction.

[2] This last feature can be explained, no doubt, by the fact that large ant-eaters seem to have no neck: their head is a direct extension of their body.

In *The Raw and the Cooked*, I emphasized on several occasions that mould and fungi have a special significance in native thought patterns. They are vegetable substances belonging to the category of the rotten, on which men fed before the introduction of the civilized arts of agriculture and cooking. As a vegetable substance, mould is therefore opposed to game, an animal food; moreover, one is rotten, whereas the other is intended to be cooked; finally, the rotten vegetable substance belongs to nature, whereas cooked meat belongs to culture. On all these levels, we see an amplification of the contrast between terms, which in the Guiana myths were initially brought together. M_{233} described the blending (within the range of purely vegetable foods) of honey, a raw, natural food, and beer, a cooked, cultural food. In the case of honey, we can say that nature anticipates culture, since it provides a food which is ready to eat: in the case of beer, it is rather culture which excels itself, since beer is not only cooked but fermented.

In moving from the initial contrast: *raw/fermented*, to the subsequent contrast: *raw/cooked*, the myths are following a regressive course: the rotten is on the hither side of the raw as the cooked is on the hither side of the fermented. At the same time, the gap between the terms has widened, because the initial polarity was concerned with two vegetable terms, whereas the one we have now arrived at consists of a vegetable and an animal term. Consequently, the mediatory nature of the polarity also follows a regressive course.

We now embark on the study of an important Guiana myth, which is extant in several different versions. Although the story is quite different, this myth can be compared to the preceding ones, if we adopt the same angle of approach, since, in it, the frog appears still more clearly as a feminine character.

M_{241}. *Warao. 'The story of Haburi'*

Long ago, there were two sisters minding themselves, for they had no man to look after them. So they were very puzzled to discover one day that starch of the palm tree, ité (*Mauritia*), they had felled the evening before was all ready prepared. Next day the same thing happened, and then it happened again and often so they decided to keep watch. About the middle of the night they saw a manicole palm tree (*Euterpe*) bend gradually over until it touched the cut they had made in the trunk of the ité tree. Both sisters rushed up and caught hold of it, begging it earnestly to turn into a man. It refused at first but, as they begged so earnestly, it did so. He became the husband of the elder of the two sisters and by and by she gave birth to a beautiful baby boy, whom she called Haburi.

The two women had their hunting-ground near two ponds; one of these ponds belonged to them, and so they used to fish there. The other belonged to Jaguar,[3] and they advised the man not to go near it. He did so nevertheless, because the jaguar's pond contained more fish than theirs. But Jaguar came along and, in order to be revenged, he killed the thief. He then took the husband's shape and returned to the spot where the two women were camped. It was almost dark. Jaguar was carrying his victim's basket, which contained the stolen fish. In a coarse, rough voice which surprised the sisters, the false husband told them they could cook the fish and eat it, but that he himself was too tired to share their meal. All he wanted was to sleep, while he nursed Haburi. They brought the child to him and, while the women were eating their dinner, he started to snore so loudly that he could be heard on the other side of the river. Several times in his sleep, he uttered the name of the man he had killed and whom he was pretending to impersonate. The dead man was called Mayara-kóto. This made the women anxious and they suspected some act of treachery. 'Our husband never snored like that,' they said, 'and he never called his own name before.' They gently removed Haburi from the arms of the sleeper, slipping in a bundle of bark in his place. They quickly made off with him, taking with them a wax light and a bundle of firewood.

While going along, they heard Wau-uta, who at that time was a witch, singing and accompanying her song with her ceremonial rattle. The women went on and on, quickly too, for they knew that, once they arrived at Wau-uta's place, they would be safe. In the meantime the jaguar had woken up. When he found himself alone, holding a bundle of bark in his arms instead of a baby boy, he became extremely angry. He changed back into his animal shape and hurried after the fugitives. The women heard him coming and hurried still more. Finally they knocked at Wau-uta's door. 'Who is there?' – 'It is us, the two sisters.' But Wau-uta would not open the door. So the mother pinched Haburi's ears to make him cry. Wau-uta, her curiosity aroused, asked: 'What child is that? Is it a girl or a boy?'

[3] TRANSLATORS' NOTE: In Roth, the animal is referred to as Tiger, which the author has translated into French as Jaguar.

'It is a boy, my Haburi', replied the mother and Wau-uta opened the door immediately and asked them to come in.

When the jaguar arrived, Wau-uta told him she had seen no one, but the beast knew by the scent that she was telling a lie. Wau-uta suggested he should find out for himself by poking his head through the half-open door. The door was covered with thorns, and as soon as Jaguar put his head in, the old woman closed it and killed him. But the sisters began to grieve for their dead husband and cried so much that Wau-uta told them to go and gather manioc in the plantation and make beer, so that they could drown their sorrow. They wanted to take Haburi, but Wau-uta insisted that there was no point in doing so and that she would take care of him.

While the sisters were in the fields, Wau-uta made the child grow by magic into a youth. She gave him a flute and some arrows. On their way back from the plantation, the women were surprised to hear music being played, for they did not remember there being a man in the house when they left. And though ashamed, they went in and saw a young man playing the flute. They asked after Haburi but Wau-uta maintained that the child had run after them as soon as they had left for the field and that she thought he was with them. All this was a lie, because she had made Haburi grow up with the intention of making him her lover. She still further deceived the two sisters by pretending to take part in the search for the little boy, having previously ordered Haburi to say she was his mother, and given him full directions as to how he must treat her.

Haburi was a splendid shot: no bird could escape his arrow, and Wau-uta directed him to give her all the big birds he killed and to give his mother and his aunt all the little ones which he had to pollute first by fouling them. The object of this was to make the sisters so vexed and angry that they would leave the place. But this they would not do: they continued searching for their little child. This sort of thing went on for many days; big birds and dirtied little birds being presented by Haburi to Wau-uta and the two women, respectively.

One day, however, Haburi did miss a bird for the first time, his arrow sticking into a branch overhanging a creek where the otters,[4] the hunter's uncles, used to come and feed. It was a nice, cleared spot and here Haburi eased himself, taking care to cover up the dung

[4] TRANSLATORS' NOTE: Roth has water-dogs, which the author has translated as otters.

with leaves. Then he climbed the tree to dislodge the arrow. Just then the otters arrived and, scenting the air, they at once suspected that their worthless nephew must be somewhere about. They discovered him on the tree branch and ordered him to come down and sit, when they would tell him a few home truths: he was leading a bad life, the old woman was not his mother, and the two younger ones were his mother and aunt respectively. They impressed upon him that it was wicked of him to divide the birds unfairly. He must do exactly the opposite, giving his real mother, the elder of the two sisters, the larger birds and tell her he was sorry and apologize for his wickedness which was due entirely to ignorance on his part.

So Haburi made a clean breast of it to his mother and gave the dirtied little birds to Wau-uta. The latter worked herself into a great passion, told Haburi that he must be mad and blew in his face [in order to drive out the evil spirits, cf. Roth 1, p. 164]; so angered and upset was she that she could eat nothing at all. All through the night she nagged Haburi. But the next morning, the latter again gave the big birds he had shot to his real mother and the dirtied little ones to Wau-uta who gave him no peace. Haburi therefore made up his mind to get out with his mother and aunt.

Haburi built a canoe from bees' wax, but by next morning a black duck had taken it away. He made another little clay canoe, which was stolen by another kind of duck. In the meantime he cut a large field and cleared it so quickly that the women could grow enough manioc for their proposed journey. Haburi would often slip away and make a boat, always with different kinds of wood and of varying shapes, but just as regularly a different species of duck would come and steal them. The last one he made was from the silk-cotton tree and this particular one was not stolen. Thus it was Haburi who first made a boat and who taught ducks to float on the surface of the water, because it was with his boats that they managed to do so. 'Indeed,' the informant comments, 'we Warao say that each duck has its own particular kind of boat.'

What was even more curious was that the next morning the last boat was found to be bigger than it was the night before. Haburi told his mother and her sister to collect all the provisions and put them aboard, while he continued to plant manioc cuttings along with Wau-uta. At the first opportunity, he slipped secretly back to the house, took his axe and his arrows and proceeded down to the waterside, having previously ordered the posts not to talk, for in those days the posts of a house could speak and, if the owner of the house were absent, a visitor could thus find out his whereabouts. Unfortunately Haburi forgot to warn the parrot in the house to keep silent, and when Wau-uta returned, the bird told her which way Haburi had gone.

Wau-uta rushed down to the landing and arrived just in time to see Haburi stepping into the boat to join his mother and aunt. The old woman seized hold of the craft screaming: 'My son! My son! You must not leave me! I am your mother!' and she refused to let go her hold, although they all repeatedly struck her fingers with the paddles and almost smashed them to pieces on the gunwale. So poor Haburi had perforce to land again and, with old Wau-uta, proceeded to a large hollow tree, where bees had built their nest. Haburi made a small hole in the trunk with his axe and told the old woman to go inside and suck the honey. As it happened, she was mad about honey and, although crying very hard at the thought of losing Haburi, she crawled through the little opening, which the latter immediately closed in upon her. And there she is to be found to the present day, the Wau-uta frog, which is heard only in hollow trees. And if you look carefully, you will see how swollen her fingers are from the way in which they were bashed by the paddles when she tried to hold on to the gunwale. If you listen you can also hear her lamenting for her lost lover: Wang! Wang! Wang! (Roth 1, pp. 122–5).

There are other variants of this myth which will be studied later. The reason why I have used Roth's variant first, and given an almost literal translation of it, is because none of the others conveys the myth's astonishing novel-like quality, nor brings out so clearly its originality, dramatic inventiveness and psychological subtleties. In fact, it was not until Rousseau's *Confessions* that French literature had the courage to broach the theme of the young boy taken in by a patroness with ulterior motives, who starts off by playing the mother figure before settling into the role of elderly mistress, while making sure that a certain ambiguity continues to hang over her equivocal sentiments. Madame de Warens was quite a young woman compared with the Guianese frog, who, because of her age and animal nature, has a depressing and repulsive appearance, that the narrator is clearly well aware of. It is stories of this kind (this one is by no means an isolated instance in the American oral tradition, although no other, perhaps, displays such brilliance) which succeed in conveying, in a sudden flash of illumination, the irrefutable feeling that these primitive peoples, whose inventions and beliefs we handle in a rather off-hand manner that would be appropriate only if they were crude productions, are capable of an aesthetic subtlety, an intellectual refinement and a moral sensibility which we ought to approach with scrupulousness and respect. However, I leave it to specialists in the history of ideas and to critics to continue these reflections on the purely literary aspect of the myth, while I turn now to its ethnographical study.

(1) The story begins with a description of the lonely life led by two sisters, who become the wives (they talk about 'our husband') of the supernatural man whose pity they have aroused. It will be remembered that the worst disasters which befell the hero of M_{238} occurred after he obtained a second wife, that the misfortunes endured by the hero of M_{235} sprang from the fact that he had two sisters-in-law, and finally that the heroine of the Chaco myths had the misfortune to have two suitors and that the rivalry between them led to disastrous consequences.

I have already drawn attention to the importance of this duplication which, on the formal level, reflects an ambiguity which seems to me to be an essential characteristic of the symbolic function (L.-S. 2, p. 216). In the myths the ambiguity is expressed by means of a rhetorical code which plays endlessly on the contrast between the thing and the word, the individual and the name he bears, the literal sense and the figurative sense. One version, which unfortunately I have been unable to consult in Paris and which I am quoting from a second-hand source, brings out the dualism of the wives, since the myth (only the initial episode is given here) claims to explain the origin of marriage between one man and two women:

M_{242}. *Arawak. 'The origin of bigamy'*

Two sisters were alone in the world. A man, the first they had ever seen except in their dreams, came down from heaven and explained agriculture, cooking, weaving and all the civilized arts to them. This explains why each Indian now has two wives (Dance, p. 102).

Now, throughout almost the whole of Guiana (and no doubt in other areas too), bigamy implies differentiation in the parts played by the two women. The first wife, who is usually the elder, has certain special duties and privileges. Even if her co-wife is younger and more attractive, the older woman retains her position as head of the household (Roth 2, pp. 687–8). There are no descriptive details about the second wife in the text of M₂₄₁: she is just a wife. The other one, how-ever, appears in such clearly defined roles as farmer, cook and mother. In bigamy, then, the dualism of the wives is not merely dual, but a polar and orientated system. The second wife is not a reduplication of the first. When she appears, endowed with mainly physical qualities, it is the first one who undergoes a transformation and becomes a kind of metaphor of the wifely function and a symbol of the domestic virtues.

I shall discuss the hero's civilizing role later.

(2) The supernatural husband makes his appearance at the time when the palm trees are being felled for the extraction of starch. About the time when *Mauritia flexuosa* begins to bear fruit, the Warao cut down the tree and split it lengthwise in order to expose the fibrous pith inside. The hollowed out trunk serves as a trough. Water is poured into it, while at the same time the fibrous substance is worked upon, so that a considerable quantity of starch is released. The fibrous particles are extracted then and, when the starch has settled as a deposit, it is put into moulds and the loaves thus obtained are then dried over a fire (Roth 2, p. 216). The other species of palm tree quoted at the begin-ning of the myth and the foliage of which turns into a man is *Euterpe edulis*, which the Indians cut down in order to facilitate the gathering of the ripe fruit. After softening them in a trough filled with tepid water (boiling water would make them hard), they pound the fruit with a mortar. The mush is drunk while fresh, sweetened with honey and diluted with water (*ibid.*, pp. 233–4).

Since we are dealing here with a myth at the end of which honey plays a decisive part, the customary association between the fruit of the palm tree and honey is all the more reminiscent of the Chaco 'honey' myths, since here, as in the Chaco, we are concerned with vegetable foods which grow wild. Even though the pith would be obtainable during the greater part of the year, the fact that the Indians choose to cut down the trees when they are beginning to fruit, suggests the end of the dry season.[5] The latter is very clearly defined in the Ori-

[5] On the subject of the seasonal fruiting of *Mauritia flexuosa*: 'The tribes ... of the Ama-zonian area greet the appearance of the ripe fruit with joy. They anxiously await this period of the year in order to celebrate their most important feasts and, at the same time, pre-arranged marriages' (Corrêa, under 'burity do brejo'). M. Paulo Bezerra Cavalcante, head of the Botany section of the *Museu Paraense Emilio Goeldi*, when consulted about the time of fruiting of several species of wild palm trees, was kind enough to reply (and I take this opportunity of thanking him) that 'according to records made over a period of years, the fruit reaches maturity mostly at the end of the dry season, or the beginning of the rainy season.' According to Le Cointe (pp. 317–32) most of the wild palms in the Brazilian area of Amazonia begin to fruit in February. M. Paulo Bezerra Cavalcante nevertheless gives

noco delta, where the rainfall is at its lowest from September to November, and reaches its maximum in July (Knoch, G 70–75). Besides, in Guiana, palm trees denote the presence of water in spite of drought, like wild fruit in the Chaco, but not in the same way: the Indians consider *Mauritia* and *Euterpe* to be a sure sign of the vicinity of water: when they cannot find water anywhere, they dig near the bases of palm trees (Roth 2, p. 227). Finally, as in the Chaco myths dealing with the origin of mead, the idea of the trough comes to the forefront. The trunk of the *Mauritia* provides a natural trough, in which the Indians prepare the soft damp substance enclosed in this ligneous outer covering which is sufficiently hard for the Warao to use the trunks of the *Mauritia flexuosa* to make the piling for their huts (Gumilla, Vol. I, p. 145). The fruit of the *Euterpe* is also prepared in a trough, but in a *different* trough, not one made from the tree *itself*, that is, the fruit is tipped into an already existing trough, instead of the trough disclosing its contents while it is in the process of being made. So, in the Warao myth, we again encounter the dialectics of container and content, of which the Chaco 'honey' myths first provided an illustration. Now, its reappearance in this new context is all the more significant in that, whereas the Chaco heroine played the part of a girl mad about honey right from the beginning, the heroine of the Haburi myth is an old woman who at the end turns out to be mad about honey and who is imprisoned in a hollow tree, in other words, in a natural trough.

As regards the sections they have in common, the versions recently published by Wilbert (9, pp. 28–44) show a striking similarity to Roth's version. It should, however, be noted that, in Wilbert's two versions, it is the younger of the two sisters who is Haburi's mother, whereas the elder sister has certain masculine characteristics: the myth lays stress on her physical strength and her ability to perform tasks normally carried out by men, such as the felling of palm trees (cf. above p. 180).

In neither of Wilbert's versions is the husband of the two sisters, who is present from the beginning of the story, of supernatural origin. No further light is thrown on the ogre's identity, nor on the reason why, in these versions, he kills the Indian, roasts him and offers the meat to the two women, who recognize the dismembered body of their husband by the penis which has been placed on top of the bundle. In spite of these differences, the ogre's paternal urge is equally stressed:

December for the *Astrocaryum* and *Mauritia* species, November for *Attalea* (whereas Le Cointe gives July, p. 332) and September for *Oenocarpus*. However, these data are not simply transposable to the Orinoco delta where a different climate prevails.

in both the Wilbert versions, as in the Roth version, he asks straight away to be given the baby. The two sisters cover their escape by obstacles magically conjured up from their pubic hair, which they throw behind them as they go. The frog kills the ogre by slashing him with a hacking knife (M_{243}) or by thrusting a lance right through his body from his anus to the tip of his head (M_{244}). The episode of the excrement takes place in the village of the Siawana, in whose cooking-pot Haburi relieves himself (M_{243}), or at the house of Haburi's 'aunt' whose food he also pollutes (M_{244}).

From this point onwards, the Wilbert versions take a distinctly different course. The transformation of Wau-uta into a frog still results from her having eaten honey, but the latter is supplied by the old woman's son-in-law, her daughter's husband, the daughter and her husband being two characters who are introduced for the first time. M_{243} then embarks on an account of further adventures which befall Haburi, and which soon take on a cosmological character. The hero encounters a skull which persecutes him (this episode recurs in one of the myths in Roth's collection and will be examined in a forthcoming volume, where I shall show that it can be interpreted as a reduplication of the frog story), then he shoots an arrow into the ground and discovers the existence of a subterranean world where abundance reigns, in the form of luxuriant palm groves and herds of wild pigs. Haburi and his companions try to reach it but a pregnant woman remains wedged in the passage leading down to it. They push her, her anus gives way and becomes the Morning Star. Those who were behind the pregnant woman were unable to reach the underworld and, as these were the best shamans, men are now deprived of their help which would have considerably improved their lot. The preparing of pith from the palm tree and the acquisition by the animals of their specific characteristics date from this period. The other shorter version (M_{244}) ends with Wau-uta's transformation into a frog. (Cf. also Osborn 1, pp. 164–6; 2, pp. 158–9; Brett 1, pp. 389–90.)

In both the Roth and Wilbert versions, therefore, the extraction of the pith from the palm tree plays a prominent part. In fact, M_{243} is to all intents and purposes a myth about the origin of this culinary process, which coincides with the arrival on earth of the Warao's ancestors, and the definitive organization of the animal kingdom. This aspect would be further confirmed if the Siawana referred to in this version were the same as the Siawani, to whom another myth refers (M_{244b}): a cannibalistic people who were subsequently changed into trees or electric eels, and whose destruction allowed the Indians to become masters of the arts of civilization, foremost among which were the technical skill and utensils which enabled them to prepare the pith of the palm tree (Wilbert 9, pp. 141–5). The importance assigned to this food can be explained if we take into account the fact that 'the moriche palm truly deserves to be called the tree of life of the pre-agricultural Warao. They make use of ten different parts, and have perfected the art of growing it. Most important of all, they consider the pith to be the only food really fit for human consumption, and even worthy of being offered to the gods as a sacrifice. The pith of the moriche palm and fish are linked under the name of nahoro witu, "the true food" ' (Wilbert 9, p. 16).

(3) When they are single, women eat vegetable pith, but once they are married, they have fish too, that is – as we have just seen from the preceding paragraph – their diet is henceforth complete. In a context which is different from the ecological point of view, the Warao group: {starch–fish–honey}, is a substitute for the group {wild fruits–fish–honey} which, as we saw, inspired the Chaco myths.

Now, the fish in question comes from two ponds. So, as in the myths of the same group which have already been studied, we are dealing here with two kinds of water – which are similar from the hydrological point of view, since both are stagnant, but are nevertheless unequal from the alimentary point of view, since one pond contains a lot of fish, the other very little. We can therefore construct the 'two kinds of water' group as follows:

$$M_{235} \left[\binom{\text{bee's 'water'}}{(= \text{honey})} : \binom{\text{women's water}}{(\text{running})} \right] :: M_{237} \left[\binom{\text{frog's water}}{\text{stagnant, high}} : \binom{\text{woman's water}}{\text{stagnant, low}} \right]$$

$$:: M_{239} \left[\binom{\text{frog's water}}{\text{stagnant, high}} : \binom{\text{woman's water}}{?, \text{low}} \right]$$

$$:: M_{241} \left[\binom{\text{women's water}}{\text{stagnant, fish } (-)} : \binom{\text{jaguar's water}}{\text{stagnant, fish } (+)} \right]$$

Honey is not water (except for Bee), but it is stagnant. The myth stresses this feature indirectly by making it clear that the opposite kind of water is running water, unlike all the variants in which the two kinds of water are described as being stagnant, and contrasted in terms of high and low, or of their relative fish content. We can therefore simplify as follows:

[stagnant : running] :: [high : low] :: [fish (−) : fish (+)]

which gives a horizontal opposition, a vertical opposition, and what could be called an economic opposition.

The *stagnant water/running water* contrast is strongly in evidence throughout the entire American continent, and first and foremost among the Warao. These Indians relate how in former times men obtained their wives from the Spirits of the Waters, to whom they gave their sisters in exchange. But they insisted on the isolation of the women at their menstrual periods, a practice to which the Water Spirits were unaccustomed and to which they strongly objected; since then, the latter have never stopped persecuting them (Roth 1, p. 241). Hence the great number of prohibitions, in particular the one forbidding the washing of the pot-spoons outside the travelling boat either on rivers or at sea. They have to be cleaned in the canoe, otherwise big storms and squalls will arise (*ibid.*, pp. 252, 267, 270). It should be noted in this connection that the Black Jaguar of the myths is supposed to cause thunder by his roaring. Farther south, the Mundurucu made a ritual distinction between running water and stagnant water. The wife of an Indian who owned a trophy head and members of the confraternity of tapirs were not allowed to use the former. Consequently these persons could not bathe in a river: water for washing was brought to them in their homes (Murphy 1, pp. 56, 61).

The Guianese taboo about washing cooking plates and dishes, or about washing them in running water, is also found in the north-west of North America among the Yurok, who stipulate that wooden dishes and greasy hands should be washed in stagnant water, never in running water (Kroeber in Elmendorf, p. 138, n. 78). The rest of the passage suggests that the taboo could be a particular application of a general relationship of incompatibility supposedly existing between food and supernatural beings. In this case, the similarity with the Guianese beliefs would be even more striking, and there would seem to be less risk in using American examples of varying origins in an attempt to explain the nature of the contrast between the two waters.

Among the Twana of Puget Sound, pubescent girls were forced to wash in running water in order to avoid the danger of contamination inherent in their condition (*ibid.*, p. 441). On the other hand, widowers and widows 'had to bathe daily in a pool made by damming a stream or small river ... This practice lasted at least for a lunar month after the burial of the deceased spouse' (*ibid.*, p. 457). The Toba of the Chaco forbade women who had just given birth to bathe in rivers: they were allowed to bathe only in the lagoon (Susnik, p. 158). Just as the Mandan contrasted running water and stagnant water, one being termed 'pure', the other 'impure' because it had no outlet (Beckwith, p. 2), so the Guarani of Paraguay considered running water to be the only 'real' water.

Unlike stagnant water, which is a kind of neutralized water, running water therefore constitutes the 'marked' term. It is more potent and more effective, but at the same time more dangerous, being inhabited by Spirits or being directly linked with them. Metaphorically speaking, we express almost the same idea when we contrast 'spring water' with 'still water'. The Yurok of California force their pubescent girls to feed near waterfalls, where the roar of the river drowns all other noises (Kroeber, p. 45); this is perhaps because they share, with the Cherokee of the south-east of the United States, the belief that noisy water 'talks' and is a medium for a form of supernatural teaching (Mooney, p. 426).

If this way of looking at the problem also applies in the South American myths, as is suggested by the similarity between the beliefs current in the two hemispheres, it follows that running water is prohibited because it might break the tenuous link established between a supernatural person and a human being. Now, we have seen that, from M_{237} onwards, the contrast between stagnant water and running water changes into another kind of contrast – that of relatively high water (since the frog looks for it in hollow trees) and relatively low water (the ponds in which humans bathe). Finally, the transformation is continued in M_{241}. Instead of there being two kinds of water, which are not at the same height, we have two kinds of water which are identical from the vertical point of view, but one of which is harmless and contains few fish, while the other is dangerous and well stocked with fish. The terms of the first contrast are reversed at the same time as this transformation takes place. From M_{235} to M_{239}, the water which was first stagnant, then high, was congruous with a supernatural and beneficent character; the water which was running at first, then low, was congruous with a human and maleficent character. In M_{241}, the reverse is the case, because of the inversion of the signs affecting the supernatural partner which, in this instance, is the Black Jaguar, a cannibalistic monster. Symmetrically, the human character is given a beneficent role. So it is the water which contains only a few fish, and which is weakly stressed in respect of the search for food, which corresponds to the relatively high water where the bee and the frog ought to have continued to bathe, and where man ought to have continued to fish. For, in that case, things would have remained as they were.

This discussion appears to be leading nowhere. Yet without it, we would never have arrived at the preceding hypothesis which, on reflection, is the only one which enables us to discover the armature common to both Wilbert's impressive version and Roth's, which are the most detailed variants of the Haburi myth available. What constitutes the apparent difference between them? Roth's version does not contain the cosmological section. On the other hand, the Wilbert versions do not have the episode of the two ponds. Now, we have just shown that this episode is a transformation of other Guianese myths which belong to the same group as the one we are busy discussing.

But in actual fact, the episode of the ponds and its system of transformations are no more than a falsely anecdotal disguise, barely concealing the cosmological theme which is developed to the full in Wilbert's lengthy version. In the episode of the ponds, the husband of the two sisters gives up safe but poor fishing in a pond which, as we have just seen, corresponds to the stagnant and relatively high water in the myth previously studied, because he prefers good but dangerous fishing in another pond, which corresponds in the same myths to running and relatively low water. Now at the end of the Wilbert version, Haburi and his companions, the forefathers of present-day Indians, make the same choice but on a much larger scale: they give up a quiet and humble life in the upper world under the spiritual guidance of their priests because, in the luxuriant palm groves and herds of wild pigs which they had glimpsed in the underworld, they see a promise of more abundant food. They do not yet know that they can only attain the food after surmounting the great dangers represented by the Spirits of the Waters and the Woods, the most formidable of which is, as it happens, the Black Jaguar.

The supernatural character in Roth's version does no more than reproduce this ancestral behaviour, when, in expectation of better fishing, he allows himself to be drawn towards a kind of water which denotes the low in the system of transformations to which it belongs, in spite of the fact that M_{241} puts it on the same level as the other, which denotes the high by virtue of the same reasoning. In this respect, there is one old version which is perfectly explicit on this point: in the underworld there is a lot of game, but on the other hand water is scarce and Kanonatu, the creator, has to create rain in order to swell the rivers (Brett 2, pp. 61–2). In all the versions, therefore, the main character (or characters) commits a moral transgression which takes the form of a fall. That which the protagonist of M_{241} suffers, since he falls into the clutches of Black Jaguar, is a metaphorical transposition of the physical and cosmic fall which led to the appearance of the first race of human beings. One signifies the other, just as the supernatural character in the first myths in the group is signified by his name (which ought not to have been uttered) and just as the water which splashes him (splashing is a declaration of love in most South American tribes, and especially among the Warao) signifies the physical desire of the sisters-in-law, at the same time as it has a metaphorical value in respect of the leading character, whom water burns *as if* it were fire.

(4) The reader will certainly have noticed that the two sisters in M_{241} are placed in the same situation as the heroine in the Chaco myths (who has a sister herself) that is, between a husband and the latter's rival. In the Chaco, Woodpecker plays the part of the husband who is a food-supplying hero. The Warao husband also supplies food, but fish and not honey. In Guiana fish is a dry-season food, just as honey is in the Chaco (Roth 2, p. 190): fishing is easier when the rivers are low. Moreover, honey reappears at the end of the story.

For the Toba, the husband's rival is Fox, for the Warao, Black Jaguar; in other words, a deceiver in the one instance, and a terrifying ogre in the other. This difference in nature has a parallel on the psychological level. Fox, as we have seen, is 'mad about women'; he is prompted by lust. No such affirmation is made about Black Jaguar in the myth. In fact Black Jaguar begins by behaving in the opposite way from Fox, since he brings the women copious supplies of food: fish in the Roth version, pieces of their husband's roasted flesh in the Wilbert versions. This last detail establishes a similarity between Black Jaguar and the Ge hero, who roasted his wife's corpse and presented it to the latter's parents, because their unfortunate daughter had been too greedy for honey: just as the man who meets the same fate in the Warao myth shows himself to be too greedy for fish. I shall return to this point.

But the main difference between Black Jaguar and Fox is the absence in the former of any erotic motivation. Almost as soon as he arrives at the woman's house, he claims to be tired and his one thought is to sleep, after the baby has been laid in his arms, at his own request. That is the normal behaviour of Indian fathers, whose one idea when they return from hunting is to stretch out in their hammocks and fondle their babies. This detail is important, because it crops up in all versions, and the reason surely is that it throws light on the jaguar's motive, which is diametrically opposed to that of the fox. Just as the latter was 'mad about women', so the jaguar proves to be 'mad about children': what prompts the jaguar is not lust, but a longing for paternity. Having displayed his gifts as a food-supplier to the two women, he settles down to being a dry-nurse to the baby.

Such an attitude seems paradoxical in an ogre, and calls for an explanation. This will be supplied in another chapter where I shall establish definitively a point that was already implicit in the Ge myths, namely, that the area of the group includes a double system of transformations: the one whose development we have been following from the beginning of this book, and another, which cuts across it, as it were, and intersects it exactly at the point we have now reached. It will then be clear that the jaguar behaves in this instance as a food-supplying father, because, in the group which is perpendicular to the one we are studying, he plays the reverse role: that of a seducer who takes mothers away from their children. Another Guianese myth, of which I shall make use later (M_{287}), provides a perfect example of the reversal of roles, since in it the deceived husbands kill Black Jaguar. So if, in M_{241}, the jaguar kills the husband, and not the husband the jaguar, he cannot be a seducer, but must be the reverse (cf. below, pp. 296–303).

As I have not yet reached the stage at which it will be possible to demonstrate this point and construct the meta-system which would integrate both aspects, I prefer to make do for the time being with a different kind of demonstration based on the comparison I have already embarked on between the fox in the Chaco myths and the jaguar in the Guianese myths, and which will be carried out *a contrario*.

Fox is a deceiver. In *The Raw and the Cooked* (pp. 309–10), I pointed out that myths which have this type of character as hero are often constructed like a mosaic, and by reciprocal overlapping of fragments of syntagmatic sequences deriving from different and sometimes opposite myths. The result is a hybrid syntagmatic sequence, the very structure of which conveys, by its ambiguity, the paradoxical nature of the deceiver. If this is so in the case we are concerned with now, we can interpret the character of *ineffectual seducer* as exemplified in Fox as a result of the juxtaposition of two antithetical characteristics, each one attributable to a person who, in his own way, is the reverse of Fox: he is either an *effective seducer*, or the opposite of a seducer, that is a *father*, but a father who (in theory) must in that case prove to be *ineffectual*:

$$\text{DECEIVER} \begin{cases} \text{seducer} \\ \text{ineffectual} \end{cases} \times \begin{cases} \text{ineffectual, but a seducer}^{(-1)} = \text{father} \\ \text{a seducer, but effectual } (= \text{ineffectual }^{(-1)}) \end{cases} \text{OGRE}$$

With the Warao myth, we discovered one of the two combinations which define the ogre in contradistinction to the deceiver. And, as I have already said, we shall encounter the other later; it will be confirmed then that the first was merely a transformation of it. From now on it is clear that the Fox of the Chaco and the Black Jaguar of Guiana are in symmetrical contrast to each other, as characters who try to impersonate their victim with intent to deceive the latter's spouse. Fox disguises himself as the women he has killed, and Jaguar assumes the appearance of the man he murdered. After being stung by an ant which had made certain of his true sex *de visu*, Fox reveals *what he is* by a physical reaction: he either utters a roar he can no longer disguise, or pulls up his skirt. Although Jaguar shows himself to be both a good father and a good husband (unlike Fox, who is extremely clumsy as a husband), he reveals, morally, *what he is not*: he utters his victim's name. The incident of the name is therefore a transposition of an episode from the Chaco myths and gives it a figurative meaning. And it also reflects, while at the same time reversing it, an incident we have already encountered in other Guianese myths belonging to the same group (M_{233}, M_{238}). There, the supernatural personage was disjoined from her human companion when her name was uttered. In the myths we are discussing now, the humans are disjoined from their supposed supernatural companion when the latter utters what (since he says it himself) *cannot be* his name.

(5) The frog is called Wau-uta. That too was the name of the frog who protected the hunter in M_{238}, and of the tree-frog into which the hero's baby changed in M_{235}. From a baby turned animal (in the form of a frog) we move therefore, through the medium of a male, hunting frog, to a female, bellicose frog (she kills the jaguar) who changes the baby into an adult. In the preceding instances, the frog belonged to the cunauaru species, and Roth suggests that Haburi's lecherous protector was of the same species, especially since the cry is phonetically the same as that attributed to the cunauaru frog in other myths.

The flight of a woman with her child, both of whom are pursued by cannibalistic monsters and who find asylum and protection with a frog, provides the theme of a Mundurucu myth (M_{143}), in which the flight is also prompted by the wife's recognizing her husband's roasted corpse. I shall study comparable North American myths in a subsequent volume.

The Warao myth and the Mundurucu myth are also alike in that the frog plays the part of shaman in both. A Tucuna myth attributes the origin of shamanistic powers to the cunauaru. This myth should therefore be quoted, if only to justify, retrospectively, the use we made of observations relating to this tribe in order to throw light on certain Guianese customs:

M_{245}. *Tucuna*. '*The origin of shamanistic powers*'

A two-year-old baby girl used to cry continuously every night. Her mother became angered by this and expelled her from the house, and the child went on weeping all by herself, until a cunauaru frog came along and took her away. The little girl stayed with the frog until she reached adolescence, and learned all the magical arts from her protectress, both those which cure and those which kill.

Then she went back to live with humans, among whom sorcery was unknown at that time. When she became very old and unable to look after herself, she asked some young girls to prepare her some food. But the latter did not like her, and refused. During the night, the old woman extracted their leg bones from their bodies. As they could not get up, the girls were forced to watch her as she ate the marrow from their bones, which was her only food.

When the crime became known, the Indians cut the sorceress's throat. She collected the blood which flowed into her cupped hands, blew it towards the sun saying: 'The soul enter into thee also!' Since that time, the soul of the victim enters the body of the killer (Nim. 13, p. 100).

The theme of the whimpering child (see later, p. 378) links the Tucuna myth with a group in which an opossum or a vixen plays the part of abducting animal (*RC*, p. 271, n. 35). The whimpering child who resists 'socialization' remains obstinately on the side of nature and awakens the lust of similarly orientated animals: those who are mad about honey, a natural food, or those mad about women or boys, which are sexual 'foods'. Taking this approach and starting from the frog which was mad about a boy, but still madder about honey, we can establish a link-up with the Chaco girl who was mad about honey and who, in her own way, was a kind of vixen (otherwise the fox would not have attempted to personify her); but at the same time, she was a girl about whom the fox was mad. We shall return later to this instance of reciprocity.

(6) In the Roth version (M_{241}), the frog kills the jaguar by trapping him in the thorny door of the hollow tree in which she lives. The

tactics used by the frog recall those used by characters in certain Chaco myths, who also take refuge in a hollow tree, in order to get rid of a cannibalistic jaguar: through the cracks in the trunk, they thrust lances on which the ogre is fatally wounded (M_{246}; Campana, p. 320), or the theme is reversed and it is the jaguar who, having sunk his claws into the trunk, finds that he cannot break free and is thus at his victims' mercy (Toba: M_{23}). In both instances we are dealing with a female jaguar whose form had been taken by a woman who had killed her husband, whereas the male jaguar of the Guiana myth appeared to the women in the guise of their husband, whom he had killed.

The Chaco myths I have just referred to deal with the origin of tobacco, which springs up from the burnt corpse of the jaguar-woman. After beginning with the contrast between honey and tobacco, and following step by step the cycle of transformations illustrated by the myths about the origin of honey, we now discover that we have come full circle since, at this appreciable distance from our point of departure, we are beginning to discern features which we know to be characteristic of the myths about the origin of tobacco.

And that is not all. The hollow tree which, in the Chaco myths, is used as a refuge against the jaguar, is a yuchan (*Chorisia insignis*), a tree of the bombax family. It is also against the spikes growing on the trunk of the yuchan that the fox is disembowelled in other Chaco myths (M_{208}–M_{209}). Although, according to the sources at our disposal, the cunauaru always seems to choose to live in a tree of a different species (*Bodelsschwingia macrophylla Klotzsch* – a tiliacea with scented flowers, the trunk of which becomes hollow when the tree reaches a certain size; Schomburgk, Vol. II, p. 334), the Warao myth appears to refer simultaneously to the physical appearance and the semantic function of the silk-cotton tree in the Chaco myths.

Looking ahead a little, this is an appropriate moment to point out that silk-cotton trees play a part in the myth we are now concerned with. After trying to build a canoe with wax, then with clay, and after experimenting with various different species of tree, the hero achieves his purpose by using the 'silk-cotton tree', which is a member of the bombax family (*Bombax ceiba, B. globosum*). The Warao did, in fact, make use of this wood which, although somewhat soft, proved to be suitable for the building of large canoes capable of taking from seventy to eighty passengers (Roth 2, p. 613). Figure 12 shows a pattern in a string game suggesting the squat and powerful appearance of the tree with its massive trunk.

It is particularly remarkable that Chaco mythology should reflect, on the imaginative level, a real-life aspect of the culture of certain Guianese Indians. The Mataco myth (M_{246}), already referred to, describes how a population which was being persecuted by the jaguar sought refuge inside an ark as high as a house, hollowed out from the trunk of a yuchan tree. But, although the Mataco myth is referring

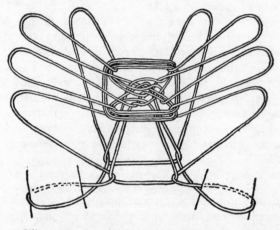

Figure 12. Silk-cotton tree. A pattern in a string game. Warao Indians.
(After Roth 2, Fig. 300, p. 553.)

imaginatively to an aspect of Warao life, in turn this aspect (and its mythical origin as suggested in M_{241}) reverses the original function of the silk-cotton tree as described in the Chaco myths. I recalled further back, when I embarked on this discussion which will be continued in a later chapter, that in the very earliest times a large yuchan tree held all the water and all the fishes of the world in its hollow trunk. The water was therefore in the trunk, whereas the technical operation which changes the trunk into a canoe creates the opposite situation: the tree is in the water. We come back here to the dialectics of container and content and of internal and external, the complexity of which is revealed with exceptional clarity in the series of oppositions (mythical/mythical, mythical/real, real/mythical) illustrated by the part played by the silk-cotton trees. Either the water and the fish are inside the tree, and human beings outside the tree, or humans are inside the tree, the water outside, and the fish in the water. Between these two extremes, the cunauaru frog's way of life occupies an intermediary position: for it, and for it alone, 'all the water in the world' (since it uses no other) is still in the tree. And when M$_{241}$ presents the canoe made from bees' wax and the one made from the wood of the silk-cotton tree as being diametrically opposed, the explanation surely is that for the bee, which is homologous with the tree-frog along the dry/wet axis (cf. above, p. 168), wax and honey replace the water inside the tree, and are not therefore interchangeable with the tree in its relationship with water.[6]

(7) There is nothing much to be said about the flute and arrows that Wau-uta gives to the boy when he reaches adolescence, except that these are normal attributes of his sex and age, the arrows for hunting, the flute for love-making, since the instrument is used in courting: so it is understandable that the women who hear it in the distance conclude that there is an unknown man in the house. The episode of the otters presents a far more complex problem.

The disgust which the stench of Haburi's excrements arouses in the otters is reminiscent of a belief held by the Tlingit of Alaska, who can hardly be considered as neighbours of the Warao: 'The land otter', they say, 'hates the smell of human excretion' (Laguna, p. 188). The species cannot, however, be the same, because of the distance between the two regions, and their climatic differences. The otters in M$_{241}$ make a collective appearance in the myth and might, because of this, belong to the species, *Lutra brasiliensis*, which lives in groups of ten or twenty, rather than to *Lutra felina* (Ahlbrinck, under 'aware-puya'): the latter is a smaller and solitary species, which the ancient Mexicans believed to possess evil powers and attributes as an incarnation of Tlaloc, being always on the look-out for bathers in order to drown them (Sahagun, Book XII, pp. 68–70, under 'auitzotl').

Yet it is impossible not to see a comparison between the Mexican beliefs and those of Guiana, especially after reading the following

---

[6] Cf. the knife made from bee's wax, homologous with 'the water which burns like fire' (M$_{235}$) in: Goeje, p. 127.

In M$_{243}$, the main contrast is between a canoe made of bone, which sinks to the bottom, and a canoe made from a species of tree called cachicamo. In M$_{244}$, the contrast is between a canoe made of wood ('sweet mouth wood'), which sinks, and a canoe made from the wood of the cachicamo.

The cachicamo (*Calophyllum callaba*) is a member of the guttifer or clusiaceae family, with a massive trunk (like the silk-cotton tree) and its wood is reputed to be rot-proof. In the Wilbert versions, Haburi also tries the wood of the peramancilla, ohori, ohoru in Warao, that is (Roth 2, p. 82) *Symphonia* sp., *Moronopea* sp., another of the guttiferae, the resin of which was gathered in vast quantities and, among other things, was mixed with bees' wax and used to caulk canoes.

passage from Sahagun: 'When the otter was annoyed – had caught no one, had drowned none of us commoners – then was heard as if a small child wept. And he who heard it thought perhaps a child wept, perhaps a baby, perhaps an abandoned one. Moved by this, he went there to look for it. So there he fell into the hands of the *auitzotl*; there it drowned him' (Sahagun, *loc. cit.*, p. 69).

This particular crying baby, who behaves like a treacherous seducer, is obviously symmetrical with the irritatingly noisy child who appears in M_{245} and other myths. Furthermore, curious echoes of the Mexican belief are found in regions of America where we had already been struck by a similarity of views on the subject of otters. The Tagish Indians of British Columbia, who are akin to the Tlingit both in language and habitat, have associated the Klondike Gold Rush of 1898 with a myth about a certain 'wealth-woman', who is also a frog-woman. Occasionally, at night, the baby she holds in her arms is heard crying. It must be taken from her and not given back to the mother who is doused with urine until she excretes gold (McClellan, p. 123). The Tlingit and the Tsimshian refer in their myths to a 'Lake Woman' who is married to an Indian, gives her sister-in-law a 'coat of riches', and will confer wealth on anyone who hears her baby cry (Boas 2, p. 746; cf. Swanton 2, pp. 173–5). Whether they are otters or frogs, these maternal sirens, whose babies utter the call, drown their victims like the Mexican otters and they share their Guianese sisters' horror of dejecta. Even the association with wealth in the form of precious metals has its Guianese equivalent; surprised at her toilet, the 'Lake woman' of Arawak mythology forgets and leaves behind on the bank the silver comb with which she was combing her hair (Roth 1, p. 242): according to popular beliefs of southern Brazil, Mboitata, the fire-snake, has a passion for iron objects (Orico 1, p. 109).

In Guiana and throughout the Amazonian area, aquatic seducers, whether male or female, often take the form of a cetacean, usually the bôto, or white Amazonian dolphin (*Inia geoffrensis*). According to Bates (p. 309), the bôto was the object of such powerful superstitions that people were forbidden to kill it (cf. Silva, p. 217, n. 47). It was believed that the animal sometimes assumed the shape of a marvellously beautiful woman, who would entice young men down to the water. But if any young man allowed himself to be seduced, she would grasp her victim round the waist and drag him to the bottom. According to the Shipaia (M_{247b}), dolphins are the descendants of an adulterous woman and her lover, who were changed into these animals by the husband – who had been ill-treated as a child – when he found them in a close embrace after prolonged copulation (Nim. 3, pp. 387–8). Nearer to the Warao, the Piapoco of the lower reaches of the Guaviar, a tributary of the Orinoco, believed in evil Spirits who lived by day at the bottom of the water but emerged at night, when they walked about 'screaming like little children' (Roth 1, p. 242).

This variation in the zoological signifier is all the more interesting in that the dolphin itself oscillates between its function as seducer and a diametrically opposite function, which it shares with the otter. A famous Baré myth (the Baré are Arawak living along the Rio Negro) about the doughty deeds of the hero Poronominaré (M_{247}) relates, in one episode, how the dolphin reduced to more modest proportions the hero's penis, which had become excessively swollen as a result of being bitten by the parasites living in the vagina of an alluring old woman (Amorim, pp. 135–8). Now, according to a Mundurucu myth (M_{248}), otters perform the same service for an Indian whose penis has been extended by a frog during copulation (Murphy 1, p. 127). The cry of this frog, of which the myth gives a phonetic transcription, suggests that it was possibly a cunauaru. Another Mundurucu myth (M_{255}), which will be analysed later (p. 206), relates that the sun and moon, as masters of fish, caused a man to revert to infancy; in spite of every kind of stimulation, his penis remained limp (Murphy 1, pp. 83–5; Kruse 3, pp. 1000–1002).

It would seem as if M_{241} were merely consolidating these two stories by expressing them in metaphorical terms: so that he may become her lover more quickly, the frog speeds up the baby Haburi's rate of growth by magical means, and so lengthens his penis. The otters' function, later will be to 'infantilize' the hero by restoring his forgotten youth to him, and by bringing him back to more filial sentiments. Now, otters are also masters of fish. According to Schomburgk (quoted by Roth 2, p. 190) these animals 'have the habit of going to the water and bringing fish after fish to their eating place, where, when a sufficient quantity has been heaped up, they start eating. The Indians turn this peculiarity to their advantage: they carefully stalk the neighbourhood of such place and wait patiently; then as soon as the otter has returned to the water after depositing its booty, they take it away.' So to defecate in such a spot as Haburi does is not only to show that you are a bad fisherman. It is also to relieve nature symbolically in the animals' 'cooking pot': this is the act which the hero commits literally (M_{243}, M_{244}) in the village of the Siawana and in his 'aunt's' house.

Most important of all is the fact that the fishing technique described by Schomburgk and commented on by Wilbert (2, p. 124) is perhaps not unconnected with the way in which Ahlbrinck (under 'aware-puya') explains the Kalina name for the otter: 'the otter is the domestic animal of the spirit of the water; what the dog is to man, so the otter is to the Spirits.' If, by combining all these points, we could conclude that the Guianese Indians consider the otter as a kind of 'fishing-dog', this would give remarkable significance to an Ojibwa myth of North America (to be discussed in the next volume), which retells the story of Haburi almost word for word, and attributes the same infantilizing role to the dog.

It follows from all I have just said that, in spite of the diversity of the species involved, certain beliefs regarding otters persist in the most remote areas of the New World, from Alaska and British Columbia to the Atlantic coast of Northern America, and southwards, through Mexico, as far as the Guiana region. These beliefs, which in each area are adapted to the local species or genera, must be very old. It is possible, however, that empirical observation may have given them a new lease of life here and there. One cannot fail to be struck by the fact that not only the myths, but naturalists as well, acknowledge that these animals, whether they are land or sea-otters, show extraordinary refinement in their habits. Ihering notes (under 'ariranha') that the great South American otter (*Pteroneura brasiliensis*) refrains from eating the heads and backbones of the biggest fish, and there exists a Guianese myth (M_{346}) which explains why the otter rejects the claws of crabs. The otter along the Arctic coasts has a very acute sense of smell and cannot tolerate any kind of filth, however minute in quantity, which would impair the insulating properties of its fur (Kenyon).

It is perhaps in this direction that we must look for the origin of that sensitivity to smells which the Indians of both North and South America attribute to otters. But, even if the advances made in animal ethology were to confirm this interpretation, it still remains true that, on the level of the myths, the empirically proved negative connection between otters and excrement becomes part of a combinatory system which operates with sovereign independence and exercises the right to effect different interchanges between the terms of an oppositional system which exists experientially in only one state but of which mythic thought gratuitously creates other states.

A Tacana myth (M_{249}) relates that the otter, the master of fish, favoured unlucky fishermen by telling them of the existence of a magic stone, which was buried in his extremely foul-smelling excrement. In order to have a good catch, Indians had to lick the stone and rub it all over their body (H.-H., pp. 210–11). Diametrically opposed to these humans who must not be put off by the otter's foul-smelling excrement are the subterranean dwarfs in Tacana mythology who have no anuses, who never defecate (they feed exclusively on liquids, mostly water) and who are extremely disgusted when they see their first human visitor relieving nature (M_{250}; H.-H., pp. 353–4). These dwarfs with no anuses are an armadillo people who live under the earth, just as the otters live under water. Elsewhere, otters are the subject of similar beliefs. The Trumai (M_{251}) relate how in the old days otters were animals without anuses, which excreted through the mouth (Murphy-Quain, p. 74). This Xingu myth refers back to one of the Bororo myths about the origin of tobacco (for the second time, then, during the analysis of the same myth, the problem of the origin of tobacco appears on the horizon): men who did not exhale tobacco smoke (that is, people who were *blocked* at the top instead of at the bottom) were changed into otters (M_{27}, *RC*, p. 105), animals which have very small eyes, according to the myth, and which are therefore also blocked and deprived of an opening onto the outside world.

If we now bring all the data together, it is possible to discern the outline of a system in which otters occupy a special place in the mythic series of characters, who are blocked or pierced above or below, or at the front or the back, and whose positive or negative disability may affect the vagina or the anus, the mouth, the eyes, the nostrils or the ears. It is perhaps because they were blocked in former times and knew nothing of the excretory functions that the otters in M_{241} are repelled by human excrement. Yet in a Waiwai myth (M_{252}), the otter is changed from a blocked to a pierced animal, when the twins who are as yet the only living people, undertake to copulate with an otter *per oculos*. The animal protests indignantly that it is not a woman and orders the two brothers to fish for women (congruous therefore with fish), who at that time had toothed vaginas which the twins had to remove so that the women should cease to be impenetrable (Fock p. 42; cf. Derbyshire, pp. 73–4), in other words impossible to pierce. The otter, which is blocked below in Trumai mythology and above in Bororo mythology, and pierced above in Waiwai mythology, undergoes a fourth transformation in Yabarana mythology where it becomes a piercing animal in respect of the low: 'Our informants remembered that the otter was

responsible for menstruation, but they could give no explanation'
(M_{253}; Wilbert 8, p. 145):

	Trumaï	Bororo	Waiwai	Yabarana
blocked/pierced	+	+	—	—
agent/sufferer	—	—	—	+
high/low	—	+	+	—
front/back	—	+	+	+

No doubt, methodical research into South American mythology
would reveal different combinations, or would make it possible, in the
case of the same combinations, to give different definitions of the 'high'
and the 'low' and 'back' and 'front' (cf. *RC*, pp. 135–6). For instance,
a Yupa myth (M_{254a}) refers to an otter which was adopted by a fisherman and which kept him supplied with big fish. But the otter refused
to fish for the women. After being *wounded in the head* by its adoptive
father, it bled copiously. To be avenged for this, it abandoned men and
took all the fish along with it (Wilbert 7, pp. 880–81). According to a
Catio myth (M_{254b}), a myocastor (?) *pierces* a man and fertilizes him
(Rochereau, pp. 100–101). For the time being, it is enough to pose the
problem, and I move on straightway to another, of which I shall also
give only a rough outline.

Although the Yabarana informants remembered only vaguely that
their myths established a relationship of cause and effect between the
otter and menstrual periods, they had a very clear recollection of a
story in which an incestuous brother, who is subsequently changed into
a moon, is held responsible for the appearance of this physiological
function (M_{253}; Wilbert 8, p. 156). This might be thought to be no
more than a discrepancy between two traditions, the one local, the
other widely known throughout both North and South America, if there
were not numerous proofs of the fact that, in native thought, the moon
and otters are often given similar roles. I have already made a comparison (p. 201) between the otter episode in the Haburi myth and
several Mundurucu myths, on which I must now dwell for a moment.
In M_{248}, a hunter allowed himself to be seduced by a cunauaru frog,
which had been changed into a beautiful young woman. But, at the
moment of orgasm, the latter resumed her batrachian form and
stretched her lover's penis by holding it fast in her vagina. When she
finally released the unfortunate hunter, the latter asked the otters for
help, but they, while pretending to put him right, inflicted the reverse

disability on him, that is, they reduced his penis to pitiful proportions. As I have already shown, this story expresses, in literal terms, the one which is told in M₂₄₁ with a figurative meaning: on the one hand, the old frog endows Haburi with a member and appetites far beyond his real age; on the other hand, the otters reverse the situation, and they go even further when they revive the hero's consciousness of his earliest childhood, thus carrying out what can be considered as the first psycho-analytical treatment in history ... [7]

The Mundurucu myth, to which I alluded very briefly, is extra-ordinarily explicit on all these points:

M₂₅₅. *Mundurucu. 'The origin of the suns of summer and winter'*

An Indian called Karuetaruyben was so ugly that his wife rejected his advances, and was unfaithful to him. One day, after a collective fishing expedition with fish-poison, he remained alone at the water's edge, sadly reflecting on his lot. The Sun and the Moon, his wife, unexpectedly arrived on the scene. They were very hairy, and their voices resembled the tapir's, and the solitary Indian watched while they threw back into the river the heads and backbones of fish, which were instantly resuscitated.

The two divinities invited Karuetaruyben to tell them his story. To find out if he were speaking the truth, the Sun ordered his wife to seduce him; K. was not only ugly, he was impotent, and his penis remained hopelessly limp. So the Sun transformed K. by magic into an embryo, which he placed in his wife's womb. Three days later she gave birth to a boy, whom the Sun turned into a young man and on whom he bestowed great beauty. When the operation was com-pleted, he made him a gift of a basketful of fish and told him to return to his village and marry another wife, abandoning the one who had deceived him.

The hero had a brother-in-law, a fine upstanding man, who was called Uakurampé. The latter was astounded by the transformation undergone by his sister's husband, and did not rest until he had learned his secret, so that he could imitate it. But when the Moon undertook to seduce him, U. had a normal relationship with her. In order to punish him the Sun had him born again ugly and hunch-backed or according to another version he made him ugly by pulling

---

[7] It is worth recalling that in another, very different part of the New World, the otter plays a didactic role in shamanistic rites of initiation, as is indicated by the joined tongues of man and the animal, depicted on many Haida rattles.

his nose and ears, and 'other parts of the body'. Thereupon he sent him back to his wife, without giving him any fish. According to the different versions, the wife either had to put up with an ugly husband, or she rejected him. 'It is your own fault,' played Karuetaruyben on his flute, 'you were too curious about your mother's vagina ... '

The two heroes became respectively the resplendent sun of the dry season, and the dull, forbidding sun of the rainy season (Kruse 3, pp. 1000–1002; Murphy 1, pp. 83–6).

This myth, of which I have chosen only those aspects which directly concern the present analysis (the others will be dealt with again later), calls for several observations. In the first place, the sun and moon appear as the hairy masters of fishing, and are in this respect congruous with otters; like otters, they respect the heads and backbones of fish, which the otters refrain from eating and which the sun and moon bring back to life again. Secondly, they recognize the hero not by the foul stench of his excrements, as was the case with Haburi, but because of a different physiological disadvantage, namely his impotence, as shown by a penis which remains small and limp in spite of every kind of stimulation. We have here, then, a double modification of the organic code, as compared with M_{241}: in the anatomical category of the low, the front replaces the back, and the reproductive functions supplant the excretory functions; on the other hand, if we make the comparison with M_{255} and M_{258}, we note an extraordinary double inversion. In M_{248}, a penis which had been excessively elongated by the frog was transformed by otters into an excessively shortened penis, whereas in M_{255}, a penis which remained diminutive in the presence of a so-called mistress, soon to be changed into a mother (unlike the frog in M_{241}, a so-called mother soon to be changed into a mistress), was extended to reasonable proportions by the sun. On the other hand, in the same myth, the second hero has a penis which is reasonably long at the beginning, but becomes too long at the end (this at least is what is implied in the Kruse version quoted above.)[8] These various points will be more clearly understood from the table of literal and figurative meanings.

Evidence of the homogeneity of the group can also be found in the names of the hero in M_{255}. Karuetaruyben means 'the red male macaw with the bloodshot eyes', but the hero is also called Bekit-tare-bé, 'the male child who grows fast' (Kruse 3, p. 1001), because his growth is

---

[8] It would be interesting to try and discover whether the Mundurucu myth might not throw some light on the obvious contrast, in the iconography of the gods of the ancient Maya, between the young and beautiful Sun-god and the old, ugly god with the long nose.

magically induced, a fact which creates an additional link with Haburi.

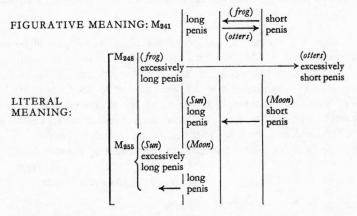

A myth from eastern Bolivia, which is extant in several variants, obviously belongs to the same group:

M256. Tacana. 'The moon's lover'

A woman's cotton plantation was pillaged every night. Her husband caught the thieves: they were two celestial sisters, the moon and the morning star.

The man fell in love with the moon, who was very pretty, but she rejected him and advised him to make advances to her sister. Finally she yielded, but she urged upon the man that, before he slept with her, he should weave a large basket. During copulation the man's penis became tremendously long, to such an extent that its owner had to put it in the basket, where it coiled up like a snake, and even protruded over the edge.

Carrying his load, the man returned to the village and related what had happened to him. At night, his penis came out of its basket and wandered off in search of women, with whom it copulated. Everyone was very frightened and one Indian, whose daughter had been attacked, mounted guard. When he saw the penis coming into his hut, he cut off the end, which changed into a snake. The man with the long penis died, and the snake became the mother of the termites which can be heard whistling today. In other versions, the penis is cut by its owner, or by the moon, or by the women who are attacked (Hissink-Hahn, pp. 81–3).

There is, then, a correlatory and oppositional relationship between the *otter/frog* pair, and other homologous pairs: *sun/moon, summer sun/winter sun* (in M$_{255}$, where the moon is sun's wife) and *morning star/moon* (in M$_{256}$), etc.

Let us now examine the question from a new angle. It will be remembered that, in M$_{241}$, the hero prepared for his escape by inventing the canoe. The first boats he made were stolen by ducks, which at that time could not swim, and which were in fact to acquire the art by using – or, one might say, by fusing with – the canoes made by Haburi. Now there are Chaco myths in which the chief characters are ducks on the one hand, and the sun and the moon on the other. They also contain the theme of the character who is unmasked by the stench of his excrement. In other words, these myths reproduce three different aspects of the Guianese-Amazonian group we have just studied:

M$_{257}$. Mataco. 'The origin of moon-spots'

The sun was hunting ducks. He changed into a duck himself and, armed with a net, dived into the lagoon and pulled the birds under the water. Every time he captured one, he killed it without the other ducks seeing. When he had finished, he shared his ducks out among all the villagers and gave an old bird to his friend Moon. The latter was not pleased, and decided to do his own hunting by using the same method as Sun. Meanwhile, however, the ducks had become suspicious. They defecated and forced Moon who was disguised as a duck to follow suit. Moon's excrements, unlike those of the ducks, were extremely foul-smelling. The birds recognized Moon and attacked him in a body. They scratched and tore his skin until he was almost disembowelled. The spots on the moon are the blue scars left on his stomach by the ducks' claws (Métraux 3, pp. 14–15).

Métraux (5, pp. 141–3) quotes two variants of this myth, one of which, a Chamacoco version, replaces ducks by 'ostriches' (*Rhea*); the other, which is Toba in origin, replaces the moon by a deceiving fox. In spite of their dissimilarities, all these myths form one group, of which it is possible to define the armature, while respecting its complexities. Certain myths explain the origin of the spots on the moon, or of the moon itself; in the natural philosophy of the American Indians, this celestial body, especially in its masculine aspect, is considered responsible for menstruation. The other myths also deal with a physiological process, which is the lengthening or shortening of the

penis, either in the literal or the figurative sense, and similarly associated with the moon considered in its feminine aspect.

These myths therefore always deal with an event which is definable
in relationship to the physiological maturity of the female sex, or
the male sex and which, in the latter case, they describe in its positive
or its negative aspect. Whether he is impotent or endowed with too
short a penis, the man is either symbolically a child or is returning to
childhood. And when he moves away from childhood either too far
or too abruptly, the extreme character of the change is shown either
by an over-long penis, or by excessively foul-smelling excrement. This
is surely tantamount to saying that the foul-smelling stools of the male[9]
correspond to the same kind of phenomenon as that which, in the
case of women, is more normally illustrated by the menstrual flow.

[9] There is a good deal to be said about the semantics of excrement. In a memorable study,
Williamson (pp. 280–81) has shown the contrast which exists in the minds of the Mafulu
of New Guinea between inedible food remnants and excrements. The polarities are reversed, according to whether the person is an adult or a very young child. Adults pay no
heed to their excrements but their inedible food waste, which is unfit for human consumption, has to be carefully preserved for fear it might be snatched away by a sorcerer, and
then it is thrown into the river in order to be rendered harmless. In the case of young
children, the opposite is true; no attention is paid to the inedible waste from food intended
for them, but great care is taken to collect their excrements and put them in a safe place.
More recent observations have revealed the existence of special buildings, in which
natives of the mountainous regions of New Guinea keep babies' excrements (Aufenanger).
It would seem as if waste, whether lying on the hither side or the far side of assimilable food,
were an integral part of the consumer, but *ante* or *post factum* according to age. This links
up with an interpretation I have given of certain customs practised by the Penan of Borneo,
who seem to consider that a young child's food forms an integral part of his person (L.-S.
9, pp. 262–3, n.):

ADULT

non-assimilable parts	assimilable parts	non-assimilable parts

CHILD

Certain facts suggest that South American Indians imagine the same kind of contrast, but
shift it from children to the dying who, in relation to the adult in the prime of life, are
symmetrical to the new-born. The Siriono of Bolivia collect the vomit and excrement of
the very sick in a basket for as long as the death agony lasts. When the dead person is
buried, the contents of the basket are emptied near the grave (Holmberg, p. 88). The
Yamamadi, who live between the Rio Purus and the Rio Jurua, may perhaps observe the
reverse practice, since they build a kind of ramp leading from the hut to the forest: it is,
perhaps, the path to be taken by the soul, but perhaps also a way of helping the sick person
to crawl outside in order to relieve nature (Ehrenreich, p. 109).

The problem of the semantics of excrement in America should be studied by starting
with the contrast between northern myths about a prodigious baby capable of eating its
own excrement and the southern versions, in which a no less prodigious baby feeds on
menstrual blood (Catio in Rochereau, p. 100). On the other hand, while it may be difficult
to separate excrement and the child's body, the same is true of noise: in terms of acoustic

If this hypothesis is true, Haburi, the hero of M_{241}, is following a cycle which is the reverse of that which a girl would follow from birth to puberty. At first a pathological adult, he is restored by the otters to the normality of childhood, whereas a young girl, through the moon's intervention, reaches normal maturity, a phenomenon which is indicated by the onset of monthly periods; these have, however, an intrinsically pathological character, since in native thought menstrual blood is considered as a form of filth and poison. The regressive movement followed by the myth corroborates a feature which I recognized from the beginning as being characteristic of all those belonging to the same group, and which I can now check by a new approach.

So far, I have not discussed ducks. They play a particularly important part in the myths of North America, and to carry out a thorough analysis would involve structuring the system to which they belong with the help of the mythology of both North and South. At the present juncture, such an undertaking would be premature, and so I shall confine myself to the South American context, in order to make two series of observations.

Firstly, in M_{241}, the hero who is the protégé of a frog involuntarily becomes the organizer of a sector of the animal kingdom. Every kind of canoe he invents is stolen from him by ducks of a particular species which, in appropriating the canoe, acquire the ability to swim, as well as their distinctive characteristics. We can thus perceive a direct link between M_{241} and M_{238}, in which another hunter, also the protégé of a frog, involuntarily became the organizer of the animal kingdom, taken this time as a whole. In M_{238}, the entire animal kingdom is graded according to size and family; in M_{241}, we move to one particular animal family, which is divided up into its various species. Between one myth

---

coding, a baby's intolerable cries, which supply the theme of myths I have summarized above (p. 195), are equivalent to foul-smelling excrement. Cries and excrement are therefore mutually interchangeable, by virtue of the basic congruence between din and stench which has already been exemplified in *The Raw and the Cooked*, and to which I shall have occasion to return in other contexts.

This connection supplies an additional piece of information about the semantic position of the otter: because a false adult ejects foul-smelling excrement, the otter sends him back to his mother; because a 'false' child (he has no reason to cry) utters loud howls, the frog, the opossum or the vixen take him away from his mother. We know already, from M_{241}, that the otter and the frog are diametrically opposed, and the preceding observation allows me to generalize the relationship. To carry the analysis further, it would be appropriate to compare the otter with other creatures (more often than not birds) which, in South as well as North America, reveal his true origin to a child who has been carried far away from his own people and brought up by supernatural beings who claim to be his parents.

and the other, therefore, the classificatory impulse diminishes and disintegrates. It remains to be seen why and how.

The natural and zoological organization supplied by M_{238} is the result of a cultural deficiency: it would never have come into being if the hero had not been an inefficient hunter. On the contrary, in M_{241}, it is the result of a cultural acquisition: the art of navigation, the invention of which was necessary so that the ducks could become fused with technical objects – the canoes – to which they owe their present appearance. This conception supposes that ducks are not a part of the animal kingdom in their own right. Having been derived from cultural operations, they provide evidence, at the very heart of nature, of a local regression of culture.

Some readers may suspect me of straining the meaning of the myth. Yet the same theory is found in a Tupi myth from the Lower Amazon (M_{326a}), which will be summarized and discussed later: for the moment, it will be enough to quote one of its themes. Because a taboo was violated, things changed into animals: the basket became the jaguar, the fisherman and his canoe changed into a duck: 'the head and beak came from the fisherman's head, the body from the canoe and the feet from the paddles' (Couto de Magalhães, p. 233).

The Karaja relate (M_{326b}) how Kanaschiwué, the demiurge, gave the duck a clay canoe in exchange for the metal motor-boat which the bird let him have (Baldus 5, p. 33). In the Vapidiana myth about the flood (M_{115}), a duck's beak is changed into a canoe, which enables a family to remain afloat (Ogilvie, p. 66).

Similarly, in a Taulipang myth (M_{326c}), a man is changed into a duck, after being deprived of the magical self-working agricultural implements. If his brothers-in-law had not been responsible for the disappearance of these marvellous tools, men would not have needed to labour in the fields (K.-G. 1, pp. 124–8). The similarity with M_{241} is obvious; in the one instance, the hero creates ducks and then disappears with the arts of civilization; in the other, the hero becomes a duck, when the arts of a 'super civilization' disappear. We shall see that this term is appropriate for the arts which Haburi denies to the Indians, since these are precisely the arts practised by the whites.[10] The comparison of these myths shows, then, that it is not by chance or through some whim on the part of the narrator that, in the first two,

[10] In connection with the re-transformation of the theme of the self-working agricultural implements into that of the revolt of the objects, the negative limit of the moon's ordering function, cf. RC, p. 299, n. 11.

ducks appear as canoes which have degenerated into animals.[11] At the same time we can understand why, in a myth the regressive movement of which I have often stressed, the hero's function as the orderer of creation is restricted to a limited field: namely, that in which, according to native thought, creation takes the form of a regression. The fact that the regression occurs from culture to nature raises a different problem, the solving of which I shall postpone for the moment in order to bring the matter of the ducks to a close.

Although ducks are congruous with canoes in respect of culture, in the natural order of things they have a correlatory and oppositional relationship with fish. The latter swim under water whereas the myths we are discussing explain why ducks, in their capacity as ex-canoes, swim on water. In the Mundurucu myths, Sun and Moon catch fish; in the Chaco myths, they fish for ducks. They are fishermen, not hunters, since the myths are careful to explain the technique used: the ducks are caught in a net by a character who has taken on their appearance and who is swimming among them. What is more, this particular form of fishing is carried out from high to low: the captured birds are dragged to the bottom, whereas fishing proper, and in particular the method practised by otters, is carried out from low to high, that is, the fish are taken out of the water and laid on the bank.

M_{241} describes Haburi purely as a bird-catcher. It is only when he misses a bird for the first time that he crouches down to release his excrement on the otters' eating place. This 'anti-fishing' operation, which produces excrement instead of food, is a movement from high to low, like duck-catching, and not from low to high. And it is offensive to the otters, in so far as they are catchers of fish.

It is important therefore to ascertain whether or not there exists a term which has a relationship with fish, correlative with that existing between ducks and canoes. A myth I have already mentioned (M_{252}) supplies such a term and, as it happens, through the agency of the otter. When the twins who know nothing about women try to copulate with an otter through its eyes, the latter explains to them that it is not a woman but that women are to be found in water, where the cultural heroes should fish for them. That the first women were fish or, after quarrelling with their husbands, decided to change into fish is a recurrent theme illustrated in so many myths that there is no need for me to draw up a list. Just as ducks are ex-canoes, so women are ex-fish.

[11] In North America, there is a correlation between ducks and canoes among the Iroquois and the Indians of the Wabanaki group.

Ducks represent a regression from culture to nature, while women constitute a progression from nature to culture, although, in either case, the gap between the two worlds remains extremely small.

This explains why otters, which live on fish, have such ambiguous and equivocal relationships with women. In a Bororo myth (M_{21}), otters act in collusion with women against their husbands, and keep them supplied with fish, on condition that they submit to their desires. Conversely, a Yupa myth, which I have already summarized (M_{254a}), states that the otter caught fish for the Indian who had adopted it, but refused to perform the same service for women. In all the myths, therefore, otters are men, or belong to the male party; this explains why the otter in the Waiwai myth was so indignant when the two simpletons tried to use it as if it were a woman, and started the wrong way round into the bargain.

We have seen that, by inventing the canoe, Haburi created the different species of ducks. He thus imposed order on nature, partially and retroactively. Yet, at the same time, he made a decisive contribution to culture, and one might suppose that the regressive character of the myth would be contradicted by this twist. The old versions quoted by Brett help to solve the difficulty. In Brett's transcription, Haburi bears the name, Aboré, and he is presented as the 'father of inventions'. If he had not had to flee from his aged wife, the Indians would have enjoyed many other fruits of his ingenuity, in particular, woven articles of clothing. One variant mentioned by Roth even relates that the hero sailed away until he finally came to the land of the White men (to the island of Trinidad according to M_{244}) to whom he taught all their arts and manufactures (Roth 1, p. 125). If it is possible to identify Haburi or the Warao Aboré with the god whom the ancient Arawak called Ahibiri or Hubuiri, we should attach a similar kind of significance to Schomburgk's remark that 'this character does not trouble himself about men' (*ibid.*, p. 120). With the exception of navigation, the only civilized art that the natives seem to claim as their own, what the myths are dealing with is undoubtedly the loss of culture, or of a culture superior to their own.

Now, Brett's versions (M_{258}), which are inferior in all respects to those of Roth and Wilbert, have the great advantage of being, in a sense, transversal to the group of Guiana myths and to the group of Ge myths in which the heroine is a girl mad about honey, as in the Chaco myths. Aboré was married to an old frog, Wowtā, which had assumed a woman's form in order to capture him when he was a little child. She was always sending him to look for honey, for which she had a great fondness. Finally, he could stand it no longer and got rid of her by imprisoning her in a hollow tree. After which, he escaped in a wax canoe that he had made in secret. His departure deprived the Indians of many other inventions (Brett 1, pp. 294–5; 2, pp. 76–83).

In concluding this excessively long variation, I must point out that, in its two consecutive parts (illustrated, respectively, by M_{237}–M_{239}, and M_{241}–M_{258}), it has a transformational relationship, worthy of special study, with an important Karaja myth (M_{177}) about unlucky hunters who fell prey to the guariba monkeys, with the one exception of their young brother, who had an ulcer-ridden body and had been rejected by his mother (cf. M_{245}) and fed on refuse by his grandfather. After being cured by a snake, he obtained protection from a frog in exchange for illusory caresses and became a miraculous hunter thanks to throwing-spears given to him by the frog. There was one for each kind of food, and their force had to be diminished by smearing them with ointment, which is the equivalent, then, of a kind of inverted hunting poison. Although the hero had forbidden anyone to touch his magic weapons, one of his brothers-in-law stole the honey throwing-spear (the gathering of honey is here likened to a hunt, whereas in the Ofaié myth, M_{192}, it is likened to agriculture) and by his clumsiness conjured up a monster, who massacred the entire village (Ehrenreich, pp. 84–6). This myth will be discussed in another context and in connection with other versions (cf. below, p. 396).

2 *Variations* 4, 5, 6

$$[\bigcirc \Rightarrow \bigcirc] \leftrightarrow [\text{frog} \Rightarrow \text{jaguar}]$$

We are now familiar with the character and customs of the cunauaru tree-frog. But I have not previously mentioned the fact that, according to the Tupi of the Amazon valley, this particular frog can be changed into a jaguar, yawárété-cunawarú (Tastevin 2 under 'cunawarú'). Other tribes share the same belief (Surára in Becher 1, pp. 114–15). The Oayana of Guiana call the mythical jaguar – which is blue according to the Tupi, but black in Guiana (cf. M$_{238}$) – Kunawaru-imö, 'Great Cunauaru' (Goeje, p. 48).

The myths make it possible to work out the analysis of this transformation in several stages:

M$_{259}$. *Warao. 'The wooden bride'*

Nahakoboni, whose name means 'he who eats plenty', had no daughter and on becoming old he began to feel anxious about his declining years, since he had neither daughter nor son-in-law to take care of him. He therefore carved a daughter out of the trunk of a plum tree; so skilfully did he cut and carve the timber that he made a wonderfully beautiful young woman, and all the animals came to court her. The old man rejected them all in turn but when Yar, the sun, came forward, Nahakoboni thought he was the kind of son-in-law whose mettle ought to be tried.

He therefore gave him several tasks to perform, the details of which I omit, apart from pointing out that one task reversed the magic technique taught by the frog in M$_{238}$; in this instance, the hero had to reach his target in spite of being ordered to aim into the air (cf. above, p. 172). At all events, the Sun acquitted himself honourably and was given the beautiful Usi-diu (literally: 'seed tree') as his wife. But on trying to prove his love, he discovered he was unable to do so, since Usi-diu's creator, in carving the young girl, had forgotten one essential detail which he confessed himself unable to add. Yar consulted the bunia bird, which promised to help. It allowed itself to be held and nursed by the young girl. Taking advantage of her innocence, it pierced the forgotten opening, from which a snake had first of all to be removed. After that, nothing interfered with the happiness of the two young people.

The father-in-law was greatly displeased that his son-in-law should have taken the liberty of criticizing his work and had called upon the bunia bird to tinker with it. He bided his time, waiting for his revenge to come. When the time for planting came, he destroyed his son-in-law's work several times by means of his 'medicine'; the latter, however, succeeded in cultivating his field with the help of a spirit. In spite of the old man's evil spells, he also finished building a hut for his father-in-law and was at last free to look after his own domestic affairs, and for a long time he and his wife lived very happily together.

One day, Yar decided to set off on a journey westwards. As Usi-diu was pregnant, he advised her to travel at her leisure. All she had to do was to follow his tracks, being careful always to take the right-hand track; in any case, he would scatter feathers on the left, so she could make no mistake. There was no difficulty to begin with, but trouble began when she arrived at a place where the wind had blown the feathers away. Then the unborn babe began to speak and told her which path to follow; it also asked her to gather flowers. While she was stooping, a wasp stung the young woman below the waist. She tried to kill it, missed the insect, but struck herself instead. The unborn babe misinterpreted her action and thought it was being smacked. It became vexed and refused any longer to show its mother which direction to pursue, with the result that the latter went hopelessly astray. She arrived at last at a large house whose only occupant was Nanyobo (the name of a large frog), who appeared to her in the form of a very old and very big woman. Having offered food and drink to the traveller, the frog asked her to clean her head, but to be careful not to put the insects into her mouth because they would poison her. The young woman, overcome with fatigue, forgot the frog's injunction. As was customary among Indians, she placed a louse between her teeth. But no sooner had she done so than she fell dead.

The frog opened up the body and extracted not one child but two:

a pair of beautiful boys, Makunaima and Pia, whom she brought up with great kindness. As the babies grew larger, they began shooting birds, then fish (with arrows) and game. 'You must dry your fish in the sun and never over a fire', the frog told them. Yet she sent them to fetch firewood and, by the time they returned, the fish was always nicely cooked and ready for them. As a matter of fact, the frog used to vomit fire from her mouth and lick it up again before the lads' return, so that there was never a fire burning for them to see. His curiosity aroused, one of the boys changed into a lizard and spied on the old woman. He not only saw her vomit out fire, but watched her take out from her neck a white substance something like the starch of the *Mimusops balata*. The brothers were disgusted by these practices and decided to kill their adoptive mother. They cleared a large field, and left in its centre a fine tree to which they tied her; then surrounding her on all sides with stacks of timber, they set fire to them. While the old woman burnt, the fire which used to be within her passed into the surrounding faggots. These consisted of wood from the hima-heru tree (*Gualtheria uregon?* cf. Roth 2, p. 70) and whenever we rub together two sticks of this same timber we can get fire (Roth 1, pp. 130–33).

Wilbert gives a short version of this myth (M_{260}), consisting only of the episode of the wooden bride, Nawakoboni's daughter, whose maidenhead several birds in turn try to break. Some fail because the wood is too hard and are left with bent or broken beaks. Another bird is successful and the young woman's blood fills a cooking pot, where several species of birds come and smear themselves with it; it is at first red but then white, then black. In this way, they acquire their characteristic plumage. The 'ugly bird' came last and that is why its feathers are black (Wilbert 9, pp. 130–31).

This variant calls for one or two comments. The theme of the bride carved out of a tree-trunk is found in very remote regions of the continent: among the Tlingit of Alaska (M_{261}), for whom the woman remains dumb, i.e. blocked at the top (high) instead of the bottom (low) (cf. Swanton 2, pp. 181–2),[12] and in Bolivia, where it provides the

---

[12] I am only quoting the Tlingit as an example. For reasons which will finally emerge in the fourth volume of this series (if it is ever written) [this has now appeared as *L'homme nu* (Paris, 1971)], I would like to draw attention to the special affinities which exist between the myths of tropical America and those of the Pacific coast of North America. But in fact, the theme of the statue or image which comes to life occurs sporadically in North America, in communities as far apart as the Eskimo of the Bering Strait, the Micmac and the Iroquois, the Plains Indians and, to the south, the Pueblo.

subject of a Tacana myth (M_{262}) which has a dramatic ending: the doll which is brought to life by the devil drags her human husband off into the world beyond (H.-H., p. 515). It is found even among the Warao ($M_{236a, b}$), in the form of a story about a young bachelor who carves a woman out of the trunk of a palm tree (*Mauritia*). She supplies him with food which he tries to pass off as refuse, but his companions discover the statue and chop it up (Wilbert 9, pp. 127–9). The kind of tree mentioned in these last myths obviously refers to the 'wooden husband', who appears at the beginning of M_{241}, thus creating an initial link with the other myths in the group.

Elsewhere, an analogy appears, at least on the semantic level, between the 'ugly bird' in M_{260} and the bunia bird in M_{259}, usually referred to as the 'stinking bird' (*Opistho comus, Ostinops* sp., Roth 1, pp. 131, 371). The position of this bird in the myths has been discussed elsewhere (*RC*, pp. 185, 205, 269, n. 33), and I shall not return to the subject. On the other hand, it is worth noting how M_{260} develops the bird theme introduced by M_{259}, so that the Wilbert version becomes to all intents and purposes a myth about the differentiation of birds according to species, thus amplifying the episode in M_{241} which is concerned with the different species of ducks. Finally, the Wilbert version links up with a group of myths about the origin of bird plumage (in particular, M_{172}, in which the last bird to arrive, a kind of cormorant, also becomes black). As I showed in *The Raw and the Cooked*, this group can be created by a process of transformation from myths dealing with the origin of hunting- or fishing-poison. Here we find the same armature, but one which results from a series of transformations, the starting-point of which was myths about the origin of honey. It follows that native thought must consider honey and poison to be in some sense homologous and this is borne out by the fact that South American varieties of honey are often poisonous. On the strictly mythical level, the nature of this connection will be disclosed later.

The Wilbert version should also be compared with a Chaco myth we have already studied (M_{175}: *RC*, pp. 305–8) which follows a remarkably similar progression, since in it the birds acquire their distinctive plumage because they open up the apertures in the deceiver's body, and blood spurts out, followed by excrement. As in the Wilbert version, the excrement turns the feathers of an ugly bird black; in this instance, it is the raven.

These parallels would be incomprehensible if they did not reflect some homology between the Toba deceiver or the Mataco fox, and the wooden bride in the Guiana myth. It is impossible to see how this homology could occur, but for the intermediary agency of the girl mad about honey, who, as I have suggested on several occasions (and shall prove conclusively), is herself homologous with the fox or the deceiver. The wooden bride must therefore be a transformation of the girl mad about honey. But we still have to explain how and why. For the moment, it is no doubt advisable to introduce further variants of the Guiana myth, without which it would be difficult to deal with the basic problems.

M_{264}. *Carib.* 'The frog, the jaguar's mother'

A long time ago, there was a woman who had become pregnant by the sun with twin children, Pia and Makunaima. While they were as yet unborn, they expressed a desire to go and see their father, and asked their mother to travel westwards. They undertook to show her the way, but as she travelled she had to pick pretty flowers for them. So she plucked flowers here and there on the way, but accidentally stumbled, fell down and hurt herself: she blamed her two unborn children as the cause. They became vexed at this and refused to tell her which road she should follow. Thus she took the wrong direction and arrived in an exhausted state at the house of Kono(bo)-aru, the Rain-frog, whose son, the Jaguar, was reputed for his cruelty.

The frog took pity on the woman, and hid her in a cassiri jar. But the Jaguar smelt human flesh, discovered where the woman was hiding and killed her. When he cut up the body, he discovered the twins and handed them over to his mother. She put them first of all in a bundle of cotton: the children grew quickly and reached man's size in a month. The frog then gave them bows and arrows, and told them to go and kill the powis bird (*Crax* sp.), because it was this bird which had killed their mother. The youths therefore went and shot powis and continued shooting them day after day. The last bird they were about to kill told them the truth, and for this reason they spared his life. The two boys were very angry and made themselves new and stronger weapons, with which they killed the jaguar and his mother, the frog.

The two lads now proceeded on their way and arrived at a clump of cotton trees (*bombacaceae*, no doubt), in the centre of which was a house occupied by a very old woman, really a frog, and where they took up their quarters. They went out hunting each day and, on their return, found some baked manioc. They could see no field anywhere about, so they kept a watch on the old woman and discovered that she extracted starch from a white spot on her shoulders. Refusing all food, the brothers invited the frog to lie down on some cotton which they teased out on the floor; then they set fire to it. The frog's skin was scorched so dreadfully as to give it the wrinkled and rough appearance it now bears.

Pia and Makunaima next continued their travels to meet their father. They spent three days at the house of a female tapir. On the third evening, the tapir returned looking very sleek and fat. The boys followed her tracks which they traced to a plum tree. This they shook so violently as to make all the fruit, both ripe and unripe, fall to the ground. The tapir was disgusted to find all her food wasted, beat both boys and cleared off. The boys started in pursuit and tracked her for a whole day. At last they caught up with her and agreed on what tactics they should follow: Makunaima was to wheel round in front and drive the creature back and, as he passed, let fly a harpoon-arrow into it. The rope, however, got in the way of Makunaima as he was passing in front and cut his leg off. On a clear night you can still see them: there is tapir (Hyades), Makunaima (Pleiades), and below is the severed leg (Orion's belt) (Roth 1, pp. 133-5).

The significance of the astronomical coding will be discussed later. In order to link this myth directly with the group about the girl mad about honey, I am going to quote a Vapidiana variation which deals with the origin of Orion and the Pleiades:

M_{265}. *Vapidiana*. 'The girl mad about honey'

One day Banukúre's wife cut off his leg. He went up into the sky, where he became Orion and the belt. In revenge, his brother shut the wicked wife up in a hollow tree, and then he too went up into the sky where he became the Pleiades. The wife was turned into a honey-eating snake (Wirth 1, p. 260).

It is clear that this version, in spite of its brevity, is situated at the point of intersection of several myths: in the first place, the Haburi story, since we may suppose that, like the old frog, the heroine is full of lewd ideas (which prompt her to get rid of her husband). And she is also mad about honey, otherwise she would not agree to go inside a hollow tree and would not change into a honey-loving animal. Moreover, the two myths end with the disjunction of the hero: horizontal disjunction in M_{241}, vertical in M_{243} (but from high to low), and vertical also in M_{265} (this time from low to high). The theme of the woman mad about honey has a more direct link with Brett's version of the myth about Aboré (Haburi), the father of inventions (M_{258}), which presents a kind of short-cut leading back to the Ge myths. The story of the man whose leg is cut off, i.e. the origin of Orion and the Pleiades, which is common to both M_{264} and M_{265}, belongs to a vast group which I was able to touch upon only very briefly in *The Raw and the Cooked*. If this group overlaps with the one whose core I saw as being formed by myths about the girl mad about honey, the reason must be an equivalence between the lewd woman, who allows herself to be seduced by a lover to whom she is too closely related (brother-in-law) or who is too far removed from her (the tapir, which is given a different function in M_{264}), and the woman mad about honey, who behaves with an indecent lack of control towards a food which is also a seducer. This complex relationship will be analysed in greater detail later, but if we are to retain it as a provisional working hypothesis, we must at least have a feeling that the four stages in the disjunction of the cultural heroes, who are separated from a female tapir, after themselves in turn leaving two frogs and being separated from their mother, is to be explained in the long run by the fact that the three animals and the woman herself are just so many combinatory variants of the girl mad about honey. I had already arrived at this hypothesis in connection with the wooden bride, and it should not be forgotten that the mother of the dioscuri in M_{259} was, in the first instance, a wooden bride.

M_{266}. Macusi. 'The wooden bride'

The Sun, finding his fish ponds too frequently robbed, set the water-lizard, then the alligator, to watch them. The latter was the thief and continued his old trade. Finally the Sun caught him in the act and slashed him with a cutlass, every cut forming a scale. Alligator begged piteously for his life and in return offered the Sun his daughter in marriage. But he had no daughter and had to sculpt the form of a woman from a wild plum tree. He left it to the Sun to infuse life into her if he liked her, then, as a precautionary measure, hid himself in the water. This habit Alligator has retained up to the present time.

The woman was imperfectly formed, but a woodpecker in quest of food pecked at her body and gave her a vagina. The Sun left her and she set out to look for him. Then follows the incident related in

M_{264}, except that, after killing the jaguar, Pia takes out of his carcass the parts of the body of his mother and makes her whole and alive again. The woman and her two sons find refuge with a frog who draws fire from her body and who scolds Makunaima, when she sees him devouring the live coals, since he has an appetite for fire-eating. Makunaima then prepares to leave. He digs a large canal into which water flows: he makes a canoe, the first of its kind, and gets into it with his mother and Pia. It is from Crane that the brothers learn the art of fire-making by striking a flint, and they also accomplish many other feats. They, for instance, were responsible for causing great waterfalls, by placing huge rocks in the rivers to detain the fishes. They thus became more successful fishermen than the crane. Pia consequently quarrelled with Crane who took up with Makunaima. Finally they separated, and Crane flew away with Makunaima to Spanish Guiana.

Pia and his mother therefore lived alone, travelling together, fishing and seeking fruit, until one day the mother complained of weariness and withdrew to the heights of Roraima. So Pia abandoned the hunt and undertook to teach the Indians the arts of civilization. By him and his teachings we have the Piai men, sorcerer-warriors. Finally Pia rejoined his mother on Roraima where he remained with her for a while. When his time of departure came, he told her that all her wishes would be granted if, while she expressed her wish, she would bow her head and cover her face with her hands. This she still does to the present hour. Whenever she is sad and sorrowful, there arises a storm on the mountain and her tears run in streams down the mountain-side (Roth 1, p. 135).

This version makes it possible to round off the group in two different respects. First of all, it refers back to M_{241}:

$$
\left[
\begin{array}{l}
M_{241}: \text{Black Jaguar} \\
\\
M_{266}: \text{Sun}
\end{array}
\right]
\begin{array}{c}
\text{master of fish} \\
\text{stolen by}
\end{array}
\left\{
\begin{array}{l}
\text{'HUSBAND made from wood} \\
\text{of } \textit{palm tree} \dots \text{'} \\
\\
\text{cayman (alligator)} \dots
\end{array}
\right.
$$

//

$$
\left[
\begin{array}{l}
M_{241}: \\
\\
M_{266}:
\end{array}
\right]
\text{exchanged}
\left\{
\begin{array}{l}
\text{for himself, by Jaguar who eats him} \\
\\
\text{for 'WOMAN made from wood of } \textit{plum tree}\text{' by} \\
\text{Sun who fertilizes her}
\end{array}
\right.
$$

//

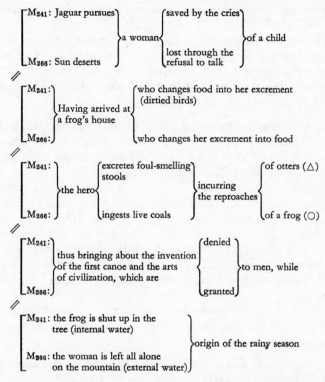

Brett gives an Arawak version (M_{267}), in which otters play a distinct part, as they did in M_{241}. The otters in the Arawak version destroy the Sun's fish ponds; the cayman tries to do likewise but is caught. To save his life, he has to give a woman to his conqueror (Brett 2, pp. 27–8). In Cubeo mythology, the cayman, the otter and the wooden bride are also linked:

M_{268}. *Cubeo.* 'The wooden bride'

Kuwai, the cultural hero, carved a woman out of the trunk of a wahokakü tree. Konéko, the bird (the hero's grandmother, in another version), made her vagina. She was a beautiful woman and Kuwai lived happily with her until one day she was carried off by a spirit, mamüwü. Kuwai sat down on a branch and wept. The otter saw him, asked him what was the matter and took him down to the bottom of the river, where the hero succeeded in winning back his wife.

However, he was chased away by an angry spirit and never came back again.

[In another version, the woman takes a boa as her lover. Kuwai finds them together, kills the snake, cuts its penis into four pieces and gives them to his wife to eat; she thinks they are small fish. On learning that her lover has been murdered, the woman changes back into a tree.] (Goldman, p. 148.)

The story in which the cayman plays a part (M_{269}) refers in all probability to another of Kuwai's wives, since it is specifically stated that this wife was the daughter of an old man of the tribe. One day when she was asleep in her hammock, Kuwai sent Cayman to look for a burning stick with which to light a cigarette. Cayman saw the woman and wanted to copulate with her. In spite of her protests, he succeeded in climbing on top of her. However, she ate the entire lower half of his stomach, including his penis. Kuwai arrived on the scene and told Cayman that he had been warned. He took a small square piece of matting and used it to mend the animal's belly. Then he threw Cayman back into the water, saying: 'It will be your fate always to be eaten' (Goldman, p. 182).

It is clear from the following equations that the two women – the one carved out of a tree, and the other one – are combinatory variants of one and the same myth:

(*a*) W^1 (carried off by a water spirit $\equiv W^2$ (attacked by a cayman);

(*b*) W^1 (seduced by a boa to whom she yields) $\equiv W^2$ (seduced by a cayman whom she resists);

(*c*) W^1 (eats the snake's penis) $\equiv W^2$ (eats the cayman's penis).

On the other hand, the group M_{268}–M_{269} allows us to establish a direct link between M_{266}–M_{267} and M_{241}:

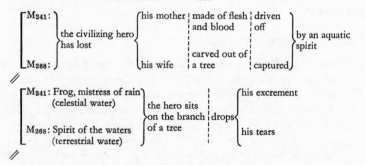

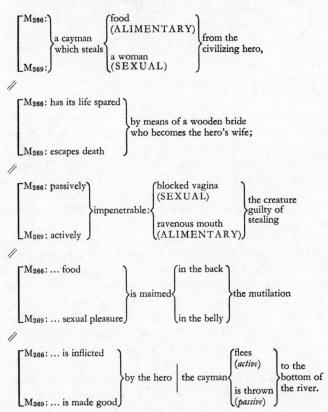

M_{241}:
M_{268}:
which arouses the anger of an otter who brings him back
to his mother / to his wife
in order to escape from the aquatic spirit
the civilizing hero disappears

Let us now link M_{266} and M_{269}:

M_{266}:
M_{269}:
a cayman which steals
food (ALIMENTARY) / a woman (SEXUAL)
from the civilizing hero,

//

M_{266}: has its life spared
M_{269}: escapes death
by means of a wooden bride who becomes the hero's wife;

//

M_{266}: passively
M_{269}: actively
impenetrable:
blocked vagina (SEXUAL) / ravenous mouth (ALIMENTARY)
the creature guilty of stealing

//

M_{266}: ... food
M_{269}: ... sexual pleasure
is maimed
in the back / in the belly
the mutilation

//

M_{266}: ... is inflicted
M_{269}: ... is made good
by the hero | the cayman
flees (active) / is thrown (passive)
to the bottom of the river.

The loop running between M_{241} and M_{266}–M_{269} is comparatively short because, in respect of both geographical location and of their places in the transformation series, these myths are close to each other. The other loop is much more extraordinary; in spite of the geographical, and what we might call the logical, distance between them, the Macusi myth refers back to the Chaco myths, whose heroine is a girl mad about honey, although this character appears to be absent from the Macusi myth:

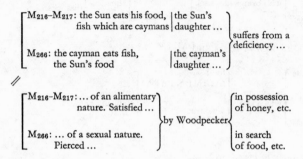

The link between the Guiana and the Chaco myths appears even more pronounced if we take into account the fact that, in the former, the relationship between the two brothers, Pia and Makunaima, is the same as that between Woodpecker and Fox in the latter: Makunaima is, in fact, the base seducer of his elder brother's wife (K.-G. 1, pp. 42–6).

So we encounter once more the equivalence, to which I have several times referred, between the wooden bride and the girl mad about honey. But easy though it is to conceive of the equivalence when the girl mad about honey is replaced by a woman who is equally mad, but about her body, it is difficult to imagine it existing in the case of the wooden bride who, being deprived of the essential attribute of femininity, ought to be afflicted with the opposite kind of temperament. In order to solve this difficulty, and at the same time make some headway in the interpretation of the myths on which this fourth variation is trying to impose some kind of order, we must go right back to the beginning.

The girl mad about honey is greedy. Now, we have seen that, in M_{259}–M_{260}, the father and creator of the wooden bride is called Nahakoboni, which means: the glutton. A glutton for what? For food first of all, no doubt, since some of the trials he imposes on the suitor consist in supplying him with enormous quantities of meat and drink. But this characteristic is not enough wholly to explain his psychological make-up, nor why he feels resentment against his son-in-law for having entrusted the bunia bird with the task of completing the girl he himself was incapable of finishing properly. The text of the myth is most illuminating on this point, provided, as always, that we read it with extreme care, taking each detail as being strictly relevant. Nahakoboni was growing old and needed a son-in-law. Among the Warao, who are a matrilocal tribe, the son-in-law sets up house with his parents-in-law and is supposed to repay them for having been given a wife by contributing labour and food. But in Nahakoboni's view, his son-in-law is not so much his daughter's husband as someone who owes him work and food. The old man wants him *all to himself*, as the mainspring of a domestic family and not the founder of a conjugal family, since what he contributed to the latter as a husband he would inevitably take from the former as son-in-law. In other words, Nahakoboni may be greedy for food, but he is even more so for services to be rendered to him: he is a father-in-law mad about his son-in-law. In the first place, it is essential that the son-in-law should never succeed in discharging his obligations; next – and this is more important – that the girl who has been given in marriage should suffer from a deficiency which, without impairing her mediatory function in the marriage, prevents her father's son-in-law becoming a husband to her. The wife, who is negativized at the outset, offers a striking analogy with the husband of the girl mad about honey, except that in Woodpecker's case the negativity occurs on the psychological level (that is, figuratively), whereas in the girl's case it occurs on the physical level, that is, literally. Anatomically speaking, the wooden bride is not a woman but rather a means whereby her father can acquire a son-in-law. Psychologically speaking, Woodpecker in the Chaco myths is not a man. The idea of marriage fills him with terror and his one concern is about the kind of reception he will be given by his parents-in-law: he is anxious only to be a son-in-law, and as a husband he is 'wooden', if we take the expression this time in its metaphorical sense.

Now, the Chaco myths are careful to present the character of the Sun in two different lights. He is shown first as a father who is unable to supply his daughter with the honey she likes; unable, therefore, to 'satisfy' her in an alimentary sense, just as the father of the wooden bride is unable to give her a sexual outlet. Secondly, the Sun in the Chaco myths is greedy, and so obsessed with one particular kind of food, the lewo fish, similar to cayman, that he sends his son-in-law to his death in order to catch them. This two-fold and fundamental inversion of the Guiana myths, in which a greedy father-in-law puts his son-in-law, the Sun, to the test, can be represented as follows:

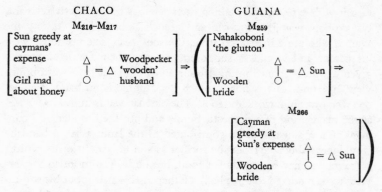

Through the Guiana myths, therefore, we glimpse, in an inverted form, the Chaco myths which were our starting-point: the Sun as father becomes Sun as son-in-law, that is, the relevant kinship bond changes from consanguinity to an affinal relationship. Sun, the examiner, becomes a Sun who is examined. The psychological apathy of the husband changes into the physical apathy of the woman. The girl mad about honey becomes the wooden bride. Lastly, and most importantly, the Chaco myths end with the drying up of the lakes and with the fish-caymans being thrown out of the water, whereas the Guiana myths conclude with the cayman either taking refuge in water, or being thrown back into the water.

I have shown on several occasions that the cayman stands in an oppositional relationship to the otters. The contrast becomes still more marked, if we note that the otters play the part of voluble animals, that is, either instruct or teach, whereas it is generally believed by the Indians of tropical America that caymans have no tongues. The belief is found among the Arawak of Guiana (Brett 1, p. 383), as is testified by the following rhymed text

> Alligators – wanting tongues –
> Show (and share) their father's wrongs.[13]

> (Brett, 2, p. 133)

The Mundurucu have a similar kind of story (M_{270}). The cayman was a glutton who devoured his sons-in-law one after the other. In order to save the life of the last son-in-law, the Indians hurled into the

---

[13] This belief is contrary to that held by the ancient Egyptians, who considered that the absence of a tongue added to the alligator's prestige: 'It is the only animal which has no tongue, because the divine word needs neither voice nor tongue' (Plutarch, § XXXIX).

monster's mouth a red-hot stone which burnt up his tongue. Since that time the cayman has been without a tongue and has a stone in its belly (Kruse 2, p. 627).

On the other hand, the otters are the rivals of the Sun in myths in which the latter appears as master of fishing or of fish ponds. In Guiana, as well as in the Chaco, fishing is an activity carried out during the dry season, as is evidenced by information from various sources, and in particular by the beginning of an Arecuna myth: 'At that time, all the rivers dried up and there was a great abundance of fish ... ' (K.-G. 1, p. 40). Conversely, the cayman, which needs water, plays the part of the master of rain in the Chaco myths. Both species are associated with water, but are also opposed to each other in respect of water; one needs a lot of water, the other very little.

In the Waiwai myths dealing with the origin of the Shodewika feast (M_{271}, M_{288}), there is a woman who has a boa as a pet. But she only gives it small rodents to eat and keeps the large game for herself (cf. M_{241}). The snake becomes angry, swallows her up and disappears to the bottom of the river. The husband gets help from the otters, which trap the snake by creating rapids and waterfalls (cf. M_{266}). They extract the woman's bones from the snake's belly and kill it. Its blood turns the river red. The birds come to bathe there and acquire a brilliant plumage, which is, however, made less brilliant again by a subsequent shower of rain against which each species protects itself as best it can. This is how birds came to acquire their distinctive plumage (Fock, pp. 63-5, cf. Derbyshire, pp. 92-3). So, the blood from the snake ($\equiv$ penis, cf. M_{268}) which devoured the woman here plays the same part as the blood of the woman, who was 'devoured' by the bird in search of food (M_{260}), when it accidentally made her a vagina. Although M_{271}, like M_{268}–M_{269}, contrasts the otters with the boa, which is a consumer and not a seducer of the woman, it is worth noting that the Tacana, who often reverse the great mythical themes of tropical America, regard otters and caymans as being in correlation with, rather than in opposition to, each other: they are not opponents but allies (H.-H., pp. 344-8, 429-30).[14]

[14] The crocodile–otter pair also appears in South-East Asia, a coincidence which appears all the more curious when we remember that many other themes are common to America and that part of the world, in particular a story about the marriage of a human and a bee-woman, who lost human form because her husband broke the rule she had laid down about not mentioning her presence (Evans, *text no. 48*). As regards the crocodile–otter pair, cf. also the following: 'They are wicked, incestuous men. They do as the horse does with the snake, the crocodile with the otter, the hare with the fox ... ' (Lafont, *text no. 45*).

The preceding discussion amounts to no more than a preliminary roughing-out of the subject. There is no point in disguising the fact that an exhaustive analysis of the group would raise serious difficulties, because of the multiplicity and diversity of the axes which would be required by any attempt to arrange the myths in order. Like all the other myths of the same group, those we are now considering depend upon rhetorical contrasts. The idea of consumption[15] is taken sometimes in the literal (alimentary) sense, sometimes in the figurative (sexual) sense, and on occasions in both senses at once. This happens in M_{269}, where the woman actually eats her seducer, while he is 'eating' her in the South American meaning of the term, that is, copulating with her. Furthermore, the links between the pairs of opposites are characterized by synecdoche (the cayman eats the fish which *form part* of the Sun's food) or metaphor (the Sun's only food is fish which are *like* caymans). Finally, these relationships, which are sufficiently complex in themselves, can be non-reflexive, but all taken literally or all taken figuratively: or reflexive, one being taken literally and the other figuratively. This situation is illustrated by the strange, partly erotic, partly alimentary marriage between the cayman and the wooden bride in M_{269}. If, for the sake of experiment, we decide to simplify the equations by disregarding contrasts of a metalinguistic nature, it is possible to integrate the most characteristic figures in the Guiana and Chaco myths by means of a diagram:

In the Chaco, the Sun feeds at the 'caymans' ' expense, and the latter at the expense of Woodpecker, Sun's son-in-law. In Guiana, the cayman feeds at the expense of the Sun and Woodpecker at the expense (but, in actual fact, to the advantage) of the latter's wife: the wooden bride. Finally, among the Cubeo, the cayman and the wooden bride feed (he, metaphorically, she, by synecdoche) on each other. Consequently, from the point of view of the spatial and temporal remoteness of the terms, the gap is greatest in the Chaco myths, and smallest in

[15] TRANSLATORS' NOTE: The author uses the French word *consommation*, which has the two meanings of 'consumption' and 'consummation'.

those of the Cubeo, while the Guiana myths occupy a middle position. Now the Chaco and Cubeo myths are also those whose respective conclusions are most exactly alike, although one gives an inverted picture of the other. At the close of M_{216}, the Sun sends his son-in-law to the lake to fish for fish-caymans, but the latter eat the bird. Sun then dries up the lake with fire, opens the monster's jaw and releases his son-in-law, who is in a sense 'de-eaten'. In M_{269}, the Sun sends the cayman to look for fire (a fire-brand) and his (the Sun's) wife eats him up. Sun closes up the victim's gaping belly and throws the cayman into the water, where, from now on, its fate will be to be hunted and then eaten.

No information is available about cayman-hunting among the Cubeo, but we are better informed in connection with Guiana, where the climatic conditions (in the eastern part at least) are practically the same as those in the Uaupés basin. In Guiana, the cayman is an important source of food; the natives eat both its eggs and its flesh, especially the tail (which is white and very delicately flavoured, as I was able to observe on many occasions). According to Gumilla (quoted by Roth 2, p. 206), the cayman is hunted in winter-time during the rise in the river when fish are scarce. We have less definite information about the Yaruro in the interior of Venezuela: it would seem that the small cayman, *Crocodilus babu*, is hunted all the year round except from May till September, when the main rainy season occurs (Leeds). However, the contrast pointed out by Gumilla between fishing and cayman-hunting seems to be indicated by Petrullo's observation (p. 200) that the Yaruro fish 'when they can find neither crocodiles nor tortoises'.

If it were legitimate to generalize this contrast[16] it would perhaps provide us with an explanation of the inversion which occurs when we move from the Chaco to the Guiana myths. The former are concerned with honey, and honey is gathered during the dry season, which in the Chaco, Guiana and the Uaupés basin is also the fishing season.

The Guiana myths effect a transformation of the Chaco myths along two axes. They state figuratively what the others state literally. And in the last stage at least, the message they transmit is not so much concerned with honey – a natural product, the existence of which testifies to the continuity of the transition from nature to culture – as with the

[16] Without, however, attempting to extend it beyond the Guiana region. The Siriono, who are skilled cayman-hunters but very poor fishermen, carry out both activities chiefly during the dry season (Holmberg, pp. 26–7).

arts of civilization, which provide evidence of the discontinuity between nature and culture, or again of the organization of the animal kingdom into graded species, which establishes discontinuity at the very heart of nature. Now, the Guiana myths lead into cayman-*hunting*, an occupation carried out during the *rainy* season, and as such incompatible with *fishing*, the masters of which are the Sun (also master of the *dry* season) and the otters (homologous with the Sun in respect of water); the otters can therefore be said to be doubly in opposition to the cayman.

However, the first Guiana myths we studied were expressly concerned with honey. We ought, then, to be able to find, at the very heart of the Guiana myths, and expressed with even greater vigour, the transformations which we first noticed when comparing the Chaco myths with certain specimens only of the Guiana myths. In this respect, particular attention must be given to the species of tree used for the carving of the bridegroom in M_{241}, and of the bride in all the others. When the theme appeared for the first time, that is in M_{241} (then in $M_{263a, b}$), the bridegroom or bride came from the trunk of a palm tree: *Euterpe* or *Mauritia*. On the other hand, in M_{259} and M_{266}, it is the wild plum tree which is mentioned (*Spondias lutea*). A great many points of contrast can be noted between these two families.

One includes palm trees, the other anacardiaceae. The trunk of the palm tree is soft inside, whereas the inside of the plum tree is hard. The myths lay great stress on this contrast, particularly the Wilbert versions in which birds twist or break their beaks on the hard wood of the plum tree (M_{260}), whereas the husband's companions have no difficulty in breaking the trunk of the palm tree ($M_{263a, b}$) with their axes. A third point is that, although the Indians eat the fruit of the *Mauritia* palm, it is the starch extracted from the trunk which provides the basic Warao diet. On the other hand, only the fruit of the plum tree can be eaten. Fourthly, the preparation of the starch is a complicated procedure, which is described in great detail in M_{243} because the acquisition of this technique symbolizes the attainment of culture. The palm tree, *Mauritia flexuosa*, exists in the wild state, but the Warao cultivate palm groves so methodically that some observers have claimed that they actually practise 'arboriculture'. It will be remembered that the starch from the palm tree is the only food common to both gods and men. In all these respects, the *Mauritia* palm contrasts with the *Spondias*, since the plum tree grows completely wild and its fruit provides food for both humans and animals, as M_{264} reminds us in the tapir episode.[17] Finally, and most important of all, the edible starch extracted from the trunk of the palm tree (which can easily be split open) maintains a seasonal contrast with the fruit of the plum tree – the trunk of which is hard to pierce.

The contrast is manifested in two ways. First, the trunk of the plum tree is not only hard, it is also believed to be rot-proof. The plum tree is said to be the only tree the tortoise is afraid to have fall on it. With other species, it is just a question of waiting patiently until the wood rots and then the tortoise is free again. The plum tree does not rot; it even goes on producing buds after it has been torn up by the roots, and new branches start growing which imprison the tortoise (Ihering, under 'jaboti'; Stradelli 1, under 'tapereyua-yua'). Spruce (Vol. 1, pp. 162–3), who gives this same member of the anacardiaceae another scientific name: *Mauria juglandifolia* Bth., stresses the fact that 'it possesses great vitality and a stake cut from this wood almost always takes root and grows into a tree'. Now it is well known that, once a palm tree has been felled, or simply had its terminal bud removed, it never grows again.

Secondly, in the case of the *Mauritia flexuosa* (which for the Warao is the most strangely 'marked' palm tree), Roth points out that the extraction of the starch takes place when the tree begins to fructify (2, p. 215). In connection with Roth's observation, I have already noted (p. 186, n. 5) that South American palms bear fruit at the beginning of the rainy season and sometimes even during the dry season. Wilbert, on the other hand, states clearly that the starch is available as a fresh food 'during the greater part of the year' (9, p. 16), but this discrepancy does not necessarily affect the semantic position of palm starch in the myths. It will be remembered that we met with a similar kind of difficulty in connection with Chaco myths, because of the tendency to associate manioc with dry-season foods, although it is available all through the year. Manioc, of course, as I said at the time, being available *even* during the dry season, happens to be more definitely connected with the dry season than with the rainy season, when the various foods available only during this latter period of the year have greater prominence. It is worth noting, in this respect, that the Warao use the same word, aru, to denote both manioc starch and starch from the

---

[17] The contrast between *Spondias* and *Euterpe* is more limited, resulting as it does from the absence of any competition between men and animals. The fruit is gathered while still hard and has to be softened in warm water, as has already been explained.

palm, and that the two products are closely associated in M_{243} and M_{244}.

As regards the ripening of the fruit of *Spondias lutea*, we have precise information concerning the Amazonian region thanks to the excellent commentary with which Tastevin follows up several Tupi myths, to which I shall have occasion to return. The etymology put forward by Tastevin and by Spruce (*loc. cit.*) of the popular name for the wild plum: tapiriba, tapereba; (in Tupi) tapihira-hiwa, 'tapir's tree', seems to me, by reason of its mythic overtones (cf. for instance, M_{264}) more probable than that derived from tapera, 'waste land, deserted area'. The fruit of *Spondias* ripens at the end of January, in other words right in the middle of the Amazonian rainy season (Tastevin 1, p. 247), and in Guiana, at the end of the rainy season (one of two) which lasts from mid-November to mid-February.

So, at the same time as we move from a tree containing an *internal* food inside its *trunk* to another which bears an *external* food on its *branches*, what we might call the meteorological 'centre of gravity' of the myths shifts from the dry to the rainy season: this is a shift similar in nature to the one we were obliged to suppose in order to account for the transition, in the Guiana myths, from the gathering of honey and fishing, which are both dry-season occupations, to cayman-hunting, which is a rainy-season occupation; similar in nature, also, to the shift we observed when comparing the Chaco with the Guiana myths: in the Chaco myths, the *water withdrawn* from the caymans (dry season) is a transformation of *imposed water* (rainy season) in the Guiana myths. Moreover, the arrival of the rainy season is announced explicitly at the end of the Macusi version (M_{266}), and implicitly at the end of the Carib version (M_{264}), since throughout the whole of the Guiana area, the appearance of the Pleiades marks the new year and the beginning of the rains.

A further aspect of the palm/plum pair of opposites is worthy of attention. When the wooden bridegroom or bride comes from the trunk of a palm tree, he or she is a provider of food. They keep their spouses supplied with starch (the bride in $M_{263a, b}$) or with fish (bridegroom in M_{241}), and we know that, from the point of view of the Warao, the starch-fish group constitutes 'real food' (Wilbert 9, p. 16). But when the wooden bride originates from the trunk of a plum tree, she plays the part of mistress and not of provider of food. Furthermore, she is a negative mistress (she cannot be penetrated) rather than a positive provider of food. The axe will destroy the provider of food, but complete the mistress. Symmetrically, although the plum tree is shown to be a source of food (in M_{264}), the food it provides exists only to be denied (to the two brothers, by the tapir).

It is at once obvious that the series of 'wooden brides', when looked at from this angle, is incomplete and must be integrated into the larger group, the study of which was begun in *The Raw and the Cooked*. The star, who is the wife of a mortal in the Ge myths (M_{87}–M_{93}), combines in her person the two roles of impenetrable mistress (because of her chastity) and provider of food (since she introduces cultivated plants, correlative with *Mauritia* which, within the category of wild vegetation, is the equivalent of cultivated plants).[18]

Now, I showed in the previous volume (pp. 179–80) that this particular group of Ge myths could be transformed into a group of Tupi-Tucuna myths, in which the supernatural wife comes from the fruit, fresh or rotten, of a tree. There is, therefore, a whole series of what might be called 'vegetable' wives:

GUIANA	TUPI-TUCUNA	GE
		STAR
		cannibalistic vegetarian
	FRUIT	
	rotten fresh	
TRUNK		
soft hard		
(palm (plum		
tree) tree)		

The central characters are negative mistresses, either psychologically or physically. One is pierced for her own good; the others are raped to their detriment. In both cases, the creature responsible is a god-opossum, a foul-smelling beast, or a bird which is called, precisely, 'stinking one'. It is all the more remarkable that the young girl who begins her human existence in this way should, in the Guiana myths, become the mother of twins who can talk while still unborn, and should be reminiscent of the heroine of a famous Tupi myth (M_{96}): the woman who loses her way because the first child with which she is pregnant refused to guide her, and who arrives at the house of an individual who makes her pregnant with a second child and is subsequently changed into an opossum. So the heroines occupying a middle position

[18] Brett had already pointed out that, among the Warao, the cultivation of the *Mauritia flexuosa* was tantamount to a genuine agricultural activity (1, pp. 166, 175).

are either deflowered or raped by foul-smelling beasts. The heroines occupying polar positions are themselves opossums. This has already been demonstrated in *The Raw and the Cooked* in connection with Star, the wife of a mortal, and we now discover that the situation is repeated at the other end of the axis: like Star, the bride carved from a palm tree is a provider of food. And both are destroyed by their husbands' accomplices: sexually in the case of Star, who is raped by her brothers-in-law; alimentarily in the case of the wooden bride, who is torn to pieces by her lover's companions who want to get at the food inside her.

A separate study of this paradigmatic group, which I have here reduced to its simplest form, but which would reveal other levels when subjected to close investigation, would be worth undertaking for its own sake.[19] I shall limit myself to calling attention to one point. The Guiana myths which have just been analysed (M_{259}, M_{264}, M_{266}), when compared with the rest of South American mythology, reveal a peculiar constructional feature in the sense that their second part – the journey made by the twins' mother – reproduces almost literally the first half of the great Tupi myth I mentioned in the preceding paragraph. This inversion provides additional proof of the fact that the course we have been pursuing from the beginning of this book is taking us round the back, as it were, of South American mythology. This has been clear ever since the reappearance, at the end of my study of the myths about the origin of honey, of the myths explaining the origin of tobacco, to which we were very close at the beginning. But the fact that we now come full circle with the myth about the twins, which has already been encountered twice in the course of our investigation, can only mean that the world of mythology is spherical, in other words, forms a closed system. However, from our present standpoint we are seeing all the major mythical themes on the reverse side. This makes the task of interpreting them more arduous and complex, rather as if we were having to decipher the theme of a tapestry from the intricate tangle of threads at the back, and which blurs a picture that was much clearer when we were looking at it on the right side, as we did in *The Raw and the Cooked*.

But what is the meaning of wrong side and right side in this context? And would the meaning of the two sides not simply have been reversed if I had chosen to begin at the other end? I hope to show that this is not

[19] Starting in particular from the complete text of a Kalapalo myth (M_{47}: in Baldus 4, p. 45), in which the following interesting transformation is to be noted: *woman without vagina* ⇒ *woman with piranha fish teeth*, which enable her to eat fish raw.

so. The wrong side and the right side are defined objectively by the native way of looking at the problem, in which the mythology of cooking develops in the right direction, i.e. from nature to culture, whereas the mythology of honey proceeds contrariwise, backwards from culture to nature; in other words, the two courses link up the same points, but their semantic charge is very different and consequently there is no parity between them.

Let us now summarize the fundamental features of this last set of myths. It relates to what might be called *misappropriation of an affine*. The story does not always concern the same kind of relative, and the culprit does not always occupy the same place in the pattern of marriage relationships. The Chaco heroine appropriates for her own use the supplies (of honey) which her husband owed first and foremost to his parents-in-law. Conversely, the greedy father-in-law in the Guiana myth (M_{259}) appropriates for himself supplies which his son-in-law would have owed to his daughter, once he had acquitted himself of his obligations towards the father-in-law. Between the two, and transposing the system of tribute-owing affines from the alimentary to the sexual level, the sisters-in-law in M_{235} try to appropriate for themselves the husband's love for his wife, and the old frog in M_{241} does the same, on the alimentary as well as the sexual plane, with the food supplies the hero owes to his mother, and with the sexual obligations he would have owed to a legitimate wife who would not have been a mistress, and would not have passed herself off as a mother. Consequently a relationship by marriage offers the culprit an opportunity of 'short-circuiting' his parents, his child or his affine. This is the sociological common denominator of the group. But there also exists a cosmological common denominator, the formula of which is more complex. According to whether the chief character is a woman (who fills a pot with the blood from her maidenhead) or a man (who does likewise with his foul-smelling excrement) – both bearing witness to the fact that the attainment of complete femininity or complete masculinity implies retrogression towards filth – a kind of structural order makes its appearance, either on the level of nature (but which gradually becomes weaker), or on the level of culture (but which gradually moves further away). The natural order grows weaker; the discontinuity which it manifests is merely a remnant of some previous richer continuity, since the birds would all have been red if the blood from the deflowering had not left behind a residue of bile and impurities, or if the rain had not washed it off in places. And culture moves upwards (M_{243}) or further into the distance (M_{241}, M_{258}), since men would have been better provided as regards spiritual help and the arts of civilization if their descent from the upper world had not unfortunately been barred by a woman pregnant with child, or if, because of a frog full of honey, the cultural hero had not been obliged to abandon them. Two females, one big with honey, the other big with child, interrupt, then, the process of mediation which the sexual discharge of blood, or the alimentary discharge of excrement, have on the contrary precipitated.

Nevertheless, in spite of this common armature, differences appear within the group and it is essential that they should be clarified.

Let us first of all compare, from the point of view of their construction, the three myths from the Roth collection, on which the fourth variation is fundamentally based. I mean the Warao myth about the wooden bride (M_{259}), the Carib myth about the frog who was the jaguar's mother (M_{264}) and, lastly, the Macusi myth about the wooden bride (M_{266}).

In the Warao myth, the heroine's adventures unfold according to an admirably regular plan: after being made complete by the bunia bird (who pierces a vagina for her), she is made pregnant by the sun (who fills her). She next swallows the parasite (which also fills her), and the frog empties her corpse of the twins which filled it.

The second and third episodes denote, therefore, a process of filling either from above or from below; one passive, the other active; and as far as the consequences are concerned, the latter is negative (involving the heroine's death), the former positive (since it makes it possible for her to give life).

Now, can it be said that episodes (1) and (4) contrast with the two intervening ones, in so far as they denote a process of emptying as opposed to filling? It seems clear that this is true of the fourth episode, in which the heroine's body is in fact emptied of the children it contained. The first episode, however, which consists of the opening up of the absent vagina, hardly seems comparable to the other in any strict sense.

It is as if mythic thought had been aware of the difficulty and had at once set about solving it. The Warao version introduces an incident, which may seem superfluous, but only at first sight. In order for the heroine to become a real woman, not only has the bunia bird to open her up, but her father has to set to work again (although he has just proclaimed his incompetence) by extracting from the freshly hollowed out vagina a snake which constitutes an additional obstacle to penetration. So the heroine was not just blocked, she was full; and the incident of the snake has no other apparent purpose than to change perforation into evacuation. Once this has been accepted, the construction of the myth can be summarized in the following diagram:

(1) heroine pierced by a bird, allowing evacuation of snake } *passive* { low anterior } heroine emptied			(+)
(2) heroine made pregnant by the sun } *passive* { low anterior } heroine filled			(+)
(3) heroine ingests a deadly parasite } *active* { high anterior } heroine filled			(−)
(4) heroine ripped open by frog } *passive* { low anterior } heroine emptied			(−)

If we remember the point, which is expressed in the diagram, that episodes (2) and (4) form a pair (since the frog *empties* the heroine's body of the very children with which the Sun had *filled* her), it follows that episodes (1) and (3) must also form a pair, that is: *snake evacuated from below, passively, with beneficial results / parasite ingested from above, actively, with maleficent results.* From this viewpoint, the myth consists of two superimposable sequences, each formed by two episodes which are in opposition to each other (*heroine emptied / filled : heroine filled / emptied*) and each in contrast to the episode in the other sequence of which it forms the counterpart.

Why this reduplication? We already know one reason, since it has been confirmed on several occasions that the contrast between the literal meaning and the figurative meaning is a constant feature of the group. In this instance, the first two episodes describe figuratively what the last two express literally: the heroine is first of all made 'eatable' (= copulable) in order to be 'eaten'. After which, she is made eatable (killed) in order to be, in fact, eaten in the other versions.

But a careful reading of the myth reveals that the reduplication of the sequences may have another function. It would seem that the first part of the myth – of which, it will be remembered, the Sun is the hero – progresses according to a seasonal cycle, the stages of which are indicated by the tasks imposed on Sun-son-in-law: hunting, fishing, burning, planting, building; whereas the second part, which starts with the Sun's journey westwards, describes a daily cycle. Expressed in this way, the hypothesis may seem unlikely, but a comparison with the other versions will give it some initial confirmation. Later, in a subsequent volume, with the help of other myths, I hope to show the importance of the contrast between seasonal periodicity and daily periodicity and to demonstrate that a close correspondence exists between this contrast and the contrast between the 'styles' in the construction of the narrative.[20]

Finally, and still in connection with M_{259}, it will be noted that, on the etiological level, the myth seems to have one function and one only: that of explaining the origin of a fire-kindling technique by friction.

Let us now consider the way in which the Carib (M_{264}) tell the same story. It will be remembered (p. 219) that they start off straight away with the second part. The daily sequence (the journey in the direction of the Sun) therefore occurs at the beginning. Furthermore, correlatively with the omission of the first part, a new part, dealing with the adventures of the two brothers at the house of another frog, then at the home of a female tapir, is added to the second. There are consequently two parts, and it would seem clear that the one which comes last in the Carib myth, and which is made up of a succession of episodes, recreates the seasonal cycle of hunting, burning and gathering of wild fruits, which start to ripen in January. If this interpretation is correct, the order of the two sequences, the seasonal and the daily, is reversed when we move from the Warao to the Carib version.

The inversion in the order of sequences is accompanied by a complete reversal of the system of contrasts which helped us to define the reciprocal relationships between the four experiences undergone by the heroine. The second experience is now put first, since the story begins when the heroine is pregnant by the Sun, whereas the fourth (the emptying out of the children from the heroine's body) remains unchanged. But between the first and fourth episodes, two new episodes are inserted – (2) the heroine hides in a jar (which she fills), and (3) she is 'emptied' out of this receptacle. This would seem to mean that the Warao version persistently treats the heroine as if she were a 'container', which is alternately emptied (episodes (1) and (4)) and filled (episodes (2) and (3)). On the other hand, the Carib version defines her by means of an oppositional relationship: *container/content*, in respect of which the

---

[20] Cf. in the meantime my report in the *Annuaire du Collège de France*, 64th year, Paris 1964, pp. 227–30. On the subject of the link between the dry season and the tasks imposed on the son-in-law, see Preuss I, pp. 476–99.

heroine plays the part of agent or victim, being herself either container or content, with beneficent or maleficent consequences:

(1) heroine made pregnant by the sun	}	container	(+)
(2) heroine filling a jar	}	content	(+)
(3) heroine emptied from the jar	}	content	(−)
(4) heroine disembowelled by jaguar	}	container	(−)

Now, it is episodes (1) and (4), on the one hand, and (2) and (3), on the other, which form pairs. Within each of the two sequences, the episodes are repeated, provided there is inversion of container and content, whereas, between one sequence and the next, the episodes which correspond to each other form a chiasmus.

The two transformations in mythical structure which we have observed as taking place at different levels, one formal, the other semantic, correspond to a third transformation which occurs on the etiological level. The Carib version merely sets out to explain the origin of certain constellations: Hyades, Pleiades and Orion,[21] which in this region are well known as heralding a change of season. To the ample information I have already given on this subject (*RC*, pp. 218–19) we can add the evidence supplied by Ahlbrink (under 'sirito'), which relates to Guiana communities who are Carib both in speech and culture: 'When *sirito*, the Pleiad, becomes visible in the evening (in April), thunder can be heard. Sirito is angry because men have cut off one of Ipétiman's (Orion's) legs. And Ipétiman is coming nearer. Ipétiman appears in May.'

Let us accept the fact, then, that M_{264} deals by implication with the beginning of the 'main' rainy season (there are four seasons in Guiana, two wet and two dry), which lasts from mid-May to mid-August. This hypothesis presents two advantages. First of all, it creates a link between the Carib version (M_{264}) and the Macusi version (M_{266}), which deals explicitly with the origin of rain and storms: these are brought about by the heroine's bouts of sadness when her tears stream down the mountain slopes after she has taken up her abode at the top

[21] As does a Tupi variant (M_{264b}) found by Barbosa Rodrigues (I, pp. 257–62), but it refers only to the Pleiades.

of Roraima. Secondly, it is possible to verify objectively, by means of astronomical and climatic references, my earlier hypothesis that the myths now being studied present the reverse side of a pattern, the right side of which we followed in our study of the Ge and Bororo myths in *The Raw and the Cooked*. The attempt to integrate the Ge and Bororo myths, which were seasonal in character, led to the following equation:

a) Pleiades-Orion : Corvus :: dry season : rainy season

We can now verify that, in the Guiana myths, the Pleiades-Orion group heralds the rainy season. What of the Corvus constellation? When it reaches its highest point in the evening in July, it is associated with a divinity responsible for the violent storms which characterize the close of the rainy season (cf. *RC*, p. 231; and in connection with the mythology of storms during the July–October period in the Caribbean Sea and the Big Dipper – the right ascension of which is close to that of the Corvus – L.-N. 3, pp. 126–8); whereas in Guiana also, the rising of Berenice's Hair (which has the same right ascension as the Big Dipper and the Corvus) denotes drought. We thus arrive at the following equation, which is the reverse of the previous one:

b) Pleiades-Orion : Corvus :: rainy season : dry season

This provides a link-up with the Macusi version (M_{266}) which, as we have just seen, deals explicitly with the origin of the rainy season. Furthermore, unlike the two myths we discussed previously, M_{266} has a double etiological function. In so far as it deals with the origin of the rainy season, it coincides with M_{264}: in so far as it explains the origin of fire-kindling by percussion (which the crane teaches to the hero) it coincides with M_{259}.

There are, nevertheless, two differences. The allusion to the rainy season found in M_{266} is *diurnal* (the tears can be seen forming torrents), whereas that in M_{264} is *nocturnal* (certain constellations are visible). And whereas M_{259} describes fire-kindling by *friction* (with two pieces of wood), M_{266} is concerned with fire-kindling by *percussion* (with two stones), a method with which the Guiana Indians are also familiar.

Consequently, as might be expected, M_{266} combines in a single myth episodes which belong by rights to each of the two other versions. It begins with the story of the wooden bride, which is missing from the Carib version, and ends with the twins' adventures after their stay in the frog's house, which are absent from the Warao version. But at the same time it reverses all the details: the father-in-law is put to the test, not the son-in-law; the heroine is pierced by the woodpecker, not by the bunia bird. Although the heroine becomes the prey of the cannibalistic jaguar, she does not die, but is restored to life again. The hero devours the red-hot coals, thus defeating the frog's purpose. It will also be noticed that the Warao bunia is prompted by lust, the Macusi woodpecker by hunger: he therefore eats the heroine in the literal sense. Symmetrically, in the second half of the Macusi version, the jaguar eats her only in the figurative sense, because he dies before he has digested his prey, and because the latter is restored to life almost as soon as she has been drawn out from the animal's belly (cf. above, p. 222).

The synthesis of the Warao and Carib versions, effected by the Macusi version by dint of a great many inversions, reveals that on the return journey we are meeting with myths which are simultaneously concerned with the origin of both fire and water, and therefore situated on the same mythological 'latitude' as the Bororo (M_1) and Sherente (M_{12}) myths we encountered on the outward journey, and which were characterized by the same etiological duality. The Macusi version therefore provides a particularly favourable opportunity to take stock of the situation.

The three myths M_{259}, M_{264} and M_{266} are concerned either with the origin of fire on the cultural level (friction or percussion), or with the origin of water on the level of nature (rainy season), or with both together.

Now, before fire was produced by means of cultural devices, it already existed in natural forms: it was vomited up by an animal, the frog, which itself is associated with water. Symmetrically (and on this point the evidence supplied by M_{266} is essential), before water was produced by natural means (rain), it already existed as a cultural achievement, since Makunaima, a veritable engineer of public works, first caused it to rise to the surface in a canal he had dug and in which he launched the first canoe.[22] Now, Makunaima, who devours red-hot coals, is associated with fire just as the frog is associated with water. The two etiological systems are symmetrical. Consequently, in the myths we are studying, the rainy season makes its appearance in the form of a transition from nature to culture. Yet, in the two instances, fire (originally contained in the frog's body) or water (subsequently contained in the mother's body) *both spread* – the former into the trees,

[22] The creation myths of the Yaruro also present the digging of rivers to be the necessary pre-condition of the appearance of water (Petrullo, p. 239).

from which sticks are taken to make fire, the latter to the surface of the earth, in the natural hydrographic system (in contrast to the artificial system first created by the demiurge). In both cases, then, we are dealing with a process of dispersion. The fundamentally regressive character of all the myths in the group has been exemplified once again.

How, then, are we to explain the ambiguity of the myths, which is clearly a result of their double etiological function? In order to reply to this question we must look more closely at the character of the crane which, in M_{266}, shows the heroes how to produce fire by percussion.

The bird referred to by Roth in English as a *crane* plays an important part in the Guiana myths. As we shall see later (M_{327}–M_{328}), it is the crane which brings back to man, or enables the humming-bird to bring back, the tobacco which was growing on a reputedly inaccessible island. Now, another Carib myth in Roth's collection (1, p. 192) begins as follows: 'There was once an Indian who was extremely fond of smoking: morning, noon and night he would bring out his little bit of cotton, strike the stones together, make fire and then light his tobacco.' It would therefore seem that, through the intermediary agency of the crane, the device of producing fire by percussion is linked with tobacco.

When it carried the humming-bird to the tobacco island, the crane placed it on the back of its own thighs, and when it relieved itself, the humming-bird's face got dirtied (Roth 1, p. 335); it is therefore a bird inclined towards defecation. Perhaps there is a connection between the crane's connotation with filth and the feeding habits of the great stilt-birds, which live on the dead fish left behind in the river-beds during the dry season (cf. M_{331} and Ihering, under 'jabiru'). During the funeral rites carried out by the Arawak of Guiana, an emblem representing the white crane was solemnly paraded when the small bones of the deceased were being burnt (Roth 2, pp. 643–50). The Umutina call one episode of their funeral ceremonies king-fisher (Schultz 2, p. 262). Lastly, since at least one myth we are dealing with uses an astronomical coding, we should not forget that farther south, among various tribes including the Bororo and the Mataco, part of the Orion constellation bears the name of a stilt-bird, while the West Indian Carib give the name 'the Boatbill' (a kind of small heron) to a star which would appear to be part of the Big Dipper and is supposed to be responsible for thunder and tempests (L.-N., *loc. cit.*, p. 129). If this coincidence is not a pure accident, it provides yet another illustration of the inversion of the pattern of constellations to which I have already drawn attention (p. 242).

Be that as it may, the appearance of the crane in M_{266} as the bird which introduces fire-kindling by percussion (and tobacco in another myth) adds weight to the supposition that myths about the origin of honey in a sense anticipate myths about the origin of tobacco, the characteristic themes of which emerge in succession in the series of transformations: a cannibalistic jaguar killed by a trunk covered with thorns, and otters playing the part of 'blocked' characters (M_{241}). The same transformations might well throw light on the ambiguity of myths which operate simultaneously as myths about the origin of fire (by friction or percussion), and myths about the origin of water (the rainy season and the hydrographic network). For, if it is true, as I hope I have been able to show, that tobacco, when smoked, has an affinity with fire and with honey diluted in water, it becomes comprehensible that myths which deal simultaneously with the etiology of honey and tobacco (and in fact change from one type into the other) manifest the ambiguity I have referred to by allowing us to glimpse the origin of fire, an element which is congruous with tobacco, through – as it were – the origin of water, an element which is congruous with honey. In the Ge myths about the origin of fire (M_7–M_{12}), the jaguar appeared as master of fire and cooked meat at a time when men had to be content with raw meat; and it was the jaguar's human wife who showed cannibalistic tendencies. The Guiana myths reverse all these data, since fire-kindling techniques (and no longer fire itself) are obtained, or invented, in the Guiana myths by human heroes, as a result of their mother having been devoured by a cannibalistic jaguar.

The myths refer to two techniques: friction or gyration, and percussion. According to M_{259}, the fire which is now produced by friction was originally the fire *vomited* up by the frog, while M_{266} tells us that it was the crane, a bird to which another Guiana myth attributes a strong tendency to defecate, which instigated fire-kindling by percussion. Between these two myths, a third occupies an intermediary position:

M_{272}. Taulipang. 'The origin of fire'

In olden times, when men still knew nothing of fire, there lived an old woman called Pelénosamó. She piled wood up in her hearth and squatted on it. Flames then spurted from her anus and the wood caught fire. She ate her manioc cooked, whereas other people left theirs out in the heat of the sun. A little girl betrayed the old woman's secret. As she refused to give the fire, her arms and legs were bound, she was placed on some wood and her anus was forced open. Whereupon she excreted the fire, which changed into wató (= fire) stones, which make fire when they are rubbed together (K.-G. 1, p. 76 and Vol. III, pp. 48–9).

If we accept the two mythical propositions that fire made by friction was originally vomited, and fire made by percussion excreted, we arrive at the following equation:

$$\text{friction} : \text{percussion} :: \text{mouth} : \text{anus}$$

But in actual fact, further deductions can be made from the material at our disposal, for it lends itself to one in particular which can serve as a test for the method I am using.

It is well known that fire-kindling techniques by gyration (or by friction) have a sexual connotation in various parts of the world, and certainly in South America: the passive wood is said to be female, the stick which is rotated, or moved backwards and forwards, is said to be male. The rhetoric used in the myth transposes this instantly and universally recognizable sexual symbolism by giving it imaginary expression, since the sexual act (copulation) is replaced by a phenomenon relating to the digestive apparatus (vomiting). Furthermore, the female who is passive on the symbolic level becomes active on the imaginary level, and the organs respectively concerned are in one instance the vagina, in the other the mouth, both definable in terms of a contrast between low and high, and both being at the same time anterior (along an axis the other pole of which is occupied by posterior orifices):

symbolical level		*imaginary level*
O, passive	⇒	O, active
anterior	⇒	anterior
low	⇒	high

In the matter of fire-kindling techniques by percussion, ethnography provides no symbolic representations, the intuitive obviousness and general validity of which are comparable to those we have just mentioned. But M_{272}, reinforced by the recurrent position occupied by the crane in the myths (the old woman who excretes, the bird which excretes, both of them masters of fire-making by percussion), enables us to deduce the unknown symbolism of this technique *from its imaginary expression, which is all we have to go by.* We merely have to apply the same transformation rules as we did in the preceding case, where they were empirically verifiable. We thus obtain the following equations:

imaginary level		*symbolical level*
O, active	⇒	O, passive
posterior	⇒	posterior
low	⇒	high

Which organ, then, can be defined as posterior and high in a system in which the posterior, low position is occupied by the anus, and the anterior, high position by the mouth? We have no choice; it can only be the ear, as has been demonstrated, moreover, in connection with another problem (*RC*, p. 136). It follows, therefore, that on the imaginary (that is the mythic) level, vomiting is the opposite correlative of coitus, and defecation the opposite correlative of auditory communication.

It is at once clear how experience confirms the hypothesis obtained by deduction; percussion is noisy, friction is silent. This explains why it was the crane which initiated the former. There is some uncertainty about the identity of the bird Roth refers to as a 'crane'. There are indications in the source-book (Roth 1, pp. 646–7; 2, p. 338) which might lead us to conclude that the bird is a species of heron, and more precisely the bittern (*Botorus tigrinus*). But even if Roth was referring to a heron as a crane, the confusion is a particularly revealing one, for throughout the entire American continent and in other parts of the world too, myths are fond of introducing the crane because of its harsh cry;[23] the ardeidae, too, which might well be the species in question, owe their scientific name, which is derived from *Botorus butor* (bittern), to their cry, which apparently is like the bellowing of an ox or bull, or even of a jungle beast. The fire-kindling technique

[23] The cranes themselves seem to share this view, since an instance is quoted in which one of these birds, on losing its mate, developed a sentimental attachment to an iron bell, the sound of which reminded it of the cry of the absent bird (Thorpe, p. 416).

As regards the harsh call of the crane in the myths of North America, cf. Gatschet (p. 102): 'of all birds the Sandhill crane is the loudest and noisiest.' The Chippewa believe that members of the crane clan have powerful voices and are the tribe's orators (Kinietz in L.-S. 9, p. 154).

As regards China, cf. Granet (p. 504, n. 2): 'The sound of the drum is heard as far away as Lo-yang when *a white crane* [italic in the text] flies right into the Gate of Thunder,' and the reference to the Pi-fang bird, which 'resembles a crane, dances on one foot and produces fire' (p. 526).

It is all the more legitimate to emphasize these parallels since there is an anatomical, hence objective, basis for the crane family's reputation for noise. 'In most species the windpipe is convoluted in the males (not always in the females), entering behind the clavicles into a hollow space in the keel of the sternum' (A. L. Thomson, p. 61).

most prominently connected with noise is, then, the work of a noisy bird.

This technique is as quick as the other method is slow. The double contrast between: *quick, noisy,* and *slow, silent,* refers back to the more fundamental one, which I emphasized in *The Raw and the Cooked,* between what I called the burnt world and the rotten world; in that context, it was found at the very heart of the category of the rotten, where it was reflected in two modalities, which were respectively the mouldy (slow, silent) and the putrid (quick, noisy), this last modality, in fact, calling for a charivari. So at the same time as we again encounter in the myths the canonical contrast between the origin of water (congruous with the rotten) and that of fire (congruous with the burnt), we note the symmetrical appearance, within the category of burnt, of two cultural modalities: friction and percussion, the respective symbolic positions of which reflect in metonymic language (since it is a matter of two real causes producing the same effect) those which were occupied metaphorically (since the meanings in that case were psychological) by the natural modalities of the mouldy and the putrid, within the category of the rotten. To be convinced of this, we have only to compare the diagram on p. 339 of *RC* with the following one, which is its exact counterpart:

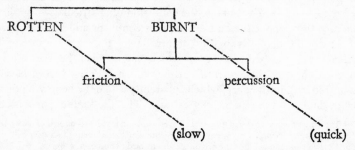

The transition from metaphor to metonymy (or the reverse), which has been illustrated in several places in the preceding pages, and to which I have drawn attention in other works (L.-S. 8, 9, 10), is typical of the development of a series of transformations by inversion when the intermediary stages are sufficiently numerous. Consequently, even in this instance, it is impossible that any real parity should appear between the beginning and the end, except for the inversion which generates the group. The group, being in a state of equilibrium along one axis, shows evidence of imbalance along another axis. This obligatory feature, which is inherent in mythic thought, protects its dynamic force while at the same time preventing it from ever becoming really static. In theory, if not in fact, there is no inertia in myth.

So, we have here an illustration, in the form of a special instance, of the canonical relationship which I described as follows in 1958 (L.-S. 5, p. 252):

$$f_{x(\text{a})} : f_{y(\text{b})} :: f_{x(\text{b})} : f_{(a-1)(\text{y})}$$

It was necessary to quote it at least once more as proof of the fact that I have never ceased to be guided by it since that time.

e. FIFTH VARIATION

[jaguar ⇒ jaguar] ↔ [○ ⇒ △]

In the preceding myths, the frog appeared as the jaguar's mother. I had already tried to solve this ethnozoological paradox in two ways: by showing that the frog and the bee have a correlational and oppositional relationship along an axis the two poles of which are formed by the rainy season and the dry season, and by revealing another correspondence, this time between the bee and the jaguar, since the latter plays the part of master of honey in the Tenetehara and Tembe myths (M_{188}, M_{189}). If the frog is congruous with the wet and the bee with the dry, it is easy to understand that the frog, in its capacity as mistress of celestial water (= the harbinger of the rainy season), could be complementary to the jaguar, whose position as master of fire has been established independently, and which is commutable with the bee.

But why do the northern Tupi look upon the jaguar as a master of honey? Let us go back and consider the four animals which the myths classify simultaneously in respect of both water and honey:

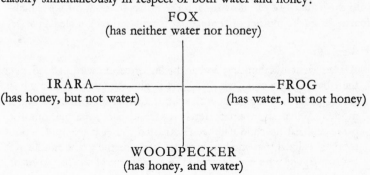

FOX
(has neither water nor honey)

IRARA
(has honey, but not water)

FROG
(has water, but not honey)

WOODPECKER
(has honey, and water)

So:

	water	honey
fox	−	−
irára	−	+
frog	+	−
woodpecker	+	+

Since the frog (in this instance, the cunauaru frog) possesses water, it must be the opposite of the jaguar, which has fire, by virtue of the equation: water = fire$^{(-1)}$ (cf. *RC*, pp. 189–91). Consequently, if the myth undertakes to relate these two animals to honey as well, it can only do so by respecting this major inversion; from which it follows that, since the frog does not possess honey, the jaguar does. This deduction restores the pattern, not only of the Tenetehara and Tembé myths, but also of the Warao myth (M_{235}), which lays down that, in respect of honey, water *is* fire (cf. above, p. 162).

My interpretation suggests that, in these same myths, there is a verifiable correspondence, on a different level, between the frog (the mistress of celestial water) and the cayman, whose semantic position is that of a master of terrestrial water (*RC*, p. 188). The cayman appears in M_{266} as a transformation of the *greedy* old man in M_{259}: and it is also symmetrical with the *greedy* frog in M_{241}: the latter steals the (future) civilizing hero from his mother in order to turn him into a husband capable of satisfying her sexually; the former gives his daughter, who is incapable of satisfying him sexually, to the (future) father of the civilizing hero.

Having clarified the rules governing the transformation of the frog into the jaguar, we can now broach the fifth variation, during which a female frog (the mother of the) jaguar is replaced by a male jaguar.

M_{273}. *Warao. 'The stolen child'*

A man went out hunting and in his absence his wife handed over their baby girl, a child who was just beginning to walk, and whose crying prevented her getting on with the cooking, to the old grandmother. When she went to fetch the child back, the grandmother protested that no child had been entrusted to her care, and the poor mother realized that she had been tricked, for the grandmother was really a jaguar who had assumed the exact form of the old woman.

All their attempts to find the child were fruitless and the parents at last gave up their quest. A few years passed and the parents began to lose things about the house: one day their necklaces, then their cotton garters; one evening all the ité starch vanished, then the bark apron-belt, then the buck-pots ... It was the jaguar who came under cover of night to steal all these things for the little girl to use, for he loved her as if she were his own kith and kin. The jaguar fed her on meat, and when she became a woman he started to lick the menstrual flow of blood, as jaguars and dogs do who like to smell the female organs. The two brothers followed his example, and the young girl found this behaviour very strange indeed.

So she made up her mind to escape and asked how to get back to her own village. The jaguar was suspicious, but she told him that, as he was getting old and would soon die, she surely ought to be returning to her parents. The jaguar, recognizing the force of her argument, was all the more willing to give her the information since he feared that, after his death, his two brothers would eat her up.

When the moment came to make the escape she had planned, she pretended that she could not remove an enormous pot full of meat from the fire, because she could not stand the heat. So without more ado, the jaguar picked up the pot between his paws and, as he held it, she dashed the boiling contents of the pot over him. The creature fell, yelled with pain and died. The two brothers heard his screams but paid no attention, because they thought he must be sporting with his girl. This was certainly not the case, since he had never had intimate relations with her.

The young girl ran to the village and made known her identity to her own people. She explained that they must all escape, because the jaguar's brothers would come for revenge and would kill them all. So the Indians got ready to leave, and loosened their hammock-ropes. One young man, a cousin of the young girl, put a heavy whetstone which he would want for sharpening in his hammock. But as he was slinging it over his shoulder in the usual manner, the unprepared-for weight broke his back and he fell down dead. His companions were in such haste to escape that they left his corpse lying there (Roth 1, pp. 202–3).

Roth makes an amusing observation in connection with this myth. When he expressed surprise at the abrupt ending, the old woman who had told him the story replied that when the two jaguars came to the village they found only the corpse there. Hence there was no one left to tell what actually did transpire subsequently.

But if we reverse the argument, the end becomes comprehensible. On arriving at the village, the two jaguars found at least one corpse there, and it may be assumed that they ate it instead of the young girl (whom, according to the myth, they were going to eat if she had stayed with them). To understand the importance of this detail, we need only recall that in the Ge myths about the origin of fire (cooking fire), the jaguar gave cooked meat to men from whom it had received a human wife. Now, here the jaguar has stolen from men (and not received as a gift) a woman who did not become its wife; correlatively, instead of men acquiring cooked animal meat, they give away raw human meat. To be convinced that this is unmistakably the meaning of the ending, which Roth held to be unsatisfactory, we have only to compare term by term the Warao myth and the group of Ge myths about the origin of fire (M_7–M_{12}), while remembering that, like most Ge tribes, the Warao have been claimed to be matrilineal, and that, contrary to what would happen in a patrilineal society, they consider the mother as a kinswoman and not as an affine:

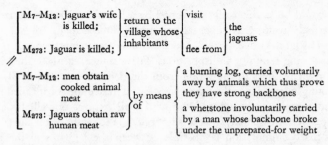

With regard to the last pair of opposites, *stone/burning log*, it will be noted that the stone in question is a whetstone, which is usually moistened before it is used (*water/fire* pair of opposites). Furthermore, it has been shown elsewhere (*RC*, p. 153) that, throughout this entire mythological system, stone is a metaphorical expression of human flesh, whereas the burning log is a metonymic equivalent of cooked meat (cause for effect). So not only the ending of M$_{273}$, but every single detail, is completely justified.

The preceding table shows M$_{273}$ to be diametrically opposed to the Ge myths about the origin of fire, with which our circular tour around South American mythology began (in *The Raw and the Cooked*). We now find ourselves, therefore, at the opposite pole from our starting-point. Whereas cooking played a doubly conjunctive role in the Ge myths (between sky and earth, and between affines), it appears twice in M$_{273}$, but always in a disjunctive capacity: it is responsible, in the first place, for a child being abandoned by her mother who is too busy cooking for her husband – and who, consequently, considers her duties as an affine (wife and cook) incompatible with those incumbent on her as kinswoman (mother and nurse); next, it is responsible for the death of the jaguar – which is neither a father nor a husband, but a foster-father; and which dies through being scalded by the contents of a pot, i.e. as the victim of a cook's intentional clumsiness.

But if, instead of casting our minds straight back to our starting-point, we try to retrace our steps slowly, other links emerge which form a series of cross-connections, making it possible to join up M$_{273}$ directly with several of the myths we have already examined. These short-cuts inevitably run through the inside of the sphere; whence it follows that the world of myths is not only round, but hollow.

Since M$_{273}$ is a Warao myth, the jaguar's partiality for the menstrual flow could be satisfactorily explained by a belief, which is peculiar to this tribal group, that supernatural spirits, unlike men, are not disgusted by it (cf. above, p. 190). It is a fact that Warao mythology is fond of describing feminine indispositions. For instance, in M_{260}, the birds dyed their feathers in the blood from the deflowering, and in M_{235} – without going as far as the jaguar in M_{273} – a masculine spirit called Bee has no scruples about lying down with a girl who is unwell: his attitude proves, incidentally, that it is not only in the myths of the northern Tupi that commutation is possible between the jaguar and the bee (cf. above, p. 249).

Nevertheless, the story of M_{273} cannot be entirely explained by reference to Warao views on menstruation. During our investigation we encountered a Tucuna myth (M_{245}), which was also concerned with a girl, weeping because she had been abandoned by her mother, and whom a frog (a transformation of the jaguar, as was shown during the fourth variation) carried off and brought up, and whom she instructed in shamanistic powers. When the girl became a fully grown woman and returned to her own people, she fed exclusively on human marrow. Here we can observe a two-term transformation of the menstrual flow in M_{273}:

(a) M_{273} [jaguar (cannibalistic animal)] $\Rightarrow$ M_{245} [frog (non-cannibalistic animal)]
(b) M_{273} ['cannibalized' heroine   ] $\Rightarrow$ M_{245} ['cannibalizing' heroine   ]

On the other hand, an additional proof of the progressive 'transparence' of the mythology of honey to the mythology of tobacco, which is additional to those I have already given, emerges from another comparison with M_{273}, this time with the Tereno myth about the origin of tobacco (M_{24}). In this myth, which has been summarized and discussed elsewhere (*RC*, p. 100 *ff*) and a Mataco variant (M_{246}, p. 197) of which I had to make use to link up the Warao myths with those of the Chaco, a woman who is subsequently changed into a jaguar (whereas the Warao jaguar began by changing into a woman) tries to poison her husband by feeding him with menstrual blood (unlike the Warao jaguar, who was partial to his 'non-wife's' menstrual blood).

Now, this Tereno myth is one of the very first (with M_{20}) in which we have encountered honey, which plays here (as I showed in the first part of this book) the role of operative factor in the origin of tobacco. This honey is, on each occasion, toxic because of some external reason (the violation of a taboo by the gatherers in M_{20}) or some internal reason (it is mixed with serpents' foetuses in M_{24}). Whether the cause mentioned is psychological or physical, this honey is consequently *filth*. On the contrary, for the jaguar in M_{273}, the menstrual blood – filth – is a kind of *honey*. Its behaviour as a jaguar which steals a little girl (who has been abandoned because she cried too much) and which is greedy for her menstrual blood, reproduces the behaviour of the frog in M_{241}, who loses no time in offering a home to a little boy (because he cried too much) and who is greedy for the honey he offers her. According to circumstances, greediness brings about or facilitates the escape of the adopted child. And it has been independently established that, in the fifth variation, the jaguar is a transformation of the frog, which is the heroine of the third.

What kind of relationship can there be between honey and menstrual blood? In the first place, they are elaborated substances, like cooked food, but through the action of what might be called 'natural cooking'. In the native system of thought, as has already been explained, honey is produced by a natural form of cooking, which belongs to the vegetable category, and it is clear that the natural form of cooking from which menstrual blood originates belongs to the animal category. We thus obtain a first correlation, to which a second can immediately be added. The jaguar in M_{273}, by avoiding any form of physical contact with the kidnapped girl other than the tasting of her menstrual blood, transposes a sexual relationship into alimentary terms. It thus simply reverses the behaviour of the two sisters in M_{235}, who tried to 'kidnap' their brother-in-law, because they experienced in sexual terms (enamoured as they were of a man called Honey) a relationship which should have remained on the alimentary level. It must be to confirm the reality of this transformation that the jaguar in M_{273} has two brothers, just as the heroine of M_{235} has two sisters. The two brothers in M_{273} are not content simply with the heroine's menstrual flow; they want to eat her up too. The two sisters in M_{235} are not satisfied with the honey produced by the hero; they want to 'eat' him too, but in the erotic sense.

We can detect a third link between honey and menstrual blood, which relates to a fact I have often stressed (and to which I shall return), namely, that South American varieties of honey are often toxic. In their case, the distance between the categories of the delicious and the poisonous is very short indeed. It is, therefore, not at all surprising that the Warao, who have metaphysical doubts about the merits of the restrictions concerning women who are indisposed (cf. above, pp. 190, 254), should see a connection between honey and the menstrual flow.

One final remark about this myth: when, in the course of the third variation, I mentioned the problem (pp. 208–9) of the menstrual flow (of the woman) and the foul-smelling excrement (of the man), I brought to light the existence of a two-fold movement the parallel nature of which is stressed in the myths. On the one hand, physiological maturation implies a regression to filth which, in terms of auditory coding, is illustrated by the state of the whimpering infant. On the other hand, the emergence of order, whether it be natural or cultural, always results from the disintegration of a higher order, only the remnants of which are retained by humanity. But is this interpretation not contradicted by M_{273}? The heroine is a whimpering baby to begin with, and far from puberty causing her to regress towards filth, it would seem on the contrary to add to her attractions. However, the attractiveness of menstrual blood affects a jaguar, as the myth is careful to point out. 'He was still a jaguar, and continued to do what jaguars and dogs do' (Roth 1, p. 202). What does this mean? Since M_{273} is diametrically opposed to the Ge myths about the origin of cooking, it must be concerned with the origin of the most completely reverse diet: a diet in which animal eats man instead of man eating animal, and in which man is eaten raw whereas the animal is eaten cooked. It is precisely over this horrible scene that the myth discreetly draws a veil, almost before it gets under way. Its aim, therefore, is to explain not the disintegration of an order which has only just been established, but the formation of a disorder which can be integrated in lasting fashion into a mythological system in which the character of the jaguar-cannibal plays a leading part. Consequently, the parallel sequence (that of physiological maturation) must also be reversed. On all counts, the new perspective envisaged by the myth is no less appalling than the previous one.

f. SIXTH VARIATION

$$[\text{jaguar} \Rightarrow \text{jaguar}] \leftrightarrow [\triangle \Rightarrow \bigcirc]$$

Let us look at the myth first of all:

M_{274}. Arawak. 'The jaguar changed into a woman'

There was a man justly noted for his skill in hunting wild pigs. He would always succeed in killing five or six, whereas the jaguar who invariably followed on the heels of the pack would catch only one or two. So the jaguar decided to change into a woman, and in this new disguise he approached the hunter and asked him to tell him the secret of his success. 'I have been trained to it since early boyhood,' the latter replied. Then the woman-jaguar expressed her desire to have him for a husband, but he, knowing her true nature, was not too anxious to give a decided answer. She overcame his scruples, however, and together they killed more pigs than it was possible to do singly.

They lived happily together for a long time. She turned out to be an exceedingly good wife, for besides looking after the cooking and the barbecuing, she was an excellent huntress. One day she asked her husband whether he had a father or mother and, on learning that his parents were still alive, she suggested they should pay them a visit, because they must surely think him dead. She knew the way, and offered to act as guide to her husband, but on condition that he promised never to reveal her origin.

So they arrived at the village, taking plenty of pigs with them. The Indian's mother at once wanted to know where his beautiful wife came from. Omitting all mention of the fact that she was really a jaguar, he merely said that he had met her by chance in the forest. Every day husband and wife went out hunting and brought back an extraordinarily large bag. The villagers became suspicious. First of all, the Indian refused to divulge the secret, but his mother became so worried that he at last made a clean breast of it to her. The husband's people made the old woman drunk and forced her to tell the secret. The woman-jaguar, who had heard everything without disclosing her whereabouts felt so ashamed that she fled growling into the bush and was never seen or heard of again. Her poor husband searched the bush in vain, calling out his wife's name, but there never, never came any reply (Roth 1, pp. 203–4).

This myth calls for two comments, one regarding form, the other regarding content.

Let us first of all examine the group of equations which provided the basis for the six variations:

$$(1) \; [bee \Rightarrow bee] \leftrightarrow [\bigcirc \Rightarrow \triangle]$$
$$(2) \; [\triangle \Rightarrow \triangle] \leftrightarrow [bee \Rightarrow frog]$$
$$(3) \; [frog \Rightarrow frog] \leftrightarrow [\triangle \Rightarrow \bigcirc]$$
$$(4) \; [\bigcirc \Rightarrow \bigcirc] \leftrightarrow [frog \Rightarrow jaguar]$$
$$(5) \; [jaguar \Rightarrow jaguar] \leftrightarrow [\bigcirc \Rightarrow \triangle]$$
$$(6) \; [jaguar \Rightarrow jaguar] \leftrightarrow [\triangle \Rightarrow \bigcirc]$$

It is clear that the last is not of the same type as the others. Instead of opening up the way to a new transformation, it merely cancels out the immediately previous operation, so that, taken together, equations (5) and (6) produce an identical transformation: one replaced a female jaguar by a male jaguar, while the other changes the male jaguar back into a female jaguar. Just as a dressmaker finishes off her work by tucking in the edge of the material and sewing it underneath to the unseen part to prevent fraying, so the group concludes by turning down the sixth variation over the fifth, like a hem.

Looking now at the content of the myth, we observe that it is not satisfied merely to complete the group at one of its extremities: it takes the group as a totality and turns it into a closed system. After a whole series of transformations, which gradually took us farther and farther away from their starting-point, we have now come back to that point. Provided only we accept the transformation of a bee-woman into a jaguar-woman, M_{274} tells exactly the same story as M_{239} and M_{234}, which provided the 'theme' for the six variations.

In all three myths, the husbands have an identical vocation: the bee's husband is the best honey-gatherer in his tribe, the jaguar-woman's husband has no equal as a hunter, but of pigs only, for he is sometimes outclassed in respect of other kinds of game. Now, if honey is obviously the mediatory term between bee and man, I have explained elsewhere (RC, pp. 83–108) why the wild pig (probably *Dicotyles torquatus* in M_{274}, where the species is not made clear; but *D. labiatus* lives in such vast herds that five or six beasts would not represent a very impressive bag) occupies a comparable position between man and jaguar. No doubt the Indian in M_{233} and M_{234} courts the supernatural woman, whereas the reverse happens in M_{274}. But in both instances, the heroines show the same concern for their affines: one before marriage, the other after. I have shown the significance of this feature, which allows us to unite in a single group the Guiana and Chaco myths in which the heroine is characterized in respect of honey (she may be either greedy for, or lavish with, honey), and which therefore provides an additional proof that M_{274} also belongs to this group.

But if the sixth variation simply brings us back to the theme, while demonstrating, through its reduplicative function, that there is no point in looking farther afield, and that the group has been blocked at one of its extremities and is furthermore a closed set, does the static character of the group thus averred not contradict the principle I recalled at the end of the fourth variation, and according to which any mythic transformation should be characterized by an imbalance, which is both a guarantee of its vitality, and a sign that it is incomplete?

In order to solve the difficulty, we should recall the very unusual course we were forced to follow by the series of transformations of the theme. All these myths, we said, deal not so much with origin as with loss. Loss of honey first of all, which in earliest times was available in limitless quantities, and which has now become difficult to find (M_{233}–M_{235}). Then loss of game, which in olden times was abundant but became scarce and widely scattered (M_{237}–M_{239}). Then, according to Haburi's story (M_{241}, M_{258}), culture and the arts of civilization were lost. Haburi, 'the father of inventions', had to abandon men in order to escape from the frog's clutches. Finally came a loss more serious than all the others: the loss of those logical categories without which man cannot conceptualize the contrast between nature and culture, nor overcome the confusion of opposites: cooking fire is vomited, food exuded (M_{263}, M_{264}, M_{266}), and the distinction abolished between food and excrement (M_{273}), as well as between the cannibalistic jaguar's search for food and man's search for food (M_{273}, M_{274}).

Consequently, like a twilight of the gods, the myths describe this inevitable collapse: from a golden age when nature was submissive and generous to man, by way of a sterner age when man was endowed with clear ideas and well-defined contrasts by means of which he was still able to control his surroundings, to a state of gloomy indistinctness in which nothing can be indisputably possessed and still less preserved, because all beings and things are intermingled.

The universal regression towards chaos, so characteristic of the myths we are dealing with, and which is also a falling back into nature explains their ultimately stationary structure. This structure testifies then, but in a different way, to the presence of a built-in gap between the content of the myth and its form: the myths can only depict decadence by means of a stable formal structure, for the same reason that some myths, which try to maintain a state of invariance throughout a series of transformations, are obliged to have recourse to an unbalanced structure. The imbalance is always present but, according to the nature of the message, it is manifested by the instability of the form to adapt itself to the inflections of the content, with regard to which it sometimes falls short: the form is constant if the message is regressive; or which it sometimes overshoots: the form is progressive if the message is constant.

At the beginning of this book, I started from the hypothesis that honey and tobacco form a pair of opposites and that consequently the mythology of honey and that of tobacco must correspond to each other symmetrically. We should now perceive that this hypothesis is not complete since, as regards their respective mythical functions, honey and tobacco entertain more complex relationships with each other. The following chapters will show that, in South America, the function of tobacco consists in restoring what the function of honey destroyed, that is in re-establishing between man and the supernatural that communication which the seductive power of honey (which is none other than that of nature) had caused to be interrupted: 'Tobacco likes listening to myths. According to the Kogi, that is why it grows near houses' (Reichel-Dolmatoff, Vol. II, p. 60). The visible changes which the six variations effected, as it were, under our very eyes therefore resemble the rapid oscillations characteristic of a strip of metal acting as a spring and one end only of which is fixed, while the other, when suddenly released by the breaking of the cable which kept it taut, vibrates in opposite directions before finding its point of rest. Only, here again, the phenomenon unfolds the wrong way round: but for tobacco, which kept it tensed in the direction of the supernatural, culture, reduced to its own resources, can only fluctuate indecisively on either side of nature. After a certain lapse of time, its impetus dies down and its inherent inertia immobilizes it at the one point at which nature and culture are, as it were, in a state of natural equilibrium, and which I have defined as being the honey harvest.

In a sense, therefore, the drama had been enacted and consummated from the very first variation, since it was concerned with honey. The others merely marked out, with ever-increasing precision, the confines of a stage left empty after the play was over. It is therefore of little importance whether they are more or less numerous. Like the chords which end Beethoven's symphonies, and always make us wonder why the composer used so many, and what made him decide not to add still more, they do not conclude a development in progress. The development had already exhausted all its possibilities, but some metalinguistic means had to be found of signalling the end of the message and the signal is obtained by enclosing its last statement in the system (made present for once) of the tones which had contributed, throughout the transmission of the music, to a more faithful rendering of the shades of meaning of the system, by modulating it in several ways.

PART THREE SUMMER IN LENT[1]

Rura ferunt messes, calidi quum sideris aestu
deponit flavas annua terra comas.
Rure levis verno flores apis ingerit alveo,
compleat ut dulci sedula melle favos.
Agricola assiduo primum satiatus aratro
cantavit certo rustica verba pede.
Et satur arenti primum est modulatus avena
carmen, ut ornatos diceret ante Deos.
Agricola et minio suffusus, Bacche, rubenti
primus inexperta ducit ab arte choros.

Tibullus, *Elegies*, I, L.II

[1] TRANSLATORS' NOTE: The French title is *Août en Carême*; the author intends this as an inversion of *arriver comme mars en Carême*, 'to happen as regular as clockwork'. The point is perhaps made clearer in English if *août* is rendered as 'summer'.

1 *Starry Night*

Unlike M_{259} and M_{266}, the Carib version (M_{264}) makes no reference to the origin of fire. The frog does no more than extract flour from a white patch between its shoulders; it neither vomits nor excretes fire and does not perish on a funeral pyre but on a bed of blazing cotton. The fire cannot therefore spread among the trees; its effects are limited to the body of the batrachian, whose scorched skin retains a rough and wrinkled appearance. This absence of an etiological factor, such as is prominent in the parallel versions, is, however, compensated for by the presence of another factor, not mentioned in M_{259} and M_{266}: this is the origin of certain constellations. It will be remembered that the tapir becomes the Hyades, Makunaima the Pleiades and his severed leg the shield of Orion.

A Guiana myth, which probably belongs to the Acawai and that I have already summarized and discussed elsewhere (M_{134}, *RC*, pp. 243–4), says that the Pleiades sprang from the viscera of an Indian, whose brother murdered him in the hope of obtaining his wife. A transition from one version to another is offered by various Guianese myths, and it is all the more plausible in that, in each case, Orion represents the severed member and the Pleiades the rest of the body; the latter, therefore, contains the viscera. In the Taulipang myth (M_{135}), the Pleiades forecast a large catch of fish, as in M_{134}, where the Pleiades correspond only to the viscera. And, in the Arecuna version (M_{136}), the amputation of the hero's limb occurs after he has murdered his grandmother who, like the frog in M_{264}, offered him excreted food. In *The Raw and the Cooked* (pp. 240–46), I discussed at length the symbolical assimilation of the Pleiades to the viscera or the part of the body containing the viscera, pointed out that it occurs in various, widespread localities in the New World and showed that, from the anatomical point of view, the relevant contrast was between: viscera (the Pleiades) and: a long bone (Orion).[2]

[2] Some Guiana variants identify the Pleiades with the head and not with the viscera, but the contrast is maintained in the form: *rounded/lengthy*.

In the Guianese area, then, the Pleiades, represented by the viscera or a part of the body containing the viscera, forecast a plentiful supply of fish. This is not our first encounter with a 'visceral' theme: it also played a part in the cycle of the girl mad about honey. For fuller details, I refer the reader back to Part Two, 2, and shall restrict myself here to mentioning the Toba and Mataco myths (M_{208}, M_{209}) in which the deceiver loses his viscera which change into edible vines, water-melons and wild fruits, or M_{210}, in which vomit (emerging from the viscera in the same way as the latter emerge from the rib-cage and the abdominal cavity) gives rise to water-melons.

In M_{134}, the disembowelling of the hero brings about the appearance of the Pleiades (in the sky) and of fish (in water). In M_{134} (and in the basic myth, M_1), the appearance of aquatic plants (on the surface of the water) is also the result of a disembowelling. Behind these metamorphoses one can discern a two-fold oppositional axis: on the one hand between the high and the low, since the stars float on high 'on the air', as the aquatic plants float down below on the water; and on the other hand between container and content, since water contains fish, whereas water-melons (and, generally speaking, the fruit and vegetables of the dry season) contain water. The disembowelling which determines the origin of water-melons in M_{208}–M_{219}, and the disembowelling which determines the arrival of the fish in M_{134} are all the more comparable in that fishing and the gathering of wild fruit take place chiefly during the dry season. It is true that M_{134} contains no more than a barely perceptible reference to the theme of the girl mad about honey: wishing to be rid of the wife after the husband, the killer Indian persuades her to get inside a hollow tree (i.e. a place where honey would normally be looked for), but under the pretext of catching an agouti (Roth 1, p. 262).[3] Whereas M_{134} does no more than establish a connection between the themes of the viscera and the origin of the Pleiades, the Taulipang (M_{135})

[3] The reference to the agouti is not accidental, since, as we know, in Guianese myths (Ogilvie, p. 65), it alternates with the tapir as master of the tree of life. But not in the same way, apparently: the tapir, the current master of wild fruit, was also master of cultivated plants when the latter, in the wild state, grew on a tree; whereas the agouti, a stealer of cultivated plants, now seems to enjoy a right of priority over them: the Rio Uaupés Indians begin gathering manioc round the outside of the field so as to deceive the agouti living in the adjoining bush, because – they say – it will imagine that there is nothing left to steal (Silva, p. 247). On the other hand, in those myths where the agouti is the first master of the tree of life, he has a grain of maize hidden in his *hollow tooth*, which can be considered as a term standing at the apex of a triangle, the other angles of which are occupied respectively by the *toothed* capybara and the *toothless* ant-eater. It is as if, in mythic thought, the agouti served to link the semantic half-value of the selfish, greedy tapir to another value, of which the capybara and the ant-eater each represent a half.

and Vapidiana (M_{265}) variants – in which the wife is in love with her young brother-in-law, contrary to what happens in M_{134} – associate the theme of the origin of the Pleiades with that of the girl mad about honey: to avenge his mutilated brother, who has been transformed into one of the Pleiades, the hero of M_{135} imprisons the widow, who has insisted on marriage, inside a hollow trunk into which she had imprudently inserted her head in order to eat honey directly from the comb. Whereupon, he transforms himself, along with his children, into an araiuág, a honey-eating animal[4] (cf. above, p. 86), after taking care to set fire to his hut (K.-G. 1, pp. 55–60). It will be remembered that in one of the Chaco myths (M_{219}), the seducer – who, according to another myth, set fire to his village (M_{219b}: Métraux 5, p. 138) – suffers the same punishment as the seductress does here.

Finally, the Arecuna version (M_{136}) combines all three themes: the floating viscera (origin of aquatic plants), the murderous wife who mutilates her husband (transported to the heavens to become the Pleiades), and the punishment of the wife who is shut up in a hollow tree (for having shown too great a greediness for honey).

The recurrence, in the Guianese and Chaco myths, of the theme of the floating or hanging viscera, allows us to apply to the group as a whole a conclusion that I had already entertained through a comparison, in a different context, of certain Guianese myths with the Chaco myths. In all these cases, as can be seen, a relationship through marriage is violated because of uncontrollable covetousness, which may be of an alimentary or sexual nature, but remains identical with itself in either form, since it is directed towards honey as a 'seductive' food or towards a seductive character, who is given the name 'Honey' in several Guianese myths.

In the Chaco version, the relationship between a son-in-law and his parents-in-law is neutralized by too greedy a wife. This is the opposite of the situation in a Guianese myth (M_{259}), where too greedy a father-in-law neutralizes the relationship between his daughter and his son-in-law. In other Guianese myths, a relationship between affines (who are respectively brother-in-law and sister-in-law) is neutralized through the elimination of the husband by his brother (M_{134}), or by his wife (M_{135}). Finally, in M_{136}, which seems out of line when approached in this way, an affine neutralizes a relationship between blood-relatives,

---

[4] But which is not eaten by men, and is therefore 'non-game'. In M_{265} it is the wife who is changed into a honey-eating creature (a snake).

since the son-in-law kills his wife's mother, who has been supplying him with food (whereas, normally, the situation is the reverse). But this inversion of the cycle of services rendered becomes comprehensible when we consider that the food is *excreted*: it is an anti-food which therefore constitutes an anti-service on the part of the mother-in-law. In short, we have arrived at the general transformational system on the basis of an exceptional foodstuff, honey, and an equally exceptional sociological situation, that of the too greedy woman, whether the object of her covetousness is honey (Chaco) or an illicit relationship (Guiana), or both at once (again Guiana).

If we try to see the system as a whole and to determine its basic characteristics, we can say, then, that its peculiarity is the simultaneous exploitation of three codes: an alimentary code the symbols of which are the typical foods of the dry season; an astronomical code which refers to the daily or seasonal movement of certain constellations; thirdly, a sociological code built around the theme of the badly brought up girl who betrays her parents or her husband, but always in such a way as to be incapable of performing the mediatory function in the marriage relationship which is assigned to her by the myth.

Codes 2 and 3 are prominent in the Guianese myths and we have seen that code 1 is doubly present, although in a blurred form: on the one hand, in the connection between the Pleiades and the movement of the fish upstream, and on the other hand, in the final transformation of the heroine, who is at first madly in love with her brother-in-law, into the woman mad about honey. In the Chaco myths codes 1 and 3 are the most obvious, but not only is code 2 discernible in the theme of the fruit and vegetables of the dry season which spring from the trickster's viscera (whereas in Guiana the viscera of the trickster's victim give rise simultaneously to the Pleiades and to fish), the possibility of the existence of an astronomical code is strengthened still further in the case that was considered above (pp. 114–15), in which the heroine, who is transformed into a capybara, represents the constellation of Aries. As it happens, Aries appears slightly before the Pleiades, and the latter slightly before Orion. We are therefore dealing with two pairs of constellations which are slightly dephased as between the Chaco and Guiana. In the case of each pair, the first constellation each time announces the appearance of the second, which is always in the most prominent position. Orion actually occupies an exceptional place in the astronomical code of Guiana, and it is well known that the tribes

of the Gran Chaco attach major importance to the Pleiades and celebrate their return with great ceremonies:

CHACO

Orion > Pleiades > Aries

GUIANA

*

All these details had to be recalled before broaching the essential
problem raised by the analysis of these myths, i.e. the reciprocal con-
vertibility of the three codes. When reduced to its simplest expression,
it can be formulated as follows: what is the common feature uniting
the search for honey, the constellation of the Pleiades and the character
of the badly brought up girl? I shall try to establish a connection
between the alimentary and astronomical codes, then between the
alimentary and the sociological codes and lastly between the sociological
and astronomical codes, and I hope that the triple demonstration will
provide proof of the homology between the three codes.

The most explicit references to the Pleiades are to be found in the
Guianese myths. It is appropriate, then, to begin by establishing the
seasonal calendar for that part of America, as we have already done for
the Gran Chaco and the Brazilian plateau. The task is not an easy one,
since climatic conditions, and particularly the rainfall, vary between the
coast and the interior, and between the western and eastern areas.
The simple contrast between a dry season and a rainy season is hardly
to be found anywhere except in British Guiana and the centre of Venezuela, where the rainfall increases up to July and then falls to its lowest
point in November. To the west of the Orinoco delta, the contrast is
less marked and the rains occur later.[5] On the other side of British

[5] At San Carlos de Rio Negro, Keses distinguishes between a rainy season (from June
to August) and a dry season (from December to March), interlinked by intermediary seasons
which he refers to as the 'rising' or the 'falling' of the waters, and which are marked by
irregular rainfall and violent storms. Also along the Rio Negro, at São Gabriel, i.e. farther
to the south and in Brazilian territory, the rainfall is apparently heaviest from December to
January and then again in May (*Pelo Rio Mar*, pp. 8–9; *Normais*, p. 2). To the west, in the
Uaupés valley, the two periods of slightest rainfall are from June to August and from
December to February (Silva, p. 245). Along the Rio Demini, a tributary flowing into the
Rio Negro on its left bank, Becher (1) distinguishes between two seasons only: rain falls
from April to September and the dry season lasts from October to March. In the territory
of the Waiwai, along the frontier between Brazil and British Guiana, it rains all the year
round; however, Fock singles out two particularly rainy periods, a major one from June
to August and a minor one in December, separated by a relatively dry season from September to November and again from January to February (cf. Knoch, p. G 85). The abundant

Guiana, the pattern is more complex since both seasons divide up into two parts. Since this four-fold rhythm is also observable inland as far as the basins of the Negro and Uaupés rivers (although in these areas rain falls all the year round and the contrasts are less definitely marked), this is the pattern I would like to draw particular attention to (Figure 13).

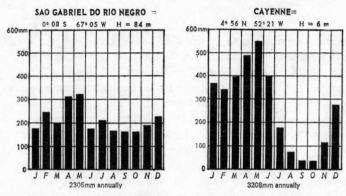

Figure 13. Annual rainfall in Guiana and the Rio Negro basin.
(After Knoch, p. G 85.)

In Guiana, the inhabitants generally distinguish between a 'little dry season' from March to May, a 'big rainy season' from June to September, a 'big dry season' from September to November and a 'little rainy season' from December to February. Since, in fact, rain falls at all periods, this pattern cannot be accepted without certain reservations. The rainfall increases or diminishes according to the time of year but, according to the area under consideration, the driest period occurs between the months of August and September, and this is also the fishing season (Roth 2, pp. 717–18; K.-G. 1, p. 40; Bates, pp. 287–9), as well as the season when various kinds of wild fruit ripen (Fock, pp. 182–4).

The Indians establish connections between the Pleiades and various points in this complex calendar and attribute to the observable conjunctions values which are equally significant although mutually contradictory. The Pleiades, which are still visible in April, in the evenings, on the western horizon, announce the approach of rainstorms

information given by such authors as Wallace, Bates, Spruce and Whiffen is not always easy to interpret, because of the relatively short periods they spent in the area, which made it impossible for them to arrive at averages.

(Ahlbrinck, under 'sirito') and when they disappear from sight in May, this is the signal for the recurrence of the rainy season (K.-G. 1, p. 29). They reappear in the mornings in the east in June (or in July at 4 a.m., Fock, *ibid.*) and announce the beginning of the dry season (K.-G., 1, *ibid.*; Crevaux, p. 215) and so determine the beginning of agricultural activities (Goeje, p. 51; Chiara, p. 373). Their rising in the east, in December, after sunset, announces the start of the new year and the return of the rainy season (Roth 2, p. 715). It can thus be seen that the Pleiades are sometimes associated with drought and sometimes with the rainy season.

It would seem that this meteorological ambivalence is reflected on another level too. Whereas they are 'hailed with joy' (Crevaux) on their reappearance in June, the Pleiades can also inspire fear. 'With the Arawaks the Pleiades are called *wiwa yo-koro*, star mother, and they believe that when the Pleiades on their first appearance (in June) are very brilliant or "bad" in fact, the other stars will follow and many people will die in the ensuing year' (Goeje, p. 27). Only through the intervention of a heavenly snake (Perseus) are men saved from mass destruction by the 'death-bearing brilliance' of the Pleiades (*ibid.*, p. 119). According to the Kalina, there were two successive constellations of the Pleiades. The first was swallowed up by a snake. Another snake pursues the second constellation and rises in the east as the constellation is setting in the west. Time will come to an end when the snake catches up with the constellation. But as long as they are in existence, the Pleiades prevent the evil spirits attacking mankind in serried phalanxes: they force them to operate incoherently and piece-meal (*ibid.*, pp. 118, 122–3).

The duality of the Pleiades makes one think immediately of certain phenomena of Andean culture. In the great temple of the sun at Cuzco, there were superposed images on either side of the centre of the altar: on the left, the sun, Venus as the evening star, and the summer Pleiades in their visible form, i.e. 'bright'; on the right, the moon, Venus as the morning star, and the winter Pleiades, hidden behind clouds. The winter Pleiades, which were also called 'the Lord of ripening', were associated with rain and abundance. The summer constellation, 'the Lord of diseases', and more particularly of human malaria, was a harbinger of death and suffering. It was because of this that the 'oncoymita' feast, which marked the appearance of the Pleiades in the spring, included confessional rites, offerings of *cavia* and llamas and anointing with blood (L.-N., pp. 124–31).

On the other hand, Kalina ideas strengthen a theory that has already been put forward about the particularly significant nature of the Orion-Pleiades pair in America and several other areas of the world. I suggested (*RC*, pp. 220–26) that, because of their respective configurations, the two constellations, which are diachronically associated since they rise within a few days of each other, are nevertheless synchronically opposed since the Pleiades are connected with the continuous and Orion with the discontinuous. It follows that the Pleiades can have a beneficent meaning in so far as they are the harbingers of Orion, without relinquishing the maleficent and morbid associations which South American thought attributes to the continuous (*RC*, pp. 279–80) and which only redound to their credit when asserted against evil spirits.

There are more direct proofs of the affinities between the Pleiades and epidemics and poison. According to an Amazonian belief, snakes lose their venom with the disappearance of the Pleiades (Rodrigues 1, p. 221, n. 2). This ambiguity puts the constellation on the same level as honey which, like it, is ambivalent and may be both desired and feared.

In the great myth of origin of the Guarani of Paraguay, the mother of the gods says: 'Under the grass tussocks of the eternal meadows, I have gathered the bees ("eichú", *Nectarina mellifica*) so that they (men) may rinse their mouths with honey when I recall them' (Cadogan 3, p. 95). Cadogan points out that the word 'eichú' refers both to a kind of bee and to the Pleiades. As a matter of fact, the *Nectarina* are wasps (Ihering, under 'enchú') and their honey is often poisonous; it is precisely this honey that the heroine of the Chaco myths is mad about and that the Sun, her father, is incapable of obtaining for her without the help of a husband. This serves to show that, in these myths, the astronomical coding is much more obviously present than could be supposed.

The honey of the *Nectarina*, which has a purifying role in the rites of the southern Guarani, had a similar function in Amazonia, where priests officiating in the cult of Jurupari used it as a vomitive. Stradelli (1, p. 416) translates the expression 'ceucy-irá-cáua' as 'a kind of bee with a very fierce sting; honey which produces heavy vomiting at certain times of the year'. The same author gives the following definition of the expression 'ceucy cipó', 'Ceucy liana': 'a kind of liana, the roots and stems of which, after being pounded in a mortar, are used in the preparation of a potion which is drunk as a purifying agent, on the eve of any feast-day, by the players of sacred musical instruments ...

this drink causes acute vomiting' (p. 415). In Amazonia, the term 'ceucy' (cyucy, ceixu; cf. Guarani: eichú) refers to the constellation of the Pleiades. We can see, then, that from Paraguay to the banks of the Amazon, honey and the Pleiades are interconnected both linguistically and philosophically.

But in Amazonia, what we are concerned with is something quite different from a natural product and a constellation. Ceucy is also the proper name of the heroine of a famous myth, which must now be adduced as evidence:

M_{275}. *Amazonia (Tupi). 'The origin of the cult of Jurupari'*

In very remote times, when the world was ruled by women, the Sun, indignant at this state of things, decided to effect a remedy by reforming mankind and submitting it to his law and then choosing a perfect woman, that he could take as his companion. He needed an emissary. He therefore arranged for a virgin named Ceucy to be fertilized by the sap of the cucura or puruman tree (*Pourouma cecropiaefolia*, of the family of moraceae) which streamed over her breasts [or lower down, according to less chaste versions]. The child, who was called Jurupari, took power away from women and restored it to men. To emphasize the latter's independence, he instructed them to celebrate feasts from which women would be excluded, and he taught them secrets to be handed down from generation to generation. They were to put to death any women who learned these secrets. Ceucy herself was the first victim of this pitiless law promulgated by her son who, even today, is still in search of a woman sufficiently perfect to become the wife of the Sun, never yet having found one (Stradelli 1, p. 497).

Many variants of this myth are on record, and some of them are considerably longer. I do not propose to examine them in detail, since they seem to belong to a different mythological *genre* from that of the more popular tales – comparatively homogeneous in tone and inspiration – that I am bringing together here to provide the subject-matter for my investigation. It would seem that some early inquirers in the Amazonian basin, prominent among whom were Barbosa Rodrigues, Amorim and Stradelli, were still able to find esoteric texts belonging to a learned tradition, and comparable in this connection to those discovered more recently by Nimuendaju and Cadogan among the southern Guarani. Unfortunately, we have little or no knowledge of the old native communities which once lived along the middle and lower Amazon. The laconic evidence supplied by Orellana, who sailed down the river as far as the estuary in 1541-2, and still more so the existence of oral traditions, whose extreme complexity, artificial composition and mystical tone suggest that they must be attributed to schools of sages and learned men, argue in favour of a much higher level of religious, social and political organization than anything that has been observed since. The study of these previous documents, which are the remains of a genuine civilization common to the whole of the Amazonian basin, would require a whole volume in itself and would involve the use of special methods in which philology and archaeology (both still in an embryonic state as regards tropical America) would have to play a part. Such a study may one day be possible. Without venturing far into this uncertain territory, I shall merely cull from the different variants miscellaneous points directly germane to my argument.

After Jurupari had ordered, or allowed, his mother's execution, because she had gazed upon the sacred flutes, he sent her up into the sky, where she became the constellation of the Pleiades (Orico 2, pp. 65-6). In the variants current among the tribes along the Rio Branco and the Rio Uaupés (Tariana, Tucano: M_{276a}), the legislator, who is called Bokan or Izy, himself reveals his supernatural origin by means of a myth within the myth, a sort of 'Graal aria', *avant la lettre*. He explains that his father before him was a great legislator named Pinon, the offspring of a secluded virgin who had escaped from her prison to look for a husband and who had been miraculously fertilized by the sun. When she returned to her family with her children, Dinari (as the woman was called) persuaded her son to put an end to the seclusion of girls, but he did not extend this benefit to his sister, Meênspuin, whose hair was adorned with seven stars. As the girl was languishing for lack of a husband, to cure her of this desire and to preserve her virtue, Pinon sent her up into the sky, where she became Ceucy, the Pleiades, and he himself was changed into a snake-like constellation (Rodrigues 1, pp. 73-127; complete text: 2, Vol. II, pp. 13-16, 23-5, 50-71).

Consequently, among the Tupi-Guarani and other populations which have come under their influence, the word 'ceucy' means: (1) a wasp producing poisonous honey which causes vomiting; (2) the constellation of the Pleiades, seen as feminine, sterile, guilty and even perhaps death-dealing; (3) a virgin withheld from the marriage relationship and who is either fertilized miraculously or changed into a star so that she cannot marry.

The triple meaning of the term would be enough in itself to establish the correlation between the sociological, astronomical and alimentary codes, since it is clear that the character of Ceucy is an inversion, on all three levels, of that of the girl mad about honey, as it is illustrated in the Guiana myths. The character in these myths, defying convention and prompted by bestial greed, swallows honey which, in the other context, is vomited up during the process of purification; she is responsible for the appearance of the Pleiades as a fertile, male entity (abundance of fish); finally, she is a mother (often even with several children) who makes a wrong use of marriage by committing adultery with one of her in-laws.

But, in fact, the character of Ceucy is still more complex. We have already seen how it can take a double form: she can be either a miraculously fertilized mother and a breaker of taboos or a virgin forced to turn into a star through the strength of the taboos preventing her marriage. Yet another Amazonian tradition presents Ceucy in the guise of a greedy old woman or of a spirit eternally subject to pangs of hunger:

M_{277}. *Anambé*. '*The ogress Ceucy*'

An adolescent was fishing by the edge of a stream when the ogress Ceucy approached. She saw the boy's reflection in the water and tried to catch it in her net. This made the boy laugh and so revealed his hiding place. The old woman drove him out by means of wasps and poisonous ants, and carried him off in her net to eat him.

The ogress's daughter took pity on the prisoner and set him free. At first he tried to appease the old woman by weaving baskets which were at once transformed into animals which she devoured (cf. M_{326a}), then he caught enormous quantities of fish for her. In the end, he fled. The ogress pursued him in the form of a cancan bird (*Ibycter americanus*?), and he sought refuge in turn with the honey-gathering monkeys, which hid him in a pot, the surucucú snakes (*Lachesis mutus*), which tried to eat him, the macauan bird (*Herpetotheres cachinans*), which saved him, and lastly the tuiuiú stork (*Tantalus americanus*), which set him down near his village where, in spite of the fact that age had whitened his hair, he was recognized by his mother (Couto de Magalhães, pp. 270–80).

This myth presents a double interest. First, it is recognizably a close variant of a Warao myth (M_{28}), which was summarized and discussed at the beginning of the first volume in this series (*RC*, pp. 109 ff) and which, significantly enough, now that we have been unexpectedly reminded of it, will have to be referred to later for the solution of a problem which it is as yet too early to broach (cf. below, p. 453). This Warao myth (M_{28}) referred to the Pleiades, the Tupi name of which is borne by the ogress in M_{277}: this name explained the origin not only of the Pleiades but also of the Hyades and Orion. In other words, it fulfilled the same etiological function as M_{264} among the Carib of Guiana, a myth which tells of another greedy female who fattens herself up on wild fruit, without leaving any for the hero.

Secondly, the ogress in M_{277}, who *is* the constellation of the Pleiades, provides a transition between the first Ceucy (in M_{275}), who is meta-phorically greedy – not for food but for masculine secrets – and the Taulipang heroine in M_{135}, who is greedy for honey in the literal sense in the second part of the myth but who also, from the outset, takes on the character of a metaphorical ogress eager for the caresses of her young brother-in-law and who, through mutilating her husband in an attempt to kill him, determines the appearance of the Pleiades in the form of a male provider of food. The man who is changed into the constellation promises the hero an abundant supply of food: 'Hence-forth thou shalt have much to eat!'

Consequently, the Taulipang heroine stands in a metonymical re-lationship to the Pleiades; the latter are the effect, she is the cause. She thus supplies the hero, unwittingly and in the form of the fish whose arrival is announced by the Pleiades, with the same food as is withheld from the hero in M_{277} by an ogress *named* 'Pleiades' (metaphor)[6] and in M_{28} by an ogress who is the *cause* of the Pleiades (metonymy), in order that they may eat it themselves. These transformations can be illustrated as follows:

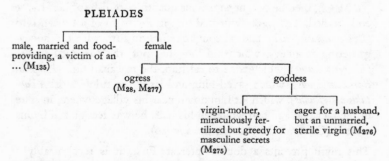

PLEIADES

male, married and food-providing, a victim of an ... (M_{135})

female

ogress (M_{28}, M_{277})

goddess

virgin-mother, miraculously fer-tilized but greedy for masculine secrets (M_{275})

eager for a husband, but an unmarried, sterile virgin (M_{276})

[6] This confirms yet again that, according to the Indian way of thought, a proper name is a metaphor of the person referred to. (Cf. above, p. 163, and below, p. 328.)

In the diagram, as can be seen, the functions situated at the two extremes (above and to the left, below and to the right) are symmetrical and inverse, whereas the others correspond to intermediary states, with an alternation of the literal and figurative senses at each shift.

I shall now try to establish a direct relationship between the alimentary and sociological codes, and shall begin with an observation. In the Guiana myths, M_{134}–M_{136}, the position of the heroine seems so unstable as to take on diametrically opposed meanings according to the context. In M_{134} she is subject to illicit approaches from her brother-in-law, whereas in M_{135} and M_{136} she is guilty of similar approaches to him. Thus she sometimes appears as a vestal virgin, sometimes as a vividly delineated bacchant.

M_{135}. *Taulipang. 'The origin of the Pleiades'* (detail)

... Waiúlale (a woman's name) was lying in her hammock. She got up on the arrival of her young brother-in-law (who had been informed by a bird about the barbarous treatment inflicted on his elder brother) and served him with beer and manioc. He asked where his brother was; she replied that he was away gathering fruit. Filled with sadness, the young man lay down and the woman stretched out on top of him. He tried to get up but she held him prisoner in the hammock. Night fell. The accursed woman would not let him out, not even to urinate.

Meanwhile, her husband was screaming with pain in the bush. But she said to the boy: 'Don't bother about your brother! Perhaps he's gone fishing. I'll get out of the hammock when he comes back!' The boy knew everything, having been informed by the bird.

During the night, he pretended to be hungry and asked the woman to fetch him some spicy stew, because he wanted to be rid of her so as to have time to urinate. Then, the wounded man, who had dragged himself as far as the hut, cried out: 'Oh my brother! This woman has chopped my leg off with an axe! Kill her!' The boy asked the woman: 'What have you done to my brother?' – 'Nothing,' she replied. 'When I left him, he was fishing and gathering fruit.' And, although her husband continued to howl with pain outside, she climbed back into the hammock and put her arms so tightly round the boy that he could not move. Meanwhile, the wounded man, who was lying on the ground in front of the hut, was calling: 'My brother! My brother! Help me, my brother!' But the brother could not get out. The wounded man continued to groan until the middle of the night. Then his brother said to him: 'I cannot help you! Your wife will not let me leave the hammock!' She had even closed the door and secured it with ropes. And the boy added, still speaking to his brother: 'I shall avenge you one day! You are out there suffering! One day your wife will have to suffer in the same way!' He struck her, but could not succeed in breaking free (K.-G. 1, pp. 56–7).

Yet it is the same woman, here presented as a ferociously lascivious evil-doer, who, in the Acawai variant (M$_{134}$), repulses her murderous brother-in-law and behaves as an attentive mother and an inconsolable widow. But this version also takes great care to dissociate her from honey: when the heroine agrees to go into a hollow tree, it is only for the purpose of getting out an agouti. The ambiguity that we have recognized in honey, partly because of its two-fold quality of being both wholesome and poisonous (the same honey having either property according to the circumstances and the season), partly because of its character as a 'ready-made food' which gives it the status of a link between nature and culture, explains the ambiguity of the heroine in the honey myths; she too can be 'entirely natural' or 'entirely cultural', and her unstable identity is a consequence of this ambivalence. For additional proof we must return for a moment to the Chaco myths about the girl mad about honey, from which we started.

It will be remembered that those myths were characterized by the simultaneous presentation of two different plots and the presence of two protagonists. We also saw that the heroine who was mad about honey – so much so, indeed, that she neutralized her husband in his function as a relation by marriage – is reducible to a transformation of the Guiana heroine who is madly in love with her brother-in-law and who – by destroying her husband – neutralizes the relationship by marriage which stands in the way of her illicit designs. The other protagonist in the Chaco myths, Fox or the trickster, combines the two roles: he is both mad about honey and madly in love with his sister-in-law (literally, when she is his wife's sister and metaphorically, when she is the wife of one of his companions). Consequently, the Chaco myths can be arranged in a manner comparable to that shown in the diagram on p. 274, which related to the corresponding Guiana myths:

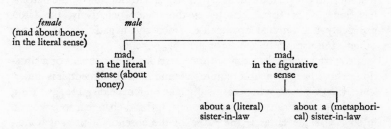

female
(mad about honey, in the literal sense)

male

mad, in the literal sense (about honey)

mad, in the figurative sense

about a (literal) sister-in-law

about a (metaphorical) sister-in-law

It may be objected that the literal sense of the word 'mad' refers to a mental disorder, with the consequence that the diagram uses it only in the figurative sense. I therefore recall my announced intention of assigning the literal meaning to the appetite for food and the figurative sense to the sexual appetite, throughout the discussion. The opposition *literal/figurative* does not refer to the word 'mad' but to the two forms of madness it serves to designate. That is why I have put a comma after the word 'mad' in each case.

A comparison of the two diagrams suggests several observations. They complete each other, since each applies the dichotomic analysis to only one of the two poles of the sexual contrast: the feminine pole in the first diagram, the masculine pole in the second. The literal and figurative senses, which alternate in one, are consecutive in the other. Lastly, the relationship connecting the masculine pole of the first diagram, or the feminine pole of the second, with the nearest term in either case, is a relationship of contiguity in one instance (the connection between cause and effect) and of resemblance in the other (the man and the woman are similarly mad about honey, in the literal sense).

It emerges from the preceding analysis that, although they are antagonistic to each other in the story, the heroine who is mad about honey and the trickster (whether animal or human in form) are really homologous: they themselves stand in a transformational relationship with each other. This is the basic explanation of the fact that the trickster can take on the appearance of the heroine and attempt to pass himself off as being her. Let us look at this point more closely.

The entire difference between the trickster (who tries to obtain both honey and his sister-in-law) and the heroine (who obtains honey but is obtained by the trickster) is connected with the fact that he is a man – an agent in respect of honey – and she a woman – acted upon in respect of honey – since the honey is transferred from the takers (of women) to the givers through the medium of the woman who establishes this relationship between them. The trickster is without honey; the heroine has honey. The former expresses the honey negatively, the latter positively but only in appearance, since she negativizes honey for others, and uses its presence for her sole benefit.

If the trickster is the negative and masculine embodiment of a situation, whose positive aspect requires a feminine embodiment, it is understandable that he should occasionally take on female disguise: as a man, he is the present cause of absent honey, and can change into a woman in so far as the latter is the cause of the absence of present honey. Therefore, if the trickster takes the place of the vanished heroine, this is because the latter is, at bottom, a female trickster, a vixen.[7] Far from constituting a problem, Fox's female disguise allows the myth to make an implicit truth manifest. The ambiguity of the Chaco heroine, who is seduced but whose character, on another level, fuses with that of her seducer, echoes the ambiguity of her Guiana opposite number.

The same demonstration can be carried out with, as the starting-point, the Ge myths which, as I have said, also stand in a transformational relationship to the Chaco myths, and therefore must have a similar relationship with the Guiana myths.

These myths raised a difficulty: why should a hero, who is chiefly remarkable for his virtues, suddenly appear to be overcome by madness in the Apinayé (M_{142}) and Kraho (M_{225}) versions, where he kills and roasts his wife, so as to offer the unfortunate woman's flesh to her unsuspecting parents? The Guiana parallels make it possible to settle the question through recourse to a different method from that used on the previous occasion, but one which will confirm the original conclusions:

M_{278}. *Warao*. '*The story of the man who was changed into a bird*'

There was once an Indian who shared a hut with his wife and her two brothers. One day, when the sky was overcast and there was a threat of rain, he remarked loudly that rain always made him sleep soundly. Whereupon, he lay down in his hammock and rain began to fall. His wife, full of good intentions, asked her brothers to help her to tie her husband up and put him outside. They left him outside in the rain all night long. When he woke at dawn, he said he had

[7] The crying baby, taken care of by a frog in M_{245} and by a frog mad about honey in M_{241}, is looked after by a vixen in other Guiana myths (M_{144}–M_{145}) and also in the myths of Tierra del Fuego (*RC*, p. 271, n. 35).

had a good sleep and asked for his bonds to be untied. He was mad with rage but concealed his anger. To get his own back on his wife, he took her out hunting, and instructed her to gather wood and build a barbecue, because he said he was going to kill an alligator which frequented a neighbouring pool. But as soon as his wife had done what he said, he killed her, cut off her head, carved up the rest of her body and smoked the pieces. He put the meat in a basket which he had woven meanwhile, and which he set down some distance from the village, as was the custom with hunters. Near the basket he drove a stake into the ground on which he propped the victim's head, with its silver brooch still in its nose and its eyes turned in the direction of the village. He brought back with him only the smoked liver, which won him a warm welcome on the part of his brothers-in-law who ate it very eagerly.

The Indian advised them to go to meet their sister because, he said, she was very heavily loaded. When they saw the head, they ran back as fast as they could to the village. The murderer had taken flight in a canoe and had taken care to untie all the others so that they should be washed downstream by the current. The brothers managed to find a boat and set off in pursuit. They had almost caught up with him when he jumped ashore and climbed up a tree, shouting: 'Your little sister is where I left her!' The brothers tried to strike him, but he had already changed into a kind of mutum (one of the gallinae, *Crax* sp.), the cry of which sounds like: 'Here little sister!' (Roth 1, pp. 201–2).

There are several known variants of this myth. In the Kalina version, which is transcribed by Koch-Grünberg following Penard (M$_{279a}$, K.-G. 1, p. 269), the hero was protected in his flight by two birds, *Ibycter americanus* (cf. M$_{277}$) and *Cassidix oryzivora*. After his brothers-in-law caught up with him, they cut off one of his legs and their victim decided to change himself into a constellation: that of Orion, 'which calls for the sun and supports it'. Ahlbrinck (under 'peti') gives other versions, one of which (M$_{279b}$) identifies the protective birds as *Crotophaga ani* and *Ibycter americanus*. The episode in which they occur will be discussed in the next volume. For a general comparison, the reader can refer to K.-G. 1, pp. 270–77. A Warao version (M$_{279d}$) ends with a massacre (Osborn 3, pp. 22–3).

It is not surprising that one of the gallinae should occur as a combinatory variant of a constellation, since I have already pointed out the 'nocturnal' character of these birds (*RC*, p. 204). In M_{28}, the shield of Orion is referred to as 'mother of the tinamidae' (Roth 1, pp. 264–5). Unfortunately we do not know whether the particular species that M_{279a} refers to is the one 'which sings regularly at two-hourly intervals throughout the night, with the result that the mutum is, for the natives, a kind of forest clock' (Orico 2, p. 174), or the one whose cry is heard at dawn, but in either case the calling of the bird can be interpreted as an appeal to the sun. On the other hand, the suggestion, in the last lines of M_{279a}, that Orion might be a nocturnal counterpart of the sun and a 'support' for it, raises the problem of the diurnal and nocturnal celestial phenomena which are correlated in the Indian way of thinking. The problem has already been encountered and partly solved in a particular instance: the connection between the rainbow and a dark area of the Milky Way (*RC*, pp. 246–7). But, for the time being, nothing would justify our extending the same argument to the sun and the whole, or part, of Orion. I shall show the same prudence in my treatment of Ahlbrinck's intriguing observation (*loc. cit.*) that the name of the hero of M_{279b} is that of a pervert.

Other myths belonging to the same area identify the mutum with the Southern Cross instead of Orion, because, according to Schomburgk (in: Teschauer, *loc. cit.*; cf. Roth 1, p. 261), one species (*Crax tomentosa*) begins to sing at the beginning of April, just before midnight, which is the time when the constellation reaches its highest point. This is why the Arecuna Indians call it paui-podolé 'the father of the mutum' (K.-G. 1, pp. 61–3, 277). Roth also mentions a constellation in the shape of a woman's severed leg, which the tinamidae greet with calls when it appears on the horizon before dawn (1, p. 173). But the birds are no longer the same in this case. However, at the period when the Southern Cross reaches its highest point before midnight, Orion is still visible on the western horizon a little after sunset. The bird heard at this time could, then, be associated with one or the other constellation.

It was not because of the astronomical implications that I introduced this group of myths, but for another reason. As it happens, the myths explicitly embody a grammatical contrast that I felt it was indispensable to have recourse to for the formulation of a hypothesis which is now seen to have been objectively justified, since M_{278} and $M_{279a, b}$, etc. tell, *ipsis verbis*, the story of a woman who has drawn the hatred of her husband upon herself *for having understood in the literal sense something that he had intended in the figurative sense*. Ahlbrinck's text is particularly clear on this point: 'There was once an Indian. One day he declared: "With rain like this I shall sleep well tonight." His wife misunderstood the remark and said to her brother: "My husband is stupid. He wants to sleep out in the rain." When night fell, the brothers tied the husband in his hammock and put him out in the rain. The next morning, he was as white as a sheet and absolutely furious ... ' (*loc. cit.*, p. 362).

We thus observe, on the rhetorical level, the final incarnation of a character who first appeared on the culinary level. The fault of the girl mad about honey lay in her exorbitant greed, which brought about the desocialization of a natural product, and caused it to be consumed immediately, whereas consumption ought to have been deferred so that the honey could be used in the exchanges between groups of affines. Still on the culinary level, the Ge transposed the situation from honey to meat, the consumption of which is postponed in this group by means of several taboos. The transformation of alimentary behaviour into linguistic behaviour which is brought about by M_{278}–M_{279}, implies then that, according to Indian thinking, the literal sense corresponds to an immediate 'consumption of the message' by natural means, and the figurative sense to a postponement of consumption, by cultural means.[8]

This is not the end of the matter. The story told by the Guiana myths confirms the link I have already established (pp. 122 *ff*) between the homologous Ge myths and the famous group of myths in which the heroine, or heroines, after being seduced by a tapir, must eat (= consume in the literal sense) the penis or the meat of the animal with which they have copulated (= that they consumed in the figurative sense). A comparison with M_{279} proves that the rule for the transformation of one group into another is even simpler than I suggested (diagram, p. 282).

If we broaden the paradigm so as to include, on the one hand, the Ge heroine in M_{142} and M_{225}, who is killed because of her greediness (for honey) and offered as meat by her husband to his affines and, on the other, the affine (mother-in-law) in M_{136} who is also killed, although for exactly opposite reasons – since she is the contrary of a greedy person: she produces fish, but by excretion, which turns them into an anti-food – we obtain a generalized system in which the relationship by marriage takes on opposite properties according to whether the

[8] A short Cavina myth (M_{279e}) tends in the same direction, since it tells how a woman changed into a monkey after scalding her little brother, whom she had thought fit to put in the boiling pot after her mother had instructed her to wash him with very hot water (Nordenskiöld 3, p. 389).

affine in question is male or female. For a woman, the male affine may be a human (according to culture) or an animal (according to nature): for a man, the female affine may be a wife (according to nature) or a mother-in-law (culturally, since the son-in-law has no physical relationship with her, only a moral one).[9] If, in this male philosophy, one of the

	CODE	FAULT COMMITTED BY THE WOMAN	PUNISHMENT
M_{156}–M_{160} (tapir as seducer)	alimentary	understanding figuratively what ought to have been understood literally	/eat/ an... .../illegitimate/... .../natural/... .../'taker'/
M_{278}–M_{279}	linguistic	understanding literally what ought to have been understood figuratively	/be eaten by/... .../legitimate/... .../cultural/... .../'givers'/

women forgets the lack of parity between the sexes, the woman's metaphorical food will be her real food, the daughter will become the food of the mother, or, alternatively, the mother will, metonymically, 'antifeed' her son-in-law and will be killed like her daughter.

The myths proclaim that the primary cause of this truly pathological distortion of the marriage relationship is an exorbitant greediness for honey. From M_{20} onwards – in which a too passionate couple, by their lust, corrupted the honey and made it unfit for use in the system of exchanges between brothers-in-law – by way of M_{24}, which reverses this pattern both on the alimentary and the sociological levels – since honey, polluted in a different and more serious way, brings about the break between the two members of an incompatible couple – in every case the myths comment persistently on the irreconcilability between the private relationship of the two spouses (i.e. the natural aspect of marriage) and their role as mediators in a relationship cycle corresponding to its social aspect.

The fox in the Chaco myth succeeds in seducing the girl; but he cannot become a son-in-law, since he is incapable of supplying his parents-in-law with honey. And the woman mad about honey in the

[9] Except, of course, in the case of a polygamous union with a woman and her daughter by a previous marriage, a practice which is not unknown in South America (L.-S. 3, p. 379), particularly in Guiana. However, the myths upon which I am basing my present argument belong to the Carib and Warao tribes, among whom the mother-in-law taboo was strictly observed (Roth 2, p. 685; Gillin, p. 76).

myths of the Gran Chaco and central Brazil, who is clever enough to find a husband, prevents him from also becoming a son-in-law and a brother-in-law, since she proposes to use for her own consumption the honey which would have enabled him to assume his position as an affine. In each case, then, the heroine is a lustful appropriator of the provisions intended for the system of exchanges between affines; and since honey is a natural product which she prevents from fulfilling a social role, she brings down the matrimonial relationship, as it were, to the level of physical union. The myths, in referring to her sad fate, thus utter a sociological condemnation (translated, however, into the terms of an alimentary code) of that *abuse of nature*, which we tolerate if it is short-lived, and which we describe in the terms of the same code, since we call it 'honeymoon'.

However, there is a difference. In our figurative speech, the 'honeymoon' refers to the short period during which we allow the bride and bridegroom to be exclusively concerned with each other: 'The evening and part of the night are devoted to pleasure; and in the day-time the husband reiterates vows of eternal love or describes in detail the delightful future that lies ahead' (*Dictionnaire des proverbes*, under 'lune de miel'). On the other hand, the (French) expressions 'lune de fiel' and 'lune d'absinthe'[10] denote the period when disagreement may begin as husband and wife take their place again in the pattern of social relationships. For us, then, honey is totally on the side of sweetness; it lies at one end of an axis at the opposite pole from bitterness or sourness, symbolized by gall and wormwood, which therefore appear as antitheses of honey.

According to the South American way of thinking, on the contrary, the opposition between sweetness and sourness is inherent in honey itself. This is partly because of the empirical distinction between bee honey and wasp honey, which are respectively wholesome and toxic in the fresh state; and partly because of the transformation undergone by bee honey, which becomes bitter when fermented, and proportionately more bitter as the process is more complete (cf. above, pp. 147–8). This attribution of ambivalence to honey occurs even in communities where mead is unknown. Thus, in Guiana, maize, manioc or wild fruit beer, which is normally bitter, is sweetened through the addition of fresh honey. And in the southern mead-drinking communities, mead is referred to as being bitter, but in comparison with fresh honey. The pole of 'fermentation' is therefore represented either

10 TRANSLATORS' NOTE: the moon of bile or gall; the wormwood moon.

by honey beer, which is bitter, or by bitter beer to which honey has not been added; the idea of honey remains present, positively or negatively, whether honey is referred to explicitly or is unmentioned.[11]

Consequently, as occasion requires, honey can be raised above its natural condition in two ways. On the sociological level, and without undergoing any physico-chemical transformation, honey fulfils a special role as the substance most appropriate for use in the system of exchanges between affines. On the cultural level, and after undergoing a physico-chemical transformation, fresh honey, which was immediately consumable without the performance of any ritual ceremonies, is changed, by fermentation, into a religious beverage the consumption of which is postponed. In one instance, honey is *socialized*; in the other, it is *culturalized*. The myths choose one formula or the other, according to the techno-economic infrastructure, or combine them, if the infrastructure so allows. Correlatively, the character whom we first encountered in the form of the woman mad about honey is defined in terms of one or other of these two dimensions; sometimes, she is properly socialized (her marriage is satisfactory), but culturally deficient (she does not allow the honey time to ferment) and desocializes her husband; sometimes she is basically a-social (in love with her brother-in-law and murders her husband) but doubly in keeping with

---

[11] The Machiguenga, a Peruvian tribe living in the region of the Rio Madre de Dios, use the same term for sweet and salty. They have a myth (M_{280}) about a supernatural being 'as sweet as salt' whose husband was always licking her. Exasperated by this, she changed him into a bee (siiro), and bees still have a great liking for human sweat.

The woman took as her second husband an Indian whom she fed on boiled fish. Surprised at being given such an abundance of food, the man spied on his wife and discovered that she brought forth the fish from her womb (cf. M_{136}), and this disgusted him. When he complained, his wife changed him into a humming-bird, which feeds on nectar from flowers and on spiders. She turned herself into a block of salt from which, since then, the Indians have got their supplies (Garcia, p. 236).

The myth shows that in a culture which does not distinguish between the flavours of salt and honey:

(1) the bee-woman of M_{233}–M_{234} becomes a salt-woman;
(2) the heroine is exasperated by her husband's greediness, instead of the husband being exasperated by his wife's generosity;
(3) the husband, not the wife, is changed into a bee;
(4) the wife is a consumer of sweat (salty) instead of being a producer of honey (sweet).

Moreover, the absence of any linguistic opposition between two flavours which are confused in the same sense category (the category of the tasty, no doubt) goes hand in hand with the fusion of the two characters who, elsewhere, are kept distinct: the bee-woman who feeds her husband on a positive substance which she secretes (honey), and the mother of the woman greedy for honey, who feeds her son-in-law on a negative substance, which she excretes (fish). An analysis of the myths about fish in North and South America would prove quite easily that, according to the Indian way of thinking, salt – a mineral yet comestible substance – stands at the point of intersection of food and excrement.

her culture, since Guiana is not a mead-drinking area and there is no reason why honey should not be consumed immediately.

The third item in my programme was the establishment of a direct correlation between the sociological and astronomical codes. To achieve this, I shall begin with a rapid review of the common features of the story of the woman mad about honey, as it occurs in the Chaco, Ge and Guiana myths, as well as in the Amazonian myth about Ceucy.

In her various incarnations, the woman mad about honey retains the same character, although it is displayed sometimes in her table-manners and sometimes in her amorous behaviour: she is *ill-bred*. The myth about Ceucy and the variants found in the Uaupés area all appear to be concerned with the definition of a particularly stern *female educational system*, a system which demands the execution of any unfortunate female who, voluntarily or accidentally, has been guilty of gazing upon the musical instruments used in the men's rites. The Rio Uaupés version (M_{276}) brings this point out very clearly since it mentions no less than three codes promulgated by successive legislators and which enumerate the various stages of the female initiation ceremonies: the obligatory shaving off of body hair, the fasting which must follow confinement, and the strict fidelity, discretion and reserve that they must maintain in their relations with their husbands, etc. (Rodrigues 2, pp. 53, 64, 69–70).

On the other hand, it should not be forgotten that, among the eastern and central Ge tribes, the story of the woman mad about honey belongs to the mythological cycle connected with the initiation rites of young men. These tales are meant as a preparation not only for military endeavour and productive labour, but also marriage; and they serve this edifying purpose by giving a description of an ill-bred woman for the benefit of inexperienced males. The myth about Ceucy operates in the same way, since it provides a single reason for the disabilities to which women are subject and those rites which are a male privilege. On all essential points, the disabilities and the prerogatives are, in fact, complementary.

The third volume in this series will complete the demonstration of the fact that this is an absolutely basic feature of the myths we are now considering, and that those myths shed light on a decisive stage in human thought, which is attested in innumerable other myths and rites the world over. It is as if, in bringing about the mystic submission of women to their authority, men had, for the first time but in a still symbolical way, grasped the principle which would one day allow them to solve the problems created by the numerical dimensions of society; as if, in subordinating one sex to the other, they had evolved a blueprint of the genuine, but as yet inconceivable or impracticable solutions, such as slavery, which would involve the subjection of certain men to the dominion of other men. We should not be misled by the *Malheurs de Sophie*[12] flavour of the story of the woman mad about honey. In spite of its apparent insipidity, which explains the scant attention the myth has so far attracted, its single central character is representative of the destiny of half of the human race, at that fatal point when it became subject to a disability the consequences of which have still not entirely disappeared and which – as the myths hypocritically suggest – might have been avoidable if an intemperate young woman had been able to control her appetite.

Let us rest content, for the time being, with having lifted a corner of the veil covering this dramatic situation, and let us proceed with the comparison. In one group of myths, the heroine briskly swallows the honey, whereas in the other she bears the name of a poisonous honey, which is no sooner eaten than it is vomited up. The Guiana variants present her as a maleficent creature who, operating from without, determines the appearance of the Pleiades in their male, food-providing role. The Ceucy cycle, on the contrary, shows her as being herself determined as the Pleiades, in their feminine form to which the Guiana Indians attribute a sinister significance. The beneficent character is linked with the abundant catches of fish obtained by the Indians through the use of poisonous plants, and the maleficent character with epidemics which kill human beings in large numbers. By way of this connection, the apparently anomalous conclusion of M_{279d} (above, p. 279), which tells of a fratricidal struggle in the course of which 'many Indians died', resumes its place in the group, at the same time as it can be added, as a further example, to the myths of the same type (M_2, M_3), which I was able to use in *The Raw and the Cooked* (pp. 279–81) for the precise purpose of demonstrating the homologous nature of fishing with poison and epidemics.

It will be remembered that the South American myths associate the rainbow, or the rainbow serpent, with the origin of fish poison and epidemics, because of the maleficent character attributed in native

[12] TRANSLATORS' NOTE: *The Misfortunes of Sophia*, a famous children's story by the Comtesse de Ségur.

thought to chromaticism, in the sense of the realm of small intervals. By means of a simple variation in the distance separating the terms, this realm can give rise to another, that of large intervals, which manifests itself on three levels of unequal extent: the universal discontinuity of living species, the havoc caused by diseases which produces a thinly scattered population, and the parallel effect on the fish population of the technique of poisoning (RC, pp. 256–81). The grouped, but apparently haphazard, arrangement of the stars forming the constellation of the Pleiades puts the latter, together with the rainbow, into the category of the continuous (RC, pp. 222–6): being similar to a fragment of the Milky Way that might have got lost in the sky, the constellation is symmetrical to the fragment of dark sky which happens, by accident, to be in the middle of the Milky Way and which, as I showed (RC, pp. 246–7), fulfils the role of nocturnal counterpart of the rainbow. Hence a triple transformation:

$$\begin{bmatrix} continuous \\ diurnal \end{bmatrix} \; 1 \left(\frac{chromatic\ light}{achromatic\ light} \right) \Rightarrow \begin{bmatrix} continuous \\ nocturnal \end{bmatrix} \; 2 \left(\frac{illuminated}{dark} \right) \Rightarrow 3 \left(\frac{dark}{illuminated} \right)$$

Moreover, we have seen (pp. 81–271) that there is a direct affinity between the first term (rainbow) and the last (Pleiades), provided we take into account the double contrast: *diurnal/nocturnal* and *daily/seasonal*. Both of them announce the cessation of rain, during a period either in the day or the year. We might almost say that the rainbow is, on a more restricted temporal scale, a diurnal constellation of the Pleiades.

I shall conclude the comparison of the two myth cycles (woman mad about honey and Ceucy) by pointing out that, in the Guiana-Amazonian versions, the first heroine is a married woman and a mother, whereas the other is a secluded virgin whom her own brother changes into a constellation in order to protect her virtue.

If we approach the matter from this angle, it becomes essential to widen the comparison. We know of a myth cycle whose heroine is equidistant from the other two: she is married but chaste, and is raped by her husband's brother or brothers. I am referring to Star, the wife of a mortal (M_{87}–M_{92}) who, in all other respects as well, is a simultaneous transformation of the woman mad about honey and Ceucy:

(1) She is a girl who is *too well bred* and who agrees to be a wet-nurse, not a wife.

(2) She vomits up maize, the prototype of *cultivated plants*, in the

face (M_{88}) or even into the mouth (M_{87a}) of her husband, instead of snatching the honey from his mouth (woman mad about honey) or being herself honey that is vomited up (Ceucy); nor must we forget that, according to Indian thought, honey is identified with *wild fruit*.

(3) Star comes down spontaneously from the sky to marry a human, whereas Ceucy represents the opposite case of a heroine who, against her will, is changed into a star *to prevent her* marrying a human, while the woman mad about honey – who is perhaps changed into a star in the Chaco myths for *having been a bad wife* to a future human (since she only allowed him to be a husband and not a son-in-law) – herself changes her husband into a star in the Guiana versions because, wishing to replace him by his brother, she condemns him to be merely an affine, not a husband.

(4) Finally, Star appears in the first instance as a food-provider, like the Pleiades in their masculine form, then as a bringer of death, like the constellation in its feminine form. Star performs the first function when she appears to men for the first time, and the second when she is on the point of leaving them – in a sense, then, at her 'rising' and her 'setting'. She thus represents an inversion of the significance of the Pleiades for the Guiana Indians, since the food-supplying constellation, which announces the arrival of the fish, seems to be the one which is visible in the evening on the western horizon, and this would seem to imply that the Pleiades are death-dealing at the time of their rising.

All these transformations, which allow us to integrate the cycle about Star, the wife of a mortal, into the group we are considering, involve an important consequence. We know that Star is an opossum, a forest animal in the first place in its food-supplying capacity and then a savannah animal in its capacity as a polluted and polluting creature, which brings death to men, after bringing them life through revealing cultivated plants to them (*RC*, pp. 164–88). Now it so happens that the character of the opossum is also expressed in terms of the astronomical and alimentary codes, to which I now return in completing the cycle of the demonstration. From the astronomical point of view, the opossum shows an affinity with the Pleiades since, according to a Rio Negro myth (M_{281}; cf. *RC*, p. 218, n. 8), the opossum and the chameleon chose the day of the first rising of the Pleiades to cauterize their eyes with pimentoes and to expose themselves to the beneficent action of the sun. But the opossum burnt its tail, which has remained hairless ever since (Rodrigues 1, pp. 173–7). Moreover, in Guiana the opossum has the same name as the rainbow (RC, pp. 249 ff), a fact which provides an additional confirmation of the equation on p. 287.

Secondly – and this is more important – the myths establish a link between the opossum and honey, as I shall show in two ways.

In one version at least of the famous Tupi myth about the twins (Apapocuva, M_{109}), the opossum plays the part of a food-supplying mother; after the death of their mother, the elder of the two boys does not know how to get food for his brother. He appeals to the opossum who, before acting as wet-nurse, is careful to clean the evil-smelling secretions from her breast. To thank her for this, the god provides her with a marsupial pouch and promises her that she will give birth without pain (Nim. 1, p. 326; Mundurucu version in Kruse 3, Vol. 46, p. 920). The southern Guarani have a variant of this myth, in which the opossum's doubtful milk is replaced by honey:

M_{109b}. *Parana Guarani. 'Honey as nourishment'* (extract)

After the murder of their mother, the elder of the twins, Derekey, did not know what to do with his brother, Derevuy, who had nothing to eat and was crying with hunger. Derekey began by trying to re-constitute the body of the dead woman, but his little brother hurled himself onto the scarcely formed breasts so voraciously that he undid Derekey's work. Then the elder boy discovered honey in the trunk of a tree and brought his brother up on it.

The bees belonged to the mandassaia or caipota variety (a sub-species of *Melipona quadrifasciata*, the honey of which is particularly sought after). When the Indians find a bees' nest of this kind, they never eat the larvae and they leave enough honey for them to live on. They do so as a mark of gratitude to the bees who fed the god (Borba, p. 65; cf. Baré, Stradelli 2, p. 259; Caduveo, Baldus 2, p. 37).

As a whole, and particularly in its conclusion, the episode offers such a close parallel with M_{109} that we may conclude that the food-supplying opossum and the bees stand in a transformational relation-ship with each other. This is brought out still more clearly by an earlier episode in the same myth, which also occurs in most other versions. At a time when it must be supposed that the opossum was still without a marsupial pouch, the mother of the twins herself behaves as if she had one, since she converses with her child or children although they are still in the womb. Communication is interrupted – in other words, the womb ceases to fulfil the same role as a marsupial pouch – after an incident which is related in the following terms in M_{109b}: 'The child in the womb asked his mother to give him some flowers. She was picking them here and there when she was stung by a wasp which was sipping honey ... ' (Borba, *loc. cit.*, p. 64). A Warao version (M_{259}), in spite of its geographical remoteness and the difference in language and culture, scrupulously preserves this reading: 'The mother had already picked several red and yellow flowers, when a wasp stung her below the waist. She tried to kill it, missed it, and struck herself. The child in the womb felt the blow and thought that it had been aimed at him; he was annoyed, and refused to continue to guide his mother' (Roth 1, p. 132; cf. Zaparo in Reinburg, p. 12).

Consequently, just as the real opossum, a good wet-nurse, is congruous with bees' honey, so the figurative opossum, who is a bad nursing-mother, is congruous with the wasp, whose honey is sour, if not poisonous. Not only does this analysis reveal a first connection between the opossum and honey; it also supplies an explanation, additional to the one I have already given on p. 236, of the recurrence of the myth about the twins in an apparently very different cycle, the starting-point of which is the origin (or the loss) of honey.

For the purposes of the second demonstration, I must refer to a series of myths which was partially examined in *The Raw and the Cooked* (M_{100}–M_{102}) and earlier in the present work (pp. 81, 82), and in which the tortoise is contrasted now with the tapir, now with the cayman or the jaguar, or again with the opossum.[13] In these stories, the tortoise or the opossum, or both of them, are buried by an opponent, or voluntarily bury themselves, to prove how well they can withstand hunger.

It is unnecessary to go into the details of the myths with which we are mainly concerned here, because they make use of seasonal points of reference: the periods of the year when such and such varieties of wild fruit are plentiful. I mentioned this (pp. 234 *ff*) in connection with plums, *Spondias lutea*, which ripen in January–February, at a time when the rain-soaked earth is already soft enough for the tapir to tread the tortoise into the ground. The latter succeeds in breaking free at the end of the rainy season, when the ground has become a quagmire (M_{282}; Tastevin 1, pp. 248–9). The same author supplies a variant which must be given more attention, since it illus-

---

[13] TRANSLATORS' NOTE. Here, and in the subsequent discussion, the author uses the masculine article, *le sarigue*, for the male or when the sex is not specified, and the feminine, *la sarigue*, whenever the female sex is indicated.

trates a type of myth to be found all the way from central Brazil to
Guiana:

M_{283a}. *Amazonia (Teffé area). 'The tortoise and the opossum'*

One day, the opossum stole the tortoise's flute. The latter wanted to
go after him, but being unable to run fast enough, changed its
mind, obtained some honey and smeared its anus with it, after hiding
its head in a hole.

The opossum noticed the gleaming honey and thought it was
water. He put his hand in, licked his fingers and realized his mistake.
But since the honey was delicious, the opossum applied his tongue to
it. At that moment, the tortoise nipped its buttocks together and the
opossum was caught. 'Let go of my tongue!' he cried. The tortoise
only agreed to do so after recovering its flute.

On another occasion, the opossum challenged the tortoise to a
contest, to see which of them could remain buried the longest
without food. The tortoise was the first to try and it remained until
the plums were ripe and began falling from the trees. Then it was the
turn of the opossum who proposed to remain buried until the wild
pineapples were ripe. When a month had gone by, the opossum
wanted to come out, but the tortoise told him that the pineapples
had hardly begun to swell. Two further months went by and the
opossum stopped answering. He was dead and only flies came out
when the tortoise opened the hole (Tastevin, *loc. cit.*, pp. 275–86).

Tastevin points out that the tortoise is the female (yauti) of the species
Testudo tabulata, which is bigger than the male (karumben). Throughout
the Amazonian area, the male and female of each species of tortoise seem
to have different names; these are, in the case of *Cinesteron scorpioides*
(?), yurari (f.) and kapitari (m.), and in the case of *Podocnemis* sp.,
tarakaya (f.) and anayuri (m.).

The origin of the tortoise's flute is the subject of another myth:

M_{284}. *Amazonia (Teffé area). 'The tortoise and the jaguar'*

After the tortoise had killed the tapir by biting its testicles (M_{282}),
it could not prevent the jaguar coming to claim its share of the feast.
Indeed, the jaguar took advantage of the fact that the tortoise was
away looking for wood, to steal all the meat, leaving only its excrements in exchange.

The tortoise went after it and encountered monkeys who helped it to climb up into the tree where they were gathering fruit. Then they left it.

The jaguar happened to pass and asked tortoise to come down. The latter asked the jaguar to close its eyes, dropped onto its head and broke its skull.

When the jaguar's carcass had rotted away, the tortoise took a shin-bone, turned it into a flute and played on it, singing: 'The jaguar's bone is my flute. Fri! Fri! Fri!'

Another jaguar came on the scene, and thought that the tortoise was threatening and challenging it. The tortoise was not successful in persuading it that it had misheard the words of the song. The jaguar made a bound, but the tortoise hid in a hole and deceived the jaguar into thinking that a foot, which was still visible, was a root. The jaguar set a toad to watch, but the tortoise blinded it with sand and took flight. When the jaguar came back, it dug up the ground in vain and consoled itself by eating the toad (Tastevin, *loc. cit.*, pp. 265–8; Baldus 4, p. 186).

By means of a transformation of this myth, it would be easy to work our way back to M_{55} (cf. *RC*, pp. 126–7). However, I shall leave this to be done by someone else, in case it should take me off in a very different direction from the one I am now proposing to follow and bring me up against the enormous problem of the mythical origin of musical instruments. As will be seen later, I shall not entirely succeed in avoiding the problem. This would certainly be a very rewarding direction in which to investigate, and it would lead us back to M_{136}, in which a mutilated hero, rising up into the sky, plays on a flute which produces the sound: tiu! tiu! tiu! (K.-G. 1, p. 57), whereas, in another story, the tortoise celebrates its victory over its opponents by crying: weh! weh! weh! and clapping its hands (M_{101}). In most of the myths of the tortoise cycle, the bone flute (which should, perhaps, be contrasted with the bamboo flute) seems to symbolize a disjunction (cf. below, p. 139).

But let us return to M_{283}, which uses other contrasts: between the tortoise and the opossum and between plums and pineapples. We know from M_{282} that plums ripen in the rainy season; it follows that the burial of the tortoise lasts from the end of the dry season to the rainy season, during the time of year when, as the myth points out, the plum trees flower, produce fruit and then shed this fruit. Consequently, the burial of the opossum must take place during the other part of the year and, as it must come to an end when the pineapples are ripe, this event must coincide with the end of the dry season. Tastevin gives no information on this point, but since I remember picking very juicy wild pineapples on the lower slopes of the Amazonian basin in August–September 1938, I think the supposition is well-founded. In the north-western part of the Amazonian basin pineapples are especially plentiful in October, which corresponds to the driest period, and this is the time of the so-called 'pineapple-feast' (Whiffen, p. 193).

The fasting contest inspired by the contrast between plums and pineapples follows on from another episode, which it reproduces in part; this is the flute-stealing episode, during which – according to the myth – the tortoise does not succeed in smearing its opponent with resin (Tastevin, *loc. cit.*, pp. 276, 279, 283) or wax (Couto de Magalhães, p. 20 of the *Curso*; the Tupi word is iraiti and, according to Montoya, who discusses the homophonous term in Guarani, the etymological meaning is 'honey-nest'), but does in the end succeed with honey. Thus we arrive at the diagram:

    (1) wax   honey
    (2) plums   pineapples

in which the left-hand column groups together entities in regard to which the opossum is in a strong position, while the right-hand column shows those in regard to which it is in a weak position: it is unable to resist honey, or unable (so far) to resist pineapples. Why are the terms themselves grouped in pairs? Like plums, wax makes it possible to hold out from the rainy to the dry season; it is the vehicle appropriate to the route leading from wet to dry: we know this from the story of Haburi or Aboré, the inventor of the first canoe which was made, precisely, of *wax*, and that men were ordered to copy henceforth in wood by 'the father of inventions' (Brett 2, p. 82). For what is a canoe, if not a means of overcoming the wet with the dry? Honey and pineapples make it possible to carry out the reverse movement, from the dry to the wet, since these are the kinds of wild fruit gathered during the dry season, as is indicated, in the case of honey, by the beginning of the verse transcription of the myth about Aboré:

Men must hunt for wild bees while the sun says they may

(Brett, *loc. cit.*, p. 26)

This is not all. Certain variants of M_{283}, in which the cayman plays the part of the flute-stealer, instead of the opossum, contain a feature exactly corresponding to the final detail in M_{283}: to oblige the cayman to give back the flute, the tortoise hides in a hole, showing only its honey-smeared behind 'from which, from time to time, there flew out a bee: zum ... ' (M_{283b}, Ihering, under 'jaboti'). There is thus a correspondence between the tortoise whose body has been 'changed into honey' and gives off bees, thus triumphing over the opossum, and the tortoise in the second part of the myth which gets the better of the opossum once and for all, because the latter's body has changed into rottenness, which is giving off flies ('meat flies', not 'honey flies'). In other words, honey makes the tortoise superior to the opossum, and rottenness makes the opossum inferior to the tortoise. As it happens, the opossum[14] is an evil-smelling creature, whereas the tortoise, a hibernating animal, is thought to be impervious to decay (RC, pp. 176–7).

What are we to conclude from these myths? The group I previously examined transformed the opossum's milk into honey and the marsupial into a bee; but on condition that the opossum first cleansed itself of the rottenness that is produced naturally by its body. Here, the opossum undergoes a reverse transformation: it is entirely assimilated to rottenness, but, in the last resort, because it first allowed itself to be seduced by honey. Yet it was able to resist wax, which represents the dry, non-perishable part of the bees' nest, whereas honey (because of the contrast that the myth establishes between the two terms) represents the wet, perishable part. The threat from wax therefore causes the opossum (*le* sarigue) to vary in a direction contrary to its nature as an evil-smelling creature, while the attraction of honey impels it in a direction in conformity with its nature, which it indeed carries to the logical limit by becoming carrion. On the one hand, honey stands in a position intermediary between wax and rottenness, thus confirming its ambivalent nature, which I have frequently emphasized. On the other hand, this ambivalence brings honey close to the opossum (*la* sarigue), which is also ambivalent in its two-fold capacity as a marsupial, i.e. a good wet-nurse, and as an evil-smelling creature. Once it is cured of this defect, the opossum tends in the direction of honey, with which it is confused through their resemblance; it becomes a wonderfully appropriate udder, producing milk as sweet as honey. When it is ravenous for honey and seeks to fuse with it, but this time by direct contact – so direct, indeed, that it plunges its tongue into the tortoise's behind – the opossum is the opposite of a wet-nurse, and since this

[14] TRANSLATORS' NOTE: The author now reverts to the feminine gender, *la sarigue*.

first attribute disappears, the other expands to the point of taking over entirely. This is precisely what the Tupi-Guarani myth-cycle about the twins is expressing in its way, since the opossum (*le* sarigue) occurs twice. First, as we have seen, as a female and in a food-supplying capacity. And later, as a man called 'opossum', who has a purely sexual role (cf. M_{96}). While the female opossum is careful to wash, her masculine counterpart stinks (cf. M_{103}).

The group that we have now considered over its whole extent comes to a close, then, on a homologous relationship between the Chaco fox and the Tupi-Guarani opossum (*le* sarigue). In the Chaco myths, the daughter of the Sun, who is abandoned by her husband when she is unwell, and whom Fox tries vainly to seduce, corresponds to the wife of the Sun, who is abandoned in a pregnant state by her husband and seduced by Opossum. Opossum is a false husband who passes himself off as the real one, Fox a false husband who passes himself off as (the wife of) the real one, and both of them give themselves away, the first by his animal stench (when he is claiming to be a human or a different animal), the second by his masculine roughness (when he is claiming to be a woman). It was therefore not entirely a mistake on the part of some early writers to apply to the opossum (*le* sarigue) the Portuguese word for fox: *raposa*. As the problem was expressed in native thought, there was an implication that one animal might be a combinatory variant of the other. They are both connected with the dry season, equally greedy for honey and, in their masculine form, endowed with the same lewd appetites; they only differ when they are considered *sub specie feminae*: the opossum (*la* sarigue) can become a good mother if it can rid itself of a natural attribute (its stench), whereas the fox, even when provided with artificial attributes (a false vagina and false breasts), only succeeds in being a grotesque wife. But is this not because Woman, eternally doomed to be opossum and fox,[15] is unable to overcome her self-contradictory nature and reach that perfection which, were it conceivable, would only serve to put an end to Jurupari's quest?

[15] As was shown on pp. 277–8, the Chaco heroine who is seduced by a fox is herself a vixen; and we have also seen (pp. 289–90) that the Tupi-Guarani heroine is, as it were, a female opossum *avant la lettre*, later to be seduced by a male opossum.

2 *Noises in the Forest*

In Indian thought, the idea of honey covers a multitude of ambiguities; first, because honey appears to have been 'cooked' by the processes of nature; then because of its various properties of being sweet or sour, wholesome or poisonous; and lastly because it can be consumed in either the fresh or the fermented form. We have seen how this substance which radiates ambiguity in all its aspects, is itself reflected in other, equally ambiguous, entities: the constellation of the Pleiades, which is alternatively male or female, food-supplying or death-dealing; the opossum (f.), an evil-smelling mother; and Woman herself, who cannot be counted on to remain a good mother and a faithful wife, since there is always a danger that she may turn into a lewd and murderous ogress, unless she is reduced to the condition of a secluded virgin.

It has also been noted that the myths are not content merely to express the ambiguity of honey by means of semantic equivalents. They also have recourse to meta-linguistic devices, when they make play with the duality of proper names and common nouns, metonymy and metaphor, contiguity and resemblance, the literal sense and the figurative sense. M_{278} establishes a link between the semantic and rhetorical levels, since the confusion between the literal and figurative meanings is specifically attributed to a character in the myth and is the mainspring of the action. Instead of affecting the structure of the myth, it is incorporated into the substance of the story. However, when a woman, who in the end is killed and eaten, makes the mistake of understanding in the literal sense something that was said figuratively, she is behaving in a fashion symmetrical to that of the tapir's mistress, whose mistake is to give the figurative meaning of copulation to that form of eating which normally can only be understood in the literal sense: i.e. the actual eating, by man, of the game he has caught. Her punishment consists in being obliged to consume, in the literal sense, i.e. to eat, the tapir's penis which she thought she would be able to consume figuratively.

But why, in some cases, must the woman eat the tapir, whereas in others she herself is eaten? I have already given a partial answer to this question (p. 123). We can go into it more deeply, however, by means of the distinction between the semantic and rhetorical codes. If we remember that the myths constantly oscillate between two levels, the symbolic and the imaginary (cf. above, p. 246), the preceding analysis can be summarized with the help of an equation:

[symbolical level]   *[imaginary level]*
    (swallowing of honey) :   (cannibalism within
                                    the family) : :

[symbolical level]   *[imaginary level]*
    (swallowing of the tapir) :   (copulation with
                                    the tapir) : :
                                 (literal sense) : (figurative sense)

Within the framework of this total system, the two mythic sub-groups – indicated by (*a*) in the case of the tapir-seducer and (*b*) in the case of the woman mad about honey – are each devoted to a local transformation:

(*a*) [*figurative* consumption of the tapir] ⇒ [*literal* consumption of the tapir]

(*b*) [*literal* consumption of honey] ⇒ [cannibalism within the family, as *figurative* consumption]

I now propose to introduce a new contrast: *active/passive*, corresponding to the fact that, in the tapir-seducer cycle, the woman is metaphorically 'eaten' by the tapir (for reasons of symmetry, since it has already been established that it is she who eats him literally), whereas in the woman-mad-about honey cycle, the heroine, who has been actively guilty of empirically observable greed, but a greed which in this instance *symbolizes* her lack of breeding, becomes the passive object of a cannibal family meal, the concept of which is entirely *imaginary*. This gives:

            (*a*) [figurative, passive] ⇒ [literal, active]
            (*b*) [literal, active] ⇒ [figurative, passive]

If, as I postulated, the two cycles stand in a complementary relationship to each other, it is essential that, in the second case, the woman, and not some other protagonist, should be eaten.

Only by understanding the myths in this way is it possible to find a common denominator for all the stories about the woman mad about honey, whether – as in the Chaco versions – she is literally greedy for the substance, or whether the myths describe her in the first place as wanting an affine (M_{135}, M_{136}, M_{298}) or an adopted child (M_{245}, M_{273}), and sometimes both at once (M_{241}, M_{243}, M_{244}; M_{258}) by carrying the idea of the honeymoon to its logical conclusion, as has been illustrated, in modern times, by Baudelaire, through a multiplication of the relationships with the loved one:

> *Mon enfant, ma sœur*
> *Songe à la douceur*
> *D'aller la-bas vivre ensemble!*

(My child, my sister
Think of the delight
Of going away to live there together!)

Once it is unified in this way, the woman-mad-about-honey cycle is consolidated by that of the tapir-seducer, which makes it possible to explain the fact that they intersect empirically. Both of them contain the theme of the character who is dismembered and barbecued and then served up to his unsuspecting family, like any ordinary game.

However, at this stage in the argument, we come up against a two-fold difficulty. It would be a waste of time to purify the substance of the myths by showing that some can be assimilated to others by the operation of transformation rules, if the effort thus expended brought to light cleavages within myths which, on a less sophisticated approach, had displayed no such complexity. Now, as it happens, while we were fusing together the characters of the tapir-seducer and the woman mad about honey in the melting-pot, each seemed to be displaying a dual nature which had not before been immediately perceptible; the simplification achieved on one level is thus in danger of being lost on another.

Let us consider first the character of the tapir. In its erotic activities, it is a representation of nature as seducer, congruous with honey. Its sexual potency, attested by an enormous penis, the size of which is amply stressed in the myths, is comparable, in the alimentary code, only with the seductive power of honey, for which the Indians have a veritable passion.

The relationship of complementarity that we discovered between the cycle of the tapir-seducer and that of the woman mad about honey shows that, according to the Indian way of thinking, honey fulfils the role of alimentary metaphor and corresponds to the sexuality of the tapir in the other cycle. Yet, when we look at the myths in which the tapir is presented as a subject in terms of the alimentary (not the sexual) code, its character is reversed: it is no longer a lover who fully satisfies his human mistress and sometimes feeds her by giving her an abundance of wild fruit, but a selfish and greedy creature. Consequently, instead of being congruous with honey as in the first instance, it becomes congruous with the woman mad about honey who, in her relationship with her parents, displays the same selfishness and greed.

According to several Guiana myths, the tapir was the first master of the food-tree and guards the secret of its location (cf. M_{114} and RC, pp. 184–8). And it will be remembered that, in M_{264}, the twins Pia and Makunaima each in turn take refuge with two animals which can be termed 'anti-food-suppliers'. The frog is so through over-abundance, since it produces a plentiful supply of food, which is really excrement; the tapir is so by default, when it conceals the location of the wild plum tree from the heroes and fattens itself on the fallen fruit.

The tapir's mistress displays exactly the same divergence. On the alimentary level, she is a bad wife and a bad mother who, being absorbed by her passion, neglects to cook food for her husband and to suckle her child (M_{150}). But, sexually speaking, she is a glutton. Consequently, far from complicating our task, the duality peculiar to the principal actor in each cycle confirms my thesis; since this duality is always of the same type, it confirms rather than contradicts the homology I postulated. This homology is certainly displayed through a relationship of complementarity: on the erotic level, the tapir is prodigal, while its human mistress is greedy; on the alimentary level, it is the tapir which is greedy, whereas its mistress, who displays a prodigal attitude towards it in one version (M_{159}), elsewhere has a negligent approach which shows that, for her, the alimentary area is 'unmarked'.

The woman-mad-about-honey cycle and the tapir-seducer cycle, when consolidated by each other, form then a meta-group the outlines of which correspond, on a larger scale, to the pattern I evolved in the second part on the basis of only one of the two cycles. The existence of the rhetorical and erotico-alimentary dimensions on the level of the meta-group was sufficiently brought out in the preceding discussion for further emphasis upon it to be unnecessary here. But the astronomical dimension is also present, and the tapir-seducer cycle refers to it in two ways.

The first reference is, no doubt, implicit. Outraged by the fact that their husbands have compelled them to eat the flesh of their lover, the women decide to leave home and change into fish (M_{150}, M_{151}, M_{153}, M_{154}). In these versions, which are all Amazonian, we are dealing with a myth about the origin or plentifulness of fish, a phenomenon that the myths of the Guiana-Amazonian area ascribe to the Pleiades. Consequently, in this sense, the tapir-seducer, like the Pleiades, is responsible for the abundance of fish. The parallel between the animal and the constellation is strengthened if we remember that the constellation of the Pleiades, i.e. Ceucy in the myths of the Tupi Amazonians, is a secluded virgin who was changed into a star by her brother *the better to preserve her virginity* (M_{275}). As it happens, the Mundurucu (who are Tupi Amazonians) say that the tapir-seducer is an incarnation of Korumtau, the son of the demiurge, who was forced by his father to take on this animal form because, as a secluded youth, *he had lost his virginity*. Such, at least, is the continuation of M_{16}, the beginning of which is to be found in *RC*, pp. 57, 85.

The preceding deduction is directly confirmed by the Guiana myths belonging to the tapir-seducer cycle, and this shows, incidentally, that Roth was too hasty in supposing that some European or African influence must be responsible for the fact that, in both the Old and the New Worlds, Aldebaran is compared to the eye of some large animal, tapir or bull (Roth 1, p. 265):

M_{285}. *Carib (?)*. '*The tapir-seducer*'

An Indian woman, who had been married only a short while, one day met a tapir which courted her passionately. It said it had assumed animal form in order to approach her more easily when she went out into the fields, but that if she agreed to follow it eastwards to the point where sky and earth meet, it would resume its human shape and marry her.

The animal put a spell on her and the young woman made a show of helping her husband to gather avocado pears (*Persea gratissima*). While he was climbing up the tree, she chopped off one of his legs with an axe and ran away (cf. M_{136}). Although he was bleeding profusely, the wounded man managed, by magic, to change one of his eyelashes into a bird, which went to fetch help. The hero's mother arrived on the scene in time. She took care of her son and he recovered.

Using a crutch, the lame husband set off in search of his wife, but the rain had obliterated all her tracks. However, he succeeded in catching up with her by following the trail of avocado plants which had sprung up in the places where she had eaten the fruits and thrown away the stones. The woman and the tapir were together. The hero shot the animal to death with an arrow and cut off its head. Then he asked his wife to return with him, otherwise he would pursue her eternally. The wife refused and hurried on with her lover's spirit still after her and her husband behind them both. When they reached the edge of the earth, the woman threw herself into the sky. On a clear night she can still be seen (the Pleiades), with the Tapir's head (the Hyades: the red eye is Aldebaran) close behind and the hero (Orion, with Rigel indicating the upper part of the sound limb) – all three in pursuit (Roth 1, pp. 265–6).

The reference to avocadoes and avocado stones raises a problem which will be dealt with in the next volume. Here I shall restrict myself to pointing out: (1) the parallel between this myth and M_{136}, in which another dissolute wife chops off her husband's leg; (2) the fact that both myths are concerned with the origin of the Pleiades, considered separately or in relation to neighbouring constellations. In one case, the body of the mutilated husband becomes the Pleiades, and his leg the shield of Orion; in the other case, the woman herself becomes the Pleiades, the tapir's head the Hyades, and Orion represents the husband (minus his severed leg) (cf. M_{28} and M_{131b}). The tapir-seducer myth is therefore using an astronomical code to convey a message which is hardly different at all from that of the myths about the origin of the Pleiades belonging to the same area.

But it is the sociological code in particular which is worthy of attention. It proves more clearly than the others the complementary nature of the two cycles, while at the same time integrating them into the much greater whole which is being investigated in this series of volumes. The woman mad about honey in the Guiana myth (M_{136}), and the tapir's mistress who figures in other myths, are both adulterous wives; but they are so in two different ways, which illustrate the extreme forms that the crime of adultery can assume: it may be committed with a brother-in-law who represents the nearest temptation, or with a forest animal representing the most remote temptation. The animal is a manifestation of nature, whereas the brother-in-law, whose closeness is the result of a connection by marriage and not of a blood relationship, which would be biological, is a purely social manifestation:

(tapir : brother-in-law) :: (remote : close) :: (nature : society)

This is not all. Readers of *The Raw and the Cooked* will no doubt remember that the first group of myths I introduced (M_1–M_{20}) – and what I am saying here is, in a sense, only a continuation of my commentary – were also concerned with the problem of relationships by marriage. But between those myths and the ones I am now considering, there is obviously a major difference. In the first group, the affines were chiefly wives' brothers or sisters' husbands, i.e. givers and takers respectively. In so far as every marriage relationship implies collaboration between these two categories, we were dealing with mutually unavoidable brothers-in-law whose action had an organic character and whose conflicts were therefore a normal expression of life in society.

In the second group, on the contrary, the affine is not an inevitable partner, but an optional competitor. Whether the brother-in-law is seduced by the wife or whether he himself plays the role of seducer, he is always a brother of the husband, i.e. a member of the social group whose existence is not essential to the marriage relationship, and who therefore figures as a contingent detail in the domestic pattern. Among the instructions given by the Baniwa to their young men on initiation is the rule 'not to go after their brothers' wives' (M_{276b}). If we take a theoretical view of society for a moment, it is clear that, to be sure of obtaining a wife, each man must be able to dispose of a sister, but he is under no obligation to have a brother. As the myths explain, a brother can, in fact, be a handicap.

Admittedly, the tapir is an animal, but the myths turn it into a 'brother' of the man, since it deprives him of his wife. The only difference is that whereas the human brother, through the mere fact of his existence, is automatically part of the pattern of relationships caused by marriage, the tapir makes a sudden and unexpected incursion into the pattern, simply by virtue of his natural attributes; he is a pure seducer, i.e. a socially void entity (*RC*, p. 276). In the social interplay of marriage relationships, the intrusion of the human brother-in-law is accidental,[16] but that of the tapir amounts to a scandal. But whether the

---

[16] The same is true of the homologous sister-in-law, i.e. the sister of the wife who figures in the Chaco (M_{211}) and Guiana myths (M_{235}), of which – as I have shown – the myths

myths are concerned with the consequences of a *de facto* situation, or with those resulting from the subversion of a *de jure* situation, what they are dealing with, as I have suggested, is undoubtedly a pathological state of the marriage relationship. There is, then, a distinct gap between them and the myths that I used as my starting-point in *The Raw and the Cooked*. The first myths, which were centred on the fundamental realities of cooking (instead of on honey and tobacco – each, in their different ways, culinary paradoxes), dealt with the physiology of the marriage relationship. Just as there can be no cooking without fire and meat, the marriage relationship cannot be established without wives' brothers and sisters' husbands, who are totally significant brothers-in-law.

It may be objected that fire and meat are not necessary conditions of cooking to the same degree; it is certainly impossible to cook without fire, but lots of other things besides game may be put into the pot. However, it should be noted that the pattern of marriage-relationships in which the brother, or brothers, of the husband figure as pathogenic elements, first appeared in connection with the cycle about Star who married a mortal, which dealt with *the origin of cultivated plants* (M_{87}–M_{92}), i.e. with something logically earlier than the origin of cooking, and which is even specifically stated in one myth (M_{92}) to have come before cooking (*RC*, p. 167).

Cooking is a mediatory process of the first order between (natural) meat and (cultural) fire, whereas cultivated plants – which are already in their raw state the result of a mediation between nature and culture – are subjected by cooking only to derivative and partial mediation. The ancients understood this distinction, since they thought that agriculture involved a form of cooking. Before the seed was sown, the upturned clods of earth had to be cooked, 'terram excoquere', through exposure to the sun's heat (Virgil, *Georgics*, II, v. 260). Thus, the actual cooking of cereals was a secondary culinary process. It is true that wild plants may also be used as food but, unlike meat, many of them can be eaten raw. They therefore constitute an indefinite category, hardly suitable for the purposes of a demonstration. This mythic demonstration, when carried out with the *cooking* of meat and the *cultivation* of food plants as simultaneous starting-points, leads, in the first instance, to the achievement of culture and, in the second instance, to the achievement of society; and the myths assert that the latter came after the former (*RC*, pp. 185–8).

---

about the husband's brother are a transformation. In the tapir-seducer cycle, transformation may also give a seductress-figure (M_{144}, M_{145}, M_{158}).

What must we conclude from this? Like cooking considered in its pure state (the cooking of meat), the marriage relationship considered in its pure state – i.e. involving brothers-in-law purely as giver and taker[17] – expresses the essential interconnection, in native thought, between nature and culture. On the other hand, the myths suggest that the birth of a neolithic economy, involving an increase in the number of communities and the diversification of languages and customs (M_{90}) gave rise to the first difficulties in social life, through population growth and a more haphazard composition of family groups than the beautiful simplicity of the models[18] would have allowed. This is precisely what Rousseau said 200 years ago in his *Discours sur l'origine de l'inégalité*, and I have often drawn attention to his profound ideas, which have been unfairly criticized. The evidence supplied by the South American Indians, and that I have shown to be implicitly present in their myths, cannot, of course, be accepted as an authoritative rehabilitation of Rousseau's views. But it not only indicates a remarkable connection between modern philosophy and these strange stories which, at first sight, would hardly seem capable of such a lofty interpretation; we should also be wrong to forget that when mankind, in reflecting upon itself, finds itself prompted to make the same suppositions, in spite of the extraordinarily different circumstances from which they spring, there is a great probability that the repeated convergence of thought with an object which is also its subject, reveals some essential aspect, if not of the history of mankind, at least of human nature with which that history is bound up. In this sense, the diversity of the paths by which Rousseau and the South American Indians – the first consciously, the second unconsciously – were led to make the same speculations about a very remote past, doubtless proves nothing about that past, but it does prove a great deal about man. If man is such that, in spite of the diversity of times and places, he cannot

[17] One always looks upon himself as the incarnation of culture, while the myths relegate the other to the category of nature; in terms of the culinary code, this gives a master of cooking fire and, according to circumstances, sometimes a consumer of raw meat (the jaguar in M_7–M_{12}), sometimes game which is to be cooked (the wild pigs in M_{16}–M_{19}). The equation:

$$(\text{giver} : \text{taker}) :: (\text{cooking fire} : \text{meat})$$

was analysed in *RC*, pp. 83–107.

[18] Therefore, these models must be essentially paleolithic in inspiration. This is not to assert, but merely to accept as a possibility, that the Indian conceptions of the marriage relationship, as they are expressed in the rules about exogamy and in the preferences for certain types of relations, go back to such a remote period in the life of mankind. I have touched on this problem in a lecture: 'The Future of Kinship Studies', *Proceedings of the Royal Anthropological Institute of Great Britain and Ireland for 1965*, pp. 15–16.

escape the obligation to entertain similar ideas about how he came into being, his genesis cannot have been in contradiction with that human nature indirectly expressed in the recurrent ideas that men, in various parts of the world, have formulated about their past.

Let us now return to the myths. We have seen that, on the level of the meta-group formed by the tapir-seducer and the woman-mad-about-honey cycles, there survives an ambiguity that had already occurred on humbler levels. Since we are dealing therefore with a structural characteristic of the meta-group, it is appropriate to pay particular attention to one of its modalities which, at first sight, seems to occur only in the tapir-seducer cycle, where it uses the resources of an acoustic code that I have not yet had occasion to consider.

Almost all the myths about a heroine who allows herself to be seduced by an animal – usually a tapir, but sometimes also a jaguar, a snake, a cayman and, in North America, a bear – carefully describe the way in which the woman sets about summoning her lover. In this respect, they can be divided into two groups, according to whether the woman pronounces the animal's name and thus addresses a personal invitation to him, or whether she is content to send an anonymous message which often consists in tapping on a tree-trunk or on a calabash-bowl placed upside down on the water.

Let me give some examples of myths belonging to the first group. Kayapo-Kubenkranken (M_{153}): the tapir-man is called Bira; Apinayé (M_{156}): the cayman's mistresses cry: 'Minti! Here we are!' Mundurucu (M_{49}): the name of the serpent-seducer is Tupasherébé; (M_{150}): the tapir-seducer appears when the women call him by his name, Anyo-caitché; (M_{286}): the hero is in love with a female sloth and calls to her 'Araben! Come to me!' (Murphy 1, p. 125; Kruse 2, p. 631). The future Guiana amazons (M_{287}) call the jaguar-seducer by his name, Walyarimé, which later becomes their rallying cry (Brett 2, p. 181). The tapir in M_{285} tells the woman to whom he is paying court, that his name is Walya (*ibid.*, p. 191). The serpent in a Waiwai myth (M_{271}, M_{288}), which is reared by a woman as a domestic pet, is called Pétali (Fock, p. 63). The cayman-seducer in the Karaja myth (M_{289}) is called Kabroro; the women make him a long speech, to which he replies since, in those days, caymans knew how to talk (Ehrenreich, pp. 83–4). The Ofaié myth (M_{159}) does not mention any name for the tapir, but his mistress calls him with the term 'Benzinho, o benzinho', literally 'blessed little one'. The Tupari myths on the same theme (M_{155}) say that the women summoned the tapir 'with a seductive call' and that, later, 'they repeated the same words' (Caspar 1, pp. 213–14). Sometimes these proper names are no more than the ordinary word for the animal used as a vocative (M_{156}, M_{289}) or as a surname (M_{285}, M_{287}).

The second group includes myths belonging in some cases to the same tribes. Kraho (M_{152}): the woman calls the tapir by striking the trunk of a buriti palm tree. Tenetehara (M_{151}): a tree-trunk, or (M_{80}), where the animal is a big snake, a calabash (Urubu) or by stamping her foot (Tenetehara). To summon their lover, the Mundurucu mistresses of the snake (M_{290}) strike a half-gourd that has been placed upside down on the water: pugn ... (Kruse 2, p. 640). Similarly in Amazonia (M_{183}), to call the rainbow-snake from out of the water. In Guiana (M_{291}), the two sisters call their lover, the tapir, by putting their fingers in their mouths and whistling (Roth 1, p. 245; cf. Ahlbrinck, under 'iriritura'). There is also a whistling call in the Tacana myths, but it is produced by the tapir- or snake-seducer (H.-H., pp. 175, 182, 217); I shall return to this inversion later (see below, pp. 330–31).

It would be easy to add other examples to this list. Those already given are enough to establish the existence of two types of call in relation to the animal acting as seducer. These types are clearly contrasted, since they can be summarized as either linguistic in nature (proper name, common noun used as a proper name, seductive words), or sonorous but non-linguistic (striking gourds, trees or the ground; whistling).

At first sight, we might be tempted to explain the dualism by reference to customs which are known to exist elsewhere. Among the Cubeo on the river Uaupés, the tapir (which the Indians say they have hunted only since they have had guns) is the only variety of large game: 'The hunters keep watch near a stream, where the ground contains salt. The tapir goes there in the afternoons, always following a customary route, and it leaves deep tracks in the muddy earth. Among the maze of these deep pathways fresh tracks and fresh dung are the signs of current use. A man who has seen a fresh track reports it. The hunters go out to kill a tapir who has already been observed, so that they may speak of him in personal terms' (Goldman, pp. 52, 57). When I was with the Tupi-Kawaib in the Rio Machado area, I myself took part in a hunt in which the tapped-out call was used: to make the wild pigs, jaguars or tapirs believe that wild fruit was falling from a tree and so head them into an ambush, the natives struck the ground with a stick at regular intervals: poum ... poum ... poum ... The peasants of central Brazil call this *batuque* hunting (L.-S. 3, p. 352).

In the most favourable hypothesis, these methods may have inspired the stories in the myths, but they do not provide a satisfactory interpretation of them. Admittedly the myths refer to hunting (men hunt the tapir), but their starting-point is different; the gourd call, which is the most frequent tapped-out call, does not correspond to any known practice; then the two types of call stand in opposition to each other, and it is the opposition which has to be explained, not each particular call.

Although the two types are contrasted, each independently has a connection with one or other of the two forms of contrasting behaviour, the function of which I discussed in relation to the Guiana myths about the origin of honey (M_{233}–M_{234}). To attract the animal lover (who is also an evil-doer), either his name has to be pronounced or something must be struck (ground, tree, gourd placed on the water). In the myths I have just referred to, on the other hand, to hold the benefactor (or the benefactress) back, his or her name must not be pronounced and the object must not be struck (in this instance, it is the water with which the seductresses try to splash him). The myths furthermore make it clear that the benefactor or benefactress are not sexual seducers, but modest, reserved and even shy individuals. We are thus dealing with a system involving two forms of linguistic behaviour, speaking and not speaking, and two forms of non-linguistic behaviour, with a positive and a negative significance. According to the particular case, the values of the two forms of behaviour are inverted within each pair; the behaviour homologous to that which attracts the tapir drives away honey, the behaviour homologous to that which holds back the honey does not attract the tapir. At the same time, it should not be forgotten that, whereas the tapir is a sexual seducer, honey is an alimentary seducer:

To effect a conjunction with the sexual seducer:	To prevent disjunction from the alimentary seducer:
(1) pronounce his name	(1) avoid pronouncing his name
(2) strike (something)	(2) do not strike (the water)

However, I pointed out that, in the animal-seducer cycle, the tapped-out call is sometimes replaced by a whistled call. In order to carry the analysis further, we must therefore also determine its position in the system.

Like the Indians of the Uaupés river (Silva, p. 255, n. 7) and the Siriono of Bolivia (Holmberg, p. 23), the Bororo communicate with each other at a distance by means of a whistled language, which, far from being limited to a few conventional signals, seems to be a thorough transposition of articulate speech, and so can be used for the transmission of the most varied messages (Colb. 3, pp. 145–6; *EB*, Vol. I, p. 824). It is referred to in a myth:

M$_{292a}$. Bororo. 'The origin of the names of the constellations'
An Indian, accompanied by his little boy, was hunting in the forest, when he noticed a dangerous sting-ray in the river and promptly killed it. The child was hungry and asked his father to cook the sting-ray. The father agreed only grudgingly, because he wanted to carry on fishing. He lit a small fire and, as soon as there were a few embers, he placed the fish on them, after wrapping it in leaves. Then he went back to the river, leaving the child near the fire.

After a while, the boy thought the fish was cooked and called his father. The latter, who was some distance away, shouted to the boy to be patient, but the boy called again and the father, by now thoroughly irritated, came back, took the fish from the fire, saw that it had not yet finished cooking, threw it in his son's face, and went off again.

Burnt and blinded by the embers, the boy began to cry. Strangely enough, echoing cries and murmurs came from the forest. The father took flight in terror, while the child, crying more loudly still, grasped a bokaddi sprout (= bokaddi, bokwadi, jatobá tree: *Hymenea* sp.) which he addressed as 'grandfather' and which he asked to rise in the air and lift him up. At once, the tree began to grow, while a terrible noise could be heard at the base of the trunk. This was caused by the Spirits (kogae) who never left the tree. By now the boy was up in the branches and, from his place of refuge there, he saw that, whenever a star or a constellation rose during the night, the Spirits hailed it by its name in the whistled language. The boy was careful to memorize all the names, which had previously been unknown.

Taking advantage of a moment of inattention on the part of the Spirits, the boy begged the tree to grow small again, and as soon as he could jump to the ground he ran off. It was from him that men learned the names of the constellations (Colb. 3, pp. 253–4).

We do not know much about the Spirits (kogae), except that an unidentified plant, which is used as a hunting talisman, as well as a reed instrument, are referred to by means of a phrase which includes the word kogae, but no doubt in the second case this is because of a connection between this particular family of Spirits, the decoration peculiar to the musical instrument and the badegeba cebegiwu clan of the Cera moiety (cf. *EB*, Vol. I, pp. 52, 740). Because of this uncertainty, and also to avoid overburdening the discussion, I shall not indicate the series of fairly simple transformations which would bring us back directly from M_{292a} to M_2, i.e. almost to our original starting-point[19] (see the table below).

Let us merely note – since the point will be needed later – that the relevant transformation seems to be:

$$M_2 \qquad M_{292}$$
$$(\text{filth}) \Rightarrow \qquad (\text{noise})$$

$$
\left[
\begin{array}{l}
\text{a young boy} \\
\text{accompanying}
\end{array}
\left\{
\begin{array}{l}
M_2: \text{his mother} \\
M_{292a}: \text{his father}
\end{array}
\right\}
\text{witnesses}
\left\{
\begin{array}{l}
M_2: \text{an aggression which} \\
\quad \text{turns into } sexual \\
\quad \text{consummation} \\[4pt]
M_{292a}: \text{a } threat \text{ of aggression which} \\
\quad \text{does } not \text{ turn into} \\
\quad alimentary \text{ consummation}
\end{array}
\right.
\right]
$$

//

[19] To justify this sudden back-reference, I should point out that the Bororo consider the sting-ray as the metamorphosis of an Indian exasperated by the jeers showered on his son by the child's young friends (Colb. 3, pp. 254–5). This myth (M_{292b}) consequently belongs to the 'vindictive father' group, which also includes M_2, M_{15}–M_{16} and M_{18}, and in which the changing of the self into a poisonous ray (skate?) corresponds to the changing of other people into wild pigs, and of the tapir into an 'other' (cf. *RC*, pp. 214–18, 278–9). It can be shown that, in both North and South America, the ray's tail represents an inverted seductive penis. For South America, cf. M_{247} (the episode in which the tapir *hostile to the hero-seducer* is killed through being impaled on the barb of a ray, Amorim, p. 139), and the Chipaya myth (M_{292c}) about a man who dies while copulating with a ray-woman, through being pierced by her barbs (Nim. 3, pp. 1031–2). The Warao of Venezuela compare the sting-ray to a young woman (Wilbert 9, p. 163). According to the Baniwa, the ray sprang from Jurupari's placenta (M_{276b}). In the Karaja myths, the sting-ray is part of a system which includes the piranha fish and the dolphin, associated respectively with the toothed vagina and the seductive penis (cf. Dietschy 2). For North America, the chief reference is the myths of the Yurok and other Californian tribes, who compare the ray to the female genital system (the body is the womb and the tail the vagina). According to one myth (M_{292d}), Lady-Skate is an irresistible seductress who captures the demigod during copulation by catching his penis between her thighs and thus succeeds in removing him once and for all from the human world (Erikson, p. 272; Reichard, p. 161). Such is also the ultimate fate of the demiurge, Baitogogo, the hero of M_2.

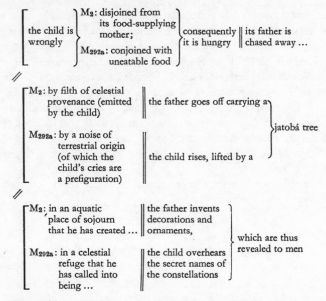

$$\left[\begin{array}{l}\text{the child is}\\\text{wrongly}\end{array}\left\{\begin{array}{l}M_2\text{: disjoined from}\\\quad\text{its food-supplying}\\\quad\text{mother;}\\M_{292a}\text{: conjoined with}\\\quad\text{uneatable food}\end{array}\right\}\begin{array}{l}\text{consequently}\\\text{it is hungry}\end{array}\|\begin{array}{l}\text{its father is}\\\text{chased away} \ldots\end{array}\right.$$

//

$$\left[\begin{array}{l}M_2\text{: by filth of celestial}\\\quad\text{provenance (emitted}\\\quad\text{by the child)}\\\\M_{292a}\text{: by a noise of}\\\quad\text{terrestrial origin}\\\quad\text{(of which the}\\\quad\text{child's cries are}\\\quad\text{a prefiguration)}\end{array}\right.\begin{array}{l}\|\text{the father goes off carrying a}\\\\\\\|\text{the child rises, lifted by a}\end{array}\left.\right\}\text{jatobá tree}$$

//

$$\left[\begin{array}{l}M_2\text{: in an aquatic}\\\quad\text{place of sojourn}\\\quad\text{that he has created}\ldots\\\\M_{292a}\text{: in a celestial}\\\quad\text{refuge that he}\\\quad\text{has called into}\\\quad\text{being}\ldots\end{array}\right.\begin{array}{l}\|\text{the father invents}\\\|\text{decorations and}\\\|\text{ornaments,}\\\\\|\text{the child overhears}\\\|\text{the secret names of}\\\|\text{the constellations}\end{array}\left.\right\}\begin{array}{l}\text{which are thus}\\\text{revealed to men}\end{array}$$

The child in M_2 who, after being changed into a bird, pollutes its
father with the excrement that it drops on his shoulder (*from above*),
in M_{292} disturbs him (*from a distance*) by untimely calls. The young hero
of M_{292} therefore provides a further illustration of the crying baby
that we have already encountered in M_{241}, M_{245}, and whom we shall
meet again later. At the same time, the *droppings* (excretion) of a very
small bird, falling from *above*, change into an *enormous* tree which causes
the father to go *far away*; symmetrically, the *tears* (secretion) of a *small*
child are changed into an *enormous* noise which causes the father to go
far away and the child himself to rise to a *high* position. The filth in M_2
plays the part of primary cause in the appearance of water, which
occupies an extraordinarily ambiguous place in Bororo culture: the
water poured over the temporary grave speeds up the decay of the
flesh, and thus engenders corruption and filth; yet when the bones have
been washed, painted and decorated, they are finally immersed in a lake
or a river which serves as their last resting place, since water is the
abode of souls, and the condition and means of their immortality.

The whistled language seems to share the same ambiguity on the
acoustic level: it belongs to spirits who produce a terrifying din (I
have just shown that this din is congruous with filth; in *The Raw and
the Cooked* it was established that noise, in the form of 'charivari',

was congruous with moral 'corruption'); and yet, although the whistled language is closer to noise than to articulate speech, it conveys information that articulate speech could not have transmitted since, at the time of the myth, men did not know the names of the stars and the constellations.

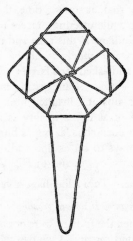

Figure 14. The sting-ray. A figure in a string game. Warao Indians.
(Taken from Roth 2, Fig. 318, p. 543.)

Consequently, following M₂₉₂ₐ, the whistled language is something more and better than a language. Another myth also explains in what way it is better but, this time, it would seem, because it is something less:

M₂₉₃. Bororo. 'Why corn-cobs are thin and small'

There was once a Spirit named Burékoïbo whose maize fields were incomparably fine. This Spirit had four sons, and he entrusted the task of planting to one of them, Bopé-joku. The latter did his best and every time the women came to gather maize, he would whistle: 'fi, fi, fi', to express his pride and satisfaction. And indeed, Burékoïbo's maize was very enviable, because of its heavy grain-loaded cobs ...

One day, a woman was gathering maize, while Bopé-joku was whistling away gaily, as usual. She was doing the work rather roughly and she cut her hand on one of the cobs she was picking. Upset by the pain, she insulted Bopé-joku and complained about his whistling.

Immediately, the maize, the growth of which depended on the Spirit's whistling, began to wither and dry on the stalk. Since that time, and because Bopé-joku took his revenge, maize no longer grows of its own accord, but men have to cultivate it by the sweat of their brows.

However, Burékoïbo promised them that he would grant a good harvest on condition that, at sowing time, they blew upwards in the direction of heaven, while uttering prayers to him. He also ordered his son to visit the Indians at this time and to ask them about their work. Any who answered rudely would have only a poor harvest.

Bopé-joku set off and asked each farmer what he was doing. They replied in turn: 'As you see, I am getting my field ready.' The last punched him in the ribs and insulted him. Because of this man's action, maize is not of as fine a quality as before. But any Indian who hopes to gather corn-cobs 'as big as bunches of the fruit of the palm tree', always prays to Burékoïbo and offers the Spirit the first fruits of his field (Kruse 2, pp. 164–6; *EB*, Vol. I, pp. 528, 774).

The Tembé, a northern Tupi tribe, have a very similar myth:

M294. Tembé. 'Why manioc is slow in growing'

There was a time when the Indians were not acquainted with manioc. Instead they cultivated camapú. One day when an Indian was preparing the ground for planting, the demiurge Maíra appeared and asked him what he was doing. Rather impolitely, the man refused to reply. Maíra left him, and all the trees surrounding the little clearing fell onto it and covered it with their branches. The man was furious and set off in pursuit of Maíra, with the intention of killing him with his knife. As he could not find the demiurge, he tried to work off his rage on something by throwing a gourd into the air and attempting to hit it before it fell. But the attempt misfired, the knife pierced his throat and he died.

Maíra came across another man, who was weeding his camapú plantation and who answered courteously when the demiurge asked him what he was doing. Whereupon the demiurge changed all the trees around the field into manioc plants and taught the man how to plant them. Then he accompanied him to his village. They had hardly got there when Maíra told the man to go and harvest the manioc. The man hesitated and pointed out that the planting had just been completed. 'All right,' Maíra said, 'you will not have manioc until next year.' And he went off (Nim. 2, p. 281).

Let us begin by clarifying the problem of camapú. The Guarayu, who are Tupi-Guarani belonging to eastern Bolivia, have a myth (M_{295a}) which tells how the wife of the Great Ancestor ate nothing but cama á pu; but this did not seem a substantial enough diet and so he created manioc, maize and the banana-vegetable, *platano* (Pierini, p. 704). In another myth (M_{296}), the Tenetehara, who are related to the Tembé, say that men used to live on kamamô, a solanaceous forest plant (Wagley–Galvão, pp. 34, 132–3). It is not certain that kamamô and

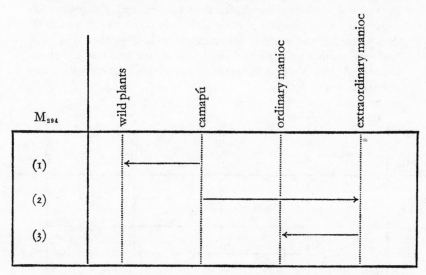

camapú are different names of the same plant, since Tastevin (2, p. 702) refers to camamuri and camapú respectively as being different plants. But camapú (*Psidalia edulis*, Stradelli 1, p. 391; *Physalis pubescens*) is also a solanaceous plant, the semantic position of which is made clearer by a Tucuna myth (M_{297}), which states that camapú are the first fruits to grow spontaneously around the edges of plantations (Nim. 13, p. 141). Camapú is therefore a vegetable food at the point of intersection of wild and cultivated plants, and it is such that man can push it towards nature or culture, according to whether or not he uses violent or temperate language. Similarly, a myth common to the Chimane and the Mosetene (M_{295b}) explains that wild animals are former human beings guilty of discourteous behaviour (Nordenskiöld 3, pp. 139–43).

When it is looked at in this light, the Tembé myth is seen to contain three sequences: the insults which bring about the transformation of the garden into fallow land and therefore of the camapú into wild plants; the polite speech which transforms the camapú into extraordinary manioc; and lastly the words of distrust which transform extraordinary manioc into ordinary manioc (see table on p. 313).

The Bororo myth comprises four sequences which cover a wider semantic field since, from the point of view of the linguistic means employed, the whistled language lies beyond polite speech and, from the point of view of the agricultural results obtained, the absence of maize is less than a harvest of camapú. We can also note a difference of division within the semantic field common to both myths: M_{293} contrasts the insult which is an exclamation with the insult in lieu of an answer, whereas M_{294} contrasts two types of insulting reply, one explicit, the other veiled:

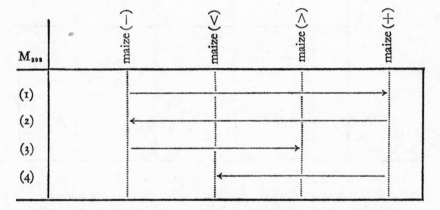

Whatever the accuracy of these shades of significance, which would repay closer analysis, the two myths stand in close parallel since they establish a correlation between acoustic behaviour and agricultural procedures. At the same time, if we take note of the fact that M_{293} is based on a major contrast between insults and the whistled language, and M_{294} on an equally major contrast between insults and polite speech (whereas M_{292a} uses only one contrast, between noise and the whistled language), we can distinguish four types of acoustic behaviour which are arranged in the following order:

1	2	3	4
noise	insulting speech	polite speech	the whistled language

but which nevertheless close a cycle since, as we have seen, whistling, in other contexts, occupies an intermediary position between articulate language and noise.

It will also be noted that all these myths refer to the loss of a miraculous form of agriculture, of which present-day agriculture is only the residue. In this sense, they reproduce the armature of the myths about the origin of honey, which also refer to such a loss and attribute it similarly to immoderate linguistic behaviour: the pronouncing of a name that should not have been uttered, and a consequent displacement of language in the direction of noise, whereas propriety would have required it to move towards silence. This allows us to glimpse the possibility of a still more extensive system, which can be made more definite through the analysis of another myth:

M_{298}. *Machiguenga*. '*The origin of comets and meteorites*'

There was once an Indian who lived with his wife and a son by a previous marriage. Being worried about what might happen between the boy and his step-mother when he was absent, the Indian decided to marry off his son, and went to a distant country to find him a wife. This country was inhabited by cannibal Indians who captured him and tore out his entrails to grill and eat them. Nevertheless he managed to escape.

Meanwhile the woman was planning to poison her husband, because she was in love with her step-son and wished to live with him. She therefore prepared a foul stew (*menjunje de bazofias*) and let ants get into it so as to poison it with their venom. But the man was a sorcerer and he guessed what she was plotting. Before returning, he sent on ahead a messenger spirit in the form of a little boy who said to the wife: 'What are you plotting against my father? Why do you hate him? Why do you want to kill him? Listen to what has happened to him: his intestines have been eaten and, although you cannot tell by looking, he has nothing in his belly. To make him fresh intestines, you must prepare a potion with a piece of mapa [a cultivated root, Grain, p. 241], cotton thread and calabash pulp.' Having said this, the messenger disappeared.

A few days later, the Indian arrived, exhausted by his journey. He asked his wife to give him something to drink, and she provided him with a beverage made from istéa (manioc beer). He at once began to lose blood and his belly was no more than a gaping wound. Terrified by this spectacle, the wife ran off and hid herself in a hollow tree (panáro: unidentified), which stood in the middle of the garden. The Indian, mad with pain, wanted to kill his wife and cried: 'Where are you? Come out, I will not hurt you!' But the wife was afraid and did not move.

In those days, edible plants could speak, but their pronunciation was indistinct. The man asked manioc and magana [*platano*, Grain, *loc. cit.*] 'where their mother was hiding', and as the plants did not reply, he tore them up and threw them into the bush. Ea, a cultivated root [Grain, *loc. cit.*], did its best to tell him, but it spoke so badly that he could not understand what it was saying. He ran in all directions, while his wife looked on from her hiding place.

In the end, the disembowelled man went back into his hut, picked up a bamboo cane and set it alight by striking the ground with a stone. He made himself a tail out of it and, looking up at the sky, said to himself: 'Where should I go? I shall be comfortable up there!' He soared up, transformed into a comet. Meteorites are the drops of incandescent blood from his body. Sometimes he snatches up corpses and turns them into comets like himself (Garcia, pp. 233–4).

This very important myth is worthy of attention from several points of view. In the first place, it is a myth about the origin of comets and meteorites, i.e. of erratic celestial bodies which, unlike the stars and constellations in M_{292a}, cannot be identified and named by the Indians. I have shown that M_{292} is a transformation of M_2, and it is clear that M_{298} is also part of the same group: it begins with an incest like M_2, and, like M_{292}, tells about a hero 'with a hollow stomach', although the expression has to be understood literally or figuratively, according to the circumstances: M_{298} has a disembowelled father, M_2 and M_{292} a famished son.

The father in M_{298}, who tries to kill his incestuous wife, comes back from afar, having lost vital organs which are an integral part of his being. The father in M_2, who has killed his incestuous wife, goes far away, loaded down with the weight of a tree which is a foreign body. This *solid* tree is a *consequence* of the murder of the incestuous woman who, in M_{298}, escapes being murdered by *means* of a *hollow* tree. M_{298} is intended to explain the cosmic anomaly caused by the existence of erratic planets. M_{292} and M_2, on the other hand, complete the order of the world: M_{292} does so on the cosmological level by enumerating and naming the celestial bodies, and M_2 on the sociological level by introducing the decorations and ornaments which make it possible to enumerate and name the clans and sub-clans (cf. *RC*, pp. 50–55).[20] Lastly, in both cases, human mortality plays a part, since it appears sometimes as the means, sometimes as the substance, of the introduction of a social order (M_2) or cosmic disorder (M_{298}).

So far we have looked at the matter from the point of view of the hero. But the heroine of M_{298} is also an old acquaintance, since she makes us think simultaneously of two characters, whom I have already shown to be one and the same. First, the adulterous and murderous wife of several Chaco myths who, in the Tereno version (M_{24}), poisoned her husband with her menstrual blood, just as the Machiguenga woman proposes to do with kitchen refuse impregnated with venom. The contrast *internal filth/external filth* is echoed by another in the myths: the Tereno heroine is caught in a pit (M_{24}) or, according to other versions, in a hollow tree (M_{23}, M_{246}). Another hollow tree serves not as a trap, but as a refuge, for the Machiguenga heroine. Consequently, according to whether the body of the heroine is, or is not, a receptacle for poison, another receptacle acts as a shelter for her victims or herself. And, in the latter case, she meets her doom outside (M_{23}) or finds salvation inside (M_{298}). I used the recurrence of the hollow-tree theme previously to connect the story about the jaguar-woman who, under the influence of stinging[21] honey (the cause of her transformation), was responsible for the creation of tobacco with the story about the woman mad about honey who triumphs over the jaguar thanks to a hollow and thorny tree (externally stinging) but changes into a frog through being imprisoned in a hollow tree full of honey (and therefore internally sweet).

The woman mad about honey is also incestuous, either with her adopted son (M_{241}, M_{243}, M_{244}; M_{258}) as in the case of the Machiguenga heroine, or with a young brother-in-law (M_{135}–M_{136}). Also like the Machiguenga heroine, she plots to kill her husband; but at this point,

[20] I have already shown, by another line of reasoning, that M_2 belongs to the tapir-seducer cycle (*RC*, p. 272, n. 36; p. 309 of the present volume) which, as we know, belongs to the same group as the woman-mad-about-honey cycle.

Although this is beyond my present scope, it would be appropriate to study certain North American parallels of M_{298}: e.g. the Pawnee myth which says that meteors sprang from the body of a man whose enemies killed him and *ate up his brains* (Dorsey 2, pp. 61–2), and certain details in the Diegueño and Luiseño myths about meteors. Generally speaking, the treatment of meteors rests on a series of transformations:

dismembered body ⇒ severed head ⇒ emptied skull ⇒ disembowelled body

which call for special study.

[21] The honey in M_{24} is stinging, in two senses: literally, since the husband has mixed young snakes in with it; and figuratively, since it causes itching.

the devices used are inverted in a very striking way which proves, if proof were needed, how narrow is the margin of creative invention in the myths.

The woman uses a knife in one case and poison in the other. By means of a knife, the Guiana heroine amputates her husband and thus reduces his body to the part containing the entrails (in connection with this interpretation, cf. above, p. 263). By means of poison, or at least the combinatorial variant of poison which consists of a non-remedy given instead of the prescribed remedy, the Machiguenga heroine causes her husband's body to remain disembowelled. In the Guiana myths (M_{135}, M_{136}), the entrails become the Pleiades, an extremely significant constellation for the Indians in the area. In the Machiguenga myth, the entrails become comets or meteors, which belong to an opposite category, because of their erratic nature. The Pleiades, in their masculine form, provide men with fish as food. The comet, in its masculine form, deprives mankind of edible plants and feeds on men, by taking toll of corpses.

A final detail will serve to complete this reconstruction. The Machiguenga hero, to turn himself into a comet, attaches to his behind a bamboo cane which he has set fire to by striking it with a stone. The Taulipang hero, while transforming himself into the Pleiades, holds a bamboo flute to his lips and plays upon it continuously: 'tin, tin, tin', as he rises up into the sky (K.-G. 1, p. 57). Since this is a bamboo flute, it stands in a relationship of correlation and opposition, not only with the *bamboo* in the Machiguenga myth, which is struck (and the importance of which will be explained later), but also with the bone *flute* of which the tortoise in M_{283}–M_{284}[22] is so proud, and with the non-instrumental whistling of the agrarian god in M_{293}; and lastly, in M_{292}, with the naming of the stars by means of the whistled language.[23]

Moreover, the Arawak of Guiana have a rite, about which it would be interesting to know more and which brings together all the inter-related elements I have just been enumerating, since it deals simultaneously with agriculture, the rising of the Pleiades and the two forms of linguistic behaviour that can be more conveniently referred to from

[22] As I do not propose to deal with this second aspect, I shall merely say here that it would be appropriately interpreted on the basis of an episode in M_{276}; the transformation of the bones of Uairy, the ant-eater, into musical instruments, cf. Stradelli 1, under 'mayua'; Uairy had revealed the secret of the masculine rites to women (cf. above, p. 272).

[23] It will be noted that, in M_{247}, the whistling of the sloth in the silence of the night is contrasted with the song that the animal tried to address to the stars when it was still capable of utterance (Amorim, p. 145).

now on as 'the whistled call' and 'the tapped-out reply':[24] 'When towards morning the Pleiades become visible the dry season is imminent, Masasikiri starts his journey and comes to warn the people it is time to prepare their fields. He makes a whistling sound to which he owes his nickname Masakiri (sic). When people hear him at night, they strike their cutlasses with something, which makes a sound like a bell; in this way they thank the spirit for his warning' (Goeje, p. 51).[25] Thus the return of the Pleiades is accompanied by an exchange of acoustic signals, the contrast between which has some formal resemblance to that between the two fire-producing techniques, friction and percussion, which I showed to have a relevant function in connection with the myths of the same area (p. 246). 'The tapped-out reply' is, in fact, a percussive noise like the other one; and, in M_{298}, it causes the object that is struck to take fire. And so there is probably nothing arbitrary about the fact that the Guiana myths about the origin of the Pleiades (which is thought of in the first place as a departure conditioning their early return) reverse the whistled call and the tapped-out call along three axes: the knife strikes instead of being struck; the reply is whistled instead of the call, but at the same time is expressed by a tune on the flute, in which the whistling of the Arawak and Bororo agrarian gods can display all its possibilities. If this suggestion is correct, it can be extended to the Tembé myth (M_{294}) in which the ill-bred farmer accidentally kills himself by trying to pierce (his knife strikes, instead of being struck, as is the polite form of reply to the god among the Arawak of Guiana) a freshly picked gourd (which is full and non-resonant and therefore in exact contrast to the sonorousness of a similar gourd dried and emptied). Lastly, it should not be forgotten that while, in most of the myths, the tapir is summoned by a tapped-out call, the Indians compare its cry to a whistle (M_{145}, RC, p. 303). In some cases, too, whistling is used to attract it (Ahlbrinck, under 'wotaro' § 3; Holmberg, p. 26; Armentia, p. 8).

Having thus found that a belief of the Arawak of Guiana provides us with an additional reason for incorporating the Machiguenga myth into the group at present under examination, it is doubtless appropriate at this point to recall that the Machiguenga themselves

[24] TRANSLATORS' NOTE: appel sifflé: réponse cognée; cogner is 'to strike hard, to thump, to bang'.

[25] According to P. Clastres (who gave me the information personally), the non-agricultural Guayaki believe in a trickster-spirit, who is master of honey and armed with an ineffectual bow and arrows made of ferns. This spirit announces his approach by whistling and is driven away by noise.

belong to a large group of Arawak-speaking Peruvian tribes. Together with the Amuesha, Campa, Piro, etc. they constitute an apparently archaic stratum of population which settled in the Montaña area at a very remote period.

Let us now return to myth M₂₉₈, which defines a form of linguistic behaviour on the part of plants towards men, instead of on the part of men towards plants (M₂₉₃, etc.), but which, in the latter respect, can be completed with the help of another Machiguenga myth. As this is a very long myth, I shall cut down the summary to a minimum except in the part directly concerned with my argument.

M₂₉₉. Machiguenga. 'The origin of cultivated plants'

In olden times, there were no cultivated plants. Men ate potters' clay which they cooked and swallowed, as hens swallow, because they had no teeth.

It was Moon who gave men cultivated plants and taught them how to masticate. He did so by instructing an indisposed young girl, whom he visited secretly and eventually married.

On several occasions, Moon caused his human wife to be fertilized by a fish, and she gave birth to four sons: the sun, the planet Venus, the sun of the lower world and the nocturnal sun (which is invisible, but provides the stars with their light). This fourth son was so hot that he scorched his mother's womb and she died while giving birth to him.[26]

Moon's mother-in-law upbraided him and said that, after killing his wife, it was only left for him to eat her. However, Moon succeeded in resuscitating her, but she was now disgusted with life on earth and decided to leave her body and betake her soul to the lower world. Moon was deeply distressed and, having been challenged by his mother-in-law, ate the body after painting the face red, thus inventing a funeral rite which still persists. He found human flesh delicious. Thus, through the fault of the old woman, Moon became a corpse-eater, and decided to go far away.

His third son elected to live in the lower world. He is a weak,

---

[26] In connection with a 'burning baby', who is the son of the sun, cf. Cavina in Nordenskiöld 3, pp. 286–7, and Uitoto in Preuss 1, pp. 304–14, where the burning sun consumes his adulterous mother who is trying to join him in the sky. This group will be discussed in another volume in connection with the North American parallels. Without going into details, we can accept the fact that the mother whose entrails are scorched by the baby to whom she is giving birth (the nearest imaginable relative) is a transformation of the disembowelled father or the man who has had his brains knocked out (by distant enemies); cf. p. 317, n. 20.

maleficent sun, which sends rain when the Indians are clearing the ground, to prevent them burning the tree stumps. With his other sons, Moon went up into the sky. But the last born was too hot; so much so that on earth he caused stones to split. His father settled him in the firmament, but so high up that we can no longer see him. Only the planet Venus and the sun now live near their father, the Moon.

Moon constructed a trap in a river and it was so efficient that it caught all the corpses floating downstream.[27] A toad kept watch and every time a corpse was caught, it informed Moon by repeatedly croaking 'Tantanaróki-iróki, tantanaróki-iróki', literally: 'the toad tantanaróki and its eye'. Then Moon would hurry to the scene and kill the corpse (*sic*) by beating it with a club. He would cut off the hands and feet and roast and eat them. The rest he would change into a tapir.

Only the daughters of Moon are left on earth; these are the plants cultivated by the Indians and their staple diet: manioc, maize, banana-vegetable (*Musa normalis*), sweet potatoes, etc. Moon continues to take a watchful interest in these plants which he created and which, for this reason, call him 'father'. If the Indians spoil or throw away manioc, scatter the peelings or clean it badly, the manioc-daughter weeps and complains to her father. If they eat manioc by itself or merely seasoned with pimentoes, the daughter becomes angry and says to her father: 'They give me nothing. They leave me all alone, or they give me nothing but pimento, which is so hot I cannot stand it.' On the other hand, if the Indians are careful not to waste any manioc and to put all the peelings into one place where it is forbidden to walk, then the daughter is pleased. And when manioc is eaten with meat or fish, which are superior foods, she says to her father: 'They are treating me well. They give me everything I want.' But what she likes best of all is to be made into beer, which is enriched with saliva and well fermented.

The other daughters of Moon have similar reactions to the treatment they receive from men. Men can hear neither their weeping nor their expressions of satisfaction, but try to please them, because they know that if the daughters were made unhappy, Moon would call them up to him and men would have to feed on earth, as they used to do (Garcia, pp. 230–33).

---

[27] The Machiguenga throw their dead, unceremoniously, into the river (Farabee 2, p. 12).

Since Rivet discovered resemblances in vocabulary between the Bororo language and the Otuké dialects of Bolivia in 1913, it has been generally accepted that Bororo culture may have affinities with that of other South American tribes living in the western areas. A comparison between M_{293} and M_{299} does a great deal to strengthen this hypothesis, since the two myths show striking analogies with each other. They both deal with the origin of cultivated plants and with the rites governing either their production (Bororo) or their consumption (Machiguenga). Five agrarian gods are associated with the origin of these rites: a father and his four sons. The Bororo myth does not mention the mother, while the Machiguenga myth eliminates her at an early stage. According to the Machiguenga, the father is the moon, and his sons 'the suns'; and the *Enciclopédia Boróro* points out, in connection with two summaries of a variant of M_{293} which will be given in the eagerly awaited second volume, that the father, Burékoïbo, is none other than the sun, Méri (Espirito denominado tambem Méri', *loc. cit.*, under 'Burékoïbo; cf. also *loc. cit.*, p. 774). In both myths, the third sun acts as a specialist in agricultural activities, either as a help (Bororo) or a hindrance (Machiguenga). However, this slight divergency is still less pronounced than at first appears since, in the Bororo myth, this sun explicitly punishes disrespectful farmers by sending them bad harvests, while the Machiguenga myth implies that the rains which occur during the slash-and-burn process, and thus cause bad harvests, may be a punishment visited upon disrespectful consumers.

The third son in the Machiguenga myth, the sun of the lower world, is a maleficent, chthonian spirit. In the Bororo myth, the third son is called Bopé-joku, from Bopé: evil spirit (cf. *EB*, under 'maeréboe': Os primeiros [espíritos malfazejos] são chamadoscomumente apenas bópe, assim que esta forma, embora possa indicar qualquer espírito, entretanto comumente designa apenas espíritos maus', p. 773). The meaning of joku is obscure, but we may note that the same sounds occur as part of the name, jokûgoe, of a species of bee which makes its nest below ground or in abandoned ant-hills (*EB*, Vol. I, under 'jokûgoe'). It does not yet seem possible to draw any conclusions from the names of the other sons in the Bororo myth, apart perhaps from the fact that the eldest's name: Uarudúdoe, corresponding to that of the Machiguenga eldest son (Puriáchiri, 'he who warms'), suggests an analogous derivation from waru > baru 'heat' (cf. Bororo barudodu 'warmed-up').

In the Machiguenga myth, there is no mention of the whistled language which, according to the Bororo, used to ensure the spontaneous growth of the miraculous maize. But, at the other end of the semantic field, the Machiguenga go further than the Bororo, since they do not rule out the possibility that cultivated plants may disappear completely if they are badly treated:

harvest:	superlatively good	good	bad	non-existent
M_{293}	whistled language	polite language	insulting language	
M_{299}		polite treatment		harmful treatment

We observe, then, as between the Bororo and the Machiguenga myths, a remarkable transformation from the more or less polite language spoken to the plants to a more or less elaborate form of cooking in which these same plants are used. There could be no better expression of the fact that, as I have often suggested (L.-S. 5, pp. 99–100; 12, *passim*), cooking is a language in which each society codes messages which allow it to signify a part at least of what it is. I have already demonstrated that, of the various forms of linguistic behaviour, insulting language is the one which approximates most closely to noise, so much so, indeed, that the two forms of behaviour appear to be interchangeable in many South American myths, as well as in the European tradition, as is attested in France by commonsense observation and numerous turns of phrase. I had occasion, in *The Raw and the Cooked*, to establish a direct homology between bad cooking and noise or din (RC, p. 293):[28] we can now see that there is a homology between refined language and more elaborate cooking. It is therefore easy to define the problematical term indicated by x in the equation on p. 311 of the preceding volume: if, in the myths, noise or din corresponds to an abuse of cooked food, this is because it is itself an abuse of articulate speech. The conclusion was predictable, and the remainder of this book will complete the proof.

However, in one way, the Bororo and Machiguenga myths, instead of echoing each other, complete each other. According to the Bororo, man could speak to plants (by means of the whistled language) at a time when the latter were personal beings, capable of understanding such messages and growing spontaneously. Now, communication has

[28] Cf. in French the double meaning of such words as 'gargote' (low-class – and therefore noisy(?) – eating-house, where the food is bad) and 'boucan' (barbecue : din). In support of the equivalence already established between the eclipse and anti-cooking (RC, pp. 296–9), we can, in the present context, refer to the Botocudo belief that eclipses come about when the sun and the moon quarrel and insult each other. They then become black with rage and hate (Nim. 9, p. 110).

been interrupted, or it is carried on through the medium of an agrarian god who speaks to man, and who is answered by men well or badly. The dialogue takes place, then, between the god and men, and plants are no more than the occasion of the dialogue.

In the Machiguenga myths, the opposite is the case. Plants, being the daughters of the god and therefore personal beings, converse with their father. Men have no means of intercepting these messages: 'Los machiguengas no perciben esos lloros y regocijos' (Garcia, p. 232); but since they are being talked about, they are the occasion of the exchange of messages. However, the theoretical possibility of a direct dialogue existed in mythic times, when the comets had not yet made their appearance in the sky. But, at that time, plants were only half-persons, with the gift of speech but so indistinct in utterance that they were unable to use it for purposes of communication.

When completed one by another, the myths are seen, then, to form a total, multi-axial system. The Salesians point out that the Bororo whistled language has two main functions: to ensure communication between speakers who are too far away from each other to conduct a normal conversation; or to prevent eavesdropping by outsiders, who understand the Bororo language but are unacquainted with the secrets of the whistled speech (Colb. 3, pp. 145–6; EB Vol. I, p. 824). This mode of communication is, therefore, both broader and more restricted. It is a super-language for the actual speakers but an infra-language for outsiders.

The language spoken by plants has exactly opposite characteristics. When it is addressed directly to man, it is an incomprehensible muttering (M_{298}), whereas when it is used clearly, it by-passes man. He cannot hear it, although it is entirely concerned with him (M_{299}). The whistled language and indistinct speech therefore form a pair of contrasts.

The absence of a multinote flute among the Bororo is all the more remarkable in that they are capable of making fairly complex wind instruments, such as horns and clarinets consisting of a tube with a reed and a sound-box, but which, like the flutes, produce only a single note. No doubt this ignorance on their part (it is, more probably, the result of a prohibition) should be related to the exceptional development of the whistled language: in other communities, the multinote flute is chiefly used for the transmission of messages. We have abundant evidence on this point, especially from the Amazon valley where hunters and fishermen used flute-tunes as leitmotiv to announce their

Bororo, M_{292}:·

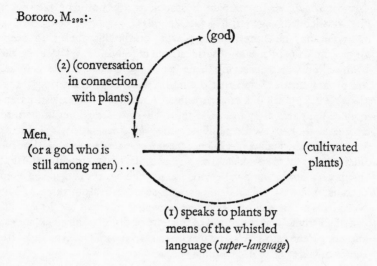

(god)

(2) (conversation
in connection
with plants)

Men,
(or a god who is
still among men) . . .

(cultivated
plants)

(1) speaks to plants by
means of the whistled
language (*super-language*)

Machiguenga, M_{298}–M_{299}:

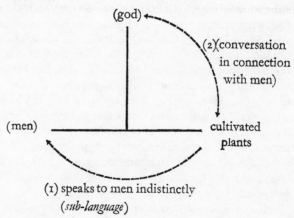

(god)

(2) (conversation
in connection
with men)

(men)

cultivated
plants

(1) speaks to men indistinctly
(*sub-language*)

Note: It will be observed that the Bororo whistled language is a *super-language* for the speakers and an *infra-language* for outsiders. Correspondingly, the plant language in M_{298}–M_{299} is an *infra-language* for the speakers (M_{298}) but a *super-language* for outsiders (M_{299}).

return, the outcome of the expedition and the nature of the catch (Amorim, *passim*). In comparable situations, the Bororo make use of the whistled language (cf. M_{26}; *RC*, p. 103).

In Tucano, the expression for playing on the flute means 'to weep' or 'to complain' by means of this instrument (Silva, p. 255). Among the Waiwai 'it is worth observing that much suggests that the flute melodies are programmatic ... and that the music itself describes various situations' (Fock, p. 280). On approaching a strange village, visitors announce their arrival by means of short, sharp whistles; but invitations to guests are conveyed by flute-playing (*ibid.*, pp. 51, 63, 87). In the language of the Kalina of Guiana, the horn 'is made to shout', but the flute 'is allowed to speak'. 'When a flute is played, or any other musical instrument producing a variety of sounds, the word that is most often used is *eruto* – to obtain language or speech for something ... The word *eti* is a personal proper name, as well as the term for the specific call of an animal and the sound of the flute or drum' (Ahlbrinck, index; and under 'eti', 'eto'). An Arecuna myth (M_{145}) uses the term 'flute' for the distinctive cry of each animal species.

These assimilations of meaning are important because, as I showed in *The Raw and the Cooked*, and precisely in connection with M_{145}, the specific animal cry is homologous, on the acoustic level, with the distinctive coat or plumage, which themselves signify the introduction into nature, through the fragmentation of what was originally continuous, of a realm of wide intervals. The reason why proper names have the same function is, then, because they establish between the persons concerned a discontinuity which replaces the confusion characteristic of a group of biological individuals limited solely to their natural attributes. Similarly, music supplements language, which is always in danger of becoming incomprehensible if it is spoken over too great a distance or if the speaker has poor articulation. Music corrects the continuity of speech by means of more clearly marked contrasts of tone and melodic patterns which cannot be mistaken, since they are perceived as a whole.

Of course, as we now know, language is by nature discontinuous, but this is not the way it is conceived of in mythic thought. It is, incidentally, a remarkable fact that the South American Indians are chiefly concerned to exploit its plasticity. The existence, in various places, of dialects peculiar to each sex proves that Nambikwara women are not alone in their tendency to distort words to make them incomprehensible, and to prefer, instead of clear utterance, indistinct mutterings comparable to those of the plants in the Machiguenga myth (L.-S. 3, p. 295). The Indians of eastern Bolivia 'like to borrow foreign words, with the result ... that their language is constantly changing; the women do not pronounce the consonant s but always change it into an f' (Armentia, p. 11). More than a century ago, Bates noted (p. 169) in connection with the Mura, among whom he had lived: 'When the Indians, both men and women, talk together, they seem to delight in inventing new pronunciations and in distorting words. Everybody laughs at these slang inventions, and the new terms are often adopted. I have observed the same thing during long sailing trips with Indian crews.'

An amusing comparison with these remarks is to be found in a letter, full of Portuguese words, that Spruce wrote from a Uaupés village to his friend Wallace, who was by that time back in England: 'Don't forget to tell me how you are progressing in the English language and whether you can already make yourself comprehensible to the natives ... ' Wallace gives the following explanatory commentary:

> When we met at São Gabriel ... we had noticed that we were quite incapable of conversing together in English, without using Portu- guese words and expressions which amounted to about a third of our vocabulary. Even when we made up our minds to speak only in English, we succeeded in doing so only for a few minutes and with difficulty and as soon as the conversation became animated or it was necessary to recount an anecdote, Portuguese reasserted itself! (Spruce, Vol. I, p. 320).

Such linguistic osmosis, with which travellers and expatriates are well acquainted, must have played a considerable part in the evolution of the American languages and in the linguistic conceptions of the natives of South America. According to a Kalina theory noted by Penard (in Goeje, p. 32): 'vowels change quicker than consonants, because they are thinner, swifter, more liquid than the resistant consonants, but in consequence their *yumi* close themselves sooner, which means they return to their source more rapidly.[29] Thus words and languages are unmade and remade in the course of time.'

If language belongs to the realm of short intervals, it is under- standable that music, which substitutes its own order for linguistic

[29] The meaning of the word *yumi* is obscure. It has been diversely translated as 'spirit' or 'father'; cf. Penard's discussion of the use of the term in Ahlbrinck, under 'sirito'. In the context, *yumi* seems to convey the idea of a cycle. On the meaning of *yumi* and its uses, cf. Goeje, p. 17.

confusion, should appear as *masked speech*, endowed with the two-fold function that is assigned to masks in non-literate societies: the concealment of the individual wearing the mask, who is at the same time given a higher significance. Like proper names which are tantamount to metaphors of the individual, since each proper name transforms an

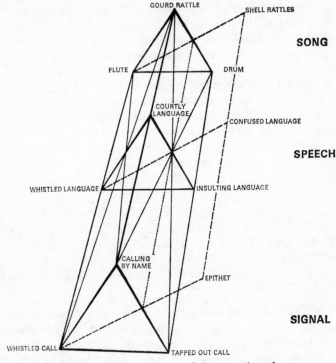

Figure 15. The structure of the acoustic code

individual into a person (L.-S. 9, pp. 284–5), a melodic phrase is a metaphor of speech.

I cannot take this analysis any further, nor do I wish to, since it raises the enormous problem of the relationship between articulate language and music. In any case, the preceding pages are adequate to indicate the general economy of the acoustic code, the existence and function of which is made manifest by the myths. The properties of this code will only appear gradually, but to make them more easily intelligible, I think it advisable at this point to give an approximate account of them, in the form of a diagram which can, as need arises, be made more precise, extended or modified (Figure 15).

The terms of the code are distributed over three levels. At the bottom are the various types of call addressed by the adulterous woman or women to the tapir-seducer (or to other animals acting as combinatory variants of the tapir): calling by name, the whistled call or the tapped-out call. They establish a connection between a human and another creature, which belongs totally to nature in its double capacity as an animal and a seducer. These three types of acoustic behaviour therefore constitute *signals*.

The middle level includes various kinds of linguistic behaviour: the whistled language, polite speech and insulting speech. This speech occurs during a dialogue between one or more men and a divinity who has assumed human shape. This is not, of course, true of the whistled speech as it is ordinarily used, but in the two Bororo myths in which it plays a part (M_{292}, M_{298}), it allows access from the cultural level (that of articulate speech) to the supernatural level, since gods or spirits use it to communicate with supernatural plants (those which once grew spontaneously) or with stars, which are supernatural beings.

Lastly, the three types of musical instrument on the highest level are connected with singing, either because they sing themselves or accompany singing, an activity which contrasts with spoken speech in the same way as the latter contrasts with a system of signals.

In spite of (or because of) its provisional nature this diagram calls for a number of observations.

First, I have established a correlation between the rattle and the drum and contrasted both of them with the flute, although the first two instruments have so far appeared only sporadically in the myths and, as it were, in a veiled form. The rattle has occurred through its reversed transformation in M_{294}: the fresh, full gourd (instead of a dry, empty one) which the hero tries (in vain) to catch on the point of his knife, in the manner of a cup-and-ball, whereas the rattle consists of a gourd threaded on a stick to which it is permanently attached. As for the drum, which I dealt with in connection with a linguistic commentary on the Kalina word 'eti', signifying the sound of the flute and the drum (p. 326), it has been obscurely present since the beginning of this volume. It is the wooden drum, made of a hollowed-out tree-trunk, split on one side, i.e. an object of the same type as the hollow tree which serves as a natural receptacle for honey and which acts as a shelter or a trap in several myths. A Mataco myth (M_{214}) expressly links the wooden drum with the hollowed-out tree-trunk which serves as a trough for the preparation of mead: 'The Indians hollowed out a larger trough and drank all the beer. It was a bird which made the first drum. It banged on it all night, and then, in the morning, turned into a man' (Métraux 3, p. 54). The full significance of this connection will soon become clear. As for the semantic position of the rattle, it will be elucidated at a later stage in the discussion.

Secondly, it was suggested above that the confused speech (addressed to the human hero by the plants in the Machiguenga myth, M_{298}) stands in direct contrast to the whistled language (spoken to the plants by the god in human shape in the Bororo myth, M_{293}, which has been shown to be symmetrical with the other). I have therefore set confused speech some distance behind the other forms of linguistic behaviour, since it is an infra-language inadequate for purposes of communication. But at the same time, its position is equidistant from those of polite speech and insulting speech, which is in keeping with the dramatic point of M_{298}: the plants, which try to initiate an impossible dialogue, want to be polite; but the recipient of the message thinks it is insulting, since he takes his revenge by tearing up the plants and eliminating them from the garden.

The question immediately arises whether there are any intermediate terms between the two extreme levels, the position of which is homologous to that occupied by confused speech on the middle level. It does in fact seem to be the case that the myths and rites provide terms which fulfil the required conditions. In the tapir-seducer cycle, the heroine sometimes calls the animal by uttering an epithet which may be either the ordinary word for the animal raised to the dignity of a proper name or a qualifying adjective solely expressive of the speaker's state of mind. Both kinds of term can lead to confusion: in one case, it is not clear whether the animal is being addressed as a person or named as an object; and in the other case, the identity of the addressee remains undetermined.

The ambiguity inherent in the epithet, whatever the type it belongs to, contrasts it with the whistled call, whose ambivalence has, on the contrary, an iconic character (in the sense in which Peirce used the adjective): the whistle which summons the tapir is a physical reproduction of the animal's own call. As we saw on p. 305, the Tucuna myths replace the whistled call by a whistled announcement. Consequently, the epithet has its proper place on the lower level of the diagram, between calling by name (when the animal has a genuine proper name) and the tapped-out call, but a little way back from both because of its ambiguity.

Passing now to the upper level, I would like to observe that South American organology includes a musical instrument, the position of which is equally ambiguous: the shell-rattles attached to dancers' legs or to a stick which is banged on the ground. From the mythological point of view, these rattles, made of nutshells or animals' hooves threaded on a string and which produce a jangling noise when they strike each other, are similar to the true rattle which produces its noise through the banging about of seeds or pebbles inside a gourd. But from the functional point of view, the shell-rattles are more closely related to the drum, since their movement – which, moreover, is less controlled than that of the hand-held rattle – is the indirect result of the stamping of the legs or the beating of the stick. Therefore, the action of the shell-rattles, which is intentional and discontinuous in its cause but haphazard in its result, is situated some way back, like confused speech; but, for the reasons that have just been given, it is equidistant from the wooden drum and the gourd-rattle.

The preceding analysis is indirectly confirmed by certain ideas about shell-rattles peculiar to the Uitoto. Shell-rattles play a considerable part in their dances, together with the flute and the drum, and are supposed to represent living creatures, especially insects: dragon-flies, wasps and hornets (Preuss 1, pp. 124–33, 633–4), which produce an ambiguous buzzing sound that is coded differently in different areas, sometimes in terms of singing, sometimes in terms of the tapped-out call (*RC*, p. 295, n. 5).

Lastly, between the three levels of the diagram, there is obviously a complicated network of cross-connections, some parallel with each other, others oblique. Let us look first at the parallel connections, each of which corresponds to a ridge of the prism. Moving upwards along one ridge, and according to a scale of increasing intensity, we find the tapped-out call, insulting language and the noise of the drum, which are the types of acoustic behaviour with the most definite affinity to noise, although it should not be forgotten that the drum manages to be, simultaneously, the most sonorous and the most linguistic term in the series: 'The wooden drums of the Boro and the Okaina ... are used to transmit messages about the dates, places and purposes of feast-days. The drummers do not seem to use a code; they try rather to represent the sounds of the words by means of the drums, and the Indians always told me that they made the words with the drum' (Whiffen, pp. 216, 253).

Along the second ridge, we find successively the whistled signal, the whistled language and the sound of the flute. This series indicates the transition from a monotone whistling to modulated whistling and then to a whistled melody. This is, then, a musical axis which is defined by the concept of tonality.

Along the third ridge are grouped essentially linguistic forms of behaviour, since calling by name is a signal made by means of a word (in this, it contrasts with the other two) and polite speech, as the myths indicate, corresponds to the most completely linguistic use of language (in contrast to insulting speech, of course, but also in contrast to whistled speech which, as we have seen, is a super-language on one level, but an infra-language on another). As for the rattle, it is, of all musical instruments, the one with the most definite linguistic function. No doubt the flute speaks, but what it utters is mainly the language of men who 'give' it the power of speech (cf. above, pp. 324–6). And although it is true that the shell-rattles and the drum transmit divine messages to men: 'the bell says its words out loud to men, here on earth' (Preuss, *loc. cit.*), this function is exercised concurrently with the different one of transmitting messages as between men: 'The sound of the drum is a summons to others' (*ibid.*). And how much more eloquent divine speech is when transmitted by a rattle, painted as a likeness of the face of the god! (Zerries 3, *passim*). According to the linguistic theories of the Kalina to which I have already referred, the phonemes of language are present on the surface of the gourd-rattle: 'The circle, encompassing six radii, is the symbol of the vowels *a, e, i, o, u,* with the *m*; … The rattle represents the globe and the stones in the rattle are the fundamental ideas, and the outside of the rattle is the harmony of speech sounds, etc.' (Goeje, p. 32).

Let us now consider the oblique connections. In the body of the prism represented by the diagram, four diagonals form two isosceles tetrahedra which interpenetrate. The one pointing upwards has, at its angles, all three varieties of call and the rattle, i.e. four terms which, as we shall see, are interlinked by a double connection of correlation and opposition. Without anticipating part of the demonstration to be given later, it will be enough to indicate here that the effect of the calls is to make an animal, a natural creature, appear within human society (and with unfortunate results, since a loss of women ensues). The rattle, on the contrary, determines the appearance of supernatural beings, spirits or gods, with a happy outcome for society.

The other tetrahedron pointing downwards has the three musical instruments at its base, while its fourth angle, after passing through the level of articulate speech, represents calling by name, which is, as it happens, the most linguistic form of call. This pattern refers back to some remarks that I made earlier (pp. 327–8). I said that music is the metaphorical transposition of speech, just as a proper name serves as a metaphor for the biological individual. The four terms thus regrouped are therefore those which function as metaphors, while the four others have a metonymical function: the rattle is the god reduced to his head, and the vocalic aspect is missing from the partial language he utters, the affinities of which are entirely with consonants, since it consists of micronoises; as for the calls, they are reduced, but in a different way, to a part or a moment of speech. Only on the middle level do the metaphorical and metonymical aspects balance each other; naturally enough, on this level we find speech in its literal sense and in three different modalities, in each of which it is entirely present.

3 *The Return of the Bird-Nester*

A long investigation into the mythology of honey has led me to establish within the framework of a wider system, which I have done no more than sketch in rough outline, a relationship of correlation and contrast between what I have found it convenient to term 'the tapped-out call' and 'the whistled call (or reply)'. But, as a matter of fact, 'the tapped-out call' ought to have attracted my attention a long time ago, and precisely in connection with one of the first myths about honey that I happened to discuss.

Let us go back, then, to p. 100 of *The Raw and the Cooked.* The Tereno Indians, who are southern Arawak living in the north-west of the Gran Chaco where the frontiers of Bolivia, Paraguay and Brazil meet, have a myth (M_{24}) about a man who discovers that his wife is poisoning him with her menstrual blood. He goes in search of honey, and mixes it with the flesh of snake embryos taken from the body of a female which has been killed at the foot of a tree which was also occupied by bees. After imbibing the mixture, the woman changes into a jaguar and pursues her husband who, to escape from her, takes over the role of the bird-nester in M_1 and M_7–M_{12}. While the ogress is chasing the parrots he has thrown down to her, the man leaves the tree and runs off in the direction of a ditch, into which his wife falls and kills herself. Tobacco springs up from her corpse.

I introduced this myth and its Mataco (M_{22}) and Toba-Pilaga (M_{23}) variants to demonstrate the existence of a cycle leading from destructive fire (of a jaguar) to tobacco, from tobacco to meat (by way of M_{15}, M_{16}, M_{25}) and from meat to cooking fire, that is, constructive fire, obtained from the jaguar (by way of M_7–M_{12}). This cycle therefore defines a closed set, in which the agents are the jaguar, the wild pig and the bird-nester (*RC*, pp. 83–107). In so doing, it was not necessary to emphasize a detail in M_{24}, which must now be brought to the fore, in the light of the remarks that have just been made: the hero knocks his sandals one against the other[30] 'in order to find honey more easily'; in other words, he addresses a 'tapped-out call' to honey, and as a result obtains not only honey but also a snake. We may now ask what the symbolic significance of this practice can be. As we shall see, echoes of it can be found in other myths, although it would seem that it cannot be directly corroborated from the available data.

Several myths found among the Tacana of eastern Bolivia, and partially used at the beginning of this study (M_{194}–M_{197}) are concerned with the quarrels between two divine brothers, the Edutzi, and meleros (in Brazil, irára, *Tayra barbara*), each of whom carries a little drum which makes a noise whenever they (male or female) are beaten. To rescue his daughters from such ill-treatment (which is, however, well deserved, since the daughters betray their divine husbands, either in their capacity of wives or cooks), the melero turns them into macaws. This is the origin of the ritual drum of the Tacana priests, which is made with irára skin and beaten during religious rites to establish communication with the Edutzi (H.-H., pp. 109–10). Here again, then, we find a link between the search for honey, of which the meleros are masters, as their Spanish name indicates,[31] and a variety of the tapped-out call.

Whether or not the great linguistic and cultural group to which the Tacana belong is connected with the Arawak family – the question still remains unsettled – it nevertheless occupies a significant position between its northern and western Arawak-speaking neighbours and the remains of an old settlement to the south and the east, of which the Tereno are the last survivors. Everything seems to indicate that the Tereno myth just referred to formed a connecting link between certain typical Chaco myths relating to the origin of tobacco and a group of Tacana myths in which the hero becomes a bird-nester but which – as far as one can tell in the case of myths that have been in contact with Christianity for more than three centuries – are concerned rather with the origin of hunting and cooking rites. In this connection, the Tacana myths refer back to the Ge myths which were studied in Part One (3 *b*.), and the heroine of which is a woman mad about honey, a role which falls to the hero's wife in the Tereno myth. The affinity between the Tacana and the Ge myths is also confirmed by the episode, which crops up here and there, about the origin of the ant-eater replacing the

[30] Most of the Chaco tribes are in the habit of using sandals with wooden or leather soles.

[31] In some Spanish-speaking areas, the ant-eater, to which we shall shortly have occasion to refer again, is also called melero, 'honey-merchant', or colmenero 'bee-keeper' (Cabrera and Yepes, pp. 238–40).

origin of the jaguar (Chaco), or the origin of the jaguar's eating habits (Ge myths about the origin of cooking fire, M_7–M_{12}), since it has been independently established (*RC*, pp. 189–91) that the animals are inverted within the group of two.

M_{300a}. *Tacana*. '*The story of the bird-nester*'

An Indian, who was a poor hunter but an expert farmer, lived with his wife and her mother and brothers. His in-laws treated him badly because he never brought home any game. However, he supplied them with manioc, maize and bananas.

One day, his brothers-in-law made him climb a tree, ostensibly to collect macaws' eggs; then they cut the liana he had used to hoist himself up and left him, after striking the roots of the tree to bring out from the hollow trunk the ha bacua, 'parrot-snake' (*Boa constrictor*), which lived there, in the confident hope that it would devour their victim.

Huddled at the tip of a branch (or hanging from the severed liana), starving and exhausted, the man nevertheless held off the snake's attacks for a whole day and night (other versions say three, eight or thirty days). He heard a noise *which at first he thought was being made by someone looking for honey* (my italics), but which in fact was being produced by the wood-spirit, Deavoavai, striking the roots of the big trees with his powerful elbows (or with his club) to bring out the boas which were his staple diet. The spirit shot an arrow which turned into a liana. The man used it to get down from the tree, but he was worried about what his rescuer might do to him. Deavoavai then killed the snake and, carrying the enormous mass of meat, went home, after inviting the man to accompany him.

The spirit lived under the roots of a big tree. His house was full of meat and his wife (a tapir or a frog, according to the versions) asked him to agree to relieve his protégé of the indolence which prevented him being a good hunter, and which the spirit drew out from his body in the form of evil-smelling exhalations or a soft mass (according to the versions).

Deavoavai presented the hero with inexhaustible supplies of food. He added a dish specially intended for the wicked in-laws and composed of fish (that the spirit had caught with timbó or by striking his legs with the backs of his hands), mixed with fat from the serpent's heart. Through eating this maleficent food they were transformed first into macaws and then into ha bacua, macaw-snakes, which

Deavoavai killed and ate on the following days (H.-H., pp. 180–83; second version, pp. 183–5: it limits the group of in-laws to the two brothers).

Before going on to examine a third and more complex version, I think it will be useful to clear the ground by means of a few remarks.

That the Tacana and Tereno myths are akin to each other cannot be doubted. In both cases the story deals with a hero who is ill-treated (physically or mentally) by an affine (his wife) or affines (his wife's mother and brothers) and who, in admittedly different circumstances, finds himself reduced to the position of a bird-nester persecuted by an ogre (jaguar or snake). In one instance, the transformation of the affine into an ogre is the result of eating a mixture of honey and snakes; in the other instance, the eating of a mixture of fish and snake-fat brings about the transformation of the affines into snakes of the same species as the ogre. The tapped-out call plays its part in every case: to obtain honey, and the little snakes into the bargain; to obtain fish which, when mixed with snake's fat, take the place of honey; and to obtain big snakes. The text of the Tacana myth strengthens the connection still further since the spirit Deavoavai's tapped-out call is at first attributed by the hero to someone looking for honey (which is actually the case in the Tereno myth). But had the noise been made by an ordinary person looking for honey, the hero would not have been rescued from his desperate situation, which demanded supernatural intervention. It follows that Deavoavai, the master of the forest (H.-H., p. 163), the initiator of techniques and rites (*ibid.*, pp. 62–3), is tantamount to a super-honey-seeker and therefore that the macaw-snakes he is looking for are themselves on the same level as a honey raised to the highest power. Conversely, with less power, the Indian honey-seeker is in the position of a master of the forest.

A Toba myth (M_{301}) tells of a giant snake which is attracted by the noise made by honey-seekers bursting open hollow tree-trunks with their axes. It demands that they should pour fresh honey into its mouth, and then devours them. This snake announces its arrival by means of a loud noise: brrrumbrrummbrum! (Métraux 5, p. 71). This noise, as it is written in the source-text, makes one think of bull-roarers, a point I shall return to. Similarly, the ogre-snakes in the Tacana myth cry or whistle as they approach, and they are also excited by the rustling of the foliage when the wind rises. Throughout all these descriptions, then, the contrast between the tapped-out call and the whistled reply or call is maintained, within the wider framework of a contrast between discontinuous and continuous noise.

The Tacana myth, a transformation of the Tereno myth, is also a transformation of the one about the bird-nester (M_1). As I am tempted to put it, in this rapid aerial survey (necessary for the purposes of this volume), of the mass of mythic material which was reviewed in the opposite direction in the previous volume, we have clearly passed directly above M_1, in approaching the other myth. M_1 and M_{300a} have the same starting-point: a conflict between affines (in the first case, a father and a son, since Bororo society is matrilineal), and the second case, a wife's brothers and a sister's husband (thus respecting the Ge transformations of M_1, but by dint of reversing the roles, since it is now the sister's husband, not the wife's brother, who plays the part of the bird-nester):

	The bird-nester:	*His persecutor:*
Bororo (M_1):	wife's son	mother's husband
Ge (M_7-M_{12}):	wife's brother	sister's husband
Tacana (M_{300a}):	sister's husband	wife's brother

This 'transformation within a transformation' is accompanied by another in the unfolding of the narrative; this other transformation brings out a contrast between the Tacana myth and the Bororo and Ge myths, as might be expected, since the Tacana are patrilineal, unlike the Bororo-Ge group (with the exception of the Sherente, with whom the predictable transformation is observable along another axis, cf. *RC*, pp. 194–5). Consequently, the different sociological coding of the Bororo and Ge myths, when looked at from this angle alone, does not express a true opposition.

Both in the Bororo myth and in the Ge myths, the hero, who has climbed to the top of a tree or a rock, or who has got half-way up a rock-face, cannot come down again because his companion has removed the pole or ladder that he used to climb up. The events in the Tacana myth are much more complex: with the help of a liana, the hero has reached the top of a big tree; his companion then climbs up another liana or a smaller tree nearby and, from this vantage point, cuts the first liana at a height from which it is impossible for his victim to jump to the ground; then he comes down again and, according to one version, even goes to the trouble of chopping down the tree by means of which he has performed the misdeed. A third version combines the two concepts: first the hero climbs to the top of a palm tree from which he can reach a liana that he uses to get to the top of a taller tree; whereupon his brother-in-law makes his return impossible by chopping down the palm tree.

It would seem, then, that the Tacana myth aims at confusing the simple relationship established by the Bororo and Ge myths between the two men: one above, the other below; and that, to achieve this end, it invents a complicated process by which one of the protagonists remains up above, while the other almost reaches the same level and then comes down again. This cannot be a random effect, because the main versions are all very particular about the point. Moreover, the theme is taken up again and developed in the following episode, where the hero tries to avoid the snake, which climbs up the tree to get at him, by coming as far as possible down the severed liana, so that he is now, relatively speaking, at a lower level than his new persecutor.[32]

A group of transformations is now immediately obvious, but they differ as between the Bororo myth and the Ge myths.

In the Tacana, as in the Bororo myth, the hero owes his safety to a liana that he has, however, put to opposite uses: either he has hoisted

[32] It is no doubt this inversion which allows the Tacana myths to link the bird-nester theme with that of the visit to the underground world. One version (M_{300b}) tells the story of an Indian who was so lazy that his brother-in-law (his wife's brother) grew tired of supplying him with food and decided to get rid of him. He therefore got him to climb *down a liana* into an armadillo's hole, ostensibly to catch the animal; then he blocked up the entrance and went off. The armadillo accepted the man's presence, and introduced him to the Idsetti deha, a community of dwarfs without anuses, living exclusively on soup and the smell of food. The hero – either because he did not manage to provide the dwarfs with the missing orifice, or because the dwarfs were disgusted by the sight of him defecating and by the foul smell – persuaded the armadillo to take him back to his own people. Before doing so, the armadillo taught him a method of hunting which consisted in plunging into a pot of boiling water, and coming out through the bottom at the same time as the water. The hunter then found himself in a land stocked with game, where all he had to do was to kill the animals and roast the meat, which his wife then withdrew from the pot, after he had re-emerged from it. The wicked brother-in-law tried to imitate him, but since he did not possess the magic comb given by the armadillo, he was scalded to death (H.-H., pp. 351–5).

It will be noted that the hero of the Bororo myth, M_1, is a bird-nester, whose fundament is devoured by vultures, so that he is incapable of retaining the food he has swallowed: he is an (excessively) pierced person, whereas the hero of M_{300b}, who excavates the armadillo's hole, is both a piercing agent and himself (well) pierced, in comparison with the dwarfs, who are (excessively) stopped up. The transformation of boiled into roast meat or, to put it more accurately, the mediation of roast meat by way of boiled meat, raises problems that cannot be tackled at this stage.

himself to the top of the rock-face (the top of the top) or he has clung to the lower extremity (the bottom of the top). In spite of this difference, the use of a liana establishes a definite kinship between the two myths, and one is even tempted to suppose they have a common origin, since one episode is practically identical in both, although the syntagmatic sequence does not seem to make it inevitable.

The Bororo hero, who has no fundament and cannot digest food after being attacked by the vultures, remembers a tale told him by his grandmother and in which the same difficulty was overcome by means of an artificial posterior made of vegetable pulp. In a version, of which I shall shortly give a summary (M_{303}), the Tacana hero remembers stories told him by his grandmother about the appropriate ways of calling for the help of the wood-spirit, which eventually sets him free. Consequently, in both cases, a form of behaviour which is anal in the one instance and oral in the other is introduced as an effect of another myth, told by a grandmother. This narrative device is sufficiently unusual to imply the existence of an actual, and not simply a logical, kinship between the Bororo and Tacana myths.

Moreover, the analysis can be carried further in this direction. When I compared M_1 with other Bororo myths, I put forward the suggestion that the hero was a 'self-confined person', i.e. a boy approaching the age at which it is customary for young Indians to join male society, and who refused to leave the feminine and maternal environment. Let us compare this with the original failing of the Tacana hero. In a community where, it would seem, agriculture proper was a female activity (Schuller; Farabee 2, p. 155, in connection with the Tiatinagua, who are a sub-group of the Tacana family), he was an inefficient hunter but an expert farmer: he thus assumed a feminine role, and disappointed the expectations of his affines who, from the functional point of view, obtained nothing more (and above all nothing different) from him than what they had got previously from the woman whom they had made over to him. The myth confirms this interpretation by supposing matrilocal residence, which is contrary to the ethnographic reality (Farabee 2, p. 156).

Another Tacana myth deals with the symmetrically opposite possibility of a woman who tries to take on a masculine role:

M_{302}. Tacana. 'The woman mad about meat'

There was once a woman who wanted to eat meat, but her husband was a poor hunter and always came back empty-handed. She therefore decided to go hunting on her own and she went off after a stag, which she chased for several days without catching up with it, and which was really a man in animal form. The latter tried to convince the woman, as her husband had done when he attempted to dissuade her from going hunting, that deer were too fast for her; and he then made her a proposal of marriage. But the woman decided to go back home, although the deer-man told her she would never get there.

Actually, she continued her hunting expedition which had already lasted, not three days, as she thought, but three years. The deer-man caught up with her, pierced her with his antlers and left her corpse lying. A jaguar ate her flesh, except for the skin, which changed into a thick cluster of marsh plants. The lice in her hair became wild rice, and from her brain sprang termites and ant-hills.

The man, who at first had been amused by his wife's pretensions, eventually went to look for her. As he was travelling, he met several birds of prey, who informed him of the fate which had overtaken the unfortunate woman. Henceforth, they added, whenever a human being passed an ant-hill surrounded by marsh grasses, he would hear the termites whistling. In spite of the advice given him by the birds, the man insisted on pursuing his quest. He came to a big river, was carried away by the current, and his body was buried in the mud. From his corpse sprang two capybaras, a male and a female, which gave off a powerful stench. This was how these animals came into being (H.-H., pp. 58–9).

This myth has a two-fold interest. In spite of the very great geographical distances involved, it allows us to establish a link between Chaco (Toba, M_{213}; Mocovi, M_{224}) and Venezuelan myths (Warao, M_{223}), about one, or several frustrated (or) disobedient women, who are subsequently changed into capybaras. Admittedly, in this case, it is the husband who is transformed into an aquatic animal, whereas the woman is changed into aquatic plants (to which – for reasons which remain to be discovered – are added the whistling termites of the marshes).[33] The Bororo myth about the bird-nester (M_1) helps us to understand this divergency in the transformational system.

[33] The metamorphosis is always a punishment for excess: in this case, a woman has tried to act the man; in another case (M_{256}), a man tries to take advantage of his long penis to behave like a superman and, in a third, a child displays shocking cruelty (H.-H., pp. 81–3, 192–3).

Indeed – and this is the second point – the myths correspond to each other partially since, in both cases, an affine (wife or father) betrays his or her function by abandoning a husband or a son, and suffers the same punishment: pierced by the antlers of a stag, devoured by cannibalistic animals (jaguar or piranha fish), and the remains (peripheral, in the case of the skin, lice and brain, central in that of the viscera) give rise to marsh plants. And while the Tacana myth makes a capybara out of the man disjoined from his huntress-wife (although he was obstinately trying to find her, in spite of the advice given by the birds), it does so after the fashion of another Bororo myth (M_{21}), in which fisher-women, disjoined from their husbands (and who wish to remain so), change the latter into pigs. The Tacana woman refuses to yield to the advances of the stag-man, although he would have supplied her with meat. In óne version of M_{21}, Bororo women receive supplies of fish from otters, which are really men, for having yielded to their advances (Rondon, p. 167).

When I compared the Bororo and Ge myths about the origin of wild pigs in *The Raw and the Cooked*, a transformation of a sociological nature enabled me to reduce the differences between them. The potential line of division which, in the Ge myths, runs between the brother and the married sister, is to be found, in the Bororo myths, between the wife and the husband:

$$[\text{Ge}](\overset{\overline{\quad/\!/\quad}}{\triangle \quad \circ} = \triangle) \Rightarrow [\text{Bororo}] (\circ \quad \# \quad \triangle)$$

If it were legitimate to postulate, on the basis of the Tacana myths, the existence of a little known social structure which seems to be no longer observable in fact, this would give us a third type of empirical situation among the Tacana, and one which would overlap with the other two. At the root of this situation there would be, instead of a state of tension, an urge to come together neutralizing the technological differences between the sexes: the man wants to be a plant-grower, like his wife; the wife wants to hunt like her husband. This desire to blur distinctions no doubt results in a cleavage, but a transformed one, since in this instance (M_{300a}) it occurs between a sister's husband and a wife's brother, the latter objecting to the fact that the wife's husband is a mere replica of the wife herself:

$$M_{300a}\left[\overset{\overline{\quad/\!/\quad}}{\triangle \quad (\circ)} = \triangle \right] \Rightarrow M_{302}\left[\text{game} \; /\!/ \; (\triangle) \equiv \circ \right]$$

(For the transformation: *brother-in-law* ⇒ *game*, cf. RC, pp. 83–92).

A comparison of the pairs of animals used respectively by M_{21} and M_{302} brings out very clearly the ambiguity of the Tacana attitude about the opposition between the sexes, since the animals concerned are mixed entities:

Bororo (M_{21}) : fish		‖	pigs
Tacana(M_{302})	capybaras ‖	deer	

The fish caught by the Bororo women in M_{21} are entirely connected with water, while the pigs into which their husbands are transformed are entirely connected with land, and may even be considered as chthonian animals. But the capybaras, which are amphibious rodents, illustrate the union of (terrestrial) water and earth; whereas the deer, considered as feminine animals by the Bororo (Colb. 1, p. 23), the Jivaro (Karsten 2, p. 374), the Mundurucu (Murphy 1, p. 93), the Yupa (Wilbert 7, p. 879) and the Guarani (Cadogan 4, p. 57), etc. – in this respect, too, in opposition to the pigs, which are masculine animals[34] – have an affinity with the sky and illustrate the union of earth and air. Perhaps the same explanation would be valid for the fact that the Tacana ogre, who replaces the Ge jaguar in the bird-nester myths, is also a mixed entity, a parrot-snake, which effects a union between earth and air and, like the deer in M_{302}, is faced with an opponent who is sometimes a man, sometimes a woman, but in either case always unwilling to give up the opposite attribute.

All these suppositions are what one might call mythico-deductive in nature; they depend upon a critique, in the Kantian sense of the word, of a body of myths in connection with which I am inquiring in what conditions they might have been produced by a supposedly unknown social structure; I am not, incidentally, under the illusion that they might be a mere reflection of that structure. But although we know very little about the ancient institutions of the Tacana, it is possible to find in them a degree of indirect confirmation of these suppositions, which gives the latter at least some likelihood of being true.

The tribes of the Tacana group practised a double initiation ceremony for boys and girls, involving ritual mutilation intended, it would seem, to stress an equivalence between the sexes in spite of their

---

[34] However, the form of the contrast is not constant, since the Kogi look upon pigs and armadillos as feminine animals, because they root about in the earth as if they were doing agricultural work (Reichel-Dolmatoff, Vol. I, p. 270).

apparent diversity. The same bamboo knife was used to cut the frenum of the penis in boys and to pierce the hymen in girls (Métraux 13, p. 446). Misbehaviour was punished by the parallel methods of exposure to ants, in the case of women, and to wasps, in the case of men (H.-H., pp. 373–4). And although Cavina women were forbidden to look upon idols or ritual objects, they enjoyed the rare privilege of playing the flute, while the men sang (Armentia, p. 13). This tendency towards sexual equality in the matter of ritual coincides with the interchangeability of the sexes to which the Tacana myths seem, in some obscure way, to aspire.

Also, it may well be that this particular form of dualism, as it finds expression in different ways in the rites and myths, is to be explained by the geographical situation of the Tacana (and their neighbours of the Panoan linguistic group) at the point of intersection of the lower cultures of the tropical forest with those of the Andean plateau. Although the myths we have considered so far have many points in common with those of the Chaco and central Brazil, they also differ from them through the presence, in the Tacana versions, of a divine protagonist, a member of a pantheon with no equivalent among the tribes of the lower cultures, and some of the gods of which even bear Quechua names. In the seventeenth century, there were still objects of Peruvian origin in the square temples erected in isolated spots by the Tacana (Métraux, *loc. cit.*, p. 447).

Because of the role that these divine beings are called upon to play, all the mythic functions are, as it were, moved one stage up; but this general upward shift does not involve any disturbance in the functions themselves, which must continue to be ensured. The Tacana myths get out of the difficulty, we might say, by making two half-terms correspond to a function. Let us consider, for instance, the following transformation: the macaws eaten by the jaguar (in the Ge myths: M_7–M_{12}) are changed into snakes eaten by a divine being (in the Tacana myths: M_{300a}, M_{303}), who therefore exemplifies the Tacana transformation of the Ge jaguar as an imaginary ogre and real saviour. This group is not homogeneous, since the transformation of the macaws into snakes is an *episode which is internal* to the Tacana myth, whereas the transformation of the jaguar into a divine being is the result of an *external operation* carried out on the myth with the help of the Ge myths. To get over the difficulty and obtain a real relation of equivalence between the myths, it has to be accepted that, because of the intervention of a divine protagonist in the Tacana series, the correspondence should be established between three Tacana terms and two Ge terms, according to the formula:

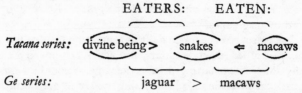

EATERS: EATEN:

Tacana series: divine being > snakes ⇐ macaws

Ge series: jaguar > macaws

As it happens, in the Tacana series, the divine being is a snake-eater and the snake a man-eater, although the humans who are changed first into macaws and then into snakes are themselves eaten by the divine being. In the Ge series, the jaguar replaces the snake (as a potential ogre) and behaves like the divine being (a real saviour), and the macaws are eaten by the jaguar in the same way as the macaw-snakes are by the divine being in the Tacana myths.

This may be the fundamental reason why the Tacana snakes must, logically, be mixed entities: snakes and birds. As snakes, they invert one term of the Ge myths (because of their subordination to a term superior to their own), and as macaws they reproduce the other term. But the main point is the renewed verification of the fact that structural analysis can be a help in historical reconstruction. Tacana specialists agree that these Indians may be of eastern origin: this would mean that they came from the area of the lower cultures and only at a later stage were exposed to Andean influence which imposed its pantheon on an older basis of belief. My interpretation tends in exactly the same direction. It may be added, on the strength of the first difference I noted between the Bororo myth and the Tacana myth with a bird-nester hero, that the complicated process resorted to by the second myth to ensure the isolation of the hero would be easily explicable if it were the result of a transformation of the corresponding episode in the Bororo and Ge myths. The complication, which is made inevitable by the respecting of an additional obligation, would appear gratuitous and incomprehensible if it were the effect of a transformation operating in the reverse direction.

Let us now return to our starting-point, i.e. M_{300a}, about which we already know that it is a transformation of three myths or groups of myths: $\{M_1\}$, $\{M_7-M_{12}\}$, $\{M_{22}-M_{24}\}$, to which we can now add a fourth group $\{M_{17}, M_{161}\}$, because of the double theme of the transformation into a great hunter of an unhappy hero, who is a prisoner at the top of a tree, from which he manages to get down thanks to a liana (which is also a *ficus* in the Tacana myths, H.-H., p. 178; cf. *RC*, p. 180, n. 20), produced by magic means.

This last aspect refers back to a fifth group of myths that has already been analysed at length in this study, and which belongs to the Guiana area (M_{237}–M_{239}). The starting-point is the same. A poor hunter is living in a matrilocal situation; his brothers-in-law try to get rid of him by delivering him up to a cannibalistic monster. A supernatural protector in the shape of a frog (like the wife of the supernatural protector in one of the Tacana versions) relieves him of the rottenness (stench, in the Tacana myths) which is causing his ill-luck, and presents him with miraculous arrows (which are shot without the archer taking aim, in the Guiana versions, or have blunt points in the Tacana myths). Therefore, whereas the bird-nester is a master of water in the Bororo myths and a master of cooking in the Ge myths, with the Tacana he becomes – like the Guiana hero – a master of hunting on whom depends the very existence of cooking, which requires meat as its material and fire (for roasting) and water (for boiling) as its means.

One version of the Tacana myth about the bird-nester brings out this new function very clearly. I shall skip the first part, which is a fairly exact reproduction of M_{300a}, and shall merely point out that in this version the divine protector is called Chibute. From the point of view that concerns us, this difference can be neglected since Chibute, the son of Deavoavai's sister and a monkey-man (H.-H., pp. 158–62) forms, with his maternal uncle, a semi-dioscuric pair, the terms of which are easily interchangeable: 'Although they are present in the Tacana pantheon as separate characters, Chibute and Deavoavai are, in this context, complementary and have the same semantic function, so that it is legitimate to use the hyphened name Chibute-Deavoavai to refer to the double personage' (*ibid.*, p. 178). After the hero's mother-in-law has consumed the maleficent food and has changed into a snake, ha bacua, her husband, accompanied by his sons, goes to look for her:

M_{303}. Tacana. 'The education of boys and girls'

The three men lost their way and, when they encountered some wild pigs, the sons followed the animals and changed into similar ones. The hero's father-in-law continued his search. He became so hungry that he ate his left arm. Suddenly Chibute appeared, chided him for his unkindness and told him that he would never again live among humans but would be done to death by them. He would be changed into a giant ant-eater, would wander aimlessly about the earth, would live without a wife and would engender and bring forth his children alone.

Moved by his wife's tears, the hero now set out after his parents-in-law. Chibute showed him the old woman who had been transformed into a snake and was doomed to die of starvation, as well as the ant-eater – showing him how to kill it, not with a bow and arrows, but by clubbing it to death. The hero then expressed the desire to learn how to.hunt, and Chibute taught him how to make a bow from the part of the trunk of the yellow chima palm tree which faces east,[35] as well as a bow-string and two kinds of arrows. And the man became the most proficient of hunters.

He in turn instructed backward pupils, with the help of Chibute. In the case of this second generation, the god abolished certain restrictions of a magical nature (the rule about making no more than two arrows a year) but introduced others of a technical nature. The myth thus moves from the art of hunting as a supernatural gift to its age-old practice, which is surrounded by all sorts of precautions and refinements that the myth describes too minutely for it to be possible to reproduce them in any detail here. I summarize: nocturnal bathing in water perfumed with the leaves of the emarepana shrub (unidentified), the scent of which will spread through the forest,[36] obligatory shooting of the first game sighted and the presentation of the stomach to the instructor's wife, while the rest of the meat goes

[35] In connection with a similar rule observed by the Yurok in California, who made their bows only of yew and from the part of the trunk facing uphill, according to some sources, or towards the river, according to others, Kroeber comments with amused condescension: 'This is exactly the kind of unpredictable restriction that Indians like to impose upon themselves' (in Elmendorf, p. 87, n. 10). But even today, in France, the basket-weavers of the Limousin know that the pliability of chestnut wood varies according to whether the trees grow in hollows or on slopes, or on slopes with different exposures (Robert, p. 158). In a rather different context, men whose job it is to float logs downstream say that the wood tends to drift towards the banks during the full moon but remains in midstream at the time of the new moon (Simonot, p. 26, n. 4). We may not understand the reasons underlying a particular piece of lore, but this is not a reason for classifying it automatically as a superstition.

[36] The Tunebo used a scented root to attract deer, and the Cuna used a plant called bisep for the same purpose (Holmer–Wassen, p. 10). Indian hunters in Virginia rubbed their bodies with angelica root, 'the hunting root', and, contrary to their usual practice, approached from upwind, in the conviction that the smell would attract the deer (B. G. Hoffman). In this case, too, the practice seems to be a positive technical device rather than a magic rite. This can hardly be true, however, of the Sherente habit of piercing little boys' ears and threading light wood sticks through them, with the intention of making the boys good hunters and immunizing them against disease.

to the aged parents of the hunters. The latter never offer meat to the instructor himself but go to help him on his plantation ...

The young hunters had two sisters, the elder of whom seemed so attractive to the hero's son that he wanted to marry her. Chibute, after being again ritually summoned by means of the call: huu! huu! which the Indians utter using their hands as a speaking-trumpet, explained that the suitor should make a pile of wood in front of the hut of his future parents-in-law, and that the girl should take wood from it, if she wanted to signify agreement. The marriage was performed according to a ritual prescribed by Chibute, and a detailed description of which is to be found in the myth.

When the woman was pregnant, her father-in-law taught her how to ascertain the sex of the child in advance and what to do to ensure an easy birth and a lusty man-child. The myth enumerates other recommendations or prohibitions, the purpose of which is to make sure that the baby does not cry continuously, sleeps at night, has no bumps on its head, etc. I again summarize: bathing in water to which juice of the rijina liana (unidentified) has been added; refraining from eating the meat of the red howler monkey (in the case of the mother), of the jaguar or the tail of the black howler monkey (in the case of the child), and from touching the blue eggs of a forest bird or the soles of the coati's feet (in the case of the child). Next come precepts about the making of arrows, hunting procedures, clues for finding one's way in the forest and the cooking of game (roast red meat, stewed pig's stomach).[37]

Also through the medium of the hero, Chibute next taught the young couple how to spin, weave and make pottery scoured with the burnt bark of the caraipé tree (one of the chrysobalanae; cf. Whiffen, p. 96, n. 3).

[With reference to the whistling termites in M_{302}, it is interesting to note that the husband must *whistle* as he cuts the wood from which the stem of the spindle is to be made and that, for the spindle to rotate more quickly, the board on which it rests must be covered by the woman with the ashes of an ant-heap that the husband has previously set fire to.]

After Chibute had advised them to summon the spider to give

[37] This different way of treating the viscera links up with a remark by Whiffen about the tribes in the region between the Rio Issa and the Rio Japura. 'It is beast-like, in their opinion, to eat the liver, kidneys and other intestines of animals, though these may be made into soup or hot-pot' (p. 130, cf. also p. 134). The parts of the animal unworthy of being roasted or smoked can still be consumed provided they are boiled.

spinning lessons to the young woman, he himself taught her how to construct a loom with its various accessories, to prepare vats of dye and to cut and sew clothes for both sexes. He also said that the hunter should adorn himself with certain feathers, carry a game-bag containing the conglomerations of hair, pebbles and fat found in the stomachs or livers of several big animals, take great care to bury the liver of the wild pig on the spot where it had been killed (so that other individuals of the same species would return there) and to make the Master of pigs an offering of a woven pouch decorated with symbols, so that he would not take his herd away but would leave it in the salt-licks where the hunters could kill a lot of animals.[38]

The passage about hunting comes to an end with the description of various signs predicting success or failure. After which, the god discusses fishing, which demands a bow and featherless arrows, made with appropriate raw materials and according to the appropriate methods. There is a lengthy disquisition on dams, nets, the preparation of fish-poison and the transport and cooking of fish. Finally, the myth ends with technical advice for the perfect hunter: daily bathing, archery practice on ant-hills (but only when the moon is waxing): forbidden foods (pig's brains, turtle's liver) or recommended foods (the brains of the *Ateles* and *Cebus* monkeys, pucarava and turtle hearts, eaten raw); correct manners (never to eat the remains of meals left in the pots); the proper way to prepare and carry one's hunting gear; body paintings, etc. The myth ends by saying that Chibute added a great many other instructions that the hero was to pass on to his son and his descendants (H.-H., pp. 165–76).

And this is only part of the complete list! Even in its fragmentary form, this myth contains more ethnographical information than an actual observer could collect during a stay of several months or even years in a tribe. Each single rite, prescription or prohibition would be worthy of a critical and comparative study. I shall give only one example which I have chosen because it is more directly relevant to the present analysis than some of the others.

To determine the sex of an unborn child, the god tells the parents to compare their dreams. If they have both dreamed about a round object, such as the fruit of a genipa (*Genipa americana*), a motacú (a palm tree: *Attalea* sp.) or an assaï (another palm tree: *Euterpe oleracea*),

[38] This passage confirms a deduction in *RC*, p. 108, where I suggested that the pig was thought of simultaneously as meat and as master of meat. Identical rules about hunting existed among the Yuracaré.

they will have a son. The child will be a daughter if their dreams were concerned with a long object, such as a manioc root or a banana.

The free association of ideas characteristic of our culture would no doubt give the opposite result: round for a girl, long for a boy. It is easy to verify the fact that, generally speaking, the sexual symbolism of the South American Indians, whatever the lexical terms it uses, is in general homologous with that of the Tacana and therefore contrary to ours. Here are a few examples relating to the sex of the unborn child. According to the Waiwai of Guiana, if the parents hear the woodpecker whistling, swis-sis, the baby will be a boy; but if the bird is tapping, tororororo, it will be a girl (Fock, p. 122; cf. Derbyshire, p. 157). In Ecuador, the Catio tease a praying mantis: if it responds by putting forward both front legs, a girl is to be expected, whereas one leg indicates a boy (Rochereau, p. 82). This symbolism can be compared with the sexual classification of the Amazonian wooden drums: the big drum producing low notes is female, while the little, high-pitched one is male (Whiffen, pp. 214–15).[39] We thus have a series of equivalences:

female : male :: long : round :: tapped :
                whistled :: whole : half :: big : little :: deep : shrill

In *The Raw and the Cooked* (p. 130), I brought out a contrast, inherent in the feminine sex, between elongated and rounded vulvae. But if it is remembered that the Mundurucu myth to which we were referring declares that the (M_{58}) pretty vulvae are the roundest ones (Murphy 1, p. 78), we arrive at the following proposition:

(*desirable woman*) more : less :: (*vulva*) round : elongated

which appears to contradict the preceding one, unless we bear in mind the latent feeling of repulsion for the female body, common among South American Indians, so that it is only desirable to them, or even tolerable, when, in respect of its odour and physiological functions, it falls short of the full manifestation of all its potentialities (*RC*, pp. 182–3, 269–71).

[39] The method of the Caingang-Coroado, which is less symbolical and more rationalized, is closer to our systematization. They hold out a club to the small ant-eater; if the animal takes it, the child will be a boy; if not, a girl (Borba, p. 25). I do not claim that the equation given above is valid for the symbolism of all tribes. For instance, the Umutina seem to be an exception, since they divide up the fruits of the bacaba do campo palm tree (*Oenocarpus* sp.) into 'male' and 'female' according to whether they are respectively long or short (Schultz 2, p. 227: Oberg, p. 108), and the Baniwa attribute 'flattened' arms to men, 'round' arms to women (M_{276b}). But it is precisely these differences in the representational systems which deserve closer study than they have so far received.

The first series of equivalences can no doubt be simplified, if we consider that the contrast between whistled and tapped echoes the other acoustic contrast between shrill and deep notes; but there remains the problem of why women are thought of as being more 'substantial' than men, if we can sum up the differences in a colloquial term. It would seem, in this connection, that the South American Indians think more or less along the same lines as the native tribes in the mountains of New Guinea, who base a strongly marked distinction between the sexes on the belief that female flesh is distributed 'vertically' along the bones, whereas male flesh is set 'horizontally', i.e. at right-angles to the axis of the bone. This anatomical difference is supposed to explain why women mature more quickly than men and marry on an average ten years earlier and, even in adolescence, can contaminate with their menstrual blood boys who remain particularly vulnerable at that age, since they have not yet been admitted to the social and psychological status of manhood (Meggitt, pp. 207, 222, nn. 5, 6).

In South America, too, a *longitudinal/transversal* contrast, formulated in different terms, was used to express differences of authority and status. Among the ancient tribes of the Rio Negro area, a chieftain could be recognized by the fact that he wore a cylinder of hard stone, pierced lengthwise, i.e. along its axis, whereas the pendants worn by ordinary people, although also cylindrical, were pierced crosswise. We shall encounter this distinction again later; it has some analogy with the difference between the dance sticks of the southern Guarani, which are hollow or solid according to the sex of the performer. It is logical to look upon a cylinder which has been pierced lengthwise as being comparatively more hollow than a similar cylinder which has been pierced across and whose mass therefore remains almost solid.

After giving this one example of the wealth and complexity of the commentaries that might be made on any of the beliefs, customs, rites, prescriptions and prohibitions listed in M_{303}, let us now consider the myth from a more general point of view. We saw that it is a transformation not only of the groups $\{M_1,\}$, $\{M_7-M_{12}\}$, $\{M_{22}-M_{24}\}$, $\{M_{117}$ and $M_{161}\}$, but also of the Guiana group $\{M_{237}-M_{239}\}$. This is not all, since, after noting in passing the fleeting reference to $\{M_{15}-M_{18}\}$ (the transformation of the wicked brothers-in-law into wild pigs), we must now examine the last transformation illustrated by the Tacana myth: that of the group of Ge myths $\{M_{225}-M_{228}$ and $M_{232}\}$, which, as the reader will remember, also deals with the origin of the ant-eater and the training of boys as hunters and (or) warriors.

In *The Raw and the Cooked*, I established an implicit transformational relationship (through the medium of M_5, itself a transformation of M_1) between one myth of this group (M_{142}) and the bird-nester myth, by means of an equivalence between the horizontal disjunction (*upstream-downstream*) and the vertical disjunction (*sky-earth*) of their respective heroes (*RC*, pp. 257–9). If we now move from the Ge myths to the Tacana myths, in which we find the bird-nester image in an undistorted form, we are still obeying the imperative which obliges us to go over the same ground in the opposite direction.

The Ge and Tacana heroes, after their voluntary or involuntary, horizontal or vertical, aquatic or celestial, disjunction, encounter ogres: various species of falcon in the Ge myths, parrot-snakes in the Tacana ones. Since the contrast between birds of prey and parrots is constant in the South American myths, in the form: *flesh-eating, fruit-eating* (birds), the ethnozoological system common to the two groups of myths would be complete if the Ge falcons could be classified as Herpetotheres, the group of snake-eaters, in the same way as the Ge and Chaco jaguars are parrot-eaters. But in at least one version, one of the birds is a *Caprimulgus*, not a falcon, and in other cases the particular kind of falcon remains unspecified.

Be that as it may, in all cases the cannibalistic animals answer to a tapped out call, which comes either, in the Tacana myths, from the hero's enemies (and then from the helpful god) or, in the Ge myths, from the hero himself (cf. also M_{177} in Krause, p. 350, where the hero beats the water: ton, ton, ton ... to cause the arrival of the killer eagles). In some cases, one or both grandparents change into ant-eaters (M_{227}, M_{228}, M_{230}), in other cases, the father, or the father and mother of the hero's wife, undergo the same fate (M_{229}, M_{303}). On pp. 132–5 I discussed the following contrasts or transformations:

(*a*) capybara (*long teeth*) | ant-eater (*toothless*);
(*b*) grandparents ⇒ ant-eaters (*eaters of ant-hills*);
    hero's head ⇒ ant-hill;
    parents-in-law ⇒ eaters of ant-eaters.

A comparable group can be found among the Tacana:

    father-in-law ⇒ ant-eater (M_{303});
    wife's brain ⇒ ant-hill (M_{302});
    hero's parents ⇒ eaters of ant-eaters (M_{303});

in connection with two myths M_{302} and M_{303}, one of which deals with the origin of the capybara, the other with the origin of the ant-eater.

Finally, in both the Tacana group and the Ge group, one myth (M_{226}, M_{303}) stands out from the others and is tantamount to a treatise in initiation. But a difference becomes apparent at the same time and it will provide the solution to a methodological and theoretical difficulty, to which the reader's attention must first be drawn.

In conducting the inquiry which has been in progress since the beginning of the previous volume, I have proceeded as if I were scanning the whole mythological field, beginning at an arbitrarily chosen point and moving methodically this way and that, up and down, from right to left and from left to right, in order to reveal certain types of relationships between myths situated consecutively along the same line or between those below or above each other on different lines. But in either case a distinction has to be drawn between the scanning operation itself and the myths it successively or periodically illuminates and which are the object of the operation.

However, in the case of M_{303}, it is as if the relationship between the operation and its object had been reversed, and in two ways. First, the scanning movement which was originally horizontal suddenly appears to be vertical. Secondly – and more importantly – M_{303} is to be defined as a group of exceptional points in the mythological field, and its unity as an object becomes intangible outside the scanning operation itself, which links the points together in its indissoluble movement: the scanning movement therefore represents the mythic substance of M_{303} and the points touched upon the series of operations to which we are subjecting it:

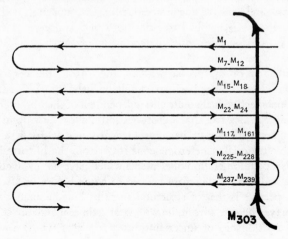

The first explanation that comes to mind when we try to account for this two-fold inversion, which is both geometrical and logical, is that a mythic system can only be grasped in a process of becoming; not as something inert and stable but in a process of perpetual transformation. This would mean that there are always several kinds of myths simultaneously present in the system, some of them primary (in respect of the moment at which the observation is made) and some of them derivative. And while some kinds are present in their entirety at certain points, elsewhere they can be detected only in fragmentary form. Where evolution has gone furthest, the elements set free by the decomposition of the old myths have already been incorporated into new combinations.

In one sense, this explanation is obvious since it depends on facts that can hardly be denied: the myths break down and, as Boas said, new myths are made out of their remains. However, it cannot be entirely satisfactory because, clearly, the primary or derivative character that we might thus be led to attribute to a given myth would not belong to it intrinsically, but would be chiefly a function of the order of presentation. As I showed in *The Raw and the Cooked* (pp. 1–6), this order cannot be other than arbitrary, since the myths cannot be judged in advance but give a spontaneous clarification of their reciprocal relationships. Therefore, had I decided to study M_{303} first, for reasons every bit as contingent as those which led me to give the number 1 to the Bororo myth about the bird-nester, M_{303} and not M_1 would have displayed the peculiar properties I am now discussing. Besides, this is not the first time we have encountered them. In connection with other myths (such as M_{139}), I had to bring into play conceptions such as intersection, cross-section and juxtaposition of armatures (*RC*, pp. 252–5).

The difficulty of the problem arises, then, from the necessity of taking two different perspectives simultaneously into account. The historical perspective is absolute and independent of the observer, since we must accept as a fact that a cross-section made at any point in the material of the myths always has a certain degree of diachronic thickness because this material, a heterogeneous mass from the historical point of view, is a conglomeration of elements which have not evolved at the same rate and cannot therefore be said to come before or after. The other perspective is that of structural analysis, but the analyst knows that, wherever he starts from, he will, after a time, inevitably come up against a relationship of uncertainty as a result of which any myth examined at a late stage in the inquiry is at once a local transformation of the myths immediately preceding it and a complete totalization of all or part of the myths included in the field of investigation.

This relationship of uncertainty is no doubt the price that has to be paid for trying to understand a closed system: at first, it is possible to learn a great deal about the nature of the relationships between the elements of a system, the general economy of which remains obscure; and in the end, relationships which by now have become redundant do more to provide information about the general economy of the system than to bring to light new types of connections between the elements. It would seem, then, that we can never know the two things at once and that we have to be satisfied with collecting information related either to the general structure of the system or to the special links between certain of the elements, but never to both at once. And yet, one kind of knowledge necessarily precedes the other, since it is impossible to inquire directly into the structure without being previously acquainted with a sufficient number of relationships between the elements. Consequently, whatever the starting-point chosen in practice, the nature of the results will change as the inquiry progresses.

But, on the other hand, it is impossible that those results should be entirely and exclusively subject to the internal limitations of structural analysis. For, if this were so, the primary or secondary character of myths belonging to very real societies would have only a relative value, and would depend on the perspective chosen by the observer. One would therefore have to give up all hope of using structural analysis to arrive at historical hypotheses. Or rather, such hypotheses would be no more than optical illusions doomed to be dispelled, if not to be reversed, whenever the mythologist chose to lay out his material differently. But, in several instances, I have put forward interpretations while at the same time claiming that, since they were irreversible, or reversible at too great a cost, they made it possible to assert, not merely relatively but absolutely, that of two given myths one represented an earlier, the other a later, stage in a transformation which could not have occurred in the opposite direction.

To try to overcome the difficulty, let us consider M_{303} in its relationship to all the other myths or groups of myths of which it is a transformation. No doubt it strikes us as being simultaneously a particular item in the group of three transformations and as an exceptional expression of the group, which it summarizes within itself as much as, or more than, we can manage to complete the group with its help. This paradoxical situation is a result of the multi-dimensional nature of the mythic field, which structural analysis explores, and at the same time establishes, by executing a spiral movement. A series, which is at first linear and recoiled upon itself, develops into a surface which in turn engenders a volume. Consequently, the first myths studied are little more than a syntagmatic chain, the message of which is to be decoded by reference to paradigmatic sets that the myths, at this stage, have not yet supplied, and which must be sought outside the mythic field, that is in ethnography. But later, and as the inquiry, through its catalysing action, brings into focus the crystalline structure of the field and its volume, a two-fold phenomenon occurs. On the one hand, the para-digmatic relationships internal to the field increase in number much more rapidly than the external relationships, which indeed reach a ceiling, as soon as all the available ethnographical information has been assembled and utilized, so that the context of each myth consists more and more of other myths and less and less of the customs, beliefs and rites of the particular population from which the myth in question derives. On the other hand, the distinction between an internal syntag-matic chain and an external paradigmatic set, which was clear at the outset, tends to disappear both in theory and in practice since, once the mythic field has been brought into being, the arbitrarily chosen axis along which the exploration is carried out, defines not only the series serving – according to the requirements of the moment – as a syntag-matic chain, but also the cross-connections which, at every point in the series, function as paradigmatic sets. According to the perspective adopted by the analyst, any series can therefore serve as a syntagmatic chain or a paradigmatic set, and the initial choice will determine the (syntagmatic or paradigmatic) character of all the other series. This, in fact, is the phenomenon that has been illustrated in the course of the analysis of M_{303}, since the syntagmatic chain formed by this myth can be changed into a paradigmatic set for the interpretation of any of the myths of which it is a transformation, while those myths in their turn would form a paradigmatic set capable of throwing light on M_{303}, if we had begun our inquiry from the opposite end.

All this is true, yet it leaves out of account an aspect of M_{303} which differentiates it absolutely from the other myths with which I have compared it, although at the present stage of the discussion I cannot suggest any historical or logical cause for the difference and therefore must not let myself be put off by the antinomy of structure and event.

All the myths that I have recognized as belonging to the same group as M_{303} refer to the education either of boys or of girls, but never of both together (or if, like M_{142} and M_{225}, they do so, it is to make the special, and therefore equally restrictive, suggestion of a similar *lack* of education). From this point of view, M_{303} introduces an innovation, since it consists of a co-educational treatise equally valid for the Emile of the Ge family and the Sophie[40] of the Guiana-Amazonian tribes.

This original feature in M_{303} confirms, in the first place, the hypothesis about the reversibility of the sexes in the Tacana institutions and way of thinking that I arrived at by purely deductive means.[41] Among these particular Indians, the admission of boys and girls to adulthood is not the result of the ritual establishment of a differential gap between the sexes, leading to a permanent belief that one is superior to the other. On the contrary, the two sexes graduate together, by means of an operation which minimizes their anatomical differences and of simultaneous instruction in the absolute necessity of collaboration (for instance, the husband is involved at several points in the making and the use of the spindle, although spinning is a female occupation).

Secondly, there is a difference between M_{303} and the other myths I have put in the same group: M_{303} is both like them and goes beyond them. The other myths consider only one aspect of a problem which, in theory, has two, whereas M_{303} tries to juxtapose both aspects and put them on the same level. It is therefore more complex, logically, and is, rightly so, a transformation of more myths than any one of the others is. We can carry the argument further: in so far as the mythology of honey, which we have used as a guiding-line, has a badly brought up

[40] TRANSLATORS' NOTE: Emile and Sophie are the pupils in J.-J. Rousseau's educational treatise, *Emile*.

[41] M_{303} provides a particularly striking illustration of this reversibility in the episode about the transformation of the father-in-law into an ant-eater which thereafter will live alone, without a mate, and will conceive and bring forth its young on its own. A common belief in South America, from the Rio Negro (Wallace, p. 314) to the Chaco (Nino, p. 37), is that there is no such thing as a male ant-eater and that the females impregnate themselves, without help from any other agent. The link between the Tacana myth and those of the Guiana area is further strengthened by the transformation of the sons of the father-in-law into pigs, since, because of a stripe on its coat, the Kalina call the giant ant-eater 'the father of the collared peccaris' (Ahlbrinck, under 'pakira'). Whatever may be the force of this last detail, the Tacana transformation of the female ant-eater, capable of conceiving independently, into a male capable of conceiving and producing young, certainly shows that the Tacana ascribe an equivalence to the sexes, which makes them commutative both ways with the same facility.

I have not found the belief in the single-sexed ant-eater among the Toba, but it is indicated indirectly by the fact that even today, when they come across the droppings of the giant ant-eater in the course of a hunt, they change their course, being convinced that the animal leads a solitary life and that there can be no other game near it (Susnik, pp. 41–2).

girl as its protagonist, as soon as it changes into a mythology of hunting, the heroine becomes a hero, a well (or badly) brought up boy.
We thus arrive at a meta-group, the terms of which are transformable
into each other, depending on the masculine or feminine values of the
chief character and the type of techno-economic activity referred to.
But all these myths remain, as it were, in the state of semi-myths, which
are still to be synthesized by the fitting of their respective series into the
framework of a single myth which would aim at filling the gap (since
an education specially conceived for one sex could only appear as a
lack to the other) by resorting to the third solution of an equal education
for all, given as far as possible in common. This is precisely the Tacana
solution, which may have been put into practice in the ancient way of
life and, in any case, imagined in their myths and justified by them.

We do not know what type of historical evolution would explain
this empirically observed fact of the coexistence of opposite educational
principles in different parts of tropical America. Does the mixed solution adopted by the Tacana (and perhaps by their Panoan neighbours
who, according to Greenberg's recent classification, belong to the
same macro-Panoan linguistic family) represent a more ancient form,
which split up to produce the masculine initiation rites of the Ge and
the feminine-biased ones of the tribes of the Guiana-Amazonian area
(and, to a lesser degree, of the Chaco)? Or have we to adopt the opposite
hypothesis of a reconciliation or synthesis of conflicting traditions
achieved by the Tacana and the Pano, in the course of a migration from
west to east? Structural analysis cannot solve such problems. But at
least it has the merit of raising them and even of suggesting that one
solution is more plausible than another, since my formal comparison
of an episode in M_{303} with the corresponding episode in M_1 and
M_7–M_{12} led to the conclusion that the Tacana myth may be derived
from the Bororo-Ge myths but that the opposite hypothesis gives rise
to enormous difficulties. This being so, the co-educational ideal of the
Tacana may result from an attempt to adapt an eastern tradition of
masculine initiation to a western tradition which laid the chief stress
on female education. The attempt may have led to the revision of
myths belonging to one or other of the two traditions so that they
could be integrated into a single system, although the reciprocal
transformational character of these myths suggests that they themselves arose, by differentiation, from a more ancient source.

PART FOUR THE INSTRUMENTS OF DARKNESS

*Nunc age, naturas apibus quas Iuppiter ipse
addidit expediam, pro qua mercede canoros
Curetum sonitus crepitantiaque aena secutae
Dictaeo caeli regem pavere sub antro.*

Virgil, *Georgics*, IV, vv. 149–52

1 *Din and Stench*

The general remarks I have just made must not cause us to lose sight of the problem which brought us back to the Tereno myth about the bird-nester (M_{24}), and which led us to compare it with the Tacana myths on the same theme (M_{300}–M_{303}). It was a question of understanding the recurrence in these myths of a 'tapped-out call', addressed in other myths to the tapir, an animal seducer, but here addressed to honey, a food which is also seductive, but which is replaced in the Tacana myths (although the link can always be discerned) by a devouring animal, the macaw-snake. Were we in need of a comparison outside Tacana mythology to confirm the group's unity, it would be amply supplied by the Tereno myth which combines the three terms: honey, snake and macaw, in order to arrive at the notion of a destructive kind of honey (by the addition of snake meat), leading to the transformation of the female consumer into a devouring jaguar – a devourer, as it happens, of macaws or parrots – and men too, whereas in the Tacana myth, it is the man (a bird-nester) who is in the position of macaw-eater.

This Tereno myth, in which honey is raised to a negative power by the addition of snake meat and functions as a means, sets out to explain the origin of tobacco, which lies on the far side of honey, just as menstrual blood (which the woman uses to poison her husband) lies on the hither side of honey. I have already referred on many occasions to the polar system constituted by tobacco and honey, and I propose to return to it later. As for the contrast between honey and menstrual blood, we have already encountered it in myths which assign variable values to the relationship between the two terms: these values may approximate to each other, when the master of honey is a male character who is not put off by a young girl who is indisposed (M_{235}); they are reversed, while still remaining far removed from each other, at the end of the series of transformations which led us from the character of the girl mad about honey (or about her own body) to the jaguar which was chaste but mad about menstrual blood (M_{273}).

Another link is observable between the Tereno myth and a group of Tacana myths to which I have referred on several occasions (M_{194}–M_{197}). In M_{197}, the daughters of the irára (the 'melero', an animal master of honey) fed their husbands on a beer into which they mixed their excrement; therefore, like the heroine of the Tereno myth, they behaved as their husbands' poisoners. When he discovered his wife's criminal machinations, the Tereno Indian set off in search of honey, the instrument of his revenge, and he knocked the soles of his sandals together in order to find it more easily. Having similarly become aware of the situation, the Tacana husbands beat their wives, thus causing the little wooden drums they had attached to their wives' backs to sound: pung, pung, pung (M_{196}).[1] On hearing this sound, and in order to prevent them being so ill-used, their father changed the women into macaws:

poison:	tapped-out call:	consequence of vengeance:
M_{24}: menstrual blood	cause (of means) of vengeance	woman changed into (jaguar) eater of macaws
M_{197}: excrement	result (of means) of vengeance	women changed into macaws

A more direct link exists between menstrual blood, excrement and honey. In M_{24}, the husband gives his wife poisoned honey in exchange, as it were, for the menstrual blood he receives from her; in M_{197}, the cook exchanges (with herself) the excrement she mixed with the beer, for the honey she should normally have used.

Consequently, however obscure the episode of the 'tapped-out' call may still appear, its presence in the Tereno myth, which is corroborated by other myths, does not seem to be explicable by exceptional or fortuitous causes. Nor would it seem to be explicable as a relic of some technical device (making a noise to drive off the swarm) or magical practice (anticipatory, imitation of the sound of the honey gatherer's axe after he has located the swarm), since such interpretations, having no ethnographical foundation, are inapplicable to the 'tapped-out call' as we have found it described by the Tacana, in a mythic context which has undergone transformation.

If the honey-gatherer's gesture of knocking his sandals together cannot be explained by accidental causes, nor by some technical or magical purpose directly linked with his search, what place can the use of an improvised instrument of noise have in the myth? In an attempt to solve this problem, which does not merely involve an ap-

---

[1] The Kalina of Guiana also use the skin of the irára to cover small-sized drums (Ahlbrinck, under 'aira').

parently insignificant detail in a very short myth, but also raises by implication the whole question of the theory of calls and, beyond that, the theory of the whole system of musical instruments, I propose to introduce two myths belonging to the Tucuna Indians who live on the banks of the Solimões river, between 67–70° longitude west, and whose dialect is now classed with that spoken by the more northerly Tucano:

M_{304}. *Tucuna*. '*The family which was changed into jaguars*'

An elderly man and his wife set off, along with other men, for an unknown destination, perhaps for the other world. The old man taught his companions how to shoot an arrow at the trunk of a tururi tree. No sooner had the arrow touched the tree than a layer of bark came away from the entire length of the trunk. Each person chose a piece of bark, and, after hammering it out to make it bigger, painted black spots on it to look like the jaguar's markings, and put it on. Having thus transformed themselves into jaguars, the hunters roamed the forest massacring and eating Indians. But others discovered their secret and resolved to exterminate them. They killed the old man while he was attacking them, disguised as a jaguar. His wife heard them utter the murderer's name. Disguised as a jaguar, she ran after him and tore him to pieces.

The old woman's son had two children. One day the old woman accompanied her son and other hunters to a place where envieira trees grew. These are fruit-bearing trees on which toucans feed. Each hunter chose a tree and climbed up it in order to kill the birds with his blow-pipe. Suddenly, the old woman appeared in the shape of a jaguar and devoured the dead birds which had fallen at the foot of the tree up which her son had climbed. After she had gone, the man came down and picked up the remaining birds. He then tried to climb back up the tree, but a thorn got caught in his foot and he bent down to remove it. At that moment the old woman leapt on his neck and killed him. She took out his liver, wrapped it in some leaves and took it back to her grandsons, claiming that it was a tree fungus. The children, however, who had become suspicious because of their father's absence, looked in the pot and recognized a human liver. They followed their grandmother into the forest, saw her change into a jaguar and devour their father's corpse. One of the boys plunged a spear, the tip of which was made from a wild pig's tooth, into the ogress's anus. She fled, and the children buried their father's remains in an armadillo's burrow.

They had already returned to their house when the old woman arrived, moaning. On their feigning concern, she explained that she had hurt herself when she fell on a tree stump in the plantation. The children, however, examined the wound and saw that it had been caused by the spear. They lit a big fire behind the house and found a hollow trunk of an ambaúva tree, one end of which they split lengthwise so that the two wooden tongues banged noisily against each other when they threw the trunk onto the ground. They thus caused such a terrible din that the old woman came out of the house, enraged that so much noise should be made in the vicinity of a sick person. They at once seized hold of her and threw her into the fire where she was burnt alive (Nim. 13, pp. 147–8).

Before analysing this myth, I shall give a few explanations of a botanical and ethnographical nature. Three kinds of tree are mentioned in M_{304}: tururi, envieira and ambaúva. The first name, which does not correspond to any clearly defined species, refers to 'several species of *Ficus* and artocarpus' (Spruce 1, p. 28); the inner layer of bark is used for making clothes and receptacles. Envieira (envira, embira) probably refers to the *Xylopia*, the fibrous bark of which is used in the making of mooring ropes, splices and shoulder-belts, and which produces aromatic seeds of which the toucans are very fond, according to the myth, and which the Kalina of Guiana use to make necklaces (Ahlbrinck, under 'eneka', 4, §c). The ambaúva or embaúba, which means literally 'non-tree' (Stradelli 1, under 'embayua'), or as French foresters would say *faux-bois*,[2] is a *Cecropia*. The Tupi name covers several species of which the most often quoted is *Cecropia peltata*, the drum tree (Whiffen, pp. 134, n. 3; 141, n. 5), thus called because its naturally hollow trunk lends itself to the making of drums, as well as dance sticks and horns (Roth 2, p. 465). Finally, the fibrous bark of the *Cecropia* makes stout ropes (Stradelli, *loc. cit.*).

The myth therefore introduces a triple pattern of trees, all used to make clothes and utensils from bark, and one of which, since it is hollowed out by nature, also supplies the raw material for several musical instruments. Now the Tucuna, who make the cylinder of their (skin) drums from embaúba wood (Nim. 13, p. 43), closely associate music and the masks of pounded bark, which play an important part in their festive celebrations, and the making of which they have carried

[2] TRANSLATORS' NOTE: Littré's dictionary defines *faux bois* as branches which do not produce fruit and cannot be used for ornament. The term implies trees without any commercial value.

to a high degree of excellence. We may already suppose that M_{304} poses a special problem (but one which for the time being remains obscure) in connection with the making of bark masks and costumes. This aspect becomes more obvious when it is recalled that, at the end of the celebrations, the visitors, who had been disguised in tunics made from the bark of the tururi tree, and decorated with fringes made from the tururi or envira (envieira) tree which almost reached the ground, handed these tunics over to their hosts in exchange for gifts of smoked meat (Nim. 13, p. 84). Now, in the myth too, the fact of wearing a bark tunic which turns him into a jaguar puts the hunter into the position of an acquirer of meat: human, not animal, meat, of course; but the bark, which provides the raw material for the tunic, belongs also to a category which is exceptional in its own way, since it was obtained by magical means, that is, was 'hunted' and not torn from the tree, and was immediately available in the form of long strips, instead of having to be laboriously peeled off the trunk (Nim. 13, p. 81).

Making allowances for the geographical distance, the regular pattern of the transformations which make it possible to move from the Tucuna myth to the Chaco myths (M_{22}–M_{24}) about the origin of the jaguar and tobacco is quite striking:

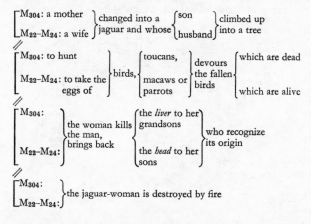

In order to interpret correctly the episode in M_{304}, in which the hero, whose foot has been pierced by a thorn, is killed by the jaguar while trying to remove the cause of the trouble, it must be recalled that, in M_{246}, which belongs to the same group as M_{22}–M_{24}, the ogress turned jaguar perishes on a tree-trunk which bristles with thorn-like spears (they are changed back into thorns in M_{241}, just as the ogress in M_{24} dies as a result of ingesting *strong* (*stinging*) honey, which makes her itch all over). It is also worth noting that, while the heroine of M_{24} poisons her husband with menstrual blood, the heroine of M_{304} brings back their father's liver to her grandsons. South American Indians

Figure 16. Toucans. (A drawing by Valette, after Crevaux, *loc. cit.*, p. 82.)

believe that the liver is an organ formed from coagulated blood and that, in women, it acts as a reservoir for menstrual blood.

In order to arrive at a satisfactory interpretation of the other transformations, it would be essential to elucidate the semantic position of toucans. This is no easy undertaking because the birds appear very infrequently in the myths. I shall do no more than suggest a theory, without claiming that it can be definitively established.

Several species of the *Rhamphastos* family are referred to as toucans. Their chief characteristic is an enormous beak which is, at the same time, very light in weight because it is porous under its horny tegument. Toucans prefer to hop from branch to branch rather than fly. Their feathers are almost entirely black, except over the breast where they are brilliantly coloured, and consequently much sought after for the purposes of ornamentation. These feathers have been prized by others besides the Indians; the ceremonial coat which belonged to Pedro II, Emperor of Brazil, and which can still be admired in the Rio de Janeiro museum, is made from the yellow, silky feathers of the toucan.

The ornamental use of feathers suggests a comparison between the toucan and the parrot and the macaw, but it is in partial contrast to the latter birds in respect of diet. The psittacidae are fruit-eating, the toucan is omnivorous and eats indiscriminately fruit, seeds and small animals, such as rodents and birds. M_{304} mentions that the toucan is particularly fond of aromatic seeds. The fact that in German it is called: *Pfefferfresser*, 'pepper-eater', is less surprising than Ihering (under 'tucano') is inclined to believe, especially since Thevet (Vol. II, p. 939a, b) refers to the toucan as a 'pepper-eater', which propagates pimentoes through the seeds in its droppings.

So far, within the range of bird species, we have consistently met with a major contrast between the psittacidae and the aquilinae (true eagles do not exist in South America). The preceding remarks about the toucan suggests that it occupies an intermediary position between these two polar terms: it can be carnivorous, like birds of prey, and part of its body is covered with feathers as brightly coloured as those of the parrot.[3] But it is obviously the subsidiary opposition between macaws and toucans which should occupy our attention, since it is the only one which plays a part in the group of myths we are studying. In this con-

[3] In support of this statement, I can quote an extract from the Vapidiana myth about the origin of death (M_{305a}). The toucan was the demiurge's pet bird and, when its master's son died, it wept so much that its plumage lost its colour: 'Has not the grief of years and the rivers of tears which he has shed dissolved some of the gaudy colours of orange and black, red and green, and left a ring of faded blue round each eye the width of the nail of a small finger?' (Ogilvie, p. 69). In respect of its plumage, the toucan thus appears as a faded parrot.

In Guiana, the small toucan seems to be subject to a taboo comparable to the one relating to opossum meat among the Ge (*RC*, p. 169): according to the Kalina, anyone who eats the flesh of this bird will die 'while still in full beauty', or as we would say, in the prime of life (Ahlbrinck, under 'Kuyakén').

nection, the toucan's fondness for the aromatic seeds of the envieira tree would seem to be the relevant feature in M_{304}.

One of the myths about the origin of honey, which we studied at the beginning of this book, describes the adventures of an Indian, who was also attacked by jaguars while robbing the nests of macaws, which feed on flowers containing sweet nectar (M_{189}). Now, we know of a myth in which the toucan plays a leading role, most probably after it has been given an exaggeratedly large beak as a punishment for greediness (Métraux 2, p. 178, n. 1). In this particular myth (M_{305b}), a honey-gatherer, thanks to the toucan's advice, succeeds in killing the demiurge Añatunpa (by lighting a fire on the back of his neck), who had offered all the honey-gatherers as food to Dyori, the ogre (Nordenskiöld 1, p. 286). So, while in M_{188}–M_{189} jaguars are changed into honey-gatherers, in M_{305b} a honey-gatherer is changed into a jaguar (which also attacks its opponents' necks). At the same time, the macaws which are being hunted are changed into a helpful toucan, a transformation which could perhaps be explained by the respective association of the macaw with sweet food and of the toucan with highly flavoured food. All the terms in M_{304} would thus reproduce those used in M_{22}–M_{24}, but would give them greater emphasis.

These remarks would be of little interest if they did not help to throw light on other aspects of the problem. In the table on p. 365 I compared only the central parts of the myths, leaving out the beginning of M_{304}, which dealt with the origin of the ability to be transformed into a jaguar, and the end of M_{23}–M_{24} (M_{22} does not contain this episode) which dealt with the origin of tobacco. Now, in these last myths, tobacco comes into existence through the jaguar, just as in M_{304} the jaguar comes into existence, as it were, through the invention of the bark tunics. The wearing of bark tunics and the absorption of tobacco are two ways of entering into communication with the supernatural world. The misuse of one of these methods brings about a woman's death by burning in M_{304}. The death of a woman by burning causes the appearance of the other method in M_{23}–M_{24}, but, according to M_{24} (cf. also M_{27}), initially as a misuse: the first men to possess tobacco wanted to smoke in isolation, that is, without sharing with others, or without trying to communicate with the spirits.

Whereas tobacco smoke sends out a courteous invitation to kindly spirits, according to another Tucuna myth (M_{318}), which will be studied later, it was thanks to the asphyxiating smoke of the pimento that men were able to exterminate a race of evil, cannibalistic spirits and examine them at leisure. The bark tunics which have been made since then were modelled on the appearance of these spirits and make it possible for men to embody them. The initiation ceremony for young girls, at which the visitors arrive in disguise and pretend to attack and destroy their hosts' houses, symbolizes a fight waged by humans to protect the young adolescent girl from the spirits which threaten her during this critical period of her life (Nim. 13, pp. 74, 89). It is clear, then, which path we have to follow if we are to re-establish a complete correspondence between the Tucuna myth (M_{304}) and the Chaco myths about the origin of tobacco. Pimento smoke is the opposite of tobacco smoke, but since it was, in a sense, given to the supernatural spirits in exchange for bark tunics (since these were obtained thanks to the application of pimento smoke), it also represents them in reverse, and the mystic use of bark tunics is therefore, ideologically speaking, on a par with the use of tobacco.

There still remains the problem of the recurrence, which is less surprising than it first appeared, of a noise-making instrument of the clapper type in M_{24} and in M_{304}. The instrument in M_{24} was a make-shift device used for locating honey, which in turn is the instrument of the ogress's successive metamorphoses, culminating in her death by burning. The noise-maker in M_{304} leads the ogress straight to the same fire. But in this case we are dealing with a real instrument, although it has no equivalent in Tucuna organology – in spite of the fact that the latter is one of the most varied in South America – and one which belongs to a type so rare in this part of the world that Izikowitz's classic work (pp. 8–9), under the heading 'clappers' – 'pieces of wood banged one against the other', gives only two references, one of which is doubtful, while the other refers to the imitation of a bird call. It would seem, then, that the Tucuna myth is referring to an imaginary instrument, the making of which it describes very carefully.[4]

The instrument nevertheless exists, if not among the Tucuna, at least among the Bororo, where it has exactly the same shape, although they make it from bamboo and not from the hollow trunk of the embaúba tree. In the Bororo dialect, the instrument is called parabára, a term which also denotes a kind of small white goose, because, according to *EB* (Vol. I, pp. 857–8), of the resemblance between the cry of the bird and the rattle of the bamboo canes. This is not a convincing explanation, because the popular name of *Dendrocygna viaduta*, irerê, is

[4] An instrument of the same type, but which is used as a catapult, has been reported among the Tucuna, the Aparai, the Toba and the Sherente (Nim. 13, p. 123, n. 23).

also interpreted as being an onomatopoeic term, although the comparison of this bird's cry with a whistle (Ihering, under 'irerê') does not make it sound much like a series of dry rattling noises.

There is some doubt, too, about the place and function of the parabára in Bororo ritual. According to Colbacchini (2, pp. 99–100; 3, pp. 140–41), these instruments, which are made from bamboo poles split longitudinally over a length of thirty to fifty centimetres and which, when shaken, produce sounds which are differently pitched according to the size of the cut, are used at the investiture ceremony for the new chief, which always coincides with funeral rites. The new chief is an incarnation of the hero, Parabára, the inventor of instruments of the same name, and he sits down on the grave while dancers of both sexes make a circle round him, shaking the bamboo poles which they finally lay on the grave. The parabára figures among the gifts presented to the new chief (who always comes from the Cera moiety) by members of the other, Tugaré, moiety.

The *Enciclopédia Bororo* states clearly that the celebration of the parabára rite is a privilege enjoyed by the Apiboré clan belonging to the Tugaré moiety. The individuals officiating at the ceremony, who personify the parabára Spirits, enter the village at the west side, each one holding in both hands a long, split bamboo cane; they move in the direction of the grave, walk round it several times, and then sit down, while the leader of the ritual, who is called Parabára Eimejera (and who is not a village chief in process of being enthroned, as was indicated in the previous sources), announces his arrival to the members of both moieties, to the accompaniment of the crackling sound of the bamboos. When he has finished, the others lay the bamboos on the grave and go away (*EB*, Vol. I, under 'aroe-etawujedu', p. 159).

Since the *Enciclopédia* does not mention the parabára in connection with the investiture of chiefs, it is probable that, because this ritual had to be performed at the same time as a funeral ceremony, the Salesian Fathers first of all thought they should associate with the one what rightfully belonged to the other. A funeral ceremony, unaccompanied by an investiture, has been observed and photographed in a village on the Rio São Lourenço (not the village in which I stayed thirty years ago, but in the same area, which is a long way from the region controlled by the missions). About a fortnight after the temporary burial on the main plaza of the village, dancers attired in ceremonial dress and personifying mythical beings inspected the corpse to see if the decomposition of the flesh had reached a sufficiently advanced stage. Several times they reached a negative conclusion, which is a necessary procedure if the ceremonies are to follow their proper course. One of the dancers, whose body was smeared with white clay, ran round the grave calling to the soul of the dead man to come out. Meanwhile, other men shook split bamboo canes, which made dry rattling noises (Kozák, p. 45).[5]

It is probable that the dancer smeared with clay personified the aigé, a frightening-looking aquatic monster, whose cry is imitated by the bull-roarers. If, as the source suggests, the object of his dance was indeed to invite the dead man's soul to leave the grave, hence the village, in order to follow the mythic beings into the world beyond, the rattling of the parabára could hasten or salute this disjunction, which is also (according to the point of view one adopts) a conjunction. I shall not attempt to go any further in the interpretation of Bororo ritual, since the second volume of the *Enciclopédia Boróro*, which may perhaps include a hitherto unknown myth about the origin of the parabára, has not yet appeared. I merely note that, according to information given to Nordenskiöld, the Yanaigua of Bolivia use an instrument of the clapper type in certain ceremonies (Izikowitz, p. 8). The Tereno of the southern part of the Mato Grosso also have a dance which involves knocking together sticks (*bate pau* in Portuguese), but its meaning is unknown (Altenfelder Silva, pp. 367–9). A festive ceremony performed by the Kayapo-Gorotiré, and which they refer to as men uêmôro, but which is also called *bate pau* by the neighbouring peasants, has been observed recently. The young men form a file two deep and move round in a ring, knocking together sticks about fifty centimetres long. The dance lasts all night, and ends with their copulating with a very young woman, who is 'mistress of the feast' and who has inherited this duty through the women on the paternal side of her

[5] Like the Bororo, several small tribes of southern California have an extremely complex burial ritual, the purpose of which is to prevent the deceased coming back among the living. It includes two dances, called respectively 'twirling' and 'to extinguish the fires'. During the latter, the shamans stamp out the flames with their feet and hands, and in both dances they knock sticks together (Waterman, pp. 309, 327–8 and Pl. 26, 27; Spier 1, pp. 321–2).

Now, California is without any doubt the area in which instruments of the parabára type are most prevalent; they are found from the Yokuts in the south as far north as the Klamath, who live in the state of Oregon (Spier 2, p. 89). The parabára is referred to as a 'clap rattle', or a 'split rattle' by American ethnographers, and its presence has also been recorded among the Pomo (Loeb, p. 189), the Yuki and the Maidu (Kroeber, pp. 149, 419 and Pl. 67). The Nomlaki (Goldschmidt, pp. 367–8) make it from elder-wood, which can play the part of the bamboo in temperate regions. Kroeber (pp. 823, 862) declares the instrument to be typical of central California, where it is supposed to be used only for dances and never for puberty rites or shamanistic ceremonies. Among the Klamath, who may have taken it over from the tribes along the river Pit farther south, its use is probably limited to the 'ghost dance', a messianic cult which appeared about 1870 (Spier 2, *loc. cit.*).

family: she inherits it from one of her father's sisters and passes it on to a daughter of one of her brothers. It stands to reason that this woman cannot claim to be a virgin. Therefore, in accordance with the Kayapo custom, she is only entitled to a second-class marriage. Yet the rite of *bate pau* is performed at those rare and much sought after marriages in which the bride, who is still under the age of puberty, is officially a virgin (Diniz, pp. 26–7). It is possible that the southern Guarani used the same type of noise-making instruments in their rites, since the Mbya describe an important divinity as holding two sticks, one in each hand and shaking them and knocking them together. Schaden (5, pp. 191–2), who gives the information, suggests that the two crossed sticks are perhaps the origin of the famous Guarani cross, which made such a powerful impression on the old missionaries.

The Uitoto believe that, when they stamp with their feet, they are establishing contact with their chthonian forefathers, who came up to the earth's surface in order to watch the feasts given in their honour, and which they themselves celebrate with 'real' words, whereas men speak by means of musical instruments (Preuss 1, p. 126). A Mataco myth (M_{306}) relates that, after the fire which destroyed the earth, a small bird, tapiatson, beat its drum near the burnt branch of a zapallo (*cucurbita* sp.) tree, as the Indians do when the algaroba (*Prosopis* sp.) ripens. The trunk started to grow and became a fine leafy tree which offered the protection of its shade to the new race of men (Métraux 3, p. 10; 5, p. 35).

This myth brings us extraordinarily close to M_{24}, in which the knocking together of the sandals was intended to hasten the conjunction of the hero and another wild 'fruit': honey. In Tacana mythology, another bird, the woodpecker – whom we know to be a master of honey – taps with its beak on a woman's earthenware pot in order to guide her husband who has lost his way (M_{307}; H.-H., pp. 72–4; cf. also the Uitoto myth in Preuss 1, pp. 304–14). In M_{194}–M_{195}, the same conjunctive role is played by the woodpecker, whether he brings a husband back to his wife or helps the divine brothers to return to the supernatural world. It would be interesting to compare more closely the conjunctive function of the tapping in M_{307} with that fulfilled in the Guarani creation myth (M_{308}) by the crackling of seeds as they burst in the fire with an explosive force capable of transporting the younger of the divine brothers to the other side of the water where his elder brother already is (Cadogan 4, p. 79; Borba, p. 67). I shall merely draw attention to the problem, and to the triple reversal of the same theme among the Bororo (M_{46}): brothers are blinded by the noisy explosion of their grandmother's bones which have been thrown into the fire, and recover their sight in water (*disj./conj.*; *animal/vegetable*; *in the water/over the water*; Kalapalo variant (M_{47}): the two brothers are respectively sun and moon, and the younger, having had his nose torn off by one of his grandmother's bones which shot out of the fire 'where they danced and made a clicking noise', decided to go up into the sky; cf. *RC*, pp. 123, 171). To be complete, the study of this theme should include references to North American sources, such as the Zuni myth about the winter ritual in which men regain possession of game which has been stolen by ravens thanks to the noisy explosion of a handful of salt that has been thrown into the fire (M_{309}; Bunzel, p. 928).[6]

So a series of discontinuous noises, which take a great variety of forms, such as tapping or drumming, the knocking together of pieces of wood, the crackling of objects in fire, or the rattling of split poles, play an obscure part in ritual and in mythic narratives. The Tucuna, one of whose myths put me on the track of the Bororo parabára, although the Tucuna themselves are unacquainted with this instrument, knock sticks together in one set of circumstances at least. It is well known that these Indians attach great importance to the puberty rites for girls. As soon as a girl detects signs of her first period, she takes off all her ornaments, hangs them in an obvious place on the posts of her hut and goes off to hide in a nearby bush. When her mother arrives, she sees the ornaments, realizes what has happened and sets off to look for her daughter. The latter replies to her mother's calls by striking two pieces of dry wood together. The mother then loses no time in erecting a partition around the young girl's bed and takes her there after nightfall. From that moment the girl remains in seclusion for two or three months without being seen or heard by anyone except her mother and her paternal aunts (Nim. 13, pp. 73–4).

This reference to the Tucuna provides a suitable opportunity for introducing another myth which is essential for any further discussion of M_{304}:

M_{310}. *Tucuna*. '*The jaguar who ate children*'

Peti, the jaguar, had been killing children for a long time. Every time he heard a child crying because it had been left alone by its parents,

---

[6] The Timbira have a dance accompanied by handclapping which is intended to keep away the harvest parasites (Nim. 8, p. 62). The Pawnee women of the Upper Missouri used to beat the water noisily with their feet at the time of planting and harvesting beans (Weltfish, p. 248).

the animal assumed the form of the mother, carried the little one off and said to it: 'Press your nose against my anus!' He then killed his victim with an emission of intestinal gas, after which he ate it. Dyai, the demiurge, decided to assume the form of a child. Armed with his sling, he sat down at the edge of a path and started to cry. Peti arrived on the scene, put him on his back and ordered him to press his nose against his anus. Dyai, however, was careful to turn his face away. The jaguar went on breaking wind, but to no purpose. Every time he broke wind, he ran faster. Some people he met asked him where he was taking 'our father' (the demiurge). Realizing whom he was carrying on his back, Peti asked Dyai to get down, but the latter refused. The animal went on his way and, passing through a cave, reached the other world. All the time he kept begging Dyai to go away.

The jaguar was ordered by the demiurge to return to the place where they had met. Here there was a muirapiranga tree, the trunk of which had a hole with very smooth sides pierced through it. Dyai forced the jaguar's fore-legs into the hole and secured them firmly. Grasping his dance stick, a hollow bamboo cane, with his hind legs which stuck out on the other side, the animal started to sing. He called on the bat to come and wipe his bottom. Other demons, also members of the jaguar clan, came running up to him in turn and gave him food. Today, you can still sometimes hear the din they make at the place called naimèki, in a small patch of secondary forest near an old plantation ... (Nim. 13, p. 132).

This myth adds a fourth tree, the muirapiranga or myra-piranga, literally, 'red wood' tree, to the botanical trio mentioned in M₃₀₄. This tree, which belongs to the leguminous family and the *Caesalpina* species, is none other than the famous '*bois de braise*' from which Brazil got its name. Being very hard and fine-grained, it can be used for many purposes. The Tucuna combine it with bone to make drumsticks (Nim. 13, p. 43). The Tucuna skin-drum is certainly of European origin, and another musical instrument appears in the myth, where it forms a counterpart to the split hollow trunk in M₃₀₄: this is the dance stick, ba:'ma, the use of which is confined to the jaguar clan and perhaps a few other clans; it is a long bamboo cane (*Gadua superba*) which may measure up to three metres. The upper extremity is split to form a groove roughly thirty centimetres long, which represents an alligator's jaw with or without teeth according to whether the instrument is said to be 'male' or 'female'. Below the jaw is a tiny demon's mask, and shell-rattles and ornaments made of falcon's feathers are fastened all the way down the cane. These instruments are always found in pairs, one male, one female. The players face each other and strike the ground at an oblique angle while crossing their bamboo canes. Since the inner dividing membranes have not been removed, the sound produced is very weak (Nim. 13, p. 45).[7]

I have already put together, in a single group, the Tembé-Tenete-hara myths about the origin of honey (the honey festival) (M_{188}–M_{189}), the Chaco myths about the origin of tobacco (M_{23}–M_{24}, M_{246}) and the myth explaining the origin of bark tunics (M_{304}, which reverses the true origin myth, as will be seen later). This operation was the result of a triple transformation:

(a) jaguars: peace-loving ⇒ aggressive
(b) birds: macaws, parrots, parakeets ⇒ toucans
(c) bird food: sweet flowers ⇒ aromatic seeds

The transformational relationship which we are about to note between M_{304} and M_{319} makes it possible, without further explanation, to strengthen the link uniting the Chaco and Tucuna myths. For if, as is already obvious, the musical instrument in M_{310} is a transformation of the one in M_{304}, they both refer back to the hollow trunk (transformed into an empty ditch in M_{24}), which in M_{23}, M_{246} acts as a place of refuge for the victims of the cannibalistic jaguar and which causes the latter's death. This can be expressed as the following transformation:

M_{23}, M_{246} M_{304} M_{310}
(hollow tree) ⇒   (split trunk) ⇒   (hollow bamboo)

This group of transformations is homogeneous as regards musical instruments: the split trunk and the hollow bamboo are both instruments of noise, and I have confirmed in another context that, in the Chaco myths, homology exists between the hollow trunk, the trough for making mead and the drum (pp. 107–8). I shall return to this aspect.

_____

[7] Very faint too, no doubt, is the noise, compared to a 'muffled roar', made by the Bororo when they beat the ground with rolls of matting in order to tell their wives and children that the aquatic monsters, aigé, have gone, and that they can safely come out of the huts where they are hiding. It should be noted that the actors personifying the aigé try to knock down the boys who are in process of being initiated and the latter are held up by their sponsors and masculine relatives, because if they fell this would be a very bad omen (EB, Vol. I, pp. 661–2). This episode would seem to be an almost literal transposition of certain details of the Tucuna initiation ceremony for girls (Nim. 13, pp. 88–9).

Let us now superimpose M_{304} and M_{310} one upon the other. At first glance a complex network of relationships appears: for while the syntagmatic sequences of both myths are reproduced in the usual way through certain transformations, they create at one point at which they meet a paradigmatic set which is equivalent to part of the syntagmatic sequence of a Bororo myth (M_5) which, as I showed at the very beginning of the previous volume, is a transformation of the key myth (M_1). It is as if my inquiry were following a spiral pattern and, after reverting to its starting-point, were now momentarily resuming its forward movement by inflecting its curve along a previous course (see table opposite).

Consequently, according to the standpoint we take, either M_{304} is linked to M_{310}, or each one is linked separately to M_5; or the three myths are all interlinked. If we ventured to form the Chaco myths about the origin of the jaguar and (or) tobacco into one 'archimyth' (just as linguists talk of 'archi-phonemes'), we would obtain another series parallel to the previous series:

| a wife and mother changed into a jaguar | devourer of husband and children | poisoner of her husband with menstrual blood | perishes *in* a ditch or *on* a hollow tree-trunk bristling with spears (or is held prisoner by its claws which have become embedded in the tree) |

So we come back to the problem, already discussed, of the mutual reversibility of a syntagmatic sequence formed by a single group, and a syntagmatic set obtained by cutting a vertical section through the superimposed syntagmatic sequences of several myths, interlinked by transformational relationships. In the present instance, however, we can at least catch a glimpse of the semantic basis of a phenomenon only the formal aspect of which has so far been examined.

It will be remembered that M_5, whose syntagmatic sequence would seem here to cut across that of other myths, explains the origin of diseases which, in a maleficent and negative sense, ensure the transition from life to death, and establish a conjunction between life here below and life in the world beyond. This is clearly the meaning of the other myths, for tobacco fulfils a similar function in a beneficent and positive sense, as does also in M_{310} the use of the dance stick (the reference may even be to its origin), a fact which can be verified in the Tucuna ritual since, in this instance, we are dealing with a real instrument. The imaginary instrument in M_{304} (but which actually has a real place in American organology) fulfils a reverse function, that is,

M_5

An unfriendly grandmother tries to kill her grandson

M_{310}: A jaguar changed into a mother

devours child

under pretext of feeding the child on anti-food (intestinal gas)

puts its arm into a pierced tree

The children bury their dead father in an armadillo's burrow

M_{304}: A grandmother changed into a jaguar

under pretext of feeding grandchildren with anti-food (fungus)

receives a spear thrust which pierces her anus

When dead, she is buried in an armadillo's burrow

it is disjunctive, not conjunctive. Nevertheless this function, like the other one, is beneficent and positive. It is not exercised against demons, who have been put to the service of man, thanks to the bark tunics which imitate their physical appearance, as in the ritual, or – according to M_{310} – against a demon who is effectively caught in a tree-trunk which grips his wrists as in manacles; it is exercised against demons who, through an excessive use of trees with bark, have got completely out of hand; they are not semblances of demons conjured up by men, but men changed into real demons.

We have, then, at our disposal a fairly solid basis for extending the comparison beyond the central zone formed by the three myths M_5, M_{304} and M_{310}, and for attempting to incorporate certain aspects, peculiar to other myths whose position at first sight appears marginal. Let us look first of all at the opening episode of the crying baby in M_{310}, since we are well acquainted with this small personage. Already, in connection with other incidents, I have made considerable progress towards understanding the part he plays, and so the reader will perhaps more readily forgive me if I indulge in a rapid excursion into a more remote region of mythology, where the character of the whimperer is more clearly discernible, because he plays a leading role there. I shall not try to justify my action, and I admit that it is irreconcilable with a sound use of structural method. I will even refrain from using as an argument, in this very special case, my deep conviction that Japanese mythology and American mythology, each in its own way, are using sources which go right back to paleolithic times and which were once the common heritage of Asiatic groups later disseminated throughout the Far East and the New World. Without putting forward any such hypothesis, which would in any case be unverifiable in the present state of knowledge, I shall merely plead extenuating circumstances: only very rarely do I allow myself this kind of digression and, when I do, the apparent divergence is meant to act as a short cut for the establishment of a point which could have been made by a different method, but a much slower and more laborious one, and one more exhausting for the reader.

M_{311}. *Japan. 'The crying "baby" '*

After the death of his wife and sister Izanami, the god Izanagi divided the world between his three children. To his daughter

Amaterasu, the sun, who had been born from his left eye, he gave the sky. To his son, Tsuki-yomi, the moon, who had been born from his right eye, he gave the ocean. And to his other son Sosa-no-wo, who had been born from his nasal mucus, he gave the earth.

At this time Sosa-no-wo was in the prime of life, and had grown a beard eight hands long. Yet he neglected his duties as master of the earth, and spent his time weeping, wailing and fuming with rage. He explained to his anxious father that he was crying because he wanted to follow his mother to the Nether Land. So Izanagi was filled with detestation of his son and drove him away.

For he himself had tried to see his dead wife again, and he knew that she was just a swollen and festering corpse, and that eight kinds of Thunder Gods rested on her: one each on her head, chest, stomach, back, buttocks, hands, feet and vagina ...

Before departing to the other world, Sosa-no-wo obtained his father's permission to say good-bye to his sister Amaterasu in the sky. But once he got there, he lost no time in defiling the rice-plantations, and Amaterasu was so shocked that she decided to shut herself up in a cave and deprive the world of her light. As a punishment for his misdeeds, her brother was banished for ever to the other world, which he reached after many trials and tribulations (Aston, Vol. I, pp. 14–59).

It would be interesting to compare this concentrated fragment of a fairly lengthy myth with certain South American tales;[8]

M_{86a}. *Amazonia. 'The crying baby'*

Yuwaruna, the black jaguar, had married a woman whose one thought was to seduce her husband's brothers. This vexed the latter, who killed her, and since she was pregnant they opened up the corpse, whence emerged a little boy who leapt into the water.

He was captured with some difficulty, but never stopped crying and howling 'like a newly born baby'. All the animals were summoned to amuse him, but the little owl was the only one able to soothe him by revealing to him the mystery of his birth. From then on, the child's one thought was to avenge his mother. He killed all the jaguars one after the other, then rose into the sky where he became the rainbow. It is because the sleeping humans did not hear

[8] And North American ones, too; e.g. the following passage in a myth belonging to the Dené Hare, which will be referred to again in the next volume: 'From his union with his sister, Kuñyan (the demiurge) had a son who sulked and cried all the time' (Petitot, p. 145).

his calls that their life-span was shortened from that time onwards (Tastevin 3, pp. 188–90; cf. *RC*, pp. 161–3).

The Chimane and the Mosetene have an almost identical myth (M_{312}): a child, after being abandoned by his mother, never stopped crying. His tears changed into rain which he himself succeeded in bringing to an end when he took the form of a rainbow (Nordenskiöld 3, p. 146). Now in the Nihongi chronicles too, Sosa-no-wo's final banishment to the other world is accompanied by torrential rain. The god asks for some form of shelter but his request is refused. As a protection, he invents the broad-brimmed hat, and the water-proof coat of green straw. This is why no one is allowed to enter the house of a person thus attired. Before he reaches his last abode, Sosa-no-wo kills a deadly snake (Aston, *loc. cit.*). In South America, the rainbow *is* a deadly snake.

M_{313}. *Cashinawa. 'The crying baby'*

One day a pregnant woman went off to fish. Meanwhile a storm broke out, and the baby she was carrying in her womb disappeared. A few months later, it appeared in the form of a quite big child, who cried persistently and gave no one any peace day or night. He was thrown into the river, which dried up the instant his body came into contact with it, while he himself disappeared up into the sky (Tastevin 4, p. 22).

Basing his arguments on a similar Peba myth, Tastevin suggests that this one may refer to the origin of the sun. It will be remembered that a Machiguenga myth (M_{299}) mentions three suns: the sun we are familiar with, the one in the underworld and the one in the nocturnal sky. In the beginning, the latter was a red-hot baby who caused his mother to die in giving birth to him, and whom his father, the moon, had to banish from the earth to avoid it being burnt up. The second Sun, like Sosa-no-wo, went to join his dead mother in the underworld where he became a master of maleficent rain. Unlike the corpse of Sosa-no-wo's mother, which was repellent, the corpse of the chthonian sun's mother was so appetizing that it provided the substance of the first cannibalistic meal.

Whether Japanese or American, all these myths closely follow an identical pattern. The crying child is a baby who has been abandoned by his mother, or has been born posthumously, which simply means that the desertion occurred earlier; or he may consider he has been unjustly abandoned, even though he has already reached an age at which a normal child no longer demands constant parental care. This excessive longing for conjunction with the family, which the myths usually situate on a horizontal plane (when it is the result of the mother's absence) involves in every case a vertical disjunction of the cosmic type: the crying child goes up into the sky where he creates a *rotten* world (rain, defilement, the rainbow as a cause of diseases, loss of immortality); or, in symmetrical variants, in order *not to* create a *burnt* world. That at least is the pattern followed by the American myths, which is duplicated and reversed in the Japanese myth in which it is the crying god who goes away, since his second disjunction takes the form of a journey. Notwithstanding this difference, we have no difficulty in recognizing, behind the character of the whimpering child, that of the anti-social hero (in the sense that he refuses to become socialized) who remains obstinately attached to nature and the feminine world: the same hero who, in the key myth, commits incest in order to return to the maternal fold, and who in M_5, although of an age to join the men's house, remains secluded in the family hut. By a quite different line of argument, we had reached the conclusion that M_5, a myth explaining the origin of diseases, was concerned by implication with the origin of the rainbow, the cause of diseases (*RC*, pp. 246–50). We now have additional confirmation of this inference, thanks to the newly discovered equivalence between the secluded boy and the crying baby, whom the myths consider to be the origin of the same meteoric phenomenon.

Before working out the consequences of this connection, we must dwell for a moment on one episode in M_{310}: the episode in which the bat comes to wipe the jaguar's bottom. As will be recalled, the latter was very fond of crying babies and asphyxiated them with his intestinal gases. It is not easy to work out the position of bats in the myths, since there is usually very little information regarding the species. Now, in tropical America, there are nine families and a hundred or so species of bats, all different in size, appearance and eating habits: some eat insects and some fruit, while others (*Desmodus* sp.) suck blood.

We may well speculate, then, about the reason for the transformation, illustrated by a Tacana myth (M_{195}), of one of the 'melero's' two daughters (who, in M_{197}, are multi-coloured macaw-women) into a bat: either the bats referred to feed on nectar, as is sometimes the case, or live in hollow trees like bees, or there is some entirely different reason for the transformation. In support of the link-up, it should be pointed out that in a Uitoto myth (M_{314}), in which the theme of the girl mad about honey makes a fleeting appearance, honey is replaced by cannibalistic bats (Preuss 1, pp. 230–70). Generally speaking, however, these animals are chiefly associated in the myths with blood and the orifices of the body. Bats drew the first burst of laughter from an Indian because they did not know about articulated speech and could only communicate with humans by tickling them (Kayapo–Gorotiré, M_{40}). Bats came out of the abdominal cavity of an ogre who devoured young men (Sherente, M_{315a}; Nim. 7, pp. 186–7). The vampires *Desmodus rotundus* sprang from the blood of the family of the demon Aétsasa; this family was massacred by the Indians whom the demon was decapitating in order to shrink their heads (Aguaruna, M_{315b}; Guallart, pp. 71–3). A demon bat was married to a human and was furious because she refused to give him something to drink. So he cut off the Indians' heads and piled them up in the hollow tree where he lived (Mataco, M_{316}; Métraux 3, p. 48).

The Kogi of the Sierra de Santa Marta, in Colombia, believe that there is a more definite link between bats and menstrual blood. In order to find out if one of their number is indisposed, women ask: ' "Has the bat bitten you?" Young men say that a young girl who has begun to menstruate is a woman, because she has been bitten by the bat. On top of every hut, the priest places a small cross made of thread, which represents both the bat and the female organ' (Reichel-Dolmatoff, Vol. I, p. 270). The Aztecs have the same sexual symbolism but in a reversed form, since they believe that the bat came from Quetzalcoatl's sperm.[9]

What has all this to do with the present argument? *The bat which is generally held responsible for a bodily aperture and a discharge of blood, is transformed, in M_{310}, into an animal responsible for closing a bodily aperture and for the reabsorption of excrement.* This threefold transformation assumes its full significance when we note that it is applied to a jaguar and, what is more, to a jaguar which kidnaps crying children. For we are perfectly familiar with this ogre: we came across him first in a Warao myth (M_{273}) where, in the form of a grandmother (a mother in M_{310}, but a retransformation of the jaguar-grandmother in M_{304}), a jaguar carried off a weeping child and, when the little girl grew up, fed on her menstrual blood (instead of breaking wind with a view to killing the child and feeding on her). Consequently, the jaguar in M_{273} behaves

---

[9] According to an Australian belief, bats spring from the foreskin when it is cut off at the time of the initiation ceremony, and the animal also denotes death (Elkin, pp. 173, 305).

towards a human as if he were a bat, whereas in M_{310} the bat adopts towards the jaguar a form of behaviour which is in correlation and opposition to the behaviour he would have adopted, had the jaguar been a human being.

Now, M_{273} belongs to the same group of transformations as the myths about the origin of honey. M_{310}, on the other hand, belongs to the same group of transformations as the myths about the origin of tobacco. In making the transition from honey to tobacco, we thus confirm the following equation:

(a) (*menstrual blood*)   (*excrement*)
       [jaguar : unwell girl] ::   [bat : jaguar]

which brings us back to a point which might have been learnt independently from a comparison between M_{273} and M_{24} (a myth about the origin of tobacco, in which a jaguar-woman poisons her husband with her menstrual blood):

(b) (*origin of honey*)   (*origin of tobacco*)
   [menstrual blood : food] ::   [menstrual blood :
                                         excrement]

In other words: honey establishes conjunction between extremes, whereas tobacco creates disjunction between intermediary terms by consolidating adjacent terms.

After this interlude about the bat, we can return to the crying baby.

The Tucuna myths M_{304} and M_{310} have two themes in common – cannibalism and filth: in M_{304}, the jaguar-grandmother tries to pass off her son's liver – an internal organ congruous with blood, and more particularly with menstrual blood – for a tree fungus, also an anti-food (RC, pp. 167, 175, 176); in M_{310}, a jaguar usurping a mother's role, forces the child to breathe in the gases it emits from its dung-soiled rear. But, whether they feed on human flesh or menstrual blood, or whether on the contrary they administer rotten substances as food, the Warao and Tucuna jaguars belong to the great family of animals with a passion for childish bawlings, which also includes the fox and the frog; the latter is also greedy for young flesh, but in the metaphorical sense since, beyond the crying baby, she coveted the adolescent whom she intended to turn into her lover.

By taking this approach, we come back to the equivalence, which had already been confirmed in a different way (p. 310) between cries – that is, din – and filth. These terms are interchangeable, according to whether the myth adopts an acoustic, alimentary or sexual coding. The problem raised by the theme of the crying baby boils down to asking why a given myth chooses to code, in acoustic terms, a mytheme – the character of the secluded boy – which, in other myths, is coded by means of actual incest (M_1) or symbolic incest (M_5).

The problem remains unsolved as regards such myths as M_{243}, M_{245} and M_{273}. In the present instance, however, a possible answer can be discerned. The two Tucuna myths about the cannibalistic jaguar give a prominent place to musical instruments, one imaginary, the other real, but which, because of their semantic function and organological type, form a pair of opposites. The instrument in M_{304}, which I compared to the Bororo parabára, is just a naturally hollow part of tree-trunk which has been split lengthwise, and which is made to reverberate by striking it on the ground at an oblique angle or by throwing it on the ground. The ensuing noise is supposed to keep away from human society a being who is himself human, but has changed into a demon. The instrument in M_{310}, a dancing stick manipulated by the captive jaguar, consists of a bamboo cane (the bamboo is a graminacea which neither South American Indians nor botanists classify as a tree), also naturally hollow, which is made to reverberate when struck against the ground while being held in a vertical position. The use of this instrument allows the jaguar to achieve a result symmetrical with that which has just been attributed to the clapper. The dancing stick establishes conjunction between a demoniacal being who has changed into a human being, and other demons: it draws the latter towards men, instead of driving the former away from men.

That is not all. The dancing stick itself has a two-fold correlational and oppositional relationship with another musical instrument, which had accompanied us discreetly from the beginning of this book and which was apparent in the background of the myths about the origin of honey: I am referring to the drum, an instrument also made from a hollow tree-trunk, to which the myths attribute a great variety of uses: it may be a place where bees nest, or a trough in which mead is prepared, a wooden drum (a transformation of the trough according to M_{214}), a place of refuge for victims of the cannibalistic jaguar and a trap for this same jaguar, as well as for the girl mad about honey ... The wooden drum and the dancing stick are both hollow cylinders, one short and squat, the other long and narrow. The drum passively receives blows from sticks or a hammer, the bamboo cane comes to life when manipulated by a performer whose gestures it amplifies and prolongs, making them reverberate right into the passive ground. The clapper is, therefore, in contrast both with the dancing stick and the drum, since the latter are hollow all the way down, whereas it is split from the outside, crosswise, but only down to a certain point. The drum and the dancing stick are also in contrast to each other, in so far as they can be respectively wider or narrower, shorter or longer, the object or the subject of the action.

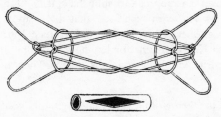

Figure 17. Honey or the hollow tree. A pattern from a Warao string game. (After Roth 2, Fig. 288, p. 525.)

In this triangular pattern, the major contrast is the one between the drum and the clapper, as can be indirectly inferred from a Warao myth, of which we need quote only one episode:

M₃₁₇. Warao. 'One of Kororomanna's adventures'

One day, an Indian called Kororomanna killed a guariba monkey. In trying to return to the village, he lost his way and had to spend the night in an improvised shelter. But he soon realized that he had chosen a bad place in which to camp, for it was right in the middle of a pathway frequented by the demons. You can always distinguish a Spirit road by the noise made by the demons occupying the trees alongside it, for they are always striking the branches and trunks, and producing short, sharp crackling noises.

It was not at all pleasant for Kororomanna, especially as the monkey's body was beginning to swell with all the noxious gases inside. In spite of the smell, he was obliged to keep the carcass near him and to watch over it with a stick, for fear the Demons might steal it from him. At last he fell asleep, only to be wakened again by the demons knocking on the trees. He had a sudden desire to mimic them, and every time they struck a tree he struck the monkey's belly with his stick. Every time he struck the animal there came a resonant *Boom, Boom,* just like the beating of a drum (the Warao use the hides of guariba monkeys to cover the ends of their skin drums).

Their curiosity having been aroused by these extraordinary noises, which were much louder than any they could make themselves, the demons at last discovered Kororomanna, who was roaring with laughter at hearing a dead animal break wind so vigorously. The leader of the demons regretted that he could not make such a splendid noise for, unlike ordinary mortals, spirits have no proper posteriors, but just a red spot: they are therefore blocked below. Nevertheless, Kororomanna agreed to split the spirit's hind-quarters. But he drove in his bow with such force that the weapon transfixed the whole body, and even pierced the unfortunate spirit's head. The demon cursed Kororomanna for having killed him, and swore that his fellow-Spirits would avenge his death. Then he disappeared (Roth 1, pp. 126–7).

This episode is taken from a very long myth and confirms the existence of the contrast between the drum, a human instrument (even endowed here with an organic nature), and the 'demoniacal' noise of sticks being struck or knocked together.[10] The dancing stick therefore must be situated between these two: it is a ritual instrument which can summon spirits, like the bark tunics which, in M_{304}, are contrasted with the clapper of the parabára type.

At this point, I would like to interpolate a few remarks on the subject of the dancing stick.

The southern Guarani believe that there is a major contrast between the stick of authority, the symbol of power and a masculine emblem, which is cut from the heart of the *Holocalyx balansae*, and the bamboo dancing stick, which is a female emblem (Cadogan 3, pp. 95–6). The masculine musical instrument is, consequently, the gourd-rattle. This contrast, which is often exemplified in literature, is illustrated most convincingly by a plate in Schaden's work, *Aspectos fundamentais da cultura guarani* (Pl. XIV in the first edition), which shows a row of five Kaiova Indians (one a small boy) holding the cross in one hand and the rattle in the other, followed by four women each one of whom is striking the ground with a piece of bamboo.[11] It would seem that,

[10] As described in the Warao myth, the noise made by the demons is not unlike the noise attributed to the jaguar by reliable observers: 'The jaguar betrays its presence by making a very characteristic series of sharp crackling noises as it nervously twitches its ears, which gives a kind of muffled version of the sound made by castanets' (Ihering, under 'onça'). According to a tale from the Rio Branco region, the jaguar makes a noise at night because its feet are shod, whereas the tapir walks barefoot and silently (Rodrigues 1, pp. 155–6).

[11] The Tacana of Bolivia call the arrow made from (hollow) bamboo 'female', and the one made from (solid) palm wood 'male' (H.-H., p. 338).

among the Apapocuva as well as among the more northerly Guarayu, the dancing stick is used for the special purpose of helping the cultural hero or the tribe as a whole to ascend into the sky (Métraux 9, p. 216). We may thus suppose the existence, among the southern Guarani, of a triple pattern of instruments, only two of which are musical instruments with additional functions: the stick of authority, which is used to assemble the men (north of the Amazon this is also the social function of the wooden drum), the rattle which brings the gods down to men, and the dancing stick which takes men closer to the gods. I have already mentioned Schaden's theory, according to which the Guarani wooden cross is supposed to represent two sticks which were once separate and knocked against each other. Finally, the Guarani contrast between a solid stick, the emblem of masculine authority, and the hollow tube, the feminine liturgical instrument, is reminiscent of the contrast (p. 351) made for sociological purposes by certain Amazonian tribes, between cylinders of hard stone which are used as pendants, according to whether they have been pierced lengthwise (and are hollow) or crosswise (and are solid).

We thus see emerging a dialectic of the hollow and the solid, in which each term is illustrated by several modalities. I have done no more than indicate certain themes and point to some possible lines of research, chiefly in order to enable us to grasp more easily the way in which the dialectic operates within the myths. Now, in their respective conclusions, the myths do much more than contrast musical instruments which are reducible to hollow tubes or solid sticks. The instrument introduced at the end of each myth has a peculiar relationship with a 'mode of the tree', which is defined at another point in the narrative.

In M_{304} and M_{310}, one or several trees are subjected to certain clearly defined operations. Trees (but only one tree to begin with) are stripped of their bark in M_{304}; in M_{310}, one tree has a hole in it. So a tree-trunk which has been stripped lengthwise is contrasted with one which has been pierced crosswise. If we complete this contrast with the one already noted between the musical instruments which appear in the two myths, and which are also 'made from trunks', we arrive at the following four-term pattern:

	M_{304}:	M_{310}:
trees :	stripped trunk	pierced trunk
percussion		
instruments :	split trunk	hollow trunk

It is obvious that this pattern of relationships forms a chiasmus. The pierced trunk and the split trunk correspond to each other, in the sense that each has an aperture perpendicular to the trunk's axis, but median in one instance and terminal in the other, and either internal or external. The symmetrical relationship linking the stripped trunk and the hollow trunk is more straightforward, since it can be reduced to an inversion of outside and inside: the tree which has been stripped of its bark remains as a cylinder with a solid interior and nothing outside, whereas the bamboo consists of an unbroken external envelope, containing only a hollow, that is, nothing:

STRIPPED TRUNK

BAMBOO

That the two-fold contrast: *empty external / solid internal*, and: *empty internal / complete external* is an invariable characteristic of the group can be clearly seen from the way in which M_{310} attempts to reverse the 'true' origin of bark masks, as it is described in a third Tucuna myth:

M_{318}. *Tucuna. 'Origin of bark masks'*

Once upon a time demons used to live in a cave. They went on a spree and attacked a village by night. They stole all the stocks of smoked meat, killed all the inhabitants, then dragged the corpses back to their den in order to eat them.

Meanwhile a party of visitors arrived at the village. They were astonished to find it deserted and followed the tracks of the gruesome procession, which led them to the mouth of the cave. The demons tried unsuccessfully to attract the intruders, but the Indians withdrew and went back home.

Another group of travellers were camping in the forest; among them was a pregnant woman who gave birth to a child. Her companions decided to stay where they were until she was strong enough to continue the journey. They were short of game, however, and had to go to sleep with empty stomachs. In the middle of the night they heard the characteristic gnawing of a rodent. It was an enormous paca (*Coelogenys paca*), which they surrounded and killed.

They all ate the paca meat, with the exception of the woman who had just given birth and her husband. The next morning the men went off to hunt leaving the mother and baby in the camp. The woman suddenly saw a demon coming towards her. He told her that the paca they had killed the night before was his son, and that the demons were coming to avenge his death. Those who had not partaken of the flesh must, if they wanted to save their lives, climb a tree of a certain species, stripping off the bark as they went up.

When the hunters returned, no one believed her story; they even made fun of her. And when, on hearing the hunting-horns and howls of the demons, she tried to warn her companions, the latter were so deeply asleep that even the red-hot resin which she dropped onto them from her torch failed to waken them. She bit her husband who finally got up and followed her like a sleepwalker. Holding the child, they both climbed the tree which the woman had taken care to locate, and tore off the bark as they climbed. When day dawned, they came down from their place of refuge and went back to the camp: there was no one left, the demons having slaughtered all the sleeping Indians. The couple returned to the village and related what had happened.

On the advice of an old sorcerer, the Indians planted a great many pimentoes. When these were ripe, they gathered them and deposited them near the demons' cave, the entrance of which they blocked with trunks of the paxiuba barriguda (a palm tree with a swollen trunk: *Iriartea ventricosa*), except in one place where they lit a big fire. They threw in enormous quantities of pimentoes, so that the smoke penetrated into the cave.

Soon a terrible din could be heard. The Indians allowed those demons who had not taken part in the cannibalistic feast to come out. But all those who had eaten human flesh perished in the cave: they can still be recognized by the red streak across their masks. When the noise stopped, and after Yagua, a slave who had been sent ahead as a scout, had been killed by a few surviving demons, the Tucuna went inside the cave and carefully noted the characteristic appearances of the various species of demons, which are reproduced today in the bark tunics (Nim. 13, pp. 80–81).

A detailed analysis of this myth would take me too far from my present theme, but I would just like to draw attention to the bark-stripping episode. A young mother ($\neq$ the old grandmother in M_{304}) and her husband, who have respected the food restrictions to which they are both subject after childbirth (Nim. 13, p. 69) ($\neq$ the elderly cannibalistic couple in M_{304}), succeed in escaping from the cannibalistic demons ($\neq$ in changing into cannibalistic demons, M_{304}), by stripping off the bark of a tree as they climb, i.e. as they move *from low to high*: whereas the humans, who turned into demons in M_{304}, achieved this result by stripping off bark *from high to low*. The major contrast on pp. 387–8 remains unchanged, and the inverted symmetry of M_{304} and M_{318} (the demons are either uncontrolled or tamed through wearing bark tunics) is dependent on an additional contrast, which has obviously been introduced for the sake of the argument: This is the contrast in the direction in which the tree is stripped, downwards or upwards.

Since the myth refers to a real-life technique, we can determine what the Indian method of bark-stripping was. According to Nimuendaju, who observed and described the Tucuna, it is done neither downwards nor upwards. The Indians fell the tree, cut off a suitable portion and hammer the bark until it is loosened from the trunk. After which they remove the bark by turning it inside out like a glove: or, more usually, they cut it lengthwise to obtain a rectangular piece which is easier to work than a cylindrical shape (Nim. 13, p. 81).[12] The Arawak of Guiana seem to employ the same technique (Roth 2, pp. 437–8), and perhaps invented it (Goldman, p. 223). As regards the techno-economical substructure, both myths, then, seem to be equally irrelevant. One is not 'truer' than the other, but since they are concerned with two complementary implications of a ritual which, if it is taken seriously, exposes the spectators (not to mention the participants) to certain danger – for what would happen if the demons impersonated by the masked dancers suddenly recovered their evil energy? – they had to invent an imaginary technique which, unlike the real-life technique, admits of opposite methods of procedure.

With the help of real or imaginary instruments, the myths, if appropriately arranged, seem to offer us the spectacle of a vast group of trans-

[12] However, Nimuendaju mentions a downwards stripping technique which is used only in the case of the matamatá tree (*Eschweilera* sp.), and which M_{304} applies to the tururi (*Comatari* sp?). Cf. Nim. 13, pp. 127, 147, n. 5.

formations covering the various ways in which a tree-trunk or a stick can *be hollow*: it can have a natural or an artificial cavity or a longitudinal or a transversal orifice; it can be used as a bee-hive, a trough, a drum, a dance stick, a bark pipe, a clapper, or a cang (a portable pillory) ... Musical instruments occupy a middle position in the series, between the objects at the two opposite extremes which take the form either of a kind of shelter, such as the hive, or of a trap, such as heavy wooden manacles. And we can say that the masks and musical instruments are themselves, each in their own way, shelters or traps, and sometimes even both at the same time. The clapper in M_{304} acts as a trap for the jaguar-demon; the jaguar-demon in M_{310}, who is caught in heavy wooden manacles, obtains the protection of his fellow-demons thanks to the dancing stick. The bark mask-like costumes, the origin of which is described in M_{318}, act as shelters for the dancers who wear them, while at the same time enabling the wearers to catch and harness the power of the demons.

From the beginning of this study, I have been constantly referring to hollow trees, used either as shelters or traps. In the myths about the origin of tobacco, the first function predominates since the people persecuted by the cannibalistic jaguar take refuge in a hollow tree. The second function prevails in the myths about the origin of honey where the fox, the girl mad about honey or the frog are imprisoned in a similar cavity. But the hollow tree only becomes a trap for these characters because it has first of all been a place of refuge for bees. Inversely, the hollow tree, which provides a providential shelter for the victims of the jaguar, in the myths about the origin of tobacco, is changed into a trap in which the jaguar perishes in trying to break through.

It would therefore be more accurate to say that the theme of the hollow tree provides a synthesis of two complementary aspects. This constant characteristic becomes even more obvious when we observe that the myths always use the same kind of trees, or trees of different kinds which are nevertheless alike in several significant aspects.

All the Chaco myths I have examined refer to the yuchan tree, the hollow bark of which shelters the children or the fellow-villagers of the woman turned jaguar, is used to make the first trough for mead, and becomes the first drum; it is in such a trunk that the demon-bat piles up the severed heads of its victims, and that the fox mad about honey is imprisoned or disembowelled, etc. The yuchan tree, in Spanish: *palo borracho*, is in Brazilian Portuguese, *barriguda*, 'the pot-bellied tree'.

It belongs to the silk-cotton tree family (*Chorisia insignis* and similar species), and has three main features – a swollen trunk, which gives it a bottle-like appearance, a profusion of long hard spikes and a white silky down which is gathered from its flowers.

The tree which acts as a trap for the girl mad about honey is more difficult to identify. We are given precise details about the species only in the extreme case in which the cunauaru, or tree-frog, is an embodiment of the heroine: this frog lives in the hollow trunk of Klotzsch's *Bodelsschwingia macrophylla* (Roth 1, p. 125), which is not a silk-cotton tree like the *Ceiba* and the *Chorisia*, but, if I am not mistaken, one of the tiliaceae. In South America, this family includes trees which provide lightweight wood and often have hollow trunks, like the bombax tree, one species of which (*Apeiba cymbalaria*) provides the Bororo with the bark that they beat and turn into loin-cloths for their women (Colb. 3, p. 60). It would seem, therefore, that the native ethnobotanical system groups into one big family trees similarly characterized by their light-weight wood and their frequent transformation into hollow cylinders, whether this transformation occurs naturally and inside the tree, or artificially and outside the tree as a result of human industry which, as it were, empties a bark tube of its trunk.[13] Within this large family particular attention should be paid to the bombax trees, since they play a leading part in the Guiana myths belonging to the same group as all those we have studied up till now:

M319. Carib. 'The disobedient daughters'

Two young girls refused to accompany their parents who had been invited to a drinking party. They remained alone in the family hut where they were visited by a demon who lived in the hollow trunk of a neighbouring tree – a ceiba tree. The demon shot a parrot with an arrow and asked the young girls to cook it. They were only too ready to oblige.

When the dinner was over, the demon slung up his hammock and called on the younger girl to join him. But not feeling so inclined, she sent her sister instead. During the night she heard strange noises and growls, which she first of all thought were caused by their love-making. However, the din grew louder so, after blowing up the fire, she went over to see what was happening. Blood was trickling from the hammock where her sister lay dead, pierced by her lover.

[13] Madame Claudine Berthe, an ethnobotanical specialist, has kindly pointed out that several modern botanists class the bombax family with the tiliaceae, or very close to them.

The girl now guessed who he really was and, in order to escape a similar fate, she hid herself under a heap of buck-corn which lay rotting in a corner, all covered with mildew. To make assurance doubly sure, she further warned the Spirit of the Rot that, if he allowed the demon to come and catch her, she would never supply him with any more corn. As it happened, the Spirit was so busy eating the corn that he did not reply to the demon's questions. The demon was unable to find the young girl's hiding place and, now that dawn was beginning to break, he had to hurry back to his home.

It was not until midday that the young girl dared to emerge from her hiding place. She rushed out to meet her people, who were returning from the drinking party. After being informed of what had happened, the parents gathered twenty basketfuls of pimentoes, tipped them round the tree and set fire to them. The demons were asphyxiated by the smoke and came tumbling down from the tree one after the other in the shape of guariba monkeys. Finally, the killer appeared and the Indians clubbed him to death. The younger sister obeyed her parents from that time onward (Roth 1, p. 231).

The armature of the above myth is clearly similar to that of the Guiana myths about the girl left alone in the camp while her people went hunting or visiting neighbours (M_{235}, M_{237}). But whereas in those myths the Spirit was a chaste provider of food and respectful of menstrual blood, the Spirit in this myth is lustful, bloodthirsty and a killer. In all the myths in this group which have a male hero, mildew plays a fatal role and is the cause of disjunction between the hunter and his game. In the present myth, where the leading character is a woman (and is looked upon as game from the demon's point of view), mildew is a protection covering the victim's and not the persecutor's body. The heroine in M_{235} chooses seclusion because she is unwell, and therefore a source of rot, whereas the two heroines in M_{319}, who have no legitimate reason for refusing to accompany their parents, are merely prompted by a spirit of insubordination. So, instead of telling the story of a well-behaved girl who is given honey as a reward, M_{319} tells the story of a disobedient girl who is avenged by the stinging smoke from the pimentoes.[14] Within this group, the two extremes of which I have just described, and which are characterized by a radical inversion of

[14] According to the Tucuna, the Spirit of the ceiba tree inflicts arrow wounds on women who are unwell: and bathing in water in which pimentoes have been cooked is the best antidote for any pollution due to menstrual blood (Nim. 13, pp. 92, 101).

all the themes, it is appropriate to place another myth occupying a middle position:

M320. Carib. 'The origin of tobacco'

A man saw an Indian with agouti paws disappearing into a ceiba tree. He was a nature-spirit. Wood, pimentoes and salt were piled round the tree and then set alight. The Spirit appeared to the man in a dream, and told him to go in three months' time to the place where he, the Spirit, had died. He would find a plant growing among the ashes. By soaking its broad leaves, he could prepare a drink to induce trances. It was during his first trance that the man learnt all the secrets of the healer's art (Goeje, p. 114).

According to a myth from the same source (M_{321}; Goeje, p. 114), the man visited by the Spirit was someone who had refused to help in preparing the fire and he was given tobacco as a reward for his compassion. Whether or not we should place the Spirit who is thus helped between the helpful Spirit in M_{235} and the unhelpful Spirit in M_{319}, it is clear that the Carib myth about the origin of tobacco closes a cycle, since the masculine character with agouti's feet (a vegetarian rodent and a perfectly harmless animal) whose ashes give rise to tobacco for drinking, after he himself has been caught in the trap of the hollow ceiba tree, links up directly with the female character in M_{24}, whose head first of all, and then her body, takes on the appearance of the jaguar, a carnivorous and dangerous animal whose ashes give rise to tobacco for smoking, after its unsuccessful attempt to kill its victims who had taken refuge in the hollow trunk of a silk-cotton tree. The circle has been completed, but only at the cost of certain transformations, which must now be examined.

In all these myths, the tree appears as an invariant term, and the fascination of native thought, from Guiana to the Chaco, with the silk-cotton family, cannot be entirely explained by such objective and noteworthy characteristics as their swollen trunks, lightweight wood and the frequency of an internal cavity. The Carib do not fell the ceiba tree (Goeje, p. 55), because, not only in their territory, but from Mexico to the Chaco, this tree has a supernatural counterpart – the tree of the world, which contains within its hollow trunk primeval water and fish, or the tree of paradise … Keeping to the method I have used up till now, I propose not to embark on these problems of mythic etymology which, in this particular instance, would necessitate extending the inquiry to the myths of Central America. Since the ceiba tree, or trees of similar species, constitute the invariant terms of the group we are concerned with, to determine their meaning we need do no more than compare and contrast the complexes of mythical contexts in which they happen to appear.

In the Chaco myths about the origin of tobacco, the hollow trunk of a silk-cotton tree is used as a place of refuge; in the Guiana myths about the origin of tobacco, it serves as a trap. But the hollow tree has a dual role in the Guiana myths in which the heroine is a girl mad about honey (whether directly or by transformation): sometimes it is a place of refuge and sometimes a trap, and occasionally both within the same myth (e.g. M_{241}). On the other hand, a secondary contrast emerges between honey which is found inside the tree, and the pimento smoke which rises up all round it.

Having evolved this first series, we can confidently construct a second. In M_{24}, the honey made bitter by the addition of young snakes has the same relationship with smoked tobacco as the stinging pimento smoke in M_{320} with a kind of 'tobacco honey':[15]

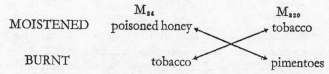

$$
\begin{array}{ccc}
 & M_{24} & M_{320} \\
\text{MOISTENED} & \text{poisoned honey} & \text{tobacco} \\
\text{BURNT} & \text{tobacco} & \text{pimentoes}
\end{array}
$$

At the same time as one circle is completed, the transfer of tobacco from the category of the burnt to that of the moistened creates a chiasmus. Two consequences ensue. First, we sense that the mythology of tobacco is two-fold, according to whether the tobacco is smoked or drunk, and according to whether its consumption is associated with the profane or the sacred, just as we had observed, in connection with the mythology of honey, the creation of a duality through the distinction between fresh and fermented honey. Secondly, we see once again that when the armature is retained, the message changes: M_{320} reproduces M_{24}, but deals with a different kind of tobacco. Mythic deduction always has a dialectical character: it moves in spirals, and not in circles. When we think we are back at our starting-point, we are never absolutely and completely there, but only in a certain respect. It would be more accurate to say that we are moving vertically over the place we set out from. But whether we are moving at a higher or a lower level,

[15] In the preparation of which salt plays a part, which explains how it comes to be mentioned in M_{321}.

there is an implied difference representing the significant discrepancy between the initial myth and the terminal myth (the adjectives being taken in a sense relating to distance covered). Finally, according to the viewpoint adopted, the discrepancy can be situated on the level of the armature, the code or the vocabulary.

Let us now look at the sequence of animals. I shall not go back over the correlational and oppositional relationship between the extreme terms, the frog and the jaguar, since this relationship has already been clarified (p. 249). But what is there to be said about the middle pair formed by the guariba monkeys in M_{319} and the agouti in M_{320}? The agouti is a rodent (*Dasyprocta aguti*), and the egotistical master of the fruit of the tree of life in the Guiana myths (cf. p. 264, n. 3). The guariba or howler monkey (*Alouatta* sp.) is a producer of filth: metaphorically, by virtue of the correlation between din and corruption, which has been demonstrated in other ways (p. 310); and literally, since the howler monkey is an incontinent animal which drops its excrement from the tops of trees, unlike the sloth which can control itself for several days and takes the trouble to climb down to the ground in order to defecate regularly in the same place (Tacana, M_{322}-M_{323}; H.-H., pp. 39–40; cf. *RC*, p. 315).[16] The Waiwai, who are a Carib tribe living along the frontier between British Guiana and Brazil, imitate various animals in the dances performed during their Shodewika festival. The dancers, dressed as howler monkeys, climb up onto the cross-beams of the collective hut and squat there, pretending to discharge banana skins onto the heads of the spectators (Fock, p. 181). This means that the agouti and the howler monkey are a pair of opposites, one being a monopolizer of food, the other a dispenser of excrement.

The part of demon-game which is assigned to the howler monkey in the Guiana myths re-emerges almost unchanged in an important Karaja myth (M_{117}), which I have so far referred to only briefly. This is a particularly appropriate point at which to return to it, since it will lead us back by an unexpected route to the problem of the clapper; its hero belongs to the family of 'unlucky hunters' who appear in M_{234}-M_{240}, and so to the group of the girl mad about honey.

M_{177a}. Karaja. 'The magic arrows'

Two great howler monkeys lived in the forest, killing and eating hunters. Two brothers tried to destroy them. On their way, they met a

---

[16] The contrast between the howler monkey and the sloth was the subject of one of my annual lecture courses at the Collège de France, cf. *Annuaire*, 65th year, 1965–6, pp. 269–70.

toad-woman who promised to teach them how to overcome monsters, but on condition that they took her as their wife. The brothers jeered at her and continued on their way. Soon they perceived the monkeys, armed, like themselves, with throwing-spears. A fight began, but both brothers were wounded in the eye and died.

A third brother lived in the family hut. His body was covered with sores and ulcers, and only his grandmother was prepared to look after him. One day, while hunting birds, he lost an arrow and tried to find it again. It had fallen into a snake's lair. The reptile came out, questioned the boy and learnt of his unhappy condition. To effect a cure, he made him a present of some black ointment, about which he was to tell no one.

He was soon better, and resolved to avenge his brothers' death. The snake gave him a magic arrow, and advised him not to reject the toad-woman's advances. In order to satisfy her, he need only simulate coitus between the poor creature's fingers and toes.

This the hero did, and in exchange was advised to let the monkeys shoot first and, when his turn came, to aim at the eyes. The dead animals remained hanging from the branches by their tails, and a lizard had to be sent to unfasten them.

The hero then went to thank the snake. The latter gave him some magic arrows which could kill and bring back all varieties of game, and which could even gather the fruits of the forest, including honey and many other things. There were as many arrows as there were animal species and different kinds of food, and also, in a gourd, a substance to be smeared on the arrows so that they should not hit the hunter too hard on returning.

With the help of the snake's arrows, the hero could now obtain all the game and fish he wanted. He got married, built a hut and cleared the ground for a plantation. But although he had urged his wife not to entrust his arrows to anyone, she allowed herself to be tricked by her own brother. To begin with, the latter shot successfully at wild pigs and fish, but forgot to smear the arrow used for gathering honey; as it came back to him, it changed into a huge head with a great many jaws all bristling with teeth. The head threw itself upon the Indians and killed them.

Alarmed by the cries, the hero ran back from his plantation and succeeded in driving the monster away. Half the village had perished. When informed of the tragedy, the snake said that it was irreparable.

He invited his protégé to a piarucu (*Arapaimua gigas*) fishing party, and told the Indian not to forget to tell him, should one of his daughters happen to push him. This is precisely what happened, but the hero forgot the snake's instructions. The latter changed into a pirarucu fish, and the man likewise. When the Indians caught them both, the snake managed to escape through a hole in the net, but the fish-man was dragged up onto the bank, where a fisherman tried to club him to death. The snake came to the rescue, helped him to get out of the net and restored him to his human shape. He explained to him that he had been punished because he had said nothing when the young girl touched him (Ehrenreich, pp. 84–6).

Krause (pp. 347–50) gives two variants of this myth ($M_{117b, c}$). The episode of the pirarucu fishing expedition does not occur in these myths or, if it does, in a scarcely recognizable form. I therefore simply refer the reader to Dietschy's interesting discussion (Dietschy 2) while at the same time pointing out, for the benefit of anyone anxious to make a complete study of the myth, that the conclusion is similar to that of M_{78}. Other differences relate to the hero's family. He is abandoned by his parents and entrusted to his grandfather who feeds him on refuse and fish-bones. In M_{177a} he marries his aunt. The two variants add another victory to the one over the monkeys: the hero vanquishes two birds of prey, after provoking them by striking the water: tou, tou ... (cf. M_{226}–M_{227}). This detail, which is common to the myths of the eastern Ge, suggests that in both cases we are dealing with a foundation myth relating to the initiation ceremony for boys which, among the Karaja, also took place in several stages (Lipkind 2, p. 187).

The interest of the myth lies in the many references linking it up with the Ge and the Guiana tribes (M_{237}–M_{239}, M_{241}–M_{258}), in particular to the Kachúyana, since, as has already been stressed, M_{177} reverses the myth about the origin of curare belonging to the Kachúyana community (M_{161}) by introducing (although with reference to fights with hostile, ill-intentioned howler monkeys) the idea of *inverted poison*, in the form of an ointment, the purpose of which is to weaken the magic arrows, so that, on the return flight, their full force should not be directed against the hunter. It is interesting to note that these super-arrows bring the collecting of wild food produce and honey into the same category as hunting, so that the myth treats these foods as game. The present state of knowledge about the Karaja does not allow us to attempt an explanation, which could be no more than speculative. Lastly, in treating the spaces between the fingers and toes as if they were real orifices, M_{177} refers back to certain Chaco myths, in which the heroine is also a batrachian (M_{175}), and to a Tacana myth (M_{324}) which likewise contains this theme.

The Krause versions modify Ehrenreich's version in one respect, which seems to me to be of vital importance. The snake (or the protector in human form in $M_{177b, c}$), instead of giving the hero magic arrows (which in fact are throwing-spears), presents him with two equally magical instruments: a wooden projectile called obiru, and an object made from two sticks of canna brava (a member of the anonaceous family), one light, one dark, stuck together with wax over their whole length, and decorated at one end with black feathers. This instrument is called hetsiwa.

When he strikes (*schlägt*) these objects or waves them in the air, the hero creates a great wind. Uohu snakes (the word also means 'wind' or 'arrow') suddenly appear and go inside the hetsiwa. Then the wind brings fish, wild pigs and honey, which the hero shares out among the villagers, keeping only the remains to eat with his mother. One day, while he is away fishing, a child gets hold of the obiru, conjures up the snakes, but is unable to make them go back into the hetsiwa. The snakes (or winds) run wild and kill all the people in the village, including the hero, who cannot control the monsters without the help of the obiru. The slaughter puts an end to the human race (Krause, *loc. cit.*).

Among the Karaja, the obiru and the hetsiwa, unlike the Tucuna clapper in M_{304}, actually exist and are known to be in current use. The obiru is a dart shot by means of a spear-thrower. M_{177} suggests that this weapon may have been used in former times for monkey-hunting, but in the early twentieth century it had become a plaything and, in the form in which it has been observed, most probably borrowed from tribes in the Xingu (Krause, p. 273, Figure 127). The hetsiwa, a purely magical object used for warding off rain, presents problems of interpretation which are extremely complex because of the unevenness in size and difference in colour of the two sticks; it also presents linguistic problems. The thicker stick, which is painted black, is called kuoluni, (k)woru-ni, a word meaning electric fish, according to Krause and Machado, but which, in this particular instance, Dietschy (*loc. cit.*) is inclined to link with the general term (k)o-woru, 'magic'. The composition of the name of the slender, whitish stick nohōdémuda is doubtful, except that the element nohō signifies penis.

According to Krause, Indians also use the term hetsiwa for a magic object made of wax, which is used for casting spells and which represents an aquatic creature that he believes to be the electric fish. Dietschy gives very convincing evidence to prove that it is the dolphin. I nevertheless hesitate to reject outright the supposed symbolical affinity between the first kind of hetsiwa, or the black stick which is one element of it, and the electric fish. In the Karaja language, the latter has the same name as the rainbow, that is, a meteoric phenomenon which, like the magic object, puts an end to rain. The use of the hetsiwa, which is strangely reminiscent of the club-spear employed by the Nambikwara to cut and dissipate storm clouds, also has a link with a more northerly Arawak myth, in which the electric fish fulfils the same function:

M$_{325}$. Arawak. 'The marriage of the electric fish'
An old sorcerer had such a beautiful daughter that he had difficulty in finding a husband worthy of her. He rejected a succession of suitors, including the jaguar. Finally, Kasum, the electric fish (*Electrophorus electricus*, a gymnotus or electric eel), appeared and boasted of his great strength. The old man jeered at him, but after touching the suitor and feeling the violence of the shock, he changed his mind and accepted him as his son-in-law, at the same time giving him the task of controlling thunder, lightning and rain. When storms approached, Kasum divided the clouds, some to the right, some to the left, and drove them respectively southwards and northwards (Farabee 5, pp. 77–8).

The comparison is interesting because of the role assigned to fish in the mythology of the Karaja, who depend almost entirely on fish for their food. The pirarucu made its appearance at the end of M$_{177a}$. This enormous fish, the only one the Karaja catch in a net (Baldus 5, p. 26), is in this respect unlike all the other species, which are caught with poison, and unlike the snake which, according to M$_{177a}$, easily escaped through the mesh net. There is a second dichotomy, which corresponds to this initial one between the snake and the pirarucu fish. One Karaja myth (M$_{177d}$) attributes the origin of pirarucu fish to two brothers who were tired of their wives and who changed into fish (*Arapaima gigas*). One was eaten by storks because it was soft (therefore rotten: cf. M$_{331}$); the other, which was as hard as stone, survived and became the laténi mask, which terrifies women and children (Baldus 6, pp. 213–15; Machado, pp. 43–5). These men who were disappointed in human love and who changed into pirarucu fish are an inversion of the woman, or women, in the tapir-as-seducer cycle, who were passionately in love with an animal and who changed into fish which, in general terms, are in contrast to the special category formed by the pirarucu.

But let us return to the hetsiwa. If we compare Ehrenreich's and Krause's versions of M_{177}, we discover that almost always two types of objects are involved. The obiru or obirus are used in $M_{177a, b}$ to 'call' game and honey, whereas, it is the function of the magic ointment, according to M_{177a}, and the function of the hetsiwa, according to M_{177b}, to neutralize the dangers inherent in this call. Provided we disregard M_{177c} (a very abbreviated version in which the hetsiwa combines both functions), it follows that the hetsiwa in M_{177b} plays the same part as the ointment in M_{177a}, which is an inverted poison.

Now the hetsiwa is itself an inverted instrument in comparison with the clapper in M_{304}, or the parabára: the two sticks of which it is made and which are fixed together over their whole length *cannot be* struck one against the other. This is by no means a unique instance. It is illustrated in a very similar form among the Sherente whose culture is, in certain respects, remarkably similar to that of the Karaja. Nimuendaju (6, pp. 68–9, Pl. III) describes and illustrates a ritual object called wabu, of which the Indians make four models, two large ones, wabu-zauré, and two small ones, wabu-rié, for the feast of the great ant-eater (cf. above, p. 132). Each one consists of two stems of burity palms (*Mauritia*) painted red and fixed together by means of projecting pegs. At either end of the upper peg hangs a very long tassel, made of bark fibres. The four wabu-bearers accompany the masked dancers to the place at which the feast is held, then divide off into pairs, one of which takes up its position to the east, the other to the west, of the dancing area.

Information is unfortunately lacking about the significance of the wabu and their function in the ritual. But their physical resemblance to the hetsiwa is all the more striking since there are two kinds of wabu, one large, one small, and since Krause (Figure 182a, b) illustrates two types of Karaja ritual instruments made of sticks fixed together.

In the present state of knowledge, the theory according to which the hetsiwa and the wabu represent, as it were, immobilized clappers, must be put forward with extreme prudence. Yet the existence of similar conceptions among the ancient Egyptians gives it a certain credibility. I am well aware that Plutarch's evidence is often suspect. I therefore make no claim to be restating authentic beliefs since, as far as I am concerned, it is of scant importance whether the imagery to which I am about to refer originated among reliable Egyptian sages, among a handful of Plutarch's informants, or in Plutarch's own mind.

In my view, the only point worthy of attention is that, after I had noted on several occasions that the intellectual processes evidenced in Plutarch's work presented a curious similarity to those I was deducing from South American myths, and that, consequently, in spite of the

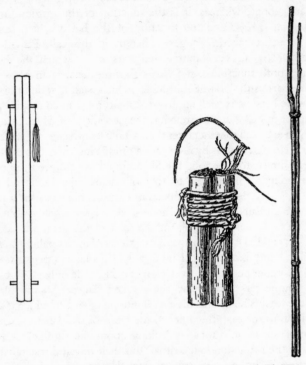

Figure 18 (*left*). Diagram of a wabu. (After Nim. 6, Pl. III.)
Figure 19. The two hetsiwa. (After Krause, *loc. cit.*, p. 333.)

time gap and geographical distance, I had to admit that in both instances human minds had worked in the same way, a new convergence should emerge in connection with a hypothesis I would not have dared to put forward, had it not made the comparison justifiable.

Here then is Plutarch's text:

Moreover, Manethus says that the Egyptians have a mythical tradition in regard to Jupiter, that because his legs were grown together he was not able to walk and so for shame tarried in the wilderness;

but Isis, by severing and separating those parts of his body, provided him with means of rapid progress. This fable teaches by its legend that the mind and reason of the god, fixed amid the unseen and invisible, advanced to generation by reason of motion. The sistrum, a metallic rattle, also makes it clear that all things in existence need to be shaken, or rattled about, and never to cease from motion but, as it were, to be waked up and agitated when they grow drowsy and torpid. They say that they avert and repel Typhon by means of the sistrums, indicating thereby that when destruction constricts and checks Nature, generation releases and arouses it by means of motion (Plutarch's *Moralia. Isis and Osiris*, 376).

Is it not extraordinary that the Karaja, whose magical practices and the problems they raise have led us to Plutarch, should have evolved a story completely symmetrical with his? They say that Kanaschiwué, their demiurge, had to have his arms and legs tied to prevent him from destroying the earth by floods and other disasters, as he would have done had his movements been unrestricted (Baldus 5, p. 29).[17]

In spite of its obscurity, the Greek text introduces a clear contrast between, on the one hand silence and immobility symbolized by two limbs normally separate yet welded together, and on the other movement and noise, symbolized by the sistrums. As in South America, unlike the first term, only the second term is a musical instrument. As in South America also, this musical instrument (or its opposite) is used to 'divert or drive away' a natural force (or it is used to attract it for criminal purposes): in one instance, it is Typhon, that is, Seth; in the other, the tapir or snake as seducers, the snake-rainbow associated with rain, rain itself or the chthonian spirits.

The sistrum proper is not a musical instrument which is widely known in South America. Among the Caduveo, I found sistrums corresponding to the description already given by other observers. They were

---

[17] In the same way, it would also be appropriate to re-examine the famous episode of Aristeus (Virgil, *Georgics*, IV) in which Proteus (who corresponds to Plutarch's Typhon) has to be bound hand and foot during the dry season: '*Iam rapidus torrens sitientis Sirius Indos*', in order to make him consent to show the shepherd how to find honey again, after it has been lost as a result of the disappearance of Eurydice, the mistress, if not of honey like the heroine of M_{233}–M_{234}, undeniably mistress of the honeymoon! Eurydice, who is swallowed by a monstrous sea-serpent (*ibid.*, v. 459), is an inversion of the heroine of M_{326a} who was born from a sea-serpent and who rejected a honeymoon, in the days when animals had the gift of speech, and therefore would not have had any use for an Orpheus.

made of a forked stick with the two branches joined by a string on which were threaded a few discs once carved from bone or shell, but nowadays made of metal. A similar instrument exists among the Yaqui of north Mexico. No other instances of it are known in America (Izikowitz, pp. 150-51).

But, in the absence of the sistrum, we have at our disposal another basis of comparison between the mythical representations of the New World and the Old. The reader will no doubt have noticed that a curious analogy exists between the means employed for the tapped-out call in the South American myths: a resonator made from a gourd or tree-trunk which is struck, sticks which are knocked against each other, or clappers, and a liturgical complex belonging to the Old World, known as the instruments of darkness. The origin of these instruments, and their use from the Thursday to the Saturday of Holy Week, presents a great many problems. As I cannot claim to participate in a complex discussion which lies outside my competence, I shall merely refer to one or two generally accepted points.

It would seem that fixed bells in churches did not make their appearance until rather late, about the seventh century. Their enforced silence from the Thursday to the Saturday of Holy Week does not seem to be recorded before about the eighth century (and then only in Rome). At the end of the twelfth and beginning of the thirteenth century, the restriction appears to have spread to other European countries. But the reason for the bells remaining silent, and for them being replaced temporarily by other sources of noise, is not clear. Their alleged journey to Rome, which accounted for their temporary absence, may be no more than an *a posteriori* explanation, founded moreover on all kinds of beliefs and imaginative suppositions connected with bells: they were thought to be animate, vocal beings, capable of feeling and acting, and fit for baptism. In addition to summoning the congregation to the church, bells had a meteorological, and even a cosmic, function. Their reverberations drove storms away, dispelled clouds and hail, and destroyed evil spells.

According to Van Gennep, whom I have followed so far (t. I, Vol. III, pp. 1209-14), the instruments of darkness which replace the bells include the hammer, the hand rattle, the clapper or hand-knocker, a kind of castanets called '*livre*', the matraca (a flat slab of wood with two moveable plates attached to either side which strike it when it is shaken) and the wooden sistrum on a string or a ring. Other instruments, such as the *batelet* and huge rattles, were quite complicated pieces of apparatus. In theory, all these devices had a definite function, but in actual practice they often overlapped: they were used to make a noise inside the church or out, to summon the congregation in the absence of bells, or to accompany the collecting of alms by children. There is, also, some evidence that the instruments of darkness may have been intended to represent the marvels and terrifying noises which occurred at the time of the death of Christ.

In the case of Corsica (Massignon), wind instruments are mentioned (the marine horn, the wooden whistle, or more simply the making of a whistling noise by blowing between the fingers), together with various percussive instruments or devices: the beating of the altar and benches in churches, the smashing of planks with clubs, the use of hand-knockers, clappers and hand rattles of various types, one of which was called raganetta, *'rainette'* (tree-frog), while another made from reeds was a sort of improved parabára, with one of the blades of split bamboo replaced by a cogged wooden wheel. The name 'tree-frog' is also found in other areas.

In France, the instruments of darkness included ordinary objects: metal pots and pans which were beaten, wooden clogs which were used for hammering on the ground, wooden mallets which were used for striking the ground and other objects; sticks with split ends or bundles of branches used in the same way; hand-clapping; and lastly musical instruments of various kinds: some with a solid wooden resonator (the knocker, the hand rattle, the clapper, the board hammered by means of an attachment and the sistrum); others made of metal (big bells, little bells and rattles) or with a membrane (the spinning, friction drum); or vibrating wind instruments (dry and wet whistles, horns, shells, hunting horns, hooters and oboes).

In the High Pyrenees, the author who gives the above classification studied the making and use of a spinning friction drum, called toulou-hou (Marcel-Dubois, pp. 55–89). An old tin with the bottom knocked out, or a cylindrically shaped piece of bark, serves as a resonator: the drum is left open at one end, while a piece of sheepskin or a bladder is secured over the other to act as a membrane. A loop of string is threaded through two holes pierced in the centre. The loose ends are fixed by means of a slip knot round a grooved stick, which is used to work the instrument. After smearing the groove with saliva, the performer grasps the handle and causes the instrument to rotate. The string vibrates and produces a kind of throbbing noise described as 'humming' or 'squeaking', according to whether the string is made of twine or horsehair.

The literal meaning of toulouhou is hornet or bumble-bee. But in other areas the instrument is called after different animals, which may be insects (the grasshopper or cicada) or batrachians (the tree-frog or toad). The German name *Waldteufel*, 'wood demon', is even reminiscent of the Warao myth (M_{317}), in which the bush spirits regret that they are so inadequately provided with musical instruments.

Although the ritual stipulates that the bells should remain silent from the Collect during mass on the Thursday before Good Friday to the Gloria on the following Saturday (Van Gennep, *loc. cit.*, pp. 1217–37; Marcel-Dubois, p. 55), it would seem that the Church has always been opposed to the instruments of darkness and has tried to restrict their use. For this reason, Van Gennep accepts the view that their origin lies in folklore. Without deciding whether or not the din made by the instruments of darkness survives as a relic of neolithic or even paleolithic customs, or whether its occurrence in widely scattered areas merely shows that man, when confronted with the same situations, reacts with the help of symbolic representations suggested to him, or perhaps even forced upon him, by the underlying processes which control his thought the world over, we can accept Van Gennep's prudently formulated thesis, and can even quote a parallel instance in support of it:

In China, every year about the beginning of April, certain officials called Sz'hüen used of old to go about the country armed with wooden clappers. Their business was to summon the people and command them to put out every fire. This was the beginning of the season called Han-shih-tsieh, or 'eating cold food'. For three days all household fires remained extinct as a preparation for the solemn renewal of the fire, which took place on the fifth or sixth day after the winter solstice. The ceremony was performed with great pomp by the same officials who procured the new fire from heaven by reflecting the sun's rays either from a metal mirror or from a crystal on dry moss. Fire thus obtained is called by the Chinese heavenly fire and its use is enjoined in sacrifices: whereas fire elicited by the friction of wood is termed by them earthly fire, and its use is prescribed for cooking and other domestic purposes ... This annual renewal of fire was a ceremony of very great antiquity in China ... since it dates from (at least) two thousand years before Christ (Frazer 4, quoting various sources: Vol. 10, p. 137). Granet (pp. 283,

514) twice briefly mentions this rite, with reference to the *Tcheou li* and the *Li ki*.

I have mentioned this old Chinese custom (which has parallels both in the East and the Far East), because it is relevant in more than one respect. In the first place, it seems to follow a relatively simple and easily discernible pattern: in order to seize fire *from above* and bring it down *here below*, there must be an annual conjunction between the sky and the earth. This, however, is a hazardous and almost sacrilegious undertaking, since celestial fire and earthly fire are governed by a relationship of incompatibility. The extinction of terrestrial fires, which is heralded or ordered by clappers, functions therefore as a necessary pre-condition. It creates the required vacuum, which allows the conjunction of celestial fire and the earth to take place without dangerous consequences. The misgivings I inevitably feel at having had to look so far afield for a term of comparison are to some extent allayed by an obvious comparison between the old Chinese rite and a recent ceremony practised by the Sherente Indians, which I have already analysed, and whose importance regarding the problems we are concerned with was indicated in *The Raw and the Cooked* (pp. 289–91, 314). Among the Sherente, too, the rite concerned the renewal of fire, which was preceded by the extinction of domestic fires and by a period of mortification. The new fire had to be obtained from the sun, notwithstanding the danger men exposed themselves to in going near it or in bringing it near to them. The same contrast is also to be observed between celestial fire, which is sacred and destructive, and terrestrial fire, which is profane and constructive, since it is the fire used in the home. To complete the comparison, we would no doubt need to discover the use of wooden clappers among the Sherente. There is no evidence of their being present, but at least we know that these Indians possess a ritual instrument, the wabu, which we recognized, for reasons very different from those that concern us at present, as being an inverted clapper (p. 401). Most important of all, the Sherente ritual of the great fast gives pride of place to another kind of noise-maker – supernatural wasps which reveal their presence to those officiating by a characteristic hum: ken! – ken! – ken-ken-ken-ken! (*RC*, p. 315, n. 19). Now, whereas the Chinese tradition refers only to the clapper, and the Sherente tradition to the wasps, we have seen that, in Europe, the rotating friction drum – which, in the Pyrenees, is called by a name signifying 'bumblebee' or 'hornet' – appears as one of the instruments of darkness alongside the clapper, and can even replace it.

Let us now proceed further with this attempt to work out a mythic ·
and ritual pattern which, as we are beginning to suspect, may be common to cultures very remote from each other, and to very different
traditions. Like archaic China and certain Amero-Indian societies,
Europe, until quite recently, celebrated a rite involving the extinguishing and renewal of domestic fires, preceded by fasting and the
use of the instruments of darkness. This series of events took place
just before Easter, so that the 'darkness' which prevailed in the
church during the service of the same name (*Tenebrae*), could symbolize
both the extinguishing of domestic fires and the darkness which covered
the earth at the moment of Christ's death.

In all Catholic countries it was customary to extinguish the lights in
the churches on Easter Eve and then make a new fire sometimes with
flint or with the help of a burning-glass. Frazer brings together numerous instances which show that this fire was used to give every house
new fire. He quotes a sixteenth-century Latin poem in a contemporary
English translation, from which I take the following significant lines:

> On Easter Eve the fire all is quencht in every place,
> And fresh againe from out the flint is fecht with solemne grace.
>
> *
>
> Then Clappers ceasse, and belles are set againe at libertée,
> And herewithall the hungrie times of fasting ended bée.

In England, the bells were silent from Maundy Thursday until
midday on Easter Sunday, and were replaced by wooden clappers
(Frazer, *loc. cit.*, p. 125). In several parts of Europe, the return of plenty
was also symbolized by 'gardens of Adonis', which were prepared as
Easter approached (Frazer 4, Vol. 5, pp. 253 *ff*).

The plenty which now returned had not just been absent since
Maundy Thursday; its loss went back much further, to the day
following Shrove Tuesday to be precise. As regards acoustic symbols and
their relationship to food, three periods can be distinguished. The
instruments of darkness accompanied the final weeks of Lent, that is
the period in which the hardships of fasting were most acutely felt,
since they had lasted longer. The bells rang out once more on Easter
Sunday to mark the end of this Lenten period. But before it even
began, an exceptional and unrestrained use of bells had summoned the
population to make the most of the last day of plenty: the bell rung on
the morning of Shrove Tuesday was known in England as the *pancake
bell*. The gastronomic excesses for which it was the signal, and indeed

rendered almost obligatory, are illustrated in the following picturesque popular ballad of 1684:

> But hark I hear the pancake bell,
> And fritters make a gallant smell;
> The cooks are baking, frying, boyling,
> Carving, gourmandising, roasting,
> Carbonading, cracking, slashing, toasting.

(Wright and Lones, p. 9; cf. pp. 8–20)

In connection with France, Van Gennep rightly insists on the culinary and ceremonial aspect, which is too often disregarded by theorists, of the Carnival-Lent cycle. But in the popular mind it has always been considered to be sufficiently important for Shrove Tuesday, or the first Sunday in Lent, to be called after the dishes associated with them: *jour des crêpes* or *crozets* (Pancake Day) in the case of Shrove Tuesday, *dimanche des beignets* or *bugnes* (Fritter Sunday) or Carling Sunday (fried peas) in the case of the first Sunday in Lent. At Montbéliard, typical Shrove Tuesday dishes were *pelai* (millet) or *paipai* (rice pudding) in the morning, and in the evening pork, ham, pig chaps or *bon-jésus* (a sort of black-pudding) with pickled cabbage. Elsewhere the Shrove Tuesday repast usually differed from other meals in that it comprised vast quantities of meat of all kinds, certain cuts being set aside specially for this particular day and prepared according to more elaborate recipes than those used for other meals. Clear meat soup, which was also used in ritual sprayings, gruel, pancakes fried in a greased pan, fritters fried in fat or oil were typical Shrove Tuesday dishes. In France, the obligatory making of pancakes is found only in the northern third of the country (Van Gennep, t. I, Vol. III, pp. 1125–36 and map XII).

If, after noting the Church's hostility towards customs it has always condemned as pagan in order to deprive them of the Christian overtones with which Europe has vainly endeavoured to endow them, we try to discover a form common to these American, Chinese and European examples, chosen from among a host of others listed by Frazer which would have served equally well, we arrive, in short, at the following conclusion:

A comprehensive inquiry into the place and function of the mythology of honey in tropical America drew our attention to an acoustic custom, which at first sight appears to be inexplicable. I am referring to the noise made by the knocking together of the honey-gatherer's sandals (M_{24}).[18] In our search for terms of comparison, we encountered first the clapper in M_{304}, which was probably an imaginary instrument, but which put us on the track of real-life instruments of the same type, whose existence in South America had passed almost unnoticed. Whether real or imaginary, these instruments are the equivalent, both from the organological and symbolic points of view, of the instruments of darkness of the European tradition, which had parallels in China, as is proved by an ancient rite.

Before proceeding further, I would like to discuss a point of organology. The European instruments of darkness include vibrating instruments with a solid body, as well as vibrating wind instruments. This then removes the objection to my interpretation which was constituted by the dual nature of the calls addressed to the animal-seducer by the heroine in a great many South American myths. These calls are either tapped out on the convex side of half a gourd placed on a watery surface, a tree-trunk or the ground, or they are whistled in imitation of the animal's cry. European ethnography notes the occurrence of the same ambiguity, sometimes in one particular place and on a clearly specified occasion. In Corsica, 'children armed with sticks beat vigorously on church pews, or, putting two fingers in their mouths, they see who can whistle the loudest. They represent the Jews hounding Christ' (Massignon, p. 276). I shall have more to say about this comment (p. 412).

This is not all. Throughout the present study, it has been noted that, in the minds of the Indians, myths about the origin of honey were associated with the dry season – or, in the absence of a dry season – with a period in the year also denoting scarcity. To this seasonal coding can be added another, acoustic in nature, and certain modalities of which I am now in a position to specify.

The conjunction of the honey-gatherer with the object of his search – a substance which is entirely on the side of nature, since cooking is not necessary in order to render it edible – or the conjunction of the woman

18 A possible analogy that comes to mind is the use of charivari to prevent swarms of bees flying away. The custom is mentioned by many writers of antiquity listed by Billiard (2, pp. 382–3), and is perhaps still practised in certain areas. But as Billiard observes, 'some people thought the noise pleased the bees, others on the contrary that they were frightened by it.' Agreeing with Layens and Bonnier (pp. 148–9), he expresses the opinion 'that it (the custom) is of no use' or rather that its only purpose is publicly to affirm the rights of the pursuer, 'which is perhaps the only plausible explanation for this time-honoured custom' (Billiard 1, year 1899, no. 3, p. 115). As will appear later, charivari in connection with bees can only be interpreted as a particular instance of the application of the instruments of darkness.

with an animal seducer, whose position is semantically the same as that of honey, an alimentary seducer, are both in danger of causing total disjunction of the human character and culture, i.e. society. It should be emphasized, incidentally, that the concept of the disjunctive conjunction is not a contradictory one, since it refers to three terms, the second of which is joined to the first by the same operation which causes its disjunction from the third. This taking over of one term by another at the expense of a third (cf. *RC*, pp. 286–9) is given acoustic expression in M_{24} in the form of the knocking together of the sandals, just as another Chaco myth (M_{301}) exemplifies the reverse operation, that of conjunctive disjunction, by means of an exactly opposite noise: the brrumbrrrummbrum! of the snake as it prepares to swallow the honey-gatherers, after consuming the honey it has extorted from them.

When I quoted this myth (p. 337), I noted that the snake's cry was reminiscent of the noise of the bull-roarers. South American myths are certainly not the only ones in which a relationship of congruence between the snake and the penis can be observed, but they systematically exploit its full resources when, for instance, they illustrate a correlational and oppositional relationship between the snake, which is 'all penis', and its human mistress, who is 'all womb': a woman who can contain within her womb her lover or her grown child, and whose other orifices are wide open, releasing menstrual blood and urine and even peals of laughter (cf. *RC*, pp. 124 ff). Of this basic pair, the tapir with the 'big penis' and the opossum with the 'big womb' (either directly in the form of a good nurse, or figuratively in the form of an adulterous woman) are simply a combinatory variant in which the terms are less clearly defined (cf. *RC*, pp. 255–6).

The fact that observations made in Melanesia and Australia led Van Baal to suggest independently a phallic interpretation of the symbolism of bull-roarers strengthens still further my own conviction that the tapped-out call of the Tereno honey-gatherer and the roaring of the Toba snake form a pair of antithetical terms. I started from the hypothesis that the former was congruous with the tapped-out or whistled call of the tapir's mistress, and the latter with the sound of the bull-roarers. This hypothesis is now given support by the identification of the former with a call, addressed by a woman with a 'big vagina' (in the metaphorical sense) to an animal which is literally endowed with a large penis, and by the identification of the latter with a warning given to women (who, however, in this instance are pursued only to be more effectively driven away) by the bull-roarer, which is a figurative penis.

Consequently, in the one instance, the power of nature conjoins the sexes to the detriment of culture: the tapir's mistress is lost to her lawful husband, and sometimes the whole female race is lost to society. In the other instance, the power of culture disjoins the sexes, to the detriment of nature which prescribes their union; temporarily at least, family links are broken in order to allow human society to be formed.

Let us return for a moment to the Pyrenees. The toulouhou revolves around an axis, like the bull-roarer, and the two instruments are alike as regards the sound they produce, although they are very different from the organological point of view. In ritualistic practices, however, the toulouhou plays a part similar to the one I have just attributed to the bull-roarer by a purely deductive process but which is confirmed by innumerable instances observed in South America (Zerries 2), Melanesia and Australia (Van Baal) and Africa (Schaeffner). The use of the toulouhou is restricted to boys who use it before and during the Good Friday mass in order to frighten women and girls. Now the bull-roarer exists among Pyrenean communities, but never as an instrument of darkness. In the Labourd and Béarn areas, it is a carnival instrument, or else it is used to keep mares away from the sheep-folds (Marcel-Dubois, pp. 70–77). On the organological level, then, the contrast is maintained between the bull-roarer and the instruments of darkness, although on the symbolic level the function assigned to the bull-roarer by illiterate societies is, in a European society, dissociated from the bull-roarer and linked with the instrument of darkness it most resembles. In spite of this minor difference, on which it would be interesting to have specialist opinion, the basic contrast remains and can be formulated in the same terms. When used outside the church and before mass, the toulouhou, unlike the other instruments of darkness, has the same function as the bull-roarer. Its aim is to disjoin women (who are thus conjoined with nature) from the society of men (culture), men being then free to assemble on their own within the sacred precincts. But when it is used inside the church during mass, concurrently with the other instruments of darkness, its function is inseparable from theirs which is (if I may be allowed to generalize on the basis of Mlle Massignon's interpretation of the Corsican data) to symbolize the conjunction of Christ's enemies (nature) with the Saviour, who is then in a state of disjunction with culture.

Let us leave the bull-roarer for the time being and look again at the two-fold coding, seasonal and acoustic, of the group we were discussing. Let us take the seasonal coding first. It can be observed all over the world; in its real form, in South America, where there is an objective contrast between two periods of the year: one characterized by scarcity, the other by plenty; in a conventional form (but which is no doubt a ritualistic expression of an actual experience) in Europe, where Lent can be seen as a period of deliberate scarcity; finally in a quasi-potential form, in Ancient China, where the period of 'eating cold food' hardly lasted for more than a few days. But, in spite of being merely potential, the Chinese contrast is conceptually the most powerful since it is between absent fire and present fire, and the same is true of the Sherente contrast. Elsewhere in South America, the contrast is between a period of plenty and a period of scarcity, which is lived through at length without being necessarily simulated during a longer or shorter space of time. We find the same contrast in Europe, but transposed into the form of a contrast between the days on which meat is eaten and the Lenten period. Consequently, as we move from China to Europe, the major contrast is weakened:

[present fire/absent fire] $\Rightarrow$ [meat/meatless]

and as we move from the New World (with the exception of one or two instances, such as that of the Sherente) to the Old World, the contrast becomes progressively slighter, since the five or six days of 'eating cold food' in China, or the even smaller number of days which make up the Christian triduum, correspond in miniature form to the longer period which, in Europe, lasts throughout the whole of Lent, from the end of Shrove Tuesday until Easter Sunday. If we disregard these differences and some possible repetitions, the underlying system can be reduced to three pairs of opposites of diminishing magnitude which can be arranged in a logical order, without the correspondences between their respective terms being obliterated:

$$\begin{cases} \text{absent fire} \\ \text{present fire} \end{cases} \begin{cases} \text{scarcity} \\ \text{plenty} \end{cases} \begin{cases} \text{meatless} \\ \text{meat} \end{cases}$$

Whether we are dealing with the absence of fire among the Ancient Chinese and the Sherente, or the period of scarcity in other parts of South America, or the absence of fire coinciding with the culminating point of Lent in the European tradition, it is clear that these various combinations of circumstances have certain features in common:

cooking is abolished either literally or symbolically; during a period varying in length from a few days to a whole season, direct contact is established between humanity and nature, as during the mythic age when fire did not yet exist and men had to eat their food raw, or after a brief exposure to the rays of the sun, which at that time was close to the earth. However, this immediate conjunction of man with nature can itself take two forms; either nature leaves man in the lurch and shortages which had at first been bearable become more acute until a state of famine is reached; or it yields a lavish supply of substitute foods, such as wild fruits and honey, in a natural instead of a cultural form (which only cooking would justify). These two possibilities, which are functions of an immediacy conceived in the negative or the positive mode, correspond to what I referred to in *The Raw and the Cooked* as the rotten world and the burnt world. And the world certainly is burnt symbolically, or is theoretically in danger of being burnt, when, by means of a burning-glass or a mirror (Old World) or by the presentation of fibres to the fire-bearing messenger of the sun (New World), men try to bring celestial fire back to earth in order to relight the fireless hearths. Similarly, that superlative kind of honey which is supposedly achieved by cultivation creates conditions of unbearable heat in the place where it grows (M_{192}). Conversely, we observed that wild, therefore natural, honey, and its metaphorical counterpart, the animal-seducer, carry with them a threat of decay.

Having reached this stage of the demonstration, I must check whether there is not a univocal correlation between the tapped-out (or whistled) call, and, on the one hand, the noise of the bull-roarers and, on the other, the burnt world and rotten world. The whole of the preceding argument would seem to establish, not only that each of these pairs of opposites is relevant in itself, but also that they are mutually concordant. However, we are about to see that serious complications arise at this point.

Let us take the case of the Bororo. They have an instrument of darkness, the parabára, and they also possess the bull-roarer. There is no doubt at all that the latter connotes the rotten world. The bull-roarer, which the Bororo call aigé, mimics the cry of a monster of the same name which is supposed to live in rivers and marshlands. The animal appears in certain rites, in the form of a dancer who is encased in mud from head to foot. The future priest learns of his vocation during a dream in which the aigé embraces him, without his experiencing fear or revulsion either at the monster's smell or at the stench of decayed corpses (Colb. 3, pp. 130, 163; *EB*, Vol. I, under 'ai-je' and 'aroe et-awaraare'). It is much more difficult to arrive at a definite conclusion regarding the symbolism of the parabára, about which practically nothing is known. The imaginary instrument in M$_{304}$, which belongs to the same family, is used to entice a demon out of the hut, i.e. to cause disjunction between him and the inhabitants of the village, and bring about conjunction with the fire in which he is to perish. On the strength of certain observations which I described on p. 370, we might be tempted to attribute the same significance to the Bororo rite of the parabára, since it features in practices which would seem to be intended to make sure that the soul has finally left the temporary grave prepared for it in the centre of the village. But it is only in the myths that the Bororo end on a funeral pyre. In real life, the bones of the dead, after being washed so as to remove all traces of flesh, are thrown into the river.

It follows that the contrast between the bull-roarer and the parabára reflects not so much the opposition between the rotten world and the burnt world as two possible procedures in relationship to the rotten world. The aigé, which is heralded by the noise of the bull-roarers, emerges from water, whereas the soul, which is conditioned by the rattle of the parabáras, moves towards water. But the water is not the same in both instances. The water in which the aigé lives is muddy and stinks of decayed corpses, whereas the bones which have been cleaned, painted and decorated with feathers cannot possibly pollute the clear waters of the lake or river into which they are dropped.

In the case of the Sherente, whose myths are strikingly symmetrical with those of the Bororo (*RC*, pp. 192–5), and present, in terms of fire, problems which the Bororo myths express in terms of water, the bull-roarer is not the voice of a Spirit who is about to appear, but the call which summons him to appear. The Spirit is celestial, not aquatic. He personifies the planet Mars, the companion of the Moon, just as Venus and Jupiter are the companions of the sun (Nim. 6, p. 85). It would seem, then, that the Sherente bull-roarer is associated with the least 'fiery' mode of the sky, and the Bororo bull-roarer with the most 'putrid' mode of water. As it happens, the Sherente also define the two modes of the sky, one diurnal, the other nocturnal, in relation to water. During the ceremonies of the Great Fast, the priests of Venus and Jupiter offer the performers clear water in bowls made from gourds (respectively *Lagenaria* and *Crescentia*), whereas the priests of Mars offer soiled water in a bowl decorated with feathers (Nim. 6, p. 97). This gives the following equivalences:

Bororo　　　　　　　　　　　　　*Sherente*

(dirty water : clean water) ::　　　[(night : day) ::

　　　　　　　　　　　　　　　　　　(dirty water : clean water)]

This is a revealing formula, in that the 'long night' described by so many South American myths certainly refers to the rotten world, just as the myths about the universal fire refer to the burnt world. This being so, are we not forced to the conclusion that it is the bull-roarer, not the clapper, which plays the part of instrument of 'darkness' in America, whereas the other instrument belongs to a contrasting category which we have been unable to identify? As we move from the Old World to the New, only the form of the contrast seems to remain constant, while the content appears to be reversed.

Nevertheless, it is impossible to be satisfied with this solution, since there is an Amazonian myth connecting darkness with an instrument which has no doubt been imagined but which, from the organological point of view, is closer to the clapper or rattle than to the bull-roarer:

M_{326a}. *The Tupi of the Amazon. 'The origin of night'*

In former times, night did not exist. It was daylight all the time. Night slept beneath the waters. Animals did not exist either, for things themselves had the power of speech.

The daughter of the Great Snake had married an Indian, who was master of three faithful servants. 'Go away,' he said to them one day, 'for my wife refuses to sleep with me.' But it was not their presence which embarrassed the young woman. She wanted to make love only at night. She explained to her husband that her father held night prisoner, and that he should send his servants to fetch it.

When they arrived in a canoe at the abode of the Great Snake, the latter handed them a tightly closed nut of the tucuman (*Astrocaryum tucuman*) palm, and told them not to open it under any pretext. The servants re-embarked and were soon surprised to hear a noise coming from the nut: ten, ten ... xi, like the sound of crickets and little toads which sing at night. One servant wanted to open the nut, but the others were opposed to the idea. After a good deal of discussion and after they had travelled a long way from the Great Snake's abode, they eventually all assembled in the middle of the canoe where they lit a fire and melted the resin sealing the nut. At once night fell and all things that were in the forest changed into quadrupeds and birds; those in the river became ducks and fish. The basket turned into a jaguar, the fisherman and his canoe became a duck: the man's head acquired a beak; the canoe became the body, the oars the feet ...

The darkness covering the world made it clear to the Snake's daughter what had happened. When the morning star appeared, she decided to separate night from day. With this end in view, she changed two balls of thread into birds – the cujubim and the inhambu [respectively of the cracidae and tinamidae families and which sing at regular intervals during the night or to greet the dawn; in connection with these 'bird-clocks', cf. RC, p. 204, n. 3]. As a punishment, she changed the disobedient servants into monkeys (Couto de Magalhães, pp. 231-3; cf. Derbyshire, pp. 16-22).

This myth raises some complex problems. Those relating to the trio of servants will be discussed in the next volume. For the time being, I am chiefly concerned with the three-fold contrast which provides the armature of the myth. The contrast between day and night is obvious, and implies two others: first, between the conjunction and the disjunction of the sexes, since day enforces the latter and night is the pre-condition of the former; then, between linguistic behaviour and non-linguistic behaviour: when there was continuous daylight, everything had the power of speech, even beasts and objects, and it was at the precise moment when night made its appearance that things became dumb and animals became unable to express themselves except by inarticulate cries.

Now, in the myth, the first appearance of night is the result of imprudent behaviour on the part of servants, who are playing on an instrument which is literally one of the instruments of darkness, since it contains darkness and since darkness escapes when the aperture is unsealed and is spread abroad in the form of noisy, nocturnal animals – insects and batrachians – which are precisely those the names of which denote the instruments of darkness in the Old World: the frog, the toad, the cicada, the grasshopper, the cricket, etc. The theory that a category corresponding to our European instruments of darkness might exist among the mythic symbols of the New World is given definitive confirmation by the presence, among these symbols, of an instrument which is precisely an instrument of darkness in the literal sense, whereas, the similar instruments in Western mythology can only be given the appellation in a figurative sense.

But, if the instrument of darkness in M_{326a} is connected with night, and if night appears in the myth as a necessary pre-condition for the union of the sexes,[19] it follows that the instrument associated with their disunion, the bull-roarer, must by implication be linked with daylight, which fulfils the same function. This would give us a four-fold correlation between night, the union of the sexes, non-linguistic behaviour and the instrument of darkness, contrasting term for term with the correlation between daylight, the disunion of the sexes, universalized linguistic behaviour and the bull-roarer. Apart from the fact that it is difficult to see how the bull-roarer could denote a form of linguistic behaviour, this way of presenting the problem merely reverses the difficulty we encountered in connection with the Bororo and the Sherente. I concluded that, among these Indians, the bull-roarer related to night, and this, in the perspective of a general interpretation, put the instruments of darkness (which we found to be in opposition to the bull-roarer) on the side of daylight. And now, the more normal linking up of the instruments of darkness with night would seem to involve relating the bull-roarer to day, and this contradicts everything we have accepted so far. The situation must therefore be examined more closely.

M_{326a} does not mention the bull-roarer. It does, however, refer to a period when night was guarded by a great snake (whose cry is believed by the Toba to resemble that of the bull-roarer) and when it 'slept beneath the waters' (like the aquatic monster which the Bororo call aigé, 'bull-roarer', and whose cry the bull-roarer imitates). We also know that, in almost every region where the bull-roarer exists, its function is to cause the disjunction of the female sex, and to put women back into the category of nature, outside the sacred and socialized world. Now M_{326a} is a myth belonging to the northern Tupi, that is, to a culture and a region whose mythology describes the great snake as a phallic being in whom all the attributes of virility were concentrated at a time when men themselves had none. They were unable to copulate with their wives, and were obliged to request the services of the snake. This state of affairs came to an end when the demiurge cut the snake's body up into pieces, which he then used to endow each man with the mem-

[19] But not in all respects. Although night is a necessary pre-condition for sexual communication, by a compensatory movement which is intended to restore the balance, night would seem to forbid linguistic communication between the partners. Such, at least, is the case among the Tucano, who allow conversation between people of opposite sexes during the day-time, but only between people of the same sex at night (Silva, pp. 166–7, 417). Individuals of opposite sexes can exchange either words or caresses, but not both at the same time, since this would be considered an abuse of communication.

brum virile he lacked (M_{80}). Consequently Tupi mythology presents the snake as a (socially) disjunctive penis, a view which had already been forced upon us by the function and symbolism of the bull-roarer. And this also is the function assumed by the Great Snake in M_{326a} in its capacity as a misbehaving father and not as a corrupt seducer: he gives away his daughter but he does not relinquish night, and without night the marriage cannot be consummated. In this respect, M_{326a} links up with a group of myths we have already studied (M_{259}–M_{269}), in which another aquatic monster presents the man it has accepted as its son-in-law – and who, in certain versions, happens to be none other than the sun, that is, daylight – with a wife who is incomplete and therefore impossible to penetrate: a girl without a vagina, symmetrical with the men without penises in M_{80}, and the reverse of the girl with the (symbolically) over-large vagina in the tapir-as-seducer cycle, the tapir being an animal with a large penis, which I showed on p. 411 to be a combinatory variant of the great snake, which is 'all penis', and which brings us back to our starting-point.

I will leave it to others to explore the complexities of this link-up, for as soon as we pause to examine mythic connections we discover that the pattern they form is so densely interwoven that the investigator who tries to grasp all the details despairs of ever making any headway. But, given the fact that the structural analysis of myths is still in a rudimentary stage, I think it preferable (since a choice has to be made) to forge ahead and mark out a path, even though we are uncertain of our aims, rather than opt for the slow and sure procedures which will one day make it possible for others to follow the same road at an even pace, and to catalogue the riches found along it.

If the comparisons just made are legitimate, we can perhaps now glimpse a possible way out of our difficulties. Let us, then, relate the bull-roarer to night of which it is the master, in the guise of the snake; and let us accept the fact that the instrument of darkness is also related to night. But the night in the one case is not exactly the same as the night in the other. They are alike only in being excessive. The night of the bull-roarer avoids daylight, whereas the night of the instrument of darkness invades daylight. It follows, strictly speaking, that neither of these 'nights' is in opposition to daylight, but rather to the empirically proved alternation in which day and night, far from being mutually exclusive, are united by a reciprocal mediatory relationship: day mediatizes the transition from night to night, and night the transition from daylight to daylight. If the terms 'night' are removed from this periodic sequence which has an objective reality, only day is left, culturizing nature, as it were, in the form of an improper extension of linguistic behaviour to animals and things. Conversely, if the terms 'day' are removed from the sequence, only night is left, naturalizing culture by the transformation of the products of human industry into animals.

The problem which was holding us up can be solved, once we recognize the operative value of a three-term system: day on its own, night on its own, and the regular alternation of the two. The system comprises two simple terms and one complex one consisting of a harmonious relationship between the first two. It provides the framework within which myths of origin, whether concerned with the origin of day or night, divide up into two distinct kinds, according to whether they place day or night at the beginning of the existing alternation. We can therefore distinguish between myths with a nocturnal preliminary and myths with a diurnal preliminary. M_{326a} belongs to the second category. The initial choice has an important consequence in that it necessarily gives precedence to one of the two terms. In the case of myths with a diurnal preliminary, which are the ones we are concerned with here, there was only day in the first instance, and although night existed, it was in a state of disjunction from daylight and remained, as it were, behind the scenes. This being so, the other possibility can no longer materialize in an exactly symmetrical form. Day was formerly where night was not; and when night replaces it (before their regular alternation is established) it can only do so by taking over where day was *before it*. We can thus understand why, by virtue of this hypothesis, the 'long day' is the result of an *initial state* of disjunction, and the 'long night' the result of a *subsidiary act* of conjunction.

On the formal level, these two situations correspond clearly to those I previously distinguished as the rotten world and the burnt world. But from the moment of my evolving this distinction, something happened in the myths. Almost imperceptibly, they moved from a spatial field to a temporal scale and, what is more, from the notion of absolute space to that of relative time. My third volume will be almost entirely devoted to the theory of this major transformation. For the time being, I am concerned merely to bring out a limited aspect of it.

In the absolute space referred to by the myths about the origin of cooking, the high position is occupied by the sky or the sun, and the low position by the earth. Before cooking fire appeared as a mediatory term between these two extremes (uniting them, while at the same time maintaining a reasonable distance between them), their relationships were inevitably characterized by imbalance: they were too near to each other or too far away from each other. The first possibility relates to the burnt world, which connotes fire and light; the second to the rotten world, which connotes darkness and night.

But M_{326a} is situated in relative time, where the mediatory term is not a being or a distinct object standing between two extreme terms. The mediation consists rather in the equilibrium between terms which are not intrinsically extreme, but which can become extreme as a result of the deterioration of the relationship linking them together. If the myth under consideration has a diurnal preliminary, the remoteness of night, that is, its disjunction from day, ensures the reign of light, and its proximity to (or conjunction with) day ensures the reign of darkness. Consequently, according to whether the myth is thought of within the context of absolute space or of relative time, the same signifieds (conjunction and disjunction) will call for opposite signifiers. This reversal is, however, no more relevant than that of the names of the notes of a scale, as a result of a change in the key-signature. In such a case, what counts in the first place is not the absolute position of the notes on, or between, the lines, but the key-signature inscribed at the beginning of the stave.

The bull-roarer and the instrument of darkness are the ritual signifiers of a disjunction and a conjunction, both non-mediatized, which, when transposed into a different tessitura, have as their conceptual signifiers the rotten world and the burnt world. The fact that the same signifieds, in so far as they consist of relationships between objects, can, when these objects are not the same, admit of contrasting signifiers, does not mean that these contrasting signifiers have a signified/signifier relationship with each other.

In formulating the above rule, I am merely extending to the domain of mythic thought De Saussure's principle of the arbitrary character of the linguistic sign, except that the field of application of the principle here acquires an additional dimension, because of the fact (to which I have already drawn attention elsewhere, L.-S. 9, p. 31) that, where myth and ritual are concerned, the same elements can equally well play the part of signified and signifier, and replace each other in each function.

In spite of, or because of this complication, mythic thought is so respectful of this principle that it is careful to assign quite distinct semantic fields to the bull-roarer and the instrument of darkness (which, from the formal point of view, constitute a pair). Why is it the bull-roarer's function, almost the whole world over, to drive women away? Is it not because it would be practically impossible for the bull-roarer to signify disjunction between night and day – the reign of daylight in the middle of night – unlike the instrument of darkness, which brings about conjunction between them? Of this conjunction, the eclipse provides at least one empirical illustration, and when we consider 'darkness' from this viewpoint it appears as a particular kind of eclipse, marked by a particular kind of charivari (*RC*, pp. 286–9). The use of the bull-roarer does more than just reverse this relationship; it transposes it by removing all the feminine terms in the periodic sequence of matrimonial unions. And is it not for this reason that the sequence presents, on the sociological level, an equivalent of the cosmological sequence formed by the regular alternation of day and night?

$$
\left(
\begin{array}{l}
\overline{\triangle = \bigcirc} \quad \overline{\triangle = \bigcirc} \quad \overline{\triangle = \bigcirc} \quad \overline{\triangle = \bigcirc} \quad \text{etc.}
\end{array}
\right)
$$

$\equiv$ (day-night, day-night, day-night, day-night, etc.)

We can say, then, that society, temporarily reduced by the bull-roarer to its masculine elements after the isolation and removal of the feminine elements, is like the course of time reduced to day only. Conversely, the Kayapo, who do not seem to have bull-roarers (Dreyfus, p. 129), use the knocking together of sticks to signify a set of circumstances which is symmetrical with that associated elsewhere with the bull-roarer: in their case, they are concerned with establishing the conjugal bond between a man and a woman, and with promiscuity rites (cf. above, p. 371). Lastly, while the instruments of darkness can denote conjunction between day and night, and between the sexes too, we already know that they denote the union of the sky and the earth. In this last respect, it would be interesting to study the part assigned to clappers and similar instruments during the festivities which greet the return of the Pleiades. I shall return later to the Chaco ceremonies, merely pointing out at this point, that, on the north-west coast of North America, rattles (used only for the winter ritual) are replaced by clappers for the spring festival, called meitla, at which the Kwakiutl wear an ornament representing the Pleiades (Boas 3, p. 502; Drucker, pp. 205, 211, 218; cf. also Olson, p. 175 and Boas 2, pp. 552–3).

2 *The Harmony of the Spheres*

It follows from what has gone before that the bull-roarer and the instrument of darkness do not effect conjunction or disjunction pure and simple. We ought rather to say that the two instruments effect conjunction *with* the phenomena of conjunction and disjunction: they conjoin the social group or the world at large to the possibility of one or other of these relationships, the common feature of which is that they exclude mediation. If the acoustic code forms a system, a third type of instrument must therefore exist, denoting the act of mediation.

We know what this instrument is in the European tradition, which establishes a complex network of relationships between the instruments of darkness and bells, according to whether the latter are absent or present and, if present, whether they are marked or unmarked:

INSTRUMENTS/
OF DARKNESS/   (BELLS:
marked/unmarked..................................absent   /present)

Shrove Tuesday...............*Lent*............*(triduum)*   /*Easter Sunday*

I propose to show, first of all, that in South America the gourd rattle or rattles (for they are normally found in pairs) represent the instrument of mediation; next, that just as the instruments of darkness appeared as being linked with honey, an excellent food for the tropical 'Lent' represented by the dry season, rattles have a symmetrical relationship with tobacco.

M₃₂₇. Warao. 'The origin of tobacco and of the first medicine-man'

An Indian had been living with a woman for a long long time; she was very good at making hammocks but could not bear a child. So he took a second wife by whom he had a child called Kurusiwari. The youngster used constantly to bother the step-mother as she was weaving her hammocks, and prevented her getting on with her work. One day she roughly pushed the child aside. He fell and cried, then

left the house unnoticed even by his parents, who were lying together in a hammock, with their minds no doubt on other things.

It was late in the day when his presence was missed. His parents
set out to look for him and found him in a neighbour's house playing
with some other children. The father and mother explained their
errand and entered into an animated conversation with their hosts.
When the Indian and his wife finally finished talking, not only had
their own child disappeared once more, but one of the children of
the house, Matura-wari, was nowhere to be seen. The same thing
happened in a third house, with the same result. The two boys had
gone, taking with them a third child called Kawai-wari.

It was a case now of six parents searching for three infants. At the
end of the first day the third couple abandoned the search, and at the
end of the second day the second couple did likewise. In the meantime, the three children had wandered on and on and had made
friends with the wasps, which in those days talked but did not sting.
It was these children that told the black ones to sting people, and
the red ones to give them fever in addition.

It was when the children arrived at the sea-shore that the first pair
of parents caught up with them. By this time they had grown into
big boys. When the parents begged them to return home, the leader
of the three, the boy who had been lost from the first house, refused,
saying that his step-mother had ill-treated him and that his parents
had paid no attention to him. Both father and mother implored him
with tears to return, but all he would promise was that he would
appear if they built him a temple (Spirit-house) and 'called' him with
tobacco. Thereupon, the three boys crossed the seas and the parents
returned to the village, where the father started building the prescribed Spirit-house. He burnt pappaia leaves, cotton leaves and
coffee leaves, but all in vain: there was no 'strength' in any of them.
But in those days men knew nothing of tobacco, which grew on an
island in the middle of the sea. The island was called 'Man-without',
because it was peopled entirely by women. The sorrowing father sent
a gaulding bird (*Pilerodius*) to fetch some of the tobacco seed: he never
returned, and the other sea-birds he sent all met with the same fate.
They were all killed by the woman guarding the tobacco field.

The Indian went to consult his brother who brought him a crane.
The bird went to roost down near the sea-shore so as to have a good
start the following morning. A humming-bird asked him what he
was doing, and suggested that he should go instead. In spite of the

crane's efforts to dissuade him, the humming-bird set off at dawn. When the crane sailing majestically along met the humming-bird, he saw him struggling in the water in great danger of drowning. The crane picked him up and placed him on the back of his own thighs. Now, this position was all very well for the humming-bird so long as no accident occurred, but when the crane commenced to relieve himself, the humming-bird's face got dirtied (cf. M$_{310}$). He decided to take to the wing again and arrived at the island well ahead of the crane. The latter agreed to wait while the humming-bird went to fetch the seeds. Since he was small and swift in flight, the watchwoman failed to kill him.

The two birds, who now had the wind behind them, flew together until they reached the village where the humming-bird delivered the seed to the crane's master, who handed them to his brother, telling him how to plant the tobacco, then how to cure the leaves and choose the bark to make the cigarettes. He also sent him to collect gourds but kept only the one which had grown on the east side of the tree (cf. p. 347 and n. 35). The man then started singing to the accompaniment of the rattle. His son and the other two lads appeared. They were now the three Spirits of tobacco and always came in answer to the call of the rattle. For the father himself had become the first medicine-man, all through his great grief at losing his child and longing so much to see him once more (Roth 1, pp. 334–6).

Another Warao myth on the same theme can be treated as a variant of the previous one:

M$_{328}$. *Warao. 'The origin of tobacco and of the first medicine-man'* (2)

An Indian called Komatari wanted some tobacco which, at that time, grew on an island out at sea. He first of all approached a man who lived alone on the shore and whom he mistakenly took to be the master of tobacco. A humming-bird joined in their conversation and suggested going to fetch some tobacco leaves. But he made a mistake and brought back tobacco flowers. So the man who lived on the shore set off for the island and succeeded in eluding the people who were keeping watch over the tobacco. He came back with his corial full of leaves and seeds, with which Komatari filled his basket. The stranger took leave of Komatari, but refused to give his name. He said the other would find it out for himself when he became a medicine-man.

Komatari refused to share the tobacco with his companions. He hung the leaves under the roof of his house and left them in charge of the wasps. The latter allowed themselves to be bribed by a visitor who offered them fish and who stole some of the tobacco leaves. Komatari noticed that some tobacco leaves were missing and drove away all the wasps except one particular kind, which he made his watch-men. Then he cleared a small area in the forest and planted his tobacco.

From four Spirits, whom he met in turn but who all refused to tell their names, he obtained the calabash tree, feathers and cotton-twine which were to decorate the first rattle, and the stones which would make it reverberate. Warned by the hero that the finished rattle would be used to destroy them, the Spirits took their revenge by causing diseases. But to no avail; thanks to the rattle, Komatari cured all the sick people, except one man whose condition was too serious. It would ever be thus: some patients would be saved, others could not be saved. Of course, Komatari now knew the names of all the Spirits. The first one he met who procured the tobacco seeds for him was called Wau-uno (Anura in Arawak) 'White Crane' (Roth 1, pp. 336–8).

These two myths, which deal with the origin of shamanistic powers, clearly consider them from two complementary points of view: the summoning-up of the guardian Spirits, or the expulsion of the evil spirits. The bird (*Pilerodius*) which, in M$_{327}$, failed to bring back the tobacco is the embodiment of one of the Spirits responsible for diseases (Roth 1, p. 349). In both cases, conjunction or disjunction is brought about through the mediation of the rattles and tobacco. It can already be seen that, as I forecast, the two terms are linked.

In both myths, the crane and the humming-bird form a pair, and the respective significance of each bird is reversed according to whether the myth considers shamanism in the one light or the other. The humming-bird is superior to the crane in M$_{327}$, but inferior in M$_{328}$. Its inferiority is shown in its naive preference, which is in keeping with its nature, for tobacco flowers rather than tobacco leaves or seeds. On the other hand, the superiority it shows in M$_{327}$ is acquired only at the cost of a denial of its own nature. Normally, it is associated with dryness (*RC*, pp. 205–6) and a pleasant smell (Roth 1, p. 371), but the humming-bird in M$_{327}$ is in danger of drowning and has its face spattered with dung. The 'tobacco road' leads through excrement. In recalling this fact, M$_{327}$ testifies to the objective reality of the progression which led us from honey (itself bordering on excrement and poison) to tobacco. In short, we took the same road as the humming-bird, and the gradual transformation of myths about the origin of honey into myths about the origin of tobacco, a transformation the various stages of which have been described throughout the present work, is reduplicated on a small scale in the Guiana myths which change the smallest bird from a *honey-eater* into a *tobacco-producer*.

Of the two Warao myths, M_{327} is certainly the more complex, and I propose to follow it rather than M_{328}. Two women play an important part in it: one is a skilful weaver, although sterile, while the other is fertile. In Tacana mythology, which I have often compared with the mythology of the northerly regions of South America, female sloths married to humans make the best weavers (M_{329}; H.-H., p. 287). The same point is made in the Waiwai myth about the origin of the Shodewika festival (M_{388}): in former times, only Indians and sloths (*Choloepus*) knew how to make fibre costumes (Fock, p. 57 and n. 39, p. 70).

How are we to explain the attribution of such a talent to the sloth, whose habits hardly predispose it for such an activity? No doubt because the usual position of the sloth, hanging upside down from a branch, is reminiscent of a hammock. Myths about the origin of sloths confirm that the resemblance has not passed unnoticed: they describe the sloth as a transformed hammock, or as a man lying in a hammock (M_{330}, Mundurucu, Murphy 1, p. 121; M_{247}, Baré, Amorim, p. 145). But two significant features in M_{327} enable us to carry the interpretation still further: on the one hand, no explicit reference is made to the sloth; on the other hand, the woman who takes its place as an expert weaver forms a pair with another woman, about whom no details are given except that she is fertile.

I have already explained above (p. 396) that the sloth is a very small eater and only defecates once or twice a week, on the ground and always in the same place. Such habits were bound to attract the attention of the Indians, who consider the control of the excretory functions to be of paramount importance. Commenting on the native custom of inducing vomiting on awakening in order to eliminate all the food which has remained in the stomach overnight (cf. *RC*, p. 241), Spruce (Vol. II, p. 454) notes that 'Indians are less keen to defecate first thing in the morning than to empty their stomachs of food. On the contrary, everywhere in South America, I have noticed that Indians who have a hard day's work in front of them and not much to eat, prefer to postpone evacuation until nightfall. They are better than white men at controlling their natural functions, and seem to respect the maxim which an Indian from San Carlos expressed to me in very approximate Spanish: *Quien caga de mañana es guloso*, 'the man who has his bowels opened in the morning is a glutton.' The Tucano takes a broader, metaphorical view of the connection, when they forbid the canoe- or net-maker to have his bowels opened before the object he is working on is finished, for fear that it might be holed (Silva, p. 368 and *passim*).

In this area, as in others, to yield to nature is to be a bad member of society. This being so, it can happen, at least in the myths, that the being most able to resist nature, will *ipso facto* be the most gifted in respect of cultural aptitudes. The retention which takes the outward form of sterility in the skilful weaver in M_{327} transposes into a different register – that of the reproductive function – the retention characteristic of the sloth on the eliminatory level. The first wife who suffered from genital constipation, although she was a good weaver, is in contrast to the second wife whose fertility seems to be offset by indolence, since she is shown disporting with her husband during the day.[20]

These observations necessitate two further comments. First, it has already been noted that, as regards defecation, the sloth stands in opposition to the howler monkey, which releases its droppings at any moment from the tops of trees. As its name implies, this monkey howls, but mostly when there is a change of weather:

> *Guariba na serra*
> *Chuva na terra*

> When the guariba monkey is heard in the hills,
> there will be rain in the land

is a popular saying (Ihering, under 'guariba'), which is in keeping with the Bororo belief that this species of monkey is a Spirit of rain (*EB*, Vol. I, p. 371). Now, a sudden fall in temperature also makes the sloth come down to the ground to defecate: 'When the wind blows, the sloth walks,' is an Arawak saying (Roth 1, p. 369), and a naturalist (Enders, p. 7) obtained stools regularly every five days from a sloth in captivity by moistening its hind-quarters with cold water. Conse-

[20] The ancients also believed there was a connection between the state of being a weaver and amorous capabilities: but they thought of it as being directly proportional, not in inverse ratio: 'The Grecians described Women-Weavers to bee more hot and earnestly luxurious than other women, because of their sitting trade without any violent exercise of the body ... I might likewise say of these that the same stirring which their labour so sitting doth give them, doth rouze and sollicit them ... ' (Montaigne, *Essays*, trans. John Florio, Vol. III, Ch. XI).

quently, the howler monkey and the sloth are 'barometric' animals, the one honouring this state by its excretions, the other by its howls. As a mode of din, the howling is a metaphorical transposition of filth (cf. p. 209, n. 9, p. 310).

This is not all. Howler monkeys cry noisily and in groups at sunrise and sunset. The sloth is a solitary animal which at night-time emits a faint musical cry 'like a penetrating whistle, beginning on D sharp above middle C and holding true for several seconds' (Beebe, pp. 35–7). According to an old author, the sloth cries 'ha, ha, ha, ha, ha, ha' at night (Oviedo y Valdes in Britton, p. 14). However, the description suggests that the animal in question may be the *Choloepus* and not the *Bradypus*, that is, the large and not the small sloth, to which the other observation referred.

If we take into account the fact that, according to the Tacana myths (M_{322}–M_{323}), any attack on a sloth engaged in the normal exercise of its eliminatory functions would cause a universal conflagration – a belief which, as we saw, is echoed in Guiana (cf. *RC*, p. 315, n. 19), where it is thought that any such attack would expose humanity to the perils resulting from the conjunction of celestial fire with the earth – it is tempting to detect, behind the acoustic aspect of the contrast between the howler monkey and the sloth, one of which is endowed with a 'terrifying' cry, according to the Acawai (Brett 2, pp. 130–32), while the other is doomed to a discreet whistle, according to a Baré myth (Amorim, p. 145), the contrast between the bull-roarer, a 'howling' instrument, and the instruments of darkness.

We now come to the second point, which takes us back to the actual text of the Guiana myths about the origin of tobacco. As it has just been elucidated, the nature of the opposition between the two women in M_{327} brings the first wife, who is sterile and gifted purely from the cultural viewpoint, into contrast with the girl mad about honey in the Chaco and Guiana myths. The second woman is homologous to the latter, since she too shows herself to be lascivious and fertile (cf. M_{135}). On the other hand, and as is normal when we move from myths about the origin of honey to myths about the origin of tobacco, the position of the whimpering child, the term common to both groups, is radically reversed. In one group, he is driven out because he is crying, in the other, he is crying because he has been driven out. In the first instance, it is the woman who can be assimilated to the girl mad about honey who drives him out, because she is exasperated by his crying: in the other instance, the woman whose role is in opposition to that played by the girl mad about honey is responsible, whereas the woman whose role is analogous remains indifferent to the child's crying. Finally, whereas the 'normal' crying baby remains near the house, calling for its mother until some animal, congruous with the girl mad about honey – a vixen or a frog – carries it off, its counterpart in M_{327} chooses to go off of its own accord and makes friends with the marabunta wasps.

This generic name is too vague to allow us to affirm that the marabunta wasps belong to a honey-producing species, and thus are in opposition to the animal abductors which the myths present as greedy consumers of honey. But it is possible to demonstrate the point in another way. Let us note, first of all, that M_{327} and M_{328}, in which wasps play almost identical parts, deal with the origin of shamanism. Now the Guiana sorcerer possesses a special power over wasps. He can drive them all out by knocking with his fingers against the nest, without a single wasp stinging him (Roth 1, p. 341).[21] I have already drawn attention to the existence among the more southerly Kayapo of a ritual battle with wasps.

According to M_{327} and M_{328}, wasps became poisonous because of their very close relationship with shamans or their guardian Spirits. The transformation which was brought about by the whimpering child in M_{327} and by the hero in M_{328} reproduces the transformation that a Botocudo myth (M_{204}) attributes to the irára, an animal which is particularly fond of honey. We thus rediscover a contrast between wasps – which have undergone a transformation through a character replacing the irára in the Botocudo myth – and the abducting animals, which are moreover honey-eaters, that is, congruous with the irára in certain conditions that have already been mentioned (p. 249).

This comparison takes us quite a long way back, but we find ourselves even further back once we have noticed that M_{327} attributes man's lack of tobacco to the unmarried women who keep watch over it on an island; they are Amazons, and 'mad about tobacco'. Now, several

---

21 But before doing so, he draws his fingers under his armpits. The Tucano do likewise, when they discover a wasp's nest. 'The smell drives the wasps out and the Indians seize the nest full of larvae; the nest acts as a plate, flour is tipped into it and eaten with the larvae' (Silva, p. 222, n. 53). The Cubeo dialect (Goldman, p. 182, n. 1) associates body hair and tobacco: 'body hair' is pwa, and underarm hair is called pwa butci, 'tobacco-hair'. The same Indians carry out a ritual burning of cut hair; they burn it in the same way as tobacco for smoking is burnt.

Guiana myths and one or two Ge myths connect the origin of Amazons with the separation of the sexes which followed on the murder of the jaguar or the cayman (combinatory variants of the tapir-seducer), which the women had taken as lovers (M_{156}, M_{287}). I have established that these women are themselves a variant of the girl mad about honey, transposed into the terminology of the sexual code. The myths we are now dealing with confirm this: on leaving their husbands, the Apinayé Amazons carry off the ceremonial axes; those in the Warao myths have sole control of tobacco which, like the axes, is a cultural symbol. In order to be conjoined with the tapir, the cayman or the jaguar – i.e. with nature – the adulterous women have recourse either to the *tapped* gourd or to the proper *name* of the animal which they imprudently *reveal*. Symmetrically, the Warao shaman's supernatural power is expressed by the rattle which is a *shaken* gourd, and by the *name* of the Spirits whose secret he has *penetrated*.

The Warao myths about the origin of tobacco contain an episode which takes us even further back, right back in fact to the beginning of our inquiry. The humming-bird's flight across a vast stretch of water to fetch tobacco growing on a supernatural island, and so that tobacco can be linked with rattles, refers back to M_1, in which we encountered the same theme for the first time, in the form of a quest, also undertaken by the humming-bird which also went to a supernatural island to fetch, not tobacco, but the rattles themselves – musical instruments which the hero must not cause to sound if he is to be successfully disjoined from the Spirits; whereas in the Warao myth, men are only able to summon the good Spirits and drive away the bad, as they wish, if they cause the instruments to sound.

A superficial study might lead to the assumption that the humming-bird's quest constitutes the only element common to both M_1 and M_{327}. But in fact the analogy between the two myths goes much deeper.

It follows from the interpretation I have already suggested of the character of the crying baby that the latter reproduces the hero of M_1 in terms of the acoustic code. Both refuse to be disjoined from their mothers, although they express their attachment by different means – one by vocal the other by erotic behaviour, passive in the first case, active in the second. The little boy in M_{327} is a whimpering child, but reversed, and so we can expect him to behave in a reverse manner to the hero of M_1. The latter is loath to join the men's house, loath therefore to become an adult member of society. The child in M_{327} shows a precocious interest in cultural activities, particularly those carried out by women, since he keeps on interrupting the making of hammocks, which is a feminine occupation.

Both heroes are boys; one is already quite grown-up, although his incestuous behaviour indicates moral infantilism; the other is still very young but his independence of spirit makes him reach physical maturity at a very early age. In each case, the father has two wives – the child's mother and a step-mother. In M_1, the child is conjoined with the mother, in M_{327} he is disjoined by the step-mother. The conjugal pair in M_{327} corresponds to the incestuous pair in M_1; the grievances of the son, whose filial rights have been encroached upon by the father, correspond to the grievances of the father, whose conjugal rights have been encroached upon by the son. It will be noted that, whereas in the Bororo myth the father complains that his son has supplanted him in an amorous capacity (and therefore as an adult), the son in the Warao myth complains that his parents are too amorously engaged with each other to pay attention to his crying.

The outraged father in M_1 tries first of all to bring about his son's death in water, but three helpful animals aid the boy, thus forming a counterpart to the three children in M_{327} who choose to cross the sea. It will be objected that the hero of M_{327} is one of these three children, whereas the hero in M_1 obtains the help of three animals without being fused with any one of them. This means that there are four characters in M_1, against three in M_{327}. But because of their inverted symmetry, a two-fold difficulty would arise if the two myths were to follow a parallel course. On the one hand, the hero of M_1 returns physically to his own people, whereas the hero in M_{327} comes back 'in spirit' only. On the other hand, the former *brings back* rain and storms, which are therefore to be the *consequence* of his return, whereas the tobacco *fetched* from a long way away is the cause of the latter's return. In the interests of symmetry the same character in M_{327} must be at one and the same time absent (since he has to be brought back) and present (since he has a mission to perform).

M_{327} solves the difficulty by reduplicating the roles. In the first part, a small child acts as the hero; in the second part, a small bird takes over the role. But if, as I am suggesting, the humming-bird is a doublet of the hero, it is clear that even in the first part, where one character virtually assumes both roles, the four characters in M_1, that is one child and three animals (one of which is a humming-bird), must correspond to the three children (one of whom will be changed into a humming-bird) since, in respect of M_{327}, the child and the humming-bird count as one character:

M_1 : (boy)	humming-bird	pigeon	grasshopper
M_{327} : boy[1]	(humming-bird)	boy[2]	boy[3]

In the rest of the story, the hero in M_1 undergoes vertical disjunction while collecting the eggs of macaws, which (M_7–M_{12}) cover him with their droppings. The hero of M_{327}, in the course of his horizontal disjunction, forms an alliance with wasps, which he turns into a poisonous species. This gives a four-fold contrast:

(*macaws/wasps*), (*hostility/friendliness*), (hero = OBJECT in respect of filth/SUBJECT in respect of poison)

The contrast between poisonous insects and filth-producing birds enabled me (*RC*, p. 315, n. 19) to effect a transformation between a Parintintin myth (M_{179}) and the Ge variants of the bird-nester myth (M_7–M_{12}), which deal with the origin of (terrestrial) cooking fire, whereas M_1, which is a transformation of these myths, deals with the origin of (celestial) water. I have just transformed another myth into M_1 and it can be observed that the initial twist shown by M_1 in relation to M_7–M_{12} is maintained in the new transformation as follows:

(*a*) M_7–M_{12} (origin of fire) $\Rightarrow$ M_1 (origin of water)
(*b*) M_{179} (object of poison) $\Rightarrow$ M_7–M_{12} (object of filth)
(*c*) M_1 (enemy of macaws) $\Rightarrow$ M_{327} (friend of wasps)
(*d*) M_{327} (subject of poison) $\Rightarrow$ M_7–M_{12} (object of filth)

Taking into account the dislocation referred to above and which, in M_{327}, results in the partial overlapping of two episodes which are consecutive in M_1, I now propose to examine the sequence in M_{327} devoted to the humming-bird's journey.

The sequence can be divided into three parts: (1) the humming-bird sets out alone, falls into the water and is nearly drowned; (2) the crane rescues it and places it between its thighs, where it continues its journey in safety, even though its face is bespattered with dung; (3) the humming-bird sets off alone once more and finally gains possession of tobacco.

A word, first of all, on the subject of the crane. In spite of the uncertainty regarding the species thus referred to in the Guiana myths, I have been able to establish (p. 247) that the bird in question is a wader with a shrill cry, which produces din, and metaphorically, filth, as the part it plays in M_{327} corroborates in its own way. But while waders are a source of noise and metaphorical producers of filth, in real life they have a correlational and inverted relationship with filth, in their capacity as carrion-eaters with a fondness for dead fish (cf. p. 244). Since they represent the *oral resorption* of filth, they are thus closely linked with the sloth, which, as we have seen, is given to *anal retention* in those myths in which it appears. The Ipurina, who believe the sloth to be their ancestor, relate that at the beginning of time storks used to collect filth and decaying matter all over the world in order to boil it in a solar pot and subsequently eat it. The pot overflowed, spilling boiling water which destroyed all living beings except the sloth, which managed to climb to the top of a tree and repeopled the earth (M_{331}; Ehrenreich, p. 129; cf. Schultz 2, pp. 230–31).[22] This story throws light on an episode of a Jivaro origin myth, in which the sloth plays the same role as ancestor of the human race. For the reason why the heron stole the two eggs, one of which was to give birth to Mika, the future wife of Uñushi, the sloth (M_{332}, Stirling, pp. 125–6) was surely that, for the Jivaro, as for the tribes of north-western Amazonia and Guiana, birds' eggs come into the category of prohibited foods, because of their 'foetal and therefore impure character' (Whiffen, p. 130; cf. Im Thurn, p. 18), which makes them congruous with filth. An Aguaruna variant (M_{333a}) seems to confirm this: according to it, the sun emerged from an egg which had been taken by the ogre Agempi from the corpse of the woman he had killed, and which was subsequently stolen by a duck (Guallart, p. 61). According to a Maquiritaré myth (M_{333b}; M. Thomson, p. 5), two of the four eggs removed from the entrails of Moon, the hero's sister, were rotten.

As carrion-eaters, aquatic birds play, in respect of water, a part which is closely homologous to that which the myths attribute to vultures in respect of land. We can therefore suppose the existence of a correspondence between the three episodes of the humming-bird's journey in

[22] The tree in question belongs to the malvaceae family, which according to modern botanical systems is closely related to the tiliaceae and silk-cotton trees (cf. p. 392, n. 13). This gives a transformation of internal beneficent water into external maleficent water, which I refrain from discussing, to avoid prolonging the demonstration.

M_{327} and the three stages of the hero's adventures in M_1. This gives:

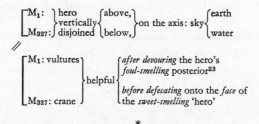

$$
\begin{array}{l}
\left[\begin{array}{l} M_1: \\ M_{327}: \end{array}\right\} \begin{array}{l} \text{hero} \\ \text{vertically} \\ \text{disjoined} \end{array} \left\{\begin{array}{l} \text{above,} \\ \text{below,} \end{array}\right\} \text{on the axis: sky} \left\{\begin{array}{l} \text{earth} \\ \text{water} \end{array}\right.
\end{array}
$$

$$
\left[\begin{array}{l} M_1: \text{vultures} \\ \\ \\ \\ M_{327}: \text{crane} \end{array}\right\} \text{helpful} \left\{\begin{array}{l} \textit{after devouring} \text{ the hero's} \\ \textit{foul-smelling} \text{ posterior}^{23} \\ \\ \textit{before defecating} \text{ onto the } \textit{face} \text{ of} \\ \text{the } \textit{sweet-smelling} \text{ 'hero'} \end{array}\right.
$$

*

So, throughout the paradigmatic set formed by myths M_1–M_{12}, which I dealt with at the beginning of my inquiry, there exist two mythologies of tobacco. The one, which I was able to illustrate by taking examples mainly from the Chaco, looks for the means of tobacco in the notion of terrestrial and destructive fire, in a correlational and oppositional relationship with cooking fire, which is also terrestrial but at the same time constructive, and the origin of which is outlined in the Ge myths (M_7–M_{12}). The other mythology of tobacco, which we encountered in the Warao myths, looks for the means of tobacco, in the notion of dominated terrestrial water (the ocean that the birds succeed in crossing), which is in correlation and opposition to celestial and dominating water (rain and storms), the origin of which is dealt with in the Bororo myth (M_1).

The two mythologies of tobacco therefore occupy symmetrical positions with regard to the initial paradigmatic set (see Figure 20 on p. 436); there is, however, one difference: the relationship between the Warao myths and M_1 presupposes a transformation with a double twist – *terrestrial/celestial dominated/dominating* water – whereas the relationship of the Chaco myths to the M_7–M_{12} group is a simpler one – *dominated/dominating* terrestrial fire – requiring only one twist. Let us dwell on this point for a moment.

At the beginning of this book, I analysed and discussed a myth belonging to the Iranxé, geographically close to the Bororo, which, in a very simple way, transformed a myth about the origin of water (M_1) into a myth about the origin of tobacco (M_{191}). So, in the Warao

[23] Since the humming-bird is by nature sweet-smelling, while in M_1 the urubus were attracted by the stench of decay emanating from the dead lizards which the hero had fastened onto his person. The reduplication: lizard, urubu-vultures in M_1, as respectively passive and active modes of decay, has its equivalent in M_{327} with the reduplication, 'gaulding bird' and crane; these are two waders associated with decay and which fail in their mission, one passively, the other actively.

myths, we are dealing with a transformation once removed. The disparity can be explained if we take certain cultural factors into account. Throughout tropical America south of the Amazon, i.e. in the areas inhabited by the Iranxé, the Bororo and the Chaco tribes, the consumption of tobacco in the form of an infusion or decoction was

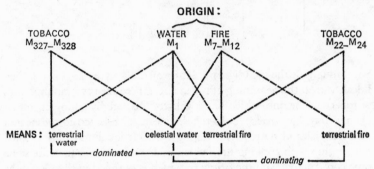

Figure 20. Pattern of relationships between myths dealing with smoked tobacco (right) and myths dealing with tobacco as a drink (left)

unknown. If we disregard tobacco-chewing, which occurred only sporadically, we can say that, in this area, tobacco was only smoked; and this makes it congruous with fire rather than with water. However, within the sub-category of smoked tobacco, I pointed out an instance of reduplication which, on the mythical level, took the form of a distinction between 'good' and 'bad' tobacco (M_{191}), or between a good and a bad use of tobacco (M_{26}, M_{27}). M_{191} even appears as being essentially a myth about the origin of bad tobacco.

As for M_{27}, it is a myth about the origin of the bad use of tobacco which in this case (and in contrast to M_{26}) comes from water. So, to the contrast between the nature of tobacco and its use (the use belonging to the category of culture), there corresponds a contrast between two kinds of relationship which tobacco can have with water, one being metaphorical (a transformation affecting certain myths), the other metonymical (the aquatic origin of tobacco, according to the myth). The relationship to water constitutes the invariant aspect, as if certain myths originating in an area where tobacco is not drunk, established the reality of the absent custom by distinguishing two varieties of smoking tobacco, or two ways of smoking them, of which one, in different ways, is always congruous with water.

The interest of these observations extends beyond the purely formal.

They no doubt contribute in no small measure to the process of reduction I am engaged upon, since they allow certain myths to be assimilated to other myths, and thus, with the help of a small set of universally applicable rules make it possible to simplify a picture, the complexity and confusion of which might at first appear discouraging. But in addition to providing a further illustration of a method, the use of which the reader may think I am extending unduly, they afford a clearer vision of the history of American communities and of the concrete relationships between them. The fact that myths belonging to very different tribes reveal an obscure knowledge of customs, evidence of which is only to be found outside their traditional habitat, proves that the distribution and state of these tribes in recent times tell us little or nothing about their past. The analysis of South American myths shows that the various communities, unconsciously no doubt, 'know' too much about each other for us not to conclude that their present distribution was preceded by different distributions, which were the result of innumerable mixings of races and cultures occurring throughout the ages. The differences we can observe between cultures and the geographical remoteness from each other of the inhabitants are not facts possessing any intrinsic significance; still less do they offer evidence in support of any historical reconstitution. These superficial differences merely reflect a weakened image of a very ancient and complex process of development, at the point where it was suddenly arrested by the discovery of the New World.

The preceding remarks will help us to overcome a difficulty raised by the analysis of the Warao myths. In accordance with their geographical origin, I assigned them to the mythological area of drunk tobacco. The distribution area of this mode of consumption, which is bounded to the south by the Amazon, presents a discontinuous aspect, with clearly marked breaks: 'The Uapés Indians smoke enormous cigars, but none of the tribes south of the Japura smoke their tobacco; it is only licked' (Whiffen, p. 143). This licking tobacco is macerated, crushed and thickened with manioc starch so as to form a kind of syrup. The actual drinking of tobacco, after soaking or boiling, is met with from the Jivaro to the Kagaba (Preuss 3, No. 107, 119), in the Montaña, and in three areas of Guiana: the Lower Orinoco, the upper reaches of the Rio Branco and the Maroni area.

Yet the Warao myths seem to be referring to smoked tobacco. M_{327} underlines this fact on two occasions: first, when the hero's father unsuccessfully burns the leaves of various plants in place of the missing tobacco; and secondly when his brother teaches him how to make a cigarette with the tobacco brought back by the humming-bird. It is well known that the cultural position of the Warao is something of an enigma. The fact that they have temples, and an organized religion with a hierarchy of priests and medicine-men, would seem to point to Andean influences. On the other hand, the groups living on the central part of the Orinoco delta have a very rudimentary culture, linking them to so-called 'marginal' tribes, and they do not consume tobacco (Wilbert 4, pp. 246–7). Whether we choose to regard them as a regressive group or as survivors from some archaic state, we cannot but be puzzled by discordant details, which prompt us to look elsewhere, among the tribes of central Guiana, for a possible term of comparison with the Warao myths:

M_{334}. *Arecuna.* '*The origin of tobacco and other magic drugs*'

A small boy had taken his four young brothers into the forest. They met djiadjia birds (unidentified) whose cry means: 'farther on, farther on!' Although they had taken food with them, the children had not eaten and they tried to kill the birds which could be easily approached. However, none was caught and as the children pursued their quarry farther and farther into the forest, they finally reached the plantation where the servants of Piai'man, the master of tobacco, worked. Terrified by the arrows, the servants asked the children to be careful not to put their eyes out. These servants, who were birds, changed into humans so that the children could have them as parents and consent to live with them.

But Piai'man claimed the children, because the djiadjia birds, which had enticed them so far, belonged to him. He undertook to turn them into medicine-men, and gave them daily doses of an emetic beverage. The children remained in isolation in a small house where the women could not see them, and vomited into a waterfall, 'to absorb its sounds', and into a large canoe. After absorbing all sorts of preparations made from the bark, or 'souls' of various trees, the children, who had become very thin and had lost consciousness, were finally given injections of tobacco juice through the nostrils and forced to undergo a painful ordeal which consisted in the threading of fine string made of human hair through their noses and out again at the mouth, by way of the back of the throat.

Towards the end of the initiation, two of the children violated a taboo, with the result that they lost their eyes and were changed into nocturnal Spirits. The three others became skilled medicine-men and grew old alongside their master. They were quite bald when the latter sent them back to their village. They had difficulty in getting their parents to recognize them. Vexed at being considered too old by a young woman whom they desired, they turned her to stone and changed the members of their own family into Spirits. These are the Spirits who now make the medicine-men's tobacco grow in ten days, without there being any need to plant it.[24] There are three varieties of this tobacco. It is very strong (K.-G. 1, pp. 63–8).

This myth introduces the theme of water in a rather discreet form – the novices absorb the voices of the waterfall which, because of their different heights, seem like the voices of three singers – but everywhere else in Guiana, tobacco and rattles are constantly associated with water, both among the Arawak and the Carib tribes. The former relate (M_{335}) how chief Arawânili obtained from Orehu, the goddess of the waters, the gourd tree, pebbles from the bottom of the sea (to put in the rattle) and tobacco, thanks to which he would be able to fight Yauhahu, the evil Spirit responsible for death (Brett 2, pp. 18–21). In Carib mythology (M_{336}), Komanakoto, the first medicine-man, one day heard voices coming from the river; he dived in and saw beautiful women who taught him their songs and presented him with tobacco, as well as with the gourd-rattle complete with its pebbles and handle (Gillin, p. 170). The Kalina fill their rattles with little black and white pebbles found in water (Ahlbrinck, under 'püyei', § 38).

Otherwise, there is no doubt about the analogy with M_{327}. Three children, or five children reduced to three, are voluntarily disjoined from their parents and travel towards the land of tobacco, being enticed there, or helped there, by birds. The land of tobacco is an island in mid-ocean, watched over by keepers; or it is a clearing in the forest cultivated by slaves. According to whether the master of tobacco is a man or a woman (or a group of women), he is welcoming or hostile. However, it should be stressed that, in the former instance, the man has a wife who tries to counteract his zeal as an initiator; 'she did not want to bother with the children'. If she had had her way, the master of tobacco would never have succeeded in obtaining it for them. Each time he tries to gather tobacco up the mountain, she manages to force him to return before he has achieved his purpose. Later in the story,

[24] Among these mauari spirits figure the Amazons who are the mistresses of tobacco in M_{327} (cf. K.-G. 1, p. 124).

another woman shows the same hostility towards the heroes when they become old men, by refusing to give them, not tobacco (which they already possess) but water.

Now it is obvious that the Arecuna myth refers to drunk tobacco, and to other narcotics taken orally. Although these narcotics are very numerous (the myth mentions fifteen or so), I am tempted to reduce them to three basic kinds corresponding to the three children, since several Guiana specialists agree that it is possible to distinguish three types of medicine-men, associated respectively with tobacco, pimentoes and the takina or takini tree (Ahlbrinck, under 'püyei' § 2; Penard in Goeje, pp. 44–5). This tree could be *Virola* sp., one of the myristicaceae family, which yields several narcotic substances (cf. Schultes 1, 2). According to a Kalina informant, the active principle of the takini is found in the milky sap which is administered to novices and is said to induce terrible delirium (Ahlbrinck, *ibid.*, § 32). Consequently, in spite of the single reference to smoked tobacco, which could be explained as being a result of distortion due to the peculiar position occupied by the Warao within the group of Guiana cultures, the presence of three children in M_{327} and several demons in M_{328} would seem to warrant the attaching of these two myths to a Guiana group about the origin of narcotic beverages, including tobacco soaked in water.

There remains a final series of remarks to be made, tending towards the same conclusion. The heroes of the Guiana myths about the origin of tobacco are children. After being disjoined from their parents, who become the initiators of shamanism by the example they set (M_{328}, M_{334}) or by the rules they lay down (M_{327}), they finally become Spirits, who only appear to men when the latter make them offerings of tobacco. We recognize here a pattern already encountered at the beginning of the previous volume, with the famous Cariri myth about the origin of tobacco (M_{25}). In that myth, the children were disjoined vertically (in the sky, and not horizontally, on land or water) and lived thereafter with a Tobacco Spirit, who had formerly shared the company of humans, but could no longer be summoned except by means of offerings of tobacco. Whereas the Warao Spirit of tobacco is a child, his Cariri counterpart is an old man. The Arecuna Spirit occupies an intermediary position between the two: he is a child who grows up, becomes old and turns bald.

The Cariri myth deals with both the origin of tobacco and that of wild pigs, into which the children are changed by the Tobacco Spirit.

I accounted for the link by showing that the myth could be inserted in a paradigmatic group about the origin of wild pigs, in which tobacco smoke plays the operative role (cf. above, p. 22). So, within the body of myths of tropical America, we can isolate an ordered series which forms a relatively closed set; the ashes of a funeral pyre give rise to tobacco (M_{22}–M_{24}, M_{26}); tobacco when burnt determines the appearance of meat (M_{15}–M_{18}); in order to render the meat edible, men obtain fire from a male jaguar (M_7–M_{12}), the feminine counterpart of which is none other than the victim who perished on the fire (M_{22}–M_{24}).

In these instances, we are concerned exclusively with smoked tobacco, as is borne out on the one hand by ethnography – the communities in which these myths originated consume tobacco in this way – and on the other by formal analysis, since these myths, in order to be arranged in this pattern, must be read, as it were, in the 'fire clef'. In *The Raw and the Cooked* (pp. 107–8), I formulated rules which made it possible to transpose the group into the 'water clef'. However, in so doing, I was merely providing a means of translating it, without establishing the actual existence of a second closed group in which water occupies, with regard to fire, a place symmetrical with that occupied by tobacco.

Supposing such a group does exist, it must be a reflection of the other in the 'water' category of M_7–M_{12}, that is, tending towards M_1, because of the transformational relationship which links these myths:

(*Origin of cooking*)
$$[M_7\text{–}M_{12} : \text{FIRE}] \Rightarrow [M_1 : \text{WATER}]$$

The water, of which M_1 traces the origin, is celestial water or, more exactly, water from tempests or storms and which puts out cooking fire: it is, then, 'anti-cooking', or 'anti-fire'. Now we know that the myths suppose a close relationship between tempests, storms and wild pigs. Thunder keeps watch over the animals; it rumbles when men hunt too freely and kill more game than they need. I have already given several examples of this relationship (*RC*, pp. 208–10); it would not be difficult to find many others scattered throughout the mythic texts. (See Figure 21, p. 442.)

If wild pigs, which supply the best meat, the highest form of cooking matter, are protected from the abuses of cooking by tempests and storms, functioning in the system as 'anti-cooking', the symmetrical group we are looking for can only exist if and when we discover a term which forms a counterpart to tobacco smoke, and, with regard to tempests and storms, has a reverse relationship from that existing between tobacco smoke and wild pigs. Tobacco smoke causes the appearance of the pigs; its counterpart must therefore cause the disappearance of tempests and storms.

Ethnography satisfies this deductive requirement. It is well known that among the northern Kayapo a divinity called Bepkororoti personifies storms (*RC*, pp. 207–10). Certain individuals called Bebkororoti

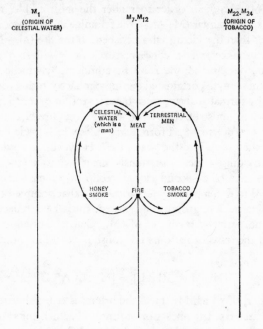

Figure 21. The pattern of relationships between myths about the origin of water, fire and tobacco

mari intercede with him on behalf of the tribe. For this purpose they use burnt bees' wax, which causes the tempest to abate (Diniz, p. 9). This is not an isolated example, as the following Guayaki invocation shows: 'He made smoke with the wax of the Choá bees in order to drive away the celestial jaguar. They struck the trees with their bows, they rent the earth with their axes, they made the smell of the choá wax rise into the sky' (Cadogan 6). When it thunders, according to the Umutina, this means that a Spirit is coming down to earth to look for honey for the celestial people; but he himself does not eat any (Schultz 2, p. 224). No doubt, in one instance, the reference is to a solar eclipse and not to a storm. But a storm is a weak form of an eclipse, and the Guayaki myth offers the additional interest of associating smoke from bees' wax with acoustic operations, to which must be added the explosion made by dry bamboo canes when thrown into the fire (Métraux-Baldus, p. 444), a noise which, as a strong manifestation of the sound of instruments of the parabára type, links up 'honey smoke' with the instruments of darkness, just as 'tobacco smoke' is linked with rattles.

In the interests of brevity, I will refrain from discussing a Uitoto myth, the length and complexity of which would justify a separate study (M_{337}). I merely mention in passing that this myth comes back to tobacco by means of a double twist: tobacco water and not smoke causes the transformation of humans into wild pigs; and the transformation punishes a hostile attitude to lightning which, at that time, was a pretty tame little creature (Preuss 1, pp. 369–403). I will also leave aside Tastevin's too fragmentary observations (4, p. 27; 5, p. 170) on the Cashinawa myths about the transformation of men into wild pigs, after they had consumed tobacco juice out of spite because a young girl did not want to marry any of them. The girl, after being left on her own, takes care of the Spirit of Tobacco, brings him up and eventually marries him; he is the ancestor of the Cashinawa (M_{338a}; cf. M_{19}, RC, p. 103). Symmetrically, in a Shipaia myth (M_{338b}), a couple who remain stuck to a nest of irapuã bees, whose honey they have been unable to ingest, are transformed into wild pigs (Nim. 3, pp. 1011–12).

On the other hand, we must pause to look at a Warao myth which, by substituting rattles for tobacco smoke, reverses both the origin and loss of wild pigs. I drew attention to this myth in *The Raw and the Cooked* (p. 85, n. 2).

M_{17}. *Warao. 'Why wild pigs are scarce'* (RC, Index of Myths: *the origin of wild pigs*)

A man, his wife and his two sons had gone to a drinking party, leaving their two daughters alone in the house, where they had chosen to remain in order to make beer from manioc and sweet potatoes (cassiri). They were visited by a Spirit, who gave them a fresh supply of food and spent the night with them without troubling either of them.

The parents came back and the daughters were unable to keep their adventure secret. The father, who was still fairly befuddled as a result of having been at the drinking party the evening before, insisted on the visitor coming back and, although he had not the slightest idea who he was, offered him his elder daughter in marriage. The Spirit took up his abode with his parents-in-law, and proved to be a good husband and son-in-law. Every day he brought back game, and also taught his parents-in-law how to hunt the wild pig. For they did not know what a wild pig really was. Until then, they had killed only birds which they believed to be pigs. The Spirit only had to shake his rattle and the wild pigs came rushing up.

Time passed. A child was born to the young couple and the husband moved his own property into his father-in-law's house. Among his property, which he had hitherto kept in the bush, were four rattles decorated with feathers, which he kept for hunting. There was a pair of rattles for each kind of wild pig, one savage, the other timid: one was used to call the beast, the other to drive it away. Only the Spirit was allowed to touch them, otherwise, as he explained, trouble would ensue.

One day, while the Spirit was in the fields, one of his brothers-in-law succumbed to temptation and borrowed the rattles. But he shook the one for the savage pigs. The beasts came rushing up, tore the baby to pieces and ate it. The other members of the family, who had escaped into the trees, shouted for help. The Spirit came running up and shook the rattle which drove the beasts away. He was so angry at his brother-in-law's disobedience and at the baby's death, that he decided to leave. From then on, Indians found it hard to get food (Roth 1, pp. 186–7).

This myth about the loss of wild pigs respects the armature of the Tenetehara (M_{15}), Mundurucu (M_{16}) and Kayapo (M_{18}) myths about the origin of pigs, while reversing all the terms. A sister's husband feeds wives' brothers, instead of the latter refusing him food. In all instances, the needy brother-in-law or brothers-in-law are bird-hunters, who are unable to obtain unaided the two existing kinds of pig (M_{17}) or the single type – in this case, the most timid – which existed at that time. The appearance of the savage species, whether absolute or relative, is the result of an abuse, committed in this case by the wife's brothers, in the other myths by the sisters' husbands: an acoustic (cultural) abuse of the rattles, or a sexual (natural) abuse of the wives. In consequence of which, the child is killed by the pigs, driven out or transformed; the savage pigs appear or disappear, and hunting becomes profitable or difficult.

Nevertheless, the Warao myth is more methodical than those belonging to the same group in its exploitation of the dichotomic principle which established an initial contrast between the two species of pig. One species represents a reward for the hunter, the other a punishment, when he makes excessive use of means which ought to be employed in moderation. Since this aspect is omitted from the Tenetehara and Mundurucu versions, we can say that, for the Warao, savage pigs punish the immoderate hunter, a role assigned by the other myths to tempests and storms, which are the pigs' avengers. The dichotomy is extended to rattles, of which there are two pairs, the terms of each pair fulfilling contrasting functions. But the two species of pigs are themselves in contrast to each other, and the four rattles form a functional chiasmus: those which are used to attract the timid species or to drive away the savage species have a positive connotation, which contrasts with the negative connotation of the two others, used to drive away the timid species (although harmless) or to attract the savage species, with the consequences already described. In terms of rattles, these antithetical values reproduce those assigned respectively by other tribes to tobacco smoke and honey smoke, one causing the appearance of pigs (which create tempests and storms), the other driving away tempests and storms (thus making possible an abusive treatment of the pigs).

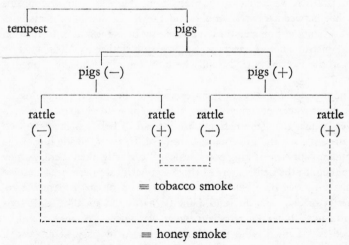

(—) wrong species of pig, wrong rattle (used to attract wrong species, and drive away right species)
(+) the reverse

Finally, and this is my third comment, the narrative of the Warao myth is linked to a paradigmatic set which has already been discussed and the initial term of which was supplied by myths dealing with the loss of honey (M_{233}–M_{239}). In changing from a myth about the origin of wild pigs to a myth about their loss, M_{17} effects two operations. One consists in substituting modes of the rattle (which are antithetical to each other) for the equally antithetical modes of smoke; in other words, it brings about a transfer from the culinary code to the acoustic code. On the other hand, within the culinary code itself, the Warao myth changes a myth about the loss of honey into a myth about the origin of meat (which thereby becomes a myth about its loss). Having been freed by the first operation, smoked tobacco becomes qualified by the second (the internal transformation of the culinary code) to occupy in Warao mythology, as is shown by M_{327}, the place allocated in other myths to drunk tobacco. The contrast between smoked tobacco and drunk tobacco reproduces, within the category of tobacco, the opposition between tobacco and honey, since in northern Amazonia, according to the locality, drunk tobacco or toxic honey are used for the same purificatory purposes.

So in its own way, that is, by preterition, the Warao myth confirms the link between tobacco smoke and the rattle. We have dealt with tobacco smoke, but we still have to show how the rattle, in relation to the instruments of darkness, fulfils a role similar to that played by bells in the European tradition, where they are instruments of mediation.

There is nothing new in this observation, because the missionaries were quick to perceive the analogy. Cardus (p. 79) describes the gourd-rattles 'which they (the natives) use instead of bells'. More than two centuries before, the Protestant, Léry (Vol. II, p. 71), made fun of the Tupinamba priests shaking their rattles: 'I can only liken them, as they were then, to the bell-ringers of those hypocritical priests who deceive ordinary people here below by carrying from place to place the reliquaries of Saint Antony and Saint Bernard, and suchlike idolatrous instruments.' If we look back to what was said on p. 403, it will be agreed that Lafitau, who was more interested by pagan equivalents, was not mistaken when he compared rattles and sistrums.

It was not the only function of the rattles to call and summon worshippers. Through them, the Spirits voiced and made known their oracles and commands. Certain models were constructed and decorated in such a way as to represent faces, while others even had movable jaws. It has been suggested that, in South America, the rattle may have derived from the idol, or the idol from the rattle (cf. Métraux 1, pp. 72–8; Zerries 3). The only point we need remember is that, both from the linguistic point of view and because of their personalization, rattles are related to bells, which were described as *signa* by Gregory of Tours, were received into the Church like new-born babies, and given godfathers and god-mothers as well as a name, with the result that the blessing ceremony could be normally treated as baptism.

There is no need to have recourse to the Popol Vuh to find evidence of the universality and antiquity of the link between the gourd-rattle and the human head. Several South American languages form the two words from the same root: iwida- in Arawak-Maipuré, -Kalapi- in Oayana (Goeje, p. 35). In Cubeo masks, the skull is represented by half a gourd (Goldman, p. 222); and Whiffen was no doubt echoing the native way of thinking when he compared (p. 122) the 'bare skulls gleaming white like so many gourds on a string'. The Cashinawa Spirit of thunder, who is bald (Tastevin 4, p. 21), has a homologue in the Toupan of the ancient Tupi, who often spoke through the medium of the rattle: 'When it is shaken, they think that Toupan is talking to them,' in other words 'the one who causes rain and thunder' (Thevet, Vol. II, pp. 953a, 910a). In this connection, it will be recalled that bells were supposed to 'tame' natural calamities.

The sacred rattle, a transmitter of messages, seems very far removed from the half-gourd placed on the water and tapped, the prototype of the instrument of darkness used by the heroine to summon the animal-seducer. And far removed it no doubt is, since one instrument ensures mediated and beneficent conjunction with the supernatural world, the other non-mediated and maleficent conjunction with nature, or (since the absence of mediatization always presents these two complementary aspects, cf. *RC*, p. 294), brutal disjunction from culture and society. Yet the distance which separates these two types of instruments does not exclude their being symmetrical; it even implies that they are. The pattern of Indian thought conceals an inverted image of the rattle which makes it possible for it to fulfil the other function.

According to the first missionaries, the Peruvians believed (M_{339}) that, in order to charm and capture men, the devil used gourds which he caused to bob alternately on and under the water. Any unfortunate person who tried to grasp them, and who was a prey to strong desire, was enticed

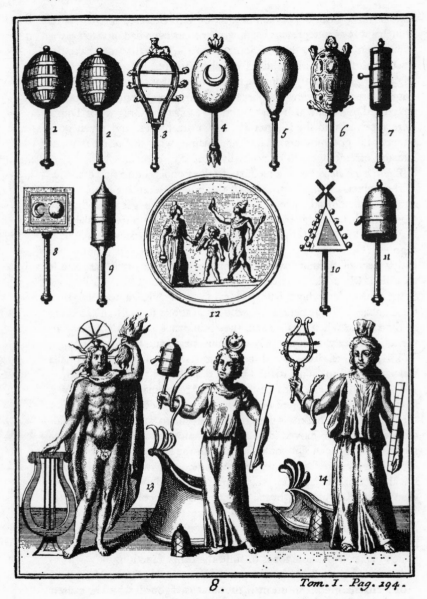

Figure 22. Ancient sistrums and American rattles. (After Lafitau, t. I, p. 194.)

a long way away from the shore and finally drowned (Augustinos, p. 15). It is remarkable that this strange notion, which seems to reflect a hallucination or a phantasm, is also found in Ancient Mexico. In Book XI of his *General History*, which deals with 'terrestrial things', that is, zoology, botany and mineralogy, Sahagun describes (M_{340}) a water-snake, called xicalcoatl, with a dorsal appendage in the form of a richly ornamented gourd, which is used to lure men. The animal allows only the decorated gourd to emerge above the surface. 'Indeed it makes it desirable as if it were going carried by the water.' 'And an ignorant one with avarice, with covetousness, considers that it has been shown to him, and that he merits a very good gourd bowl; then he descends into the water. When he wishes to take it, it only goes drifting away; he goes to follow it there: little by little it makes him reach for it in the depths of the water. Thereupon the water churns up: it foams over him so that there he dies. The serpent's body is black, only its back is intricately designed like a gourd vessel' (Sahagun, Part XII, pp. 85–6).

The same theme occurs here and there from Mexico to Peru. A Tumupasa myth (M_{341}) relates that a boy, a deaf-mute who had been unjustly beaten by his father, set off towards the river, carrying a gourd for drawing water which he had slung across his back. However hard he tried to dive into the water, the gourd made him float on the surface. So he took it off, sank to the bottom and changed into a snake (Nordenskiöld 3, p. 291). A Uitoto myth (M_{342}) describes a battle between the Spirits of the gourd trees and the first men. The latter perished in a flood which spared no one, not even two fishermen who were swept along by the current when they tried to seize hold of a small pottery jar which was floating on the water and eluding their grasp. According to another myth (M_{343}), the conflict which gave rise to the flood occurred on the occasion of the marriage of a Spirit of the waters to a shy young girl, the daughter of the 'Gourd-man' and who was called 'Gourd-under-water' (Preuss 1, Vol. I, pp. 207–18).[25]

[25] An ancient Colombian rite is no doubt linked to the same group, but unfortunately its mythic context is not known: 'They used to practise the following superstitious custom to find out whether children were going to have happy or unhappy lives. At weaning time, a small coil of esparto grass was prepared with, inside it, a piece of cotton dampened with the mother's milk. Six young men, all good swimmers, went to throw it into the river. Then they in turn dived into the water. If the coil disappeared below the surface before they reached it, they would say that the child in question would be unhappy. But, if they had no difficulty in retrieving it, they believed that the child would be very lucky' (Fr P. Simon in Barradas, Vol. II, p. 210).

Whether ancient or contemporary, all the myths establish a relationship of incompatibility between gourds and water. Like the sacred rattle, the gourd is by nature 'in the air', hence 'outside water'. The union between the gourd and water, symbolized by the water-snake's appendage, or by the marriage of a gourd-girl with a Spirit of the waters, is diametrically opposed to the contradictory idea – since a gourd usually floats (M$_{341}$) – of a receptacle *full of air* and *in water*. This, of course, relates to the dried gourd, from which a rattle can be made. Evidence of the contrast between a fresh gourd and a dried gourd in respect of water is found in a Ge myth which, like the Uitoto myth, considers Sun, the demiurge, as being the protector of gourds or gourd-men: either he tries to rescue them from the flood by providing them with poison intended for the Spirits of the water (M$_{343}$), or (M$_{344a}$) he prevents Moon, his mother, from gathering gourds, before they are ripe, from a plantation in a clearing made by the snail.[26] According to this myth, which belongs to the Apinayé, the demiurges, Sun and Moon, threw their (*fresh*) gourds into the water, where they instantly changed into humans. When the flood came, some humans managed to stay afloat on a raft which was equipped with (*dried*) gourds as buoys; these men became the ancestors of the Apinayé. Others were carried along by the flood, and gave rise to various other communities. Those who had taken refuge in the trees became bees and termites (Oliveira, pp. 69–71; cf. Nim. 5, pp. 164–5). The contrast between the fresh gourd and the rattle has already been encountered in another myth (M$_{294}$).[27]

The contrast between the serpent and the gourd-receptacle, which the myths regard as a complete antithesis, is therefore primarily a contrast between the wet, long, solid and soft, and the dry, round, hollow and hard. But this is not all. Whereas the dried gourd supplies the material for a musical instrument, the rattle, the snake (as I showed on p. 418) provides the 'material' of the bull-roarer, which reproduces

[26] 'When the Indian women have planted the gourd tree, they afterwards strike themselves with the hands on the breasts in the belief that thus the fruit of the gourd tree will grow large like the breasts of the women. When the tree has grown big the Canelos women are in the habit of hanging the shells of the forest snail (called churu) upon its branches, in order that it shall bear large and abundant fruit' (Karsten 2, p. 142).

[27] It may be wondered whether the Apinayé myth does not, in its turn, reverse the more widespread South American version, of which a good example is found among the Maipuré of the Orinoco (M$_{344b}$). In this myth, humanity is reborn from the fruits of the *Mauritia* palm, which are thrown from the top of the tree by the survivors of the flood. This would give a pair of opposites – *gourd*/(palm) *fruit* – congruous, on the acoustic level, with the organological pair *gourd-rattle*/*shell-rattle*.

its cry. In this sense, the snake-gourd illustrates the contradictory union of the bull-roarer and the rattle, or, more accurately, it is the bull-roarer in the guise of the rattle. There is another Chaco myth which, when compared with the Tereno myth (M_{24}) – in which the hero sounds a clapper, an instrument of darkness, in order to find honey more easily – seems to suggest that the same relationship of incompatibility exists between the rattle and the instrument of darkness. In this Toba myth, which I have already made use of (M_{219b}), Fox takes advantage of the absence of the villagers, who are away looking for honey, to set fire to the huts. The Indians are very angry, kill Fox and cut his body up into pieces. Carancho, the demiurge, takes possession of the heart in order to go 'where he hopes to find honey'. The heart protests and declares that it has become a ceremonial rattle: it bounces like a ball, and the Indians give up looking for honey (Métraux 5, p. 138). Consequently, just as the instrument of darkness in M_{24} helps in the search for honey, the transformation of the heart into a rattle has the opposite effect.

There is a group of Guiana myths which I do not propose to analyse in detail, so as to avoid embarking on an examination of the 'rolling head' theme, the study of which would require a whole volume to itself. These myths (M_{345}–M_{346}) belong to the unlucky brother-in-law group which has already been dealt with. Ill-treated by his wife's brothers, because he did not bring back any game, a hunter obtains possession of magical objects which make him a master of hunting and fishing, provided he uses them in moderation. His brothers-in-law spy on him, steal the objects, use them immoderately or clumsily and bring about a flood in which the hero's son perishes; fish and game disappear. According to some versions, the hero changes into a 'rolling head' and attaches himself to the neck of the vulture, which thus turns into a two-headed bird; according to others, he becomes the father of wild pigs (K.-G. 1, pp. 92–104).

The first two magical objects of which the hero takes possession are of particular interest for our inquiry. One is a small gourd, which he must only half fill with water. This causes the river to run dry and all the fish can be picked up. The water returns to its normal level when the contents of the gourd are emptied back into the river bed. The brothers-in-law steal the gourd and make the mistake of filling it to the top. The river overflows, and carries away the gourd as well as the hero's child, who is drowned. However allusive the text of this myth may be, it is certainly linked to the Tumupasa and Uitoto myths I have already quoted, and beyond them to Peruvian and Mexican beliefs, because, according to the other version we know of, the gourd belongs in the first place to the otter, which is a Water Spirit. In this version, the lost gourd is swallowed by a fish and becomes its air-bladder, i.e. an – internal, not external – organ, symmetrical with the Mexican serpent's dorsal appendage.

The second magical object is an oar, which later becomes a joint of the crab's claw. The hero uses it to churn up the water near the bank, and the river dries up below the point where the water had been disturbed. The brothers-in-law imagine they will obtain better results if they stir up the water where it is deep. As on the previous occasion, the river overflows and carries away the magic object. From the organological point of view, the two objects are connected, one to a gourd-receptacle: i.e. a rattle; the other to a beater or clapper: i.e. an instrument of darkness. But each, within its category, admits of only one limited mode of use: the gourd must be only partially filled, in other words, the water *it contains* must be shallow, like the water into which the oar is plunged, that is, which *contains it*. Otherwise, the instruments instead of being beneficent become maleficent. The line of demarcation does not run between the rattle and the instrument of darkness, but between two possible methods of using each type of instrument:

	RATTLE (*mediation present*)	INSTRUMENT OF DARKNESS (*mediation absent*)
moderate use of one or other (*mediation present*)		
immoderate use of one or other (*mediation absent*)		

Unlike the rattle, the gourd which is half-full of water is only half-full of air; unlike the clapper, the oar is a stick which is struck not against another stick but on water. So the two magic objects in M_{345}–M_{346} represent, in respect of water, a compromise similar in type to that which characterizes their use. This observation leads on to the consideration of a further point.

According to whether the gourd is more or less full, the water it contains makes more or less noise as it is tipped into the river. Similarly, the oar makes more or less noise according to whether it is shaken

at a greater or lesser distance from the bank. The myths are not explicit about this acoustic aspect of the various kinds of behaviour towards water. But it is very apparent from Amazonian beliefs, which
are found even in Guiana: 'Take care not to ... leave your gourd lying
upside down in the boat: the gurgling noise made by the air as it
comes out from underneath the gourd when water enters it, has the
power to make the Bóyusú (a large water snake) appear immediately;
this is an encounter people are on the whole anxious to avoid' (Tastevin 3, p. 173). What I said in *The Raw and the Cooked* (p. 294) about the
word *gargote* and the fact that it had an acoustic connotation before
acquiring a culinary one, will have prepared the reader for the fact
that the same consequences can also follow from unclean cooking
methods: 'You must not ... throw pimentoes into the water, nor
tucupi (manioc juice) containing pimento nor remains of food seasoned
with pimento.[28] The Bóyusú would not fail to stir up waves, bring
about a storm and cause the boat to sink. So, when a fisherman draws
in to the bank to spend the night in his boat, he does not wash the plates
that evening: to do so would be much too dangerous' (Tastevin, *ibid.*).

Similarly in Guiana you must not spill fresh water into the canoe,
or wash the pot spoon in the river, or plunge the pot directly into the
river either to draw water, or in order to clean it, otherwise big squalls
and storms will arise (Roth 1, p. 267).

These culinary restrictions, which are also acoustic restrictions,[29]
have their equivalent on the linguistic level, and this confirms the
homology of the meta-linguistic contrast between the literal meaning
and the figurative meaning with the contrasts relating to other codes.
According to the Guiana Indians, there is no surer way of offending the
Water Spirits and thereby getting caught in storms, and being ship-
wrecked or drowned than to utter certain words, most of which are
of foreign origin. Thus, instead of arcabuza, 'gun', Arawak fishermen
must say kataroro, 'foot', and instead of perro, 'dog', kariro, 'the
toothed one'. Similarly, they are careful not to refer to certain things
by their right names, but by paraphrases: 'that which is hard' is rock,
'the beast with a long tail' the lizard. It is also dangerous to name little

[28] 'Spirits (p. 182) ... burnt tortoise shell' (p. 183), i.e. everything with a strong smell or
taste. To act differently would be to 'throw pimento in his (Bóyusú's) eyes. Hence his fury,
and those terrifying storms accompanied by torrential rain, which immediately punish any
such reprehensible act' (*ibid.*, pp. 182–3).

[29] And, as such, take us straight back to the crying baby by a much shorter loop than the
one I have chosen to follow: 'A pregnant woman tries not to make any noise as she works;
for instance, she avoids knocking the gourd-bowl against the inside of the jar when she
goes to draw water. Otherwise, her unborn son will cry all the time' (Silva, p. 368).

islands and streams (Roth 1, pp. 252–3). If, as I have tried to show in the course of this book, the literal meaning connotes nature, and the meta-phorical meaning culture, a system which puts metaphors and para-phrases, careful cooking, moderate noise or silence into one category, and the word 'raw', dirtiness and din into the other, can be declared coherent. Especially since the gourd, which includes within itself all these aspects, acts at one and the same time as speaker (in its capacity as a rattle), culinary utensil (as spoon, scoop, bowl or water bottle), and as a source of intentional or involuntary noise, either because it is used as a resonator for the tapped-out call, or because air rushes in when water pours out.

We come back, then, to the gourd which made its first appearance in *The Raw and the Cooked* in a very unusual role. A Warao myth (M_{28}) tells of an ogress who wears half a gourd as a head-dress, which she often removes and throws into the water in such a way as to make it spin like a top. Then she stands and watches it for a long time.

When I analysed the myth (*RC*, pp. 109–11, 116–20 and *passim*), I left aside this detail, which now takes on greater importance. It should be noted, in the first place, that, among certain tribes at least, it is to some extent a reflection of actual behaviour. Apinayé women 'in-variably take with them a gourd-bowl when they go off into the savan-nah. When empty, this receptacle is usually placed on their heads like a cap, and it is used as a container for anything worth keeping. Men never observe this custom ... A young child's hair would fall out if his parents ate agouti meat, or if the mother put a gourd of the *Crescentia* species on her head instead of one of the *Lagenaria* species, which involves no risk' (Nim. 5, pp. 94, 99).

We have already encountered, among the Sherente, a contrast between *Crescentia* and *Lagenaria*, subsidiary to the one between the gourd receptacle and the receptacle made of some indeterminate sub-stance – and not of earthenware, as I inadvertently stated (*RC*, p. 291) – but perhaps of wood, since bowls made of *Spondias* wood figure among the characteristic emblems of the Sdakran moiety (Nim. 6, p. 22), which is associated with the planet Mars, personified by an officiant who proffers muddy water in a bowl. The two species of gourd which contain clear water are associated, one (*Lagenaria*) with the planet Venus, the other (*Crescentia*) with the planet Jupiter. These two planets are in contrast to each other in so far as one is 'big' (suffix: -zauré) and male (M_{138}), the other 'small' (suffix: -rié) and female (M_{93}). The Jupiter myth describes this planet in the form of a miniature woman whom her husband hides, precisely, in a gourd. The contrast between Mars on the one hand, and Venus and Jupiter on the other, corresponds among the Sherente to the contrast between the moon and the sun (Nim. 6, p. 85). The Apinayé distinguish between the two demiurges thus named according to the good or bad use they make of gourds (M_{344}), which in this case belong to the *Lagenaria* species (Oliveira, p. 69). By uniting the Apinayé and Sherente beliefs, we arrive at the following tentative pattern:

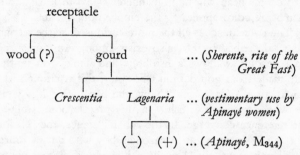

The receptacles used in the Sherente ritual of the Great Fast contain respectively unclean water (which is rejected) and clean water (which is accepted); the gourds used by the Apinayé women can serve both as receptacles and head-dresses if they belong to the *Lagenaria* species, but as receptacles only if they belong to the *Crescentia* species; the latter are, then, just as unacceptable as headgear as soiled water is unacceptable as a beverage. And, when Sun and Moon throw *Lagenaria* gourds into the water, the latter are changed into human beings, who are either successes or failures. Logically, all the terms along the oblique line to the left should have a lunar and nocturnal connotation, and those along the oblique line to the right a solar and diurnal connotation, and this, in the only case where this relationship has not been independently proved, has the following implication:

Crescentia : *Lagenaria* :: (moon, night) : (sun, day).

In order to carry the process of reconstruction further, we would have to know more about the respective positions of *Crescentia* and *Lagenaria* in technology and ritual, and be surer of the interpretation of the Apinayé terms formed from the root gó (Timbira Kō-): gócráti, *Crescentia*, gôrôni, *Lagenaria*, and gôtôti, the ceremonial rattle. Almost everywhere in South America, except perhaps in the Chaco, ceremonial rattles seem to have been made, in former times, from *Crescentia*.

There is some uncertainty in the matter, however, since the American origin of *Lagenaria* remains debatable.

I propose, therefore, to examine the restrictions concerning the gourd as headgear from a more general point of view, and as they can still be observed in Amazonian folk-lore: 'Children usually wash in the house by taking water from a pail with a gourd and pouring it over their bodies. But if they happen to put the scoop over their heads, the mothers at once utter a warning, for it is said that a child who puts a gourd on his head will be ill-mannered, slow to learn and stunted. The same prejudice applies to the empty flour basket ... ' (Orico 2, p. 71). The coincidence is all the more curious since the second use of the gourd described by M_{28} also exists among Amazonian peasants: 'When someone swallows a fish-bone and chokes on it, the plates (usually made from gourds) must be spun; this is enough to remove the obstruction' (*ibid.*, p. 95). Now, the heroine of M_{28} is a greedy female who devours raw fish. On this precise point, folk-lore and mythic reference converge. In the other instance, the relationship is rather one of symmetry: an Amazonian boy who puts a gourd on his head will not grow; the Apinayé child, whose mother commits the same offence, will become bald – i.e. he will grow old before his time. Baldness being very rare among the Indians, a more accurate expression of the native way of thinking would no doubt be to say that the first child will remain 'raw', whereas the other will 'rot'. There are, in fact, a great many myths which give this explanation for the loss of body hair or hair from the head.[30]

In order to classify the transformations undergone by the gourd, we have, then, at our disposal a double coding system, culinary and acoustic, which frequently combines the two aspects. Let us begin by considering the ceremonial rattle and its inverted form, which I described as the 'diabolical gourd'. One produces sounds, the other is silent. The first enables men to catch the Spirits, who come down into the rattle and speak to men through it; the second enables the Spirits to capture men. And this is not all. The rattle is a container of air, contained in air; the diabolical gourd is a container of air, contained in water. The two instruments are therefore in opposition to each other

---

[30] A man became bald through having lived inside the belly of the great snake, which had swallowed him (Nordenskiöld 1, p. 110: Choroti 3, p. 145: Chimane), or through having touched the rotten corpses in the monster's entrails (Preuss 1, pp. 219–30: Uitoto). Chthonian dwarfs become bald because human excrement fell on their heads (Wilbert 7, pp. 864–6: Yupa). The theme of the person who becomes bald after being swallowed is found even on the north-west coast of North America (Boas 2, p. 688).

in respect of the container, which is either air or water. One introduces the supernatural into the world of culture; the other – which is always described as being elaborately decorated – seems to cause culture to emerge from nature, symbolized in this instance by water.

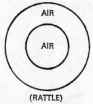

(RATTLE)

(DIABOLICAL GOURD)

Next come four modalities which, still through the agency of the gourd, illustrate the same number of logical operations which have to do with both air and water. The call tapped out on a bowl which has been turned over and placed on the surface of the water, thus causing air to be enclosed inside the gourd by the pressure of water, forms a contrast with the gurgling noise made by the gourd, full of water, as it empties, thus involving the exclusion of water by air:

(TAPPED-OUT CALL)

(GURGLING GOURD)

These two operations, although reversed in relationship to each other, produce a noise which is caused either by air or water. The other two operations are similarly reversed but silent, either relatively (very little water is poured out gently, near the bank) or absolutely (the gourd is made to spin). The first puts half water and half air in the gourd (M_{345}–M_{346}); the second excludes all water from the gourd and includes no air in the water. This can be shown diagrammatically as follows:

(GOURD AS FISHING CHARM)

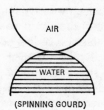

(SPINNING GOURD)

In spite of their formal aspect, which would almost justify recourse to a Boole-Venn kind of algebra to give it adequate expression, these operations have clearly defined, and in each case unambiguous, relationships with the mythology of cooking. Let us examine the last four operations I have just listed. The first devolves upon the mistress of the tapir or of the snake-seducer who, in her eagerness to rejoin her lover, neglects her duties as nursing mother and cook, thus annihilating the art of cooking. The second operation, also connected with the snake – but which has become a devouring monster instead of a seducer – results from a form of cooking which over-manifests its presence by scattering its refuse without thought or care. This gives the following opposition:

(*a*) *non-existent cooking/exorbitant cooking*

The third operation allows the person who performs it to replenish a cooking-pot which had remained empty through his fault. It therefore confers a practical existence on fish and meat, which are themselves pre-conditions of the practical existence of cooking. The fourth operation, which is equally beneficent, cancels out a disastrous consequence of cooking: that which results from an over-greedy eater choking himself. The two noisy operations are therefore connected with anti-cooking, characterized by deficiency or excess; the two silent operations belong to cooking, one of them ensuring the desired means towards it, while the other palliates a foreseen and dreaded consequence:

(*b*) *positive means of cooking obtained/negative consequence of cooking eliminated*

There still remains to be interpreted one last use of the gourd. It is a permissible use for Apinayé women, provided the gourd is a *Lagenaria*, but taboo if it is a *Crescentia* and, in the case of either species, taboo also for children, among the peasant communities of Amazonia. In M_{28}, it is attributed to a supernatural creature.

At first glance, the use of the gourd as a head-dress has no place in a system in which we have found no other vestimentary symbols. Only much later, in the fourth volume of the present series, do I intend to show that this new code is homologous with the culinary code, and to put forward rules for their mutual conversion. At this point, it is enough to stress the *anti-culinary* connotation of the use of a utensil as an article of clothing, the final detail in an ogress's portrait which, if it were imitated by humans, would transfer them from the category of consumers of cooked and prepared food into that of the raw substances which are put into the gourd to be eaten later. On either side of the central category of the cooked, and along two axes, beliefs and myths express, then, by means of the gourd, several antithetical ideas relating either to cooking which is *present*, by establishing a contrast between its positive conditions (meat and fish) and its negative consequences (choking on ingested food); or to cooking which is *neglected* by default (negative) or through excess (positive); or finally, in the *absence* of cooking or in consequence of its symbolic rejection, to the two modes of anti-cooking constituted by the raw and the rotten.

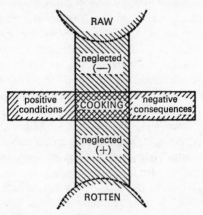

Figure 23. The system of culinary operations

*

Consequently, as the field of inquiry widens and as new myths force themselves upon our attention, myths which were studied a long while back re-emerge and throw into prominence certain of their details, previously neglected or unexplained, but which now appear like pieces of a puzzle that have been put to one side until the gaps in the almost completed pattern reveal the shapes of the missing parts and their inevitable positions; then, when the last piece has been fitted into place, we are vouchsafed – like an unexpected gift or additional bonus – the hitherto undecipherable meaning of some vague shape or indefinite colour, whose relationship to the neighbouring shapes and colours eluded comprehension, whichever way we tried to think of it.

This may be the case with a detail in a myth (M_{24}) I have often referred to in the course of this book; however, it is so tiny a detail that I did not even include it in my summary of the myth (*RC*, p. 100). The hero, a Tereno Indian and a honey-gatherer, is a victim of the machinations of his wife who is slowly poisoning him by mixing her menstrual blood with the food she prepares for him: 'After he had eaten, he walked with a limp and had no zest for work' (Baldus 3, p. 220). After being informed of the cause of his infirmity by his young son, the man sets out to look for honey; and it is at this point that he takes off his sandals made of tapir hide and knocks the soles together 'to find honey more easily'.

So, the hero of M₂₄ is lame. This detail might seem pointless, if limping did not happen to have a very conspicuous place in Tereno ritual. The most important of the Tereno ceremonies took place towards the beginning of April, to celebrate the appearance of the Pleiades and to ward off the dangers of the dry season, then about to begin. After assembling the participants, an old man, facing in succession to the east, the north, the west and the south, proclaimed himself the ancestor of the chiefs of the four cardinal points. Then he raised his eyes to the sky and begged the Pleiades to send rain, and to spare his people from war, disease and snake-bites. When he had finished his prayer, the other persons present set about making a great din which lasted until daybreak. The next evening, at sunset, in preparation for festivities which lasted the whole night through, musicians took up their positions in the four or six huts which had been built for them in the dancing area. The next day was given over to often brutal contests between opponents belonging to opposite moieties. When these were finished, and when everybody had assembled in the chief's hut, a musician, ornately dressed and holding a stag's antlers in his right hand, limped towards a previously chosen hut. He knocked the antlers against the panels of the door and, still limping, returned to the spot he had come from. The owner of the hut came out and asked what was wanted of him. He was asked to give an ox, a cow or a bull, which had been acquired jointly by the community. He then handed over the animal, which was forthwith killed, roasted and eaten (Rhode, p. 409; Colini in Boggiani, pp. 295–6; cf. Altenfelder Silva, pp. 356, 364–5; Métraux 12, pp. 357–8).

In Vancouver Island, an old woman would pretend to limp when she went to throw into the sea the bones of the first salmon, after it had been ritually consumed by children (Boas in: Frazer 4, Vol. 8, p. 254). It is well known that, along the north-west coast of the Pacific, the salmon, which constitute the natives' staple diet, arrive each year in the spring (L.-S. 6, p. 5). All the myths belonging to this region of Northern America associate limping with seasonal phenomena. Winter can be vanquished and spring made to come only by a crippled girl (M_{347}: Shuswap; Teit, pp. 701–2). A child with twisted legs causes the rain to stop (M_{348}: Cowlitz; Jacobs, pp. 168–9) or the sun to shine (M_{349}: Cowlitz and other Salish coastal tribes; Adamson, pp. 230–33, 390–91). A lame man brings back the spring (M_{350}: Sanpoil-Nespelem; Ray, p. 199). Moon's lame daughter marries the new moon; henceforth the weather would be less warm, because the Sun would move (M_{351}: Wishram; Sapir, p. 311). And I end this brief list with a Wasco myth, which brings us back to our starting-point (cf. M_3), since it describes a cripple who was the only dead man capable of coming to life again and of remaining among the living; since then, the dead have no longer been able to come to life again, like the trees in spring (M_{352}: Spier–Sapir, p. 277).

The northern Ute of the Whiterocks region (Utah) performed a 'limping dance', sanku'-ni'thkap, the symbolism of which had been forgotten by the time its characteristic movements and the songs and music which went with it, came to be recorded. This exclusively feminine dance imitated the gait of a person limping with the right leg and dragging it along so as to bring it into line with the left, every time the left foot took a step forward. The dancers, who were about a hundred in number, formed two parallel lines about ten yards or so apart, and faced west, the direction in which the drummers had taken up their positions and, behind them, the singers. Each file moved towards the musicians, then swerved round and came back. The drums beat out a characteristic rhythm, peculiar to this dance, each drummed note being slightly out of phase with the note as sung. A contrast could be observed between the 'drumbeats, which recur with mechanical regularity, and the voice, which has a varying accent and rhythm' (Densmore, pp. 20, 105, 210).

Ritual limping has also been noted in the Ancient World where it was similarly linked with seasonal changes. In Britain, the bundle of sheaves which a farmer, who had finished his own harvest, would set up in his neighbour's field where there was still corn standing, was called the 'Crippled Goat' (Frazer 4, Vol. 7, p. 284). In certain parts of Austria, it was customary to give the last sheaf to an old woman who had to limp on one foot as she took it home (*ibid.*, pp. 231–2).

The Old Testament describes a ceremony for overcoming drought, which consisted in dancers limping round the altar. A Talmudic text suggests that in Israel, in the second century A.D., the limping dance was still used to obtain rain (Caquot, pp. 129–30). As with the Tereno, it was a question of bringing a dry period to an end – '*tardis mensibus*', to quote Virgil's expression (*Georgics*, I, v. 32) – as is the general wish in the country districts of Europe once the harvest has been gathered in.

In archaic China, all the themes we have successively encountered in the course of this book were associated with the limping dance. First of all, it had a seasonal character, which is admirably expounded by Granet. The dead season, which was also the season of the dead, began with the arrival of hoar-frost. This put an end to agricultural occupations, which had been carried out in anticipation of the winter drought during which men were confined to the villages: everything had at that time to be closed up for fear of plagues. The instrument used at the Great No, a winter feast, which was chiefly or exclusively masculine, was the drum. It was also the festival of ghosts, celebrated for souls 'who, since they no longer received any form of worship had become maleficent Beings' (Granet, pp. 333–4). These two aspects are found among the Tereno, the chief purpose of whose funeral rites was to cut the bridges between the living and the dead, for fear the latter should come back to torment the former, or even to abduct them (Altenfelder Silva, pp. 347–8, 353). Yet the feast held at the beginning of the dry season was also an invitation to the dead, who were roused by calls to come and visit their relatives (*ibid.*, p. 356).

The ancient Chinese believed that with the arrival of the dry season the earth and sky ceased to communicate (Granet, p. 315, n. 1). The Spirit of drought was personified by a little bald woman[31] with eyes at the top of her head. While she was present, the sky refrained from sending rain, so as not to harm her (*ibid.*, n. 3). Yu the Great, the founder of the first royal dynasty, inspected the cardinal points and caused thunder and rain to return. Just as bells proclaim the coming of autumn and hoar-frost (*ibid.*, p. 334), the instruments of darkness, which we have already discussed (p. 407), forecast the first rumblings of thunder and the arrival of spring (*ibid.*, p. 517). The Chang dynasty was founded thanks to Yi Yin, who sprang from a hollow mulberry

[31] Hills and rivers are the first to suffer from drought. It deprives hills of their trees, i.e. their hair, and rivers of their fish, which are their people (Granet, p. 455). This is a symmetrical inversion of the concept of baldness found in South American myths (cf. above p. 456, n. 30). The same word, *wang*, means mad, deceitful, lame, hunchbacked, bald and Spirit of drought (Schafer).

tree, the tree of the east and the rising sun. The hollow tree, perhaps originally a mortar, was used to make the most precious of all musical instruments, a drum shaped like a trough and beaten with a stick. The hollow mulberry and paulownia trees (i.e. one of the *moraceae* – like the American *Ficus* – and a member of the family of *scrophulariaceae*) were cardinal trees associated respectively with the east and north (*ibid.*, pp. 435–44 and 443, n. 1). The founder of the Yin dynasty, T'ang the victorious, fought against drought. Yu the Great, on the other hand, the founder of the Chang dynasty, managed to check the flood which Kouen, his father, had been unable to control. These two heroes were half-paralysed, therefore hemiplegic, and they limped. 'Yu's step' is an expression used for a way of walking in which 'the steps (of each foot) never project beyond each other' (*ibid.*, p. 467, n. 1 and pp. 549–54; Kaltenmark, pp. 438, 444).

The Chinese legend is reminiscent of a Bororo myth I summarized at the beginning of the previous volume and to which I have just referred again (M_3). The hero, who is lame, escapes from the flood and repeoples the earth, which has been laid waste by the baleful sun, by beating on a fish-shaped drum, kaia okgeréu, that is, a wooden mortar hollowed out by fire and with an ovoid base (*EB*, Vol. I, under 'kaia', 'okogeréu').[32] According to a Karaja myth (M_{353}), whose link with the previous myths (M_{347}–M_{352}) is obvious in spite of the geographical distance between them, the sun, the moon and the stars all had to have a leg broken, so that they would limp and move slowly. Otherwise men would not have enough time, and work would be too hard (Baldus 5, pp. 31–2).

To my knowledge, the American data have never before been compared with the information relating to the Ancient World that I have just briefly mentioned. It is clear that, in both contexts, we are dealing with something more important than a mere recurrence of limping. Limping is everywhere associated with seasonal change. The Chinese data seem so close to the facts we have studied in this book that even the brief account I have given involves a recapitulation of several themes, such as the hollow tree, which is a trough and drum, sometimes

[32] Perhaps we should also compare Yu the Great, who sprang from a stone, with one of the Edutzi gods of Tacana mythology (M_{196}). Edutzi, who was first imprisoned in a stone cavern 'at a time when the earth was still soft', then freed by a squirrel which gnawed through the wall, married a human by whom he had a son resembling a stone. After assuming human shape, the son married, and he slung over his wife's back a little wooden drum which reverberated every time he beat her (H.-H., p. 109). The theme seems to be Arawak in origin (cf. Ogilvie, pp. 68–9).

serving as a place of refuge and sometimes as a trap; disjunction between sky and earth, as well as their conjunction, mediated or non-mediated; baldness as a symbol of imbalance between the dry element and the wet element; seasonal periodicity; and finally the contrast between bells and instruments of darkness symbolizing respectively extreme abundance and extreme scarcity.

Whenever these phenomena occur, either together or separately, it would seem, then, that they cannot be explained by particular causes. For instance, the limping dance of the ancient Jews cannot be accounted for by Jacob's dislocated hip (Caquot, p. 140), nor that of Yu the Great, the master of the drum, by the fact that, during the classical period, Chinese drums rested on a single foot (Granet, p. 505). Unless we accept the fact that the ritual of the limping dance goes back to paleolithic times and was part of the common heritage of the Ancient and the New World (a theory which would solve the problem of its origin but leaves its survival unaccounted for), a structural explanation alone can throw light on the recurrence in such widely differing periods and regions, but always within the same semantic context, of a custom whose strangeness is a challenge to the speculative mind.

It is precisely because of the remoteness of the American phenomena, which makes it unlikely that they can have been influenced by some obscure link with customs elsewhere, that it is possible to re-open the question. In the present instance, the observations are unfortunately too few and fragmentary for us to draw a definite conclusion from them. I propose merely to sketch out a theory, without concealing the fact that it must remain vague and uncertain, as long as we are lacking in further information. But if, always and everywhere, the problem is how to *shorten* one period of the year to the advantage of another – either the dry season to hasten the arrival of the rains, or the reverse – may not the limping dance be seen as a reflection, or more accurately as a diagrammatic expression, of the desired imbalance? A normal gait, characterized by the regular alternation of the left and right feet, is a symbolical representation of the periodicity of the seasons; supposing there is a desire to give the lie to this periodicity in order to extend one season (for instance, the salmon months) or to shorten another (the hardships of winter, 'the slow months' of summer, extreme drought or torrential rain), a limping gait, resulting from an inequality in length between the two legs, would supply a suitable signifier in terms of the anatomical code. Incidentally, it is in connection with calendar reform that Montaigne embarks on a discussion of lameness. 'Two or three yeares are now past since the yeare hath beene shortened tenne days in France. Oh how many changes are like to ensue this reformation! It was a right removing of Heaven and Earth together ... '[33]

By quoting Montaigne in support of an interpretation of customs occurring in scattered regions of the globe and about which he knew nothing, I am well aware of taking a liberty which some people may consider to cast a doubt on my whole method. It would be appropriate to dwell on this point for a moment, especially since the problem of comparison and its legitimate limits is discussed with remarkable lucidity by Van Gennep, precisely in connection with the Carnival–Lent cycle which is at the centre of the argument.

After emphasizing the need to state the geographical location of rites and customs, in order to resist the temptation to reduce them to certain hypothetical common denominators – as he would no doubt have accused me of doing – Van Gennep goes on: 'What in fact happens is that so-called common customs turn out not to be common.' This being so, there arises the question of the differences; 'If we accept the fact that carnival-like customs, in most cases, go no further back than the early Middle Ages, with very few instances of survival from the Greco-Roman, the Gallo-Celtic or the Germanic, we may well wonder why, since the Church everywhere banned the same forms of licence and prescribed the same forms of abstentions, rural communities every-where did not adopt the same attitudes.' Have we to suppose that these attitudes have simply disappeared? But where they were already absent at the beginning of the nineteenth century, there is rarely evidence in ancient sources that they were once present. The hypothesis of survival comes up against the same kind of difficulty: 'Why should certain ancient pagan customs, whether classical or barbarian, have been handed down and preserved in some regions, and not in others, when the whole of Gaul was subjected to the same administrative system, the same religions and the same invasions?'

The agrarian theory put forward by Mannhardt and Frazer is just as unsatisfactory. 'Everywhere in France, at dates which vary according to altitude and climate, winter comes to an end and spring is reborn: can it be that the people of Normandy, Brittany, Poitou, Aquitaine, Gascony and Guyenne took no part in this rebirth which, according to

[33] Montaigne, *Essays*, trans. John Florio, Vol. III, Ch. XI. The late Brailoiu made a study of a very common irregular rhythm in popular music, the bichronous rhythm, based on a ratio of 1 to 2/3 or 3/2, and variously called 'limping', 'clogged' or 'jolting'. These adjectives and Montaigne's comments bring us back to the observations I made on pp. 401–3.

the agrarian theory, was the determining cause of the ceremonies of the Cycle?'

'Lastly, Westermack's general theory which stresses the sacred, hence prophylactic and multiplicatory, character of certain days, does not help us much either: we have only to transpose the terms of the preceding question to ask why the French throughout France did not all in the same way regard the days around the spring equinox as being alternately maleficent or beneficent.' And Van Gennep concludes: 'A solution certainly exists. The one usually accepted is that the annual date is of no importance and that different communities chose at random to hold their ceremonies at the equinox or the solstice. This moves the difficulty back a stage without solving it' (Van Gennep, t. I, Vol. III, pp. 1147–9).

It might be thought that the method I have followed, since it involves comparisons between customs originating in both the Old and the New World, puts me in an even worse category than Van Gennep's predecessors. Were they not less blameworthy in looking for the common origin of French customs, and even trying to reduce them to an archaic model, which was, however, much closer in time and space than the models with which I have ventured to compare them? Yet I do not think I am at fault, since to compare me with the theoreticians rightly criticized by Van Gennep would be to fail to recognize that I am not apprehending the facts at the same level. By bringing together, after analyses which in every instance are localized in time and place, phenomena between which there was previously no apparent link, I have given them additional dimensions. And, what is more important, the enrichment, which is evident from the multiplication of their axes of semantic reference, brings about a change of level. As their content gradually becomes more detailed and more complex, and as the number of their dimensions is increased, the truest reality of the phenomena is projected beyond any single one of these aspects with which we might at first have been tempted to confuse it. Reality shifts from content towards form or, more precisely, towards a new way of apprehending content which, without disregarding or impoverishing it, translates it into structural terms. This procedure gives practical confirmation of a statement I made in a previous work: 'it is not comparison that supports generalization, but the other way round' (L.-S. 5, p. 21; translated by Claire Jacobson and Brooke Schaepf).

The errors condemned by Van Gennep all derive from a method which disregards this principle or is unaware of it. But when it is applied systematically and care is taken, in each particular case, to define all its consequences, we find that none of these cases is reducible to any one of its empirical aspects. So if the historical or geographical distance between the various phenomena under consideration is too great, it would in any case be futile to try to link one aspect with others of the same kind, and to claim that a superficial analogy between aspects, whose meaning has not been thoroughly and independently elucidated by internal criticism, can be explained as an instance of borrowing or survival. The analysis of even a single instance, provided it is properly carried out, leads us to mistrust pronouncements such as the one made by Frazer and accepted by Van Gennep (*ibid.*, p. 993, n. 1): 'The idea of a period of time is too abstract for its personification to have been achieved by the primitive mind.' Without discussing the particular phenomena the two authors were thinking of, I shall confine myself to the general principle and declare that nothing is too abstract for the primitive mind, and that the further back we go towards the common and essential conditions of the exercise of all thought, the truer it is that these conditions take the form of abstract relationships.

It is enough to have raised the issue, since I do not propose at this point to embark on a study of the mythical representations of periodicity, which will be the subject of the next volume. In moving now towards the conclusion of the present work, let us simply take advantage of the fact that the Chinese theme of the hollow mulberry tree refers us back to that other hollow tree which occupies such an important place in the Chaco myths about the origin of tobacco and honey that were discussed at length at the beginning. We saw the hollow tree first as a natural hive for South American bees, the 'hollow thing' (as the Ancient Mexicans used to say), as is also, in its own way, the rattle. But the hollow tree was also the primeval receptacle containing all the water and all the fish in the world, and the mead trough which could be changed into a drum. As a receptacle filled with air, or water, or pure honey or honey diluted with water, the hollow tree, in all these modalities, acts as a mediatory term in the dialectic of container and content, the extreme terms of which, in equivalent modalities, belong either to the culinary code or to the acoustic code; and we know that these two codes are linked.

The fox is better qualified than any other character to bring out the significance of these multiple connotations. When imprisoned in a hollow tree (M_{219}), the fox is like honey; when crammed full of honey, which is consequently enclosed within it, the fox is like the tree (M_{210}); when it slakes its thirst with water which fills its stomach, later changed into a water-melon, it contains within its body an internal organ which contains the water (M_{209}). In the series of foods illustrated by these myths, fish and water-melons are not only symmetrical because they belong respectively to the animal and vegetable kingdoms: considered as dry-season foods, fish is food enclosed in water, and the water-melon (especially in the dry season) is water enclosed in a food. Both are in contrast to aquatic plants, which are *on* the water and, by maintaining a relationship of contiguity between the dry element and the wet element, define them by mutual exclusion rather than by mutual inclusion.

A homologous, and similarly triangular, system can be discerned in connection with the hollow tree. The naturally hollow tree is in contrast to the tree which has been stripped of its bark. But, since one consists of a longitudinal cavity enclosed within a solid, and the other of a cavity longitudinally excluded by a solid, they are both in contrast to the tree which is bored and holed transversally, just as the clapper stick of the parabára type is split transversally; it is not surprising, then, that the clapper stick should be in correlation and opposition to two musical instruments, which in turn present the same contrast as the hollow tree and the stripped tree: the drum, which is itself a hollow tree, comparatively squat and broad and with a thick outer casing, and the dance stick, which is also hollow, but not a tree, and comparatively longer and less broad, and with a thin outer casing; one is associated with sociological and horizontal conjunction (the summoning of guests from neighbouring villages), the other with cosmological and vertical conjunction (causing the ascension of the worshippers towards the Spirits), while the clapper stick is used to disjoin the Spirits horizontally by driving them away from humans.

The six main modes of the gourd that I have listed assemble these culinary and acoustic contrasts around an object, which is a receptacle like the hollow tree, transformable like the tree into a musical instrument, and capable of acting as a hive. The table on p. 469 will avoid the necessity of a lengthy commentary.

In diagram form, the gourd system, with its six terms, can be illustrated more satisfactorily than it was in the incomplete and provisional sketches on pp. 456–7 (see Figure 24, p. 470).

The three left-hand terms imply silence and the three right-hand terms noise. The symmetry between the two terms in the middle position is obvious. The four terms occupying the outside positions form a chiasmus, at the same time as they are horizontally united as pairs. Terms (1) and (2) endow the gourd's shell with a relevant function, which is either to establish within itself a union between air and water, or to create disunion between the air inside and the air outside. In (5), the shell does not prevent a union between the air (inside) and the air (outside). In (6), where the shell fulfils the same function with regard to air as it does in (2), it does not ensure the same union between air

culinary triads		triad of the hollow tree	acoustic triads	
gourds:	foods:		noise-makers:	gourds:
fishing charm (M_{345})	fish	hollow tree	drum	rattle
diabolical gourd (M_{339}–M_{340})	water-melon	tree stripped of bark	dance stick	gurgling gourd
spinning gourd (M_{28})	aquatic plants	bored tree	clapper stick	tapped gourd

and water as in (1). Consequently, in (2) and (5), air is disjoined or conjoined in respect of air; in (1) and (6), air is conjoined to water, with or without the action of the shell.

Figure 24, as the culminating point of the present work, calls for certain comments. In *The Raw and the Cooked*, my main theme was South American myths about the origin of cooking, and it led me, in the end, to more general remarks about charivari as a mode of din, and eclipses as the equivalent, on the cosmological level, of the upsetting of affinal, i.e. social, relationships. The present work, which has dealt with the mythology of honey and tobacco, has moved away from cooking in order to investigate the consumable substances peripheral to the meal. This is because of the relative positions of honey and tobacco: the former lies on the hither side of cooking, in the sense that nature offers it to man in the state of an already prepared food and concentrated nutriment, which only needs to be diluted, while the latter lies beyond cooking, since smoked tobacco has to be more than cooked; it has to be burnt before it can be consumed. Just as the study of cooking led us to a discussion of charivari, so the study of the substances surrounding cooking, also obeying what I am inclined to call the curvature of mythological space, has had to deflect its course in the direction of another custom, the widespread distribution of which has also been brought home to us; this is the use of the instruments of darkness, an acoustic modality of din and which also have a cosmological connotation since, wherever they are found, their use is associated with a change of season.

In this instance too, the link with economic and social life is clear. First, because the myths of cooking are concerned with the presence or

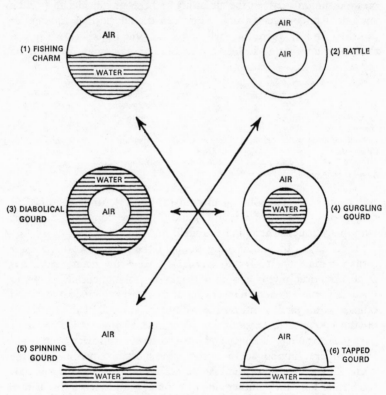

Figure 24. The gourd system

absence of fire, meat and cultivated plants *in the absolute sense*, whereas the myths about the substances surrounding cooking deal with their *relative* presence or absence, in other words, with the abundance or shortage characteristic of one or other periods of the year. Next, and this is the main point, as I have shown (p. 302), the myths about the origin of cooking relate to a physiology of the marriage relationship, the harmonious functioning of which is symbolized by the practice of the art of cooking, whereas, on the acoustic and cosmological levels, charivari and eclipses refer to a social and cosmic pathology which reverses, in another register, the meaning of the message conveyed by the introduction of cooking. Symmetrically, the myths about the circumstances surrounding cooking elaborate a pathology of the marriage relationship, the embryo of which is symbolically concealed in culinary and meteorological physiology: this is because, just as the marriage relationship is constantly threatened 'along its frontiers' – on the side of nature by the physical attractiveness of the seducer, and on the side of culture by the risk of intrigues between affines living under the same roof – cooking, too, because of the availability of honey or the discovery of the use of tobacco, is in danger of moving entirely in the direction of nature or of culture, although hypothetically it should represent their union.

This pathological condition of cooking is not simply linked with the objective presence of certain types of food. It is also a function of the alternation of the seasons which, by being characterized, as they are, sometimes by abundance and sometimes by shortages, allow culture to assert itself, or force mankind to move temporarily closer to the state of nature. Consequently, whereas, in one case, culinary physiology is reversed so as to become a cosmic pathology, in the other case, culinary pathology looks for its origin and objective basis in cosmic physiology, that seasonal periodicity which is distinguished by its regularity and is part of the given nature of things, unlike eclipses which, at least according to the native way of looking at them, are non-periodic accidents.

It would have been impossible to unravel the complexities of this problem if we had broached it simultaneously at all levels; in other words, if, like someone deciphering a text on the basis of a multi-lingual inscription, we had not understood that the myths transmit the same message with the help of several codes, the clues of which are culinary – that is techno-economic – acoustic, sociological and cosmological. However, these codes are not strictly equivalent to each other, and the myths do not put them all on the same footing. The operational value of one of them is superior to that of the others, since the acoustic code provides a common language into which the messages of the techno-economic, sociological and cosmological codes can be translated. I showed in *The Raw and the Cooked* that cooking implies silence and anti-cooking din, and that this was the case for all the forms that might be assumed by the contrast between a mediated relationship and a non-mediated relationship, independently of the conjunctive or disjunctive character of the latter. The analyses contained in the present book confirm this finding. While the myths about the origin of cooking establish a simple contrast between silence and noise, those concerned with the substances surrounding cooking go more deeply into the contrast and analyse it by distinguishing between several of its modalities. This being so, we are no longer dealing with din, pure and simple, but with contrasts within the category of noise, such as those between continuous and discontinuous noise, modulated or non-modulated noise, and linguistic or non-linguistic behaviour. As the myths gradually widen and specify the category of cooking, which was originally defined in terms of presence or absence, they widen or specify the fundamental contrast between silence and noise, and introduce between these two opposite poles a series of intermediary concepts which mark out a frontier that I have done no more than reconnoitre, taking great care not to cross it in either direction, so as not to find myself venturing into two foreign fields: the philosophy of language and musical organology.

Last but not least, it is necessary to emphasize a formal transformation. If any reader, exasperated by the effort demanded by these first two volumes, is inclined to see no more than a manic obsessiveness in the author's fascination with myths, which in the last resort all say the same thing and, after minute analysis, offer no new opening but merely force him to go round in circles, such a reader has missed the point that a new aspect of mythic thought has been revealed through the widening of the area of investigation.

To work out the system of the myths about cooking, I had to make use of oppositions between terms which practically all referred to tangible qualities: the raw and the cooked, the fresh and the rotten, the dry and the wet, etc. But now, the second stage of my analysis reveals terms which are still contrasted in pairs but whose nature is different in that they refer less to a logic of qualities than to a logic of forms: empty and full, hollow and solid, container and contents, internal and external, included and excluded, etc. In this new instance, the myths still proceed in the same way, that is, by the establishment of simultaneous correspondence between several codes. The reason why tangible representations, such as the gourd and the hollow trunk, play the central role that I have illustrated, is that, in the last resort, these objects in practice fulfil several functions, and the functions are homologous: as a ceremonial rattle, the gourd is an instrument of sacred music, used conjointly with tobacco, which is seen in the myths as an inclusion of culture in nature; but, as a receptacle for food and water, the gourd is a non-sacred cooking utensil, a container intended to hold natural products, and therefore an appropriate illustration of the inclusion of nature in culture. The same is true of the hollow tree which, as a drum, is a musical instrument whose sound acts as a summons and is therefore eminently social, and which, as a receptacle for honey, is part of nature if the honey is fresh and enclosed within it, and part of culture if the honey, instead of being in a naturally hollow tree, has been put to ferment in an artificially hollowed out trunk.

All my analyses show – and this is the justification for their number and monotonousness – that the demarcative features exploited by the myths do not consist so much of things themselves as of a body of common properties, expressible in geometrical terms and transformable one into another by means of operations which constitute a sort of algebra. If this tendency towards abstraction can be attributed to mythic thought itself, instead of being, as some readers may argue, wholly imputable to the theorizing of the mythologist, it will be agreed that we have reached a point where mythic thought transcends itself and, going beyond images retaining some relationship with concrete experience, operates in a world of concepts which have been released from any such obligation, and combine with each other in free association: by this I mean that they combine not with reference to any external reality but according to the affinities or incompatibilities existing between them in the architecture of the mind. We know, as it happens, that just such a dramatic change took place along the frontiers of Greek thought, when mythology gave way to philosophy and the latter emerged as the necessary pre-condition of scientific thought.

But, in the case with which we are now concerned, we cannot speak of progress. First of all, because the change-over, which actually took place in Western civilization, has never occurred among the South American Indians. Secondly, and more importantly, because the logic of qualities and the logic of forms that I have distinguished on the theoretical level, in fact belong to the same myths. It is true that, in this second volume, I have presented a great many new documents, but they are not different in kind from those that I analysed previously: they are myths of the same type, belonging to the same tribes. They have allowed us to move forward from one kind of logic to another, but this progress does not result from some new and different contribution to be found in them. It would be truer to say that the new material has acted on the myths already discussed in the fashion of a photographic developer, bringing out latent, but hidden, properties.

By obliging me to broaden my perspective in order to embrace a greater number of myths, those newly introduced have replaced one system of connections with another, but this does not abolish the original system, since we only have to reverse the operation to make it reappear. If we did so, we should, like an observer adjusting his microscope in order to ensure greater magnification, see the previous pattern reappear as the field of vision was reduced.

The lesson to be drawn from the South American myths is then of specific value for the resolving of problems relating to the nature and development of thought. If myths belonging to the most backward cultures of the New World bring us to this decisive threshold of the human consciousness which, in Western Europe, marks the accession to philosophy and then to science, whereas nothing similar appears to have happened among savage peoples, we must conclude from the difference that in neither case was the transition necessary, and that interlocking states of thought do not succeed each other spontaneously and through the working of some inevitable causality. No doubt, the factors which determine the formation and the respective growth-rates of the different parts of the plant are present in the seed. But the 'dormancy' of the seed, that is, the unforeseeable time which will elapse before the mechanism begins operating, does not depend upon its structure, but on an infinitely complex pattern of conditions relating to the individual history of each seed and all kinds of external influences.

The same is true of civilizations. Those which we term primitive do not differ from the others in their mental equipment but only by virtue of the fact that nothing in any mental equipment ordains that it should display its resources at a given time or utilize them in a certain direction. The fact that, on one occasion in human history and in one place, there occurred a pattern of development which we see, perhaps arbitrarily, as being the cause of subsequent events – although we cannot be sure of this, since there is not and never will be any term of comparison – does not give us authority to transmute one historical occurrence, which can have no meaning beyond its actual happening at that place and in that time, into a proof that such a development should be demandable in all places and at all times. If such were the case, it would be too easy to conclude that, wherever such an evolution has not taken place, its absence is to be explained by the inferiority or inadequacy of societies or individuals (L.-S. 2).

In stating the claims of structural analysis as vigorously as I have done in this book, I am not therefore rejecting history. On the contrary, structural analysis accords history a paramount place, the place that rightfully belongs to that irreducible contingency without which necessity would be inconceivable. In so far as structural analysis, going beyond the apparent diversity of human societies, claims to be reaching back to common and fundamental properties, it abandons the attempt to explain, not of course particular differences which it can deal with by specifying in each ethnographical context the non-varying laws according to which they are being produced, but the fact that these differences, which are all potentially possible at the same time, do not all occur in practice and that only some of them have actually occurred. To be valid, any investigation which is entirely aimed at elucidating structures must begin by submitting to the powerful inanity of events.

Paris, May 1964 – Lignerolles, July 1965

Bibliography

In the numbered entries, works already listed in the Bibliography of the preceding volume retain their original numbers; works appearing here for the first time are added at the end of the entry, regardless of date of publication.

ABBREVIATIONS:

ARBAE	*Annual Report of the Bureau of American Ethnology*
BBAE	*Bulletin of the Bureau of American Ethnology*
Colb.	Colbacchini, A.
EB	Albisetti, C. and Venturelli, A. J., *Enciclopédia Boróro*
H.-H.	Hissink, K. and Hahn, A.
HSAI	*Handbook of South American Indians*
JAFL	*Journal of American Folklore*
JSA	*Journal de la Société des Américanistes*
K.-G.	Koch-Grünberg, Th.
L.-N.	Lehmann-Nitsche, R.
L.-S.	Lévi-Strauss, C.
Nim.	Nimuendaju, C.
RC	Lévi-Strauss, C., *The Raw and the Cooked*, London, 1970
RIHGB	*Revista do Instituto Historico e Geographico Brasileiro*
RMDLP	*Revista del Museo de la Plata*
RMP	*Revista do Museu Paulista*
SWJA	*Southwestern Journal of Anthropology*
UCPAAE	*University of California Publications in American Archaeology and Ethnology*

ABREU, J. Capistrano de. *Rã-txa hu-ni-ku-i. A Lingua dos Caxinauas*, Rio de Janeiro, 1914.

ADAMSON, T. 'Folk-Tales of the Coast Salish', *Memoirs of the American Folk-Lore Society*, Vol. XXVII, 1934.

AHLBRINCK, W. 'Encyclopaedie der Karaiben', *Verhandelingen der Koninklijke Akademie van Wetenschappen te Amsterdam, afdeeling Letterkunde Nieuwe Reeks Deel 27*, 1, 1931 (French translation by Doude van Herwijnen, mimeograph, Institut Géographique National, Paris, 1956).

ALTENFELDER SILVA, F. 'Mudança cultural dos Terena', *RMP*, n.s., Vol. 3, 1949.

ALVAREZ, J. 'Mitologia ... de los salvajes huarayos', *27ᵉ Congrès International des Américanistes*, Lima, 1939.

AMORIM, A. B. de. 'Lendas em Nheêngatu e em Portuguez', *RIHGB*, t. 100, Vol. 154, Rio de Janeiro, 1928.

ARMENTIA, N. 'Arte y vocabulario de la Lengua Cavineña', ed. S. A. Lafone Quevedo, *RMDLP*, t. 13, 1906.

ASTON, W. G. (ed.). 'Nihongi. Chronicles of Japan from the Earliest Times to A.D. 697', *Transactions and Proceedings of the Japan Society*, London, 2 vols., 1896.

AUFENANGER, H. 'How Children's Faeces are Preserved in the Central Highlands of New Guinea', *Anthropos*, t. 54, 1–2, 1959.

AUGUSTINOS. 'Relación de idolatria en Huamachuco por los primeiros — ', *Informaciones acerca de la Religión y Gobierno de los Incas* (Colección de libros y documentos referentes a la Historia del Peru, t. II), Lima, 1918.

AZA, J. P. 'Vocabulario español-machiguenga', *Bol. Soc. Geogr. de Lima*, t. XLI, 1924.

BALDUS, H. (2) *Lendas dos Indios do Brasil*, São Paulo, 1946.

——. (3) 'Lendas dos Indios Tereno', *RMP*, n.s., Vol. 4, 1950.

——. (4) (ed.) *Die Jaguarzwillinge. Mythen und Heilbringersgeschichten Ursprungssagen und Märchen brasilianischer Indianer*, Kassel, 1958.

——. (5) 'Kanaschiwuä und der Erwerb des Lichtes. Beitrag zur Mythologie der Karaja Indíaner', *Sonderdruck aus Beiträge zur Gesellungs-und Völkerwissenschaft, Festschrift zum achtzigsten Geburtstag von Prof. Richard Thurnwald*, Berlin, 1950.

——. (6) 'Karaja-Mythen', *Tribus, Jahrbuch des Linden-Museums*, Stuttgart, 1952–3.

BANNER, H. (1) 'Mitos dos indios Kayapo', *Revista de Antropologia*, Vol. 5, No. 1, São Paulo, 1957.

——. (2) 'O Indio Kayapo em seu acampamento', *Boletim do Museu Paraense Emilio Goeldi*, n.s., No. 13, Belém, 1961.

BARRADAS, J. Perez de. *Los Muiscas antes de la Conquista*, 2 vols., Madrid, 1951.

BARRAL, B. M. de. *Guarao Guarata, lo que cuentan los Indios Guaraos*, Caracas, 1961.

BATES, H. W. *The Naturalist on the River Amazon*, London, 1892.

BECHER, H. (1) 'Algumas notas sôbre a religião e a mitologia dos Surára', *RMP*, n.s., Vol. 11, São Paulo, 1959.

——. (2) 'Die Surára und Pakidái. Zwei Yanonámi-Stämme in Nordwestbrasilien', *Mitteilungen aus dem Museum für Völkerkunde in Hamburg*, XXVI, 1960.

BECKWITH, M. W. 'Mandan-Hidatsa Myths and Ceremonies', *Memoirs of the American Folklore Society*, Vol. 32, New York, 1938.

BEEBE, W. 'The Three-toed Sloth', *Zoologia*, Vol. VII, No. 1, New York, 1926.

BILLIARD, R. (1) 'Notes sur l'abeille et l'apiculture dans l'antiquité', *L'Apiculteur*, 42nd–43rd year, Paris, 1898–9.

——. (2) *L'Agriculture dans l'Antiquité d'après les Géorgiques de Virgile*, Paris, 1928.

BOAS, F. (2) 'Tsimshian Mythology', *31st ARBAE*, Washington, D.C., 1916.

——. (3) 'The Social Organization and the Secret Societies of the Kwakiutl Indians', *Reports of the United States National Museum*, Washington, D.C., 1895.

BOGGIANI, G. *Os Caduveo*. Translated by Amadeu Amaral Jr., São Paulo, 1945 (Biblioteca Histórica Brasileira, XIV).

BORBA, T. M. *Actualidade Indigena*, Coritiba, 1908.

BRAILOIU, C. *Le Rythme aksak*, Abbeville, 1952.

BRETT, W. H. (1) *The Indian Tribes of Guiana*, London, 1868.

——. (2) *Legends and Myths of the Aboriginal Indians of British Guiana*, London [1880?].

BRITTON, S. W. 'Form and Function in the Sloth', *Quarterly Review of Biology*, 16, 1941.

BUNZEL, R. L. 'Zuni Katcinas', *47th ARBAE* (1929–30), Washington, D.C., 1932.

BUTT, A. 'Réalité et idéal dans la pratique chamanique', *L'Homme, revue française d'anthropologie*, II, 3, 1962.

CABRERA, A. 'Catalogo de los mamiferos de America del Sur', *Revista del Museo Argentino de Ciencias Naturales, Zoologia 4*, 1957–61.

CABRERA, A. L. and YEPES, J. *Mamiferos Sud-Americanos*, Buenos Aires, 1940.

CADOGÁN, L. (1) 'El Culto al árbol y a los animales sagrados en la mitologia y las tradiciones guaraníes', *America Indigena*, Mexico, D.F., 1950.

——. (2) *Breve contribución al estudio de la nomenclatura guaraní en botánica*. Asunción, 1955.

——. (3) 'The Eternal Pindó Palm, and other Plants in Mbyá-Guaraní Myths and Legends', *Miscellanea P. Rivet, Octogenario Dicata*, Vol. II, Mexico, D.F., 1958.

——. (4) *Ayvu Rapyta. Textos miticos de los Mbyá-Guaraní del Guairá*, São Paulo, 1959.

——. (5) 'Aporte a la etnografia de los Guaraní del Amambás Alto Ypané', *Revista de Antropologia*, Vol. 10, Nos. 1–2, São Paulo, 1962.

——. (6) 'Some Animals and Plants in Guaraní and Guayaki Mythology', MS.

CAMPANA, D. del. 'Contributo all'Etnografia dei Matacco', *Archivio per l'Antropologia e l'Etnologia*, Vol. 43, fasc. 1–2, Firenze, 1913.

CAQUOT, A. 'Les Danses sacrées en Israel et à l'entour', *Sources orientales VI: Les Danses sacrées*, Paris, 1963.

CARDUS, J. *Las Misiones Franciscanas entre los infieles de Bolivia*, Barcelona, 1886.

CASCUDO, L. da Camara. *Geografia dos Mitos Brasileiros*, Coleção Documentos Brasileiros 52, Rio de Janeiro, 1947.

CHERMONT DE MIRANDA, V. de. 'Estudos sobre o Nheêngatú', *Anais da Biblioteca Nacional*, Vol. 54 (1942), Rio de Janeiro, 1944.

CHIARA, V. 'Folclore Krahó', *RMP*, n.s., Vol. 13, São Paulo, 1961–2.

CHOPARD, L. 'Des Chauves-souris qui butinent les fleurs en volant', *Science-Progrès La Nature*, No. 3335, March 1963.

CIVRIEUX, M. de. *Leyendas Maquiritares*, Caracas, 1960, 2 parts (Mem. Soc. Cienc. Nat. La Salle 20).

CLASTRES, P. *La Vie sociale d'une tribu nomade: les Indiens Guayaki du Paraguay*, Paris, 1965 (typescript).

COLBACCHINI, A. (1) *A Tribu dos Boróros*, Rio de Janeiro, 1919.

——. (2) *I Boróros Orientali 'Orarimugudoge' del Mato Grosso, Brasile* (Contributi Scientifici delle Missioni Salesiane del Venerabile Don Bosco, 1), Torino [1925?].

——. (3) Cf. next entry:

COLBACCHINI, A. and ALBISETTI, C. *Os Boróros Orientais*, São Paulo–Rio de Janeiro, 1942.

CORRÊA, M. Pio. *Diccionario das Plantas uteis do Brasil*, 3 vols., Rio de Janeiro, 1926–31.

COUMET, E. 'Les Diagrammes de Venn', *Mathématiques et Sciences humaines* (Centre de Mathématique sociale et de statistique E.P.H.E.), No. 10, Spring 1965.

COUTO DE MAGALHÃES, J. V. *O Selvagem*, 4th edn., São Paulo–Rio de Janeiro, 1940.

CRÉQUI-MONTFORT, G. de and RIVET, P. 'Linguistique bolivienne. Les affinités des dialectes Otukè', *JSA*, n.s., Vol. 10, 1913.

CREVAUX, J. *Voyages dans l'Amérique du Sud*, Paris, 1883.

DANCE, C. D. *Chapters from a Guianese Log Book*, Georgetown, 1881.

DEBRIE, R. 'Les Noms de la crécelle et leurs dérivés en Amiénois', *Nos Patois du Nord*, No. 8, Lille, 1963.

DELVAU, A. *Dictionnaire de la langue verte*, Paris, new edn., 1883.

DENSMORE, F. 'Northern Ute Music', *BBAE 75*, Washington, D.C., 1922.

DERBYSHIRE, D. *Textos Hixkaryâna*, Belém-Para, 1965.

Dictionnaire des proverbes, Paris, 1821.

DIETSCHY, H. (2) 'Der bezaubernde Delphin von Mythos und Ritus bei den Karaja-Indianern', *Festschrift Alfred Bühler, Basler Beiträge zur Geographie und Ethnologie. Ethnologische Reihe*, Band 2, Basel, 1965.

DINIZ, E. Soares. 'Os Kayapó-Gorotíre, aspectos sóció-culturais do momento atual', *Boletim do Museu Paraense Emilio Goeldi*, Antropologia, No. 18, Belém, 1962.

DIXON, R. B. 'Words for Tobacco in American Indian Languages', *American Anthropologist*, Vol. 23, 1921, pp. 19–49.

DOBRIZHOFFER, M. *An Account of the Abipones, an Equestrian People*, transl. from the Latin, 3 vols., London, 1822.

DORNSTAUDER, J. 'Befriedigung eines wilden Indianerstammes am Juruena, Mato Grosso', *Anthropos*, t. 55, 1960.

DORSEY, G. A. (2) *The Pawnee; Mythology* (Part 1), Washington, D.C., 1906.

DREYFUS, S. *Les Kayapo du Nord. Contribution à l' étude des Indiens Gé*, Paris-La Haye, 1963.

DRUCKER, Ph. 'Kwakiutl Dancing Societies', *Anthropological Records*, II, Berkeley, 1940.

EB: ALBISETTI, C. and VENTURELLI, A. J., *Enciclopédia Boróro*, Vol. 1, Campo Grande, 1962.

EHRENREICH, P. 'Beiträge zur Völkerkunde Brasiliens', *Veröffentlichungen aus dem Kgl. Museum für Völkerkunde*, t. II, Berlin, 1891. (Portuguese translation by E. Schaden in *RMP*, n.s., Vol. 2, 1948.)

ELKIN, A. P. *The Australian Aborigines*, 3rd edn., Sydney, 1961.

ELMENDORF, W. W. 'The Structure of Twana Culture', *Research Studies, Monographic Supplement*, No. 2, Washington State University, Pullman, 1960.

ENDERS, R. K. 'Observations on Sloths in Captivity at higher Altitudes in the Tropics and in Pennsylvania', *Journal of Mammalogy*, Vol. 21, 1940.

ERIKSON, E. H. 'Observations on the Yurok: Childhood and World Image', *UCPAAE*, Vol. 35, Berkeley, 1943.

EVANS, I. H. N. *The Religion of the Tempasuk Dusuns of North Borneo*, Cambridge, 1953.

FARABEE, W. C. (1) 'The Central Arawak', *Anthropological Publications of the University Museum*, 9, Philadelphia, 1918.

——. (2) 'Indian Tribes of Eastern Peru', *Papers of the Peabody Museum, Harvard University*, Vol. X, Cambridge, Mass., 1922.

——. (4) 'The Amazon Expedition of the University Museum', *Museum Journal, University of Pennsylvania*, Vol. 7, 1916, pp. 210–44; Vol. 8, 1917, pp. 61–82; Vol. 8, 1917, pp. 126–44.

——. (5) 'The Marriage of the Electric Eel', *Museum Journal, University of Pennsylvania*, Philadelphia, March 1918.

FOCK, N. *Waiwai, Religion and Society of an Amazonian Tribe*, Copenhagen, 1963.

FOSTER, G. M. 'Indigenous Apiculture among the Popoluca of Veracruz', *American Anthropologist*, Vol. 44, 3, 1942.

Q

FRAZER, J. G. (3) *Folk-Lore in the Old Testament*, 3 vols., London, 1918.

——. (4) *The Golden Bough. A Study in Magic and Religion*, 13 vols., 3rd edn, London, 1926–36.

GALTIER-BOISSIÈRE, J. and DEVAUX, P. *Dictionnaire d'argot*. Le Crapouillot, 1952.

GARCIA, S. 'Mitologia ... machiguenga', *Congrès International des Américanistes*, 27th session, Lima, 1939.

GATSCHET, A. S. 'The Klamath Indians of Southwestern Oregon', *Contributions to North American Ethnology*, II, 2 vols., Washington, D.C., 1890.

GILLIN, J. 'The Barama River Caribs of British Guiana', *Papers of the Peabody Museum* ... Vol. 14, No. 2, Cambridge, Mass., 1936.

GILMORE, R. M. 'Fauna and Ethnozoology of South America', *HSAI*, Vol. 6, *BBAE 143*, Washington, D.C., 1950.

GIRAUD, R. 'Le Tabac et son argot', *Revue des Tabacs*, No. 224, 1958.

GOEJE, C. H. de. 'Philosophy, Initiation and Myths of the Indian of Guiana and Adjacent Countries', *Internationales Archiv für Ethnographie*, Vol. 44, Leiden, 1943.

GOLDMAN, I. 'The Cubeo. Indians of the Northwest Amazon', *Illinois Studies in Anthropology*, No. 2, Urbana, 1963.

GOLDSCHMIDT, W. 'Nomlaki Ethnography', *UCPAAE*, Vol. 42, No. 4, Berkeley, 1951.

GOUGENHEIM, G. *La Langue populaire dans le premier quart du XIXᵉ siècle*, Paris, 1929.

GOW SMITH, F. The Arawana or Fish-Dance of the Caraja Indians, *Indian Notes and Monographs, Mus. of the American Indian, Heye Foundation*, Vol. II, 2, 1925.

GRAIN, J. M. 'Pueblos primitivos – Los Machiguengas', *Congrès International des Américanistes*, 27th session, Lima, 1939.

GRANET, M. *Danses et légendes de la Chine ancienne*, 2 vols., Paris, 1926.

GREENHALL, A. M. 'Trinidad and Bat Research', *Natural History*, Vol. 74, No. 6, 1965.

GRUBB, W. Barbrooke. *An Unknown People in an Unknown Land*, London, 1911.

GUALLART, J. M. 'Mitos y leyendas de los Aguarunas del alto Marañon', *Peru Indigena*, Vol. 7, Nos. 16–17, Lima, 1958.

GUEVARA, J. 'Historia del Paraguay, Rio de la Plata y Tucuman', *Anales de la Biblioteca*, t. V, Buenos Aires, 1908.

GUMILLA, J. *Historia natural ... del Rio Orinoco*, 2 vols., Barcelona, 1791.

HENRY, J. (1) *Jungle People. A Kaingáng Tribe of the Highlands of Brazil*, New York, 1941.

——. (2) 'The Economics of Pilagá Food Distribution', *American Anthropologist*, n.s., Vol. 53, No. 2, 1951.

HÉROUVILLE, P. d'. *A la Campagne avec Virgile*, Paris, 1930.

HEWITT, J. N. B. Art. 'Tawiskaron', in 'Handbook of American Indians North of Mexico', *BBAE 30*, 2 vols., Washington, D.C., 1910.

HISSINK, K. and HAHN, A. *Die Tacana, I. Erzählungsgut*, Stuttgart, 1961.

HOFFMAN, B. G. 'John Clayton's 1687 Account of the Medicinal Practices of the Virginia Indians', *Ethnohistory*, Vol. 11, No. 1, 1964.

HOFFMAN, W. J. 'The Menomini Indians', *14th ARBAE*, Washington, 1893.

HOFFMANN-KRAYER, E. *Handwörterbuch des Deutschen Aberglaubens*, 10 vols., Berlin and Leipzig, 1927–42.

HOHENTHAL Jr, W. D. (2) 'As tribos indígenas do médio e baixo São Francisco', *RMP*, n.s., Vol. 12, São Paulo, 1960.

HOLMBERG, A. R. 'Nomads of the Long Bow. The Siriono of Eastern Bolivia', *Smithsonian Institution, Institute of Social Anthropology, Publication No. 10*, Washington, D.C., 1950.

HUDSON, W. H. *The Naturalist in La Plata*, London, 1892.

HOLMER, N. M. and WASSEN, S. H. (2) 'Nia-Ikala. Canto mágico para curar la locura', *Etnologiska Studier*, 23, Göteborg, 1958.

IHERING, H. von. (1) 'As abelhas sociaes indigenas do Brasil', *Lavoura, Bol. Sociedade Nacional Agricultura Brasileira*, Vol. 6, 1902.

——. (2) 'As abelhas sociaes do Brasil e suas denominações tupis', *Revista do Instituto Historico e Geografico de São Paulo*, Vol. 8 (1903), 1904.

IHERING, R. von. *Dicionário dos animais do Brasil*, São Paulo, 1940.

IM THURN, E. F. *Among the Indians of Guiana*, London, 1883.

IZIKOWITZ, K. G. 'Musical and Other Sound Instruments of the South American Indians. A Comparative Ethnographical Study', *Göteborgs Kungl-Vetenskaps-och Vitterhets-Samhälles Handligar Femte Följden*, Ser. A, Band 5, No. 1, Göteborg, 1935.

JACOBS, M. 'Northwest Sahaptin Texts', *Columbia University Contributions to Anthropology*, Vol. XIX, Part 1, 1934.

KALTENMARK, M. 'Les Danses sacrées en Chine', *Sources orientales VI: les Danses sacrées*, Paris, 1963.

KARSTEN, R. (2) 'The Head-Hunters of Western Amazonas', *Societas Scientiarum Fennica. Commentationes Humanarum Litterarum*, t. 7, No. 1, Helsingfors, 1935.

KENYON, K. W. 'Recovery of a Fur Bearer', *Natural History*, Vol. 72, No. 9, November 1963.

KESES, M., P. A. 'El Clima de la región de Rio Negro Venezolano (Territorio Federal Amazonas)', *Memoria, Sociedad de Ciencias Naturales La Salle*, t. XVI, No. 45, 1956.

KNOCH, K. 'Klimakunde von Südamerika', in *Handbuch der Klimatologie*, 5 vols., Berlin, 1930.

KOCH-GRÜNBERG, Th. (1) *Von Roroima zum Orinoco. Zweites Band. Mythen und Legenden der Taulipang und Arekuna Indianer*, Berlin, 1916.

KOZÁK, V. 'Ritual of a Bororo Funeral', *Natural History*, Vol. 72, No. 1, January, 1963.

KRAUSE, F. *In den Wildnissen Brasiliens*, Leipzig, 1911.

KROEBER, A. L. 'Handbook of the Indians of California', *BBAE, 78*, Washington, D.C., 1925.

KRUSE, A. (2) 'Erzählungen der Tapajoz-Munduruků', *Anthropos*, t. 41-4, 1946-9.

——. (3) 'Karusakaybë, der Vater der Munduruků', *Anthropos*, t. 46, 1951; 47, 1952.

LABRE, A. R. P. 'Exploration in the Region between the Beni and Madre de Dios Rivers and the Purus', *Proceedings of the Royal Geographical Society*, London, Vol. XI, No. 8, 1889.

LAFITAU, J. F. *Mœurs des sauvages américains comparées aux mœurs des premiers temps*, 4 vols., Paris, 1724.

LAFONT, P. B. *Tóló i Djvat, Coutumier de la tribu Jarai* (Publication de l'École française d'Extrême-Orient), Paris, 1961.

LAGUNA, F. de. 'Tlingit Ideas about the Individual', *SWJA*, Vol. 10, No. 2, Albuquerque, 1954.

LAUFER, B. 'Introduction of Tobacco in Europe', *Leaflet 19, Anthropology, Field Museum of Natural History*, Chicago, 1924.

LAYENS, G. de and BONNIER, G. *Cours complet d'apiculture*, Paris, Libr. gén. de l'enseignement (no date).

LEACH, E. R. 'Telstar et les aborigènes ou "La Pensée sauvage" de Claude Lévi-Strauss', *Annales*, November-December, 1964.

LE COINTE, P. *A Amazonia Brasileira: Arvores e Plantas uteis*, Belem-Pará, 1934.

LEEDS, A. *Yaruro Incipient Tropical Forest Horticulture. Possibilities and Limits.* See Wilbert, J., ed., *The Evolution of Horticultural Systems.*

LEHMANN-NITSCHE, R. (3) 'La Constelación de la Osa Mayor', *RMDLP*, t. 28 (3rd series, t. 4), Buenos Aires, 1924-5.

——. (5) 'La Astronomia de los Tobas (segunda parte)', *RMDLP*, t. 28 (3rd series, t. 4), Buenos Aires, 1924-5.

——. (6) 'La Astronomia de los Mocovi', *RMDLP*, t. 30 (3rd series, t. 6), Buenos Aires, 1927.

——. (7) 'Coricancha. El Templo del Sol en el Cuzco y las imagenes de su altar mayor', *RMDLP*, t. 31 (3rd series, t. 7), Buenos Aires, 1928.

——. (8) 'El Caprimúlgido y los dos grandes astros', *RMDLP*, t. 32, Buenos Aires, 1930.

LÉRY, J. de. *Histoire d'un voyage faict en la terre du Brésil*, ed. Gaffarel, 2 vols., Paris, 1880.

LÉVI-STRAUSS, C. (0) 'Contribution à l'étude de l'organisation sociale des Indiens Boróro', *JSA*, n.s., t. 18, fasc. 2, Paris, 1936.
——. (2) *Les Structures élémentaires de la parenté*, Paris, 1949.
——. (3) *Tristes Tropiques*, Paris, 1955.
——. (5) *Anthropologie structurale*, Paris, 1958.
——. (6) 'La Geste d'Asdiwal', *École pratique des hautes études, Section des Sciences religieuses*, Annuaire (1958–9), Paris, 1958.
——. (8) *Le Totémisme aujourd'hui*, Paris, 1962.
——. (9) *La Pensée sauvage*, Paris, 1962.
——. (10) *The Raw and the Cooked*, London, 1970 (*RC*).
——. (11) *Race et histoire*, Paris, 1952.
——. (12) 'Le triangle culinaire', *L'Arc*, No. 26, Aix-en-Provence, 1965.
LIPKIND, W. (2) 'The Caraja', *HSAI, BBAE 143*, 7 vols., Washington, D.C., 1946–59.
LOEB, E. 'Pomo Folkways', *UCPAAE*, Vol. 19, No. 2, Berkeley, 1926.
LORÉDAN-LARCHEY. *Nouveau Supplément au dictionnaire d'argot*, Paris, 1889.
MACHADO, O. X. de Brito. 'Os Carajás', *Conselho Nacional de Proteção aos Indios. Publ. no. 104, annexo 7*, Rio de Janeiro, 1947.
McCLELLAN, C. 'Wealth Woman and Frogs among the Tagish Indians', *Anthropos*, t. 58, 1–2, 1963.
MARCEL-DUBOIS, C. 'Le toulouhou des Pyrénées centrales', *Congrès et colloques universitaires de Liège*, Vol. 19, *Ethno-musicologie*, II, 1960.
MASSIGNON, G. 'La Crécelle et les instruments des ténèbres en Corse', *Arts et Traditions Populaires*, Vol. 7, No. 3–4, 1959.
MEDINA, J. T. 'The Discovery of the Amazon', transl. by B. T. Lee, *American Geographical Society Special Publication no. 17*, New York, 1934.
MEGGITT, M. J. 'Male-Female Relationships in the Highlands of Australian New Guinea', in J. B. Watson, ed., *New Guinea, the Central Highlands, American Anthropologist*, n.s., Vol. 66, No. 4, part 2, 1964.
MÉTRAUX, A. (1) *La Religion des Tupinamba*, Paris, 1928.
——. (3) 'Myths and Tales of the Matako Indians', *Ethnological Studies 9*, Göteborg, 1939.
——. (5) 'Myths of the Toba and Pilagá Indians of the Gran Chaco', *Memoirs of the American Folk-Lore Society*, Vol. 40, Philadelphia, 1946.
——. (8) 'Mythes et contes des Indiens Cayapo (groupe Kuben-Kran-Kegn)', *RMP*, n.s., Vol. 12, São Paulo, 1960.
——. (9) *La Civilisation matérielle des tribus Tupi-Guarani*, Paris, 1928.
——. (10). 'Suicide Among the Matako of the Argentine Gran Chaco', *America Indigena*, Vol. 3, No. 3, Mexico, 1943.
——. (11) 'Les Indiens Uro-Čipaya de Carangas: La Religion', *JSA*, Vol. XVII, 2, Paris, 1935.

——. (12) 'Ethnography of the Chaco', *HSAI, BBAE 143*, Vol. 1, Washington, D.C., 1946.

——. (13) 'Tribes of Eastern Bolivia and Madeira', *HSAI, BBAE 143*, Vol. 3.

——. (14) 'Estudios de Etnografia Chaquense', *Anales del Instituto de Etnografía Americana. Universidad Nacional de Cuyo*, t. V, Mendoza, 1944.

MÉTRAUX, A. and BALDUS, H. 'The Guayakí', *HSAI, BBAE 143*, Vol. 1, Washington, D.C., 1946.

MONTOYA, A. Ruiz de. *Arte, vocabulario, tesoro y catacismo de la lengua Guarani* (1640), Leipzig, 1876.

MOONEY, J. 'Myths of the Cherokee', *19th ARBAE*, Washington, D.C., 1898.

MOURA, José de, S.J. 'Os Münkü, 2a Contribuição ao estudo da tribo Iranche', *Pesquisas, Antropologia no. 10*, Instituto Anchietano de Pesquisas, Porto Alegre, 1960.

MURPHY, R. F. (1) 'Mundurucú Religion', *UCPAAE*, Vol. 49, No. 1, Berkeley–Los Angeles, 1958.

MURPHY, R. F. and QUAIN, B. 'The Trumai Indian of Central Brazil', *Monographs of the American Ethnological Society*, 24, New York, 1955.

NIMUENDAJU, C. (1) 'Die Sagen von der Erschaffung und Vernichtung der Welt als Grundlagen der Religion der Apapocúva-Guarani', *Zeitschrift für Ethnologie*, Vol. 46, 1914.

——. (2) 'Sagen der Tembé-Indianer', *Zeitschrift für Ethnologie*, Vol. 47, 1915.

——. (3) 'Bruchstücke aus Religion und Überlieferung der Šipaia-Indianer', *Anthropos*, t. 14–15, 1919–20; 16–17, 1921–2.

——. (5) 'The Apinayé', *The Catholic University of America, Anthropological Series, no. 8*, Washington, D.C., 1939.

——. (6) 'The Šerente', *Publ. of the Frederick Webb Hodge Anniversary Publication Fund*, Vol. 4, Los Angeles, 1942.

——. (7) 'Šerente Tales', *JAFL*, Vol. 57, 1944.

——. (8) 'The Eastern Timbira', *UCPAAE*, Vol. 41, Berkeley–Los Angeles, 1946.

——. (9) 'Social Organization and Beliefs of the Botocudo of Eastern Brazil', *SWJA*, Vol. 2, No. 1, 1946.

——. (13) 'The Tukuna', *UCPAAE*, Vol. 45, Berkeley–Los Angeles, 1952.

NINO, B. de. *Etnografia chiriguana*, La Paz, 1912.

NORDENSKIÖLD, E. (1) *Indianerleben, El Gran Chaco*, Leipzig, 1912.

——. (3) *Forschungen und Abenteuer in Südamerika*, Stuttgart, 1924.

——. (4) 'La Vie des Indiens dans le Chaco', translated by Beuchat, *Revue de Géographie*, Vol. 6, 3rd part, 1912.

——. (5) 'L'Apiculture indienne', *JSA*, t. XXI, 1929, pp. 169–82.

——. (6) 'Modifications in Indian Culture through Inventions and Loans', *Comparative Ethnographical Studies*, Vol. 8, Göteborg, 1930.

Normais Climatológicas (Ministerio da Agricultura, Serviço de Meteorologia), Rio de Janeiro, 1941.

Normais Climatológicas da área da Sudene (Presidência da Républica, Superintendência do Desenvolvimento do Nordeste), Rio de Janeiro, 1963.

OBERG, K. 'Indian Tribes of Northern Mato Grosso, Brazil', *Smithsonian Institution, Institute of Social Anthropology*, Publ. no. 15, Washington, D.C., 1953.

OGILVIE, J. 'Creation Myths of the Wapisiana and Taruma, British Guiana', *Folk-Lore*, Vol. 51, London, 1940.

OLIVEIRA, C. E. de. 'Os Apinayé do Alto Tocantins', *Boletim do Museu Nacional*. Vol. 6, No. 2, Rio de Janeiro, 1930.

OLSON, R. L. 'The Social Organization of the Haisla of British Columbia', *Anthropological Records II*, Berkeley, 1940.

ORBIGNY, A. d'. *Voyage dans l'Amérique méridionale*, Paris and Strasbourg, Vol. 2, 1839–43.

ORICO, O. (1) *Mitos amerindios*, 2nd edn, São Paulo, 1930.

——. (2) *Vocabulario de Crendices Amazonicas*, São Paulo-Rio de Janeiro, 1937.

OSBORN, H. (1) 'Textos Folklóricos en Guarao', *Boletín Indigenista Venezolano*, Años III–IV–V, Nos. 1–4, Caracas, 1956–7 (1958).

——. (2) 'Textos Folklóricos en Guarao II', *ibid.*, Año VI, Nos. 1–4, 1958.

——. (3) 'Textos Folklóricos Guarao', *Anthropologica*, 9, Caracas, 1960.

PALAVECINO, E. 'Takjuaj. Un personaje mitológico de los Mataco', *RMDLP*, n.s., No. 7, *Antropologia*, t. 1, Buenos Aires, 1936–41.

PARSONS, E. C. (3) 'Kiowa Tales', *Memoirs of the American Folk-Lore Society*, Vol. XXVII, New York, 1929.

PAUCKE, F.: *Hacia allá y para acá (una estada entre los Indios Mocobies)*, *1749–1767*, Spanish translation, Tucumán-Buenos Aires, 4 vols., 1942–4.

Pelo rio Mar – Missões Salesianas do Amazonas, Rio de Janeiro, 1933.

PETITOT, E. *Traditions indiennes du Canada nord-ouest*, Paris, 1886.

PETRULLO, V. 'The Yaruros of the Capanaparo River, Venezuela', *Anthropological Papers no. 11*, *Bureau of American Ethnology*, Washington, D.C., 1939.

PIERINI, F. 'Mitología de los Guarayos de Bolivia', *Anthropos*, t. 5, 1910.

PLUTARCH. 'De Isis et d'Osiris', *Les Œuvres morales de –*, translated by Amyot, 2 vols., Paris, 1584.

POMPEU SOBRINHO, Th. 'Lendas Mehim', *Revista do Instituto do Ceará*, Vol. 49, Fortaleza, 1935.

PREUSS, K. Th. (1) *Religion und Mythologie der Uitoto*, 2 vols., Göttingen, 1921–3.

——. (3) 'Forschungsreise zu den Kagaba', *Anthropos*, t. 14–21, 1919–26.

RAY, V. F. 'The Sanpoil and Nespelem', *Reprinted by Human Relations Area Files*, New Haven, 1954.

REICHARD, G. A. 'Wiyot Grammar and Texts', *UCPAAE*, Vol. 22, No. 1, Berkeley, 1925.

REICHEL-DOLMATOFF, G. *Los Kogi*, 2 vols., Bogotá, 1949–50 and 1951.

REINBURG, P. 'Folklore amazonien. Légendes des Zaparo du Curaray et de Canelos', *JSA*, Vol. 13, 1921.

RHODE, E. 'Einige Notizen über dem Indianerstamm der Terenos', *Zeit-schrift der Gesell. für Erdkunde zu Berlin*, Vol. 20, 1885.

RIBEIRO, D. (1) 'Religião e Mitologia Kadiuéu', *Serviço de Proteção aos Indios*, Publ. 106, Rio de Janeiro, 1950.

——. (2) 'Noticia dos Ofaié-Chavante', *RMP*, n.s., Vol. 5, São Paulo, 1951.

RIGAUD, L. *Dictionnaire d'argot moderne*, Paris, 1881.

RIVET, P. Cf. CRÉQUI-MONTFORT, G. de and RIVET, P., *and* ROCHE-REAU, H. J. and RIVET, P.

ROBERT, M. 'Les Vanniers du Mas-Gauthier (Feytiat, près de Limoges) depuis un siècle', *Ethnographie et Folklore du Limousin*, No. 8, Limoges, December, 1964.

ROCHEREAU, H. J. and RIVET, P. 'Nociones sobre creencias, usos y costumbres de los Catios del Occidente de Antioquia', *JSA*, Vol. 21, Paris, 1929.

RODRIGUES, J. Barbosa. (1) 'Poranduba Amazonense', *Anais da Biblioteca Nacional de Rio de Janeiro*, Vol. 14, fasc. 2, 1886–7, Rio de Janeiro, 1890.

——. (2) *O Muyrakytã e os idolos symbolicos. Estudo da origem asiatica da civilizacão do Amazonas nos tempos prehistoricos*, 2 vols., Rio de Janeiro, 1899.

——. (3) 'Lendas, crenças e superstições', *Revista Brasileira*, t. X, 1881.

——. (4) 'Tribu dos Tembés. Festa da Tucanayra', *Revista da Exposicão Anthropologica*, Rio de Janeiro, 1882.

RONDON, C. M. da Silva. 'Esbõço grammatical e vocabulário da lingua dos Indios Boróro', *Publ. no. 77 da Comissão ... Rondon. Anexo 5, etnografia*, Rio de Janeiro, 1948.

ROSSIGNOL. *Dictionnaire d'argot*, Paris, 1901.

ROTH, W. E. (1) 'An Inquiry into the Animism and Folklore of the Guiana Indians', *30th ARBAE* (1908–9), Washington, D.C., 1915.

——. (2) 'An Introductory Study of the Arts, Crafts and Customs of the Guiana Indians', *38th ARBAE* (1916–17), Washington, D.C., 1924.

ROYDS, Th. F. *The Beasts, Birds and Bees of Virgil*, Oxford, 1914.

Roys, R. L. (1) 'The Ethno-botany of the Maya', *Middle Amer. Research Ser. Tulane University*, Publ. 2, 1931.

——. (2) 'The Indian Background of Colonial Yucatan', *Carnegie Institution of Washington*, Publ. 548, 1943.

Russell, F. 'The Pima Indians', *26th ARBAE* (1904–5), Washington, D.C., 1908.

Saake, W. (1) 'Die Juruparilegende bei den Baniwa des Rio Issana', *Proceedings of the 32nd Congress of Americanists* (1956), Copenhagen, 1958.

——. (2) 'Dringende Forschungsaufgaben im Nordwestern Mato Grosso', *34e Congrès International des Américanistes*, São Paulo, 1960.

Sahagun, B. de. *Florentine Codex. General History of the Things of New Spain.* In 13 parts. Transl. by A. J. O. Anderson and C. E. Dibble, Santa Fé, New Mexico, 1950–63.

Sainéan, L. *Les Sources de l'argot ancien*, Paris, 1912.

Saint-Hilaire, A. F. de. *Voyages dans l'intérieur du Brésil*, Paris, 1830–51.

Salt, G. 'A Contribution to the Ethnology of the Meliponidae', *The Transactions of the Entomological Society of London*, Vol. LXXVII, London, 1929.

Sapir, E. 'Wishram Texts', *Publications of the American Ethnological Society*, Vol. II, 1909.

Schaden, E. (1) 'Fragmentos de mitologia Kayuá', *RMP*, n.s., Vol. 1, São Paulo, 1947.

——. (4) *Aspectos fundamentais da cultura guarani* (1st edn in Boletim no. 188, Antropologia, no. 4, Universidade de São Paulo, 1954; 2nd edn, São Paulo, 1962).

——. (5) 'Caracteres especificos da cultura Mbüá-Guarani', nos. 1 and 2, *Revista de Antropologia*, vol. II, São Paulo, 1963.

Schaeffner, A. 'Les Kissi. Une société noire et ses instruments de musique', *L'Homme, cahiers d'ethnologie, de géographie et de linguistique*, Paris, 1951.

Schafer, E. H. 'Ritual Exposure in Ancient China', *Harvard Journal of Asiatic Studies*, Vol. 14, Nos. 1–2, 1951.

Schomburgk, R. *Travels in British Guiana 1840–1844*, translated and edited by W. E. Roth, 2 vols., Georgetown, 1922.

Schuller, R. 'The Ethnological and Linguistic position of the Tacana Indians of Bolivia', *American Anthropologist*, n.s., Vol. 24, 1922.

Schultes, R. E. (1) 'Botanical Sources of the New World Narcotics', *Psychedelic Review*, 1, 1963.

——. (2) 'Hallucinogenic Plants in the New World', *Harvard Review*, 1, 1963.

Schultz, H. (1) 'Lendas dos indios Krahó', *RMP*, n.s., Vol. 4, São Paulo, 1950.

——. (2) 'Informações etnográficas sôbre os Un utina (1943, 1944 e 1945)', *RMP*, n.s., Vol. 13, São Paulo, 1961–2.

——. (3) 'Informações etnográficas sôbre os Suyá (1960)', *RMP*, n.s., Vol. 13, São Paulo, 1961–2.

SCHWARTZ, H. B. (1) 'The Genus Melipona', *Bull. Amer. Mus. Nat. Hist.*, Vol. LXIII, 1931–2, New York, 1931–2.

——. (2) 'Stingless Bees (Meliponidae) of the Western Hemisphere', *Bull. Amer. Mus. Nat. Hist.*, Vol. 90, New York, 1948.

SÉBILLOT, P. 'Le Tabac dans les traditions, superstitions et coutumes', *Revue des Traditions Populaires*, t. 8, 1893.

SETCHELL, W. A. 'Aboriginal Tobaccos', *American Anthropologist*, n.s., Vol. 23, 1921.

SILVA, P. A. Brüzzi Alves da. *A Civilização Indígena do Uaupés*, São Paulo, 1962.

SIMONOT, D. 'Autour d'un livre: "Le Chaos sensible", de Theodore Schwenk', *Cahiers des Ingénieurs agronomes*, No. 195, April, 1965.

SPEGAZZINI, C. 'Al través de Misiones', *Rev. Faculdad Agr. Veterinaria, Univ. Nac. de La Plata*, Series 2, Vol. 5, 1905.

SPIER, L. (1) 'Southern Diegueño Customs', *UCPAAE*, Vol. 20, No. 16, Berkeley, 1923.

——. (2) 'Klamath Ethnography', *UCPAAE*, Vol. 30, Berkeley, 1930.

SPIER, L. and SAPIR, E. 'Wishram Ethnography', *University of Washington Publications in Anthropology*, Vol. III, 1930.

SPRUCE, R. *Notes of a Botanist on the Amazon and Andes* ... , 2 vols., London, 1908.

STAHL, G. (1) 'Der Tabak im Leben Südamerikanischer Völker', *Zeit. für Ethnol.*, Vol. 57, 1924.

——. (2) 'Zigarre; Wort und Sach', *ibid.*, Vol. 62, 1930.

STEWARD, J. H. and FARON, L. C. *Native Peoples of South America*, New York-London, 1959.

STIRLING, M. W. 'Historical and Ethnographical Material on the Jivaro Indians', *BBAE 117*, Washington, D.C., 1938.

STRADELLI, E. (1) 'Vocabulario da lingua geral portuguez-nheêngatu e nheêngatu-portuguez, *etc.*', *RIHGB*, t. 104, Vol. 158, Rio de Janeiro, 1929.

——. (2) 'L'Uaupés e gli Uaupés. Leggenda dell' Jurupary', *Bolletino della Società geografica Italiana*, Vol. III, Roma, 1890.

SUSNIK, B. J. 'Estudios Emok-Toba. Parte 1ra: Frasearío', *Boletín de la Sociedad científica del Paraguay*, Vol. VII-1962, Etno-linguistica 7, Asunción, 1962.

SWANTON, J. R. (2) 'Tlingit Myths and Texts', *BBAE 39*, Washington, D.C., 1909.

TASTEVIN, C. (1) *La Langue Tapïhïya dite Tupï ou N'eêngatu*, etc. (Schriften der Sprachenkommission, Kaiserliche Akademie der Wissenschaften, Band II), Vienna, 1910.

———. (2) 'Nomes de plantas e animaes em lingua tupy', *RMP*, t. 13, São Paulo, 1922.

———. (3) 'La Légende de Bóyusú en Amazonie', *Revue d'Ethnographie et des Traditions Populaires*, 6e année, No. 22, Paris, 1925.

———. (4) 'Le fleuve Murú. Ses habitants. – Croyances et mœurs kachinaua', *La Géographie*, Vol. 43, Nos. 4–5, 1925.

———. (5) 'Le Haut Tarauacá', *La Géographie*, Vol. 45, 1926.

TEBBOTH, T. 'Diccionario Toba', *Revista del Instituto de Antropologia de la Univ. Nac. de Tucumán*, Vol. 3, No. 2, Tucumán, 1943.

TEIT, J. A. 'The Shuswap, *Memoirs of the American Museum of Natural History*, Vol. IV, 1909.

TESCHAUER, Carlos S. J. *Avifauna e flora nos costumes, supersticões e lendas brasileiras e americanas*, 3rd edn, Porto Alegre, 1925.

THEVET, A. *Cosmographie universelle illustrée*, 2 vols., Paris, 1575.

THOMPSON, d'Arcy Wentworth. *On Growth and Form*, 2 vols:, new edn, Cambridge, Mass., 1952.

THOMPSON, J. E. 'Ethnology of the Mayas of Southern and Central British Honduras', *Field Mus. Nat. Hist. Anthropol. Ser.*, Vol. 17, Chicago, 1930.

THOMSON, M. 'La Semilla del Mundo', *Leyendas de los Indios Maquiritares en el Amazonas Venezolano, Recopiladas por James Bou, Presentadas por*·–. Mimeograph.

THOMSON, Sir A. Landsborough (ed.). *A New Dictionary of Birds*, London, 1964.

THORPE, W. H. *Learning and Instinct in Animals*, new edn, London, 1963.

VAN BAAL, J. 'The Cult of the Bull-roarer in Australia and Southern New-Guinea', *Bijdragen tot de taal-, land- en Volkenkunde*, Deel 119, 2e Afl., The Hague, 1963.

VAN GENNEP, A. *Manuel de Folklore français contemporain*, 9 vols., Paris, 1946–58.

VELLARD, J. *Histoire du curare*, Paris, 1965.

VIANNA, U. 'Akuen ou Xerente', *RIHGB*, t. 101, Vol. 155, Rio de Janeiro, 1928.

VIMAÎTRE, Ch. *Dictionnaire d'argot fin-de-siècle*, Paris, 1894.

VIRGIL. *Géorgiques*, text edited and translated by E. de Saint-Denis, Paris, 1963.

WAGLEY, Ch. and GALVÃO, E. 'The Tenetehara Indians of Brazil', *Columbia Univ. Contributions to Anthropology*, 35, New York, 1949.

WALLACE, A. R. *A Narrative of Travels on the Amazon and Rio Negro*, London, 1889.

WATERMAN, T. T. 'The Religious Practices of the Diegueno Indians', *UCPAAE*, Vol. 8, No. 6, Berkeley, 1910.

WEISER, F. X. *Fêtes et coutumes chrétiennes. De la liturgie au folklore* (French translation of *Christian Feasts and Customs*, New York, 1954), Paris, 1961.

WELTFISH, G. *The Lost Universe*, New York, 1965.

WHIFFEN, Th. *The North-West Amazons*, London, 1915.

WILBERT, J. (2) 'Problematica de algunos métodos de pesca, *etc.*', *Memorias, Sociedad de Ciencias Naturales La Salle*, Vol. XV, No. 41, Caracas, 1956.

——. (3) 'Los instrumentos musicales de los Warrau', *Antropológica*, No. 1, pp. 2–22, Caracas, 1956.

——. (4) 'Rasgos culturales circun-caribes entre los Warrau y sus inferencias', *Memorias, Sociedad de Ciencias Naturales La Salle*, t. XVI, No. 45, 1956.

——. (5) 'Mitos de los Indios Yabarana', *Antropológica*, No. 5, Caracas, 1958.

——. (6) 'Puertas del Averno', *Memorias, Sociedad de Ciencias Naturales La Salle*, t. XIX, No. 54, 1959.

——. (7) 'Erzählgut der Yupa-Indianer', *Anthropos*, t. 57, 3–6, 1962.

——. (8) *Indios de la región Orinoco-Ventuari*, Caracas, 1953.

——. (9) 'Warao Oral Literature', *Instituto Caribe de Antropologia y Sociologia, Fundación La Salle de Ciencias Naturales*, Monograph No. 9, Caracas, 1964.

WILBERT, J. (ed.) *The Evolution of Horticultural Systems in Native South America. Causes and Consequences, A Symposium*, Caracas, 1961.

WILLIAMSON, R. W. *The Mafulu. Mountain People of British New Guinea*, London, 1912.

WIRTH, D. M. (1) 'A mitologia dos Vapidiana do Brasil', *Sociologia*, Vol. 5, No. 3, São Paulo, 1943.

——. (2) 'Lendas dos Indios Vapidiana', *RMP*, n.s., Vol. 4, São Paulo, 1950.

WRIGHT, A. R. and LONES, T. E. *British Calendar Customs. England*, Vol. II. *Fixed Festivals, Jan.–May Inclusive* (Publ. of the Folklore Society, CII), London, 1938.

ZERRIES, O. (2) 'The Bull-roarer among South American Indians', *RMP*, n.s., Vol. 7, São Paulo, 1953.

——. (3) 'Kürbisrassel und Kopfgeister in Südamerika', *Paideuma*, Band 5, Heft 6, Bamberg, 1953.

Indexes

Index of Myths

Numbers in boldface indicate complete myth

1. Myths listed in numerical order and according to subject-matter

a. New Myths

2. Myths listed by tribe

General Index

Abipones, the, 53
Abreu, J. Capistrano de, 132
Acawai, the, 263, 276, 429
Acoustic code, 328–9
Adamson, T., 461
Affines, 237–8, 265, 281–2, 302, 342
Agouti, 264 and n., 276, 394, 396
Aguaruna, the, 382, 434
Ahlbrinck, W., 113, 168, 173, 174n., 199, 202, 241, 269, 279, 280, 306, 319, 326, 327n., 357, 364, 367n., 439, 440
Aigé, 375n., 415
Alaska, 199, 202, 217
Aldebaran, 300, 301
Algaroba, 67, 101, 372
Alimentary and linguistic behaviour, 281–2
Altenfelder Silva, F., 76, 371, 460, 472
Amazonian region and tribes, 51–2, 55, 58, 59, 64, 67, 82, 87, 90, 112, 117, 132, 139, 140, 157, 162, 178, 186, 200, 208, 211, 234, 270–73, 285, 287, 291–3, 300, 306, 324, 357, 358, 379–80, 387, 416–17, 430–31, 434, 436, 437, 439n., 453, 456, 458
Ambaúva tree, 364
Amorim, A. B. de, 201, 271, 309n., 318n., 427, 429
Amuesha, the, 370
Anacardiaceae, 231, 233
Andean culture, 269, 344, 345, 438
Ant-eaters, 63, 65, 131–6, 145, 149, 264n., 335n., 347, 350n., 351, 352, 357n.
Ants, 344
Apapocuva, the, 387
Apiburé clan, 370
Apinayé, the, 116n., 119–21, 123, 125–7, 137, 138, 149, 278, 431, 450, 455, 456, 458
Aquilinae, 367
Arapuã bee, 122, 124, 130
Araticum plant, 83
Arawak, the, 153–4, 166–7, 185, 200, 201, 213, 223, 228, 244, 256–7, 269, 318–20,
334, 335, 390, 400, 428 429, 439, 447, 453, 463n.
Archery and arrows, 169–73, 177, 178, 182, 183, 188, 199, 217, 219, 346–9, 363, 396–8, 438
Ardeidae, 247
Arecuna Indians, 229, 263, 265, 280, 326, 438–40
Argentina, 121
Aries (constellation), 169–15, 135, 266, 267
Arizona, 113
Armadillo, 339n., 343n., 377
Armentia, N., 319, 327, 344
Ashluslay, the, 53, 102
Aston, W. G., 379n., 380
Astronomical and sociological codes, 285–9
Australia, 382n., 411, 412
Avocado pears, 300–301
Axes, 431, 442
Aztecs, the, 382
Azywaywa tree, 35

Babylonians, the, 17
Baldness, 456 and n., 462n.
Baldus, H., 211, 236n., 289, 400, 403, 443, 460, 463
Bamboo, 369–71, 374–5, 386 and n., 443
Banana, 321, 336
Baniwa, the, 302, 309n., 350n.
Banner, H., 124, 135
Baré, the, 201, 289, 427, 429
Bark masks, 388–9
Bark stripping, 390, 469
Bate pau, 371–2
Bates, H. W., 51–2, 200, 267n., 327
Bats, 382–3
Batuque hunting, 307
Baudelaire, 298
Beans, 305
Becher, H., 215, 267n.
Beckwith, M. W., 190
Beebe, W., 429